TRIANGLE CLASSICS
ILLUMINATING THE GAY AND LESBIAN EXPERIENCE

And the Band Played On
by Randy Shilts

Another Mother Tongue
by Judy Grahn

The Autobiography of Alice B. Toklas
by Gertrude Stein

The Beebo Brinker Chronicles
by Ann Bannon

Before Night Falls
by Reinaldo Arenas

Bertram Cope's Year
by Henry Blake Fuller

Borrowed Time/Love Alone/Becoming a Man
by Paul Monette

A Boy's Own Story/
The Beautiful Room Is Empty
by Edmund White

Brideshead Revisited
by Evelyn Waugh

The Celluloid Closet
by Vito Russo

City of Night
by John Rechy

Dancer from the Dance
by Andrew Holleran

Death in Venice and Seven Other Stories
by Thomas Mann

Family Dancing
by David Leavitt

The Family of Max Desir
by Robert Ferro

The Front Runner
by Patricia Nell Warren

Gay Spirit/Gay Soul
by Mark Thompson

The Gilda Stories/Bones & Ash
by Jewelle Gomez

Giovanni's Room
by James Baldwin

A Home at the End of the World/Flesh and Blood
by Michael Cunningham

I've a Feeling We're Not in Kansas Anymore/
Buddies/Everybody Loves You
by Ethan Mordden

The Little Death/Goldenboy/How Town
by Michael Nava

The Lord Won't Mind/One for the Gods
by Gordon Merrick

The Lure
by Felice Picano

The Naked Civil Servant/How to Become a Virgin/Resident Alien
by Quentin Crisp

Nightwood/Ladies Almanack
by Djuna Barnes

Olivia
by Olivia

Oranges Are Not the Only Fruit
by Jeanette Winterson

Orlando
by Virginia Woolf

The Picture of Dorian Gray
by Oscar Wilde

The Price of Salt
by Patricia Highsmith

Rubyfruit Jungle
by Rita Mae Brown

Sexual Politics/Sita
by Kate Millett

A Single Man
by Christopher Isherwood

Skinflick/Gravedigger/Nightwork
by Joseph Hansen

The Sophie Horowitz Story/Girls, Visions and Everything/After Dolores
by Sarah Schulman

Stone Butch Blues
by Leslie Feinberg

Surpassing the Love of Men
by Lillian Faderman

The Swimming-Pool Library
by Alan Hollinghurst

The Well of Loneliness
by Radclyffe Hall

What Is Found There/An Atlas of the Difficult World/The Fact of a Doorframe
by Adrienne Rich

Zami/Sister Outsider/Undersong
by Audre Lorde

THE LITTLE DEATH

GOLDENBOY

HOW TOWN

THE LITTLE DEATH

GOLDENBOY

HOW TOWN

MICHAEL NAVA

INTRODUCTION BY GREG HERREN

InsightOut Books
New York

The Little Death
Copyright © 1986, 2001 by Michael Nava

Golden Boy
Copyright © 1988, 1996 by Michael Nava

How Town
Copyright © 1990 by Michael Nava

Introduction copyright © 2001 by Greg Herren

This edition was especially created in 2001 for InsightOut Books by arrangement with Alyson Publications and HarperCollins, Inc. This edition copyright © 2001 by Bookspan. All rights reserved.

Printed in the United States of America

Introduction

As a lifelong fan of the mystery genre, it gives me a great deal of pleasure to have this opportunity to write an introduction to the first three books in the Henry Rios series. I cut my teeth on the Hardy Boys and Nancy Drew; as I got older I made the natural progression to Agatha Christie, Ellery Queen, Dashiell Hammett, Raymond Chandler, and many others far too numerous to mention. As I also became aware of my nascent sexuality, I began to notice that when gays and lesbians made their infrequent appearances in these books, they were villains and/or helpless victims held in contempt by the protagonists. I longed to read mysteries where the hero of the story was a gay man. When I began to pursue my own dream of being a mystery writer, my initial attempts into the field were with heterosexual characters. It never even dawned on me that writing a "gay mystery" was even possible.

That changed when I discovered Michael Nava's work.

It was one of those life-changing moments. A gay and lesbian bookstore had opened in the town where I was living, which meant no more searching in vain in the chain stores for books with queer content. I walked in one hot afternoon and asked the cashier if there were any mysteries in stock. He smiled and replied, "Have you read Michael Nava?" I said no, and he immediately walked to the floor of the store and returned with three books: *The Little Death*, *Goldenboy*, and *How Town*. I bought them and there was no turning back. Since that day, I have eagerly awaited the publication of each new book in the Henry Rios series. Each book is a gay bestseller, and Nava has legions of fans.

So, who exactly is Henry Rios, and why is he so popular?

Raised in a poor family in a rural town by an abusive father and an enabling mother, Henry was driven to become a success. He was a star runner in high school and made it all the way through law school with financial aid and scholarships. But the scars and wounds of his childhood did not heal with his successes; rather, they have been kept open by dealing with his homosexuality in a world, and profession, that is largely homophobic. An outsider because of his Hispanic heritage, a sexual outsider because of his same-sex attraction, he champions the downtrodden.

When the series opens in *The Little Death*, Henry is working as a public defender in San Francisco and living alone. His battles with alcohol have left him dissatisfied and somewhat embittered, and he is unhappy with the system that employs him. His own puritanical streak about the law keeps him from taking a position with a high-powered law firm, with all the money and privilege that would come along with it. After a chance encounter with a handsome young man arrested for drug possession, Henry tries to help him. His help comes to naught when the young man—the heir to a huge fortune—winds up dead.

Goldenboy, the second novel in the series, takes a grim look at the effects of homophobia and the dangers of the closet. Henry, now living in Los Angeles, becomes the attorney for a teenaged waiter accused of murdering a coworker, another young waiter. The motive for the crime? According to the police, the victim was threatening to "out" the killer, who came from a deeply religious (and equally intolerant) family. Henry believes that his client is innocent and begins digging into the crime. Before long, the trail leads him to Hollywood's gilded closets, and he exposes the hypocrisy extant in that system.

Goldenboy is also important in that it is the volume where Henry meets Josh, the attractive, intelligent college student infected with HIV, and begins the long, sometimes heartbreaking relationship that colors every decision that Henry makes in the future books.

It is in *How Town* that we really get to know Henry, as he does, indeed, come home again to the small San Joaquin Valley town where he was raised, in order to represent an old high school buddy now accused of murder. Henry's past was always merely hinted at before; in *How Town* we are exposed to it in all of its bleak ugliness. The abusive father, the complacent mother, the poverty, the racism, and his sexual confusion all come flooding back as Henry investigates this murder. The sexual attraction he felt for his old friend when they were teenagers is probed in Henry's mind, and reading those heartbreaking passages is like touching an exposed nerve.

We've all been there.

That is perhaps the key to Nava's popularity. For while at times Henry can seem almost insufferably priggish and self-righteous, Nava is a master of creating character. And though we as readers might disagree with Henry's decisions or actions, we *understand* him, because his experiences are universal. Whether it is facing up to the reality of a relationship with an HIV-positive lover, fighting his alcoholism, or dealing with the painful bitter memories of child abuse, Henry, through Nava's mastery, becomes real to us. He lives, he laughs, he cries, he loves . . . all in the face of overwhelming odds against him. We share his pain, we share his laughter, and we root for him because we want him to succeed, because if he can, by extension, so can we. He fights the legal system, which in Nava's work is a metaphor for the society it strives to protect: classist, racist, sexist, and homophobic. Henry is a gay hero in a world without them.

The recently released *Rag and Bone* is, according to Nava, the final Henry Rios novel. I hope that isn't true, because I don't want to say goodbye to Henry. But if I must, I would like to thank him and his creator for allowing me to share in their world.

It's been a pleasure.

—Greg Herren
Editor, *Lambda Book Report*

THE LITTLE DEATH

I wish to thank Paul Gillette, without whom
I would not have finished this book,
and the Wednesday Night regulars—*in vino veritas.*

For Bill

Preface to the 15th Anniversary Edition

I began writing *The Little Death* in the summer of 1980, just after I had graduated from law school at Stanford and while I was studying for the bar exam. I was working at the Palo Alto, Calif., jail, located, like the jail in the novel, in the basement of the courthouse. My job was to interview arrestees after they were booked to determine whether they should be released on their own recognizance or held overnight until a judge could set bail. My hours were from 10 P.M. to 6 A.M. Palo Alto is an affluent university town without much serious crime, and often my only clients were a couple of drunk drivers or an inept burglar or an unfortunate prostitute. I had a lot of time on my hands. The cops who ran the jail had little use for someone whose job was to release prisoners, and they scorned my attempts to fraternize.

Inevitably, I found myself at my desk in the corner of a small room with a pile of legal outlines in front of me and the bar exam breathing down my neck. After three years of law school, however, I was unable to motivate myself to study the rule against perpetuities, the 18 exceptions to the hearsay rule, or the ins and outs of the ex post facto clause. I started, at some point, simply to write descriptions of what I saw and heard at the jails. Those descriptions eventually coalesced into the beginnings of the story that would become this book.

This kind of literary doodling was a habit so deeply ingrained in me that I did it almost unconsciously. I composed my first poem when I was 8 years old. By the time I was 12 I was writing almost every day, releasing onto the page all the words I dared not say aloud about the discovery of my homosexuality. Poetry was the form of my first work because poetry is a coded language and it suited my purposes; I could convey my anguished teenage emotional state without specifying its cause.

I came out when I was 17, and I gradually accustomed myself to this mysterious difference that seemed to set me apart from most people. As I did, I doodled less in verse and more in prose, and I began to think maybe being homosexual was a subject worth writing about. By the time I began the jottings that became this book, I was 24, in a relationship (with a lovely man named Bill Weinberger, to whom this book is dedicated), and out to everyone who mattered to me. When I got serious about turning my notes into a novel, there was no question in my mind that the still-nameless narrator would be an openly gay man.

But why a mystery instead of the usual semiautobiographical first novel? This had to do with the time and my temperament. In the late '70s, the landscape of gay fiction, such as it was, was dominated by a group of New York writers whose books depicted the hermetic world of the homosexual demimonde of Manhattan. Although billed as "post-Stonewall" writers, they were, in fact, a generation older than those of us who actually came of age in the late '70s, and the attitudes and assumptions that prevailed in their novels were distinctly unliberated. There was precious little difference between the doomed queens in Andrew Holleran's 1978 *Dancer From the Dance* and the doomed hustler in John Rechy's 1963 *City of Night;* they were all equally self-loathing, sexually compulsive, and morally irresponsible.

I failed to recognize anything on the pages of Holleran's book, or the works of Edmund White or Larry Kramer, that bore the remotest resemblance to my life. I was gay, true, but I was also a third-generation Californian from a working-class Mexican-American family, upwardly mobile but morally serious; determined to make for myself a better place in the world than I had been born into but without compromising my ideals. I was not tormented about being homosexual, and I knew what I wanted from being gay—not erotic adventures but love, a partner, a shared life. I was looking for a way to live in the world, not a gay ghetto in which to hide away from it, and in this pursuit not one of the fashionable gay writers—ghetto dwellers to a man—was of any use to me.

I had stumbled across only one writer, Joseph Hansen, who had created a gay character who lived in the larger world with courage, if not ease. Beginning with 1970's *Fadeout,* Hansen had written a series of mysteries featuring an insurance investigator named David Brandstetter. Brandstetter was not only openly gay but calmly masculine, competent at his work, compassionate even toward those who reviled him, and a romantic. He was altogether an admirable hero, and his creator, Hansen, was a superlative writer who, as an added bonus, wrote about California with as deep a love for the place as I felt. Hansen's novels also showed me that the mystery could broach large questions of morality and justice and paint a broad canvas of contemporary life. I also thought that writing a mystery would help me overcome the great stumbling block of all first-time novelists: creating a plot. Writing *The Little Death*, I learned the rudiments of my craft in a way I might never have if I had tried to write a book closer to my actual life.

It took me four years to finish the book. By then Bill and I had moved to Los Angeles, where I worked as a prosecutor. Bits and pieces of that experience worked their way into the novel, and somewhere along the line my nameless narrator acquired a name, Henry Rios. I also found a writers' workshop run by a man named Paul Gillette, a marvelous teacher of great generosity and no pretensions who shepherded me through the final draft. The book was completed in August 1984. Thirteen publishers rejected it before Sasha Alyson enthusiastically accepted it. The book did well enough that Sasha asked for a sequel. I had never intended to start a series, but I was still interested in the character and the possibilities of crime fiction, so I obliged him with *Goldenboy* and thus became a full-fledged mystery writer.

My career as a mystery writer was inadvertent, but my association with Rios over the next 17 years proved to be one of my more enduring relationships. Quite without design, I ended up chronicling the life of a man not unrepresentative of my generation of gay men. In the process I may have also written a kind of spiritual autobiography.

Michael Nava
San Francisco
March 2001

The Linden Family Tree

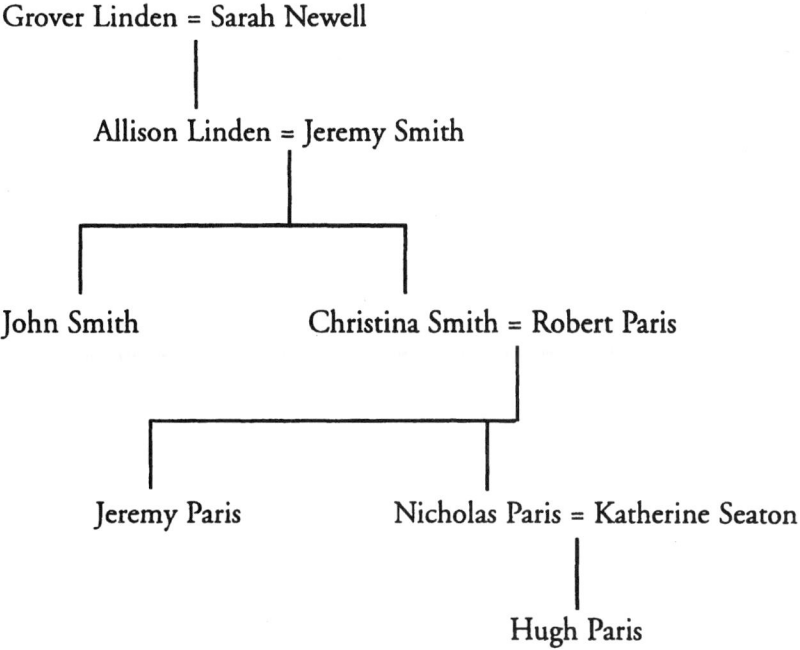

— 1 —

I stood in the sally port while the steel door rolled back with a clang and then I stepped through into the jail. A sign on the wall ordered the prisoners to proceed no further; more to the point, the word STOP was scrawled beneath the printed message. I stopped and looked up at the mirror above the sign where I saw a slender dark-haired man in a wrinkled seersucker suit, myself. As I adjusted the knot in my tie, a television camera recorded the gesture on a screen in the booking room.

It was six-thirty in the morning but the jail was as loud as if it had been six-thirty at night. The jail was built in the basement of the courthouse, and there were, of course, no windows, only the intense, white fluorescent lights that buzzed overhead. The jail was a place where people waited out their time and yet without day or night time stood still; only mealtimes and the change of guards communicated the passage of time to the inmates.

I moved out of the way of a trustie who raced by carrying trays of food. Breakfast that morning, the last day of July, was oatmeal, canned fruit cocktail, toast, milk and Sanka. Jones stepped into the hall from the kitchen and acknowledged me with an abrupt nod. He had done his hair up in cornrows and his apron was splattered with oatmeal. Jones cooked for the population. He was also a burglar and an informant and his one great fear was coming to trial and being sentenced to time at the state prison in Folsom. Several of his ex-associates were there, thanks to his help. I had just been granted a further continuance of his trial, delaying it for another sixty days. Our strategy was to string out his case as long as possible so that when he inevitably pled guilty he would be credited with the time he served in county jail and avoid Folsom altogether. The district attorney's office was cooperative; the least they owed him was county time — easy time, the prisoners called it. County was relatively uncrowded and the sheriffs relatively benign. On the other hand, county stank like every other jail I'd ever been in. The stink was a complex odor of ammonia, unwashed bodies, latrines, dirty linen and cigarette smoke compounded by bad ventilation and mingled with a sexual musk, a distinctive genital smell. The walls were faded green, grimy and scuffed. The floor, oddly enough, was spotless. The trusties mopped it at all hours of the day and night. Busy work, I suppose.

Everyone in the public defender's office avoided the jail rotation. If the law was a temple, it was built on human misery and jails were the cornerstones. I minded the jail less than most, finding it — psychologically, at least — not so much different from a courtroom. So much of crime and punishment consisted of merely waiting for something to happen, for a case to move. But it was different, the jail, from the plush law school classroom, just a few miles away, from which I graduated ten years earlier determined to do good, to be good. I achieved at least one of those things. I was a good lawyer, and most days that was enough. I was aware, however, that I took refuge in my profession, as unlikely as that seemed considering the amount of human suffering I dealt with. It offered me a role to escape into, from what I no longer knew; perhaps nothing more significant than my own little ration of suffering.

I went into my office, a small room tucked away at the end of a corridor and where it was almost possible to hear yourself think. I picked up a sheaf of papers, arrest reports and booking sheets, the night's haul. There was the usual array of vagrants and drunk drivers, a couple of burglaries, a trespass. One burglary, involving two men, was the most serious of the cases so I gave it special attention. The two suspects were seen breaking into a car in the parking lot of a Mexican restaurant on El Camino. The police recovered a trunkful of car stereos, wires still attached. The suspects were black men in their early twenties with just enough by way of rap sheets to appeal to a judge's hanging instinct. I gathered the papers together and went into the booking office.

"Good morning, Henry," Novack drawled, looking up from the sports page. He had a pale, pudgy face and a wispy little moustache above a mouth set in a perpetual smirk. Novack treated me with the same lazy contempt with which he treated all civilians, not holding the fact that I was a lawyer against me. This made us friends of a sort.

"Good morning, deputy," I replied.

"We had ourselves a little bit of excitement here last night," he said, folding his paper. "Los Altos brought in a drunk — that's what they thought he was, anyway — and it took three of us to subdue him."

"What was he on?"

"Well we took a couple of sherms off of him when we finally got him stripped and housed, so it was probably PCP."

"Why didn't I see an arrest report for him?"

"We couldn't book him until he came down enough to talk. Here's his papers."

I took the papers and asked, "Where's he at now?"

"In the drunk tank with the queens. He's a fag."

"That's no crime," I reminded him.

"Good thing, too, or we'd have to charge admission around here."

I read the report. The suspect's name was Hugh Paris. He stood five-foot ten, had blond hair and blue eyes. He refused to give an address or answer questions about his employment or his family. He had no criminal record. I studied his booking photo. His hair was in his face and his eyes went off in two different directions, but there was no denying he was an exceptionally handsome man.

"How do you know he's gay?" I asked.

"They picked him up outside of that fag bar in Cupertino," Novack said.

"He was arrested for being under the influence of PCP, possession of PCP, resisting arrest and battery on an officer. Geez, did the arresting officer go through the penal code at random?" Novack scowled at me. "Was anyone hurt?"

"Just scuff marks, counsel."

"Was he examined by a doctor to determine whether he was under the influence?"

"Nope."

"Did you ask him to submit to a urine test?"

"Nope."

"Then all you can really prove against him is drug possession."

"Well," Novack said, "I guess that's a matter of interpretation between you and the D.A. Are you going to want to see the guy?"

"I'll talk to him," I replied, "but first I'll want to interview these two," and I read him the names of the burglars.

☐

I interviewed the burglary suspects separately. They were bored but cooperative. They knew the system as well as I did. They had nothing by way of defense so the best I could do for them was try to plead them to something less serious than burglary. I'd observed that repeat offenders were the easiest to deal with, treating their lawyers with something akin to professional courtesy. All they wanted was a deal. It was only the first timers who bothered to tell you they were innocent. After the interviews ended, I walked back to the booking office and poured myself a cup of Novack's coffee. I flipped him a quarter and asked to see Hugh Paris.

They brought him in in handcuffs and a pair of jail blues so big that they fell from his shoulders and nearly covered his bare feet. His eyes were focused but he still looked disheveled. I thought, irrelevantly, of a picture of a saint I had seen as a boy, as he was being led off to his martyrdom. There was a glint of purity in Hugh Paris's eyes completely at odds with everything that was happening around him. The guard sat him down in the chair across from mine. I took out a legal pad and set it down on the table between us. I introduced myself as Henry Rios, from the public defender's office.

"A lawyer?" he asked, thickly.

"That's right," I said. "How do you feel, Mr. Paris?"

He gave me a puzzled look as if how he felt should be obvious, and asked, "Are the handcuffs necessary?"

"The sheriffs think so," I said, studying him. "Do you think you'd be all right without them?"

"I'm not going to hurt you."

I had decided he was down from whatever drug he had taken. I called in the deputy and asked him to remove the handcuffs. He resisted but, in the end, the handcuffs went. He stationed himself outside the door. I got up and closed it.

"Better?" I asked.

Paris smiled, revealing a set of even, white teeth. He rubbed his wrists and smoothed his hair, buttoned the top buttons of the jail jumpsuit and pulled himself up in the chair. He looked less dazed now, and he fixed me with a look of appraisal.

"Thank you," he said. "I feel terrible. Why am I here?"

"You were arrested," I replied, and read him the charges.

"Mr. Rios," he said, "I don't remember much about last night, but I do know that I didn't take any drugs."

"None?"

"I smoked a joint and then I went to this bar."

"What's the last thing you remember?"

"I was having a drink," he said, "and then I heard this horrible, rasping noise. It scared the hell out of me. And then I realized it was my own breathing. Then I went outside, I think, because I remember the lights. And then I woke up here. That's it."

"The police found a couple of sherms in your clothes," I said, testing him.

"What's a sherm?" he asked.

"Cigarettes dipped into PCP."

"I don't smoke," he replied, conversationally. It was possible he was telling the truth.

"Were you alone at the bar?"

"I came with an ex-boyfriend," he said, calmly, "but he left before any of this happened."

"You smoke the joint with him?"

"Yes."

"Did you know anyone else at the bar?"

"Not that I remember."

"How many drinks did you have?"

"Two or three. Not more than three."

"What's your friend's name?"

"I don't want him involved."

I had been taking notes. I put down my pen and leaned back into the chair. "There isn't anyone in this room but you and me," I began. "Anything you say to me is privileged. The resisting and battery charges won't stick and they have no evidence you were under the influence of PCP because they didn't bother to have you examined by a doctor. That just leaves the possession charge. If you were just holding it for someone, I might get the charge reduced or even dismissed."

"You don't believe me," he said.

"I have to argue evidence," I said, "and the evidence is, first, you were high on something last night and, second, the police found PCP on you. It shouldn't be hard to see what inference can be drawn from those two facts."

"I know what PCP is," he said, "but I've never used it and I've certainly never carried it on me."

"It could've been in the joint you smoked with your friend," I said. "Let me at least talk to him."

He shook his head. "I have to take care of this my own way."

"You have money to hire your own lawyer?"

"Money isn't the problem," he said, dismissing the thought with a shrug. He looked away from me and seemed to withdraw into himself. I could hear the deputy outside the door shouting at a trustie. Paris looked back at me without expression. The silence went on for a second too long. "You're gay," he said.

Still looking into his eyes, I said, "Yes, I am."

"I didn't think so at first."

"What gave me away?"

"You didn't react at all when I mentioned my boyfriend. You didn't even blink. Straight men always give themselves away."

I shrugged. "There probably isn't anything you could tell me about yourself or your boyfriend that would surprise me. So why not level with me about last night?"

"I have," he said, wearily. "Look, it was Paul's joint and

maybe it was laced with PCP. He could've given me the cigarettes. I just don't remember."

"Then let's call him and clear it up."

"I can't."

"Why?"

"I'm hiding," he said. "I shouldn't have called Paul in the first place. I can't risk seeing him again."

"Who are you hiding from?"

"I'm sorry," he said. "I can't tell you, although I'd like to."

"Then take my card," I said, digging one out from my wallet, "and call me when you want to talk."

He studied the card and said, "Thanks. I'd like to make a phone call."

"I'll take care of that," I said. I reached across the table to shake his hand. This we did very formally. Then the deputy knocked and I called him in to take the prisoner back to his cell.

☐

Outside it was a bright and balmy morning. A fresh, warm wind lifted the tops of the palm trees that lined the streets and sunlight glittered on the pavement. I put on my sunglasses and headed toward California Avenue where I was meeting my best friend, Aaron Gold, for breakfast. He had told me he had a business proposition to make. A couple of kids cycled by with day packs strapped to their shoulders. The Southern Pacific commuter, bound for San Francisco, rumbled by at the end of the street. I felt a flash of restlessness as it passed. Another summer passing. In two months I would be thirty-four.

"Henry," I heard Gold call. I looked up from where I'd stopped, in front of a pet store. He approached rapidly, his intelligent, simian face balled into a squint against the sunlight. He was tall, pale, a little thick around the waist, but he still carried himself like the college jock he'd been.

"Morning, Aaron."

"What were you thinking about?" he asked.

"Nothing really. Getting older."

He made a derisive little noise. "You're still a kid. Look at me, I'm pushing forty. Am I worried?"

"You're in your prime," I said, not altogether jokingly. In his tailored suit, Gold looked sleek and prosperous from his polished shoes and manicured nails to the fifty dollar haircut that tamed his curly, black hair.

"You never went to my tailor," he said, looking me over critically. "Come on, let's eat." He took me by the elbow and led me across the street into the restaurant where all the waitresses knew him by name. We found a table at the back, ordered breakfast and drank our first cups of coffee in silence.

Thirteen years earlier, Gold and I had been assigned as roommates in the law school dormitory our first year there. We had not liked each other much at first. He mistook my shyness for arrogance and I failed to see that his arrogance masked his shyness. Things sorted themselves out and we became friends. He was one of the first people I told I was gay. It would be an exaggeration to say he took it well, but we remained friends on the levels that counted most, respect and trust. Lately, he had even relaxed a little about my homosexuality — joking that I needed to meet a nice Jewish boy and settle down.

He was saying, "Did you run into anyone I know at the jail?"

"You don't go to county jail for SEC violations," I replied.

"Trading stock on insider information isn't the only criminal activity my clients engage in."

"Doubtless, but they wouldn't stoop to the services of a public defender."

"Actually," he said, "that brings me to the subject of this meeting, your future."

"It's secure as long as there's crime in the streets."

"There's crime in the boardrooms, too, Henry. My firm is interested in hiring an associate with a criminal law background. I've circulated your name. People are impressed."

"Why would your firm dirty its hands in criminal practice?"

Gold put his coffee cup down and said, "Corporations consist of people, some of whom are remarkably venal. Others still are just plain stupid. Anyway, they've come to us often enough needing a criminal defense lawyer to make it worth our while to hire one. We'd start you as a third-year associate, at sixty thousand a year."

I answered quickly, "Well, thanks for thinking of me, but I'm not interested."

Gold said, "Look, if it's the money, I know you deserve more, but that's just starting pay."

"You know it's not the money, Aaron," I said, reflecting that the sum he named was almost double my present wage.

He sighed and said, "Henry, don't tell me it's the principle." I said nothing. "You're wasting yourself in the public defender's office. You knock yourself out for some little creep and what you get in return is a shoebox of an office and less money than a first-year associate at my firm makes."

"So I should exchange it for a bigger office and more money and the opportunity to defend some rising young executive who gets busted for drunk driving?"

"Why not? Aren't the rich entitled to as decent a defense as the poor?"

"You never hear much public outcry over the quality of legal representation of the rich."

"What is it you want?" he asked, his voice rising. "The rosy warm glow that comes from doing good? You're not dealing with political prisoners, you're dealing with crooks and murderers."

"It's true they don't recruit criminals from country clubs, but if they're outsiders, so am I."

"Because you're gay," he said, flatly, dropping his voice. "If you're gay."

"That's settled."

"I won't argue the point now," he said, "but you let it run your life, closing doors for you. If you really were gay and accepted it, you would make your choices on other grounds than whether someone would object."

"I can think of plenty of reasons for not joining your firm," I replied, "none of them related to being gay."

"They aren't why you'll turn me down," he said.

I laid my fork aside and glanced out the window. It was luminous with summer light. Gold and I had a variation of this conversation nearly every time we talked. Since each of our positions was set in stone, the only thing our talking accomplished was to get us angry at each other.

"Every choice closes doors," I said, "and at some point you are left in the little room of yourself. I think most people who get to that room go crazy because they're surrounded with missed possibilities and no principle to explain or justify why they made the choices they did. I don't invite unhappiness, Aaron. Avoiding conflict may not be the noblest principle, but it works for me."

"Can you say you're happy?"

"No, can you?"

"No, but there are substitutes."

I didn't need to ask him what his substitutes were, I knew. Work was at the top of the list. In fact, work was the whole of his list. It had been mine, too, but recently I'd lost a big case and word had it I was burned out. Maybe I was, but if so, what was my alternative to work? I had never thought to cultivate any. The waitress came around and I offered her my cup for coffee, promising myself I would sit down later and think about the future, hoping it would creep up on me before I had the chance. I told Aaron about my jailhouse interviews.

"Hugh Paris," Gold said, "that name is familiar."

"Think he trades stock on insider information?"

"Maybe he's rich." I shook my head. "You'd be surprised," Gold continued, "at the number of the rich in our little town. They may not control their money, or know exactly where it comes from, but it dribbles in, from trusts, stocks, annuities."

"Whether or not he was rich," I said, "I wish he'd talked to me. He looked like he was carrying a secret he needed badly to unload."

"Another missed possibility?" Gold asked as he reached for the check. I let him take it.

☐

It was a little after eight when I got to my office on the fourth floor of the courthouse. There were already people waiting in the reception room, thumbing through the inevitable packets of official looking papers that criminal defendants seem to generate as they go through the system. The receptionist had not yet come in, so they stopped me as I walked through and I tried to answer their questions. Finally, I made it to the door that seperated us from our clients. I walked down the narrow corridor, made narrower by the presence of file cabinets, for which there was no other space, pushed against the walls. I passed my small, sunless office and headed toward the lounge.

Frances Kelly, the supervising attorney, sat at a table with the daily legal journal spread out in front of her. She let a cigarette burn between her fingers, lifting it to her lips just as the ash fell, dropping on the lapel of her jacket.

She looked up at me as I poured myself some coffee. "Did you know Roger Chaney?" she asked.

"Not well," I answered. "He left the office just as I was coming in."

"Excellent lawyer," she said. "He and I trained together, shared an office. He helped me prepare for my first trial."

"Is there something about him in the journal?" I asked, sitting across from her as she lit another cigarette.

"He's being arraigned today in federal court in San Francisco," she said, "on a conspiracy to distribute cocaine charge."

"Roger Chaney?" I asked, incredulously. "I thought you were going to tell me he'd been elevated to the bench."

"With Roger," she replied, "it could've gone either way."

"Are the charges true, then?"

"I know he had a very successful practice defending some big dealers, and he was making a lot of money, but that was never the lure of the law for him."

"No? Then what?"

She rose heavily, an elegant fat woman in a linen suit with black hair and beautiful, clear eyes, and ambled to the coffee urn. "He was an intellectual virtuoso," she said, "convinced he could talk circles around any other lawyer or judge, and he was right. But the courtroom isn't the real world."

"He thought he could get away with something?"

"We must presume him innocent," she said, piously, "but he had that kind of vanity." After a second she added, "So do you."

She headed for the door and motioned for me to follow. We went into her office, the only one with a window. Outside, a thin layer of smog rose in the direction of San Jose, but the view to the brown hills surrounding the university was clear as they rolled beyond the palm trees and red tile roofs.

Frances was saying, "I sometimes think really brilliant people shouldn't be permitted to practice law. They get bored too easily and cause trouble."

"Are you about to pass along some advice?"

She laughed. "I just wanted to know how you are, Henry. You've been with us three months and we haven't had much chance to talk." She referred to my forced transfer from the main office in San Jose to this branch office. The topic of conversation, my mental health, now came into focus as sharply as the yellow rose in the vase at the edge of Frances' desk. I was annoyed by both.

"Considering that my transfer was against my will, I'm fine."

"I had nothing to do with the transfer," she said. "You're not being put out to pasture, just given a rest after your last trial."

"Which I lost," I said. "That was the real reason I got kicked down from felony trials to arraignments."

"The jury convicted him," she said, "and no one faults your work which, considering the circumstances, was excellent." I didn't know whether by circumstances she referred to the fact that only a few I.Q. points separated my client from a vegetable or the fact that he used an axe handle to bludgeon his elderly parents to death. A series of coroner's photographs passed through my mind. Pained by the recollection, I touched my fingers to my forehead. She caught the gesture and tactfully looked away.

"The circumstances were of no interest to the jury," I said. "They sent him to Death Row."

"That's on appeal."

"And I was farmed out here, to rusticate."

"You object to my company?" She expelled a gust of cigarette smoke that passed through the sunlight like a cloud.

"But seriously," I replied.

"To rest," she said, "from the pressures of trial court. I could see the burn-out on your face when you first got here."

"Send me back," I said. "I've done nothing but interview clients for other lawyers and sit in arraignment court haggling with the D.A. over public nuisance cases."

"Whether you go back is not my call."

"Whether?" I demanded. "Not when? Call San Jose and tell them that I didn't crack up, after all. Tell them I'm burned out from the other end. I mean, you all think I'm demoralized or exhausted from my work, but I'm not. It's the rest of my life I'm burned out on. This job keeps me going." I heard the tremor in my voice so I cut myself short.

"I'm not proposing to take your job away," she replied. "Everyone in the office knows you're one of the best lawyers we have." She put out her cigarette in an onyx ashtray and lit another. "The office has just hired a dozen new lawyers, most fresh out of law school. They're looking for someone to train them. The job is yours if you want it."

"That's the second-best offer I've had this morning," I said. She looked puzzled. "It's nothing. I don't see myself as a teacher."

"You have so much to pass along."

"I'm thirty-three, Frances, not sixty-three. I'm not ready to sit on the veranda and tell war stories."

"Think about it," she said. She noticed me looking at the rose and she plucked it from the vase and handed it to me.

"And if I don't take the job, my exile continues."

"The rose is from my garden," she replied.

"My favorite flower," I said, standing.

□

In my office, I dropped the rose into the trash can and sat down. There was a pile of cases to be reviewed before I went down to arraignment court that afternoon. There was also a list of clients to be interviewed and advised, and cases to be assigned to other lawyers. I opened the first file and thought, immediately, of Hugh Paris sitting in his cell downstairs. And here, I told myself, I sit in my cell upstairs. I dismissed the thought as self-pity compounded with a pang of lust. But the little room was too warm, suddenly, and I could not concentrate on the papers before me.

I got up and went into the bathroom where I washed my face in cold water. Looking at the mirror, I studied that face carefully. I pressed my fingers, lightly, at the corners of my eyes, smoothing out the wrinkles and I looked, almost, twenty-five again. I could quit and start over, I told the reflection in the mirror. My eyes answered, start what over? What is there?

Another lawyer came in, and I turned from the mirror, said hello to him and went back to my office.

The morning dragged on as I shuffled files from one side of my desk to the other. Outside my office, I heard the babble of voices as the other lawyers interviewed clients and witnesses or hurried off to court shouting last minute questions about a legal issue or a particular judge's temperment. I felt the excitement but did not share it.

There comes a point in the career of every criminal defense lawyer when he realizes that what keeps him in practice are his prejudices not his principles. Suspicion of authority and contempt for the platitudes with which injustice too often cloaks itself can take you a long way but, ultimately, they are no substitute for the simple faith that what you are doing is right. It came to me, as I sat there buried in papers, that I had lost that faith.

I left a message with Frances's secretary that I wanted to see her after lunch, then went off to a nearby bar and had a couple of drinks. As I sat on the barstool cracking peanuts and sipping my bourbon, my thoughts veered back to Hugh Paris.

It was nothing as trivial as lust. Seeing him had precipitated this crisis because I had not been able to help him, though I wanted to. And, after all, what did my help amount to? Getting someone less time in jail than otherwise or even getting him off were often temporary respites in long-term downward slides. That was the extent of the assistance I could offer — dispensing placebos to the terminally ill.

Frances was in her office when I knocked at the door. She beckoned me in and I sat down, swallowing the mint I'd been chewing to mask the bourbon on my breath. It was important that she not know I had been drinking.

"Frances, I've made a decision."

"You'll teach the class?"

"No." I gripped my hands together in my lap. "I'm quitting."

"What?" She stared at me.

"I called San Jose and told them. I wanted to tell you, too. I wanted to thank you for your many kindnesses—" I stopped. The air between us buzzed with inarticulate feeling.

"Henry, you can't mean this. Take a few days off, a few weeks if you want. Travel."

I shook my head. "I hate traveling. I have no hobbies. I'm thirty-three years old and all I know about life is what I learned in law school or the inside of a courtroom. And it's pathetically little, Frances." She reached for a cigarette. "I know I'm a little old for it, but I believe I'm having an identity crisis."

"That's no reason to quit your job," she replied.

"This is more than my job, it's my life. And it's not enough." I rose. "Do you understand?"

"No. Do you?"

"Not very clearly." I sat down again. "I met a man in the jail this morning, an inmate. I wanted to help him, to offer him some kind of comfort, something human. But all I knew how to do was deliver speeches."

"We offer people what no one else can give them," Frances said, "a possible way out of their trouble. Is that so insignificant?"

"Of course not, when it works. But so often it doesn't, and anyway," I laid my hands on her desk, "what does that give me?"

She sighed. "Well that's the key, isn't it? If you've reached the point of asking that question then whatever you're getting from it is obviously not enough."

"Wish me luck."

"No," she said. "I'll wish you'll change your mind."

"I won't."

"All right," she said, "then good luck."

I went back to my office and cleaned out my desk. Some of the other lawyers drifted in, stood around nervously, said a few well-intended words. By three o'clock I'd done nearly everything I needed to do to extricate myself from my job. Just before I left I called down to the jail. Hugh Paris had been bailed out by someone who signed the bail receipt as John Smith. I gathered up the last of my papers and left.

– 2 –

I was awake the second I heard the movement in the shrubs outside the bedroom window. I glanced at the clock on the bedstand; it was a little after three a.m. The soft but distinctive shuffle of footsteps echoed outside and then I heard a quick rap at the front door. I got out of bed, pulled on a pair of pants and went into the living room. I stood near the door and listened. The last time I had been awakened at that hour was by a disgruntled, drunken client who wanted to break my legs. He might have, too, had he not passed out while we were talking.

There was another knock, louder and more urgent. I peered through the peephole. Hugh Paris stood shivering in the dark. He wore a pair of jeans and a gray polo shirt. I was startled to see him but not surprised. In the two weeks since I'd seen him at the jail, I'd thought of him often, the way one thinks of unfinished business. The thought of him nagged at the back of my mind for a lot of reasons, not the least of which was his beautiful, calm face. One could ascribe any kind of character, from priest to libertine, to his remote and handsome face. A breeze blew his hair across his forehead. He touched his knuckles to the door and rapped harder. I opened it enough for him to see me.

"Don't turn on any lights," he said. "I think I was followed."

"Come in." I opened the door a little wider and he slipped through. I ordered him to stand still and patted him down for weapons. He wasn't even carrying a wallet. "All right," I said. "Come over to my desk. I have a reading lamp that will give us enough light without attracting attention." He followed me and sat down. I touched the light switch and his face leapt forward from the darkness like a flame.

He said, "I could use a drink."

"First tell me how you got my address."

"I called your office yesterday, and when they told me you quit I convinced the receptionist that we'd gone to college together and I was passing through town and wanted to surprise you." He shivered I went over to the kitchen counter and brought back a bottle of Jack Daniels and two glasses. As he drank, I noticed for the first time that he was about my age — not younger, as I'd remembered. The skin beneath his eyes was pouched with fatigue, as though he had awakened from a long sleep. He set his empty glass on the desk, and I moved the bottle toward him. The liquor brought the color back to his face.

"When someone comes to visit me at this hour, I assume it's not just to chat," I said.

"I need a place to stay tonight."

"And you don't have any better friends?" He poured himself another drink. I caught the glint of his watch. It was very thin and elegant, mounted on a black leather strap. I had seen watches like that before. They went along with trust funds, prep schools and names ending with Roman numerals.

Hugh was saying something. I asked, "What?"

"You asked me if I had any better friends and I said no. I came down from the city."

"And you were followed? By whom?"

"It's a long story," he said, and, as if as an afterthought he added, "I only need the bed for the night." His inflection was sexual and I thought about it for a second before responding.

"As flattering as it is, I can't believe you came here to proposition me," I said, "which is not to say that couldn't be part of the deal. But why don't you tell me what you really want."

He smiled, charmingly, ruefully. "All right, Henry. I may not look like it but I come from money. Old and famous money. A lot of it has been spent to keep me out of San Francisco."

"Why?"

"My grandfather controls the money, and he hates me."

"Because you're gay?"

"That probably has something to do with it," he said, lightly. "There have been other problems through the years."

"Drugs?" I guessed, remembering the circumstances of his arrest.

"You've seen hypes before?" I nodded. He held his right arm out beneath the dim yellow light. I saw bluish bruises clustered at intervals up and down his vein. They were faint and there were no recent marks or scabs.

"You stopped using?"

"Six months ago. I told my grandfather. He was not impressed."

"Who is he?"

"Robert Paris," he said, as if each syllable was significant.

I thought for a second the name meant something to me but recognition faded as quickly as it came.

"The name is not familiar."

"No? It doesn't mean anything to most people but I thought you might recognize it." I shook my head and he shrugged. "I think he had me followed tonight."

"Why? If he hates you, why should he concern himself with your whereabouts?"

"Money. I have certain rights to the family fortune," he said, lifting his glass. "My grandfather would like to extinguish them."

"You mean with some legal action?"

"No," he replied, softly, "I mean murder." He drained his glass. I knew at once that he believed what he was saying, but I did not believe it. From my experience, I did not believe in premeditated murder any more than an agnostic believes in God and for the same reason; there never was any proof. Whether a killing occurs in an instant or years after some remembered slight, no killer is ever in his right mind when he kills. For me, that ruled out premeditation.

"You're exaggerating," I said.

"No. He's killed before." He smiled, bleakly. "I'm not making this up. You don't know my grandfather."

"Rich people don't go around planning to kill each other. They use lawyers, instead."

Hugh laughed and said, "Not someone who thinks he's above the law. Henry, I don't mean he's going to kill me himself or hire someone to shoot me in broad daylight. I'm sure it would be arranged to look like an accident or a suicide."

I shook my head. "That's unbelievable. I've known murderers. I've represented them and one or two I even got off. The perfect passionless murder does not exist. Killing is a sloppy business."

"Have any of your murderers been rich?" I told him no. He continued, "I didn't think so. Money buys a lot of insulation and silence. My grandfather could have us both killed and no one would ever suspect him." He poured himself another drink and said, "I see by your face you don't believe me."

"I believe that you think you're in danger. I'm not sure what you want from me."

"You heard me out," he said. "That's all I wanted. And a bed. Wasn't that the deal?"

"I guess so," I said, aware, suddenly, of the nearness of his body and the noise of his breathing and the darkness of the room around us. We rose, wordlessly, and went into the bedroom.

◻

I woke up alone and lay back, watching the shadow of the tree outside the window sway across the wall. The only noises were the clock ticking and the wind. The sheets and blankets were kicked back and over the foot of the bed. A wadded up towel lay crumpled on the floor among Hugh's scattered clothes. The detritus of passion. I sat myself up against the wall and studied my nakedness impassively. I kept myself in shape out of habit and thought about my body only when it was sick, hurt, or hungry.

Once as an adolescent and twice as an adult, I had been in love, the last time having been four years earlier. Except for those times, sex was largely a matter of one-night stands. It wasn't the best arrangement, but, I told myself, it was all that I had time for. Now that my career had come to an abrupt halt, there was a lot of time, more time than I'd ever had as an adult. Enough time to go crazy, or fall in love again. I got out of bed and dressed.

Stepping into the living room I saw him, wearing an old blue robe of mine, pacing the patio. From where I stood, he looked like a figure projected on a screen, luminous, distant and larger than life. He seemed to me at that moment the sum of every missed opportunity in my life. I let the feeling pass. He saw me, smiled, drew open the door and came into the room.

"You're finally awake."

"Yes, I like watching you. Hungry?"

"No, but how about some coffee?" I told him I would brew a pot. "I guess I should get dressed." He disappeared into the bedroom emerging a few minutes later pulling on his shirt.

I handed him a mug of coffee and said, "Let's go back outside." We stepped out on the patio to a brilliant day. The smells of the potted plants hung in the air, musky and carnal. "What are you going to do?"

"Go back to the city."

"And your grandfather?"

"He'll find me when he wants to." He sipped his coffee. "And you?"

"I've decided to set up my own practice and there's a lot to be done to get ready."

He nodded as if I'd said something significant. The air between us was thick with unspoken words. I reached over and touched his arm briefly. He smiled.

"Did you always want to be a lawyer?"

"No, I drifted into it from graduate school. I wanted to change the world and law offered more opportunities than history."

"Did you know you were gay when you started law school?"

"I've always known."

"It doesn't seem to be a problem with you."

"Is it with you?"

"No one ever prepared me for it," he said, "or the experience of feeling different even though you don't appear different to other people."

I nodded. The sexual aspect of homosexuality was, in many ways, the least of it. The tough part was being truthful without painting yourself into a corner: I am different, but not as different as you think.

Aloud, I said, "It's schizophrenic, isn't it?" At once Hugh's face changed. The placid blond handsomeness dissolved and was replaced by anger.

"Don't use that word around me. You don't have any idea of what schizophrenia is like."

"I just meant—"

"That it's an identity crisis? It's the end of identity. It's death."

Startled by his outburst, I mumbled an apology. The fierceness went out of his eyes but not the distance. The intimacy between us was shattered and I could not think of any words to call him back.

"I'm all right, just sort of keyed up, I guess. I should be going now."

"I'm really sorry, Hugh," I said, again.

"You couldn't've known," he said, more to himself than me. "I'd like to see you again. I'll call."

"Sure. I'd like that." We stood facing each other, but it seemed absurd to shake hands, so we just smiled, like two strangers who had collided by accident.

□

A week after Hugh's nocturnal visit, I met Aaron Gold for drinks at a bar on University Avenue called Barney's to talk about my future, again. Gold had been in solo practice in San Francisco for a couple of years before joining his current firm, and I relied on him for advice on setting up on my own. His years as an associate with a rich, prestigious firm had not eradicated his memories of the privations of his first practice.

Gold liked advising me. It allowed him to relive his days on his own when he expected to build a powerful firm from his own ambition and drive. In the end, he decided the world was insufficiently impressed and he signed on with a firm in town. A good firm, the best in the area and successful enough to have branch offices, but, after all, not a New York firm or even one in San Francisco.

His choice puzzled me. As an editor of law review, Gold could have written his ticket anywhere in the country, but he stayed in our backwater university town far from the centers of the power and influence he'd once set out to dazzle. And he had become a real company man, absolutely dedicated to the firm and annoyingly secretive about his work.

We were getting along pretty well, Gold and I, I thought as I stepped into the bar from the muggy August afternoon. However, some aspects of my life remained a problem for him as I discovered again when I brought up the subject of Hugh Paris.

"You went to bed with a client?" he asked incredulously as the startled cocktail waitress brought our drinks.

"He's not a client," I said after she'd gone. "I didn't take his case."

"It's the appearance of impropriety you should be concerned about."

"Look, I haven't exactly advertised the news. I was just telling you."

He set his drink down and asked, "Why?"

"You asked what was new with me. I told you."

"Some things you can omit."

"Listen, Aaron, I get to thrill to your accounts of your latest girlfriend, but you treat me like a eunuch. You confide in me, but I can't confide in you? Are we friends, or what?"

He rubbed his forehead and sighed, dramatically. "Yes, we're friends. It's just that — well, in addition to the fact that you're gay — this Paris guy sounds like trouble. You should marry or something."

"Hugh's all right," I said, defensively, and added, "and as for marriage, you're nearly six years older than me and not married."

"That's different. I got into law late and I have to make up for lost time if I want to make partner before I'm forty. Then I'll marry. A man can marry at any time."

"If it makes you that uncomfortable for me to talk about being gay, I'll stop talking about it."

He waved his hand as though waving away a fly. "It's part of your life. It's just difficult. Give me time."

"I told you ten years ago."

"What, in law school? Everyone was something in law school. Marxists, feminists, homosexuals — I was a socialist. It was all theory, then. It didn't mean anything. I never thought you were serious. Let's have another drink." He summoned the waitress.

"Did we sell out?"

"Sell out what?" He lifted an eyebrow. "What did we have to sell? Nothing. We had nothing. It's now that we all have something to sell, and to lose." He raised his glass and touched it against mine in an ironic toast.

□

For the next two days, I reviewed my options. Setting up practice in San Francisco was out of the question because of the expense and the fact that there were too many criminal defense lawyers there already, scrambling for a living. When I'd been transferred out of the Public Defender's office in San Jose, I had burned too many bridges to find my way back. So, for the time being, I decided to stay where I was.

I rented a suite in an office building within walking distance of the courthouse. I bought a desk, installed a phone, and had a nameplate nailed to the door. My business cards were in the process of being printed. All I needed were clients. Since my practice had centered in San Jose, I had very little local reputation and knew I would have to rely, initially, on appointments to criminal cases from which the public defenders disqualified themselves. I had already decided that I did not want a civil law practice.

Appointments represented a steady source of income. Lawyers were appointed from a list maintained by the judges; one applied to be placed on the list. Appointments were sought after and placement on the lists was dictated by political considerations, which, in the world of a small town, meant appeasing those in a position to make life difficult for you. For the judges that meant the D.A. and the public defenders who not only belonged to the same union, but, between them, handled virtually all the criminal matters. The judges were unlikely to appoint any lawyer who had antagonized one or the other office. Therefore, I found it necessary to go make my peace with my ex-employer. I had set up an appointment to see Frances Kelly, to ask her pardon and to get her as a reference.

I climbed the five flights of stairs to the public defender's office in the courthouse. By the time I got there I was sweaty from exertion and nervousness. The reception room was almost empty as I stepped up to the counter and gave my name. The receptionist was new. It had been a little less than a month since I'd quit but it seemed like a year, chiefly because nothing had changed. Even the calendar on the wall was still turned to July. A couple of my ex-colleagues passed through on their way to court. They saw me but said nothing. Omerta, I thought — apparently, I had become a nonperson.

Fifteen minutes later, Frances's secretary appeared and led me to her office, never once acknowledging that she knew me. I wondered if I would get the same reception from Frances. I knocked at her door and entered on her command.

She greeted me with friendly curiosity, rising slightly from behind her desk, extending a braceleted hand. "You look well," she said.

"Thanks. So do you." And, in fact, she looked as sleek and opulent as ever, carrying her avoirdupois like a summer parasol. We exchanged civilities and a little office gossip and then, mentally clearing my throat, I shifted subjects. "I have a favor to ask." She smiled. "But first I want to apologize for the abruptness of my departure."

"You're forgiven," she said.

"I'm going to open my own practice."

"Congratulations," she murmured.

"I don't have any clients yet. I plan to apply to the appointments' list."

"That's wise." I grimaced, mentally. This was like pulling teeth.

"I know the politics of the courthouse," I said. "The presiding judge will know my name immediately, probably remember hearing that I quit, and call you for your opinion."

"And you want to know what I'll tell him."

"No," I said. "I'd like you to recommend me."

She smiled. "I see. Well, your old spirit seems to be returning." She lit a cigarette. "Do you need the money?"

"What?"

"Do you need the money, or do you just want to go back to work?"

"It's not the money," I said. I knew I could live for a year on my savings. "I want the work. I'm good at it."

"Yes, of course, but I'm confused. A month ago you left the office saying you needed time to think over your life."

"I've thought about it."

"And all that led to is concluding that you want to go back to doing the same thing you just left? Has anything really changed?" The question was rhetorical. She went on, "I would tell the presiding judge that you're a brilliant lawyer but a troubled man. I would tell him that if I was a defendant I would gladly entrust you with my case but if I was a judge I would be concerned about saddling a client with a potentially sick lawyer."

"Those are hard words, Frances," I said.

"You could try a case with no preparation and do a better job than another lawyer with unlimited time to prepare, but that's not the point. Frankly, I think you would be tempted to wing it because your heart's not in it anymore."

"You're wrong," I said. "I have never walked into a courtroom unprepared."

She pointed to a stack of files sitting on top of a bookcase. "Your last cases," she said. "Nothing had been done on them."

"I carried them in my head."

"That's the problem, Henry. You're carrying too much in your head."

I stood up. "I can't change your mind?"

"Take all the time you need," she said, "and then come back to me. Not only would I recommend you to the list, I'd help you come back to the office if you wanted."

"How am I supposed to know how much time is enough?"

"You'll know," she said, as though making a promise to a child.

☐

I sat at my desk watching the sun set from my new office. The air was dense with a buttery light; the golden hour we used to call it at school. I could see the ubiquitous red tile roofs of the university. The undergrads would not be arriving for another month, but the law school would start up again in a week or two. When I had graduated from there, ten years earlier, it seemed my life was a settled thing. I would rise in the public defender's office, do important political work, and there would be a judgeship at the end, perhaps. I started out with all the right credentials, but somewhere along the line the ambiguities of my profession bogged me down. Truth and falsehood, guilt and innocence, law and equity — this was the stuff of my daily bread. Just as I came to see that there were few clear answers in the law, I also saw there were even fewer such answers in my life.

Frances was right. I wasn't ready to step back into the swamp. I wasn't, but I couldn't think of anything else to do with my life. I opened the side drawer and pulled out a bottle of bourbon and a glass. I kept the sunset company a little longer.

□

It was late when I stumbled in and the red light on my phone machine blinked a welcome. I navigated my way to it and played the messages. There were two of them, both from Hugh, a couple of hours apart. The first was brief, tentative, a greeting. The second asked me to meet him in the city the next day, at a bar in the Castro. I erased the messages, took off my shoes, stretched out on the couch and fell into a sodden sleep.

When I awoke it was light out but the room was shadowy. I inhaled the fumes of last night's liquor and sat myself up. My body ached and my head felt as if someone was tightening a wire around my temples. I got myself into the bathroom and swallowed some aspirin. I went into the bedroom and changed into my running clothes. Outside, I forced myself to stretch and set off toward the university.

The first mile was torture. I passed beneath the massive stone arch at the entrance to the school, pulled off the road and threw up. I felt better and ran down the long palm-lined drive to the Old Quad. Lost somewhere in the thicket to my left was the mausoleum containing the remains of the family by whom the university had been founded. Directly ahead of me loomed a cluster of stone buildings, the Old Quad.

I stumbled up the steps and beneath an archway into a dusty courtyard which, with its clumps of spindly bushes and cacti, resembled the garden of a desert monastery. All around me the turrets and dingy stone walls radiated an ominous silence, as if behind each window there stood a soldier with a musket waiting to repel any invader. I looked up at the glittering facade of the chapel across which there was a mosaic depicting a blond Jesus and four angels representing Hope, Faith, Charity, and, for architectural rather than scriptural symmetry, Love. In its gloomy magnificence, the Old Quad never failed to remind me of the presidential palace of a banana republic.

Passing out of the quad I cut in front of the engineering school and headed for a back road that led up to the foothills. There was a radar installation at the summit of one of the hills called by the students the Dish. It sat among herds of cattle and the ruins of stables. It, too, was a ruin, shut down for many years, but when the wind whistled through it, the radar produced a strange trilling that could well be music from another planet.

The radar was silent as I slowed to a stop at the top of the Dish and caught my breath from the upward climb. I was soaked with sweat, and my headache was gone, replaced by giddy disorientation. It was a clear, hot morning. Looking north and west I saw the white buildings, bridges and spires of the city of San Francisco beneath a crayoned blue sky.

The city from this aspect appeared guileless and serene. Yet, when I walked in its streets what I noticed most was how the light seldom fell directly, but from angles, darkening the corners of things. You would look up at the eaves of a house expecting to see a gargoyle rather than the intricate but innocent woodwork. The city had this shadowy presence as if it was a living thing with secrets and memories. Its temperament was too much like my own for me to feel safe or comfortable there.

I looked briefly to the south where San Jose sprawled beneath a polluted sky, ugly and raw but without secrets or deceit. Then I stretched and began the slow descent back into town.

When I got to San Francisco that afternoon, it was one of those days that arrives at the end of summer just as the last tourists are leaving complaining about the cold and fog. The sky was cloudless. I parked my car on 19th and headed down into the Castro.

The sidewalks were jammed and the crowds drifted slowly past bars from which disco music blared and where men sat on barstools looking out the windows. The air smelled of beer and sweat and amyl nitrate. At bus benches and on strips of grass in front of buildings, men sat, stripped of their shirts, sunbathing and watching the flow of pedestrians through mirrored sunglasses. Approaching the bar where I was meeting Hugh, I smelled marijuana, turned my head and saw a couple of kids sharing a joint as they manned a voter registration table for one of the gay political clubs. I stepped into the bar expecting to find more of the carnival but it was nearly empty. The solitary bartender wiped the counter pensively.

I ordered a gin-and-tonic and took it to a table at the back of the room. Plants hung from the ceiling in big ceramic pots and the lighting was so dim that the atmosphere was nocturnal. Here and there in the darkness I saw a glint of polished brass or a mirror. Suspended from the center of the room was a large fan turning almost imperceptibly in the stale air. It was a place for boozy meditation — emotion recollected in alcohol, as someone once told me in another bar — and I was in a contemplative mood. For the first time in my adult life, I could not see any farther into the future than the door through which Hugh now entered.

I watched him step from the brightly-lit doorway into the dimness of the room, weaving slowly between tables as he approached me. He came up to the table, mumbled a greeting and sat down. He'd had some sun since I'd seen him last. His skin was now the color of dried roses, and his hair was a lighter blond than before but just as disheveled. I restrained an impulse to touch him. He leaned back into his chair, into the shadows. The bartender drifted over and stood in front of us a moment before taking Hugh's order. Hugh looked up, ordered mineral water, and turned away, missing the bartender's bright, yearning smile.

"I didn't actually think you'd come," he said in a low, slow voice.

"You could've called sooner. It's been a couple of weeks."

"Too risky," he said, vaguely, as the bartender set a bottle of Perrier before him. "I have to limit my contacts with outside people."

"Still in hiding?"

"You still don't believe me?"

"I don't think anyone's trying to kill you. Something else has got you scared."

"Junkies are fearless," he replied. He reached out to pour from his bottle into his glass, but his hand shook so violently that he spilled the water on the table. He very slowly set the bottle down. Then, swiftly, everything fell into place for me.

I reached across the table and pulled him forward into the light. He did not resist. His skin was feverish to the touch. His pupils were tightly balled up and too bright. I laid his right arm on the table and spotted the mark almost immediately, a reddish pinprick directly above the vein a few inches above his wrist.

"When did you shoot up?"

"Not long ago," he said, licking his lips.

"You told me you were clean."

"I was. I ran into a friend."

"When?"

"I don't remember. Last week? After I saw you."

"Why didn't you call me?"

"I thought I could handle it. I can't. I need help." The princely face was covered with a film of sweat and its muscles sagged as though they were being pulled downward.

"I didn't come here to babysit a hype," I said, standing.

He reached out and grabbed my arm. He opened his mouth but nothing came out. I saw slow motion panic spread across his face. I stood above him for what seemed like a long time. Then, slowly, I eased back down into the chair beside him.

— 3 —

Outside it was dusk. I turned from the window back to the room, fumbling for a light switch. I pushed a button and three lights flickered on, unsteadily, from a brass fixture in the center of the room. Hugh was asleep in the bedroom at the end of the long, narrow entrance corridor. The toilet gurgled from the bathroom where I'd poured out his vomit and flushed it away.

From my law practice I knew that a heroin addict could stay clean long enough to clear his body of the addiction. If he began to use again it took him awhile to become readdicted. Some addicts used casually — chipping, they called it — but sooner or later their habit caught up with them. Hugh was in the first stage of readdiction. His body, recognizing the opiate for what it was — poison — struggled to reject it, making him sick. If he continued using, the sickness would stop and the body would make its lethal adjustments. That he was sick was encouraging because it meant there was still time to prevent his readdiction.

Not that I knew how to prevent it. I poured myself a drink from the bottle of brandy I'd found in the kitchen. When a hype came to me, it wasn't for medical advice or psychological counseling, but simply to stay out of jail. If I did that much for one of them, got him into a hospital or a drug program, then I considered myself successful. As to why someone became addicted or how he rid himself of the habit, those things remained mysteries to me. The only thing I was pretty sure about was that when dealing with an addict, the fact of addiction was more important than the drug. Thinking about Hugh I wished, for his sake, that I knew more.

I wandered aimlessly across the big, bare room. The house had the dank, decaying smell of so many Victorian houses, as if the walls were stuffed with wet newspaper. Hugh's house, only a couple of blocks from Castro, was in a neighborhood undergoing renovation; many of the neighboring houses looked freshly painted or were in the process of reconstruction or were for sale. His house was untouched by this activity. Strips of paint peeled from the banister of the stairs leading up to the porch. Inside, the rooms were painted white, badly, in some spots barely covering the last application of gaudy wallpaper. The wooden floors were scarred and dirty. From the kitchen, the refrigerator shrieked and buzzed, then subsided to a low whine. It wasn't the house of an heir.

Yet there were incongruous, aristocratic touches. There were dazzlingly white sheets on his bed and freshly laundered towels piled in the bathroom. The few pieces of furniture scattered around the house were of obvious quality. The brandy I was drinking was Courvoisier VSOP, and the glass from which I drank it appeared to be crystal.

I found myself at the bookshelves which held a couple of dozen books. Many of them were worn-out paperbacks, Tolkien, Herman Hesse, a volume of Ginsberg — the library of a college sophomore of the sixties. I opened the Ginsberg. Written on the flyleaf were Hugh's name, the year 1971, and the words New Haven. Inspecting the second shelf, I saw the books were poetry, mostly, and by people I'd never heard of. The spine of one volume was cracked and when I opened it a sheaf of pages fell out, fluttering to the floor. I knelt down to pick them up and saw, on the bottom shelf, a framed photograph laid face down. I picked it up with the pages, put the book back together and turned the picture over.

It was the portrait of a woman, a lady, I thought. She may have been as young as fifty. It was hard to tell from the black and white photo whether her hair was white or an ashy shade of blond. Light and darkness had been tactfully deployed on the plain background behind her. The obvious effect was timelessness and the apparent reason was the woman's age. Still, there was an elegance in her angular, handsome face quite apart from the photographer's craft, and a kind of luster in the brightness of her hair and eyes. I thought she must have once been beautiful.

"My mother," a voice commented behind me. I nearly dropped the picture in surprise and turned to find Hugh standing at the edge of the room, just outside the light. He stepped forward, white-faced, his eyes exhausted. "Sorry. I didn't mean to come up on you like that." He held out his hand for the photo and I gave it to him. He studied it a moment then returned it. I laid it back on the bookshelf.

"Nice picture," I said. "Looks professional."

"The official portrait," he said, with a trace of contempt in his voice. "It appears on all the dustjackets."

"She writes?"

He nodded, seating himself on a corner of the couch, drawing a thick sweater across his bare chest. I noticed for the first time, watching him, that the room was cold. "What has she written?"

"Poetry, mostly."

"I didn't notice any of her books on your shelves."

"I don't have any."

"You're not close to her?"

"I haven't seen her in years."

"Does she live in San Francisco?"

"No, in the east. Boston, I think."

"With your father?"

He hesitated a second before saying, "He's dead."

I heard his hesitation with a lawyer's ear and something about it was not quite right, so I asked, "Are you sure?"

"Don't cross-examine me." He shivered and reached to the table for the brandy, swigging it directly from the bottle. Then he put it down and ran a hand through his already disheveled hair. He looked fragile and unhappy.

"I'll make you some coffee," I said, still standing by the books, "if you'll tell me where it is."

"Blue canister in the refrigerator," he said, shivering again.

When I returned to the living room he was standing at the window, which was now black with night, facing himself — a ghostly reflection. I set the mugs of coffee down and went over.

"Something out there?"

"A car passed by, slowly, without its lights on."

"Has that happened before?"

"No," he said, "and maybe it wasn't meant for me." I made a noise in the back of my throat. "You still don't believe that I'm in danger of being killed."

"You're doing a pretty effective job of killing yourself." He turned away, abruptly, went to the table and picked up a cup of coffee.

"I'm sorry about today."

"Do you want to talk about it?"

"I was bored and lonely."

"Some would call that the human condition."

He laughed mirthlessly. "My coping mechanism is easily overwhelmed."

"That sounds like a diagnosis."

"My last analyst," he replied, carelessly, "who also told me that intimacy is difficult for me."

"I hadn't noticed."

"Sex is not the same thing."

"I see. Thank you for setting me straight."

"Wait," he said. "Let's start over. I asked you to come up because I wanted to see you again, not to score points against you."

"All right," I said, crossing over to the couch and sitting down beside him. I lay my hand, tentatively, on his. "Tell me what happened between last weekend and today."

He looked at me intently through cloudy blue eyes, then said, "Have you ever heard of a poet named Cavafy?" I told him no. "A Greek poet. Gay, in fact. He wrote a poem about a young dissolute man who tires of his life and resolves to move to a new city and mend his ways. The poet's comment is that moving away is futile because, having ruined his life in one place, he has ruined it everywhere."

"And?"

"I had so many good reasons for leaving New York and coming home, but when I got here they — evaporated. I was the same person, it was the same life."

"People overcome addictions."

"But not self-contempt." He poured brandy into his coffee cup and leaned back as if to tell a bedtime story. "My grandfather, who raised me after my father died, had very primitive and set notions about what a man is. He never missed an opportunity to let me know that I didn't measure up."

"Let it go," I said, thinking back to my own father. "You'll live to bury him. That changes everything."

"He poisoned my childhood," Hugh said, ignoring me, "and I looked for causes, not knowing they didn't exist, believing that I deserved his abuse."

Something in his tone made me ask, "What kind of abuse, Hugh?"

"He said I was too pretty to be a boy," Hugh replied, his eyes bright with defiance and shame. Slowly, I understood.

"He assaulted you — sexually?"

"The joke is that I already knew I was gay. Knew I was different, anyway. What took me years to learn is that it didn't have—" he paused, searching for words — "to be so demeaning."

"What did he tell you?"

"That I led him on, that I wanted it." He smiled, bitterly. "I was the seductive twelve year old. A few weeks after it happened he sent me to a prep school in the east. Eighteen years ago. I can count on my fingers the times I've seen him since."

"Why have you come back?"

"I'm living on my anger, Henry. It's the only life I've got left in me, and I've come back to confront him. But I need to be strong when I see him, and I'm not strong yet."

"In the meantime, you brood and destroy yourself."

"I thought, in the meantime, you and I could become friends." I heard the ghost of seduction in his voice, yet it was not meant seductively. It was a plea for help. "If only I had met you — even five years ago."

"What's wrong with now?" I asked and drew him close.

☐

The next morning I woke to find Hugh standing perfectly still in a wide sunny space near the window, facing the wall above my head, wearing only a pair of faded red sweatpants. He held his hands at his side, fingers splayed, but not stiffly. He breathed, slowly, deeply. His breath filled his entire torso with quivery tension as he inhaled, bringing his chest and abdominal muscles into sharp relief. As he exhaled, his chest fell with delicate control. The color of his skin darkened as the blood rushed in a torrent beneath the skin. Each muscle of his body was elegantly delineated, like an ancient statue that time had rendered human.

He lifted his chin a little, drew his shoulders even straighter and parted his legs, one forward and one back. I watched as he sank to the floor, raising his arms at his side until he was fully extended in a split. There was the slightest tremor in his fingertips giving away the effort but no other part of his body moved. He pulled his back straighter, closed his eyes and held the position until the tremor in his fingers died. Then, he carefully brought his back leg forward in a wide arc, lowering his arms at the same time, until he was sitting. He opened his eyes.

"That was amazing," I said.

"I was so much better once," he replied, shaking his head vigorously, scattering drops of sweat from his hair. "I studied dance in college."

"Where?"

"Where?" he repeated, smiling. "I was at Yale for a couple of years, and N.Y.U. for a semester or two and Vanderbilt for a few months. I moved around."

"Without ever graduating?"

"I never did, no." He stood up, crossed over to the bed, a mattress laid against a corner, and extended his hand. "Get up and I'll take you to breakfast."

I let him pull me out of bed and our bodies tangled. He was flushed and a little sweaty and his hair brushed against the side of my face like a warm wind as we drew each other close.

An hour later we were sitting at a table in a dark, smoky corner of a coffeehouse on Castro. The waiter cleared our breakfast plates and poured more coffee.

"So you still consider yourself a hype?" I asked, pursuing our conversation.

"Of course. I'm addicted whether I use or not because being high is normal for me and how I function best. When I'm not using, I'm anxious."

"I'm pretty anxious myself, sometimes, but I've never felt the desire to obliterate myself."

"It's not just the sedative effect a hype craves. It's also the rush, and the rush is so intense, like coming without sex."

"I've heard that before from my clients. One of them said it was like a little death."

Hugh looked at me curiously and asked, "Do you know what that means?"

"I imagine he meant you lose yourself."

"Exactly. La petite mort — that's what the French called orgasm. They believed that semen is sort of concentrated blood so that each time a man came he shortened his life a little by spilling blood that couldn't be replenished."

"And women?"

"Then, as now, men didn't much concern themselves with how women felt." He finished his coffee. "Let's go for a walk."

Walking down Castro toward Market, Hugh reached over and took my hand. Self-consciously, I left it there. It perplexed me how sex with other men seemed natural to me but not the small physical gestures of affection and concern. What I remembered most clearly from my first sex with another man was the unexpected tenderness. It disturbed me — disoriented me, I guess. I had expected homosexuality to be dark and furtive, but it wasn't. It was shattering but liberating to come out and it ended a lot of doubts that had been eroding my self-confidence. I remember thinking, back then, so this is it, one of the worst things I can imagine happening has happened. And life goes on.

As we rounded the corner of Castro and crossed over to Market, he gently let go of my hand. We were out of the ghetto. I reached over and put my hand back into his. He looked over at me, startled, then tightened his grip. And life went on.

□

There were three messages from Aaron Gold on my answering machine when I got to my apartment, each a little more frantic than the last. I couldn't blame him. I had gone to San Francisco for a day and stayed a week. Finally, tired of wearing Hugh's clothes and needing a little time away from the intensity of our developing relationship, I drove home to pick up the mail and for a change of clothes.

I called Gold's office. His first words were, "Are you all right? I was ready to start calling the hospitals."

"I'm fine. Why are you so alarmed?"

"We were supposed to have dinner on Monday night. It is now Friday."

"Jesus, Aaron. I completely forgot. I should've called from the city."

"The city? Is that where you've been?"

"Yes, at Hugh Paris's."

"He lives there? Where?"

"Why?" There was a long silence on the other end of the line. "Aaron, are you still there?"

"Are you going back up?"

"Tonight," I said.

"I need to see you before you go," he said in a strange voice.

"Sure. When?"

"I'll meet you in an hour at Barney's," he said.

He was already at the bar when I got there, staring, a bit morosely over a tall drink with a lot of fruit jammed into the glass.

"You look like you've lost your best friend," I said, sitting down. Touching his glass, I said, "What's that you're drinking? A Pink Lady?" He said nothing. I added, to provoke him, "Jews really don't have the hang of ordering alcohol."

"You're pretty chipper," he said, sourly. The waitress came over and I ordered a Mexican beer.

"I'm happy, Aaron."

"Hugh Paris?" he asked, with almost a sneer in his voice. "Tell me, what do you really know about him?"

"I'm not sure I understand what you mean."

He waited until I had my drink, then said, "You've heard of Grover Linden."

"In this town," I said, "you might as well ask me if I know who my father is."

"Great-great-grandfather," he said. "That's his relation to Hugh Paris."

"You're not serious."

Gold merely nodded.

The first time I heard Grover Linden's name I was a fourth-grade student in Marysville. His picture appeared in my social studies book and the caption beneath it identified the broad-faced bearded man as the man who built the railroad. The railroad that connected the west and the east, I learned in high school, took ten years to construct and cost the lives of hundreds as an army of Chinese coolies worked feverishly to break through the Sierras during three of the coldest winters in the nineteenth-century. It was the railroad that raised San Francisco from a backwater village to an international city. It was the railroad from which Grover Linden, who began his adult life as a blacksmith in Utica, derived the wealth that made him the richest man in America.

Linden rose to become a United States senator and bought the Democratic nomination to the presidency. He lost that election, too opulent and corrupt even for that opulent and corrupt era, the Gilded Age. Popular opinion turned against him and he was forced to divest himself of his railroad in a decision by the Supreme Court that I read in my law school anti-trust course. He died in 1920, having nearly lived a century, leaving an immense personal fortune. Almost incidentally, he donated a vast tract of land on the San Francisco peninsula to found the university that bore his name. The first president of the school, Jeremiah Smith, Linden's son-in-law, raided the Ivy League luring entire faculties to California with the promise of unlimited wealth to support their research. In less than a century, Linden University had acquired an international reputation as one of the country's great private schools. The year Gold and I graduated from the law school, the commencement speaker, a United States Supreme Court justice, addressed a distinguished audience that included half the California Supreme Court as well as the sitting governors of three states, all of them alumns. And Linden, statues and paintings of whom were everywhere, lay entombed on the grounds of the school in a marble mausoleum along with his wife, daughter and son-in-law.

"Hugh hasn't told you who his family is?" Gold asked.

"No, not really. I mean — he mentioned money, but I had no idea."

"He didn't tell you his grandfather was Judge Paris?"

"Robert Paris, you mean?"

Gold nodded.

"He told me that, but it's a far cry from someone named Robert Paris to Grover Linden."

"It's complicated," Aaron said. He pulled the slightly soggy cocktail napkin from beneath his drink and got out his pen. "Look," he said. "This is Linden's family tree."

At the top of the tree were Linden and his wife, Sarah. The next generation consisted of their daughter, Allison, who married Jeremiah Smith.

"Then," Gold said, "there were two kids, John Smith and Christina Smith, Linden's grandchildren. Christina married Robert Paris."

"John Smith never married?"

"No," he shrugged. "Linden's descendents aren't prolific. Christina and Robert Paris had two sons, Jeremy and Nicholas." He traced the tree down into that generation. "Nicholas married Katherine Seaton. Hugh is their son."

He tucked his pen back into his coat pocket. I studied the napkin.

"Hugh's the last living descendant of Grover Linden?"

"No, John Smith is very much alive. He controls the Linden Trust," Gold said, referring to the megafund, the income of which supported the university's research which ranged from cancer cures to bigger and deadlier nuclear bombs, with the emphasis on the latter.

"John Smith," I repeated, and, suddenly, it came to me. "He bailed Hugh out of jail."

Gold lifted an eyebrow but said nothing.

"Are there any other descendants?"

"Hugh's father, Nicholas."

"Hugh told me his father was dead."

"He might as well be," Gold said. "Nicholas is locked up in an asylum. A basket case."

"And Hugh's mother, Katherine?"

"The parents divorced twenty years ago. I don't know anything about her."

"You seem to know a lot. Why?"

"Robert Paris is one of my firm's clients," he said glumly. "I'm telling you more than I should have as it is."

"Why tell me this much?"

"For your own good. Hugh's a black sheep."

"Meaning?"

"He has a serious drug problem." I nodded and sipped my beer. "And he's been hospitalized for — I guess you'd call them emotional problems." This I hadn't known but, swallowing my surprise, I nodded again.

Gold looked annoyed, probably having expected shock from me.

"I know about those things."

"And you still plan to see him?"

"I'm not an eighteen-year-old coed," I said, to irritate him further. "What I want to know is your source of information Robert Paris?"

"Don't ask me to violate a client confidence."

"A strategic attack of ethics, Aaron?"

"Look, Henry, I'm going out on a limb for you. The guy's crazy. He's been threatening his grandfather, calling day and night, writing nutty letters."

"I don't believe you," I said, not without a twinge of anxiety that the allegations were true.

Gold dug into his breast pocket and withdrew a wad of rubber-banded letters. He tossed them at me. "Read them," he commanded.

I leafed through the envelopes. They were postmarked San Francisco, addressed to Robert Paris in Portola Valley but gave no return address. It occurred to me that I did not know what Hugh's handwriting looked like. Clinging to that thread of doubt, I dropped the letters on the table.

"Where did you get these?"

"Afraid to read them?"

"Go to hell," I said, rising, but Gold was on his feet first.

"Fine," he said. "You can shut me out but you have your own doubts about the guy, don't you?" It was a fair statement but I was not inclined to concede the point. "Keep these," he said, indicating the letters. "They make enlightening reading." He drew himself up and walked out. I saw him pass in the window, looking straight ahead. I resisted the impulse to go after him — since I wasn't sure what I wanted to say — and finished my drink. Then, I gathered up the letters and put them in my coat pocket as I rose to leave.

The letters were heavy in my pocket as I walked to my car. There had not been enough time to know Hugh well, particularly since I saw him through the haze of infatuation, but my mind hadn't gone entirely out of commission. Hugh was a troubled man, troubled enough to make threats if not to carry them out. His hatred with his grandfather was fused with his sexual awakening, and his grandfather remained for him a figure who was frightening but seductive. Then, too, the years of drug addiction had taken their toll. Beneath the charm and humor, there was ruin. I saw all this and it made my feeling for him more intense and protective. The letters — and really, I had little doubt he'd written them — complicated matters. They were a sign that the sickness was deeper than I thought, but, even so, he deserved the chance to explain or deny them.

I called Hugh as soon as I got back to my apartment. The phone rang and rang; I pictured the empty room in his house, the phone wailing into the silence. The anxiety I felt in the bar was increasing by the minute and growing more diffuse; fed by emotional and physical exhaustion, it now verged on simple, unthinking panic. Throwing some clothes into a duffle bag, I hurried out to my car and headed for the city.

I was hardly aware of the other traffic on the road or the fading light of late afternoon. By the time I got to Hugh's house it was sunset. The first thing I noticed was that the lights were out. Walking up the stairs to the porch, my hands shook. I searched the door quickly for signs of forced entry but found none. I knocked, much too loudly and for too long. There was no answer. I craned my neck around the side of the porch and looked into the front window. The living room filled with shadowy gray light and the emptiness of the place was an almost physical force. I knew no one was there.

I went back to my car and got in, telling myself he would have to come back eventually. All I had to do was wait. So I waited. The streetlights came on. A police car rolled by. I heard a dog bark. A man and a woman walked by, hand in hand, glancing into my car as they passed. I checked my watch. It was ten. The next time I checked it was nearly six in the morning and I was cramped up behind the steering wheel. My panic had dissipated but, as I looked at the house, it seemed to emanate a kind of deadness.

I went back up the stairs to the porch and knocked on the door. I waited a few minutes, watching the neighborhood awaken to another perfect end of summer day. Defeated, I turned away, went down to my car and left. The drive home seemed endless.

A tall, sandy-haired policewoman was leaning against the wall outside the door to my apartment. She asked me if I was Henry Rios, and, when I agreed that I was, she asked me to step over to her patrol car.

"What's going on, officer?"

"A man died," she said, simply, "and he had your business card on him."

"Who was he?" I asked, as a chill settled along my spine. The bright morning light suddenly seemed stale and unreal.

"We don't know," she said, briskly. "He wasn't carrying a wallet. We'd like you to come down to the morgue and see if you can identify the body."

We went over to the patrol car. Her partner was standing alongside the car drumming his fingers on the roof. He opened the back door for me and I got in. They got into the front and we swept down the quiet street.

"You're a hard man to track down," she said. "We've been trying since last night."

"I was out," I said.

"A bachelor," her partner said, smiling into the rearview mirror. I smiled back.

The coroner was a black man, his dark skin contrasting with his immaculate white frock. He had a round, placid face and his eyes were black and bright. It was a decent face, one that kept its secrets. He led me down a still corridor that stank of chemicals. The officers followed a few steps behind, talking softly. We came to the room and he instructed the police to wait outside. He and I went in.

"They're like kids in here," he said, speaking of the officers. "They get into everything."

I merely nodded and looked around the room. One wall had several metal drawers in it. On the drawers, just below the handles, were slots into which there had been fitted squares of cardboard with names typed on them. There was a row of steel tables, set on casters, lined up against another wall. It was quite cold in the room. A white room. White lights overhead. The coroner moved around quickly and efficiently.

"When did all this happen?" I asked as he put his hand on the handle of a drawer marked John Doe.

"Estimated time of death around 10:30 last night. They found him in San Francisquito Creek just below the footbridge leading out of campus. Drowned."

"In three feet of water?" I asked incredulously.

"We took some blood," he explained quietly. "There was enough heroin in his system to get five junkies off." I opened my mouth but nothing came out. "Are you ready now?"

"Yes."

He pulled at the handle. The drawer came out slowly, exposing first the head, and then the torso, down to the sunken genitals. The coroner stopped and took a step back, as if inspecting death's work.

The elegant body was as white as marble. I could see a dark blue vein running up the length of his arm, and a jagged red mark just beneath his armpit where the needle went in. There were bruises on his chest. His head rested on a kind of pillow. Death had robbed his face of its seductive animation but I recognized him.

"His name is Hugh Paris," I said, and the coroner took a pencil and pad of paper from his pocket and wrote. "His grandfather's name is Robert Paris and he lives somewhere in Portola Valley. I don't know where." I heard the pencil scratching but I could not take my eyes off of Hugh's face.

"Is that it?"

"Yes, that's all."

"The police will want a statement." I looked at the coroner. The dark eyes were impassive but remotely sad as he studied Hugh. "Such a young man. It's a shame."

I agreed that it was a shame and excused myself, hearing, as I left, the drawer slide shut. The two officers were at the far end of the corridor, smoking. They looked up when they saw me and the woman smiled. As I approached, I saw the smile leak from her face. I stopped, ran the back of my hand across my eyes and inspected it. It was wet. I hadn't realized I was crying.

– 4 –

"The coroner says it was an accident."

"The coroner also said he was drugged."

"The guy was a hype. Whaddaya expect?" Torres blew a cloud of cigar smoke across the small, windowless room, then tilted back in his swivel chair revealing an enormous stomach that poured over a heavy metal belt buckle fashioned from the letters USMC. The desk between us was piled high with papers but he had cleared enough space for the plastic nameplate that identified him as Samuel Torres, Detective, Homicide.

Torres and I went back a long way. I had once dissected his testimony on cross-examination in a murder case on which he was the investigator. He was lucky the jury hadn't hissed him when he got off the stand. Neither of us had forgotten his humiliation. Now he studied me with small, dark eyes. On the wall, above his pitted, jowly face, there was a calendar distributed by some policeman's association. It was a drawing showing two cops standing against a flowering tree of some kind. They were dressed in black uniforms, riot helmets on their heads, jaws adamantly set against the future. Fine art, cop style. That calendar drawing spoke volumes to me about the cops – they were menacing and paranoid, and not very bright.

"A hype knows how much he can handle," I said, resuming my conversation with Torres. It was three in the afternoon, and I had not been home since I was brought to the morgue that morning from my apartment.

"Hey, everyone makes a mistake. The guy was just partying. And anyway, counsel" — he said the last word sneeringly — "we got this one figured out."

Now it was my turn to sneer. "Right. You have him wandering around the university at ten at night, shot up with dope, losing his balance, tumbling down the embankment and drowning in three feet of water. It happens every day."

"You're wasting my time," Torres said.

"I don't think that's possible, detective."

"Watch it, Rios. This ain't a courtroom. No judge is gonna take your punches for you."

"I'm terrified."

"Ormes, get him out of here."

The only other person in the office, a woman who had been quietly listening to us, rose from her desk and came over to me. Her nameplate identified her as Terry Ormes, also a homicide detective. She was tall and slender, and she wore a dark blue dress cut so austerely that I had thought it was a uniform at first. She had an open, plain face made plainer by the cut of her hair and the absence of makeup. It wasn't the kind of face that compelled a second look, but if you did look again you were rewarded. Her face radiated intelligence. She studied me for a second with luminous gray eyes.

"Come on, Mr. Rios," she said in a friendly voice, "I'll walk you out."

I shrugged and followed her out of the office, down a bright corridor, past the crowded front desk to the steps of the police station. It was a cool afternoon, cloudy.

"Your colleague's an asshole," I said out of frustration.

"Sam's been around a long time and he's set in his ways. He's not a bad cop, just tired."

The mildness of her reply knocked the air out of my anger. "Well, thanks — Detective."

"Terry," she said, extending her hand.

"I'm Henry," I said, shaking hands.

"I think you're right about Hugh Paris," she said. "I think someone killed him. I just can't figure out who or why."

I looked at her. "Can you talk now?" She nodded. "Let's get a cup of coffee, then." I gestured to a Denny's across the street.

"You look beat," she said, once we were seated in an orange vinyl booth. I took a sip of coffee, tasting nothing but hot.

"It's been a long day and it started at the morgue. Why do you think Hugh was murdered?"

"I was the first one from homicide at the scene this morning," she said. "Are you familiar with the footbridge?"

I said yes. San Francisquito Creek ran along the eastern boundary of the campus at the edge of the wood that fanned out in both directions from the entrance to the school. As the creek flowed north into the bay, it descended, ultimately becoming subterranean as it crept into town. By the time it reached the edge of campus, there was a six-foot embankment down to the water.

Across from the creek was the edge of a shopping center. The footbridge forded the creek at this point, allowing pedestrians access to the shopping center from the walking paths through the wood. The area around the bridge, some of the densest wood on campus, had a bad reputation since it had been the scene of a couple of rapes a few years earlier. It wasn't the kind of place people visited at night.

Terry Ormes was saying, "I was there before they lifted the body out of the water. It was just at dawn and I was watching from the bridge. I swear I saw footprints down there on the bank, and they weren't made by just one pair of shoes."

"How many pairs of shoes?"

"At least two pair. The sand kept the impressions pretty good."

"Anyone take pictures?"

"I went back to my car to radio for a photographer," she said, "but by the time I got back, the paramedics had gone charging down the embankment and pulled him out of the water. They walked all over the place. There was no way to tell."

"That doesn't help much," I said glumly.

She lowered her coffee cup. "That's not all. I walked up that embankment six or seven times. I didn't see anything, not a scrap of clothing or blood or hair or even any broken grass. If Hugh Paris slipped down the embankment, he was awfully careful not to leave any traces behind. And there's one other thing. You saw the body?" I nodded. "Did you see his back?"

"No."

"There were bruises around his shoulders. I think someone held him face down in the water until he drowned."

All I could manage was, "Jesus." There was a long, still moment between us. "Did you tell any of this to Torres?"

"Sure," she said, "but it didn't make it into his report. Like I said, Sam's tired. This one just looked too tough to make out a murder."

I sighed. "Well, he's right, maybe. A jury wouldn't convict a guy of a parking ticket on the evidence we've got."

She gazed at me, coolly. "Why do you care?"

"Hugh was my friend. He told me someone was trying to kill him, but I didn't believe him. Now I owe him the truth, whatever it may be."

"Is that all?"

"You really want to know?"

"No," she said abruptly. "If it's personal, keep it to yourself, but if it's something I can use to investigate, don't hold back. Is that fair?"

"Very fair, detective," I said. "I need more time before I can tell you anything else."

She took out a business card and scribbled a number on the back of it. "My home number," she explained. "This investigation is officially closed, so don't call me at the office." She handed the card to me. "I'll help you if I can."

"Why?"

"I'm a cop," she said, a little defiantly. "We're not all like Sam."

I finished my coffee then found a phone and called the coroner's office to ask when they'd release the autopsy report and their official findings. I was informed that the body had been claimed by the family and there would be no autopsy. The preliminary findings — death by misadventure — would stand. It was hard to get additional information from the sexless bureaucratic whine on the other end of the line but, finally, it told me that Hugh's body had been turned over to his mother, Katherine Paris, who gave a local address and listed the university as her place of employment.

It was dark as I drove home. The tree-lined street where I lived was still and from the windows of my neighbors' houses came the yellow glow of light and domesticity. My own apartment would be dark and chilly. For a moment I considered driving past my building to the nearest bar but I was too tired. I felt the weight of the day and its images like an ache that wracked my brain. Surely we were never meant to live in the appalling circumstances in which we so often found ourselves, alone, fearful, mute. I parked, got out of my car and stood indecisively in the driveway. With whom could I share this loss?

I could think of no one. I walked to my apartment and slipped the key into the lock. I pushed the door open, walked through the living room into the bedroom and lay on the bed, fully clothed. Despite my exhaustion I made myself relive the last day I spent with Hugh, scouring my memory for clues to his death. He'd risen early, put on a tie and blazer. He said he was going out on business and asked me to meet him at the St. Francis around noon. I'd become accustomed to Hugh's solitary comings and goings and once I was satisfied they didn't involve drugs, I relaxed.

I'd arrived at the St. Francis early and had just turned the corner from Geary when I spotted Hugh, his back turned to me, engaged in emphatic conversation with a tall old man. They'd talked for a moment and then the old man got into a silver Rolls.

Uncle John. John Smith.

That's how Hugh referred to the old man, as Uncle John. But he wouldn't tell me anything more and we argued over lunch about it.

"I'm protecting you," I heard him say. Uncle John. That afternoon we made love. And then—

I woke up four hours later, rolled myself over onto my back and sat up. I was certain someone else was in the apartment. I switched on a lamp and made a lot of noise getting out of bed. Then, like a frightened child, I went, noisily, from room to room talking to the darkness as I turned on every light in the apartment. Eventually, I found myself standing in the middle of the living room. I was alone. I stood there for a few minutes, not feeling or thinking anything, not knowing what to do. Then, my stomach, which had been patient all day, roared and demanded food.

I rummaged through the refrigerator coming up with a shriveled apple and a carton of spoiled cottage cheese. In the end, I made my meal out of a bottle of Jack Daniels and a packet of peanuts left over from some long-forgotten airplane trip. I sat down to think. It seemed a waste of time to devise fancy theories about a crime when the evidence was barely sufficient even to establish that a crime had occurred. I believed Hugh had been murdered, but the basis of my belief consisted of Hugh's unsupported assertions and Terry Ormes's unrecorded observations. Clearly, I needed to know more about the Paris family and Hugh's last few months.

The latter I would leave to Ormes — with the resources of the the police department behind her, she could tap into the paper trail that we all generate as we go through life. As for the Paris family and Hugh's relations with it, two names immediately came to mind, Aaron Gold and Katherine Paris. Then I drew a blank. Finally, a third name did occur to me. Grant Hancock. I turned the name over in my mind and mentally wrote beside it, "last resort." Then I poured another drink.

☐

The law office of Grayson, Graves and Miller, Aaron Gold's firm, occupied the top three floors of the tallest building in town. A carpeted, wood-paneled elevator whisked me up to the twentieth floor and deposited me in a reception room the size of my entire apartment and considerably better furnished. A middle-aged woman sat behind a semi-circular desk, beneath a Rothko, manipulating the most elaborate phone console I had ever seen. Wading through the carpet, and between the heavy chairs and couches scattered around the room, I approached her and asked for Aaron. She took my measure with a glance and invited me to wait.

Instead, I walked over to a huge globe of the world and spun it. She cleared her throat censoriously and I drifted to the window. The window faced south to the foothills and beyond, where behind rustic stone walls and elaborate electronic alarm systems, the firm's rich clients kept the twentieth century at bay.

Grayson, Graves and Miller was just another weapon in their armory. The receptionist called my name and directed me through the door beside her desk and down the hall. I went through the door and found myself looking down a seemingly endless, blue-carpeted corridor lined with closed doors. I heard a lot of frantic voices coming from behind those doors. The refrigerated air blew uncomfortably as I made my way down the hall looking for Gold's office. This, it occurred to me, was my idea of hell. Just then, a door opened and Gold stepped out and came toward me. The stride was a touch less athletic today, I noticed, and the stomach muscles sagged a bit beneath his elegantly tailored shirt. He was tired around the mouth and eyes and his shaggy hair looked recently slept on.

As we stepped into his office, he instructed his secretary that we were not to be disturbed. On his desk was yesterday's paper turned to the story of Hugh's death. I sat down on a corner of the desk while Aaron stood irresolutely before me.

"I was going to call you," he said.

"I've saved you the trouble." I lifted a corner of the newspaper. "Hugh told me he was in danger of being murdered. I didn't believe him."

Gold said nothing.

"He even told me who the murderer would be, his grandfather, Robert Paris. A client of your firm."

Gold shook his head.

"That can't be true," he said, unconvincingly.

"Then what were you going to call me about?"

Gold wandered over to the liquor cabinet and poured himself some scotch. He held the bottle at me. I shook my head.

"You got Hugh's letters from someone," I continued, "presumably the recepient. If Robert Paris is involved in Hugh's death and you're protecting him, you're already an accessory."

"Don't lecture me about my legal status," Aaron snapped. "I just want to talk."

"I'm listening."

"Judge Paris's account is managed by the two most senior partners in the firm," he began, "but there's enough so that some of it trickles down to the associates. I've done my share of work on that account and I'd heard of Hugh Paris, knew he was the judge's grandson. I'd heard he was bad news," Aaron shrugged. "I really didn't give it much thought."

He sipped his drink.

"Still," he continued, "when you told me he was in jail, I thought that was important enough to mention to one of the partners on the judge's account. I thought we might want to do something for him."

You did, I thought, but said nothing.

"I got the third-degree," Aaron said. "The two partners questioned me for more than an hour. When they were satisfied I wasn't holding back anything they explained to me that Hugh had made threats against the judge's life. I was shown the letters and asked to report back to them anything else that I might learn from you of Hugh's activities."

"And did you?"

"Of course I did," he replied, emptying his glass. "The partners had me convinced that Hugh was dangerous. They told me that he was a drug addict, that his father was crazy. There were disturbing reports from private investigators who'd been hired to keep an eye on him in New York. I not only believed Hugh was a threat to his grandfather but also to you."

I shook my head. "You never met him." Aaron wasn't listening.

"But the more they confided in me," he said, "the stranger it seemed that the judge would go to such lengths and to such expense to keep track of Hugh. It seemed completely out of proportion to any possible threat Hugh may have posed to Robert Paris."

"And now Hugh is dead."

"Yes." He rose from the couch and went back to the liquor cabinet, pouring another drink. "Three days ago I had a meeting with the partners on the Paris account. They asked me a lot of questions about you — questions that contained information they could have got only by having had you followed."

"What kind of questions?"

"They wanted to know the nature of your relationship with Hugh."

"And did you tell them?"

"No, but I think they already knew."

We looked at each other.

"Three days ago," I said, "and the next day we had lunch and you tried to talk me out of seeing Hugh. And that night he was killed."

"I swear I had nothing to do with that," he said.

"But your client — the judge did."

"I don't think it's that simple," Aaron said. "I've been doing some research. Something's going on that goes back a long time and involves a lot of people."

"You're talking in riddles."

"I can't speak more clearly — yet." He looked at me. "I'm going to stay here," his gesture encompassed the entire firm, "until I find out. But I don't want to see you. It's not safe for either of us."

"This is no time to split up," I said.

"They're watching you, Henry. But they're not worried about my loyalties. You're my diversion."

"Why are you doing this, Aaron?"

"I won't be an instrument of crime," he said. "I either have to clear my client of this murder or urge him to turn himself in. That's my obligation."

"Then our interests are different," I said, "because I want justice for my friend."

He nodded. "I'll be in touch, Henry. Wait for my call."

"You have to give me something, Aaron. Something to go on."

"All right," he said. "Robert Paris inherited his wife's estate after she was killed in a car accident. She had a will but she died intestate."

"That doesn't make sense."

"If you can make sense of it," he said, "you'll know who killed Hugh Paris."

I heard the tremor in his voice and I was frightened for both of us.

◻

I was sitting on the patio of the student union at the university having left Gold's office an hour earlier. I had come to find Katherine Paris. I stared out across the empty expanse of grass and pavement. Misty light hung from the branches of the trees. A white-jacketed busboy cleared away my breakfast dishes.

School had not yet started for the undergraduates so there was none of their noise and traffic to shatter the stillness. I was thinking about Hugh. The same money that raised this school was responsible for his death. The money was everything and nothing, something that overwhelmed him and which, perhaps, could only be contained by the institution. It had not done Hugh any good, but was merely the background noise against which he played out his unhappiness.

I got up and walked across the plaza to the bookstore. It was a two-story beige box with a red tile roof, a far cry from the excesses of the Old Quad. But then, as the campus moved away from the Old Quad the architecture became purely utilitarian as conspicuous displays of wealth, whether personal or institutional, went out of style. I entered the store and stopped one of the blue-frocked salesclerks, asking where the poetry books were shelved. I was directed to the back wall of the second floor. The poetry books covered a dozen long shelves and it took me a minute to figure out that they were arranged alphabetically.

There had been a brief time in college when I wrote poetry. It was, like most sophomore verse, conceived in the loins rather than the mind. It was a notch better than most such verse, perhaps, but it was no loss to literature when I stopped writing. My brush with poetry, however, left me with a permanent respect for those who wrote it well. Seeing familiar names again, Auden, Frost, Richard Wilbur, took me back to sunny autumn afternoons when I sat in my dorm room writing lame couplets.

Katherine Paris had published a half-dozen slender volumes over the past twenty years and one thick book of collected poems. Each book was adorned with the same photograph I had seen at Hugh's house and beneath it was the same paragraph of biographical information. She was born in Boston, graduated from Radcliffe, took a master's degree from Columbia and currently divided her time between Boston and San Francisco. Her work had won the National Book Award and been nominated for the Pulitzer Prize. She had been translated into twelve languages — they were listed — and had once been mentioned by T.S. Eliot who found her work elliptical. Nothing about a crazy husband and a homosexual son; apparently, that information was private.

I struggled with about a dozen of her poems before I saw Eliot's point. Her work was indeed elliptical, she left out everything that was essential, including logic and meaning. Her words neither described nor observed things. They were just words scattered across the page. This was braininess of the highest order, the verbal equivilant of the white canvas passed off as a painting; so abstract that to have expected some sense from it would have insulted the artist. As my attention wandered from the poems, it seemed to me that I was being watched. I closed the book and looked around. The boy standing next to me quickly directed his attention to his feet.

He wore a baggy pair of khaki shorts rolled up at the bottom over a long sinewy pair of legs. He had on a white sweatshirt with a red paisley bandana tied around his neck and a small button with the lambda — the symbol of gay liberation — on it. He had a round cherubic face, short hair of an indeterminate dark color. He looked about twenty. He raised his eyes at me and I realized that I was being cruised, not spied on.

"Hello," I said, pleasantly.

Pointing at the book in my hand he said, "I took a creative writing course from her last quarter." Almost as an afterthought, he added, "My name is Danny."

"Henry," I said. "Did you like the course?"

"Actually," he confided, pushing his hair with slender fingers, "she's a good poet but a very neurotic woman."

"Don't the two go together?"

"No," he said, "I reject the notion of the doomed artist. I mean, look at Stevens, he sold insurance and Williams was a doctor."

"Sorry," I said, "It's been a long time since I read poetry. Who are Stevens and Williams?"

He looked slightly shocked. "Wallace Stevens? William Carlos Williams?" I shook my head. Looking at me intently he said, "Aren't you a student? A grad student maybe?"

"I'm a lawyer and my interest in Katherine Paris is professional, not literary."

"A lawyer," he repeated as though describing a virus. "Don't lawyers wear suits when they're working?" I was wearing a pair of jeans and a black polo shirt.

"Not on house calls," I replied. "Where can I find Mrs. Paris?"

"Third floor, English department in the Old Quad. I'll walk you there if you like, okay?"

"Sure, just let me pay for the book."

Between the bookstores and the Old Quad I learned quite a bit about Danny's tastes in poetry, his life and his plans as well as receiving a couple of gently veiled passes. I steered the conversation around to Katherine Paris.

"She had this great lady persona," he was saying, "but don't cross her."

"You did?"

"Anyone with any integrity does sooner or later. Her opinions are set in stone."

"Not writ in water?"

"That's Shelley. That was pretty good. Anyway, she doesn't let you forget who has the power." We had reached the English department. He smiled at me, sunnily. "What do you want with her anyway?"

"Her son was killed on campus a couple of days ago. He was a friend of mine. I want to ask her some questions."

"You mean the guy that they found in the creek?" I nodded. "That's too bad. Was he a good friend?"

I reached out and touched the button on his chest. "We were good friends."

His look said, "And here I've been cruising you." Aloud, he said, "You must think I'm a real jerk."

"How could you have known?" I asked, reasonably. "And thanks for the help." We shook hands, he a little awkwardly and I remembered how rare the gesture was among students. "The poem with the phrase writ in water, that was about Keats, wasn't it?"

"Yes," he said. "Shelley wrote it when Keats died. He called it Adonais." He started to say something else, thought better of it, smiled again and walked away. I watched him go and then turned and climbed up the stairs to the third floor.

☐

Katherine Paris did not look like a woman anyone ever called mother. Her small feet were encased in gold slippers and she wore a flowing white caftan that obliterated any sign of a body beneath it. The string of blue beads around her neck was probably lapis lazuli. It was the only jewelry she wore. Her face had the false glow of a drinker but none of a drinker's soft alcoholic bloat. It was a hard angular face I saw as I entered her office; deeply wrinkled, deeply intelligent. She instructed me to sit down. I sat. She continued writing.

The walls of the office were bare. The curtains were drawn against the afternoon light and the only source of light was her desk lamp. She worked at an elegant writing table whose spindly legs hardly seemed able to bear the weight of the books piled on top. At length, she looked up at me from beneath half-glasses evidently surprised to find that I was still there.

I introduced myself, to her obvious pleasure, as an admirer of her work. She accepted the volume of her collected poems and signed it for me.

"How were you introduced to my poetry?" she asked. Her voice was a low, whisky rumble.

"Your son, Hugh," I replied and, at once, the pleasure vanished. Her eyes narrowed.

"I see. Tell me, Mr. Rios, which of my poems is your favorite? Or have you actually opened this — brand new book?"

"In fact I have, Mrs. Paris, but you're right, I didn't come here to discuss them. I'm a lawyer."

"Is that a threat?"

"Mrs. Paris, I was Hugh's friend—"

"Hugh was rather generous in that regard. He had altogether too many friends. Were you one of his — special friends?" she asked archly.

"I cared for Hugh," I said.

"Mr. Rios," she said, mockingly, "spare me the homosexual sentimentality. What is it you want from me?"

"I believe Hugh was murdered. I'm not sure by whom but the

first thing to do is determine the exact cause of death. The body was moved before an autopsy—"

"That's enough," she said. "You walk in from nowhere, tell me someone killed my son and ask permission to cut open his body?" These last words were delivered in a tone of rising incredulousness. "Just who the hell are you? One of his boyfriends? Do you think there's money for you in this?"

Unable to suppress my hostility, I said, "Mrs. Paris, I sympathize with your deep grief, however, I'm talking about a crime."

"My deep grief? Getting himself killed was the most unselfish thing Hugh ever did. As for the body, it was cremated yesterday. As for crimes, Mr. Rios, you're now trespassing and in one minute I'm going to call campus security and have you thrown out." She picked up the phone.

"Why was he cremated?" I asked, rising.

"That is not your business," she said, "now get out."

"Thank you for your time, Mrs. Paris." She put the phone down and went back to her writing.

☐

Sitting on my patio an hour later, I finished a gin-and-tonic, watched clouds move in from the ocean and counted up my leads. They amounted to about nothing. There were Hugh's allegations against his grandfather and the coincidence of his death under odd circumstances. Gold knew more than he was saying, but either he could not say any more or really believed that our interests were sufficiently different for him not to confide in me. Katherine Paris was a dead end. I needed something tangible. It seemed to me that Hugh Paris moved through life like a nomad, using life up as he lived it, and leaving very little behind.

And then I remembered the letters. They were still in the pocket of the coat I had worn three days earlier. I finished my drink and went to the closet to retrieve them. Even as I spread them out on my desk a voice within begged me not to read them. I was afraid of what they might contain. I made myself another drink and circled my desk, vaguely, looking at them — thirteen in all, arranged from the earliest, in June, to the most recent, only a couple of weeks earlier. Finally, I sat down and started reading.

They were not exactly the rantings of a lunatic. On the other hand, there was little in them that could be called civilized discourse. Mostly, they were excruciatingly detailed invective of a psychosexual nature — literate but profoundly disturbed. I refolded the last letter and tucked it back into its envelope. It seemed impossible these could come from Hugh, but the details told. I said to myself that I was now his advocate, not his lover, and an advocate accepts revelations about his client that would send the lover running from the room. It's part of the masochism of being a criminal defense lawyer to want to know the worst, in theory so the worst can be incorporated into the defense, but in actuality to confirm a blighted view of humanity. If I believed that people are basically good, I would have gone into plastics. People are basically screwed-up and often the best you can do for them is listen, hear the worst and then tell them it's not so bad.

It wasn't so bad, Hugh, I said, silently. I've seen worse. And the letters contained solid information. Hugh believed his grandfather was responsible for the deaths of his grandmother and his uncle, Jeremy. He also accused the judge of imprisoning his father, Nicholas, in an asylum. Finally, he accused the judge of depriving him of his lawful inheritance. There wasn't much elaboration since, obviously, Hugh expected his grandfather to understand the allusions. It wasn't evidence but it was something. A lead. A theory. Hugh's death was part of a cover-up of earlier murders. All right, so it was melodramatic. Most crime is.

I collected my thoughts and called Terry Ormes. Her crisp, friendly voice was a relief after the dark muttering voice of the letters. I told her, briefly, editing out the lurid details, what the letters contained.

"That's still not much," she said.

"Well, it's something. Apparently, Hugh's grandmother and his uncle were killed up near Donner Pass on interstate 80 about twenty years ago. Can you contact the local police agency in the nearest town up there with a hospital?"

"Sure," she said, "but if it happened on 80, it was probably a CHP case. What am I asking for?"

"Everything you can find out about the circumstances of their deaths. Any reports, death certificates, anything. And find out anything you can about Hugh's life the last six months. Rap sheets, DMV records, any kind of paper."

"Call me in two days," she said. "What will you do?"

"I have one other card to play," I said. "I'll be in touch."

The line went dead. I gathered up the letters and buried them beneath a pile of papers in the bottom drawer of my desk. I closed and locked it. For a long time I sat, nursing my drink, thinking about the hole where my heart had been.

— 5 —

The next morning I sat down to dial a number I'd not called in four years. The receptionist I reached announced the name of the law firm in the hushed tones appropriate to old money. I gave her the name I wanted and waited the couple of minutes it took to work through the various intermediaries until a deep unhurried male voice spoke.
"Grant Hancock here."
"Grant, this is Henry Rios."
There was the slightest pause before breeding won out and he said, "Henry, it's been a long time."
"Four years, at least."
"Are you in the city?"
"No, I'm calling from my apartment. Grant, I need your advice."
"Surely you don't need the services of a tax lawyer on what you make with the public defender."
"I'm not a P.D. anymore," I replied, "and what I want to talk about is death, not taxes."
"Anyone's in particular?"
"Yes, Hugh Paris. I thought since you're both — well, old San Francisco stock — that you might have known him."
"Indeed I did," Grant said slowly. "How well did you know him?"
"Well enough to think that he was murdered." The line buzzed vacantly. "Grant? Are you still there?"
"Yes," he said. "I don't want to discuss this over the phone. Can you come up here tonight?"

"About nine?"

"Fine. I'm still at the same place. You know the way." I agreed that I did.

"Henry, did Hugh mention me? Is that why you called?" His voice was, for Grant, agitated.

"No, he never said anything about you. It was my own idea to call. I know how thick the old families are with each other."

"I knew him a long time ago," Grant said in a far-off voice, and then stopped himself short. "I'll talk to you tonight." The line went dead.

Grant Hancock, along with Aaron Gold, had been one of my two closest friends at law school. His name was the amalgamation of two eminent San Francisco families and he grew up in a mansion in Pacific Heights. He was one of those San Francisco aristocrats who, for all their culture and worldliness, never move a psychological inch from the tops of their hills. Among those families that gave the city its reputation for insularity, "provincial" was a compliment.

In the normal course of existence, I would never have met someone like Grant since his world was far removed from mine and hardly visible to the untrained eye. Its tribesmen recognized each other by certain signs and signals meaningless to the outsider. However, Linden University was an extension of that world and the law school was a kind of finishing school from which he entered a law practice so leisurely and refined that it would have befitted one of Henry James's languid heros.

Grant cultivated a certain languor and part of it was real, growing out of a sense of belonging that was deep and unshakable. Part of it was an act, a way of masking real passion and a strong if confused decency. His decency was as simple as the desire to treat everyone fairly and civilly but it was undercut by his knowledge that, from his position of privilege, he could afford to act decently at no cost to himself. He wondered how he would treat others had he not been so privileged, and, I think, he assumed the worst about himself.

The fact that he was gay added to his confusion because acknowledging his homosexuality was an opportunity to take a moral risk and he passed it up. He rigidly separated his personal and professional lives and spent great amounts of energy policing the border between them. And for all that, I had once loved him and he had loved me. There had even been a time when it appeared that we might live together, openly, but that time came and passed, and he could not bring himself to do it. We drifted apart, he back to his hill and I back to real life.

I was thinking about all this as I finished dressing and made a pot of coffee. There was something of Grant in Hugh Paris as if Hugh had been a version of Grant more comfortable with himself and more distant from that insular world of old money and unchanging attitudes. I let the comparison lie. There was work to be done.

The weather was beautiful, almost cruelly so, I thought as I walked across the parking lot to the courthouse. The deep and broad blue sky and the dazzling morning sun which should have looked down upon an innocent landscape instead shone above cramped suburban cities and cramped suburban lives. The sunlight brushed the back of my neck as if it were fingers wanting me only to stop for a moment and do nothing but breathe and be grateful that I was alive. Another time, I thought as I pushed open the glass door to the courthouse.

I walked up the stairs to the clerk's office on the second floor. Telephones screeched and voices rose in frustration at the service counter. This was the place where court records relating to criminal cases were kept. By the time I got a sullen clerk's attention, I had forgotten the weather and gratitude was the farthest thing from my mind. Having already located the case number on a master index, I ordered the court docket on Hugh's case to see what had happened to it. Fifteen minutes later, the docket was regurgitated from the bowels of the bureaucracy by the same clerk, who warned me three times not to remove the file from the room.

I went over to the reading counter and flipped through the pages of the docket. The criminal charges filed against Hugh the day after his arrest were possession of PCP, being under the influence of PCP and resisting arrest — all misdemeanors. His arraignment had been set for a week after his release from jail. On that day, he appeared through his attorney, Stephan Abrams, and the D.A. moved to dismiss all charges against him. The court granted the motion and that was the end of the case. I made a mental note of the D.A.'s name: Sonny Patterson, an old courtroom adversary. I had the docket copied and went down the hall to the office of the District Attorney.

Sonny Patterson rattled the docket sheet and dropped it on his desk. He took a drag from his cigarette, scattering ashes on his pale green shirt and bright orange tie. Hick was written all over his puffy potato face, but it was an act, like his carefully mismatched clothes. He got juries to like him by letting them think that they were smarter than he. But Sonny had a mind for detail and one that made connections. A good mind. Evasive when circumstances required evasion. He was being evasive now.

"Come on Henry, I handle twenty cases a day in the arraignment court. You're talking a thousand cases ago."

"It's not every day that you dismiss a three-count complaint involving drugs and resisting arrest."

"Misdemeanors," he replied disdainfully.

"Being under the influence carries a mandatory thirty day jail sentence."

"So?" he said, shrugging. "With good time/work time figured in you're out in twenty."

"That's still twenty days longer in county than I'd care to spend."

"I know your position on determinate sentencing, counsel," he said stiffly.

I held up my palms. "Sorry," I said. "I didn't come here to debate the point. I just want to know why you dumped the case."

"What was the defendant's name again?" he drawled in a vaguely Southern accent. Another affectation. The furthest south Sonny had ever been was Castroville.

"Hugh Paris," I replied.

"Isn't he the guy they pulled out of the creek about a week back?"

"The same."

"You know him pretty well?"

"Yes," I said.

"The papers say it was an accident."

"So do the cops."

"I know," he said, "I had Torres up here to tell me about it. He mentioned — in passing — that you identified the body." He leaned forward on his desk. "Do you know anything about this man's death that the police don't know?"

Police, I thought. Did he mean the cops? Any moment now he'll be calling them peace officers. Aloud I said, carefully, "I don't know anything about Hugh's death the cops don't know. I just added up the information differently."

"So did I," he said, picking up the phone and pushing a button. He reeled off a string of numbers into the receiver. A couple of minutes later there was a knock on the door and his secretary entered with a thick file. Hugh's name was written across the outside of the manila folder. She put the file on the desk and Sonny flipped through the arrest report to the three sheets of yellow paper on which the complaint appeared. He turned the last sheet over to some writing. This was the alibi, so-called because every time a D.A. dismissed a case he was required to set out his reasons on the back of the complaint in the event someone — like a cop or irate citizen — took exception to the dismissal down the road.

"Insufficiency of the evidence," Sonny said, lifting his face from the sheet.

"That's meaningless. What was the problem?"

"The alleged PCP cigarette was analyzed by the crime lab and came back as creatively rolled oregano, dipped in ether to give it the right smell. Mr. Paris's pusher misled him. Street justice, I guess."

"And the other charges?"

"We won't pursue the under the influence charge unless the defendant was examined by a doctor at the time of his arrest. The cops didn't do that."

"What about the resisting arrest count?"

"That was plain, old-fashioned contempt of cop. A little chickenshit charge. Not worth the paper it was written on." He glanced at the complaint with an expression almost of distaste. I wasn't surprised by his reaction. The D.A.'s know better than anyone what cops can be like — touchy, hostile, self-righteous.

"Have you ever heard of that lawyer, Abrams, before?"

"Nope. He's not a local. He's got himself a fancy address up in the city. You want it?"

I nodded.

He scrawled an address on a sheet of legal paper and pushed it across the desk.

"Thanks," I said, rising to go. "You don't think Hugh's death was an accident, either, do you?"

"If I did," he said, suddenly grim, "I wouldn't have given you the time of day."

"Then why are you?"

"The cops botched this one," he said. "I know it, but I can't prove it. I've already beefed Torres but even if they reopen the investigation now, the trail's cold. You seem to know something about this case. Better you than no one. Good luck and remember," he said, as I opened the door, "you're an officer of the court."

"Meaning?"

"If you find out who did it, let me know the bastard's name. He won't get away with it."

But so often criminals do, I nearly said, but I kept the thought to myself.

At the end of the day I drove to San Francisco on highway 280, the serpentine road that wound through the foothills behind the posh peninsula suburbs and within view of the hidden houses of the rich. The twisted eucalyptus trees stood high and elegantly on those hills and the air was moist with the fragrance of their leaves. Deer grazed those hills and now and then a jeep went flying along the dirt roads with no apparent destination. A line of horses appeared on the horizon and then disappeared behind a clump of oak.

I was passing through some of the wealthiest communities in the country, and the only sign of money was its absence. The developer's hand was stayed from these hills and woods to perpetuate a view of California as it had existed a hundred years earlier. Even the Southern Pacific commuter train, whose whistle I heard in the distance, was a subsidized prop, reminding listeners of the pristine age before Henry Ford gave wheels to the masses. A hundred years earlier, Grover Linden raised monuments to his wealth, but his heirs bought privacy, the ultimate luxury. Judge Paris lived somewhere in those hills, as safe as money could make him. Like God, he moved a finger and the sparrow fell. To him, a little death. But not to me. I floored the accelerator as if physical speed could make time move faster. I would bring this death home to him, whatever it took.

I followed a curve in the road and when I looked up, the darkened skyline burst across the rose-colored sky of dusk, vaguely Oriental in shape and pattern and decidedly sinister. This was the first time I had returned to San Francisco since Hugh's death. Those untroubled summery days seemed far more remote than a mere ten days ago. I exited near the Civic Center and came up Market, now nearly deserted as downtown emptied, toward the bay. For all its magnificence the city seemed shabby to me as little gusts of winds kicked up scraps of newspaper and blew them across the street and the bag ladies stood shapelessly in front of dark windows muttering invectives. It would be cold later. I had not thought to bring a coat.

Stephan Abrams's office was on the fifth floor of a highrise on Montgomery Street. Having called him earlier, I followed his directions and got to his office a few minutes before I was expected. His secretary told me he was on the phone and asked me to sit and wait. I took a look around the office. Chrome-and-leather furniture, off-white walls, industrial gray carpeting, an unnumbered Miro lithograph; all the indicia of unspectacular success. He entered the room and confirmed my image of him.

Abrams was bulky but not fat. He had sharply etched features, a receding hairline he made no attempt to disguise, and eyes that shone from deep within their sockets. He wore a dark gray suit, a white shirt, red silk tie. He looked solid, not one to start a fight but not one to run from a fight either. The perfect all-purpose family lawyer. We shook hands. His grip, predictably, was firm.

"Mr. Rios?" he said. "I'm sorry to make you come up so late in the day but I was booked solid."

"That's fine. I have another appointment a little later."

"Oh? Well, then, there's no problem, is there? You said something over the phone about a client we had in common."

"Yes, Hugh Paris."

"Maggie," he said to his secretary, "why don't you go on home, now. I'll close up here. Step into my office Mr. Rios."

I went into his office and he followed me in, closing the door behind him. There were the usual framed degrees on the wall, one from Berkeley and another from Hastings Law School, full of seals and flourishes; a little vulgar, I thought. Abrams stepped over to a small roll-top desk against a wall, fiddled with the lock and opened it to reveal a bar. He motioned me to one of the two armchairs in front of a large plain desk in the center of the room. Without asking, he poured two glasses of scotch, Chivas Regal, and carried them over. He sat down in the other chair and handed me a glass.

"So," he said, "Hugh Paris. At what point did you represent him?"

"I didn't, actually. I offered but he turned me down. Then you picked up the case and got the charges dismissed."

"It wasn't hard, considering the lab report. Your cops have itchy fingers down there, but then that's true of cops in most college towns when it comes to drugs."

"The voice of experience?"

"I was a P.D. too, in Berkeley, back in the 'sixties." He took a healthy swallow of his drink. I swilled mine around in my glass, to be sociable. I hate scotch. "But the fires burn out."

"You're doing well."

"I have no complaints," he said. "So, what's on your mind, Mr. — look, do you have a first name? Mine's Steve." He smiled engagingly. I was beginning to dislike him.

"Henry," I said. "Did Hugh hire you?"

"I was retained on his behalf."

"By whom? Robert Paris? Aaron Gold?"

"I have to claim the privilege, counsel. But if you speak frankly, then perhaps I can, too."

"Hugh was murdered," I said. "That's to the point, isn't it?"

"Brutally," he replied, smiling. "Do you have any evidence to support your assertion?"

"None that I can share with you." His eyebrows shot up. "But it seems to me that someone who cared enough to hire a lawyer on his behalf might also care enough to assist me in finding his murderer."

"Anything you say to me, Henry, I assure you will reach the right ears."

"I don't deal with middlemen," I said, tasting the scotch.

"Then why did you come here? To insult me?"

"To give your client a message," I said.

"A message, Henry?" he asked softly. "If you want to deliver a message, I suggest UPS. Their rates are lower than mine."

"Tell your client I know who killed Hugh Paris. The police are cooperating and it's just a matter of time before we nail him. He's not safe. And neither are you. You may not answer my questions but you'll answer to a subpoena and, if you're helping to cover up a crime, I'll have you brought up before the Bar."

"Get out of here, Henry, before I throw you out," he said, rising. "Now."

I stood up. "All right. Thank you for your time — Steve. And here's my card." I flicked it on the desk.

I shut the door behind me, and stood outside waiting to see if he picked up the phone. He didn't. I went out into the street. I'd blown it. My purpose in coming to Abrams was to find out for whom he worked and the extent of his relationship to Hugh. Instead, I'd implied misconduct on his part and threatened him. Those were courtroom tactics, not the way to handle an investigation. But then, I'd been thrown out of a number of offices during this investigation. I seemed to be making people uncomfortable. That was some progress. Now, if I could only get them to talk. I set off in the darkness to find Grant Hancock.

☐

Grant lived in a twenty-eighth floor condominium in a building that rose above Embarcadero Plaza. I walked there from Abrams's office through the early evening. Seagulls squawked overhead as I approached the blue awning that marked the entrance. A doorman stood just outside the double glass doors. He wore a blue blazer over gray flannel trousers. I noted the bulge beneath his jacket where he strapped his holster. It was an odd neighborhood for a luxury high-rise, but there were spectacular views of the bay from the condos and, at night, it was as quiet in the streets as a graveyard. In the noisy, cramped city in which new construction was constantly obliterating someone's view, peace and a vista of Sausalito from the living room were reason enough to pay the toney prices for a few hundred square feet of condo.

I identified myself to the doorman and he called up to Grant's apartment. A moment later I boarded a dimly-lit elevator that carried me to the twenty-eighth floor.

I rang the bell and he opened the door. Behind him, in the darkness, candles were burning, and his window framed the bridge and the lights of Marin blazing across the bay. He still wore the slacks from his suit and a button-down shirt the shade of pearl; purchased, no doubt, from one of those men's shops that sell to you only if your great-grandfather had an account with them. The three top buttons of his shirt were undone, revealing a patch of tanned and expensively maintained flesh. His sandy hair was clipped short above his ears and the handsome, expressionless face was as mysterious and self-contained as ever. He smelled of bay rum, and his clear blue eyes took me in with a long detached look. I could see myself in that look; disheveled, thin, dark beneath the eyes and getting grayer, liquor on my breath. I heard, for the first time, music playing softly in the room, guitar and flute.

"Come in, Henry," he said stepping back. I took it all in and smiled. The room was a joke. The candles were set in a pair of silver candlesticks atop an orange crate. There were some pillows stacked against the wall and an elaborate stereo system but no other furnishings. There was, I remembered, a mattress on a box spring in the bedroom and a butcher block table and two chairs in the kitchen. The refrigerator was apt to be stocked with wine, fruit juices, vitamins, some apples and cheese. The kitchen shelves contained a few mismatched plates of heirloom china and beautiful old wine glasses. He was holding one in his hand. The years had faded for a moment and all my feeling for him came back with an intensity that made my heart pound. And then he took a step and the feeling passed as quickly as it had come.

"I see the decorator hasn't been in yet," I said, more edgily than I'd intended.

Grant shrugged. "When I get lonely for furniture I go to my father's house. A glass of wine? Or do you want to stick to whiskey?"

"Wine," I said. "I was drinking scotch with a lawyer."

"A seemingly innocent pursuit," he observed drily, pressing a glass into my hand. "You're awfully thin, Henry. Still forgetting to eat?"

"As always. You look — very well, Grant."

Aloud he said, "Thank you," but he was thinking something else. Bad feelings have a life of their own.

I wanted desperately to say something that would wipe away the stain from our last, angry conversation four years earlier but for me that was all history. I had lost the scent of the emotions that led to the breakup. I had almost forgotten that I was the one who stopped returning calls. I could only think of how well he looked and how it was good to see him.

He sat on the floor, cross-legged. Candlelight blazed through his hair. Theatrical, I thought, but effective. I lowered myself to the floor until we were face to face. "I wanted to ask you about Hugh," I began, tentatively.

"Yes, of course."

"What did you know about him?"

He shrugged. "The Paris family is peninsula and seldom ventures up to the city. I didn't really know Hugh until we were undergrads at Yale. He was younger than I by a couple of years and I took him under my wing." He looked into his wine glass. "I was in love with him," he added simply.

"What happened?"

"Hugh was eighteen and not out of the closet. Neither was I, for that matter. He was tactful enough to overlook my infatuation. We behaved toward each other," he said, suddenly bitter, "like perfect young gentlemen. And at night I lay in bed praying to God to make me different or kill me or, preferable to either, put Hugh beside me."

"You never told me any of this."

"It was ancient history by the time I met you and, besides, I hadn't seen or heard from Hugh in years. Not until about six months ago when I ran into him on the streets. He saw me and tried to slip by but I stopped him. He wasn't particularly friendly but he agreed to have a drink with me that night."

"And did you?"

"Yes, and he spent the night here." A twinge of jealousy constricted my chest for a second. "It was nothing like I'd imagined it would be when I was nineteen," Grant added. "It wasn't memorable and yet—" he poured wine into his glass from the bottle beside him — "I've thought of him almost every day since then. He's one of those people who live less in your memory than your imagination. Like a symbol."

"Of what?" I asked.

"I suppose it's different for everyone who knew him," Grant replied. "For me, he was a symbol of being young and unknowing."

"I've never thought that was an enviable state."

"No? Then maybe life has spared you some of the things I know about."

"I don't think I've been spared much of life's nastiness," I said, "but I don't take it personally. And as for Hugh, I preferred the flesh-and-blood human to the symbol. Tell me, what do you know about the judge?"

"What does anyone know about Robert Paris? The poor boy who made good by marrying into the right family. My father thinks he's the ultimate nouveau riche, but no one denies that he's a brilliant and ruthless man. Of course, that was before the stroke. Now I hear he's half-dead but he hasn't actually been seen in town for months."

"What stroke?"

"He had a series of strokes about a year ago. Since then, he's stayed up on the Linden estate in Portola Valley. He sees no one, and no one sees him."

"What about a man named John Smith?" I asked.

"Are we going to explore every branch of the Linden family tree?" Grant asked mockingly.

"Hugh saw him the day he was killed."

"Well, he is Hugh's great-uncle," Grant replied. "So surely there's nothing unusual about Hugh having seen him."

"I don't know. Is there? What kind of man is John Smith?"

"He's a stuffy old zillionaire," Grant said, "nominally a banker but only in the sense that he owns banks. He's Robert Paris's brother-in-law and controls the other half of the Linden fortune. He and the judge don't get along."

"Really? Do you know that as a fact?"

"Good Lord, Henry, half of the city knows that as a fact."

"Then he's someone Hugh might have gone to for help."

"Help for what?"

"I don't know. I'd like to talk to him though."

"It's easier to see the Pope," Grant said, "and probably more fun."

"What do you mean?"

"Smith is a recluse. You'd never get past the palace guard."

"Could you?"

"I'd have to know why I'm trying."

"I think Robert Paris had Hugh murdered."

Grant sipped his wine. "You're crazy," he remarked cheerfully. "Smith would throw you out the minute you uttered those words." Grant shook his head. "Sorry, I can't help you."

He finished his wine and set the glass down on the floor.

"I'm perfectly serious, Grant."

"That's your forte," he said, "but even so you don't go to someone like John Smith to accuse a member of his family of homicide. That's what the police are for."

"They're not interested."

"Then perhaps you should take your cue from them," he said, rising. "I'm going out to get some dinner. Want to join me?"

"I can't tonight, but I'll take a rain check."

"Suit yourself," he said. "I'll call you."

Rising to leave I said, "It was good to see you again, Grant."

A smile, at once cynical and tender, flickered across his lips. "What amazes me most about you," he said, "is your sincerity."

"I'm afraid that it's my only social skill."

"Good night, Henry," he said, letting me out.

I stepped out of Grant's building, passing the doorman who acknowledged my departure with the slightest of nods. I had parked down by the piers on Embarcadero and had walked, first to Abrams' office and then to see Grant. Now as I returned to my car, walking beneath the freeway, the streets around Embarcadero Plaza were deserted. It was only the racket from the freeway and the lumbering noise of the buses as they screeched to a halt at the nearby bus yard that gave an illusion of activity.

It was the road noise that kept me from making out my name the first time it was shouted by a voice behind me. The second time I heard it distinctly, stopped, and turned around. A man, my height but considerably more muscular, hurried toward me. He wore tight levis and a leather bomber jacket over a white t-shirt. As he stepped beneath a streetlight, I saw he was carrying something in his right hand. A gun. Aimed at my stomach.

"Henry," he said in a friendly voice, "I've been shouting at you for the last block." His dark hair was cut short and he wore a carefully clipped moustache. He was good-looking in an anonymous sort of way. A Castro clone.

"I don't think I know you," I said.

"Well, we're going to be good friends before the night is over."

He kept the gun on me while he raised his left hand in the air and motioned toward us. A moment later a car — black, Japanese, four-door, with its lights out and no license plate — crept up beside us. Two other men were in the front seat and one in the back. The two in the front and my friend with the gun were not only dressed identically but, as far as I could see, might have been a set of triplets. The man in the back seat differed from the others only in that he was a blond. He stepped out of the car and approached us.

"Hello, Henry. Just relax and do what you're told and everything will be fine."

"Sure," I said, as the car came up directly behind me.

The blond reached into his back pocket and pulled out a black bandana, of the kind allegedly used by some gay men to indicate their sexual specialties. I didn't think that he was signaling me for a date. Smiling, he brought the bandana over my eyes and tied it at the back of my head.

"Put your hands out, please," he said.

I put my hands out slowly. They were bound with rough twine. I was led by the arm into the back seat, where I was wedged between the two men. Lest I forget who was in charge, the dark-haired man pushed the nozzle of the gun against my side, just below my ribs.

The motor started and the car jumped forward. It was pretty quiet outside, so I assumed we were traveling on the periphery of the city. I had no sense of time. Finally, we stopped and the only noise I heard was the sound of the sea as someone unrolled a window and the wind swept in.

It occurred to me that I was about to be killed. I wondered if it would hurt. I wondered if there was an after-life. I supposed that I was about to find out. It was too bad I hadn't gone to dinner with Grant.

"Who sent you?" I asked.

A voice that I recognized as belonging to the blond said, reasonably, "Don't ask questions you don't expect answers to."

My arms were pulled out in front of me. I felt something cold and liquid dabbed at the inside of my arm at my elbow. The smell of alcohol filled the car.

"Nice biceps," the blond said. "You lift weights, Henry?"

"No," I said. "It's heredity."

"You're lucky then," he replied. "I have to lift pretty hard to stay in shape."

The needle hit me with a shock, and I jerked my arms back.

"Steady," the dark-haired man said, holding the gun against my neck. "Stay cool."

"What is it?" I asked.

"We have some questions for you," the blond replied. "This will make it easier for you to answer them."

Minutes, or hours, passed. My tongue felt heavy in my mouth. Things stopped connecting in my head. I struggled to stay awake but it was like trying to keep my exhausted body afloat in a warm sea. It was so much easier just to give up and go under.

"Sodium pentothal," I muttered in a voice that I vaguely recognized as my own. "Truth serum."

"Very impressive," the blond said. "Now relax."

"It doesn't work," I murmured, half to myself. "Results aren't admissible in court. I won't tell you — anything I — don't want to—"

"Quiet now," one of them was saying. I couldn't tell which anymore. "Rest. Later we'll talk."

I heard a roaring in my ears that was either the ocean or the sound of my blood.

— 6 —

Something scampered across my ankles. I opened my eyes in time to watch a rat's tail disappear between one of the two garbage cans I was wedged between. It was still dark. There was a wall behind me, a street-lamp far away, and even more distant, the noise of traffic. My head felt like glass, as if the slightest unplanned move would shatter it. I turned my wrist and slowly brought my watch to my face. It was one-thirty. I had left Grant's apartment just before ten — three and a half hours lost. I tried to remember. We had driven around a lot and someone asked me a lot of questions but I couldn't remember what had been said or whether I'd responded. And then I passed out. And now I was awake.
  Sort of.
  I lifted myself up and found that I was standing in an alley that dead-ended into a brick wall. At the other end, I saw a light and started moving toward it. The light seemed to move away and I kept running into things, trash cans, piles of boxes, the wall. This is not a dream, I told myself, though the atmosphere was as fetid as a nightmare. Finally, I reached the lamp-post and hugged it, closing my eyes and waiting for things to stop spinning. When I looked again, everything was more or less still as I tried to get my bearings.
  There was a wide, dimly lit street beside me and warehouses all around. The spire of the Transamerica pyramid, surrounded by the other downtown skyscrapers, loomed ahead of me. Judging by distance, I concluded that I was somewhere south of Market. I made my way up to the first intersection and read the

street signs, Harrison at Third; one block south of Folsom and about eight blocks east of the gay bars where I might find help. I headed north to Folsom and turned left, feeling worse with each step as I became more conscious of my nausea and my aching body. The street was full of shadows and silences, and the darkness seemed unending. Had I been in less pain, I would have been terrified.

As I walked down the street, I attempted to puzzle out the identity of my abductors. All roads led to Robert Paris. They had been waiting for me when I came out of Grant's building. Whether Abrams had called them or they'd followed me into the city, it was clear that my nosing around had not gone unnoticed. Aaron had warned me I was being watched. Until this moment I hadn't believed him. The judge wanted to know how much I knew about Hugh's murder. Apparently, I didn't know enough to be gotten rid of. Yet.

Ahead of me I saw men walking up and down the street. I came to a corner and looked up. There was a red neon sign on an angle above a door. It said Febe's. I crossed the street and stood at the open doorway. Directly inside the entry was a brown vinyl curtain that reached to the floor, and beyond it I heard muffled noises. I pushed through the curtain just in time for last call at one of the most notorious leather bars in the city.

Two men were playing at a pinball machine on my left. One of them wore black leather pants, shiny in the dim light, and a leather vest. The other wore jeans, a t-shirt and a collar around his neck studded with metal spikes. He sipped from a bottle of Perrier. To my right there was a curved bar bathed in red lights. All heads turned toward me. In my slacks and gray polo shirt I was in the wrong clothes for Febe's. The atmosphere began to change from curiosity to hostility.

I had now been standing at the door for more than a minute. The bartender, undoubtedly thinking I was a tourist, scowled and started to come out from behind the bar. I took a couple of steps toward him and then passed out.

I was awakened with a hit of amyl nitrate.

"Jesus Christ," I muttered, pushing the donor's hands out of my face. "Enough."

The hands withdrew and a voice asked, "You all right?"

"I'm better," I said, sitting up from the floor.

The bartender knelt beside me. He was wearing a tight pair of levis and a pink bowling shirt with the name Norma Jean stitched above the pocket. Most of his face was lost behind a thick beard, but the concern in his wide blue eyes would have done justice to my mother.

"Good," he said. "I'll just call a cab and you can go back to the St. Francis or wherever you're staying and sleep it off."

"I'm not drunk," I said, slurring my words. "Drugged. I was drugged."

"Against your will?"

I nodded.

"Honey, that musta been some scene." He smiled. "He hurt you?"

I shook my head.

"Did he take your money?"

"No," I said, "they just drove me around and asked me questions."

"Now that's bizarre. Should I get the cops?"

"No, I'd like to call a friend."

"Oh, are you a local?"

I nodded.

"Hell, the way you came in here staring I thought you were a tourist who'd taken the wrong turn at Fisherman's Wharf."

"Next time," I mumbled, "I'll remember you have a dress code. Help me to the phone, okay?"

"Sure," he said, rising to his full height. I grabbed his extended hands and he raised me up, effortlessly. The bar was empty and all the lights were on, revealing a homey and rather shabby tavern. Apparently I'd cleared the place out. He led me around the bar to the house phone. "You make your call. I've got to clean up."

"Thanks. I know your name's not Norma Jean."

"Dean," he said, grabbing a broom.

"Thanks, Dean. I'm Henry." He nodded acknowledgement while I dialed Grant's number.

Grant picked up the phone on the second ring, and I remembered he was a light sleeper. I told him, briefly, what had learned and asked if he would come and pick me up. Wide awake, he told me to wait and that he was on his way. I hung up.

Dean brought me a glass of brandy and had me sit on a stool behind the bar as he went back to his work. I watched him lifting boxes of empty beer bottles and stacking them against the wall.

Someone was knocking at the front door. Dean glanced over at me and then went to answer it, behind the curtain. He emerged a second later followed by Grant Hancock. With his Burberry overcoat and perfectly groomed hair, Grant looked as if he had just stepped off the pages of a fashion magazine. Dean winked at me, approvingly.

Grant came up and inspected me. "You look terrible, Henry. Should we get you to a hospital?"

"I think everything's working," I said. "I just need a ride back to my car."

"Your car? What you need is sleep. Come on."

I got up and followed him out. Dean walked us to the curb where Grant had parked.

"Thanks, Dean." I reached out and patted his arm awkwardly, wanting to say more but not sure what.

"Come back sometime," he said, smiling. I climbed into Grant's car. We drove through the soundless streets to his building.

"I really should get back home tonight," I said.

"Henry, it's three-thirty in the morning," Grant replied as he steered into the underground garage and parked in a numbered stall. "No one has to do anything at three-thirty, especially you. You're hardly awake now. I doubt that you could make it all the way back."

"You're probably right," I said. "I'll stay."

"Of course you will," he replied, getting out of the car.

When we got to his condo, I took a hot shower, changed into borrowed clothes and asked for a drink. We sat on the floor in the living room drinking brandy by candlelight. The room was very still as Grant had me explain the events which occurred after I left his apartment.

"I think," he said, "that you are lucky to be alive."

"I agree, and now I know, beyond any doubt, that the judge was responsible for Hugh's death."

"So now you can stop and go on with your life."

"What?"

Grant swirled the brandy in his glass, watching it streak and run down the sides. "The mystery is solved."

"But I still have to prove the solution."

"To whom?"

"The police, to begin with, and maybe, at some point, a jury."

"Are you serious?" he asked, putting his glass down. "You think you can prove this against Robert Paris? Do you know anything about the man?"

"As a general proposition? No."

"You're talking about one of the most powerful men in the state," he said. "You're talking about a man who declined appointment to the United States Supreme Court."

"I didn't know that," I said.

"That's the point. Think of it this way, Henry. You and the judge both have piles of stones to throw at each other. You've pretty much used yours up but he hasn't even started. He's been playing with you."

"Schoolboys throw rocks at frogs in sport," I quoted, "but the frogs die in earnest."

"No," Grant said. "Not for sport. For power. I know Robert Paris," he continued, staring into his glass. "You don't stand a chance."

"Is this the voice of experience talking?"

Grant looked up. "My father," he began, "got it into his head that he wanted to be mayor of this city. Have you met my father?" I nodded. My recollection was of an elegant but rather dim patrician whom Grant inexplicably idolized. "Robert Paris was backing another candidate who would have trounced my father anyway. But just to make sure," he set his glass down and looked away, "they told my father I was gay and that if he persisted, the whole town would know. That's how my father found out his only son was homosexual. My father is a man," he continued, "who still thinks gay is a perfectly acceptable adjective for divorcees. Or did, anyway. It broke his heart," Grant said. "It really did."

"Grant, I'm sorry."

He shrugged. "That's water under the bridge," he said, "but the moral is: Don't fuck with Robert Paris. Hugh's dead. You're not." And then he added softly, "I'm not."

"But if it had been you rather than Hugh, I'd do the same."

He smiled a little. "You miss my meaning."

"No," I said, reaching out to touch his hand, "I don't."

☐

"What time is it?" Grant mumbled, turning over in bed.

"A little after six," I replied, buttoning my shirt.

"You're leaving?"

"Yes, there's someone I have to see."

"Your associates keep odd hours." He sat up in bed, watching me tie my shoes.

"Will you call Smith for me?" I asked.

He thought about it a second.

"I still don't see the point of it," he said.

"The police wouldn't reopen their investigation without pressure from somewhere. Who better than Smith?"

"If you could only give me something more concrete," he said.

"If I didn't know you better, Grant, I'd say John Smith intimidates you."

"He does. It's not often I ask for an audience with a local deity."

"Okay," I said, "then don't."

"I'm sorry, Henry. I just can't see getting involved at this point."

"You've already been helpful, Grant."

"Thanks."

We looked at each other.

"Is this it, then?" he asked.

"No," I replied. "No."

I leaned over and kissed him.

"All right," he said.

☐

An hour later I was finishing breakfast in Terry Ormes' kitchen. She cooked well for a cop, I thought as I swallowed a forkful of scrambled eggs. It occurred to me that I could not remember when I had eaten last. The eggs were good — she put tarragon in them. She was talking on the phone, explaining to someone why she would be late for work. I got up and cleared the table, rinsing dishes and stacking them in the dishwasher. Her kitchen was long, sunny and narrow. Everything was in its place but this bespoke an orderly presence rather than a fussy one. She finished her call and came back into the kitchen carrying a manila folder. She sat down at the kitchen table. I joined her there.

"More coffee?" she asked, pouring herself a cup.

"Sure," I said, noticing for the first time that the backs of her hands were covered with faint freckles.

"How long have you been a cop?" I asked, continuing our earlier conversation.

"Seven years, going on twenty."

"Tough life?"

"It's what I always wanted. My dad was a cop. He got as high up as captain before he retired."

"Did he want you to join the force?"

"He never came out and said it, but he was happy that I did."

"And your mother?"

"She'd have been happier if I'd gone into something more feminine. Schoolteaching, for instance, like my brother." She sipped her coffee. "What about you? Was your dad a lawyer?"

"No, he was foreman of the night crew at a cannery in Marysville. I'm the only lawyer in my family."

"The scuttlebutt around the station is that you're good."

"I am," I said.

"But you're not a great cop," she said, "judging from what happened to you last night. The first thing we learn is not to take unnecessary risks."

"And how do you know when a risk is unnecessary? I was playing a hunch going to see Abrams. I didn't think much would come from it. I was wrong."

"I'll say. Why don't you run your next scheme by me and let me decide if it's an unnecessary risk?"

I laughed. "Are you my partner or my mother?"

"I guess that depends on what you need most," Terry said. "Let's get to work."

She opened the manila folder and handed me a thin sheaf of papers.

"What's this?"

"Hugh Paris," she said. "Everything I could get on him."

"Doesn't seem like much."

"It isn't. He didn't have a California driver's license so I ran his name with DMV and came back with nothing. The only criminal record he has was his arrest in July. No credit cards, no known bank accounts. He leased his house from something called the Pegasus Corporation, one of those companies that owns companies."

I'd been going through the papers as I listened to her. "These are his phone bills?"

"For the last six months. Service was in his name. An unlisted number."

A fair number of the calls were to Portola Valley — the judge — and even a couple to my apartment. It was odd to see my phone number there and I wondered if anyone else had obtained these records. And then I noticed a number of calls made to Napa. I asked Terry about them.

"They were made to a private mental institution called Silverwood. You know anything about that?"

"His father is a patient there," I replied, writing the number down. I came to the last page. "I thought there'd be more."

"So did I. I get the feeling he was deliberately lying low." I nodded agreement. She took out a bundle of papers from the folder and pushed them across to me. "I had better luck with the grandmother and uncle," she said. I had asked her to find out what she could about the car crash which had killed Hugh's grandmother, Christina, and his uncle, Jeremy, twenty years earlier. Hugh had maintained that his grandfather was responsible for those deaths.

Terry had obtained copies of the accident report prepared by the CHP, written within a couple of hours of the collision. She had also gotten the coroner's findings based on an inquest held in San Francisco three days after the accident.

The CHP concluded that the car, driven by Jeremy Paris, had been headed east into Nevada on highway 80 at the time of the crash. It was dusk, a few days before Thanksgiving, the road was icy, traffic was light and there had been a snowstorm earlier in the week. The Paris car had been in the far left lane, nearest the center divider, a metal railing about four feet high. There was reason to believe that Jeremy Paris had been speeding.

About twenty miles outside of Truckee, disaster overcame the Parises. Their car suddenly went through the center divider, skidded off the side of the road across four lanes of westbound traffic, nearly hit a westbound car, and plunged off the road where its fall was broken by a stand of trees. Within a matter of moments, the car burst into flames. Christina Paris was dead when the police got to her, having been summoned by the driver of the car who had narrowly avoided being struck by the Paris car. Jeremy Paris died in the ambulance.

The driver of the other car, Warren Hansen, was the only witness and had provided details of the accident to the police. Hansen had been returning home to Sacramento from a week's skiing. He, the report noted in cop talk, was HBD — had been drinking, shorthand for drunk. Hansen claimed that the Paris car was going too fast for the road and that it appeared to be followed by another car, tailing it from the next lane over. He remembered that the second car was dark and its lights were off. He said that just before the accident the dark car had been striking against the back bumper of the Paris car.

All these statements were duly noted by the cop who took the report. They were then dismissed by the sergeant who signed off on the report and who remarked that Hansen was drunk and further disoriented by the shock of nearly having been in a serious collision. The sergeant concluded that Jeremy Paris had simply lost control of his car as he sped down the icy roads at dusk, the most treacherous hour for motorists. It was plausible. I could almost hear the sergeant sighing with relief as he filed the report; another mess averted.

I turned to the coroner's report. Sitting without a jury, he accepted the findings of the CHP as to the circumstances of the accident, based upon the brief testimony of a single witness, the sergeant. He added some information from the autopsies; charred meat is essentially all that had been left of Christina and Jeremy Paris. Finally, he fixed the times of their deaths. According to the coroner, given the circumstances of the accident and the conditions of the bodies, the deaths could be characterized as essentially simultaneous. When I came upon that phrase, simultaneous death, something clicked in the back of my mind.

I went on to the next page. It was a death certificate, made out for Warren Hansen who died on April 27, of a self-inflicted gunshot wound. Six months after the accident. I looked up at Terry.

"Up to this," I said, holding the death certificate, "I could almost believe it was just an accident."

"Me, too," she said. "But as soon as I got it, all the loose ends unraveled again." She explained that it made no sense to hold the inquest without calling the only eye-witness to the accident, or the paramedics who brought the bodies up from the crash and who could have testified to the times of death. "But then," she continued, "it dawned on me that that was the whole reason for the inquest. To set the times of death. There's no other reason to hold a coroner's inquest for a simple car accident. They don't usually call the coroner unless there's some question about the deaths."

"But there wasn't any question here," I said. "And certainly no reason to hold the inquest hundreds of miles from where the accident occurred and three days afterwards. The only difference between the police report and the coroner's inquest were the times of death. Someone wasn't happy with the fact that Jeremy Paris was still alive when they pulled him from the car."

"Naturally," she said, "I thought it was the judge who requested the coroner but I was wrong. It was John Smith, Christina's brother, who arranged it."

I thought for a moment. "Well, maybe he suspected," I replied, "and wanted a coroner's independent examination of the accident."

Terry laughed derisively.

"What?" I asked.

"That's not what Smith got," she said. "The examining coroner was Tom Fierro. Do you know about him?" I shook my head. "He's the guy they discovered with the suitcases of money under his bed. My dad used to talk about him and said that Tom was everyone's favorite coroner. When you bought him, he stayed bought."

"Do you think he was paid off?"

She sighed eloquently. "Of course I do, but who am I going to ask about it?" She gathered up the papers and stacked them neatly. "What's our next move?"

"All this means something," I mused, "and if I just sat still long enough it would come to me. But I can't sit still. These calls to Napa," I said, lifting the phone bills. "Maybe Hugh said something to his father that could help us. That's where I'm going. You work on finding out more about John Smith. He may hold the key."

"I don't know," she said, "I think there are too many doors for just one key. Stay in touch."

☐

The street sign was so discreetly placed that I missed it the first time and drove on until I found myself at a dead end. I turned around and drove slowly until I saw that the narrow opening between clumps of dusty bushes was, in fact, a road; a back road off a back road at the edge of Napa's suburban sprawl.

It was one of those luminescent autumn days. The sky was radiantly blue and the air was warm and silty. You drank rather than breathed it. At my right, a white picket fence appeared and beyond it, orchards and pasture. These gave way to a large, formal lawn, arbors, tennis courts, and a rose garden, looking for all the world like the grounds of a country club.

Only there was no one around.

I looked over to my left and saw a white antebellum mansion shimmering like a mirage in the heat of the day. Smaller bungalows surrounded it at a respectful distance, each in the shade of its own great oak. One or two people moved slowly down a walk between the big house and one of the smaller ones. I turned into a circular driveway and drove up to a parking lot at the side of the house. I got out of my car and went up the steps of the great house, crossed the veranda and touched the doorbell.

Above the bell was a small brass plate with the word "Silverwood" etched into it.

A husky young man dressed in orderly's white appeared at the door. "May I help you?"

"I've come to see Mr. Nicholas Paris," I said, extracting a business card from my breast pocket and handing it to him.

He studied it.

"Are you expected?"

"I was his late son's lawyer," I replied. "He'll know who I am."

The attendant looked at me and then opened the door. I stood in a massive foyer. There was a small table off the side of the staircase where he had been sitting. He went to the table, picked up the phone and dialed three numbers.

"There's a lawyer out here to see one of the patients." He paused. "Okay, clients, then. Anyway, he's out here now." He hung up and said, "Have a seat," gesturing me to a sofa against the wall beneath a portrait of a seventeenth-century gentleman. I sat down. The attendant went back to his book, something called The Other David. The house was still, but the air was nervous.

"Where are the patients?" I asked.

"Everyone takes a nap after lunch," he replied, looking up, "just like kindergarten."

"You a nurse?"

"Do I look like a nurse?" His muscles bulged against his white uniform. "I keep people out there," he gestured to the door, "from getting in and people in here from getting out."

"Nice work if you can get it," I observed.

He grunted and went back to his book.

A moment later, a short, bald man stepped into the foyer from a room off the side. He wore a white doctor's coat over a pale blue shirt and a red knit tie. He looked like an aging preppie and I was willing to bet that he wore argyle socks. The attendant handed him my business card.

"Mr. Rios," he said, "I'm Dr. Phillips, the director. Why don't we step into the visitor's lounge?"

I followed him into the room from which he had emerged. It was a long, narrow rectangle, paneled in dark wood, furnished in stiff-backed Victorian chairs and couches clustered in little groups around coffee tables. The view from the windows was of a rose garden. A dozen long-stemmed red roses had been stiffly arranged in a vase on the mantel of the fireplace. A grandfather clock ticked away in a corner. Except for us, the room was deserted.

Phillips lowered himself in a wing chair and I sat across from him. The little table between us held a decanter filled with syrupy brown fluid and surrounded by small wine glasses. He poured two drinks. I lifted a glass and sniffed, discreetly. Cream sherry. I sipped, crossing my legs at my ankles like a gentleman.

"Now, then, Mr. Rios, what can we," he said, using the imperial, medical we, "do for you?"

"I represent the estate of Hugh Paris, the son of one of your patients—"

"Clients," he cautioned.

"Clients," I agreed. "At any rate, Hugh Paris died rather — suddenly, and there are some problems with the will I believe I could clear up by speaking to his father, Nicholas."

Phillips shook his head. "That's quite impossible. You must know that Nicholas Paris is incompetent."

"Doctor, that's a legal conclusion, not a medical diagnosis. I was told he has moments of lucidity."

"Far and few between," Phillips said, dismissively. "Perhaps if you told me what you need, I could help you."

"All right," I said. "I drafted Hugh Paris's will which, as it happens, made certain bequests that violate the rule in Shelley's case, rendering the document ineffective. I had hoped that Mr. Paris, as his son's intestate heir, would agree to certain modifications that would effect the testater's intent, at least as to those bequests which do not directly concern his interests in the estate."

Phillips's eyes had glazed over at the first mention of the word will. He now bestirred himself and said, "I see."

"Then you understand my problem," I plunged on, "I am responsible for drafting errors in Hugh's will. There's some question of malpractice—"

Phillips perked up. "Malpractice?" He was now on comfortable ground. "I sympathize, of course, but Mr. Paris is hardly in any condition to discuss such intricate legal matters."

"I only need ten minutes with him," I said.

"Really," Phillips said, lighting a cigarette, "you don't understand. Mr. Paris is not lucid."

I could tell our interview was coming to an end. I tried another tack. "But he's being treated."

Phillips lifted an eyebrow. "We can do very little of that in Mr. Paris's case. We try to make him comfortable and see that he poses no danger to himself or others."

"Is he violent?"

"Not very."

"Drugs?"

"The law permits it."

"You know, doctor," I said, "even those who cannot be reached by treatment can sometimes be reached by subpoena."

Phillips sat up. "What are you talking about?"

"A probate hearing, with all the trimmings. You might be called to testify to Paris's present mental condition and the type of care he's received here. It might even be necessary to subpoena his medical records. I understand he's been here for nearly twenty years. That's a long time, doctor, time enough to turn even a genius into a vegetable with the right kind of — treatment."

Phillips fought to keep his composure.

"I could have you thrown out," he said softly.

"And I'll be back with the marshal and a bushel of subpoenas."

In an even softer voice he asked, "What is it you want?"

"I want to make sure he's too crazy to sue me."

Phillips expelled his breath, disbelievingly. "Is that all?" He rose from the chair. "Ten minutes, Mr. Rios, and you'll go?"

"Never to darken your doorway again."

"Wait here," he said abruptly and left the room. I poured my sherry into a potted plant.

When Nicholas Paris entered the room, the air went dead around him. He wore an old gray blazer over a white shirt and tan khaki slacks. No belt. He might have been a country squire returning from a walk with his white-blond hair, ruddy complexion and composed features — there was more than a hint of Hugh in his face. But then you looked into his eyes. They were blue and they stared out as if from shadows focusing on a landscape that did not exist beneath the mild California sun. I felt the smile leak from my face. Phillips sat him down in a chair, scowled at me and said, "Ten minutes."

I approached him. "Nicholas?"

He inclined his head toward me.

"My name is Henry. I was Hugh's friend."

He said nothing.

I knelt beside the chair and looked at him. It was as if he were standing behind a screen: the thousand splinters refused to add up to a human face. I saw that his pupils were moving erratically. Drugs.

"I was his friend," I continued. "Your son Hugh."

He looked away, out the window.

He said in a voice hoarse from disuse, "Hugh."

"Hugh," I said.

I kept talking, softly. I told him how I had met Hugh and how much I had cared for him. I told him that I believed Hugh's death was a murder. I was telling him that I needed to know what, if anything, Hugh had said to him when he visited here.

Nicholas Paris stared out the window as I spoke, giving no indication that he heard anything but the loud chirping of a bird outside.

And then, suddenly, I saw a tear run from the corner of his eye. A single, streaky tear.

He said, "Is Hugh dead?"

He hadn't known.

"Oh, God," I muttered. "I'm sorry."

"That's enough," a woman spoke, commandingly, above me. I looked up. Katherine Paris stood, coldly composed, beside me. Her face was red beneath her makeup, and her small, elegant hands were clenched into fists. I glanced up at the doorway. Phillips was standing there and, behind him, two burly orderlies.

I rose from the floor. "Good afternoon, Mrs. Paris."

She raised a hand and slapped me. "Get him out of here," she ordered Phillips.

He gave a signal and the orderlies moved in.

— 7 —

It was dusk when Katherine Paris's bronze-colored Fiat came off the road that led from Silverwood and turned onto the highway. I switched off the radio, started my car, and followed her. There was no reason to think she would recognize my car; blue Accords are so common as to be almost invisible on the roads of California. She led me past vineyards, orchards, farm houses, and a desolate-looking housing tract with street names like Chardonnay and Pinot Noir. It was getting chilly out, a sign of autumn in the air. We drove on and on, deeper into the country between gently wooded hills now gloomy in the thick blue light of early evening. She turned her lights on and I turned on mine. A truck roared by and then a motorcycle and then it was just the two of us again, and the dense smell of wet earth rising from the darkened fields around us.

It would have been nice, I thought, had Hugh Paris been beside me. There was a restaurant in St. Helena that I'd been to once and liked. We could have driven there for dinner and stayed overnight somewhere and visited the wineries the next day. Eliot had it wrong about memory and desire; they smelled like wet earth on an autumn night and had nothing to do with spring.

My thoughts drifted back to the task at hand. The Fiat's turn signal flashed on and we went down a narrow road. A brightly-lit three-story building rose just ahead of us. A sign above the entrance identified it as the Hotel George. The hotel was constructed of wood, painted white with green trim, a charming old place. A wide porch surrounded the first floor and chairs were lined up near the railing. They were mostly empty now. She parked and I watched her climb the steps and walk quickly across the porch into the building.

I waited in my car to see whether she would come out. There were some hot springs in the vicinity and I imagined that the George was a place from which people commuted to them. There were only three other cars in the lot; business, apparently, was slow.

When she failed to come out after five minutes, it occurred to me that Mrs. Paris might be meeting someone. Who? A member of the family? It was a small family to begin with and events had savaged it.

Of Linden's grandchildren, John and Christina Smith, only Christina married. She and Robert had two sons, Jeremy and Nicholas. Of the two sons only Nicholas married and he and Katherine had produced only one child, Hugh. Of these four generations, the only survivors were John Smith, the judge, mad Nicholas and Katherine herself. The decimation of Grover Linden's descendents proceeded as if in retribution. I shook myself out of my musing and realized that another five minutes had passed. I decided to go in after her.

The lobby was a little rectangular space, the floor covered with a thick gray carpet, the furnishings dark Spanish-style chairs and tables. A polished staircase beside the registration desk led to the upper floors. Across from the desk was an open door with a small neon sign above the doorway identifying it as the bar. I went over and looked in. Through the dimly-lit darkness I could see her, sitting on a high stool at the end of the bar. I walked in and approached her from behind. She was alone.

I took the stool next to her, ordering bourbon and water. I wished her a good evening.

Her head swiveled toward me until we were face to face. I saw exhaustion in her eyes so deep that it quickly extinguished the flash of anger that registered when she recognized me. There was contempt in her look and disdain and beneath it all a plea to be left alone. I regretted that I could not comply.

"May I buy you a drink, Mrs. Paris?"

"Why not," she said mockingly. "I'm sure they'll take your money here and I never refuse a drink." I summoned the bartender and ordered refills. "You follow me here?"

"Yes."

"Why?"

"To talk."

"About Hugh?"

"Not necessarily. We could talk about you. Or your husband. Or your ex-father-in-law."

"I find none of those subjects appealing," she said. The darkness of the room cast shadows that hid all but the deepest lines in her face and she looked like a much younger woman. She was small, her feet not reaching to the metal ring at the bottom of the barstool, and, for an instant, as she lifted her drink she looked as fragile as a child.

"Then tell me about your poetry."

She looked sidewise at me. "Mr. Rios, I once had a talent for writing, a very small talent. I used it up a long time ago, or drank it up, perhaps. At any rate, that subject is the least appealing of all." After a moment's silence, she asked abruptly, "Do you like your life?"

"You mean, am I happy?"

'Yes, if you want to be vulgar about it." She finished her drink. Another soldier down.

"I have been, from time to time."

"A lawyer's answer," she said disdainfully. "Mincing — oh, pardon me. Equivocal. What I mean is," and her voice was suddenly louder, "on the whole, wouldn't you rather be dead?"

"No."

"Well I often think I would," she said softly.

"Why?"

She shook her head. "Every drop of meaning has been squeezed from my life. I hardly expect you to understand."

"Your husband?"

"My husband," she said. Another drink had appeared in front of her. I realized that I was about to be the recipient of the drunken confidences of an old, depressed woman. Common decency almost got me out of the bar, but not quite. "I married

Nick Paris in my sophomore year at Radcliffe. I had an old Boston name and no money. He was rich and crazy. I knew about the rich but not the crazy." She scraped a fingernail across the surface of her glass. "I wanted to be Edna St. Vincent Millay, Mr. Rios. Instead, I became a crazy rich man's wife. And a minor poet." She stared at me as if trying to remember who I was. "What is it you want from me?"

"Who killed Hugh?"

"Oh, that. Why do you think anyone killed Hugh. He was quite capable of killing himself."

"And you would rather be dead but here you are, alive and well."

"Alive, perhaps. I can't help you, darling. I was bought and paid for long ago."

"By whom?"

"Surely you know enough about this family to know by whom. When I married Nick his parents were horrified by my poverty, tried to buy an annulment but by then I was pregnant with Hugh. We came out to California and things were fine for awhile. Christina, my mother-in-law, treated me quite well. And Jeremy, of course, I was quite fond of."

"Your brother-in-law."

She nodded. "Then it went bad." She lit a cigarette.

"What happened?"

"Christina wanted a divorce. Her husband wouldn't hear of it."

"The judge."

"Of course. The marriage was working for him. He had what he wanted from the family — money, power, prestige. And he treated her like a chattel and his sons like less than that. He is, you know, a malevolent human being."

"I gathered."

She looked at me. "Hugh tell you some stories? I assure you, there are worse." She expelled a stream of cigarette smoke toward her reflection in the barroom mirror. "Then they were killed, Christina and Jeremy."

"Do you know where they were going at the time?"

"To Reno. Christina was to obtain a divorce. Jerry went for

moral support. It was all very conspiratorial. They left early in the morning without telling the judge, but he found out. The next day they brought the bodies back."

"He killed them."

"Do your own addition," she said. "Nicholas was already sick by then. He really loved Jeremy and after Jeremy's death he deteriorated pretty quickly. Perhaps not so quickly as to warrant that lunatic bin, but that's a matter for the doctors to dispute."

"And what happened to you?"

"I was having an affair at the time," she said, "and Paris — the judge — hired an investigator to document my indiscretion. He demanded that I agree to a divorce and renounce my rights to Nick's estate. Unfortunately, I had acquired a taste for wealth, so I was desperate to salvage something. And, as it happened, I had a pawn to play." She touched a loose strand of hair, tucking it back.

"Hugh?"

"Yes. His father's heir. I gave Paris custody of my son and got in exchange—"

"Your thirty pieces of silver," I said bitterly.

"Considerably more than that," she said. "And what right do you have to judge me? He was nothing to you but a trick."

"No," I said. "I loved him."

She looked away from me. A moment later she said, "I have never understood homosexuality. I can't picture what you men do with each other."

"I could tell you but it would completely miss the point."

"I'm sorry, Mr. Rios, and about so many things it's hardly worth while to begin enumerating them now."

"Would you like me to drive you back into the city?"

"No, thank you. The bartender cuts me off at ten and I take a room in the hotel. I'll be fine." She had stepped down from the barstool. "Goodnight, Mr. Rios."

"Goodnight, Mrs. Paris."

Then she was gone, weaving between tables toward a door marked Ladies. I went out into the darkness and the chilly autumn air, drunk and depressed.

◻

The next morning I was at the county law library when it opened and spent the next hour ploughing through treatises on the law of trusts and estates. The coroner's phrase, that Christina and Jeremy Paris had died simultaneously, had been ticking away in the back of my mind. I'd thought about it all the way back from Napa. There had to be a reason for the discrepancy between the times of death recorded at the scene of the accident and the coroner's finding. The coroner's report was a legal document and there were only two areas of the law to which it pertained, criminal and probate. Since, at the time, there was no issue of criminal liability arising from the accident, the coroner's findings must have been sought for the purposes of the probate court. When I got to that point, I remembered simultaneous death, a phrase I recollected dimly from my trusts and estates class.

I picked up a red-covered casebook, *Testate and Intestate Succession*, eighth edition, by John Henry Howard, Professor Emeritus at Linden University School of Law. Professor Howard had been my teacher for trusts and estates. Back then, he was only up to his fifth edition. I opened the book to the general table of contents. The book was divided into the two main sections, intestate and testate succession. Seeing the two concepts juxtaposed in type on facing pages, I suddenly realized my research mistake. Aaron Gold had told me that Christina Paris had left a will but her estate, nonetheless, passed through intestacy. I had focused on whether there could be a drafting error that would invalidate a will and which, somehow, involved times of death. But the rule of simultaneous death was a concept of intestate succession and it functioned whether a will was properly drawn or not; the issue was not whether a will was correctly drafted, but who it named as a beneficiary. I turned to the more detailed table of contents and, under intestate succession, buried near the bottom of the page, saw the words simultaneous death.

It was not a not a hot topic in the law of estates, rating little more than a page and a half. One page was a general discussion of the concept, with case citations. The other half-page presented a hypothetical situation and a number of questions arising from it. I remembered that Professor Howard's hypos were never as easy as they first looked.

Given the byzantine complications of most estate law, the concept of simultaneous death was relatively simple and straightforward. The underlying premise was that neither a dead person nor his estate should be permitted to inherit a bequest by one living. Consequently, if a woman left her estate to her daughter but her daughter predeceased her, the gift was void. Upon the mother's death the gift reverted to her estate rather than passing to the daughter's heirs.

But what happened if mother and daughter died in such a manner that it was impossible to tell who died first? Did the gift revert to the mother's estate or pass to the daughter's? It was for such a contingency that the rule of simultaneous death arose. Using this rule, the law presumed that where the testator and beneficiary died simultaneously, the beneficiary died first. Consequently, the gift reverted to the estate of the giver and was distributed according to the rest of her testamentary scheme.

So it made no difference whether the will was properly written or not. For instance, a father might make a will leaving everything he owned to his son, but if the son died before the father the will became just a scrap of paper and the father's estate was divided as if the will had never existed. I was beginning to think that something very similar to that had occurred in the case of Christina Paris.

There was one other point about the rule of simultaneous death that had special meaning for me. The presumption, that the testator survived the beneficiary, was rebuttable. This meant that it could be disputed in court by competent evidence. The testimony, say, of the paramedics at the scene of the accident. But if all the probate court had before it was the coroner's report, it was not likely to look further; a court may believe or disbelieve the evidence submitted to it, but it has no means by which to conduct its own investigations.

I turned to the hypothetical. At first glance the facts seemed simple enough, but I read the hypo more carefully the second time looking for land mines. Halfway through it occurred to me that the facts were suspiciously familiar: a wealthy woman left her entire estate to one of her two sons who, subsequently, was killed in the same car accident that killed her. Was it possible that Professor Howard had based this hypo on the facts of Christina Paris's death? Beneath the hypo, Professor Howard provided six additional facts, each of which changed the disposition of the woman's estate. Number six asked whether it would make any difference to the distribution of her wealth if one of her intestate heirs — her husband, perhaps — had arranged the deaths precisely to invalidate the will. *Her husband, perhaps!*

☐

Two hours later I was walking alongside a dusty hedge on a dead-end street in an obscure wooded pocket of the campus where retired professors lived in university-subsidized houses. While it was generally acknowledged at the law school that John Howard, who'd retired eight years earlier, was still alive, he was seldom seen and even more rarely contacted. Finally, some antiquarian in the alumni office had found an address for me.

I came to a white picket gate. Across a weedy, dying lawn and in the shade of an immense oak tree stood a stucco house. It was remarkably still and peaceful-looking, like a ship harbored in calm waters. I pushed the gate open and went up the flagstones to a green door. There was a brass knocker in the shape of a gavel. I knocked, twice.

The door was opened by a middle-aged Asian woman wearing a green frock. She wiped her hands on her apron and eyed me suspiciously. "Yes?"

"I've come to see Professor Howard. Are you Mrs. Howard?"

"Housekeeper," she replied. "You want professor?"

"Yes, does he live here?"

"Sure," she said, "but long time no one comes."

"Well, I'm here," I pointed out.

"I'll get," she said, hurrying away. She'd left the door open so I stepped inside.

There was an odd smell in the house, musty and faintly sweet, a mixture of cigar smoke and furniture polish. I was standing at the end of a long dark hall. An arched entrance led off to a little living room. The furniture, old and very ugly, was too big for the room, as if purchased for some other house of grander proportions. A vacuum cleaner had been parked between two brick-red sofas. There were ashes of a fire in the fireplace. A pot of yellow chrysanthemums blazed on a coffee-table near a tidy stack of legal periodicals. The walls exuded an elderly loneliness. He probably never married, I thought.

The housekeeper appeared, touched my arm and told me to come with her. I followed down the hall and into a bright little kitchen. She opened the door to the back yard and I stepped outside. I saw an empty ruined swimming pool, the bottom filled with yellow leaves. Facing the pool were two white lawn chairs — the old-fashioned wooden ones — and between them a matching table. There was a fifth of vodka, a pint of orange juice and two glasses on the table. One of the chairs was occupied by an old man wearing a sagging red cardigan frayed through at the elbow.

He turned his face to me. His thick gray hair was greasy and disheveled. He now sported a wispy goatee. He held a cigar in one hand as he reached for a glass with his other. Professor John Henry Howard, latest edition.

"You wanted to see me?" he asked in a voice thickened with the sediment of alcohol and old age.

I nodded.

"Well, boy, introduce yourself."

"Henry Rios, sir. Class of '72. I took trusts and estates from you."

He peered at me intently as I approached, hand outstretched. He put down the cigar, shook my hand and motioned me to sit beside him. "'72? A good class, that. Not that many of you cared for probate. No, you belonged more to the quick than the dead. Where did you sit, Mr. —"

"Rios. In the back row."

"Ah, one of those. What was your final grade?"

"An A-minus."

He lifted his shaggy eyebrows and for a second I thought he was going to demand to see my transcript.

"Well, you must've learned something. Have a drink."

"No, I—," but before I could finish he'd filled the glass with vodka and added, as an afterthought, a splash of orange juice. I sipped. It was like drinking rubbing alcohol.

"The smart cocktail," the professor said touching his glass to mine. "One of my remaining pleasures. I have a system, you see. I allow myself only as much vodka as I have orange juice. Through judicious pouring I can make a pint of orange juice last all day."

"The legal mind at work," I said.

Professor Howard chuckled. "Indeed. So, Mr. Rios, what are we going to talk about?"

"I want to ask you about a hypo that appears in your casebook."

"You a probate lawyer?"

"No."

"Good, because if you were I'd charge you, and I ain't cheap. Proceed." He tilted his head back.

I withdrew from my pocket a xeroxed copy of the page in his book with the illustration of simultaneous death. "It's this," I said, handing it to him.

"What's the question?" he asked as he skimmed the page.

"A wealthy woman and her oldest son are killed in an auto accident. She'd devised her entire estate to that son. The court uses the rule of simultaneous death to invalidate the will and her estate passes, through intestacy, to her husband. Now here, in number six, you ask what effect it would have on the distribution of the estate if her husband had actually arranged the accident."

"Well, think, Mr. Rios," he prodded. "If you killed your old mother to obtain the family jewels, do you think the court would reward your matricide?"

"I take it from your tone the answer is no."

"If the law was otherwise it would be open season on every person of means. That answer your question?"

"One of them. These facts are based on the deaths of Christina and Jeremy Paris, aren't they?"

He picked up his cigar from the edge of the table and lit it.

"I'm investigating the death of her grandson, Hugh Paris, who was a friend of mine. I believe he knew or suspected that her death and the death of her son, Jeremy, was arranged by Robert Paris. I think you know something about that."

"What kind of law did you say you practice?"

"I didn't. Criminal defense."

He shook his head. "Criminal is a troublesome area. No rules. Might makes right, with only the thin paper of the Constitution between the fist and the face."

"Why did he have them killed?"

Howard regarded me through narrowed eyes, as if deciding whether or not to lie.

"She was on her way to obtain a divorce. That would've extinguished his intestate rights. She'd already cut him out of her will."

"How do you know that?"

"I drafted the will," he said, tremulously.

"What else do you know, professor?"

"About the will or the marriage? They were intertwined. The marriage was hell for her but she put up with it for the children and because she was Catholic and, not least of all, because she was Grover Linden's granddaughter and the Lindens don't acknowledge defeat. But she hated Robert. He used her, robbed her. So she came to me one night and told me to write her a will that would cut him off from the Linden money in such a way that he would lose if he contested it."

"How did you do it?"

"We gave him all the community property, his and hers. It was not an insignificant amount. That was the carrot. Everything else went to their sons. Jeremy was given his share outright and Nicholas's was put in a trust to be administered by Jeremy and his uncle, John Smith. That was the stick."

"I don't see it."

"Robert could hardly complain he wasn't provided for since he got everything they'd accumulated in thirty years of marriage. And should he contest the will that would put him in the position of challenging the rights of his own sons as well as his brother-in-law, a man richer even than he. For good measure, we threw in an in terrorem clause providing that he would lose everything if he unsuccessfully challenged any clause of the will."

"You thought of everything," I said, admiringly.

"Except one thing. His intestate rights. As long as they remained married, he was her principal intestate heir. So, from his perspective it was just a question of invalidating the will."

"Did he know about it, then?"

"Yes. She made the mistake of taunting him with it. Two weeks later she and Jeremy, who had dined together at her home, became seriously ill with food poisoning. It may have been a fluke that Robert, who ate the same things, was unaffected." The professor shrugged. "It frightened her. By then I had discovered the hole in our scheme. I advised her to get a divorce."

"She never made it," I said.

He breathed noisily and sucked at his now unlit cigar.

"I have only one other question. Why did she come to you?"

"Mr. Rios," he said, "that's ancient history."

"Please?"

"Almost sixty years ago," he said, "I attended a reception at this university given by Jeremiah Smith who was then in the thirtieth year of his presidency. His wife was dead and so his daughter, Christina, functioned as his hostess. I was nine months out of law school, just hired as a part-time lecturer in property law. Robert Paris was also at the reception, my colleague at the law school with about three months more experience than I. Well, Robert and I dared each other to approach the grand Miss Smith and ask her to dance. I did, finally. I got the dance, but he got the marriage, four years later. She and I became friends, though. We were always friends."

"I'm sorry."

He smiled, crookedly and without humor. "You know, Mr. Rios, there is one aspect of this case which you have failed to examine adequately."

"Sir?"

"Jeremy's death. Why was it necessary to kill the two of them in such a manner that simultaneous death could be found? Robert, as Jeremy's father, was Jeremy's principal intestate heir, since Jeremy had neither wife nor children. He could've picked Jeremy off at his leisure unless what?"

"Unless Jeremy had also executed a will that named a beneficiary other than the judge."

"Precisely."

"And did he?"

"Yes. It was still in draft form but it would've sufficed."

"Who was Jeremy's beneficiary?"

"His nephew, Hugh Paris."

"What became of Jeremy's will?

"I have it, somewhere. I brought it out only six months ago to show Hugh."

"Hugh was here?"

"Yes. He came to me knowing less than you do but enough to have guessed the significance of the fact that his uncle and grandmother were killed at the same time."

"They weren't, you know," I said. "She died before him by fifteen minutes. That's what the police report said, but the coroner was bribed to find otherwise."

He closed his eyes. "If I had known that twenty years ago, I would've gone to the police. How could Robert have been so clumsy?"

"I think he was desperate," I said. "Unnerved. If he'd been accused then, he might have fallen apart."

"And your friend would be alive," he said. "Now, I'm sorry."

And after that, there didn't seem to be anything left to say.

□

I left the professor and walked back to the student union where I found a phone and called Terry Ormes at the police station. She was out in the field so I left a message. Sonny Patterson at the D.A.'s office was out to lunch. I set up an appointment to see him the next morning. No one was answering at Aaron Gold's office. I hung up the phone feeling cheated, like an actor robbed of his audience. I stood indecisively in front of the phone booth until the smells from the cafeteria behind me reminded me it was time to eat.

I bought two hamburgers and two plastic cups of beer and took them to a corner table. As I ate, I put the case together the way I would present it to Sonny the next day.

It was a simple tale of greed. Robert Paris had been disinherited by his wife, Christina, in favor of his two sons, Nicholas and Jeremy. Nicholas posed no problems. He was mentally ill and could be easily controlled by the judge. Jeremy, however, had to be gotten rid of. Paris had to invalidate Christina's will in such a way as to strike her bequest to Jeremy, and any of his heirs, so that he himself might inherit that portion of Christina's estate through intestacy. Christina and Jeremy were killed in an accident to which there was but one witness who himself was later killed. A crooked coroner presided at the inquest and manipulated the times of death, making it appear that Christina and Jeremy died simultaneously. By operation of the rule of simultaneous death, Christina's estate passed to her remaining family, half to the judge through intestacy and half to his younger son, Nicholas, by operation of Christina's bequest which was not affected by the invalidity of the bequest to Jeremy.

Nicholas was then committed to an asylum and his wife, Katherine, blackmailed into a divorce. I had no doubt that the judge had been appointed conservator of Nicholas's estate. By the time the wheels of his machinations came to a stop, Judge Paris had secured control of his wife's fortune.

There was only the smallest of hitches: Hugh. In Hugh's case the judge acted more subtly. He took the boy from his mother, sexually abused him, and then set him adrift in a series of private schools far from his home. The judge made sure that Hugh had all the money he could spend. Rootless, without direction, with too much money and not enough judgment, Hugh became a wastrel, a hype. He very nearly self-destructed. But not quite. He came home, pieced together the story of his grandfather's crimes and suddenly became a serious threat to Robert Paris. So he too was killed.

That was the story. The evidence would not be as seamless or easily put together. It would come in bits and pieces, fragments of distant conversations, scribbled notes, fading memories. The investigation would be laborious and involve, undoubtedly, protracted legal warfare. Sonny might look at it, see the potential quagmire and look the other way. But I doubted it. I knew, from trying cases against him, that he didn't run from a fight. And he liked to win.

At least my part would be over. I would finally be able to exorcise that last image of Hugh lying in the morgue.

I got up and went back to the phone. This time Terry was in her office.

"Listen, I'm glad you called back," she began.

"I'm seeing Patterson in the morning. I'm going to lay out the whole story for him and I'd like you to be there."

"What story is that?"

"Robert Paris killed his wife, his son and his grandson. I know exactly how it happened and why. I'm sure Patterson will order the investigation into Hugh's death reopened."

"I don't think so," Terry said softly. "Where are you?"

"At the university. The student union. Why?"

"Have you seen this morning's paper?"

"No, not yet. I've been on the move since I got up."

"You better take a look at it."

"Why?"

"Robert Paris is dead. The judge is dead."

"What?"

"Early this morning. A stroke. Henry? You still there?"

"Yeah," I mumbled, looking across the patio of the student union to the courtyard. There were three flag poles there, one for a flag of the United States, one for a flag of California and the third for the university's flag. Having spent most of the day on campus I'd passed those poles maybe four or five times not noticing until this moment that the three flags flew at half-mast.

— 8 —

There was a burst of organ music as the doors to the chapel opened and the archbishop of San Francisco, flanked by red-skirted altar boys, stepped blinking into the bright light of midday. The university security guards who had been lounging in the vicinity of the doors now closed ranks, forming a loose cordon on either side of the funeral procession.

I was standing against a pillar next to a camera crew from a local T.V. station. A blond woman spoke softly into a microphone. The television lights exploded at the appearance of the first dignitaries emerging from the darkness of the church.

The mayor of San Francisco, an alumna, came out on the arm of the president of the university. Following a step or two behind came the governor, a graduate of the law school, walking alone, working the crowd with discreet waves and a slack smile. Next came a coterie of old men who, even without their robes, had the unmistakable, self-important gait of judges. For a moment afterward the threshold was empty. Then came eight elderly men dressed in similar dark suits, white shirts and black ties, shouldering the gleaming rosewood coffin.

Inside that box were the mortal remains of Robert Wharton Paris, who had been eulogized that morning by the San Francisco Chronicle as one of the most distinguished Californians of his time. No mention was made that the judge's sole surviving descendant, his son, was locked up in an asylum in Napa. Instead, the newspapers looked back on what was, inarguably, a dazzlingly successful life.

Robert Paris, who was born into a poor family of farmers in

the San Joaquin valley eighty years earlier, worked his way through Linden University, went to Oxford as a Rhodes scholar, and returned to the United States to take a law degree from Harvard, all before his twenty-fifth birthday. Hired as an instructor in property law at the university law school he quickly rose to the rank of full professor. In the process, he married Christina Smith, the granddaughter of Grover Linden and daughter of Jeremiah Smith, the university's first president.

Paris left the law school to form, with two of his colleagues, a law firm in San Francisco that now occupied its own building in the heart of the financial district. He resigned from the firm to accept appointment to the United States Court of Appeals for the Ninth Circuit. He was a distinguished jurist frequently mentioned as a potential candidate for the U.S. Supreme Court but he was too conservative for the liberal Democrats who then occupied the White House. When he was finally offered a position on the Court by a Republican president, he was forced to decline, citing age and physical infirmity. Shortly afterwards he left the court of appeals and spent the last decade of his life in virtual seclusion. Now, he was dead.

Greater than the man was what he represented, the Linden fortune. The media estimated the extent of that fortune at between five-hundred million and one billion dollars, but so cloaked in secrecy were its sources and tributaries that no one really knew. There was so much money that it had acquired an air of fable as though it were stored not in banks, trust companies and investment management firms, but hidden away in caves as if it were pirate treasure.

Famous money. Money gouged out of the Sierra Nevadas by the tens of thousands of picks that laid out the route of the transcontinental railroad. Ruthless money. Money acquired at the expense of thousands of small farmers forced from their farms by the insatiable appetite of Grover Linden's land companies.

Corrupt money. Money paid in subsidies to Grover Linden's railroad from the Congress in an era when the prevailing definition of an honest politician was one who, when bought, stayed bought.

Endless money. Money flowing so ceaselessly that during a

financial crisis in the 1890's, Grover Linden essentially guaranteed the national debt out of his own fortune and the government averted bankruptcy.

Robert Paris was steward to that fortune and only I, and perhaps one or two others, knew at what cost he had acquired his stewardship. I watched them carry him across the courtyard, and I was thinking not of the family of a nineteenth-century American railroad baron but of the Caesers, the Borgias, the Romanovs. Only on that dynastic scale could I begin to comprehend how a man might kill his wife, his child, his grandchild to satisfy an appetite for power.

I remembered a painting by Goya that I'd seen, years earlier, in the Prado called *Saturn Devouring His Children*. Saturn consumed his sons and daughters to avoid the prophecy that one son would reach manhood and depose his father. The mother of Zeus substituted for the infant Zeus a stone wrapped in swaddling clothes, which Saturn ate. Hidden away, Zeus grew and ultimately fulfilled the prophecy. Had Robert Paris feared the same end from his male descendants? Or was he simply mad? Or had that family of farmers in San Joaquin been poorer than anyone could imagine?

Meanwhile, the funeral had become a party for the rich. The crowd spilled out from the church, sweeping across the courtyard of the Old Quad to the driveway where I had earlier observed a fleet of limosines lined up behind a silver hearse. So loud and jovial were the mourners that I expected, at any moment, to be offered a cocktail or a canapé from a roving waiter. There were no signs of real grief; only, now and then, a ceremonial tear dabbed at with an elegant, monogrammed handkerchief. The rich are different, I thought: condemned to live their lives in public, they go through their paces at the edge of hysteria like show dogs from which every trait has been bred but anxiety. The body was to be interred in the Linden mausoleum, a quarter-mile distant. Judging from the snarl of cars in the driveway, I'd be able to walk there before the internment began.

The heat was slow and intense, a pounding, relentless, unseasonable heat. I set off down the road sweating beneath my fine clothes like any animal. In a way it was pointless for me to have come to the funeral. Lord knows there was nothing more to be done about Robert Paris except, perhaps, drive a stake through his heart.

I beat everyone to the mausoleum but the press. This was a historic event. No one had been laid to rest in Grover Linden's tomb since the death of his son-in-law, Jeremiah Smith, first president of the university, fifty years earlier. The lesser members of the Linden-Smith-Paris clan, including the judge's wife and eldest son, were buried in a small graveyard two hundred feet away. Hugh, however, was not there. I had never learned what became of his ashes.

I removed my jacket, positioned myself in the shade of an oak tree and studied Grover Linden's resting place. The legend was that Linden wanted his tomb patterned after the temple of the Acropolis. What he got was a much smaller building constructed from massive blocks of polished gray granite adorned on three sides with Ionic columns. At the entrance there were two steps which led to a bronze screen and beneath it two stone doors. On each side, the entrance was flanked by a marble sphinx.

In front of the tomb was an oval of grass bounded by a circular pathway, a tributary of the footpaths that criscrossed the surrounding wood. That wood was a popular trysting place, and it was not unusual to find the grounds near the tomb littered with beer cans, wine bottles, marijuana roaches, and used condoms. Today, however, the groundskeepers had been thorough.

I heard cars pulling up and then the cracking of wood as people surged forward from the road trampling the dry grass and fallen twigs; the more-or-less orderly procession across the Old Quad had become a curiosity-seeking mob, red-faced and sweaty, converging from all directions as the university security guards fought to keep open a corridor from the road to the steps of the tomb. I watched a photographer shimmy up one of the venerable oaks and stake out her position among its branches.

Finally the pallbearers appeared, walking slowly and stumblingly across the uneven dirt path. They were preceded by the school's president, who climbed the steps of the tomb and opened the doors. As he fiddled with the locks, one of the pallbearers, an old man, started to sink beneath the weight of his burden. Two security guards hurried to his side and propped him up. His mouth hung open and a vein beat furiously at his temple.

"Welcome to necropolis," a voice beside me murmured. I turned to find Grant Hancock standing beside me, cool and handsome in a light gray suit. "Do you see that gentleman there?"

I followed his gaze to a shadowy corner at the far edge of the crowd from where a tall thin old man surveyed the chaos from behind a pair of dark glasses.

"John Smith," I said. "I hadn't noticed him at the church."

"He wasn't in attendance," Grant said. The old man slipped away. "One titan buries another," Grant remarked.

"Cut from the same cloth?"

"God, no," Grant said. "Robert Paris was so vulgar he had buildings named in his honor while he was still alive. The only thing for which Smith has permitted use of his name is a rose."

"A rose?"

"He's an amateur horticulturist," Grant said. "Incidentally, what are you doing here?"

"I wanted to make sure he was dead."

He picked a fragment of bark from my shoulder and said, "It was open casket. He's dead."

"Open casket? That was vulgar."

"Robert Paris never did anything tastefully except die in his sleep. As for me, when I die I'll direct my family to bury me without fanfare."

I smiled. "When you die, Grant, the tailors and barbers will declare a day of national mourning."

"And when you die," he said, not quite as lightly, "I'll miss you." We began walking. "In fact, I've missed you the past four years."

I said nothing, feeling the sun on my neck, thinking of the funeral, thinking of Hugh, thinking as usual of too many things.

Grant said, "I've changed."

"Only very young people believe that change is always for the better," I said. "I'm mostly interested in holding the line, which is, I guess, the difference between thirty and thirty-four."

"Am I being rejected? Again?"

"No."

We had reached his car. He leaned against it and we looked at each other.

"I feel very old today," I said, "as though I've dissipated my promise and my capacity to love. I've felt that way since Hugh died. I don't know what there is left of me to offer."

"Let me decide that."

I nodded. "I'll drive up this weekend."

"Good, I'll see you then."

I walked back to my car and got in. I loosened my tie and rolled up my sleeves, tossing my jacket into the back seat. On the front seat was a book I'd bought that morning, *The Poems of C.P. Cavafy*, the poet Hugh had mentioned to me that distant summer evening in San Francisco. I glanced at my watch. It was almost one, time to drive to the restaurant where I was meeting Terry Ormes for lunch. I picked up the book. Flipping through it at the bookstore I'd marked a page with the little poem that I now read aloud:

The surroundings of the house, centers, neighborhoods
which I see and where I walk; for years and years.
I have created you in joy and in sorrows:
out of so many circumstances, out of so many things.
You have become all feeling for me.

The words had a liturgical cadence, almost a prayer. You have become all feeling for me. I had not come to see Robert Paris buried, but to bury Hugh. And still I was dissatisfied. I put the book down and started up the car.

☐

Terry ran her fingertip around the rim of her glass of wine as I ordered another bourbon and water. The lunchtime crowd at Barney's had thinned considerably since we'd been seated an hour earlier. The plate of pasta in front of me was mostly uneaten, but I'd refused the waiter's attempts to clear it away. The presence of food helped me justify the amount of bourbon I was drinking.

Terry wore a satiny cotton dress, white with thin red and blue vertical stripes. A diamond pendant hung from her slim neck. Looking at her I wondered if she had a lover. I didn't imagine many men could accept her calm self-possession and luminous intelligence without feeling threatened. And, just now, she also looked beautiful to me.

"I should be getting back to work," she said, making no effort to move. Instead she poured the last of the wine from the bottle into her glass. Continuing our conversation, she asked, "What is it you can't accept?"

I shrugged. "Robert Paris's death, I guess. I wanted a confrontation and he ups and dies on me."

"But you don't think he was killed?"

"No. Apparently he's been in bad health for years and he died of natural causes."

"Then let it rest," she said. She sipped her wine. "What are you going to do with yourself now?"

"I don't know. I'm completely unprepared for anything other than the practice of law."

"That sounds like a good reason to do something else."

"I agree, but the details of my new life are — elusive."

The waiter deposited my drink in front of me and made another play for my plate. This time I let him take it.

"Just watch the whiskey intake," she said.

"I have to get my calories somewhere."

"You might come to my house for dinner some night."

"I'd like that."

We looked at each other.

"I'm offering as a friend," she said.

"I know. I accept."

I saw her look away. What did she see when she looked at me, I wondered. An alien or just a lonely man? The latter, I thought. Her dinner invitation came out of compassion, not curiosity.

"We're both different, Terry. We play against expectation and we're good at what we do. It's our competence that makes us outsiders, not the fact that you're a woman cop or I'm a gay lawyer."

She nodded, slightly, and made a movement to leave. I rose with her.

"Take care of yourself, Henry. Go away for a few days, meet someone new, and when you get back, call me."

"I promise," I said and watched her go.

I should have gone, too, but instead I stayed another hour at the bar. Finally, when the first wave of the office workers from the surrounding business washed in, I asked for the check, paid it and left.

☐

I put the key into the lock, turned it, pushed the door and nothing happened. The dead-bolt was bolted. I fumbled on my key chain for the dead-bolt key and jammed it into the lock. I leaned my shoulder against the door and pushed. It opened. I stood for a moment staring at the door. I didn't remember bolting it. In fact, I never did.

Stepping into my apartment I suddenly stopped. There was something wrong. I looked around. Everything appeared as it had been when I set off for the university that morning, but was it? Had I closed the book lying on the coffee table? I walked around the room.

The dead-bolt. I knew I hadn't bolted the door. There was no point. There were so many other ways to break into my apartment that it never occurred to me that someone might try using the front door. But someone had, and he had very carefully turned both locks when he left.

Slowly, starting with my bedroom, I methodically went through every room of the apartment, taking inventory. It took more than an hour to make the search. In the bedroom, I lifted from the wall my framed law school diploma. I opened the wall safe beneath. There I found intact my grandfather's pocket watch, my birth certificate, my passport, my parents' wedding rings — optimistically bequeathed to me — and five thousand dollars cash, some of the bills twenty years old, the sum of my father's estate. Everything was accounted for.

It was the same in the bathroom and the kitchen and in the hall closet. I sat down at my desk and began going through the drawers. Then I discovered what was missing: Hugh's letters to his grandfather, which Aaron Gold had given me.

I closed the bottom drawer. Robert Paris was dead but someone had stolen the only evidence I had which linked him to the murder of his grandson. The apartment seemed suddenly very quiet. I felt as if I were in the presence of ghosts. As much to get out as to learn whether she'd seen or heard anything I went to my neighbor.

I pushed the doorbell beneath her name, Lisa Marsh. She came to the door in a bathrobe. This was not unusual, since she was a resident at the university medical school and worked odd hours. But her face was flushed, her hair disheveled and her eyes bright; it wasn't the appearance of sleep.

"Hi," I began, waiting for recognition to register with her. She smiled.

"Sorry to get you out of bed but someone broke into my house this afternoon."

She stepped back. "Oh, no. When?"

"I left at ten this morning and got back an hour ago." I looked at my watch. It was about six. "I was wondering if you'd seen or heard anything."

"You better come in," she said. I did, closing the door behind me. All the curtains were drawn, but a lamp shone in a corner, revealing the remnants of a meal for two people laid out on a long coffee table. "Excuse me for a minute, Henry."

She went into her bedroom, and I heard her talking to someone. A few minutes later she returned with a man who was stuffing his shirttails into his jeans.

"I don't think you've met Mark," she said.

"Um, how do you do?" I said.

He smiled. "Fine."

"I am really sorry to disturb you," I said to both of them.

Lisa shrugged. "This is an emergency. Have you called the police?"

"No, not yet. I'm trying to figure out what happened first."

We went into the living room and sat down. I told them about the dead-bolt, the neatness of the search and the fact that only one thing had been taken. They did not ask, and I did not tell them, exactly what that thing was.

"What I was thinking," I concluded, "was that you may have heard something or seen someone."

They looked at each other and then back to me.

"We had lunch at around noon," Lisa said, "and were done by twelve-thirty. I'm afraid that after that we weren't paying much attention."

Mark frowned thoughtfully. "Wait. I heard a phone ringing next door. It woke me, and I looked over at the alarm clock thinking it might be the hospital — I work there, too. It was about three-thirty or a little before. Then I got up to use the bathroom and get a glass of water from the kitchen."

"Did you hear anything else?"

He shook his head.

The three of us looked at each other. Lisa touched her finger to her lip.

"But I did," she said. "The sound of silver rattling as somone opened a drawer. But I thought it was Mark."

"No, I got a glass from the counter. I didn't open any drawers."

"All this happened around three-thirty?"

"I'm sure of it," Mark said, "because I had to check in with the hospital at four."

I got up to leave. It was six-thirty. The burglar had been in my apartment only three hours earlier.

"What did he take?" Lisa asked.

"Some letters."

"Were they important?"

"The fact that they were stolen makes them important again," I said, then thanked them for their help.

Back in my apartment I headed for the phone. I hadn't noticed earlier that the answering machine had been shut off. I switched it back on. The recording dial was turned to erase. I moved the dial back to rewind, listening as the tape sped backwards. The message had not been rewound before my visitor attempted to erase it. Consequently, he had only succeeded in erasing blank tape. I turned the dial to play. There was the noise of someone trying to clear his throat and then the voice of a very drunk Aaron Gold.

"Henry . . . secretary said you called the other day . . . need to talk to you . . . s'important . . . s'about Hugh . . . Judge Paris . . . you got it wrong. Remember, no cops. I'm at home." The line went dead. I fast forwarded the tape to see if he'd called again. There were no other calls.

Mark said he heard the phone ringing at about three-thirty. A few minutes later, Lisa heard someone in my kitchen. Aaron's call must have come in while the burglar was in the apartment. If he was in the kitchen, which was just a few feet from the phone, the burglar heard the message. In fact, he not only tried to erase the message but turned the machine off so that the red light wouldn't immediately attract my attention. Shutting off the machine had also prevented any further messages from Aaron. Suddenly, I was very worried for him.

The phone rang at Aaron's house three times before his answering machine clicked on. I waited for the message to finish knowing that Aaron often screened his calls, and hoping that he was doing that now.

"Aaron, this is Henry," I said, practically shouting, "if you're at home, pick up the phone." The tape ran on. I tried calling his office but was told he hadn't been in that day. I put the phone down, got my car keys and hurried out of the apartment.

☐

Aaron lived in a small wooden house on Addison, set back from the road by a rather gloomy yard that was perpetually shaded by two massive oaks. There was a deep porch across the front of the house. The overhanging roof was supported by four squat and massive pillars completely out of proportion to the rest of the building. Gold and I referred to the place as Tara. The recollection of that mild joke dispelled some of my uneasiness as I opened the gate and stepped into the yard.

It was dusk and the shadows were at their deepest. Aaron's brown BMW was parked, a little crookedly, in the driveway. There were lights on behind the drawn curtains but the house was still. I heard a noise, a movement on the side of the house in the narrow strip of yard between the building and the fence that bounded the property.

Abruptly I stopped, turned and sped toward the side yard, moving as quietly as I could. When I reached the edge of the building I stopped and listened. Another noise, fainter. Breathing? I slowed my own breath. Someone had been coming up the side yard when he heard me open the gate. Now he was standing still, wondering, as I had wondered, at the source of the noise. I crouched, walked to the very edge of the building, and then sprang.

For an instant no longer than a heartbeat we saw each other through the evening shadows. He raised his arm to his chest, holding something in his hand. I balled my hand into a fist and brought it down on his wrist as hard as I could. Startled, he dropped what I now saw was a gun. He gasped, turned, and started running. I stooped down, retrieved the gun and ran after him. He was scrambling over the redwood fence when I got to the back yard.

"Stop," I shouted, training the gun at his back. I squeezed the trigger and then released it. It seemed suddenly darker as a burst of adrenilin rushed to my head. He was wearing — what? — dark pants, a dark shirt, taking the wall like an athlete. I knew that in another second it would be too late to stop him. I had to stop him. But shoot him? I was going to shoot a man? This wasn't even remotely a situation of self-defense. I held on to the gun and ran for the fence. He was nearly over the top. With my free hand, I reached up and grabbed his ankle. He kicked free. In another second I heard him drop to the ground on the other side. I clambered up the fence, trying to get footholds on the rough wood. Reaching the top, I looked down at the alley, which ran the length of the street. He was gone. He had run to the end of the block or else had gone into someone's back yard. I let myself drop back. Try to remember his face, I thought, as I made my way back to the house. The back door was ajar.

I entered the house through the kitchen.

"Aaron," I said in a whisper.

There was no answer. I groped for a light switch, found it and turned it on. The fluorescent light blinked on, filling the room with a white electric glare. From the doorway of the kitchen I could see into the dining room and to the arched entrance that led into the living room. There was a light on in there. I stepped into the dining room and repeated Aaron's name. There was no answer.

I crossed the room to the archway, holding the gun loosely at my side. Aaron Gold slumped forward in a brown leather armchair, his chest on his knees, his fingertips scraping the floor. Blood dripped steadily from his lap to a bright circle beneath him. On the table beside the chair was an empty bottle of Johnny Walker Red, a glass, and a small pitcher of water. The strongest smell in the room was of alcohol.

He'd probably been too drunk to know what was happening. I took no comfort from this.

I started toward him. There was a loud noise out on the porch, the sound of footsteps and voices. Someone was pounding on the door.

"This is the police. Mr. Gold. Open up. This is the police."

Numbly I went to the door and pulled it open. A young officer was flanked by three other cops. I opened my mouth to speak, but before I could utter a word, one of them said, "He's got a gun."

As soon as the sentence was out, there were four guns on me.

"Drop it," the first officer said. I let the gun slip from my hand to the floor. "Now step outside nice and easy."

"All right," I said, regaining my composure, "but my friend is hurt in there."

"We'll take care of him in a minute." One of the other officers directed me to turn, put my hands up against the wall and spread my legs. The felony position. I did as I was told. Another of the officers stepped into the house and I heard him mutter, "Jesus Christ." To the officers outside he said, "Get the paramedics."

I was searched, handcuffed and ordered to remain standing against the wall.

"This is a mistake," I said to the officer watching me.

"It sure is," he replied.

Now I heard the shriek of sirens as the paramedics' unit shattered the stillness of the night. I had often heard that noise and wondered to what tragedy they were being summoned. This time I knew.

The officer who had first come to the door approached me, pen and pad in hand.

"What's your name?"

"Henry Rios," I said.

He looked me over. Perhaps out of deference to the fact that I was still wearing most of my suit from the funeral, he called me mister.

"I'm going to read you your constitutional rights. Listen up." He began to read from the Miranda card in the dull drone that I had heard so many times before when I was a public defender. I had about fifteen seconds in which to make up my mind whether to talk to him or not.

"Do you understand these rights?" he was asking.

"Yes," I replied.

"Do you want a lawyer?"

"I am a lawyer," I said.

The answer startled him and then he searched my face carefully. "I've seen you before," he said.

"I was a public defender."

He whistled low beneath his breath. "Then you know the script," he said. "Do you want a lawyer?"

"Yes. Sonny Patterson at the D.A.'s office. I'll talk to him."

He nodded. "We're going to take you down to county," he said. "I'll radio ahead and have them rouse Patterson."

"Thank you."

He turned to one of his fellow-officers. "Take him."

"What charge?" the other asked.

"One eighty-seven," the first officer replied. Penal Code section 187 — murder.

Out in the street the paramedics had arrived.

— 9 —

It took Sonny Patterson two hours and seven phone calls to get me out of jail. Most of the time I sat on one of the three bunks in a holding cell watching soundless reruns of *Fantasy Island* while he wheedled on the phone in the booking office for my release.

The last time I'd been at county was as a public defender the morning I met Hugh Paris. Nothing at the jail had changed, including the inmate population. Several trusties who recognized me from back then drifted past the cell, not saying anything but just to stare. I smiled and said hello and they moved on.

The sheriffs let me keep my own clothes but they did not spare me any other part of the booking process. I was strip-searched, photographed, finger-printed and locked up, all the while thinking, this is unreal. The worst part was the strip-search. Until then it had never occurred to me to make the distinction between nudity and nakedness. Now I knew. Nudity was undressing to shower, or sleep, or make love. When you stripped in a hot closet-sized cell that smelled of the previous fifty men and under the indifferent stare of four cops, then you were naked. I still felt that nakedness. It was like a rash; I couldn't stop rubbing my body.

I made my mind into a blank screen across which flickered the images of the day from Robert Paris's casket to Aaron Gold's fingertips dipped in a dark pool of his own blood. These pictures passed through me like a shudder, but it was better than trying to suppress them.

This entire affair began with the murder of one man, Hugh Paris. Now it was assuming the dimensions of a massacre. No one connected with the Paris family seemed safe, including, perhaps, Robert Paris himself. Had the judge's death been purely coincidental to the fact that I'd begun to develop evidence that implicated him with three murders? Was there a gray eminence in the shadows directing events, or did the dead hand of Robert Paris still control the lethal machinery? Until that afternoon I had believed the investigation into Hugh's death was closed. The killing of Aaron Gold changed all that. I was back at the starting line, but with this difference: I was exhausted.

I lay back on the bunk and closed my eyes. Maybe it was the ever-present atmosphere of sexual tension in the jail or just my own loneliness, but I thought back to the last time Hugh and I had made love. Once again I saw the elegant torso stretched out beneath me as I lowered my body to his, and felt that body responding, resisting, yielding. The image of his face came to me with such clarity that I could see the fine blond hairs that grew, almost invisibly, between his eyebrows. And I could see his eyes and in those eyes I saw, with more regret than horror, the face of Aaron Gold bathed in blood.

I sat up. Sonny Patterson was watching me from just outside the cell.

"You all right?"

"Yeah, I must have fallen asleep."

"You look bad, pal."

"I've had better days." I rose from the bunk and walked to where he was standing. "Well?"

"It didn't look so good at first. Two shots fired from the gun, and your fingerprints all over the place. Fortunately for you, the same neighbor who called the cops also saw the guy going into the yard, and it wasn't you."

"Saw the guy?"

"Well, saw a guy. Blond, about your height. Good build. Good looking. Couldn't be you."

"I do what I can."

He lit a cigarette and offered me one. I hesitated and then accepted it. The last time I smoked I was eighteen.

"Incidentally, does that description sound like anyone you know?"

I shook my head.

"What about the guy you saw on the side of the house?"

I took a puff. It went down pretty smoothly. "It happened too fast. All I really saw was the gun."

"You're sounding like a witness for the prosecution. How come your defense witnesses always had such better memories?"

"Clean living, Sonny," I said, dropping the cigarette to the floor and crushing it with my heel. The second drag had made me want to vomit.

"Well, that's something I'll never be accused of." He smiled. "Hey, Wilson," he yelled to one of the jailers, "release the gentleman. He owes me a couple of drinks."

"I owe you a case."

"No," he said, suddenly serious. "You owe me an explanation."

"Did you call Terry Ormes?"

"Yeah, she's up in my office. That's where we're going."

□

It was only around ten but if felt like midnight. Sonny brewed a pot of coffee and brought out a fifth of Irish whiskey from the deep recesses of his desk. Terry yawned, accepted coffee but laid her hand across the cup when he started to pour the whiskey in. He shrugged and poured me a half-cup of coffee, a half-cup of whiskey. For himself, he dispensed with the coffee.

"Now that we're all comfortable," he began, settling into his armchair and his affected Southern drawl, "why don't you begin at the beginning?"

Between the two of us, Terry and I told Patterson the history of the Linden-Smith-Paris clan from the end of the nineteen twenties to the burial of Robert Paris that very afternoon. Patterson listened without comment, moving only to lower the level of fluid in the whiskey bottle now and then. There wasn't a lot left when we finished.

He looked back and forth between us and shrugged. "So," he said, "what crime has been committed that I can prove?"

Terry looked at him. "How about four murders, a burglary, and conspiracy to obstruct justice?"

"A crime that I can prove," he repeated. "In the murders of

Christina and Jeremy Paris, the eyewitness is dead, the coroner is dead, and the deaths have the appearance of being an accident. The remaining evidence — the will — is grist for speculation but not nearly enough to make out a murder. And the trail is twenty years old. The officers who wrote these reports might be dead themselves, and you know as well as I do that their reports are inadmissible hearsay. The death of Hugh Paris—" he glanced over at me. I'd told him that Hugh and I were lovers. "Put out of your head how much you liked the guy. Let me put it as crudely as I can — a hype O.D.'s and drowns. No one sees the death, no traces of murder survive except in Ormes's recollection. So maybe we can impute a motive to the judge, after a lot of circumstantial fandangoes, but so what? The judge is dead. Even assuming he arranged Hugh's murder, I doubt very seriously that he jotted it down in his appointment book." He looked at us.

"Aaron," I said.

"Yes, Aaron Gold. After I persuade the cops that you didn't do it — and you didn't, did you—?" I shook my head, "what do you think they're gonna conclude?"

"A break-in," Terry said wearily, "that got out of hand." Contemptuously, she added, "All the pieces fit."

"Detective," Patterson said, "cops are like prosecutors in this respect: we have to play the facts we're dealt. We can't engage in cosmic theories, because we're bound by the evidence we gather and the inferences we can draw from it. You can't expect me to put Robert Paris on trial for a murder that was committed four days after he died. All that the evidence will support in the case of Aaron Gold is a bungled burglary."

"The perfect crimes," Terry muttered.

"Exactly," Patterson said, shaking the last drops of liquor out of the bottle, "the perfect crimes. No witnesses, no evidence. Plenty of motive — if the murders could be connected, but nothing connects them except a few bits of circumstantial evidence and one hell of a lot of conjecture." He looked at us again and sighed. "Drink up."

"Drink up? Is that the D.A.'s position on these murders?"

"Jesus Christ, Henry, think of this case as a defense lawyer. Wouldn't you love to be defending Robert Paris? With the case I have against him?"

"Paris didn't physically kill Hugh, and he didn't pull the trigger on Aaron," I said. "The murderer is still alive."

"Then bring him to me," Patterson said, "and we'll talk."

I said, "This is a police matter."

Patterson shook his head. "You know as well as I do that the police don't have the time or interest to pursue this investigation. They've got their hands full. And as for you," he said, turning to Terry, "my advice is that if you place any value on your career on the force, you'll discontinue your interest in closed cases."

She lifted her eyebrows. "What do you mean?"

"I mean Hugh Paris," Patterson said. "I've been known to bend elbows with Sam Torres. He knows that you've been assisting Rios, and he doesn't like it. In fact, he considers it a personal affront that his subordinate would use police resources on a case that he closed and on behalf of a civilian."

"Christ," I muttered. Terry looked stricken and I knew why. A woman detective, even a good one — no, especially a good one — would always be walking the line. A misstep could have disastrous consequences on her career. I couldn't ask her to risk it for me.

"You're on your own, Henry," Patterson said. "Take my advice and forget it. Go away until things cool down. You're not safe."

"Then you believe the murders are all connected?"

"Of course I do. I believe every word of it. The rich are malignant." He held out his empty coffee cup to me. "Now what about those drinks?"

☐

I woke late the next day, having closed a bar with Patterson the night before. Terry had begged off early. Sonny and I remained, getting drunk, swapping trial stories and he complaining about his marriage. Boys' night out, except that Aaron Gold was dead.

I went out for the papers. The San Francisco *Chronicle* made no mention of the murder, but the local daily put it on page one. I read it while the coffee brewed — burglary suspect, unidentified man detained and then released, no other suspects, would anyone having any information kindly notify the police.

As I drank my coffee, I wondered who there was to mourn Aaron. His law firm associates? A few ex-girlfriends? He had family in L.A. that he had spoken of maybe twenty times in all the years I'd known him. After all those years and all the people he'd known, I probably was still his closest friend. It disturbed me to think that he'd gone through life so alone. That image of opulent self-worth that he projected to the world was shadow play. My grief was real.

I needed to think, but the effort was painful; all the easy connections between Hugh's death and Aaron's led to a dead man, the judge. But there it was. Aaron had information he wanted to share with me about Hugh's death. The man who broke into my house was also interested in that information — not gaining access to it — but suppressing it. He also had taken the only proof I had linking Robert Paris to his grandson's death, so I'd assumed that Aaron's information further implicated the judge. But the judge was dead. What difference would it make to anyone whether his reputation was ruined?

And then it came to me. No one cared about the judge at this point. The break-in and Aaron's murder were the acts of someone with something left to lose should it become public knowledge that the judge had arranged his grandson's death. And who was that someone? Hugh's actual killer — the man or men hired by the judge to carry out the murder. Robert Paris's death hadn't really solved the crime. Hugh's murderer was still at large and I believed that that person was more than a goon employed for the occasion but someone upon whom the judge had relied pretty often. Who would know about the inner-workings of Paris' staff? Only a peer who had frequent dealings with that staff. John Smith.

And who was John Smith?

I had done a little research on Smith, gleaning the few facts I knew about him from the back issues of the *Chronicle* and my conversations with Grant. He was eighty-one years old, unmarried, a banker by profession, and something of a philanthropist. Four months out of the year he lived in Geneva where he was associated with various banks headquartered there. He was also chairman of the Linden Trust and, by virtue of his control of the disbursements of that fund, was more responsible for the development and course of nuclear research than any other private citizen. He gave money to Catholic charities, had had a rose named in his honor, had never graduated from college. In virtually every respect his life was opposite that of his brother-in-law, Robert Paris. Yet Smith, who lived in relative anonymity, was by birth something that Robert Paris never became, a member of the American aristocracy.

Nor, apparently, did the two men like each other. There was never anything as obvious as a public falling out. As stewards of the Linden fortune, their economic interests frequently converged and were too important to allow personal feelings to stand in the way of greater enrichment. Nonetheless, Grant had spoken as if the enmity between the two ancient tycoons was public knowledge.

All this made Smith a potential ally. Someone in Robert Paris's retinue had killed Hugh and Aaron. I could not interest the police in pursuing the investigation but Smith, with his money and influence, could. What remained was to make an appeal to him. I needed entree into his world. Once again I would have to rely on Grant Hancock whose family, though perhaps poorer, was as distinguished as Smith's.

I picked up the phone and dialed Grant's number.

Grant was at work. I reached his secretary who made it clear to me that unless I was a paying client I could leave a message. Finally, after lengthy negotiation, she agreed to give Mr. Hancock my name. He was on the phone a moment later.

"Henry, I was going to call you. I just heard a very disturbing rumor about Aaron from one of our classmates who was working on a case with him."

"It's true, Grant. Aaron's been murdered."

"Jesus."

"And I was arrested for his murder and spent half the night in jail."

"What?"

"And the same day he was murdered, someone broke into my apartment and stole the letters that Hugh had written to his grandfather. Aaron called my apartment while the break-in was in progress. He said he had information about Hugh's death. Whoever was in my apartment — and I think it was Hugh's killer — heard the phone message and tried to erase it. Then the killer went to Aaron's. When I got to Aaron's house, he was dead."

"Wait — Hugh's killer killed Aaron? The judge killed Hugh."

"No, the judge had Hugh killed. An important distinction, Grant. The man who did the actual killing is still at large and probably in a panic since the death of his employer."

"Didn't you also just say you'd been arrested for Aaron's murder?"

"Yes."

"How did that happen?"

"I was holding the gun." I heard Grant make a noise, and I explained how it was I came to be at Aaron's house when the police arrived. I also told him that the police were treating the case as a burglary and that the district attorney considered any other interpretation of the events leading to Aaron's death unprovable.

"But you think differently."

"Yes."

"I was afraid of that. I take it, then, this is not a social call."

"Grant, I've respected your wish to be left out of this, until now."

"Is that the sound of chips being cashed I hear?" he said.

"The police are prepared to write off Aaron's death the same way they wrote off Hugh," I continued, ignoring his joke. "I want to make contact with John Smith."

"You're obsessed with Smith," Grant said. "He's just a private citizen — albeit a rich one."

"Money makes things happen," I replied, "and if even you feel intimidated by John Smith, imagine his effect on a chief-of-police. Or the mayor."

There was a thoughtful silence on the line.

"First," Grant said, "you'll have to engage his attention."

"All I want is my foot in the door."

"I'm going to put you on hold," Grant said, and the line went blank. Five minutes later he came back on. "Sorry," he said, "I had to make a call. I want you to call this number and ask for Peter Barron. He's one of Smith's aides at Pegasus."

"At what?"

"Pegasus. Smith's corporate flagship. A holding company." He gave me the number. I thanked him. We hung up.

A company that owns companies. That's how Terry Ormes had described the corporation that held title to the house in San Francisco that Hugh had leased and was living in at the time of his death. Pegasus Corporation.

I dialed the number Grant had given me.

"Good morning. Mr. Barron's office," a woman said.

"Is Mr. Barron in?"

"Yes. Who may I say is calling?"

"Henry Rios."

"May I tell Mr. Barron what this call is in reference to?"

"Hugh Paris," I replied.

"One moment." I was back on hold.

"Good morning, Mr. Rios," a male voice said. For the briefest moment I thought I recognized the voice.

"Mr. Barron? I'm a friend of Grant Hancock. He gave me your number—"

"How is Grant?"

"He's fine. Look, I have some information about Hugh Paris's death that I think might interest your employer, Mr. Smith."

"Such as?"

"Hugh was murdered at the direction of his grandfather, Robert Paris, and whoever performed the killing is still at large."

There was a long skeptical pause. "I see," he said finally. "Have you shared this information with the police?"

"The police take the position that Hugh's death was accidental."

"Oh, is that the position the police take?" His tone was mocking. Once again, his voice sounded familiar. "Well, Mr. Rios, I doubt that Mr. Smith is in any position to do what the police can't or won't do. He was deeply affected by Hugh's death, and I think, at his age, he should be spared these speculations which would only make Hugh's loss harder to accept."

"It's not speculation. I have proof."

"Mr. Rios, give the old man a break. He doesn't need to hear that members of his family killed each other off. Take your story back to the police or, better yet, keep it to yourself."

Switching to a different tack I asked, "Who arranged for the lease of Hugh's house from Pegasus?"

"What are you talking about?"

"Hugh leased his house from Pegasus. Who was his contact there?"

"Pegasus isn't in the real estate business."

"I saw the lease."

There was silence on the other end. At last he said, "Can't be. Look, Henry, I really must go."

"Have we ever met?"

"I don't think so," he replied, sounding, I thought, nervous.

"I know your voice."

"Well, maybe we've met through Grant. Goodbye, Henry."

The line went dead.

A moment later I was back on the phone to Grant asking him what Peter Barron looked like.

"I've only seen him a few times. He's about our age. Blond. Handsome. Gay."

Blond, good-looking — that's how Aaron's neighbor described the man he saw in Aaron's yard the night of the murder. Was that also the man I saw? I closed my eyes, but I was unable to picture the face. Still, his hair — it was blond, wasn't it? And I knew I had seen him somewhere before.

"Gay?" I asked Grant. This, too, seemed significant.

"I've run into him at Sutter's Mill," he said, naming a bar popular with professionals. "Did he say something to you?"

"No, nothing like that. Is there any chance I might've met him through you?"

"I hadn't seen you in four years until two weeks ago," Grant said. "Hardly enough time to introduce you to my friends, much less a cocktail party acquaintance. Do you know Peter Barron?"

"I'm sure of it, but I can't figure out where. He knows we've met, too. He lied to me about that and about Hugh's relation to Pegasus. I think I'd better drive up to the city. Where is Pegasus?"

Grant gave me an address on Montgomery Street.

"I'll call you," I said and hung up.

□

Pegasus Corporation was housed on floors thirty-eight, thirty-nine and forty of a Japanese bank building near the Embarcadero freeway. I called up to Barron's office from the street to make sure he was in, then I entered the building. It was close to noon and I explained to the security guard that I was meeting someone for a lunchtime conference but had misplaced his office number. I gave the guard Peter Barron's name and he made a call.

"He's on thirty-nine, sir," the guard said. "Take one of the elevators to your right."

On the thirty-ninth floor I played a variation of the same trick with the receptionist, a stern-looking young Chinese woman who sat at a desk beneath a large brass engraving of Pegasus in flight.

"Hello. Do you know if Mr. Barron's gone out to lunch yet?"

She glanced at a sheet of paper. "No," she said, reaching for the phone. "You have an appointment?"

"Wait," I said, briefly laying my hand over hers as she touched the phone. "Peter and I roomed together in college ten years ago and I haven't seen him since. I'm in town for the week and wanted to surprise him. Understand?"

She nodded.

"Do you know when he goes out to lunch?"

"Any minute now. You can wait here."

"Okay, but — well, when I saw Peter he still had hair to his shoulders and was as skinny as a pole. I'm not sure I'd recognize him."

She nodded again as gravely as if I were administering a quiz. Or maybe it was my antiquity that intimidated her. Her own college years could hardly be more than a few months behind her.

"Can you describe him to me?" I asked.

She looked at the wall behind me, thinking. "He's about six

feet," she began hesitantly, "blond hair and blue eyes. Nice build." She giggled. "Very handsome."

Her description added nothing to what Grant had already told me and it fit about ten thousand men in the financial district alone.

"Thank you," I said. "I'll sit here with a magazine pulled up over my face and wait for Peter. You just carry on with your job. All right?"

"All right," she said and answered a call.

I looked at my watch. It was twelve-five. Six minutes later, behind a flock of secretaries, a blond man stepped into the room from a door beside the receptionist's desk. I recognized him at once. He informed the receptionist that he would be out for the rest of the day.

She replied loudly, "Thank you, Mr. Barron."

He started walking out into the corridor. I put my magazine down and fell into step beside him.

"Hello, Peter."

He glanced at me and stopped. "Henry. I was just going to pay you a visit."

He spoke in the same soft reasonable tone of voice with which he had addressed me only three weeks earlier, the night he and his three friends abducted me as I was leaving Grant Hancock's apartment and shot me up with sodium pentothal. Peter was the one who wielded the needle and told me he wanted information for his employer, who I had then thought was Robert Paris.

"You work for Smith," I said.

"You're surprised?"

"It doesn't make sense to me, especially if you also killed Aaron Gold."

"Killed who?"

"You killed Hugh Paris and you killed Aaron Gold."

"Henry," he said with a small, hurt smile. "I have never killed anyone and as for our last meeting, you might at least give me a chance to explain."

"One doesn't explain away two murders."

He sighed impatiently, "Damn it, Henry, I don't know what you're talking about. All right, Hugh was murdered, but not by me. This other guy I've never even heard of."

My curiosity overcame me. "Then who killed Hugh?"

He shook his head. "We — Mr. Smith and I — have been trying to find out. I don't know. That's why I — what did you call it — abducted you — that night."

I looked at him. We were standing in the corridor while people rushed around us. He seemed calm and rational for someone just accused of two murders. I, by contrast, was beginning to sound hysterical even to myself. And he worked for Smith. Smith, in my scheme of things, was a good guy.

Perhaps sensing my uncertainty he said, "There's a lot I have to tell you about Hugh's death, Henry, and you have the most urgent right to know. You were his lover."

"How did you know that?" I demanded.

"We've been working the same field. You know about me. I know about you." He reached out and laid a hand on my shoulder. "I'm gay, too, Henry. I understand."

I didn't want to believe him but no one, not even Grant, had acknowledged my right to grieve. The weight of Hugh's death and the frustration I felt at not knowing who killed him all closed in on me. I brushed aside a tear. Barron tactfully looked away.

"All right," I said. "Let's go somewhere and talk."

We walked to an elevator and stepped inside.

"What exactly do you do for Smith?" I asked.

He reached his hand into his jacket, pulling out a gun.

"Special assignments," he replied. "Now, we're going down to the garage, and then we'll get off, you first with me following. You behave yourself, Henry, and maybe I'll let you live."

I looked into his eyes, felt his breath on my face. He smiled and then stepped behind me, against the wall of the elevator.

"You're crazy," I said. "You killed Hugh and Aaron Gold."

"An interesting thought," he said. "But why would I've done that? Who was I working for?"

"Maybe no one," I replied. "You might just be a freelance psychopath."

"Let's not call names," he said nudging the nozzle of the gun into the small of my back.

At that moment the elevator stopped. A dozen people crowded on. The gun pressed harder against my back.

I clenched my hands into fists. "This man's got a gun," I shouted and jerked away from Barron.

A woman screamed.

"Get him," someone shouted.

The elevator stopped again. The doors flew open. Barron pushed his way to the front as hands reached out trying to stop him. He broke clean and ran down the corridor. Perhaps aware that he was still armed, no one followed. The elevator door closed.

"Who was he?" a man asked me.

"A nut with a gun," I replied.

Three hours later I was sitting on the floor in Grant Hancock's apartment drinking a glass of wine while he went to the door to pay for a delivery of Chinese food. He took the small white cartons from a brown bag and set them on a tea tray between us. We opened them up and ate from them with wooden chopsticks.

I had just told him that after getting the names of the other people on the elevator I'd gone to the police.

"What did they do?"

"What cops always do, they took a report and promised to look into it. By the time that report reaches the appropriate desk, Peter Barron could be in Tierra del Fuego."

Grant chewed a bit of shrimp.

"I don't understand why Barron pulled a gun on you. He works for Smith. Smith is supposed to be on our side."

"Does he work for Smith? I mean, he does, ostensibly, but in actuality I think he was working for Robert Paris."

"That sounds complicated."

"But it fits the evidence. What I think happened is that Hugh contacted Smith to let Smith know he was back in town. Maybe he even enlisted Smith's help in exposing Robert Paris as the murderer of Christina and Nicholas. Smith leased the house for him, probably gave him money. Peter Barron works for the security section of Pegasus — I think Smith might have entrusted him to keep an eye on Hugh and make sure he stayed out of trouble. In fact, I remember that it was Smith who bailed Hugh out of jail when he was arrested in July."

"Are you positive?"

"Yes, I called the jail and had them check." I finished my wine and poured another glass. "At the time I thought John Smith was an alias used to avoid notoriety by whoever bailed Hugh out."

"Well, it is hard to believe there are men in the world actually named John Smith."

I poked at the carton of rice.

"Anyway," I continued, "Barron was supposed to protect Hugh but instead he betrayed him to Robert Paris."

"How would Barron have known about the bad blood between Hugh and Robert Paris?"

"I'm sure Hugh told him," I said. "It was a subject to which he often returned."

Grant nodded.

"So Barron went to Robert Paris with the information that Hugh was in the city and that he, Barron, knew where Hugh was. Paris then paid Barron to murder Hugh. And that's how it was done."

"And Smith? Don't you think he was a little suspicious about the circumstances of Hugh's death?"

"I'm sure he was. He probably had Barron conduct an investigation. You can imagine Barron's conclusion."

Grant put down the carton from which he'd been eating. "And Aaron? Why kill Aaron?"

"Aaron worked for the firm that handled Paris's legal work. He must've learned something very damaging that implicated Barron with Hugh's murder."

"Such as?"

"Pay-offs, maybe. Reports. I don't know. Aaron never had a chance to tell me."

"How much of this do you think Smith knows?" Grant asked, pouring me the last of the wine.

"My impression of Smith from reading the newspapers," I said, "is that information reaches him through about three dozen intermediaries. Everything is sanitized by the time it touches his desk. He probably knows next to nothing about what really went on."

"And you're going to tell him."

"Yes." I picked up a bit of chicken with my chopsticks. "It's strange that Hugh never talked to me about Smith."

"From everything you've said, it doesn't sound like Hugh told you much about his family."

"That's true."

"He wanted to protect you. Knowing how potentially dangerous the situation was, he wanted to keep you out of it." After a pause he added, "He loved you."

"Instead of protecting me, Hugh left me ignorant — and vulnerable."

Grant sighed. "When do we ever do the right thing by the people we love?"

When, indeed, I wondered, looking at him from across the room.

☐

The next day I went back to Pegasus, this time to see Smith but I got no closer than his secretary. She, unlike the gullible receptionist, was not inclined to let strange men without appointments loiter in her office. She threatened to have me ejected. Taking the hint, I went out into the corridor to ponder my next move. There didn't seem to be any. Two middle-aged men in dark suits came out of Smith's office and passed. Their jowls quivered with self-importance. I watched them walk to a door at the end of the corridor — what I'd assumed was a freight elevator.

One of the two withdrew a key from his pocket and fit it into a lock on the wall. The door slid open, revealing a small plushly appointed elevator.

The executive elevator. Of course.

It would hardly do for Smith and his retinue to waste expensive time waiting for the public elevator or to endure the indignities of making small talk with file clerks. Smith would have to leave at some point, and, if I couldn't wait for him in his office, I'd wait here.

So I waited. I waited from ten in the morning to nearly six at night, fending off the occasional security guard with my business card and an explanation that I was meeting a friend from

Pegasus's legal staff. I thought that Smith might emerge for lunch until I saw a food-laden trolley wheeled off the executive elevator by a red jacketed waiter. About an hour later the waiter reappeared with the now empty trolley and boarded the elevator. Just as the doors closed I saw him finish off the contents of a wine glass.

At about four a few lucky employees began to leave, singly, or in groups of two or three. By five, the corridor was packed. By five-forty-five when it seemed that everyone who could possibly work at Pegasus had left for the day, the doors were pushed open and two beefy bodyguard-types strode out flanking a third man. The third man was tall, thin and old. The blue pinstriped suit he wore fell loosely on his frame and was shabby with many wearings, but he wore it as if it were a prince's ermine. They walked rapidly past me to the executive elevator. The key went into the lock. I rushed over to where they were standing.

"Mr. Smith."

The tall old gentleman turned toward me slowly, examining me without particular interest.

"My name is Henry Rios. I have to talk to you about Hugh Paris."

At the mention of my name, the old man raised his eyebrows a fraction of an inch, indicating, I thought, either recognition or surprise. However, he said nothing. The two men closed ranks in front of him.

"Don't come any closer," one of them said, allowing his jacket to fall open, revealing a shoulder holster.

John Smith's employees, it seemed, were issued sidearms along with their Brooks Brothers charge plates. I stepped back.

"All I want is ten minutes of your time," I said to Smith.

The elevator door opened and he stepped into it. The bodyguards followed him in. I lunged forward trying to keep the doors open. "Ten minutes," I shouted.

The same man who'd just spoken to me now lifted a heavy leg and booted me in the chest, throwing me backwards to the floor.

I lifted myself up.

John Smith was staring at me. He opened his mouth to speak just as the doors shut.

— 10 —

The wine was cold and bitter. A white-jacketed busboy moved through the darkness of the restaurant like a ghost. Outside, a freakish spell of blisteringly hot weather had emptied the streets but here it was cool and dark and the only noise was the murmur of conversation and the silvery clink of flatware against china, ice against glass. It was two o'clock in the afternoon. Aaron Gold had been buried that morning in Los Angeles.

Grant asked, "Should we have sent flowers?"

"I've never understood that custom," I replied. "Are the flowers intended as a symbol of resurrection or are they just there to divert attention from the corpse?"

But Grant wasn't listening. His glance had fallen to the front page of the *Chronicle* laid out on the table between us. The contents of Robert Paris's will had been made public. His entire estate, five hundred million dollars, was bequeathed to the Linden Trust of which John Smith was chairman. Would it matter to Smith now that Robert Paris was a murderer or was half a billion dollars sufficient reparation?

As if he read my thoughts, Grant looked up at me unhappily and said, "There's no justice in this. You must do something."

"I've tried everything," I said to Grant, "everything I could think of doing."

A waiter set down shallow bowls of steaming pasta before us. The fragrance of basil rose from the dish reminding me of summer. I picked up my fork.

"You haven't tried what you're trained to do," Grant said.

I lifted an interrogatory eyebrow.

"I've been thinking about this," Grant said. "The first thing you have to do is ask yourself what it is you want. You don't want the identity of the killer, you already know who that is, but what you do want is to bring the killer to justice. And I'm not talking about Barron — he was just the instrument — I'm talking about Robert Paris. You want there to be a public record of his guilt."

I nodded.

"Who is better able to make that record than a lawyer in a court of law?"

"Unfortunately," I said, "Judge Paris is no longer within any court's jurisdiction."

"Wrong," Grant said. "You're thinking of the criminal side."

I put my fork down. "What are you thinking of?"

"Well, I'm not a litigator, of course, but it occurred to me that you should sue him."

Grant picked up his fork and speared a clam. I watched him chew and swallow. My brain was buzzing. Why hadn't I thought of this before?

"Of course," I said. "Wrongful death. I'll sue Robert Paris's estate for the wrongful death of Hugh Paris."

"And Aaron too."

I shook my head. "The judge was already dead when that happened. We'd never be able to prove it."

Grant buttered a bit of bread. "You think we could prove it as to Hugh's death?"

"I don't know but we'll do a hell of a lot of damage to Robert Paris's reputation in the attempt."

I thought some more.

"In fact," I continued, "we can do some damage to John Smith while we're at it, or at least get his attention."

"How?"

"Well, if a suit is pending against Paris's estate which involves money damages, there should be enough money set aside from the estate to cover those damages in the event the suit succeeds."

Grant dabbed his mouth with a napkin and smiled.

"You mean we can obtain some kind of injunction to prevent the judge's executors from disbursing the estate."

"Exactly. The Linden Trust won't get a penny until the suit's resolved. And as for the executor," I continued, "which happens to be Aaron's law firm, we'll plaster them with discovery motions and compel them to produce every scrap of paper they have that involves Hugh or Peter Barron or Robert Paris. We'll depose everyone from the senior partner to the receptionist."

"Those depositions will make the front page of the *Chronicle*," he said.

"For months," I replied, "if not years." Smiling, I reached across the table and patted his head. "Good thinking for someone who's not a litigator. It's perfect, Grant."

Grant looked at me and smiled nervously. "Well, not quite perfect," he said. "As I understand it, the only people entitled to bring the suit would be Hugh's executors or his heirs."

It took a moment before I understood. "Katherine Paris."

"I'm afraid so," he said.

☐

Katherine Paris lit a cigarette and eyed me suspiciously from across my desk. We were in my office. This was the first time I'd used it for business since I'd leased it three months earlier. There was a film of dust on the bookshelves and the file cabinets. Both were empty. The only objects of my desk were three newly purchased volumes of the code of civil procedure, the probate code and the evidence code, a yellow legal tablet, my pen and the plastic cup into which Mrs. Paris tapped her cigarette ash.

"Tell me again how this works," she said, "preferably in English. I cannot follow you when you start quoting the law at me."

I smiled as charmingly as I knew how. Her hard, intelligent face showed no sign of being charmed. I had virtually pulled her off a plane to Boston to get her to talk to me. Her baggage had gone on without her. Now she planned to leave that night on another flight. The clock was ticking away.

"It's called a wrongful death action," I said, "and it's a law suit brought by the heirs or estate of someone who died through the negligence or wrongful act of another. The most common instance is a suit brought by the family of someone killed in a car accident or on the job."

"I would hardly classify homicide as an instance of neglect," she remarked impatiently.

"But it is a wrongful act."

"Oh, at the very least," she snickered.

"Mrs. Paris, please — I know it sounds like hair-splitting, but there are precedents in the case law that permit the heirs of a murder victim to bring an action against his murderer."

"So you want my consent to bring this wrongful death action against Robert's estate."

"Exactly."

"And you intend to ask for two hundred and fifty million dollars in damages?"

"Yes."

She stubbed out her cigarette. "What you want is permission to conduct a circus."

I began to respond but she cut me off.

"Mr. Rios, you are a very clever man and I have no doubt that you were devoted to Hugh but this idea of yours is absurd."

"It's not absurd," I said. "It's entirely plausible." She remained unimpressed. "Mrs. Paris, you stand to gain by this suit whether we get to trial or not."

"What are you talking about?"

"I know that you were left nothing in Robert Paris's will. There's enough truth to this suit that even if we can't prove the allegation that the judge had Hugh murdered, the suit has considerable harassment value."

"I beg your pardon?"

"It takes five years to get a relatively simple civil lawsuit to trial. A case of this magnitude could drag on for a decade, easily. At some point the judge's executors will simply decide to pay you off and settle the suit."

"But what would you get out of that, Mr. Rios? Surely you have other motives for wanting to sue Robert's estate than my further enrichment."

"I intend to pursue this case through the pages of the *Chroni-*

cle so that even the fact of a settlement will be an admission of Robert Paris's guilt. That will satisfy me, Mrs. Paris," I said with rising emotion, "even if it takes the next ten years of my life to accomplish it."

Visibly startled by my vehemence, she sat back in her chair.

"It won't bring Hugh back to life," she said softly.

"Mrs. Paris, do you have any doubt that Hugh was murdered?"

"No," she said, without hesitation.

"And do you have any doubt that Robert Paris was his murderer?"

In a softer voice she said, "No."

"But the police say Hugh killed himself, shot himself full of heroin and drowned in three feet of water. You saw the body."

Her face went white. Her cigarette burned unheeded. She nodded.

"How can you allow your son to be slandered with this ridiculous explanation of his death? It's as if you left his body to the vultures. Doesn't he deserve a decent burial, a peaceful rest?"

"Spare me," she whispered.

"I can't," I said. "I loved him."

She lit another cigarette and proceeded to smoke it, all the while looking out the window as dusk gathered in the sky. Once she lifted a long finger to the ivory cameo at the neck of her blouse. Perhaps her husband had given it to her, perhaps, even, it had been given to her by Hugh. At length she turned her face back to me and studied me for a long time. I did not avoid her eyes but looked back into them.

"You loved him," she said, at last, echoing me. "I told you once I didn't understand that kind of love."

"That love differs only in expression but not quality from the love you felt for him."

"No," she said. "The quality is different. Yours — it's much finer."

"May I proceed with the suit?"

She said, "All right."

The words fell like two smooth pebbles and clattered on the desk between us.

"Thank you, Mrs. Paris."

"But I intend to catch that flight for Boston tonight. You'll be on your own."

"I understand that."

"Yes, I imagine you do," she said. "You strike me as someone who was born to be on his own. I know I was." These last words were spoken with sadness, resignation. Recovering herself, she said, "I suppose you want me to sign something."

"No," I said. "You'll either be good at your word or you won't. If not, a piece of paper won't compel you."

"You needn't worry about my word. I never give it unless I intend to honor it."

I nodded, slightly, in acknowledgment.

"However," she continued, "I wish to add one condition of your employment by me. You may take your thirty percent if and when we win. In the meantime—" she dug into her bag and withdrew a leather checkbook, "you'll need money to proceed."

I watched her write out a check for ten thousand dollars and lay it on the desk between us.

"I'll expect an accounting, of course," she said. "If you need more money notify me at the address on the check. But do remember, Mr. Rios, while I may be well-off I'm counting on you to make me truly rich, so spend wisely."

"I will."

She rose and gathered up her things. "Now tell me, Mr. Rios, truthfully, if we do get to trial what are our chances of winning?"

"Let me give you a legal answer," I said. "I would say we have two chances, fat and slim."

She let out a low, throaty laugh that echoed in the room even after she'd left.

☐

The next morning I stepped up to the counter of the clerk of the superior court, wrote out a check, handed it over with a stack of papers to a young black woman, and with those actions commenced the suit of *Paris versus Paris*. Along with the complaint and summons, I filed a request for discovery and a restraining order against the disbursement of Robert Paris's estate pending the outcome of this action. Simultaneously, a courier service I'd hired with some of Mrs. Paris's money served copies of the documents upon Grayson, Graves and Miller as executors of the judge's estate. The clerk stamped my copies of the papers and handed them back to me, wishing me a good day as she did. I thanked her and stepped out into the hall and into the glare of television cameras.

"Sir, look this way, please," a voice called to me. I turned to the camera. A blond man in a gray suit spoke into a microphone, explaining that I had just filed a two hundred and fifty million dollar lawsuit against the estate of Robert Paris claiming that Paris had murdered his grandson. He spoke with no particular urgency and in a normal tone of voice, but to me it was as if he was shouting his words to the world through an amplifier on the tip of the Transamerica pyramid.

At length the blond, introducing himself as Greg Miller, turned to me and said, "Mr. Rios, why have you filed this lawsuit rather than going to the police?"

I cleared my throat and told my story.

☐

When I woke the next morning the phone was already ringing. I let my answering machine take the message as I got out of bed and wandered into the kitchen to start the coffee. I caught the tail end of the message — a reporter from the L.A. *Times* requesting an interview.

I'd gotten to bed at three that morning, having spent the previous twelve hours talking to reporters from newspapers and television stations from Sacramento to Bakersfield. I put on a bathrobe and stepped outside to pick up the *Chronicle* and the local. I'd made the front page of both. I glanced at the stories — they were the usual jumble of fact and fantasy but the slant was decidedly in my favor.

I skimmed the rest of the *Chronicle*. On the next-to-the-last page, in the society section, I saw a picture of John Smith. He'd attended a charitable function the night before and was shown arriving at the Fairmont. By his expression I saw that he was used to having his picture taken but not particularly tolerant of the practice. He looked away from the camera, both his eyes and his mind visibly occupied on another matter. I had a good idea of what it was.

I folded the paper across Smith's face and went to the window. Outside the sky was clouded over. Knots of red and yellow leaves waved back and forth in the trees like pennants. There was a lot to be done that day. Grant was expecting me for lunch where we would map out our litigation strategy. The phone messages would have to be responded to. I needed to hire a secretary and have a phone installed in my office. Abruptly, I had become a practicing lawyer. It felt good.

I rinsed out my coffee cup and went to the bedroom where I changed into my sweats and running shoes. I stretched in the living room for a couple of minutes and then went out. It was about seven and there weren't many other people on the road. A Chinese boy came flying by, long, skinny legs pounding the sidewalk, black hair flapping like silk at the back of his head. We nodded acknowledgment as we passed each other.

It had been some time since I'd last run and it took longer than usual to catch my stride. I swiveled my head back and forth, trying to relax my neck. It was then that I noticed the silver Rolls.

It was gliding a few feet behind me, too slowly and with too little sense of direction. I increased my speed and turned a corner. I looked over my shoulder, and it was still following. Suddenly, the car sped up, turned the corner ahead of me and stopped in my path. I slowed to a trot. The front passenger window was soundlessly lowered. I felt a surge of prickly heat across my chest as my blood rushed not from exertion but from fear. I stopped. The only person in the car was the driver. He was a middle-aged man with silver hair, wearing a black suit, white shirt, black tie and a visored black cap. He turned his face to me and smiled.

"Mr. Rios?" he called out. "I'm sorry if I startled you."

Cautiously, I approached the car close enough to talk without shouting.

"How do you know who I am?"

"Your picture's in the papers," he said. "Mr. Smith wonders if he could see you."

"John Smith?"

The driver nodded.

"Now?"

"Yes, sir."

I looked at him. He seemed harmless but then I couldn't see his lower body from where I was standing.

"And where does Mr. Smith propose we have this meeting?"

"He's waiting for you at the Linden Museum on the university campus."

"Step out of the car, please, and come around to my side."

"Sir?"

"Please."

I heard him sigh as he opened the door and got out. When he came around I told him to turn his back to me, put his hands on the top of the car, and spread his legs.

"Is this really necessary?" he asked as I patted him down for weapons.

"Don't take it personally," I replied, "but the last time I got into a small enclosed space with one of Mr. Smith's employees he pulled a gun on me."

"I'm not armed," the driver replied.

"So I see," I said, turning him around by the shoulders. "On the other hand you've got twenty pounds over me and it feels like muscle. Do you know where you are now in relation to the museum?"

"Yes."

I looked into the car and saw the key was in the ignition. "Then you won't mind walking there."

"Come now, Mr. Rios—" he began.

"Look," I said. "I'll drive myself to the museum alone, or I won't go at all. Understood?"

After a moment's pause, he said, "Understood. But be careful with the car."

"I hear they drive themselves," I said, getting into the driver's seat.

I calculated that it would take the driver at least a half hour to walk back to campus. Smith, or whoever had dispatched him, was probably not even certain I could be lured to the museum, much less at a fixed time, but he would begin to get nervous if too much time passed without word from the driver. I could cover the distance to the campus in about ten minutes. This gave me, I decided, about fifteen minutes of dead time before anyone got jittery. Fifteen minutes was more than enough time for the plan that now suggested itself to me.

I made a stop. When I started up again, ten minutes later, I noticed the white van a car-length behind me. I began to whistle. The van's lights flickered on and off. I relaxed.

I drove beneath the stone arch and onto Palm Drive. Just before I reached the oval lawn that fronted the Old Quad I turned off a rickety little side street called Museum Way. When I looked in my mirror, the van was gone. I followed the road for a few hundred yards until it ended, abruptly, at the voluminous steps of a sandstone building, the Grover Linden Museum of Fine Art. I parked the car and got out.

The edifice, reputedly inspired by St. Peter's, consisted of a domed central building and two wings jutting off on each side at a slight angle. As a law student, I had sometimes come here to study since it was as deserted a spot on campus as existed. It was deserted now as I made my way up the steps to where a uniformed university security guard stood. Behind him, the museum's hours were posted on the door and indicated, quite clearly, that the museum was closed on Tuesdays. Today was Tuesday.

"Mr. Rios?"

"That's right."

"Go right in, sir. Mr. Smith is up on the second floor in the family gallery. Do you know where that is?"

"Yes."

The monster was surprisingly graceful inside. Sunlight poured into the massive foyer from a glass dome in the ceiling. A beautiful staircase led up from the center of the foyer to the second floor. Walkways on that floor connected the right and left wings of the museum. The staircase and interior walls were white marble, the banisters of the staircase were polished oak and the railings were bronze. All that glare of white and polished surfaces made me feel that I was inside a wedding cake.

I started up the stairs to the second floor, got to the top and turned right. Above the entrance to the gallery at my right were chiseled the words "the Linden Family Collection." On each side of that entrance stood an armed security guard. They weren't wearing the university's uniforms. I stepped past them into the room.

The family gallery was a long and narrow rectangular room. Along one of the long walls were six tall windows looking out over a garden. Along the other were paintings of the various buildings of the university as they existed on the day the university opened its doors for business. There were also a dozen standing glass cases that displayed such memorabilia as Grover Linden's eyeglasses, Mrs. Linden's rosary and a collection of dolls belonging to the Linden's only daughter.

I strolled past these treasures toward the end of the room. There, alone on the wall, hung the only well-known work in the room, a six foot portrait of Grover Linden himself painted by John Singer Sargent. Beneath it, on a wooden bench, sat an old man, John Smith.

There was no one else in the room and the only noise was the soft squish of my running shoes as I walked across the marble floor. Smith rose as he saw me approach. At six foot four he had five inches over me but was thin and frail-looking. The tremulous light that fell across his face washed it of all color. Even his eyes were faded and strangely lifeless as if they'd already closed on the world. He extended his hand to me. His grip was loose and perfunctory and the hand itself skeletal and cold. And yet, even that touch conveyed authority. He sat down again and motioned me to sit beside him. I did. The two guards at the other end of the room moved to just inside the gallery. I felt their eyes on us.

"Thank you for coming," Smith said in a surprisingly firm voice. He elongated his vowels in the manner of Franklin Roosevelt, I noticed; the accent of wealth from an earlier time.

"You're welcome. Though I must say this is an odd meeting place."

"My lawyers," he said, "advised me not to speak to you at all, since it's likely that I'll become involved in this lawsuit of yours, but I had to talk to you."

"So we're hiding from your lawyers?"

"Exactly," he replied. We watched dust motes fall through the air. "You know I haven't been to this museum since it was dedicated sixty years ago. Of course I was just a boy then. But for years I dreamed about this portrait of my grandfather."

"Is it a fair likeness?"

"It errs on the side of tact," he said, smiling a little. He cleared his throat with a murmur. "Now, Mr. Rios, perhaps we can discuss our business."

"Which is?"

"This — lawsuit." He looked at me and said, "What will it cost me to persuade you to drop it?"

"Well, to begin with, an explanation of why you would make such a request."

"My family's good name," he said.

"Robert Paris was a member of your family by marriage only," I said, "and, from what I understand, no friend of yours. Additionally, my information is that he was responsible not only for the murder of Hugh Paris but also your sister, Christina, and your nephew, Jeremy."

"Your information," Smith said with a trace of contempt. "Are you so sure your information is correct?"

"I'm positive of it. Aren't you?"

"As to my sister and nephew," he said, rising, "yes. As to Hugh," he shrugged, slightly, and moved toward a window. I rose and followed him over.

"How long have you known about Christina and Jeremy?" I asked.

"Twenty years," he replied. "John Howard sought me out after they were killed and brought me the wills. I had some of my men conduct an investigation of the accident and the subsequent coroner's inquest. They established that the accident had been arranged and the inquest rigged for the purpose of a finding of simultaneous death. It wasn't difficult, Robert was inept as a murderer and left a trail of evidence that would have sent him to the gas chamber but the evidence was scattered through half a dozen police jurisdictions and the police were even more inept than he."

"But you had the evidence. Why not use it against him?"

He regarded me coolly as if deciding that I was not as bright as he'd been led to believe. "I did use it, Mr. Rios."

"Not to go to the police."

"No," he said, laying a fingertip against the windowsill. "My investigators obtained the evidence as," he smiled at me, conspiratorially, "expeditiously as possible. Their methods were not the police's methods and, consequently, my lawyers informed me that Robert would've been able to suppress enough of the evidence to weaken the case against him, perhaps fatally."

"Nonetheless," I insisted, "it was worth a try."

"You don't understand," he said, impatiently. "There were higher stakes to play."

"Something greater than justice for the dead?" I asked.

He raised an eyebrow. "I was told you had a lawyer's way with words," he said, not admiringly.

"You were talking about higher stakes."

"Yes, there was the money to think about, Christina's estate, one-half of my grandfather's fortune. It had fallen into Robert's hands. Robert was many things, most of them contemptible, but he was good with money. I had to think ahead about what would've happened to that money had Robert been removed from the picture."

"It would've gone to its rightful heirs."

"Who at that time," Smith said, "were my lunatic nephew, Nicholas, and his ten-year-old son, Hugh."

"Why couldn't you have had yourself appointed their guardian?"

"Because there was someone with a much stronger claim to that office."

"Who?"

Smith snorted. "Your client, Mr. Rios. Katherine Paris."

I said, "Ah."

"Katherine Paris," he said with recollected scorn, "a writer." It was the ultimate epithet. "She didn't know the first thing about money."

"Whereas the judge knew all about money."

"And, more importantly, I had a lever with which to control him."

"So you took the evidence that linked him to the murders and used it to blackmail him."

·159·

Smith looked out the window. A few late roses clung tenaciously to life. Perhaps they were the ones that had been named in his honor. "Yes," he said, defiantly. "Yes."

"And what did you get in return for not exposing him?"

"An agreement." He began to walk across the room. I walked with him. "At Robert's death, his entire estate was to revert to the Linden Trust, of which I am chairman. In the meantime, his affairs were controlled by my lawyers. He couldn't invest or spend a cent without my approval."

"And if he had?"

"My lawyers would've seen to it that criminal proceedings were initiated against him the second he deviated from our agreement."

"Other than your lawyers, who knew about the agreement?"

"His lawyers, of course."

Grayson, Graves and Miller — Aaron's firm. In the remote reaches of my mind something fell into place but was still too distant for me to articulate.

"So you see, the blackmail — your word, not mine — was a necessary evil."

"That seems to be your forte."

"That was cheap, Mr. Rios," he said, stopping in front of a painting that depicted the original law school.

"A moment ago you indicated that I was right about the murders of Christina and Jeremy Paris but not about Hugh's. What did you mean?"

The color, what there was of it, seeped from his face. "Robert Paris didn't have Hugh murdered," he said.

"You mean Peter Barron acted on his own?"

"No."

I was about to speak when, staring at his gaunt ancient face, the bones so prominent that I could have been addressing a skull, I realized that I was staring at Hugh's murderer.

"You," I said. "Robert Paris was your creature. He couldn't have employed an assassin with you controlling his money, unless you agreed to it."

Smith looked away.

"And of course you agreed to it. You had as much or more to

lose as Robert Paris had his earlier murders been exposed. You knew that Paris killed his wife and son and you knew that Hugh was the rightful heir to the judge's share of the Linden fortune. For twenty years you helped cover up those murders and defraud Hugh of his inheritence." I advanced toward Smith, who moved a step back. "But Hugh thought you would help him and he came to you. You leased him the house so you could keep an eye on him. He trusted you. You betrayed him."

The two guards had come up behind Smith, their hands on their guns. I stopped. Smith glanced over his shoulder and ordered them to retreat. They stepped back.

"Hugh hated his grandfather almost to the point of psychosis," Smith said, "and he knew that I was no friend of Robert's." He smiled, bitterly. "You see, Mr. Rios, I made a pact with the devil, but I could never bring myself to enjoy his company."

"That makes no difference."

"Perhaps not. Still, I encouraged Hugh's hatred of his grandfather — partly, I suppose, to deflect any suspicion from myself but also because Hugh gave vent to the hatred I felt for Robert Paris, my sister's murderer, my nephew's murderer."

"But you danced to his tune."

"Yes, I see that clearly now, but at the time, I was blind. One's own motives are always lost in mists of rationalizations. Hugh found out about the murders and expected my help in exposing his grandfather. If I refused to help him he would become suspicious of me, perhaps even guess my complicity. But I could hardly agree to help him expose Robert without also exposing myself."

"Did you tell him about your part in the cover-up?"

"Yes." Smith said.

"And he went berserk."

"Yes."

"Threatened to expose you as well."

"Yes."

"So you had him killed."

"Yes."

Smith brought his hand to his throat, as if protecting it. Suddenly, I saw the scene that had occurred between Smith and

Hugh when Smith revealed his part in the cover-up. Hugh must have responded like a madman, physically attacking his great-uncle. In a way, that might have made it easier for Smith to give the order to have Hugh killed; to regard Hugh as a madman on the verge of bringing the entire family to ruin and obloquy. Smith believed he served a legitimate purpose in having Hugh murdered, but in fact he was merely acting as Robert Paris's agent.

Smith and I had squared off, facing each other tensely across a few feet of shadowy space.

"That's not the end of the story," I said. "You had Hugh killed by Peter Barron. But where is Peter Barron?"

"Dead," the old man muttered.

"His life for Hugh's?"

"Is that so rough a measure of justice?"

"Yes, from my perspective, especially when you weigh Aaron Gold's death in the balance."

Smith shook his head. "That was unintentional. Mr. Gold worked for the firm that handled Robert's personal accounts. Shortly after Hugh's death, the partner who worked closest with Robert discovered certain documents missing that showed the extent to which I controlled all of Robert's transactions. There were also some personal papers missing, among them, Hugh's letters to Robert. The partner conducted a quiet investigation. The documents were found at Mr. Gold's home and the letters, as you know, at your apartment."

"Aaron had discovered that Paris wasn't in control of his affairs but that you were," I said, "and he reasoned that you, not Paris, were behind Hugh's death."

"Something like that," Smith said. "No one ever had an opportunity to talk to Mr. Gold."

"You saw to that," I said.

"No," Smith repeated wearily. "That was Peter Barron acting on his own. He told me he'd gone to talk to Mr. Gold, that there was a struggle and the gun went off."

"There was no struggle," I said, "Aaron was shot as he sat in an armchair getting drunk."

"I didn't believe Barron," Smith said, "since he had reasons of his own for wanting the identity of Hugh's killer secret."

"He was the trigger man."

Smith nodded. "So now you know everything," he said, "and I repeat my original question: What will it cost me to persuade you to drop the lawsuit?"

I shook my head. "It's never been a matter of money. I want an admission of guilt. I want that admission in open court and for the record. I want the law to run its course. No secret pay-offs, no cover-ups."

"My lawyers were right," Smith said, "I shouldn't have spoken to you. And yet I'm glad I did." He hunched his shoulders as if suddenly cold. "I'm not an evil man, or at least, I can still appreciate an act of human decency. I appreciate your devotion to Hugh, Mr. Rios, but you must understand that I too will have the law run its course and I will fight you with every resource to which I have access."

"I understand that," I said, "but I have two things on my side that you do not."

"What?"

"Time," I said, "and justice."

A ghostly smile played across Smith's withered lips. "Good-bye, Mr. Rios," Smith said, "and good luck."

He turned and strode the length of the gallery. The two guards fell in behind him. I waited a moment and then followed him out. I got to the top of the steps outside the museum in time to watch the silver Rolls slip away into the wood. I jogged down the steps.

I turned down the collar of my sweatshirt and spoke into the thin metal disc attached there. "He's gone," I said. "I hope you got it all down."

A moment later the white van moved into view from behind the museum. The passenger door swung open and Terry Ormes got out, followed by Sonny Patterson pushing his way out from the back of the van. Terry had insisted that I be wired for sound in the event that I was being led into a trap, so that the cops could respond. Neither of us had expected the conversation we had just heard. Patterson had signed on at the last minute, in the event that something useful was said. He walked toward me looking like a man who'd just heard an earful.

"Your little speech about time and justice," Patterson said, "ought to play real well in front of the grand jury."

"You recorded it?"

"The whole thing."

"Then there will be a grand jury."

"You bet," he said, "and if they don't come back with an indictment, I'm washing my hands of this profession."

Terry who had come up beside us, said, "Good work, Henry."

"It's not exactly how I thought it would go down."

"I'll guess you'll be amending the complaint in your lawsuit to allege Smith as a defendant," Patterson said.

I shrugged. "I'll talk to my client. She may not want to pursue the case after the grand jury concludes its business."

"You wanted it to be Robert Paris, didn't you?" Terry said.

"Yes."

"Why?"

"Smith is as much a victim as Hugh. Smith was a moderately good man who chose expediency over justice the one time it really mattered. But Robert Paris was the real thing, he was evil. I pity Smith."

Patterson looked at me disdainfully. "That old public defender mentality," he said. "People don't commit crimes, society does. You know Latin?"

I shook my head.

He said, "Durum hoc est sed ita lex scripta est — It is hard but thus the law is written."

"Where's that from?"

"The Code of Justinian, and it was engraved over the entrance of the library of my law school — which was not as big a deal as your law school here at the university, but those of us who went there were hungry in the way that justice is a hunger."

He turned from us and walked away. Terry and I looked at each other. What Patterson wanted was clear: a fair trial and a guilty verdict. My own motives were hopelessly confused — my hunger had never been as simple as Sonny's.

"Maybe," I said to Terry, "I never wanted justice but just to vent my grief about Hugh."

She shook her head. "Grief is half of justice," she said, and added, a moment later, "the other half is hope."

GOLDENBOY

I want to thank Kelly McCune for her advice and assistance,
Mike and Alan for their last-minute insights,
my friends on Deloz Avenue,
Bill, of course, and Sasha.

— Foreword —

Goldenboy is the second book in Michael Nava's now-classic series of mystery novels that feature California lawyer Henry Rios. The first book in the series, *The Little Death*, was published by Alyson in 1986. *Goldenboy* followed two years later and had immense popularity and critical acclaim. The book won Lambda Literary Awards for Best Mystery and Best Small Press Publication, and it has been reprinted numerous times. In addition to English, the book has appeared in Japanese and German.

Nava's legal background—like the character Henry Rios, Nava is a lawyer—lends an air of authenticity to the legalistic and investigative aspects of his writing. Yet the investigation, the unfolding of plot—the mystery, if you will—is not what makes Nava's work special. What makes his novels so tremendously interesting are the characters.

In *Goldenboy* we cross paths with famous actors, not-so-famous actors, Hollywood hustlers of all types, grizzled investigators, the amazingly rich, and the incredibly mundane. And every one of these characters is intensely real, drawn with a depth and clarity seldom seen in modern literature. Each individual has fears, joys, and loves. Each individual has a present, a past, and dreams of the future. Michael Nava's characters are mirrors; in them we see ourselves. We might like what we see. We might not. But we always understand.

It gives me great pleasure to include *Goldenboy* in the Alyson Classics Library collection.

Thank you for reading.

Scott Brassart, Associate Publisher
Los Angeles, 1998

> Ah, Spencer
> Since words are crude and only stand between
> Heart and heart, and understanding fails us
> There's nothing left amid such deafness but bodily
> Contact between men. And even that is very
> Little. All is vanity.
>
> *The Life of Edward the Second of England*
> —Bertolt Brecht

— 1 —

"You have a call."

I looked up from the police report I had been reading and spoke into the phone intercom. "Who?"

"Mr. Ross from Los Angeles."

"Put him through." I picked up the phone thinking it had been at least a year since I'd last talked to Larry Ross.

"Henry?" It was less a question than a demand.

"Hello, Larry. This is a surprise."

"Are you free to come down here and handle a case?"

I leaned back into my chair and smiled. Born and bred in Vermont, Larry retained a New England asperity even after twenty years in Beverly Hills where he practiced entertainment law. His looks fit his manner: he was tall and thin and beneath the pink, nude dome of his head he had the face of a crafty infant.

Rejecting a sarcastic response — Larry was impervious to sarcasm — I said, "Why don't you tell me about it."

"It's the Jim Pears case. Have the papers up there carried anything about it?"

I thought back for a minute. "That's the teenager who killed one of his classmates."

"Allegedly killed," Larry replied, punctiliously.

"Whatever," I said. "I forget the details."

"Jim Pears was working as a busboy in a restaurant called the Yellowtail. One of the other busboys named Brian Fox caught Jim having sex with a man. Brian threatened to tell Jim's parents. A couple of weeks later they found the boys in the cellar of the restaurant. Brian had been stabbed to death and Jim had the knife."

"Airtight," I commented.

"No one actually saw Jim do it," he insisted.

I turned in my chair until I faced the window. The rain fell on the green hills that rose behind the red-tiled roofs of Linden University. That last weekend of September, winter was arriving early in the San Francisco Bay.

"That's his defense — that no one actually saw him do it? Come on, Larry."

"Hey," he snapped, "whatever happened to the presumption of innocence?"

"Okay, okay. Let's presume him innocent. What stage is he at?"

"The Public Defender has been handling the case. Jim pled not guilty. There was a prelim. He was held to answer."

"On what charge?"

"First-degree murder."

"Is the D.A. seeking the death penalty?"

"No," Larry replied, uncertainly, "I don't think so. But isn't that automatic if you're charged with first-degree murder?"

"No." I reflected that, after all, criminal law was not Larry's field. "The D.A. has to allege and prove that there were special circumstances surrounding the murder which warrant the death penalty."

"Like what?" Larry asked, interested.

"There are a lot of them, all listed in the Penal Code. Lying in wait, for instance. There's also one called exceptional depravity."

"Not just your garden-variety depravity," Larry commented acidly. "Only a lawyer could have written that phrase."

"Well, figuring out what it means keeps a lot of us in business," I replied, glancing at my calendar. "When does Pears's trial begin?"

"Monday."

"As in two days from today?"

"That's right," he said.

"I'm missing something here," I said. "The trial begins in

two days and tne boy is represented by the P.D. Am I with you so far?"

"Yes, but — " he began, defensively.

"We'll get to the buts in a minute. Isn't it a little late to be calling me?"

"The P.D.'s office wants to withdraw."

"That's interesting. Why?"

"Some kind of conflict. I don't know the details."

Almost automatically I began to take notes, writing 'People v. Pears' across the top of a sheet of paper. Then I wrote 'conflict.' To Larry I said, "You seem to know a lot for someone who isn't involved in the case."

"Isn't the reason for my interest obvious?"

I penned a question mark. "No," I said, "better explain."

"Everyone's abandoned him, Henry. His parents and now his lawyer. Someone has to step in — "

"I agree it's a sad situation. But why me, Larry? I can name half a dozen excellent criminal defense lawyers down there."

"Any of them gay?"

"Aren't we beyond that?"

"You can't expect a straight lawyer to understand the pressures of being in the closet that would drive someone to kill," he said.

I put my pen down. "What makes you think *I* understand?" I replied. "We've all been in the closet at one time or another. Not many of us commit murders on our way out."

There was silent disappointment at his end of the line and a little guilt at mine.

"Look," I said, relenting, "how does Jim feel about me taking the case?"

"I haven't spoken to him."

"Recently?"

"Ever."

"Customarily," I said, "it's the client who hires the lawyer."

"His P.D. says he'll go along with it."

"Go along with it? I think I'll pass."

"Jim needs you, Henry," Larry insisted.

"Sounds to me that what he needs is a decent defense. I'm not about to take a case two days before it's supposed to go to trial even if Jim himself asked me. I'm busy enough up here."

"Henry," Larry said softly, "you owe me."

In the silence that followed I calculated my debt. "That's true," I replied.

"And I'm desperate," he continued. Something in Larry's voice troubled me — not for Jim Pears, but for Larry Ross.

"Are you telling me everything?" I asked after a moment.

"I need to see you, Henry," he said. "I'll fly up tonight and we'll have dinner. All right? I'll be there on the five-fifteen PSA flight."

"That'll be fine, Larry." I said goodbye.

After I hung up, I went across the hall to Catherine McKinley's office. She and I had both worked as public defenders and had remained friends after leaving the P.D. Now and then we referred clients to each other, though this happened less often as she took fewer and fewer criminal defense matters, preferring the greener pastures of civil law. I had remained in the trenches.

Her secretary, a thin young man named Derek, was taping a child's drawing to the side of his file cabinet. The drawing depicted a green house with a lot of blue windows, a red roof, a yellow door and what appeared to be an elephant in the foreground.

"Is your daughter the artist?" I asked.

He turned to me and smiled. "It's our house," he replied.

"And your pet elephant?"

"That's the dog. You want to see her?" he asked, gesturing toward Catherine's closed door.

"If she's not busy."

He glanced at the phone console. "Go ahead," he said, and handed me a bulky file. "Would you give this to her?"

"Sure."

I knocked at the door. Catherine said, "Come in."

In contrast to my own office which could charitably be described as furnished, Catherine's office was decorated. The color green predominated. Dark green wallpaper. Wing chairs upholstered in the same shade. All the green, she told me, was to provide subliminal encouragement to her clients to pay their bills. It must have worked because she looked sleeker by the day.

She glanced up at me with dark, ironic eyes. Catherine was a small, fine-boned woman, not quite pretty but beside whom merely pretty women looked overblown. I set the file at the edge of her desk.

"What's this?" she asked, laying an immaculately manicured finger on the folder.

"Derek asked me to bring it in."

She smiled. "I didn't think he was your type."

"I was on my way in anyway," I said, dropping into one of her money-colored chairs. "I may need a favor."

She raised a pencilled eyebrow.

As I told her about Larry's call the eyebrow fell and the shallow lines across her forehead deepened. When I finished she said, "You can't really be thinking about taking the case."

"I'm afraid I really am," I replied. "Larry wouldn't have called me if it wasn't important, much less remind me that I owe him..." I let the sentence trail off.

Catherine filled in the blank. "Your life?"

I shrugged. "My professional life, anyway."

"Still," she said dismissively. "Sounds like a slow plea to me."

"Maybe."

"What's the favor?"

"If I take the case I'll need someone to stand in for me on my cases up here. Just to get continuances."

"It'll cost you, Henry," she warned.

I smiled. "My professional life?"

"We'll start with lunch," she replied. "Get me a list of your cases and we'll discuss them then. Is that it?"

I stood up. "For now. Thanks, Cathy."

She looked at me. "Don't you ever get tired of losing, Henry?"

I thought about this for a second. "No," I said.

◻

It was still raining when I left my office at six to meet Larry's plane at the San Francisco airport. The wind was up, scattering red and yellow leaves like bright coins into the wet, shiny streets. A stalwart jogger, wrapped in sweats, crossed the street at the light and I felt a twinge of regret. The only kind of running I did these days was between courts. Still, a glance in the mirror reported no significant change in my appearance from my last birthday — my thirty-sixth. The light flashed green and I jostled my Accord forward onto the freeway ramp.

I entered a freeway that was clogged with Friday night traffic. Sitting there, watching the rain come down, gave me time to think. It wasn't true that I never got tired of losing. Only three years earlier I had been tired enough of it to resign from the P.D.'s office, expecting to abandon law altogether. But I had fallen in love with a man who was murdered. Hugh Paris's death led me back into law though I took a lot of detours getting there. One of them was through the drunk ward of a local hospital. I might have been there yet had it not been for Larry Ross and the United States Supreme Court.

The summer I entered the drunk ward was the same summer that the Supreme Court, in a case involving Georgia, upheld the right of states to make sodomy — a generic term for every sexual practice but the missionary position — illegal. Within weeks there was a move to reinstate California's sodomy law, which had been repealed ten years earlier, by a special election. A statewide committee of lawyers was organized to fight the effort. Larry Ross, a hitherto closeted partner in a well-known Los Angeles firm, chaired the committee. He needed a lawyer from northern California to lead the effort up here. After asking around, he found me, or rather, what was left of me.

We went into the campaign with the polls running against us. Larry poured all his energy and a quarter of his net worth — which was considerable — into trying to change the numbers. Halfway through, however, it was plain that we would lose. Since we couldn't win the election, we decided to try to knock the sodomy initiative off the ballot with a lawsuit. We went directly to the state Supreme Court, arguing that the initiative violated the right to privacy guaranteed by the state constitution.

Two days before the ballot went to the print shop, the court ruled in our favor. It looked like a victory but it wasn't. We had merely prevented things from getting worse, not improved them. Since then, some part of me had been waiting for the next fight. Maybe Larry had found it in this Pears case.

I pulled into a parking space at the airport and hurried across the street to the terminal. I was nearly twenty minutes late. Coming to the gate I saw Larry in a blue suit, raincoat draped over one arm and a briefcase under the other. He was far away yet I could hardly fail to recognize his spindly stride and the gleaming dome of his head.

Then, coming closer, I thought I had made a mistake. The man who now approached me was a stranger. The flesh of his face was too tight and vaguely green in the bright fluorescent light. But it was Larry. The edges of his mouth turned upward in a smile.

"Henry," he said embracing me, or rather, pulling me to his chest, which was as far up on him as I came.

I broke the embrace and made myself smile. "Larry."

He looked at me and the smile faded. I looked away.

It was then I noticed the odor coming off his clothes. It was the smell of death.

— 2 —

To cover my shock at his appearance I asked, "Do you have any luggage?"

"No, I'm catching the red-eye back to L.A. Where are we eating?"

I named a restaurant in the Castro. As we talked, he looked less strange to me, and I thought perhaps it was only exhaustion I saw on his face. He worked achingly long hours in the bizarre vineyard of Hollywood. We talked of small things as I drove into San Francisco. We came over a hill and then, abruptly, the city's towers rose before us through the mist and rain, glittering stalagmites in the cave of night, and beyond them, sensed rather than seen, the wintry tumble of the ocean.

We rolled through the city on glassy streets shimmering with reflected lights. On Castro, the sidewalks were jammed with men who, in their flak jackets, flannel shirts, tight jeans, wool caps and long scarves, resembled a retreating army. I parked and we walked back down to Nineteenth Street to the restaurant. Inside it was dim and loud. Elegant waiters in threadbare tuxedos raced through the small dining rooms with imperturbable poise. We were seated at a table in the smaller of the two dining rooms in the back with a view of the derelict patio just outside. Menus were placed before us.

"It's really good to see you," Larry said, and picked up his menu as if not expecting a response. I ventured one anyway.

"You've been working too hard," I said.

"I suspect you're right," he replied.

I dithered with the menu as I tried to decide whether to pursue the subject.

"What you want to say," Larry said, "is that I look terrible."

"You look—" I fumbled for a word.

"Different?" he asked, almost mockingly. He lit a cigarette and blew smoke out of the corner of his mouth away from me. I waited for him to continue. Instead, the waiter came and Larry ordered his dinner. When it was my turn I asked for the same.

We sat in nervous silence until our salads were brought to us. The waiter drizzled dressing over the salads. Larry caught my eye and held it. When the waiter departed, Larry picked up his fork, set it down again and relit his discarded cigarette.

"I'm dying, Henry," he said softly.

"Larry—"

"I was diagnosed eight months ago. I've already survived one bout of pneumocystis." He smiled a little. "Two years ago I wouldn't have been able to pronounce that word. AIDS has taught me a new vocabulary." He put out his cigarette.

"I'm so sorry," I said stupidly.

The waiter came by. "Is everything all right?"

"Yes, fine," Larry said.

"Why didn't you tell me sooner?" I asked.

"There was nothing you could have done then," he said, cutting up a slice of tomato.

"Is there now?"

"Yes. Defend Jim Pears." He put a forkful of salad in his mouth and chewed gingerly.

"I don't understand."

"I'm going to die, Henry," he said slowly. "Not just because of AIDS but also because the lives of queers are expendable. Highly expendable." He stopped abruptly and stared down at his plate, then continued, more emphatically. "They hate us, Henry, and they'd just as soon we all died. I'm dying. Save Jim Pears's life for me."

"Don't die," I said, and the words sounded childlike even to my own ears.

"I won't just yet," he replied. "But when I do I want it to be my life for Jim's. That would balance the accounts."

"But it's entirely different," I said.

"It's the same disease," he insisted. "Bigotry. It doesn't matter whether it shows itself in letting people die of AIDS or making it so difficult for them to come out that it's easier to murder."

"Then you do think he did it."

"Yes," he said. "Not that it makes any difference to me."

"It will to a jury."

"You'll have to persuade them," he said, "that Jim was justified."

"Self-defense?"

Larry said, "There might be a problem there. Jim's P.D. told me Jim doesn't remember anything about what happened."

"Doesn't remember?" I echoed.

"She called it retrograde amnesia."

The waiter came and took Larry's salad plate. He cast a baleful glance at my plate from which I had eaten nothing and said, "Sir, shall I leave your salad?"

"Yes, please."

We were served dinner. Looking at Larry I reflected how quickly we had retreated into talk of Jim Pears's case as if the subject of Larry's illness had never been raised.

"I want to talk some more about you," I said.

Larry compressed his lips into a frown. "I've told you all there is to know."

"How do you feel about it?"

"Henry, I've turned myself inside out examining my feelings. It was painful enough the first time without repeating the exercise for you."

"Sorry." I addressed myself to the food on my plate, some sort of chicken glistening with gravy. A wave of nausea rose from my stomach to my throat.

Larry was saying, "But I won't go quietly. Depend on that."

We got through dinner. Afterwards, we went upstairs to the bar. Sitting at the window seat with glasses of mineral water we watched men passing on the street below us in front of what had been the Jaguar Bookstore.

Abruptly, Larry said, "I wondered at first how I could have been infected. It really puzzled me because I thought AIDS was only transmitted during tawdry little episodes in the back rooms of places like that." He gestured toward the Jaguar. "All my tawdry little episodes were twenty years in the past, and then there was Ned." Ned was his lover who had died four years ago.

"Were you monogamous with Ned?"

He smiled grimly. "I was monogamous, yes."

"But not Ned."

"You don't get this from doorknobs, Henry." He frowned.

"Do you think he knew?"

"He killed himself didn't he?" Larry snapped. "At least now I know why," he added, quietly.

"Who have you told?"

"You."

"That's all?"

He nodded. "My clients are movie stars. Having a gay lawyer is considered amusing in that set but a leper is a different matter."

"But — your appearance."

"You haven't seen me in, what? A year? And even you were willing to accept the way I look as the result of overwork. It's not really noticeable from day to day."

"But you must have been in the hospital?"

"With the flu," he said. "A virulent, obscure Asian flu with complications brought on by fatigue."

"People believed that?"

"People are remarkably incurious and besides..." He didn't finish his sentence. He didn't have to. I knew he was going to say that people preferred not to think about AIDS, much less believe that someone they knew had it. I was struggling with my own disbelief and, at some deeper level, my terror.

"How long can you keep it a secret?"

"Henry, you're talking to a man who was in the closet for almost thirty-five years. I know from secrets." He yawned. "I'd like to go for a walk down by the water, then we have to talk some more about Jim Pears."

It had stopped raining by the time we reached Fisherman's

Wharf but that loud, normally crowded, arcade of tourist traps and overpriced fish restaurants was deserted anyway. We walked around aimlessly, jostling against each other on the narrow walks, stopping to comment on some particularly egregious monstrosity in the shopfront windows. We walked to the edge of the pier where the fishing boats were berthed, creaking in the water like old beds. A rift in the clouds above the Golden Gate revealed a black sky and three faint stars. Larry looked at them and then at me.

"Do you wish on stars, Henry?" he asked.

"Not since I was a kid."

"I do," Larry replied. "Wish on stars. Pray. Plead. It doesn't do any good." We stood there for a few more minutes until he complained of the cold.

I drove us to Washington Square and we found an espresso bar. Tony Bennett played on the jukebox. We each ordered a caffe latte. Larry brought out a bulky folder from his briefcase and put it on the table between us.

"What is it?" I asked.

"My file on Jim Pears. You're taking the case, aren't you?"

I hesitated. "Yes. I'll fly down on Monday morning. Will I have a chance to talk to Jim before the hearing?"

"I don't know. You'll have to ask his P.D. A woman named Sharon Hart." He paused and sipped his coffee. "She's not a bad lawyer but something's not working out between her and Jim."

"It happens. I'm always running up against the expectations of my clients. You learn to be tactful."

Larry wasn't listening. He was looking at his reflection in the window. When he looked back at me, he asked, "Do I seem hysterical to you?"

I shook my head.

"I do to myself sometimes." He rattled his cup. "I'm so angry, Henry. When I wake up in the morning I think I'll explode from rage."

He tightened his jaw and clamped a hand over his mouth.

"Don't you expect that?" I asked, awkwardly.

He lowered his hand, revealing a faintly hostile smile. "You've been reading too much Kubler-Ross," he said. "There are only two stages to dying, Henry. Being alive and being dead. We treat death like a bad smell. I'm supposed to excuse myself and leave the room."

His eyes were bright. It was the only time I had ever seen Larry even approach tears and it was frightening.

"Why should you care what other people think? You never have before."

"Well, that's not true," he snapped. "I was the original closet queen, remember?" He expelled a noisy breath, then sipped from his coffee. "I don't know why I'm taking it out on you."

"Because I'm here?"

He shook his head. "Because I love you." He tried to smile but his face wouldn't cooperate. "I'll miss you."

He lowered his face toward the table and I watched the tears slide down his cheeks and splatter on the table top. I reached for his hand and held it. After a moment or two it was over. He looked up, drew a dazzlingly white handkerchief from his breast pocket and wiped his face.

He glanced at his watch. "It's the witching hour. You'd better get me back to the airport."

I pulled up in front of the terminal and helped Larry gather his things. He put his hand on the door handle.

"Wait," I said.

He looked over at me. I leaned across the seat and kissed him.

"I love you, too," I said.

"I know."

A moment later he was gone.

— 3 —

It was nearly one when I pulled into the carport and parked in my allotted space. It was raining again and a heavy wind rattled the treetops filling my quiet street with creaks and wheezes. I grabbed the bulky folder Larry had given me and made a run for my apartment, stopping only to collect my mail and a soggy edition of the evening paper.

Inside I was greeted by silence. The only unusual thing about this was that I noticed it at all. I put the folder on my desk, added the paper to the stack in the kitchen and leafed through the bills and solicitations that comprised my mail. I turned on a burner and poured water into the tea kettle, set it on the flame, opened a bag of Chips Ahoy and ate a few. When the water was boiling I poured it into a blue mug with "Henry" emblazoned on it — the gift of a client — and added a bag of Earl Grey tea. Then there was that silence again. It seemed to flow out of the electrical outlets and drip from the tap.

Only the silence was not quite silent enough. It was filled with my loneliness. I had lived alone long enough and I did not want to die this way. These days, death no longer seemed like such a distant prospect to me. I sipped my tea. I thought of my empty bed. I opened the folder and found the transcripts of Jim Pears's preliminary hearing.

◻

The purpose of a preliminary hearing is to see whether the prosecutor can establish probable cause to bring the defendant to trial — to "hold him to answer," in the arcane language of the law. For the defense, however, the prelim is an opportunity to preview the prosecution's evidence so as to prepare to refute it at trial. Consequently, the prosecutor puts on as little evidence as possible to show probable cause, holding what he can in reserve.

The transcripts of Jim's prelim consisted of two slender volumes. The events leading up to Brian Fox's death were narrated by two witnesses who had also worked at the restaurant. The first was a waiter named Josh Mandel. I set my cup down and began reading:

Frank Pisano, D.A.: At some point prior to Brian Fox's death, did you have a conversation with Brian about Jim Pears?

Mrs. Sharon Hart, P.D.: Objection, calls for hearsay.

Pisano: This statement is admissible under section 1350 of the Evidence Code. We filed some papers —

The Court: I have them here.

Pisano: Yes, Your Honor. Uh, we expect Mr. Mandel will testify that he was told by Brian Fox that he — Brian — saw Jim Pears engaging in sex with a man. That's relevant to the issues here and Brian Fox is certainly unavailable, thanks to Mr. Pears.

The Court: Mrs. Hart?

Hart: There're a lot of conditions here that have to be satisfied before 1350 applies. Like — for example, the statement has to have been written down or tape-recorded.

The Court: Where is that? Oh, all right, I see it. What about that, Mr. Pisano?

Pisano: It also says it's okay if the statement is made under circumstances that indicate its trustworthiness. That's an alternative to a taped or written statement.

Hart: No it's not. That's in addition to.

The Court: Well, I tend to agree with the prosecutor on that. I'm going to let the statement in.

Hart: Defense objects.

The Court: Understood. The objection's overruled.

Pisano: Do you remember the question, Josh?

Josh Mandel: Yeah. Brian told me he had proof that Jim was gay.

Pisano: Do you mean homosexual?

Hart: Objection, leading.

The Court. We're wasting time. Overruled. Answer.

Mandel: Yes.

Pisano: Did he tell you what this proof was?

Mandel: Yes.

Pisano: What was it?

Mandel: He said he saw Jim having sex with some guy in a car out in the restaurant parking lot.

Pisano: How long before Brian was killed did you have this conversation with him?

Mandel: A couple of weeks.

Pisano: Now, did you ever overhear a conversation between Brian and Jim Pears regarding this incident in the parking lot?

Mandel: Well, I think. Yeah. They were talking about it.

Pisano: What was said?

Hart: Objection, hearsay.

Pisano: This is an admission, Your Honor.

The Court: Let's hear it. Answer the question, Mr. Mandel.

Mandel: Brian was asking Jim how would he like his mother to know that he was— (Inaudible.)

Pisano: You'll have to speak up, Josh.

Mandel: A cocksucker. I'm sorry, Your Honor, but that's what he said.

The Court: I've heard worse things in this court, Mr. Mandel. Next question, counsel.

Pisano: Okay. Did Jim Pears say anything in response?

Mandel: Yeah.

Pisano: What?

Mandel: He said something like, 'I'll kill you before that happens.'

Pisano: And how soon before Brian's murder did this conversation take place?

Mandel: It was two days.

(Cross-examination by Mrs. Hart)

Hart: Now you say that Brian Fox told you he saw Jim having sex with a man that night, is that right?

Mandel: Yes.

Hart: This was in a private car in the parking lot at night?

Mandel: Yeah, I guess.

Hart: Did Brian explain how he happened to be there?
Mandel: Not to me.
Hart: Well, isn't it true that Brian Fox followed Jim and then snuck up on him?
Pisano: The People will stipulate that Brian was not asked to join in on the festivities.
The Court: Why don't we let the witness answer, Mr. Pisano?
Mandel: I don't know.
Hart: Now, Mr. Mandel, what words did Brian use to describe what he had seen?
Mandel: I don't remember, exactly.
Hart: Well, did he say he'd seen Jim having sex or making love?
Mandel: No. It was more like he saw him getting a blow job.
Hart: Okay. Did you ever hear Brian Fox call Jim a faggot?
Pisano: Objection, irrelevant.
The Court: Overruled. Answer the question.
Mandel: Yes.
Hart: More than once?
Mandel: Yes.
Hart: Did you ever hear Brian Fox call Jim a queer?
Mandel: Yes.
Hart: More than once?
Mandel: Yes.
Hart: How many times did you hear Brian Fox call Jim either a faggot or a queer?
Mandel: I don't remember.
Hart: Isn't it true that you don't remember because that was how Brian normally referred to Jim?
Mandel: He called him that a lot.
Hart: Around other people?
Mandel: Yes.
Hart: Now, Mr. Mandel, isn't it true that, in addition to being a waiter at the Yellowtail, you are also a manager?
Mandel: Manager-trainee.
Hart: And isn't part of your job to supervise the busboys on the shifts that you manage?

Mandel: Yes.

Hart: And did you ever manage a shift where Brian and Jim were working?

Mandel: Yeah.

Hart: And during one of those shifts did you hear Brian call Jim a queer or a faggot?

Mandel: I'm not sure. Maybe.

Hart: But you never stopped Brian, did you?

Mandel: I don't remember.

Hart: In fact, isn't it true that you also called Jim a faggot once?

Mandel: I don't remember.

Hart: Isn't it true that you told Jim to start acting like a man?

Mandel: That was just because he was letting Brian get to him.

Hart: Then shouldn't you have talked to Brian?

Mandel: Yeah. (Inaudible) I'm sorry, Jim.

Hart: I have nothing further, Your Honor.

(Examination by Mr. Pisano of Andrea Lew, a cocktail waitress at the Yellowtail.)

Pisano: Who was working at the Yellowtail between eleven-thirty p.m. and midnight on the night Brian was killed?

Lew: It was just me and Frank — that's the bartender — and Jim was the busboy.

Pisano: Besides the bar was any other part of the restaurant open?

Lew: No, the kitchen closes at ten.

Pisano: How many people were in the bar at that time?

Lew: Not many. It was Monday, you know. Slow night. Maybe a dozen.

Pisano: Between eleven-thirty and midnight did you see anyone enter the bar?

Lew: Just Brian.

Pisano: Now, would you have noticed if anyone else had come in?

Lew: Well, yeah, because you have to cross in front of the bar to get to the dining rooms or the kitchen.

Pisano: Was Jim Pears in the bar when Brian came in?

Lew: Yes.
Pisano: Did he see Brian?
Mrs. Hart: Objection, calls for speculation.
The Court: Sustained.
Pisano: Okay. Was Brian working that night?
Lew: No, just Jim.
Pisano: Do you know what he was doing there?
Lew: (Shakes head.)
Pisano: You're going to have to answer yes or no for the reporter.
Lew: No.
Pisano: Did you see Brian leave the bar at some point?
Lew: No, but he was gone.
Pisano: Did you see Jim Pears leave the bar?
Lew: Yes.
Pisano: When was this?
Lew: Maybe around midnight.
Pisano: Where did he go?
Lew: Back toward the kitchen.
Pisano: Did you also go back to the kitchen at some point?
Lew: Yes.
Pisano: Why?
Lew: There's a movie theater next door and around midnight the last show gets out. Some people came in for a drink and Frank needed some more ice so he told me to have Jim bring him up some.
Pisano: Where is the ice kept?
Lew: In the walk-in — that's the refrigerator — in the kitchen.
Pisano: About what time was it when you went back into the kitchen?
Lew: A quarter after twelve.
Pisano: Did you see Jim back there?
Lew: No.
Pisano: What did you do?
Lew: It's hard ... I ...
Pisano: One step at a time, Ms. Lew, and we'll get through this. He wasn't in the kitchen. Then what?

Lew: I looked in the locker room. I looked outside, out the back door, but he wasn't there.

Pisano: Was the back door unlocked?

Lew: Yeah.

Pisano: Okay. He wasn't in the kitchen, the locker room, or outside. Then what did you do?

Lew: I looked in the walk-in. He wasn't there. That left, the only place was the cellar. That's where I went.

Pisano: I want you to describe the cellar, Ms. Lew.

Lew: There's a big room where the wine's kept. Then there's two little rooms, one for the manager's office. The other one is where we keep the hard liquor.

Pisano: Did you go into the cellar?

Lew: Yes.

Pisano: What did you find in the big room?

Lew: Nothing. I called Jim but he wasn't there.

Pisano: What did you do then?

Lew: It was kinda creepy down there. I was going to get Frank's ice myself but then—

Pisano: We're almost done, Ms. Lew.

Lew: I'm sorry. The manager's office was closed up. I saw that the door to the liquor room was open a little and the light was on. I went over and then — there was this noise, like a whimper. Like a puppy makes. I thought maybe Jim was lifting boxes and hurt himself so I went in.

Pisano: What did you see?

Lew: The first thing was just Jim. He was kinda hunched over and leaning against some boxes. There was a funny smell, like a bottle of liquor got broken so I looked down at the floor. That's when I — saw him.

Pisano: Saw who, Ms. Lew?

Lew: Oh, God, I didn't know at first. His face was all — but then it was the clothes Brian was wearing in the bar. There was blood. I looked back at Jim. He was holding one of the kitchen knives and his hands were bloody. There was blood on his shirt and his pants like he tried to wipe the knife clean.

Pisano: Did he speak to you?

Lew: No. I don't know. I ran out of there and started screaming for Frank as soon as I was upstairs.

Pisano: Then what happened?

Lew: Frank came to the back and there was some other guys with him, from the bar, I guess. I told them what was downstairs. We piled things up against the cellar door and called the police.

Pisano: And when did they arrive?

Lew: Five, ten minutes. It seemed like forever before I heard the sirens.

Pisano: That's all, Ms. Lew. Thank you.

The Court: Cross-examination, Mrs. Hart.

Hart: I have no questions of this witness.

☐

The bloody images of Brian Fox's murder remained with me even after I set the transcripts aside and made myself another cup of tea. Coming back to my desk, I picked a looseleaf binder out of the folder Larry had given me and opened it up. Inside were press accounts of the Pears case from the day Jim was arrested to the day after he'd been held to answer. I flipped the pages until I came to a story that had a picture.

The headline proclaimed "The Tragic Death of Brian Fox." Beneath the headline was a black-and-white of Brian that startled me for no better reason than his youth. I had cast someone older and sleazier for the role of the boy who tormented Jim Pears. Instead, I found myself looking at a handsome boy with light hair whose features had not yet set on his slightly fleshy face. His half-smile revealed either shyness or surprise. There was a caption beneath the picture: "His mother called him golden boy."

I read the story. It consisted of lachrymose interviews with Brian's mother, teachers, and fellow students. You'd have thought he was in line for sainthood, at least. I looked back at the face. No hint of sainthood there. Maybe the twist of the smile was neither shyness nor surprise. Maybe it was sadism. I wondered, would a jury buy that? Probably not.

I went back and read the stories in chronological order. Jim had not fared nearly as well as Brian. The only picture of him showed him lifting his handcuffed wrists to his face as he was led into court for arraignment. The first spate of stories were more or less straightforward accounts of what had occurred at the Yellowtail that night. They tallied with the cocktail waitress's testimony.

Subsequent stories, ignoring the possibility of Jim's innocence, dwelt on his motive for killing Brian. Much was written about what were termed Brian's "teasing" remarks about Jim's homosexuality. There were inaccurate reports of the parking lot incident. According to one paper, it was Brian himself to whom Jim offered sex. Another paper got most of the details right but the reporter termed Brian's activities a "prank." The upshot was that Jim was a psycho closet case with a short fuse that Brian accidentally ignited.

The last batch of stories was the worst. Oddly enough — or perhaps not — Jim's father, Walter Pears, was responsible for these stories. Jim's parents had resisted the media until just before the prelim. Then his father had talked. Walter Pears's explanation for Jim's crime was "demonic possession." He announced that since Jim was apparently in the thrall of Satan, the best that could be done was, as the elder Pears said repeatedly, to "put him away for everyone's good."

The press took up the notion of satanism. There were rumors about the alleged disfigurement of Brian Fox's body. A priest made the connection between homosexuality — an abomination before God — and worship of the devil by whom, presumably, such practices were tolerated. At length, the coverage grew so outrageous that the chief of police himself felt constrained to deny that any evidence of devil-worship or demonic possession existed in the case.

I reached the end of the binder. A first-year law student could predict the result of this case. Jim's trial would merely be a way station on the road to prison. Keeping him off death row would be as much victory as anyone could reasonably expect. It was nearly three in the morning. I finished my tea and got ready for bed.

— 4 —

The storm that passed through San Francisco on Friday had worked its way through Los Angeles by the time I stepped off the plane on Monday. It was a distinctly tropical eighty degrees that last morning of September. I threw my overcoat into the back of my rented car and made my way downtown to the Criminal Courts Building.

The vast city was just awakening as I sped eastward on the Santa Monica Freeway. I had spent a lot of time in Los Angeles when I worked with Larry on the sodomy lawsuit two years earlier. I knew the city as well as anyone who didn't live there could, and I liked the place. Between the freeway and the Hollywood Hills the feathery light of early morning poured into the basin and it truly did seem, at that moment, to be the habitation of angels. The great palms lifted their shaggy heads like a race of ancient, benevolent animals. Along the broad boulevards that ran from downtown to the sea, skyscrapers rose abruptly as if by geologic accident but were dwarfed by the sheer enormity of the plain.

I parked in the lot behind the Criminal Courts Building across from City Hall and walked around to the courthouse entrance on Temple. In the space between the entrance platform and the ground lay the charred remains of a campfire, with people sleeping in rags and old blankets. Inside, the walls of the foyer were covered with gang graffiti. After an interminable wait, an elevator picked me up and ascended, creaking its way to the floor where the Public Defender had his offices. I walked into a small reception room, announced myself to the receptionist and sat down to wait. The room was crowded with restless children and adults sitting nervously on plastic chairs. A little boy came up and stared at me with wide, black eyes.

"Are you my mama's P.D.?" he asked.

I smiled at him. "No."

"Then how come you wear a suit?"

A stout woman called from across the room, "Leave the man alone, Willie."

"I'm waiting for my P.D., Willie," I said.

"Nah," he replied, and went back to his mother.

The door beside the receptionist's desk opened. A short, heavy gray-haired woman in a bright floral dress said, "Henry Rios."

I stood up.

"I'm Sharon Hart," she said. "You want to come into my office?"

I followed her through the door and we picked our way down a hallway lined with metal file cabinets into a small office. There was a calendar on one wall and framed degrees on the other. Sharon Hart sat down behind her government-issue desk and motioned me to sit on one of the two chairs in front of it. She pulled an ashtray out of her desk and lit a cigarette.

"So," she said. "You're the famous Henry Rios."

There was nothing particularly hostile in her tone so I ventured a smile.

"I hope you can walk on water, Mr. Rios, because that's the kind of skill you're going to need on this case."

"Is that why you're getting out?"

She looked at me sharply. "I'm not afraid of tough cases."

"Then why withdraw?"

"This case is indefensible on a straight not-guilty plea."

"There are alternatives."

She shook her head. "Not with this client. He won't agree to any defense that admits he did it."

"Any chance he didn't do it?"

Her look answered my question.

"Then that could be a problem," I said.

"He's also going to make a lousy witness," she said offhandedly. "Not that there's much for him to say. He doesn't remember what happened."

"So I was told. Retrograde amnesia, is that it?"

She nodded. "I had the court appoint a shrink to talk to him. You'll find his name in the files." She gestured to two bulky folders lying at a corner of her desk. "The doctor says it's legitimate. Jim doesn't remember anything between opening the cellar door and when that girl — the waitress — came down and found him with Brian Fox."

"Is he crazy?"

She smiled slightly, showing a crooked tooth. "My shrink will say that he was at the time of the murder."

"Not quite the question I asked," I murmured.

"Is he crazy now? Let's say the pressure's getting to him."

"Where's he being held?"

"County jail," she said.

"You've told him what's going to happen this morning?"

"Yes," she said. "He'll agree to it." She stubbed out her cigarette and lit another. "We don't get along," she added. "Call it ineffective empathy of counsel. But I do feel sorry for the kid. I really do." She stood up. "Take the files. You'll find my investigator's card in them. He can fill you in. We better get downstairs. Pat Ryan runs a tight ship."

"The judge."

"Patricia Ryan."

"Irish."

Sharon smiled. "Black Irish, you might say."

Television cameras were set up in the jury box and the gallery was packed with reporters. To avoid the press, we had come in through the corridor that ran behind the courtrooms. As soon as we reached counsel's table, though, the cameras started rolling. At the other end of the table a short, dark-haired man was unpacking his briefcase.

"The D.A.," Sharon whispered. "Pisano."

"What's he like?" I asked.

She shrugged. "He's decent enough until you get him in front of the cameras."

"A headline grabber?" I asked.

"The worst."

As if he'd heard, the D.A. smiled at us, then turned his attention to a sheaf of papers that he was marking with a red pen.

"Where's Jim?" I asked.

"In the holding cell, I guess," she said. "They won't bring him out until she takes the bench."

I looked over my shoulder at the reporters. "This is quite a circus," I said.

"Better get used to it."

A middle-aged woman with stiffly coiffed hair and dressed in black stared at Sharon Hart and me with intense hostility from the gallery.

"Who's that?" I asked.

Sharon glanced over. "Brian Fox's mother. She comes to every hearing. You'll like her."

"What about Jim's parents?"

"Oh, them," she said venomously. "They're just as nice as Mrs. Fox."

In a seat across the aisle from Brian's mother sat a young man in a blue suit, wearing horn-rimmed glasses. My eye caught his for a moment, then he looked away.

"That's Josh Mandel," Sharon said.

"Oh," I replied, glancing at him once again.

She looked at me. "Do you know him?"

"No," I said, and yet he seemed somehow familiar.

The bailiff broke the silence of the courtroom with his announcement. "Please rise. Department Nine is now in session, the Honorable Patricia Ryan presiding."

The judge came out from behind the clerk's desk through the same door by which we had entered. Patricia Ryan was a tall black woman whose handsome face was set in a faintly amused expression.

In a pleasant, light voice she said, "Good morning, counsel. Please be seated." She looked down at her desk. "People versus Pears. Is the defendant in court?"

A blond court reporter clicked away at her machine taking down every word.

"He's coming," the bailiff said.

The door to the holding cell opened and the TV cameras swung away from the judge over to the two marshals who escorted Jim Pears into the courtroom. I had just enough time to glance at him before the judge started talking again. They sat Jim down beside Sharon Hart at the end of the table.

"We were to begin the trial of this matter today," the judge said. "However, ten days ago the Public Defender's office filed a motion to withdraw from the case. Is that correct Mrs. Hart?"

"Yes."

The judge looked at me quizzically and said, "Who are you, sir?"

"Henry Rios, Your Honor. I've been asked to substitute in should the Public Defender's motion be granted."

"Thank you, Mr. Rios. All right. The defendant is now present and represented. The People are represented and are opposing this motion."

"That's right, Your Honor," Pisano said.

"Mrs. Hart, you go first."

Sharon Hart stood up. "The People complain about delay," she began, "without showing that their case would be prejudiced by the delay. They don't say either that witnesses or evidence would become unavailable to them if the trial is postponed. My client, on the other hand, has a constitutional right to effective representation. My office can't provide that at this point. So it seems to me, Your Honor, that if you weigh his rights against the prosecution's pro forma objection, it's clear the motion should be granted."

The judge said, "Mr. Pisano."

"Your Honor," he said. "the D.A.'s office is not a lynch mob. We want Mr. Pears to get a fair trial. Our objection is that the P.D.'s office has completely failed to tell anyone why it can't handle this case. Now," he said, stepping back from the table and coming up behind Sharon Hart, "we saw how well Mrs. Hart conducted the defense during the prelim—"

"Thanks," Sharon whispered mockingly.

"—so what's the problem now? They say they have a conflict. What conflict?" He shrugged eloquently. "Surely we all want to see that justice is done as expeditiously as possible."

"I'm sure," Judge Ryan replied with a faint smile. She was clearly aware that Pisano was playing to the press.

Undeterred, he continued. "We don't know what the conflict is and I would hate to suspect that this motion is only to delay things, but..." He left the end of the sentence dangling, with another shrug of his shoulders. "And what about our friend, Mr. Rios," Pisano continued. "He's not going to be ready to start trying the case today. No, he'll be asking for time. Maybe a lot of time. Maybe, considering the People's evidence, forever."

Sharon Hart seethed. I composed my face into the mask I reserved for such occasions.

"Or maybe," Pisano said, "there's another reason for this motion. Mr. Rios here is not unknown. He was one of the lawyers who knocked the sodomy initiative off the ballot a couple of years ago. He represents a powerful constituency."

"I hardly see—" the judge began.

"Your Honor, if I may finish," Pisano cut in, his voice darkening theatrically. "Let me suggest that this motion is the result of political pressure on the P.D.'s office by the gay community to let Mr. Rios try the case..." Again Pisano let the end of his sentence trail off suggestively.

I heard the rustling of papers in the gallery as the reporters scribbled their notes. Pisano would make the news tonight.

"I really must object," Sharon Hart said. "That remark is completely improper."

The judge glowered at the D.A. "Mr. Pisano, that comment is not well taken."

"My apologies," the D.A. said smoothly. "Perhaps I spoke out of turn. But the court must understand the People's frustration. This motion is so mysterious, Your Honor. I'm completely at a loss as to why a perfectly competent lawyer like Mrs. Hart wants off this case."

"Mrs. Hart."

"Your Honor, it took me a minute but I finally understand what the D.A. is up to. He wants me to put on the record why my office can't represent Mr. Pears. We obviously can't do that without compromising the defense. This court will simply have to accept my representation that an irreconcilable conflict exists between me and Mr. Pears."

The judge's eyebrows darted up. Judges do not appreciate being told what they must accept.

"Nonetheless," the judge observed, "the motion is discretionary with me."

Seeing her mistake, Sharon said, "I didn't mean to suggest otherwise, Judge. I'm just saying the prosecution wants a sneak preview of the defense. They're not entitled to that."

Pisano broke in. "Your Honor, as you point out, granting or denying this motion is your choice. I just don't see how you can make a fair decision based on some vague representation of irreconcilable conflicts. We're not talking no-fault divorce here."

"Anything else?" Judge Ryan asked, looking at Hart and Pisano.

"Submitted," both lawyers said in unison.

The judge stared uneasily into space.

"What's she thinking?" I whispered.

"She's thinking that if she grants the motion she'd better have a good reason because the D.A. will file a writ petition in the Court of Appeal before the ink is dry on her order," Sharon whispered back.

I heard the clink of metal and remembered that Jim Pears, who had been ignored during the hearing, was still sitting at the end of the table.

"What does Jim—" I began.

"Shush," Sharon snapped. The judge had begun to speak.

"...concerned, Mrs. Hart, that I don't have enough of a basis to rule intelligently on your motion. Now I can appreciate you not wanting to tip your hand to the prosecution. So what I think I'll do is take Mr. Rios, you and the reporter into chambers and have you put the conflict on the record. I will then order that portion of the transcript sealed. Is that acceptable?"

I watched the struggle in Sharon's face. She clearly thought her word that a conflict existed should be enough, but she also wanted to win.

"Yes, Judge," she said.

"What about the People?" the D.A. asked.

"What about the People?" the judge repeated with exasperation.

"Well, I thought—"

"Nice try, Mr. Pisano," the judge said. "Court's in recess. Mrs. Hart, Mr. Rios."

We followed her back across a corridor into her chambers and sat down while she took off her robe and hung it up. There was a framed law degree on the wall from Stanford and, next to it, a picture of the judge shaking hands with the Democratic governor who had appointed her to the bench. The windows of her office overlooked City Hall and the Times-Mirror Building. She sat down behind a vast rosewood desk.

"All right," she began briskly. "We're in chambers on People versus Pears. Mrs. Hart, tell me about this conflict." The reporter's fingers flew across the keyboard of her machine as the judge spoke.

"My client refuses to cooperate in preparing a defense," she said.

"He wants to plead guilty?" the judge asked.

"No, he insists he's not guilty."

Judge Ryan grinned. "Most defendants do, Mrs. Hart."

"That's not a tenable defense," Sharon insisted.

The judge nodded, thoughtfully. "Unless you have a secret weapon, the evidence presented at the prelim seems pretty conclusive."

"There is no secret weapon," Sharon said. "At least in regards to whether he did it. But, as to why he did it..." She let the sentence trail off.

"I understand," the judge said.

We were at a delicate point. Since Judge Ryan would be presiding at the trial there was a limit to what Sharon Hart could disclose to her about the defense without laying the judge open to a charge of being less than completely impartial.

"Anyway," Sharon continued, "I feel very strongly that I cannot continue to represent Mr. Pears and I think he feels just as strongly that he can't work with me, either."

The judge turned to me. "Mr. Rios."

"I'm willing to try the case on terms set by my client."

The judge arched an eyebrow. "Have *you* read the transcript of the preliminary hearing?"

"Yes. However, Judge, whatever the state of the evidence, there comes a point when you have to do what your client wants — if, in good conscience, you can."

The judge frowned but said nothing.

"He's right, Judge," Sharon said, coming to my rescue. "It's Jim who's on trial here."

The judge looked at the reporter and said, "This is off the record." The reporter stopped typing and the judge said, "Do you really think Jim Pears has the wherewithal to call the shots in this case?"

Sharon and I exchanged surprised looks.

"Now I know I'm speaking out of turn," the judge continued, "but when I look at Jim Pears all I see is fear. I'm going to grant your motion, Sharon, and I'll give you some time to prepare for trial, Mr. Rios, but I want you to know that I feel very strongly that this is not a case that should be coming to trial. There should be a disposition."

"The D.A.'s not giving an inch from murder one," Sharon said sourly.

Judge Ryan set her mouth into a grim smile. "The D.A.," she said, "can be persuaded. All right. You think about what I've said, Mr. Rios. Now let's go out and do this on the record."

"Yes, Judge," we both chimed.

We preceded her into the court. I asked Sharon what that was all about.

"It sounds to me like she doesn't want a jury to get their hands on Jim. If I were you, I'd consider waiving a jury and having a court trial."

I stopped at the table where Jim was sitting and leaned over. "Jim, my name is Henry," I whispered.

He looked up at me and said, "I didn't do it."

— 5 —

Sharon Hart's motion was granted and I was substituted in as Jim Pears's attorney of record. The trial date was continued to December first to give me time to prepare. After the ruling was made the D.A. stood up.

"Yes, Mr. Pisano," the judge said.

"The People wish to move to amend the complaint."

The judge looked annoyed. "This isn't exactly timely notice, counsel."

"The Penal Code says the People can move to amend at any time," Pisano replied blandly.

"There's a difference between what's permissible and what's fair," she snapped. "What's your amendment?"

Sharon Hart moved to the edge of her seat. Pisano took out a stack of papers and passed a set of them to me. The other set he handed to the bailiff who took them to the judge. I glanced at the caption. It was a motion to amend the complaint and allege special circumstances to the murder charge.

"You're seeking the death penalty?" the judge asked. Behind us, the gallery murmured. The bailiff called the courtroom into order.

"Yes, Your Honor," Pisano replied.

Sharon Hart said, audibly, "Bastard."

"At the preliminary hearing you said this wasn't a special circumstances case," Judge Ryan said.

Contritely, Pisano replied, "I was wrong. We have reviewed the transcripts of the prelim and looked at our evidence. We now think we can show special circumstances."

I got to my feet. "Your Honor, I'm not prepared to respond to this motion at this time. I'd ask that it be put over for a couple of weeks to give me time to file an opposition."

"Fine," she said. "File your papers within twenty-one days. I will hear arguments a month from today. Court is adjourned."

The judge left the bench and the bailiff cleared the courtroom of reporters. The deputies who had been standing beside Jim got him to his feet.

"When can I talk to my client?" I asked one of them.

"He'll be back at county this afternoon."

"Jim, I'll be there later."

He stared past me and nodded. They led him off.

The courtroom cleared out quickly, until only Sharon Hart and I were left.

"You coming?" I asked her.

"Not through that door," she said, indicating the front entrance. I remembered the reporters and the TV cameras. "You?" she asked.

"If I don't," I said, "Pisano will have the boy convicted and sentenced by the six o'clock news."

"See you," she said, and slipped out the back.

⁋

"Mr. Rios, can you answer a few questions?" I stood in a semicircle of reporters, the TV cameras running behind us in the busy corridor outside the courtroom. Pisano — to his chagrin, I imagined — commanded a smaller group down the hall.

"Sure," I said. I heard the clicking of cameras as a couple of photographers circled.

"What do you think about the D.A. seeking the death penalty?"

"It's an obvious attempt to extort a guilty plea from my client," I replied.

"Why did the Public Defender withdraw from the case?"

"Irreconcilable conflicts," I said.

"What were they?"

"That's information protected by the attorney-client privilege," I replied.

"What's your defense going to be?"

"Not guilty."

"What about the evidence?"

"What about it?"

"It's pretty strong."

"Strong is not good enough," I said. "It has to be," and I repeated the ancient charge to the jury, "beyond a reasonable doubt and to a moral certainty. I expect to show that it's not."

"How?"

Good question, I thought. To my interrogator, though, I said, "I'm not free to disclose the details of our investigation."

"What about the political pressure by gays that the D.A. talked about? Is that true?"

"As counsel for the People conceded, he was speaking out of turn."

"Then it's not true?"

"Of course not."

"But you are gay aren't you?"

I turned to face the person who had asked the question. It was Brian Fox's mother. She was trembling with anger.

"Yes, I am, Mrs. Fox, for what that's worth."

"You're all thick as thieves," she said while the cameras turned on her. "All of you — faggots. What about my boy? He's dead."

"Yes, I know," I said, and stopped myself from expressing condolences. It would only give her another opportunity to attack. "I expect the facts surrounding his death will come out at trial. All of them, Mrs. Fox."

We glared at each other. Her face was rigid. She pulled her head back, drew in her cheeks and spat, hitting my neck. The TV cameras recorded the incident. I wiped my neck with my handkerchief. She turned away and clicked down the hall.

"There's your lead," I told the reporters.

□

From the courthouse I drove to Larry Ross's house. Though he worked in Beverly Hills he lived in Silver Lake, a hilltop community east of Hollywood and far from the currents of fashion on the west side of the city. Silver Lake was a reservoir named in honor of a turn-of-the-century water commissioner, but the fortuitous name aptly described the metallic sheen of the water which was not quite a color but a quality of light.

There were hills on both the east and west sides of the lake. Larry lived in the west hills on a street where the architecture ran the gamut from English Tudor to Japanese ecclesiastical. Stucco was the great equalizer. Larry's house was sort of generic Mediterranean. From the street it appeared as a two-storey white wall with an overhanging tile roof, small square windows on the upper floor and a big, dark door set into an arched doorway on the lower. I parked in the driveway and let myself in.

From the small entrance hall, stairs led up to the guest rooms on the second floor. The kitchen was off to the right. To the left there was an immense boxy room that terminated in a glass wall overlooking a garden composed of three descending terraces and the reservoir at the bottom of the hill. The room was furnished with austere New England antiques but its austerity was lightened by elegant pieces of Chinese pottery, Oriental carpets, and wall-hangings like the parlor of a nineteenth-century Boston sea captain made prosperous by the China trade. It was a room designed for entertaining but its stillness indicated that it had not been used for that purpose for a long time, since Ned's suicide.

After Ned's death, Larry had built another wing onto the house, where he now lived. It consisted of a loft bedroom that looked out over his study and the garden.

I went upstairs where I would be staying while I was in town. In a study on the second floor I read rapidly through the files that Sharon Hart had given me. I noted the name of her investigator, Freeman Vidor. I also found the name of the psychiatrist, Sidney Townsend, who had examined Jim. There was no report from the psychiatrist. I called him, reaching him just as he was about to begin a session. He told me to come by in an hour. Freeman Vidor was out, but I left a message on his machine. Finally, I called Catherine McKinley, who had spent the morning in court attempting to continue my cases and then in my office fending off clients.

"What happened in court?" I asked her.

"I got three continuances and disposed of two other cases.

That frees you up for at least a couple of weeks. How are you?"

"Trial's set in six weeks. My client wants a straight not guilty defense."

"On the facts you told me?"

"That's right."

"The kid has a death wish."

"Then he may get it," I replied. "The D.A. wants to amend and add special circumstances."

"That just occurred to him?" she asked, incredulously.

"He's playing to the press," I replied. "I don't know how serious he actually is about amending."

"Any chance the kid's not guilty?"

"I asked the very same question of the P.D. who was handling the case. She rolled her eyes."

"That must mean no," Catherine said. "What are you going to do, Henry?"

"Larry Ross sees Jim as a victim of bigotry against gays," I said. "That's what he wants to put on trial."

"I don't see how that changes the evidence."

"Agreed. But it might change the way the jury looks at the evidence."

"I don't know, Henry," she said. "I think people are tired of being told they have to take the rap when someone else breaks the law."

"Larry's point is that in this society it's easier to kill than to come out. That's not so far-fetched."

"Not if you're gay," she replied. "Most people aren't."

"Would you buy it, Catherine?"

"Yes," she said after a moment's pause. "And I'd still vote to convict."

"You're a hard-hearted woman," I joked.

"That's right," she said seriously. "And I'm not even a bigot."

We said our goodbyes and I sat at the desk in the study looking out the window to the lake below.

□

Sidney Townsend looked exactly like what I imagined someone named Sidney Townsend would look like. He concealed the shapelessness of his body in an expensive suit but his face was big, florid, and jowly. His hair was swept back against his head and held fixedly in place by hairspray. Small, incurious eyes assessed me as he smiled and shook my hand.

He led me into his office, a tastefully furnished room that was nearly as dark as a confessional. Perhaps he specialized in lapsed Catholics, I thought, or maybe the dimness was evocative of a bedroom in keeping with psychiatry's obsession with sex. I sat down on a leather sofa while he got Jim's file. He joined me, sitting a little too close and facing toward me, his jacket unbuttoned and his arm draped across the back of the sofa, leaning toward me. The perfect picture of candor. I drew back into my corner.

"So," he said, "you're taking Jim's case to trial."

"So it appears. Do you get many appointments from the court?"

"It's probably a quarter of my practice," he said. "Does that bother you?"

"I just like to know," I said. "I wouldn't want the D.A. to be able to call you a professional witness."

"I have a whole response worked out for that," he said with a confident smile.

I bet you do, I thought. Aloud I said, "I'd like to know something about Jim Pears."

"Oh," Townsend said, offhandedly, "a typical self-hating homosexual."

"Typical?"

He shrugged. "I know that the A.P.A. doesn't consider homosexuality to be a mental disease," he said, "but let's face it, Mr. Rios, many if not most homosexuals have terrible problems of self-esteem. I see a lot of instability among them."

"You think being gay is a mental disorder per se?" I asked, keeping my voice neutral.

"That's not what I said," he replied tightly, then added, "You're gay yourself, aren't you?"

"Is that relevant?"

He smiled and shrugged. "To whether you retain me, probably." He studied me. "I'm not the enemy, Mr. Rios."

I looked back at him warily. "Okay, you're not the enemy. Why don't we talk about Jim."

He picked up a folder and opened it. "Jim says he's known about his homosexuality from the time he reached puberty," Townsend said. "He's had sexual relations with men for the last couple of years. Typical bathroom pickups, parks, that sort of thing. The incident in the restaurant was consistent with his pattern of sexual behavior."

"Which incident?"

"The man he was discovered with," Townsend said, "was a customer in the restaurant who picked him up and took him out to his car for sex. That's where this other boy — Fox? — found them."

"These sexual encounters sound risky," I said.

"They are. Maximally so, but then, Jim wanted to get caught."

"Is that what he says?"

"No, but it's obvious, isn't it?"

"What seems obvious to me," I said, "is that the reason a gay teenage boy has sex in public places is because he has nowhere else to go."

Townsend looked as if the thought had not occurred to him. "Possibly," he said.

"I was told that Jim doesn't remember anything about the actual killing," I said.

"That's right," Townsend replied. "It's a kind of amnesia induced by the trauma of the incident. It's fairly common among people who were in serious accidents."

"Not physiological at all?"

"He was given a medical examination," Townsend said. "Nothing wrong there. It's psychological."

"Aren't there ways to unlock his memory?" I asked.

"As a matter of fact," Townsend said, "I tried hypnosis."

"Did it work?"

"No. People have different susceptibilities," he explained. He thought a bit. "There are drugs, of course. Truth serums. I doubt they would work, though. He's really built a wall up there."

"Are you treating him at all?"

"That's not really my function, is it? My examination was entirely for forensic purposes."

"What about his parents? Have you talked to them?"

"They wouldn't talk to me. They're strict Catholics who don't trust psychiatry."

"They'd rather believe their son is possessed by the devil," I observed, bitterly.

"Which is simply an unschooled way of describing schizoid behavior," Townsend explained.

"Who's schizoid?"

"Jim, of course. He's completely disassociated himself from his homosexuality."

"Can you blame him?"

"I've given you my views on homosexuality," Townsend replied tartly.

"No doubt you shared them with Jim as well."

His small eyes narrowed. "I said I wasn't the enemy."

"Because you're not actually malicious?"

"Do you want me to testify or not?" he snapped.

"No, I don't think so."

He looked at me, then shrugged. "I still have to bill you for this time."

"Sure." I got up to leave.

"Mr. Rios," he said, as I reached the door. "You're making a mistake, you know. I'm the best there is."

"So," I said, "am I."

— 6 —

The sheriffs brought Jim into the conference room and seated him across from me at a table divided by a low partition. The walls were painted a grimy pastel blue that made the room look like a soiled Easter egg. The lights were turned up to interrogation intensity and I got my first good look at Jim Pears.

His fingernails were bitten down to ragged stubs. His face was white to the point of transparency and a blue vein pounded at his temple as if trying to tear through the skin. Splotches of yellow stubble spotted his chin and cheek. His hair, unwashed and bad-smelling, was matted to his head. The whites of his eyes were streaked with red but the irises were vivid blue — the only part of his face that showed life.

His eyes were judging me. It was as if I was the last of a long line of grown-ups who would fail him. It annoyed me. His glance slipped away.

"I'm sorry I wasn't able to talk to you this morning," I said. "Do you understand what happened in court?"

In a soft voice he answered, "You're my lawyer now."

"That's right. We have to be ready to go to trial in six weeks."

He shrugged and stared at the partition between us. After a moment his silence became hostile.

"Is anything wrong, Jim?"

"I don't like lawyers," he announced.

"You've got lots of company."

His face remained expressionless. "She didn't believe me," he said. "Do you?"

"That you didn't kill Brian Fox?"

He nodded.

I make it a point not to lie to my clients, but this can involve something short of the truth. I said, "I'm willing to start from that assumption."

His face was suspicious. "What do you mean?"

"What matters is convincing a jury that you're innocent," I explained.

Now he understood. "You don't believe me, either."

"I have an open mind," I replied.

He withdrew again into a sulky silence. I decided to wait him out and we sat there as the minutes passed.

"I can't sleep at night," he said abruptly.

"Why?" I wondered if he was going to confess.

"They leave the lights on. It hurts my eyes."

"It's just so the guards can keep an eye on things."

"Nothing happens in there." He looked at me. "I'm with the queens. That's what they call them."

"You're safer there than in the general population."

"They're like women," he continued, ignoring me. "They say things that make me sick." He shuddered. "I'm not like that."

"Not like what, Jim?"

"Gay." He spat out the word. Once again, his eyes drifted away. He seemed unable to look directly at anything for longer than a few seconds.

"Whether you're gay doesn't make any difference in jail," I said. "There are guys here who would claw through the walls to get at you."

His face shut down. "You're gay," he said.

"That's right."

"Gay lawyer," he said, mockingly. "Do you wear a dress to court?"

The taunt was so crude that at first I thought I'd misheard him. It was something that a six-year-old might say.

"I don't give a damn whether you think you're gay or not, Jim. That's the least of your worries."

"I'm sorry," he mumbled. "You made me mad," he added. "I didn't kill Brian."

"Then who did?" I demanded.

His shoulders stiffened. "Someone else."

"Someone else is not going to be on trial. You are. And you are also the only witness to what happened in the cellar. So unless you cooperate with me, I'd say your chances of getting out of here are pretty damn slim."

"I don't remember," he whined.

"Then you might as well fire me and plead guilty," I replied.

His face began to disintegrate into a series of jerks and twitches. At that moment, his father's theory of demonic possession seemed almost plausible.

"My head hurts," he whimpered. "I want to go back to my cell."

"All right. We're not getting off to a very good start but I'll be back tomorrow. I'll be back every day until you remember what happened that night."

"I'll try," he said.

I sat in my car in the parking lot beneath the jail surprised at the violence of my dislike of Jim Pears. I didn't usually speak to a client the way I had spoken to Jim. Part of my anger was a response to his childish insult which would have been comical except for what it revealed about the state of his self-awareness. He told me he wasn't gay with the desperation of someone who could not allow himself to believe anything else. His panic had calcified and become brittle. He was on the verge of shattering. But instead of sympathy for him I felt impatience. With his life at stake there was no time to waste while he sorted himself out.

Then I thought of how he had been unable to even look at me, and my impatience thawed a little. He had been alone in the dark for a long time and now, abruptly, he'd been yanked into the light. All he wanted was to cover his face as if he could make the harsh world disappear simply by closing his eyes to it. Perhaps he could be reached by a simplicity equal to his own. But simplicity was not among my bag of tricks.

☐

Larry's Jaguar was already in the garage when I pulled in. I found him in the kitchen watching a portable TV as he chopped boiled potatoes into cubes.

"You're a star," he said.

I watched myself on the TV. A reporter explained that Jim's trial had been continued because he changed lawyers. Larry washed lettuce in the sink, drowning out the set. I turned it up.

" ... accused of the brutal slaying of Brian Fox. Today, prosecutors moved to seek the death penalty."

Larry shut off the water. "The death penalty?"

"Wait. I want to hear this."

"The D.A. also questioned the motives behind the change of attorneys. Pears's new lawyer is Henry Rios, a prominent Bay Area attorney who is also openly gay. The D.A. suggested that pressure from the gay community to have a gay lawyer try the case led to today's hearing."

"Asshole," Larry said.

"Meanwhile," the reporter continued, "there was a dramatic confrontation outside the courtroom between Rios and the victim's mother, Lillian Fox."

We watched Mrs. Fox spit at me. I shut the television off.

"You've had quite a day," Larry said, arranging lettuce leaves in a big wooden bowl.

"I'm thinking that it was a mistake for me to have taken the case," I said.

He opened a can of tuna fish, drained and chopped it and added it to the salad. "Because the D.A. called you a carpetbagger?"

"No," I said. "It's the client. I talked to him this afternoon."

"And?" He quartered tomatoes, sliced green beans.

"He says he's not gay."

Larry looked over at me. "The kid killed someone rather than come out of the closet. What did you expect him to say?"

"He also says he didn't do it. That's why the P.D. got out of the case. He won't plead to anything."

Larry added the finishing touches to the salad and put a couple of rolls into the microwave.

"You of all people should know that there are ways of bringing clients around," Larry said.

"I don't like him."

"Oh." He wiped his hands on a towel and poured himself a

glass of water. "Why?"

"He makes me feel like a faggot," I replied.

"Well," Larry smiled. "Aren't you?"

"Come on, Larry. You know what I mean. His self-loathing is catching."

"Let's eat," Larry said. "Then we'll talk."

After dinner we sat on the patio. The wind moved through the branches of the eucalyptus trees that lined the lake. A yellow moon rose in the sky. A string of Japanese lanterns cast their light from behind us. Larry lit a cigarette.

"Those can't be good for you, now," I said.

"They never were," he replied. "Did I tell you about the cocktail party tomorrow?"

"If you did I don't remember."

"It's a fundraiser for Jim's defense."

"I suppose I have to go," I said, unhappily.

"I'm afraid so," he replied. He shrugged. "These people want to help Jim."

"He's not much interested in helping himself."

"What's bothering you about this case?"

"I told you."

"You don't have to like him."

"He tells me he didn't do it," I said. "Which means he's either not guilty or he can't bring himself to admit his guilt. The first possibility is remote."

"Maybe he thinks he was justified," Larry offered.

I shook my head. "No, I believe he thinks he didn't do it. This amnesia—"

"That's deliberate?"

"It certainly allows him to deny knowledge of the only evidence that could resolve this case one way or the other."

The smoke from Larry's cigarette climbed into the air. A faint wind carried the scent of eucalyptus to us from the lake.

"What bothers me," I said, "is that he insists he's innocent when he so clearly isn't."

"It must be a pretty horrible thing to admit you killed someone," Larry said quietly.

"Not someone like Fox," I said, "who made Jim suffer and who he must hate."

"Then maybe it was death," Larry said. "Being in that room with a man he had killed. Once you've seen death unleashed, it pursues you." He sat forward, his face a mask in the flickering light of the lanterns. "Maybe that's what he's running from, Henry."

☐

The next morning I went to see Freeman Vidor, who had been investigating Jim's case for the Public Defender. His office was in an old brownstone on Grand Avenue which, amid L.A.'s construction frenzy, seemed like a survivor from antiquity. The foyer had a marble floor and the elevator was run by a uniformed operator who might have been a bit player when Valentino was making movies.

Freeman Vidor was a thin black man. He sat at a big, shabby desk strewn with papers and styrofoam hamburger boxes. A couple of framed certificates on the walls attested to the legitimacy of his operation. I also noticed a framed photograph — the only one on the wall — that showed a younger Vidor with two other men, all wearing the uniforms of the L.A.P.D. He now wore a wrinkled gold suit and a heavy Rolex. He had very short, gray hair. His face was unlined, though youth was the last thing it conveyed. Rather, it was the face of a man for whom there were no surprises left. I doubted, in fact, whether Freeman Vidor had ever been young.

We got past introductions. He lifted the Times at the edge of his desk and said, "I see you made the front page of the Metro section."

"I haven't read the article," I replied and glanced at it. There was my picture beneath a headline that read: "S.F. Lawyer to Defend Accused Teen Killer."

"Teen killer," I read aloud.

"Sort of jumps out on you, doesn't it?" he replied. "Listen, you want some coffee? I got a thermos here."

"No, thanks."

He poured coffee into a dirty mug, added a packet of Sweet

'n Low and stirred it with a pencil.

"I read the report you prepared for Sharon Hart," I said.

"That's one tough woman," he replied.

"She jumped at the chance to dump Jim's case."

"I said tough, not stupid." He sipped the coffee and grimaced.

"Is there an insult in there for me?"

He smiled. "Only if you're in the market for one. All I meant is, that boy's only hope is to get a jury to feel sorry for him because this Fox kid was harassing him about being a homosexual." He finished the coffee. "But first you got to convince them it ain't a sin to be gay."

"This is Los Angeles, not Pocatello."

He lit a cigarette. "Yeah, last election a million people in this state voted to lock you guys up."

"That was AIDS."

"You tell someone you're gay," he replied, "and the first thing they do after they shake your hand is get a blood test."

"Including you?"

"It's not on the list of my biases," he said. "You want to tell me about yours?"

"Some of my favorite clients are black."

He thought about this, then laughed. "You want me in the case?"

I nodded.

"A hundred-and-fifty a day plus expenses."

"That's acceptable."

He blew a stream of smoke toward a wan-looking fern on a pedestal near the window. "Who's paying?"

"There are some people who would like to see Jim Pears get off on this one."

He smiled. "Your kind of people?"

"That's right."

"If my mama only knew." He opened a notebook and extracted a black Cross pen from the inner pocket of his jacket. "What do you want me to do?"

"I want background on Brian Fox."

He raised a thin eyebrow. "Background?"

"Whatever you can find that I can use to smear him," I explained.

He nodded knowingly. "Oh, background. What else?"

"I read in the prelim transcript that there's a back entrance to the restaurant."

"The delivery door. It was locked."

"Lock implies key, or keys. Find out who had them and what they were doing that night."

"You're fishing," he said.

"I want to know."

He made a note and shrugged. "It's your dime."

— 7 —

The cocktail party for Jim's defense fund was being held in Bel Air. I heard Larry pull into the driveway at a quarter of six, straightened the knot in my tie, put on my jacket and went downstairs to meet him. He was just entering the house as I came down.

He looked up at me and smiled. "You sure you don't mind this?"

"What, the party?"

He nodded and tossed a bundle of mail on a coffee table. He looked tired.

"Are you feeling okay?" I asked as he dropped into a chair.

"No, not really," he replied. He rubbed his temples and shut his eyes. His breath was shallow and strained. I switched on a lamp and sat down on the sofa across from him.

"I could go alone," I said.

Without opening his eyes, he smiled. "It's asking a bit much for the lamb to lead itself to slaughter," he replied.

"It can't be that bad. Who's going to be there?"

He opened his eyes. "Just the L.A. chapter of HomIntern."

"HomIntern?"

"Homosexual International," he replied and yawned. "I told a few of my friends about Jim's case and a couple of them volunteered to kick in money to help pay the legal costs. One thing led to another and the next I knew Elliot Fein was calling and offering his house for a fundraiser."

"Elliot Fein, the ex-judge?" I asked, impressed. Fein was a retired court of appeals judge and a member of a wealthy family whose patriarch had made his money in movies.

"The same," Larry said, kicking off his huge penny-loafers. He put his long, narrow feet on the table. "I could hardly refuse. Really all they want to do is get a look at you," he added. "See what they're getting for their money."

"You think they'll be satisfied?"

He gave me the once-over. "I guarantee it. How was your day?"

I told him about my meeting with Freeman Vidor. "You know what's beginning to bother me?" I said. "The fact that everybody — including his ex-lawyer, his shrink, and now Vidor — is so quick to write Jim's chances off."

Larry's smile was fat with satisfaction. "I knew I'd hired the right man for this job."

"Well," I said defensively, "the presumption of innocence has to mean something."

The smile faded. "Oh, he's an innocent, all right," Larry said, and drew out a cigarette from his pocket.

"I wish you wouldn't smoke so much."

"Please." He lit the cigarette with his gold lighter.

"Obviously he killed Brian," I said, picking up the thread of my earlier thought, "but killing is not necessarily murder."

Larry put his shoes on. "And that's what you're here to prove. We better get going."

"You're sure you want to go?"

"I'll be fine."

The sun had already set but, as we headed west on Sunset, there was still a dreamy light at the edge of the horizon and above it the first faint stars. We passed UCLA. Larry signaled a turn and we entered the west gate of Bel Air, up Bellagio. We passed tall white walls as we ascended the narrow, twisting road. From my window I watched the widening landscape of the city below and the breathless glitter of its lights. As with most cities, Los Angeles was at its most elegant when seen from the aeries of the rich.

At the top of the hill, Larry began a left turn past immense wrought iron gates opened to reveal a driveway paved with cobblestones. A moment later a house came into view. It seemed to consist of a single towering box though, as we slowed, I could see there were two small wings, one on either side. A boy in black slacks, a white shirt and a lavender tie directed us to stop. Another boy, similarly dressed, opened my door.

"Good evening, sir, how are you?" he asked as I stepped out of the Jaguar.

"Fine, thanks, and you?"

"Oh, fine, sir." He seemed startled that I'd bothered to reply.

Larry came around to me and said, "Ready, counsel?"

"Let's go."

The first thing I noticed when we stepped into the house was the size of the room we had entered. Its walls were roughly the dimensions of football fields and to say that the space they enclosed was vast exhausted the possibilities of the word. The second thing I noticed was that the far wall, except for a fireplace that could easily have accommodated the burghers of Calais, was glass. The city trembled below.

"Where do the airplanes land?" I whispered to Larry as we entered the room. Little clumps of people, mostly men, were scattered amid the white furnishings.

"None of that," he replied. "Here comes our host."

I expected the owner of the house to be dwarfed by it, but Elliot Fein didn't even put up a fight. He was a shade over five feet and his most distinctive feature was his glasses. They were perfectly round and bright red. His skin was the color of dark wood, his hair was glossy black and his face was conspicuously unlined. I guessed, from his effort to conceal it, he must be nearing seventy.

"Larry," he said in a wheezy voice. They exchanged polite kisses.

"This is Henry Rios," Larry said.

"Why haven't I met you before?" Fein asked by way of greeting.

I couldn't think of any reason except the absence of twenty or thirty million dollars on my part. This didn't seem to be the tactful answer so I said, "I don't know, but it's a pleasure, Justice Fein."

He took my extended hand and held it. "Elliot to my friends. We're all so glad you agreed to take the boy's case."

"Thank you." I attempted to regain possession of my hand but he wasn't through with it yet.

"You know," he said confidentially, "I sat in the criminal division of superior court for years before I was elevated. From what I know about Jim Pears's case, it's going to be rough sledding."

"An unusual metaphor for Los Angeles," I observed.

He looked puzzled, then dropped my hand. "Comments like that go right over a jury's head," he said with a faked smile.

I made a noise that could be interpreted as assent.

"Who's the judge?" he asked.

"Patricia Ryan."

"Good. Very good," he replied judiciously. "I'll call her for lunch next week." He beamed at us. "I'm neglecting my duties. Let me get you a drink."

"Thanks, but I don't drink," I said.

His eyes narrowed and he nodded. "Oh, that's right. Perrier, then?"

"Nothing, thank you," I replied. I felt a flash of irritation at Larry who had obviously told Fein I was an alcoholic.

"What about you, Larry?" Fein asked.

"Not just yet. I think I should take Henry around."

"Of course," Fein said, and stepped aside. "I'll talk to you later."

We started across the hall and Larry said, in a low voice, "I know what you're thinking but I didn't tell him."

"Then how did he know?"

"He's like God, only richer. So I'd watch the wisecracks if I were you."

For the next hour we worked the room. The crowd consisted of well-dressed, expensively scented men and a few women all of whom, like Fein, had found ways to slow time's passage. Larry and I fell into a routine. He would introduce me. Someone would inevitably ask what I thought of Jim's chances. I would launch into a lengthy explanation of the concept of presumption of innocence. At some point — before a member of the

·57·

audience actually fell asleep — Larry would break in to make a pitch for money. As we moved away from one group, I heard a man stage whisper, "She's pretty but someone should tell her to lighten up."

I turned to Larry, who had also heard, and said, "I need a break."

"I'll come and find you."

When he left I found myself near the center of the room. A short, stocky man stood a few feet away staring up at the ceiling. I followed his gaze to the chandelier. It was a sleek metallic thing lit with dozens of silvery candles. The man and I exchanged looks. He smiled.

"At first," he said, "I wondered why Elliot couldn't afford electricity. Then I realized the candles must be much more expensive."

There were faint traces of an English accent in his voice. His face was square and fleshy and showed its age. His was the first truly human visage I'd seen all night.

"It's less conspicuous than burning hundred-dollar bills, I guess."

He laughed. "I heard you introduced, Mr. Rios. My name is Harvey Miller."

"Henry to my friends," I replied, shaking his hand. "Are you part of this crowd?"

"Am I rich? No. I work at the Gay and Lesbian Center on Highland. Elliot's on the board. Do you know about the Center?"

"Sure," I said. "You do good work."

"So do you, I hear." He accepted a glass of champagne from a passing waiter.

I shrugged. "It's my Catholic upbringing. The world's troubles weigh on my heart. *Mea culpa.*"

He sipped from the glass and lowered it. "You seem a bit brittle, Henry."

"This isn't my natural habitat. I was going outside for some air. Join me?"

"I'd like that."

We made our way through the clumps of oversized furnishings and past the squadrons of rented waiters carrying trays of food and drink, to a door that let us out onto an immense patio. We walked to its edge and looked out over the city. Streams of light marked the major boulevards which were crammed with the tail end of rush-hour traffic. The spires of downtown probed the ashen sky. Lights of every color — red, blue, silver, gold — twinkled in the darkness as if the city were an enormous Christmas tree.

I made this comparison to Harvey.

"It is like a Christmas tree," he replied, "but most of the boxes beneath it are empty. For a lot of gay people, anyway."

I looked at him as he finished off the contents of his glass. "What exactly do you do at the Center?"

"I'm a psychologist," he replied, smiling at the city.

"Well," I said, "for a few gay people some boxes, like this house, are crammed full."

"No, not really." He set the glass down on the ledge of the wall. "It's not easy for anyone in this society to be gay."

"I wouldn't waste much sympathy on the rich," I said. "Even compassion has its limits."

He moved a step nearer. "Are you always the life of the party?"

I smiled. "Sorry. Yesterday I was sitting in a filthy little room trying to pry some truth out of Jim Pears and tonight I'm at Valhalla meeting the gay junior league. When the altitude changes this fast I get motion sick."

"Why do you have such a low opinion of us?"

"I don't. It's just that it's not my profession."

"What?"

"Homosexuality."

"No," he said, feigning a smile. "You're a lawyer, right? Never mind that the law oppresses us."

"I thought we were going to be friends, Harvey."

"You can't isolate yourself in your work."

"I'm not trying to," I said. "But Jim Pears is a client, not a cause. If I can save his life, I've done my job."

"And if not?" he asked, leaning against the wall. "Have you still done your job?"

"By my lights," I replied.

He picked up his glass. "I'm disappointed that your lights have such a narrow focus."

I shrugged. "In my work, someone is usually disappointed."

"Good luck," he said and went back inside.

When I went back in, the party was breaking up. I spotted Larry standing with a fat man in a shiny suit. Not an old suit. A shiny one. Larry signalled me to join them. The fat man's face shone like a waxed apple. A fringe of dyed hair was combed low over his forehead. He fidgeted a smile, revealing perfect teeth.

"Henry, this is Sandy Blenheim," Larry said.

I shook Blenheim's hand. It was soft and moist but he compensated with a grip that nearly broke my thumb. Before I could say anything, Blenheim started talking.

"Look, Henry, I'm running a little late." He jabbed his hand into the air, as if to ward off time's passage. "So if we could just get down to business."

"What business is that?"

"I'm an agent. I have a client who's interested in buying the rights to the trial."

"Jim's trial?" I asked.

Blenheim gave three rapid nods.

"Why?"

"To make a movie," Larry interjected.

I looked at Blenheim. "A movie?"

"It's great. The whole set-up. Gay kid exposed. We could take it to the networks and sell it like that." He snapped his pudgy fingers. "We tried talking to the kid's parents but they won't deal. The kid won't even talk to me. So you're our last hope."

"I really don't understand," I said.

Blenheim spread his hands. "We buy your rights, see, and if you can bring the kid and his folks around, that just sweetens the deal. What about it?"

"It's a bit premature, don't you think?" I said. "There hasn't actually been a trial."

"But there will be," Blenheim insisted. "We can give you

twenty," he continued. "Plus, we hire you as the legal consultant. You could clean up."

"I'm sorry," I began, "but this conversation is not—"

"Okay," Blenheim said, affably. "I've been around lawyers. You guys are cagey. Tell you what, Henry. Think on it and call me in a couple of weeks. Larry's got my number. See you later."

He turned, waved at someone across the room, and walked away. I looked at Larry. "Have I just been hit by a truck?"

"No, but you might check your wallet."

"What was that all about?"

"Just what the man said," Larry replied. "He wants to make a movie."

"About Jim? That's a little ghoulish, isn't it?"

Larry shrugged. "He gave me a check for five hundred dollars for Jim's defense," he said. "I figured that was worth at least a couple of minutes of your time."

"Okay, he got his two minutes." I looked at Larry; he was pale and seemed tired. "I think we should get you home."

"Fein's invited us for dinner," he replied. "There's no tactful way out."

"Then let's not be tactful," I said.

He began to speak, but then simply nodded. "I am tired," he said.

Fein accepted my excuses with a fixed smile and later when I said good-night he looked at me seemingly without recognition. But the boy who had parked our car remembered me.

"Enjoy yourself?" he asked, opening the car door for me.

Thinking of Fein and Harvey Miller and the fat agent, I said, "It wasn't that kind of party."

— 8 —

I returned to the jail day after day to talk to Jim Pears. We sat at the table in the room with the soiled walls beneath the glaring lights. As far as I knew, he had no other visitors. Jim showed no interest in preparing for the coming trial beyond repeating his stock claim of innocence. He answered my questions with the fewest words possible unless I asked him about the events leading up to the killing. Those he wouldn't answer at all, maintaining loss of memory.

One late afternoon a week after our first interview, I said, "Tell me the last thing you remember about that night."

His blue gaze drifted past my face. "I was at the bar."

"Before Brian got there."

"Yes."

"Do you remember seeing him arrive?"

Jim shook his head. I drew a zero on my legal pad. A blue vein twitched at his temple. His eyes, the same throbbing blue, scanned his fingertips.

"Did Brian ever threaten you?"

He looked up, startled. "No."

"Demand money?"

"No."

"Did you tell him to meet you at the restaurant that night?"

His eyes were terrified. "No."

"Did he tell you he was coming there?"

"No," he replied, drawing a deep breath.

"But once he got there you assumed it was to see you, didn't you?"

"I don't know."

"Don't know what?"

"What I thought." He shifted in his seat.

I drew another zero on the pad. "Tell me about the guy who picked you up the night Brian saw you in the car. Had you ever seen him before?"

"No," he replied.

"What did he look like?"

"That was a long time ago."

"You must remember something," I snapped.

He slumped in his chair. "He was old," he said finally, and added, "Like you."

Ignoring the gibe, I asked, "Was he tall or short?"

"Average, I guess."

"I'm not interested in your guesses. What color was his hair?"

"Dark."

"What about his eyes?"

He was quiet for a moment, then he said, in a voice that was different, almost yearning, "They were blue."

"Like yours?" I asked.

"No, different," he replied in the same voice. He was seeing those eyes.

"Tell me about his eyes," I said, quietly.

"I told you," he replied, the yearning gone. "They were blue."

"How did you end up in his car?"

"He told me to meet him."

"Where?"

"In the lot behind the restaurant."

"Then what happened?"

He stared at me, color creeping up his neck.

"You got in the car and then what happened?"

"We talked." It was almost a question.

"Is that what you were doing when Brian came up to the car, talking?"

He shook his head. "He was — sucking me."

"That's what Brian saw?"

"Yeah."

"What did Brian do?"

"He opened the car door," Jim said, talking quickly, "and yelled 'faggots'. Then he ran back across the lot of the restaurant."

"What did you do?"

"I got out of the car. The guy drove off. I went home."

"Did he tell you his name?"

"No."

I looked at him. No, of course not. Names weren't important.

"Brian threatened to tell your parents," I said. "Did that worry you?"

"Sure," he said, "but—" He stopped himself.

"But what?"

"He didn't."

"The D.A. will say that he didn't because you killed him. What's your explanation?"

"I didn't kill him."

"Why didn't he tell your parents?"

"I don't know," he replied, his voice rising. "Ask him."

"He's dead, Jim. Remember?"

"Yeah, I remember. Why aren't you trying to find the guy that killed him?"

"Why don't you tell me the truth?"

"Fuck you," he replied.

"This isn't getting us anywhere," I observed in a quiet voice. "Are you sleeping better?"

"They give me pills," he said, all the anger gone.

I frowned. I had had Jim examined by a doctor to see what could be done to relieve his anxiety. Apparently the doctor chose a quick fix.

"How often?"

"Three times a day," he said.

"I'd ease up on them," I cautioned.

He shrugged.

"You need anything?"

He shook his head.

"I'll see you tomorrow, then," I said.
His face showed what he thought of the prospect.

☐

There was a knock at the door. I got up from the desk and went downstairs. It was Freeman Vidor, whom I had been expecting. I let him in, found him a beer, and led him up to the study.

"Nice place," he commented, sitting on the sofa and looking around the room. He glanced at the piles of paper on the desk. "How's it going?"

"The good news is that there won't be any surprises from the prosecution at trial," I replied. "The bad news is that they don't need any."

He lit a cigarette and looked around for an ashtray. I gave him the cup I had been drinking coffee from.

"What about you?" I asked. "Any surprises?"

He dug into the pocket of his suit and extracted a little notebook. He flipped through pages filled with big, loopy handwriting. "Maybe."

"Fox?" I asked, setting a fresh notepad on the desk in front of me.

"Uh-huh," he said, and sipped his beer. "There's a private security patrol in the neighborhood where his folks live. Seems about a year ago they started getting complaints about a Peeping Tom. They kept a look-out and, lo and behold, they find Fox in someone's back yard. There's a girl lives there he went to school with. It was just about her bedtime."

"What was his story?"

"He wanted to talk to her," Freeman said, dropping his cigarette into the coffee cup and pouring a little beer over it. "Only they caught him with his pants down."

"What?"

"Jerking off. He said he was just taking a piss."

"Anyone press charges?"

"Not in that neighborhood," he said. "Security took him home and told his parents." He belched softly. "Excuse me. There was some other stuff, too," he continued. "Seems like Brian was the neighborhood pervert."

"I'm listening."

Freeman shrugged. "Now these are just rumors," he cautioned. "He spent a lot of time with kids who were younger than him — thirteen, fourteen."

"Boys? Girls?"

"Both," he replied, and finished off the beer. "'Course, less time with little girls because their folks got kind of suspicious that a high school senior was hanging around them. So mostly he was with the little boys. They thought he was kind of a creep."

"And why is that?"

"A couple of them came over to his house to go swimming when his folks were gone. He gave them some beer and tried to get them to go into the pool naked."

"What happened?"

"They split," he replied and thumbed through the notebook. "After that, they all pretty much avoided him."

"Did they tell their parents?"

He shook his head.

An interesting picture was beginning to develop. I asked, "What about kids his own age? Did he have a girlfriend?"

"Nope," he said. "Didn't go out much with girls. He was kind of a loner except for his computer buddies."

"The stories in the papers make him sound like the most popular kid in his class," I observed.

Freeman lit another cigarette. "The kids didn't write those stories, grown-ups did. They see a young guy, not bad looking, smart enough, killed by some — excuse the expression — faggot. What do you think they're going to make of it?"

"'Golden boy,'" I said, quoting the description from one of the newspaper accounts.

"Yeah," Freeman said, dourly, "Golden boy. Hell," he added, "the only thing golden about that boy's his old man's money. There's a lot of that."

"Rich?"

"Real rich," he replied.

"Then why was he working as a busboy?" I asked.

Freeman shrugged. "Not because he needed the money. His counselor at the school says he told Brian's folks to put him to work. Teach him to fit in — no, what did she say?" He flipped through the notebook. "Learn 'appropriate patterns of socialization,'" he quoted. He grinned at me. "Some homework."

"Did it work? What did they think of him at the restaurant?"

"That he was a lazy little shit," Freeman replied. "They fired him once but his old man got him the job back."

"Speaking of the restaurant, what did you find out about the keys to the service door?"

"There's four copies," he replied. "One for the manager and his two assistants and one they leave at the bar."

"Were they all accounted for?"

"Everyone checks out, except for one. The day manager, a kid named Josh Mandel."

"The prosecutor's star witness," I said.

"That's him."

"No alibi for that night?"

Freeman nodded, slowly. "He says he was out on a date."

"You have trouble with that?"

"Let's just say he don't lie with much conviction."

— 9 —

The next day I called the Yellowtail and learned that Josh Mandel was working the lunch shift. I headed out to Encino at noon on the Hollywood Freeway. October brought cooler weather but no respite from the smog that hung above the city like a soiled, tattered sheet. Hollywood Boulevard looked more derelict than usual, as if the brown air above it were its own gasps and wheezes. The movie money had migrated west, leaving only this elegant carcass mouldering in the steamy autumn sunlight.

The air was clearer in the valley but there was decay here, too; but with none of the fallen-angel glamour of Hollywood. Rather, it lay in the crumbling foundations of jerry-built condominium complexes, condemned drive-ins and bowling alleys, paint blistering from shops on the verge of bankruptcy. The detritus of the good life. It was easy to feel the ghost town just beneath the facade of affluence.

The Yellowtail anchored a small, chic shopping center comprised of clothing boutiques and specialty food stores, white stucco walls, covered walkways, tiled roofs, murmuring fountains, and grass the color of new money. I pulled into the parking lot beside the restaurant and walked around to the entrance. Heavy paneled doors led into a sunlit anteroom. A blonde girl stood at a podium with a phone pressed to her ear. She looked at me, smiled meaninglessly, and continued her conversation.

I walked to the edge of the anteroom. The restaurant was basically a big rectangular room with two smaller rooms off the main floor. The first of these, nearest to where I stood, was the bar. The other, only distantly visible, seemed to be a smaller dining room. The entire place was painted in shades of pink and white and gray. Behind the bar there was an aquarium in which exotic fish fluttered through blue-green water like shards of an aquatic rainbow.

There were carnations in crystal vases on each table. Moody abstracts hung from the walls. Light streamed in from a bank of tall, narrow windows on the wall opposite the bar. The windows faced an interior courtyard, flowerbeds, and a fountain in the shape of a lion's head. Above the din of expense-account conversation I heard a bit of Vivaldi. The waiters were as handsome as the room they served. They seemed college-age or slightly older, most of them blond, wearing khaki trousers, blue button-down shirts, sleeves rolled to the elbows, red silk ties. The busboys were similarly dressed but without ties. They swept across the tiled floor like ambulatory mannequins.

"Excuse me, are you waiting for someone?" It was the girl at the podium. I looked at her. She was very nearly pretty but for the spoiled twist of her lips.

"I'd like to see Josh Mandel."

"Are you a salesman?" she asked, already looking beyond me to a couple just leaving.

"No, I'm Jim Pears's lawyer."

Her eyes focused on me. Without a word, she picked up the phone and pressed two numbers. There was a quick, sotto voce conversation and when she put the phone down she said, "He asked for you to wait for him in the bar."

"Fine. By the way, is Andrea Lew working today?"

The girl said, "She quit."

"Do you know how I can reach her?"

"No," she said in a tone she probably practiced on her boyfriend.

"Thanks for your help," I replied, and felt her eyes on my back as I made my way to the bar. I found an empty bar stool and ordered a Calistoga water. Andrea Lew was right; it was impossible for anyone to enter the restaurant without being seen from the bar. Assuming, of course, that someone was watching.

I was about to ask the bartender about Andrea when I heard someone say, "Mr. Rios?"

I looked up at the dark-haired boy who had spoken. "You're Josh," I said, recognizing him from court.

He nodded. In court he had seemed older. Now I saw he was very young, two or three years out of his teens, and trying to conceal the fact. The round horn-rimmed glasses didn't help. They only called attention to green-brown eyes that had the bright sheen of true innocence. His hair was a mass of black curls restrained by a shiny mousse. He had a delicate, bony face, a long nose, a wide strong mouth and the smooth skin of a child. "Why don't we go down to my office," he said, and I was suddenly aware that we had been staring at each other.

"You mind showing me around the place first?" I asked, stepping down from the bar stool. I was about an inch taller than he.

He frowned but nodded. "You've already seen all this," he said, jutting his chin at the dining room. "I'll show you the back."

We made our way across the big room and pushed through swinging double doors.

"This is the waiter's station," he told me. We were in a narrow room. The kitchen was visible over a counter through a rectangular window on which the cooks placed orders as they were ready and clanged a bell to alert the waiters. In one corner was a metal rack with four plastic tubs filled with dirty dishes. A busboy took the top tub and carried it out through another door behind us. Pots of coffee bubbled on the counter. Cupboards held coffee cups, glasses, napkins, and cutlery. One of the blond waiters walked in, lit a cigarette and smoked furiously.

"Put it out, Timmy," Josh said as we passed through the door where the busboy had gone and stood at the top of a corridor that terminated at the back door. Josh walked toward it. I followed.

"Dishwasher," he said, stopping in front of a small room where a slender black man wearing a hair net pushed a rack of dishes into an immense machine.

We walked back a little farther. "Employees' locker room," Josh said. There were three rows of lockers against a wall. Opposite the lockers were two doors, marked men and women. A bench completed the decor. "This is where we change for work," he said.

We went back into the corridor.

"Back door," he said, pointing.

I looked at the door and realized, for the first time, that the lock which Andrea Lew had talked about was an interior lock. Inspecting it further I saw that it could not be unlocked from outside at all but only from within. I asked Josh about it.

"It's for security," he replied. "It can't be picked from outside."

"You keep it unlocked during the day?"

"Uh-huh, for deliveries. Night manager locks it up when the kitchen closes at ten."

"So if anyone was back here after ten he'd need a key to get out?"

"Uh-huh," he said.

"But there's a key at the bar."

He looked at me and blinked. "Yeah, for emergencies."

"Show me the cellar," I said.

I followed him back down the corridor and around the front of the walk-in refrigerator. We passed briefly through the kitchen and then went down a rickety flight of stairs into the cellar. We stood in a big, dark room that had a damp, fruity smell. Behind locked wooden screens were hundreds of bottles of wine. The room was otherwise bare. He showed me two smaller rooms adjacent to each other. The door to one of them was open, revealing a cluttered desk. The door to the other was closed.

"That's where they found Jim," he said. "You want to go in?" His voice indicated clearly that he didn't.

"Maybe later," I said, giving him a break.

We went into his office. He sat in a battered swivel chair behind a desk made of a thick slab of glass supported by metal sawhorses. There was a phone on the wall, its lights flashing.

He closed a ledger on the desk before him and offered me a cup of coffee. I declined.

"How's Jim?" he asked.

"Surviving."

"I'm really sorry about what happened," he said, defensively. "They told me I had to testify."

"Of course you did," I said soothingly. "You seem pretty young to be managing this place."

"I'm twenty-two," he protested, and must have caught my smile. "I usually just manage the floor but Mark — he's the head guy — he's out sick today."

"Have you worked here long?"

"Six years. I started as a busboy."

"You go to school?"

He picked up a paper clip. "Two years at UCLA. I dropped out."

"Why?"

He flattened out the paper clip. "Is that important?"

"I won't know until you tell me."

He set the paper clip aside. "I didn't know what I was doing there," he said. "I never was much for school."

I accepted this, for the moment. "What was Jim like to work with?"

He was visibly relieved by the change of subject. "He was a hard worker," Josh said. "Reliable."

"You ever see him outside of work?"

He shook his head and picked up a pencil.

"Were you surprised to find out he was gay?"

Our eyes caught. "What do you mean?"

"Didn't Brian tell you Jim was gay?"

"Yes."

"Did you believe him?"

He put the pencil down. "Yes."

"Why?"

He looked at the desk. "I don't know. I just did."

I let his answer hang in the air. He picked up the paper clip again.

"And later you heard Brian threaten to tell Jim's parents."

"It wasn't exactly like that," he said, softly.

"No?"

"It was more — like a joke," he said, raising his head slowly. "Brian said something like, 'You want your mama to know you suck cock?' like the way little kids insult each other."

"And Jim? Did he know it was a joke?"

"I think so," he replied. "He kind of laughed and said, 'I'll kill you first.'"

"Where did this happen?"

"The locker room. We were all changing for work."

"This was the only time you ever heard them say anything to each other like this?"

"Yes," he said, and bit his lower lip.

"You know, Josh," I said, "this sounds entirely different than it did when you testified at the prelim."

"I told the prosecutor but he kept saying that Jim really meant it because, you know, he did kill Brian. I guess he convinced me."

"Do you think Jim killed Brian?" I asked.

"That's what they say. All the evidence looks pretty bad for Jim."

"Do you think he did it?" I asked again.

Josh took off his glasses and cleaned them with his handkerchief. "I don't know," he said, finally.

"Can you think of anyone else who would have a reason to kill Brian Fox?"

He shook his head quickly.

"Where were you the night he was killed?"

He looked shocked. "On a date."

I looked at him until he looked away. He was lying. "Who with?"

Recovering himself he said, "The D.A. said I don't have to talk to you."

"But you are going to have to testify again," I said.

"I'll tell the truth," he replied, his face coloring. It was useless to push him.

"You won't have any choice, Josh," I said. I wrote Larry's number on a slip of paper. "If you want to talk later you can reach me here."

He looked at the paper as if it were a bomb, but took it and slipped it into his pocket.

□

Larry's car was in the driveway though it was only two-thirty. That worried me. Except for a certain gauntness, Larry gave no sign of being gravely ill, but his condition was never far from my mind. I knew it preoccupied Larry, too. Sometimes he became very still and remote. It actually seemed as if some part of him were gone. When I mentioned it, he smiled and said he was practicing levitation. What he was actually doing, I think, was practicing dying.

I found him in his study on the phone. He saw me and motioned me to sit down.

"Sandy," he said to his caller, "you really can do better than Rogers, Stone."

I recognized this as the name of a well-known entertainment law firm. Larry put on his patient face. I could hear his caller's voice across the room.

"That's true," Larry said, "but I'm not available." He listened. "I know you think he walks on water, Sandy, but the guy's a one-season sensation. Next year you'll be pushing someone else." He picked up a pen and started to doodle on a legal pad. "Look," he said finally, "I'll think about it, and get back to you. No, I really will think about it. What? Yeah, he's right here." He pushed the mute button on the phone and said, "It's Sandy Blenheim. He wants to talk to you."

"The fat guy at Fein's party?"

Larry nodded. "The one who wants to make you a star."

Reluctantly, I took the phone. "Hello, this is Henry Rios."

"Henry," Blenheim said, all oily affability. "You think about my proposal?"

"No, not really. I haven't had much time."

There was a disappointed silence at his end of the line. "What is it, Henry? The money?"

"Look, Mr. Blenheim ... "

"Sandy."

"Sandy. I don't think this is going to make a good movie."

"There's a lot of kids out there in Jim's position," Blenheim said. "Kids in the closet. Kids getting picked on. This picture could show them there's a right way to come out and a wrong way. You know what I'm saying?"

I shot a glance at Larry. He smiled. "Sure, I understand," I said. "But this isn't the right—" I searched for the word. "—vehicle," I said.

Larry nodded approvingly.

"Come on, you've talked to the kid. You know what's going through his head. That's the good stuff. Like how did he feel when he pulled the trigger—"

I cut him off. "Actually, he doesn't remember."

"What do you mean he doesn't remember?"

"Just what I said," I replied, "and I've really told you more than I should but it's just so you know that this isn't the story you think it is."

"Maybe if we talked some more," he suggested.

"I'm sorry," I replied. "It wouldn't serve any purpose. Do you want to talk to Larry?"

"Yeah, put him back on."

I handed the phone to Larry. "It's for you."

"Yes, Sandy," he said. I heard the angry buzz of Blenheim's voice complaining about my intransigence. Larry broke in and said, "He doesn't want more money, Sandy. He wants to try his case in peace." More angry buzzing. "Well," Larry said, shortly, "I think it's called integrity. You might look it up in the dictionary." There was a click on the other end. "If you can spell it," Larry added.

"I didn't mean for him to get mad at you, too," I said.

Larry put the phone down. "Big finishes are a way of life around here. He'll be over it by tomorrow."

"You're home early."

He lit a cigarette. "Yeah. I was having a terrible day — about the two millionth since I passed the bar, and then it occurred to me, what the hell am I doing?" He smiled and drew on his cigarette. "I'm not into terrible days anymore."

"Maybe you should just quit."

"And do what, die?" He looked at me and smirked. "Was that tactless?"

"Yes," I replied. "A sure sign you're getting better."

"Did you see the waiter?" Larry asked, putting out his cigarette. I noticed that he had only smoked it half-way down.

"Yeah."

"And was he a rabid queer-baiter?"

"Didn't seem the type," I said, thinking of Josh Mandel's eyes. "I could be wrong, of course. He did lie to me."

"About anything important?"

"It was about what he was doing the night Brian was killed," I replied. "I don't know yet if that's important. On the other hand, I've figured out why Jim insists he didn't kill Brian Fox."

"Why?" Larry asked.

"Because they were lovers."

— 10 —

"Really?" His eyebrows flicked upwards.

I told him what I had learned about Brian Fox's sexual escapades. A penchant for voyeurism, and budding pedophilia was of a different order than fumbling in the back seat with more-or-less willing partners of the same age. Yet how different were these activities from Jim's excursions into bathrooms and parks? To me, they revealed a kind of sexual despair. I could understand that in Jim's case; he was gay and his fear drove him underground. But what about Brian Fox? Maybe it didn't matter. What was important was that Brian was unusually sensitive to Jim's sexual secret. My guess was that what drew Brian to Jim was not antipathy as much as fascination — one sexual loner's recognition of another.

"I don't think Brian followed Jim out into the parking lot because he wanted to embarrass him," I said. "I think he wanted to know for sure whether Jim was gay."

"Are you saying Brian was gay, too?" Larry asked.

"God, I hope not. Let's just say he was—"

"A pervert?"

"That'll do for now."

"That's the pot calling the kettle beige."

I walked to the window and looked past the terraced garden to the shimmering lake. "Jury trials demand a sacrifice," I said. "And if it's not going to be Jim, it has to be Brian."

"You still haven't explained why you think they were lovers."

"The first thing is why Brian didn't tell anyone about Jim."

"Didn't he tell Josh Mandel?"

"But not Jim's parents," I replied. "The obvious reason seemed to be blackmail, but there's a limit to how much you can extort from an eighteen-year-old busboy."

"To how much money," Larry said, revelation in his voice.

"Exactly. But the other thing that might've interested Brian was sex. Sex on demand."

"You think it didn't matter to him that it was another guy?"

"A blow job is a blow job is a blow job."

"*Pace* Gertrude Stein," Larry murmured and leaned back into his chair. "You said lovers, Henry. This scenario is not my idea of a romance."

"Agreed, but then — what did Auden say — 'The desires of the heart are as crooked as the corkscrew.' Josh Mandel described the scene where Jim supposedly threatened to kill Brian." I related Josh's version from that afternoon.

"Puts things in a different light," Larry said, extracting a cigarette from his pack of Kents.

"Doesn't it," I agreed. "It sounds like post-coital banter."

"Who have you been sleeping with?"

"You know what I mean."

Larry lit the Kent. He blew out a jet of smoke and nodded. "You think some affection developed between those two."

"It adds up."

"So am I to infer that Jim didn't kill Brian?" Larry asked, tapping ash into a crystal ashtray.

"No, the evidence is inescapable. It only explains why he can't bring himself to admit it. He didn't hate Brian."

"Then why kill him?"

"It was still blackmail," I said. "Brian had power over Jim. At some point Jim must have realized that Brian was using him and would go on using him whether Jim consented or not."

"That must've been hard if he cared at all about Brian."

"And it added to his guilt about being gay. Being gay meant being a victim."

Larry put out the cigarette and rose from behind his desk. "What are you going to do?"

"Go back to Jim. Let him know that I know."

"I suppose you have to," Larry said, gathering his cigarettes.

"You think I shouldn't?"

Larry shrugged. "He hasn't told you because he wanted to keep it a secret. Think of his pride."

"That's a luxury he can't afford," I replied.

☐

Jim came out and sat at the table, focusing on my left ear. His face was slack and tired.

"Were you asleep?" I asked.

"Who can sleep around here," he muttered.

"The tranquilizers don't help?"

His shrug terminated that line of conversation.

"I wanted to talk to you about Brian."

"Okay," he said, indifferently.

The indifference stung. "You were lovers," I said.

He gave me a hard look. "Guys don't love each other," he said.

"But you had sex with him."

His face colored but he didn't look away. "He wanted it," he said slowly.

"Did you?"

His narrow fingers raked his hair.

"Was having sex with him the price Brian charged for not telling your parents about you?"

He nodded. He looked at me again, his childishness gone. "Brian always wanted to make it with me," he said, knowingly. "He just needed a reason—"

"An excuse, you mean."

"—so he wouldn't have to think he was a faggot."

"How did you feel about being with him?" I asked.

"I don't know," he said, out of the side of his mouth. "Sometimes he was a jerk about it. Sometimes it was — okay."

"Did you like him?"

"Once when his parents were gone, we slept at his house," Jim said. "That was really nice, in a bed and everything."

"Where did you usually meet Brian for sex?"

"His car," Jim said. "The park. The locker room at the restaurant."

"The wine cellar?"

His eyes showed fear.

"Was that why he was there that night?"

"I don't know why he was there," Jim said. His voice trembled.

"But you assumed that's why he was there," I said. "Didn't you?"

After a moment's hesitation he said, "Yeah."

"Did Brian like you as much as you liked him?" I asked quietly.

He shook his head slowly, surprise in his face. "He never stopped calling me a faggot when other guys were around. Even after we made it. He told Josh Mandel about me."

"And you still liked him?" I continued.

"He was different when we were alone," Jim said, almost mournfully. He sounded less like the jilted lover than the slightly oddball child other children avoid; the mousy-haired boy lingering at the edge of the playing field watching a game he was never asked to play.

"So," I said, in a matter-of-fact voice, "one part of you really liked him and another part of you hated him because he was using you, Jim. Isn't that how it was?"

He opened his mouth but nothing came out. He nodded.

"Part of you loved him—" I waited, but he didn't react. "And part of you wanted—"

As if continuing a different conversation, he broke in, "Everything was so fucked up. I was tired." I heard the exhaustion pouring out from a deep place. "I wanted to kill—"

"Brian," I said.

"Myself," he replied. "I wanted to kill myself. Not Brian. I didn't kill Brian."

"But Brian's the one who's dead, Jim."

"No," he said, his face closing. "You think I killed him, but I didn't. I wanted to kill myself."

"That's what you wanted, Jim, but think about it," I said,

quickly. "Wanting to kill anyone means that there's violence inside of you. You can't always control that violence or direct it the way you planned. It's like a fire, Jim."

He was shaking his head violently, and his body trembled. "No, no, no," he said. "It wasn't me. I swear it wasn't."

"Think back, Jim. Try to remember that night."

"I don't remember," he said in a gust.

"You do remember," I said. "You have to, Jim."

His body buckled and then he started to scream. The guard ran up behind and restrained him, looking at me with amazement. As quickly as he had started, Jim stopped and slumped forward. Tears and snot ran down his face. He lifted his face and looked at me with such hatred that I felt my face burn.

"You're like everyone else," he said. "You want me to say I killed him. To hell with you." To the guard he said, "Get me out of here."

"We have to talk," I said.

"No more talking. You're not my lawyer anymore."

He jerked up out of the chair. The guard looked at me, seeking direction.

"Okay, Jim. I'll be back tomorrow."

"I won't be here," Jim Pears said.

☐

A phone was ringing.

I opened my eyes and tumbled out of bed, hurrying to pick the phone up before it woke Larry.

"Hello," I said, shaking from the chill.

A drunken male voice slurred my name.

"Yes, this is Henry. Who is this?"

"I know who killed Brian whatsisname," the voice continued.

I sat down at the desk. "Who are you?"

"It's not important," he said. "It wasn't that Pears kid. I'll tell you that much."

I was trying to clear my head and decide whether this was a crank call. I still wasn't sure.

"Were you at the bar that night?" I asked.

"Not me. Shit, you wouldn't catch me dead in the valley," he said and chuckled.

"Then how do you know?"

"I saw you on the news," he said. "You're kinda cute, Henry. You gotta lover?"

"Tell me about Brian Fox."

I heard bar noises in the background and then the line went dead.

I put the phone down. If it was a crank call, the caller had gone to a lot of trouble to find me. He would have had to call my office up north to get Larry's phone number. Unless he already had it. Josh Mandel? As I tried to reconstruct the voice, the phone rang again. I picked it up.

"Hello," I said, quickly.

"Mr. Rios?" It was a different voice, also male but not drunk.

"Yeah. Who am I talking to?"

"This is Deputy Isbel down at county jail," he said. "We got a bad situation here with Jim Pears."

"What happened?"

"Seems like he overdosed."

I stared at my faint reflection in the black window. "Is he dead?" I watched myself ask.

"No," the deputy replied cautiously. "They took him down to county hospital. Thought you'd want to know."

"Did you call his parents?"

"His dad answered," the deputy said, grimly. "Thanked me and hung up before I could tell him where the boy was."

"I see," I replied. "Where's the hospital if I'm coming from Silver Lake?"

I scrawled the directions on the back of an envelope and hung up. In the bathroom, I splashed water on my face, subdued my hair, rinsed my mouth, and dressed. I crept down the stairs. Just as I was closing the front door behind me, I heard the phone ring again. By the time I got to it, the caller had hung up.

— 11 —

Jim was still alive at daybreak. His doctor set her breakfast tray on the table in the hospital cafeteria where I had been waiting for her. She took a bite of scrambled eggs and made a face.

"They should make hospital cooks take the Hippocratic oath," she said. " 'First, do no harm.' That part."

I smiled, not too convincingly to judge from her expression. Her face was the color of exhaustion. She turned her attention to her meal, and ate with complete concentration as if taking a test. When she lifted her head, she looked almost relieved to be done with it.

"How are you feeling?" she asked.

I smiled again, this time genuinely. No matter how casually a doctor asked, this question always sounded like an accusation to me.

"I'm tired," I replied.

She nodded understandingly. "Go home."

"If he's all right."

Her narrow, studious face tensed a bit. "I didn't say that."

"No," I agreed, "you didn't."

"He's alive, Henry, but not all right." She rubbed her eyes. "He was unconscious for a long time, not breathing well. There's brain damage. How did he get those barbituates in jail?"

"They were prescribed," I answered. "To relieve anxiety. He must have stockpiled them."

"If they'd found him five minutes later, he'd be dead."

"It seems that was his plan." In my head I heard him telling me that he wouldn't be at the jail when I returned to see him.

According to the guards who'd brought him into the hospital, one of Jim's cellmates had been awakened by a gurgling noise. It was Jim, choking on his own vomit.

"You never said what he was in for," the doctor said.

"Murder," I replied.

"That little guy?"

"Yes," I said. He had also told me that he had wanted to kill himself, not Brian. Well, maybe he killed part of himself when he killed Brian. He decided to finish the job. Thanks to me.

She curled her elegant fingers around a chipped coffee mug. "Well, he did manage to do a lot of damage to himself, so I guess murder's not impossible."

"Will he live?"

"Parts of him." She wore a thin gold wedding band. She saw me notice it and said, "You were one of the lawyers on that sodomy case a couple of years back."

"I'm surprised you remember."

"I recognized your name as soon as you told me. You're his lawyer, or what?"

"His lawyer," I said, shaking the grounds at the bottom of my coffee cup.

"No parents?"

"He has parents," I said, setting the cup down. "They couldn't be bothered."

"That's rough," she said, blinking the tiredness from her eyes. She studied me. "Was his situation so bad?"

I nodded. "He got backed into a corner. I helped put him there."

"Working in emergency," she said, "I see a lot of suicide attempts. The ones who survive, they didn't mean to succeed." She pushed her tray away. "The ones who don't make it — it's not that they give up, Henry. They fight, but they fight to die. That's what Jim's doing. You can murder someone, but you can't make him kill himself. You understand?"

I studied the pattern of the grounds at the bottom of my cup. "Yes," I said, lifting my tired eyes to hers.

"Go home," she said. "I'll call you if anything happens."

□

It was cold and gray outside the hospital. The sun was like a circle of ice, lightening the sky around it. The silvery towers of downtown shimmered through the morning mist. In this weather the palm trees seemed wildly incongruous, like tattered banners of summer.

I had read, years ago, of the Japanese poet who commented upon suicide, "A silent death is an endless word." Should I read Jim's attempt to kill himself as a reproach, as release, as an admission of guilt? Of love? I could understand why he did it but I didn't approve. It was the drama that disturbed me. The most basic rule of survival is to wait things out. It was a rule Jim was too young to have learned. With almost twenty years on him, I knew that the great passions — love, fear, hope, terror — merge with the clutter of the day-to-day, and become part of it. A truer symbol of justice than the blindfolded goddess was a clock.

A clock was ticking in the kitchen of Larry's house as I let myself in. He was sitting at the table with a cup of coffee in front of him. He looked up when I entered.

"I heard your car when you left," he said. "That was six hours ago."

"You've been awake since?"

"Off and on," he replied. "It's Jim, isn't it?"

"He tried to kill himself," I said, sitting down.

In a gray voice, Larry asked, "Is he dead?"

"No. He's in a coma."

"How did it happen?"

I explained.

Larry raised the cup to his lips without drinking. The robe he wore fell away, revealing his thin, hairless chest, the skin as mottled as an autumn apple. A few sparse white hairs grew at the base of his neck. His face showed nothing of what he felt but the white hairs trembled.

"How stupid," he muttered. "What a stupid thing to do."

"He was afraid," I said.

"Well I know a few things about fear," Larry snapped. He shut his eyes for a moment. When he opened them he said, "I'm sorry I said that."

"Who better?"

"No," he shook his head. "It's not the same at all. I've had my life, but to throw it all away at eighteen..." He lifted his fingers from the table in a gesture of bewilderment.

"If you can't imagine the future," I said, "it must not seem like you're throwing much away."

Larry nodded. "You'll have to do something about the trial."

"I'll ask for a dismissal."

"Then what?"

"I suppose he'll revert to the custody of his parents."

Larry frowned. "The perfect son at last."

I went upstairs to get some sleep. As I undressed I remembered the call I received the night before. I called my office and reached my secretary. I asked whether anyone had requested my number in the last day or so.

She went through the telephone log. There had been someone, a man named King who had insisted on getting my number in Los Angeles. The name meant nothing to me. I thanked her and hung up.

I got into the rumpled bed, naked between the cold sheets. Outside, a bird cawed. Inside, there was silence. I closed my eyes and slept a long, black sleep.

◻

Three days later I was back in court. The press was out in full force. Pisano, the D.A., told the court he would not dismiss the charges against Jim Pears as long as Jim remained alive. He put Lillian Fox on the witness stand. She demanded that the prosecution proceed. I informed Judge Ryan that Jim had suffered permanent, catastrophic brain damage and was unlikely ever to revive. I asked the judge to dismiss the charges on her own motion, as the law permitted, in the interests of justice. However, as she had just finished pointing out, those interests were complex.

"Your Honor," I said, "the medical evidence is that my client is, for all intents and purposes, dead. I don't see what more could be accomplished by hounding him to the grave."

Pisano was on his feet. "The medical evidence is not conclusive," he said.

"It's as conclusive as it's going to get," I snapped. "Jim Pears isn't going to get much deader, short of driving a stake through his heart."

"So dramatic," Pisano said, mockingly.

"You're just trying to squeeze another headline from this, aren't you?"

The judge broke in. "Gentlemen, some restraint."

"Speaking of restraints," I said, angry now, "my client's wrist is handcuffed to the railing of his hospital bed. Do the police really think he's going to rise up and go on a crime spree? This entire hearing is ghoulish. Regardless of what Jim is charged with, what he may or may not have done, we've reached a point where simple decency demands that this matter be ended."

"Is that true about the handcuffs?" the judge asked.

"Yes," I replied.

"It's standard operating procedure," Pisano put in, in his best bureaucratic drone.

"Even so," Judge Ryan said to him, "it's a little gratuitous, counsel, don't you think?"

"Not at all," he replied.

"The motion, Judge," I said, "is pending."

"Thank you, I'm aware of that," she replied, sharply. Then, looking down at some papers before her, she said, "This matter is scheduled for trial in four weeks. I will continue it until that date for a status hearing. In the meantime, the defendant's motion to dismiss is denied without prejudice to renew it at that point. That's all, gentlemen." She rose swiftly and departed the bench.

I turned to Pisano. "Think the streets are safer now?" I demanded.

He capped the pen he had taken notes with. "This isn't personal, Henry. It's business. Learn that and you'll live a lot longer."

"Calling it business doesn't make it right."

He smiled faintly. "You shouldn't be a lawyer, Henry. You should be God." He walked away to talk to Lillian Fox who was hissing his name behind us.

"Henry?"

It was Sharon Hart, looking like a giant bumblebee in a black suit and a yellow silk blouse.

"Hello, Sharon. I didn't see you come in," I said, closing my briefcase.

"I slipped in halfway through," she said. "I'm in trial next door."

"How's it going?" I asked without real interest.

She shrugged. "My guy's found Jesus."

I smiled, in spite of myself. "What?"

"He admits everything but says that Jesus has forgiven him and the jury should, too."

"Think they'll buy it?"

She grinned. "Not Mrs. Kohn," she said. "Juror number six. You were real good, just now."

"Didn't seem to help."

"Don't blame yourself, or Pat Ryan. Judges are elected, too, and if you're black and a woman someone's always gunning for you. She's got to be careful."

"The fact that the lynch mob has the franchise, instead of a rope and a tree, doesn't make this justice. She should understand that."

"I'm sure she does," Sharon said, frowning. "Trust me, she'll do the right thing. Anyway, it's not like Jim's innocent."

"At this point his guilt or innocence is irrelevant," I replied. "He's removed himself from the court's jurisdiction."

"Tough way to do it," she commented, sticking an unlit cigarette into the side of her mouth. The bailiff cleared his throat censoriously. The cigarette went back into her pocket.

"But effective," I replied.

"Yeah," she said. "I've got a couple of clients I'd like to tell to kill themselves."

I shook my head.

"I've got to get back to my trial," she said, and looked at me steadily. "But there's one thing I've got to ask you. Do you think Jim killed Brian Fox?"

"Yes," I replied, without hesitation. "I do."

She looked relieved. "Well, I guess this is goodbye," she said, and stuck her hand out at me.

I shook it. "Goodbye, Sharon."

"Good luck," she replied. I watched her leave the courtroom. I began to follow but remembered the press outside. In no mood for further combat, I slipped out through the back.

☐

Larry drove me to the airport and pulled up in front of the Air California terminal. We got out and I took my things from the trunk.

"You're sure you don't want me to see you off inside?" he asked.

"I'm sure," I replied. We looked at each other. "You wanted me to balance the accounts. I didn't do it, did I?"

Larry looked worn and frail. "I guess Jim showed us that people aren't numbers."

"No," I agreed. "I'll be back in a month."

"Until then."

We embraced and he kissed my cheek. I stood at the curb and watched his Jaguar melt into the frantic Friday afternoon traffic.

On the plane I thought about the loose ends: a drunken phone call from someone who claimed Jim wasn't the killer, Jim's own insistence that he hadn't done it, the fact that Jim and Brian had been something akin to lovers, and Josh Mandel's obvious lie about where he had been the night of the murder. Grist for speculation but hardly enough to take to the jury. Not even enough to change my own mind, really. Jim Pears had killed Brian Fox. That much was inescapable. And yet...

I looked out the window. The sea was white with light, an enormous blankness beneath a gentle autumn sky.

— 12 —

On Monday, December first, I found myself back in the courtroom of Patricia Ryan where the case of People versus Pears was about to end — not with a bang, but a whimper. The previous week I had worked out an arrangement allowing the D.A. to designate a neurologist to examine Jim for the purpose of assessing his chances of recovery. The doctor, a sandy-haired man with a vague air about him, sat beside the prosecutor, a young woman named Laura Wyle, the third prosecutor I had dealt with in the past month. The case was now of such low priority that it had trickled down through the ranks to the most junior member of the D.A.'s homicide unit.

It was as cold in the court as it was outside in the rainy streets, the result, I was told, of the heat having been off over the weekend. The bailiff wore a parka over his tan uniform and the court reporter sat with her hands beneath her legs while we waited for the judge to take the bench. The only other people in the court were a middle-aged couple, the man very tall and the woman very short. Jim's parents. Walter Pears wore a black suit, a brilliantly white shirt and a dark blue tie. Light gleamed off the lenses of his wire-rimmed glasses. His long, stern face was set in a look of sour distaste that I associated with religious fanatics and tax lawyers; Walter Pears was both. His wife was, for all intents and purposes, invisible. Even now, looking at her, I was more aware of the color of her dress — an unflattering shade of green — than her face. They were here to reclaim their son. Poor Jim, I thought again, turning away from them. The bailiff stood up and said, "All rise."

Patricia Ryan emerged from her chambers, seated herself and said, "Good morning, ladies and gentlemen."

We bid her good morning. The reporter started to click away.

"People versus Pears," the judge said. "Let the record reflect that the parties are represented but Mr. Pears is not present." She shuffled some papers. "I have received a medical report in this case by a Dr. Connor—"

"Uh, present," the doctor said.

"Yes, hello, Doctor," the judge said. "From what I gather it is your conclusion that Jim Pears suffers from permanent and irreversible brain damage, is that right?"

Doctor Connor drew himself up and surveyed the room as if he had just awakened in Oz. He saw me and blinked furiously.

"Doctor," the judge said.

"Right," he said. "Uh, yes, Your Honor. Did you say something?"

In a voice of practiced patience, she repeated her original question.

Connor's arms jerked up to his sides and backwards as if pulled by wires. "That's kind of the village idiot explanation," he said, cheerfully.

Judge Ryan squinted and said coldly, "Doctor, I'd like you to answer my question, not assess my intelligence."

The D.A. tugged at Connor's coat. He leaned over and she whispered, fiercely, into his ear. He jerked upright and said, "The answer is yes." He plopped back into his chair.

"Thank you," she said. "Now, it's my understanding that the People wish to make a motion pursuant to Penal Code section 1385."

Laura Wyle stood up. "In view of the unlikelihood that James Pears will ever be fit to stand trial, the People move to dismiss the action in the interests of justice."

"Mr. Rios?"

"No objection, Your Honor."

"Motion granted. The action is dismissed. Mr. Pears is remanded to the custody of his parents. Are they in court?"

"Yes, Your Honor," I said, rising. I turned to the gallery.

Sometime during Connor's disquisition Josh Mandel had entered the courtroom and now sat behind me. Surprised, I wondered why the D.A. had ordered him in. "Mr. and Mrs. Pears are present."

"I am ordering Jim's release," she said to them. "You'll have to make arrangements to move him through the sheriff's office. My clerk will assist you."

Walter Pears rose, all six-foot-six of him. "Thank you," he bellowed, mournfully.

"Court is in recess," Patricia Ryan said. "Thank you for being here, Mr. Rios."

"My pleasure."

She smiled charmingly and left the bench. I turned to Laura Wyle. "You have a witness here," I observed.

She looked around. "Where?"

"Josh Mandel."

"I didn't tell him to be here," she replied.

Connor came around and said, loudly, "Can I go now? I have appointments all morning."

"Certainly," she said. "Thank you."

"A waste of my time," he muttered, and pushed his way past the railing and out of the court.

I raised a sympathetic eyebrow at the D.A.

"He's a real ass, isn't he," she said. "Well, excuse me, Henry. Lillian Fox is upstairs in my office having hysterics."

"My sympathies," I said.

Walter Pears came up to the railing, leaned over and said, "Mr. Rios, if I might have a word with you? Privately."

I looked at him. "Sure. Now?"

"If you please."

"There's a small conference room just outside the courtroom," I said. "I'll be there in a minute."

"Yes, that'll do," he said, as if bestowing a favor.

I turned around in my chair. Josh Mandel was looking directly at me. "Hello, Josh."

"Hi," he said. Today he wore a yellow rain slicker over jeans and a red crew neck sweater. Not witness apparel, I thought.

"You came in for the last act?"

"Can I talk to you?"

"I think the Pears have first dibs. Can you stick around?"

He shook his head. "I've got to get to Encino."

"You want to tell me what it's about?" I asked, standing up and straightening my coat.

"It's kind of personal." He was forcing himself to keep his eyes on me.

"Is it about Jim?"

"Sort of," he said, now standing too. The railing separated us by a few inches. "I don't think he killed Brian."

"You have some evidence?"

"Maybe. I'm not sure — look, can I see you tonight?"

"I have plans, I'm afraid."

His face was adamant. "It doesn't matter when. I'll be home all night."

"Give me your number," I said, after a moment's hesitation. "I'll call you."

"Okay." He pulled out his wallet and extracted a bank deposit slip, jotting his number on the back. "It's in Hollywood," he said.

"I'll call," I said, accepting the paper.

"Thanks," he said, and stuck his hand out. I shook it. I watched him go. Handsome kid, I thought, and felt disloyal to Jim for having thought it.

◻

Walter Pears folded his hands in front of him. They were big hands with stubby, hairy fingers. He wore a heavy gold band on one finger and what looked like a high school graduation ring on another. His wife, introduced as either Leona or Mona, sat a few inches behind him as watchful as a little bird. I sat down in the only other chair in the room and closed the door behind me.

I waited for Pears to speak.

"As I told you earlier," Pears began after a few uncomfortable seconds, "I am also a lawyer. A tax specialist."

"Yes," I replied. "You told me."

"I know nothing of litigation."

It was clear that he expected congratulations.

"Well, some lawyers just aren't cut out for it," I said.

A bit of color crept into his neck. "That's not precisely why I introduce the subject."

"Do I get three guesses or are you going to tell me?"

He straightened himself in his chair. "I take exception to your tone."

"You're wasting my time," I replied. "And, as one lawyer to another, you know what billing rates are like these days."

For a moment he simply stared at me while his knuckles went white. Then he cleared his throat and said, "My wife and I wish to file a suit against the county. That is, I believe, the proper governmental entity responsible for the maintenance and operation of the jail."

"That's right," I said, outrage beginning to flicker in some dim corner of my brain. "What cause of action do you have against the county?"

"I have undertaken a preliminary investigation of the circumstances surrounding my son's suicide attempt," he announced. "It appears that the medication he took was prescribed to him by a physician at the jail."

"There's no mystery about that."

"Then you will agree that the authorities at the jail failed to monitor whether James was, in fact, taking that medication when it was given to him?"

"I wasn't there," I said. "The fact is that he managed to stockpile it. You can draw an inference of negligence by the jailers if you want."

"I do," he said. "Indeed, I do, Mr. Rios. Not merely negligence, but gross negligence." He pushed his glasses back against his face from where they had slipped forward on his nose. Only his eyes reminded me of Jim. "As a proximate result of that gross negligence, I have been injured."

"You?" I asked.

He corrected himself. "My son has been directly injured," he said, "but certain interests of mine are also implicated."

Leaning forward, I said, "Mr. Pears, will you stop talking like a Supreme Court opinion and tell me what the hell it is you want from me?"

"I told you," he said, stiffening. "I intend to sue the county.

I want you to represent me or, rather, to represent Jim since the suit would be brought on his behalf."

I stared at him. "You son-of-a-bitch."

"Don't you dare address me in that manner."

"The night your son tried to kill himself you didn't even have the decency to show up at the hospital. I know that because I was there. And now you think I'm going to help you pick his bones?" I had leaned further across the table until I was within spitting distance of Pears. His face was aflame.

"We're not rich people," a tiny voice ventured from a corner of the room. I looked at Mrs. Pears. "Hospital care for Jim will be so expensive."

"Don't tell me you don't have medical insurance," I snapped. "Besides, if you had any respect for Jim you'd pull the plug and let him die."

"We're Catholics," she peeped.

"I was raised Catholic, Mrs. Pears," I said, "so I know all about Catholics like you who can't take a shit without consulting a priest."

Suddenly, Walter Pears jumped up, sending his chair skidding across the floor with a metallic shriek. I got up slowly until we faced each other.

Pears said, "If you were a man I'd kill you."

"If you were a man," I replied, "your son wouldn't be a goddamn vegetable in the jail ward of a charity hospital."

The door opened behind me. Judge Ryan's bailiff stuck his head into the room. "Everything okay here, folks?"

Mrs. Pears got to her feet. "Yes, officer. We were just leaving. Let's go, Walter." She tugged at his sleeve.

Pears seethed and stalked out of the room ahead of his wife. She stopped at the door and said to me, "There's a special place in hell for people like you."

After she left, the bailiff looked at me. "What was that all about?"

"Theology," I replied.

— 13 —

As I approached the door to Larry's house I heard the unmistakable noise of gunfire. I let myself in and called his name.

"In here," he shouted back.

I followed his voice to the study where I found him in his bathrobe, sitting on the sofa, watching a cassette on the TV. The cassette was frozen on the image of a man in a cop's uniform holding a gun.

"That sounded like the real thing."

"Stereo," Larry replied. He reached for a glass containing about a half-inch of brown fluid. Brandy. It disturbed me that he had taken up drinking again. He looked much the same as he had in October and insisted that his disease was still in remission. But he went into his office less and less often. My impression was that he now seldom left his house. It was even more difficult to talk to him about being sick, because he seemed to have reached a stage more of indifference than denial.

He had asked me to spend a few days with him. Since we were entering the holiday season and prosecutors were unwilling to face Christmas juries, it was a good time for me to get away.

"How did it go in court?" he asked.

I sat down beside him. "The charges were dismissed."

"Free at last," he muttered bitterly.

"When are you going to forgive Jim, Larry?"

He lifted his bony shoulders, dropped them and stared blankly at the frozen action on the screen.

"His parents asked me to sue the county," I said.

Larry made a disgusted noise. "Why?"

"For not preventing their little boy from trying to kill himself."

"Vultures," he said without heat.

"I thought so, too. Jim's dad and I got into a little scuffle."

"You draw blood?"

I shook my head.

"Too bad." He pushed a button on the remote control and the action on the screen began again.

"What are you watching?"

"Do you remember Sandy Blenheim?"

I nodded. "The agent."

"There's an actor he wants me to represent. Tom Zane. He's one of the stars of this show."

The cop on the screen raced down a dark alley in pursuit of a shadowy figure ahead of him. He commanded the figure to stop, then fired his gun. He came to the prone body, knelt and flipped it over. He saw the face of a boy and said, "Oh my God, Jerry."

"Who's the corpse?" I asked.

"The cop's son," Larry replied. "I've seen this one before."

On the screen the cop was sobbing. Then there was an aerial view of Los Angeles and the words "Smith & Wesson" appeared as music began playing. The screen split and displayed the faces of two men, one on each side. The man on the left was a white-haired, elegantly wrinkled old party who smiled benignly into the camera. On the right was one of the handsomest men I had ever seen. At first it was like looking at two different men. His slightly battered nose — it looked like it had been broken, then inexpertly set — and firmly moulded jaw gave his face a toughness that kept him from being a pretty boy. But there was prettiness, too, in the shape of his mouth, the long-lashed eyes. At second glance, though, the parts fit together with a kind of masculine elegance that reminded me of dim images from my childhood of an earlier period of male stars, Tyrone Power or John Garfield. Only his dark hair seemed wrong, somehow.

Larry stopped the picture. "The fellow on the right is Zane."

"Who's the other?"

"Paul Houston. He's been on the tube for twenty years in

one series after another. This was supposed to be his show but Tom Zane's edged him out."

"Why? His looks?"

Larry sipped his brandy. "Watch."

He fast-forwarded the tape until he reached a scene in which Tom Zane was standing in the doorway of Paul Houston's office. Larry turned off the sound. Even with the sound off, Paul Houston was clearly an actor at work. His face was full of tics and pauses meant to convey, by turn, cranky good humor, concern, exasperation, and wisdom. It wasn't that his acting was obvious but merely that it was unmistakable. He was trying to reach the audience beyond the camera.

Tom Zane, on the other hand, hadn't the slightest interest in anything but the camera. He opened his face to it and the camera did all the work. It amounted to photography, not acting, and yet the effect was to intimate that, next to Tom Zane, Paul Houston looked like a wind-up toy. Larry shut off the tape and turned to me.

"See?" he said.

"He has a lot of charisma," I observed. "But can he act?"

Larry said, "He couldn't act his way out of the proverbial paper sack, but the camera loves his face."

"Well, it's some face. I've never heard of Tom Zane before."

"He came out of nowhere about a year ago and got a bit part in the pilot of this show. The response to him was so overwhelming that they killed off the actor who was originally supposed to play Houston's partner and replaced him with Zane."

"What's he want with you?"

"He's putting together a production company."

"I thought you weren't taking new business."

"Sandy's persistent," Larry said. "In fact, he was just here a while ago to drop off the cassette and," he picked up a paperback, "this."

I looked at the cover. "*Edward the Second* by Bertolt Brecht. Why?"

"Zane's performing the title role in a little theater on Santa Monica. Sandy wants me to come tonight."

"Are you?" I asked. We'd planned to have dinner out and take in a movie.

"If you'll come, too," he said, setting the book down.

"Sure," I said. "Did Sandy say anything about Jim Pears?" Larry shook his head. "That was last week's sensation."

"Tough town you got here," I said. I picked up the book. "Isn't Brecht sort of ambitious for an actor who can't act?"

"I guess we'll find out tonight," Larry said. "It's kind of a vanity production."

"What does that mean?" I asked, flipping the pages of the play. It was in verse.

"Zane's producing it himself. It's not to make money but to show people in the industry what he can do as an actor. I suspect his wife's behind it."

"Who's that?"

"Irene Gentry."

"Irene Gentry?" I put the book down. "I saw her in *Long Day's Journey Into Night* three years ago. She's wonderful."

"Yeah," Larry said dubiously.

"What does that mean?"

"It's not about her acting. She really is a fine stage actress but in this town she has—" he smiled "— a reputation."

"What sort?"

"Nothing specific, just that she's difficult to work with. Not that she ever got much work here. She's always had too much going against her."

"For instance?"

"She's plain, she's now past forty, she's New York, and she's too damned good an actress."

"That's ridiculous."

"Which part?"

"All of it."

He lit a cigarette. "The days when movies could tolerate a Katherine Hepburn or Bette Davis as a leading lady are over. The public wants candy for the eyes. Irene Gentry is a five-course meal."

"I wrote her a fan letter once," I said.

"Henry, you surprise me."

I shrugged. "I was a lot younger, then," I offered, by way of explanation. "She was doing Shaw's *Caesar and Cleopatra*."

"Yes," Larry said, exhaling a stream of smoke, "I saw her in that, too."

We were both silent.

"Well, you may get to meet her tonight," he said, finishing his drink. "I'm going to take a nap, Henry. Wake me in an hour or so, all right?"

"All right." After he left I turned the tape back on, with the sound, and listened to Tom Zane deliver excruciatingly bad lines with all the animation of a robot. He was such a bad actor that it was almost possible to overlook his face. Almost. After a minute or two, I shut the tape off and picked up the Brecht.

◻

Edward the Second was an English king who ruled from 1307 to 1324. His calamitous reign culminated in a thirteen-year civil war that ended with his abdication. Two years later he was murdered by order of his wife's lover, a nobleman named Mortimer. Much of Edward's misfortune resulted from a love affair he conducted with a man named Piers Gaveston in an age when sodomy was a capital offense. Edward's homosexuality was less disturbing to his vassals than his insistence on carrying on openly with Gaveston. Parliament twice exiled Edward's lover only to have Edward recall him. Eventually, the nobility split between those who were loyal to the king and those who were repelled by him. This led to the civil war.

The notes in the Brecht book said that Edward's life had been the subject of an earlier play by Christopher Marlowe, the Elizabethan playwright who was himself homosexual. Marlowe's work was the source of much of Brecht's play. In Brecht's version, Edward — vain, frivolous, proud, willful, and incompetent — was more like the degenerate scion of the Krupp family than a fourteenth-century monarch. This characterization was emphasized by the way Brecht portrayed Gaveston, the object of Edward's passion. Gaveston was essentially a whore; a butcher's son who, for reasons inexplicable even to himself, was plucked from his low station by the whim of an infatuated king.

Gaveston was canny and fatalistic: the real hero of the Brecht play.

Though Edward was no hero he did have a certain grandeur which was mostly evident at the end of the play when he is held in captivity. In defeat and squalor, he repented nothing, becoming more of a king than when he actually governed.

The cost to Edward of his homosexuality was a gruesome death. While Brecht's stage directions indicated death by suffocation, the accompanying notes discussed the actual circumstances of Edward's murder. A red-hot poker was thrust into his anus. His last lover, who according to the historical record was not Gaveston, was castrated; his genitals were burned in public and then the man was decapitated.

□

The play was being performed in West Hollywood on Santa Monica Boulevard just east of La Cienega. Since I planned to see Josh Mandel after the play, Larry and I took separate cars. The rain had stopped at dusk and the skies had cleared. They were flooded with the lights of the city but, for all that, Santa Monica seemed dark and uninhabited as I waited at a traffic light just east of the Hollywood Memorial Cemetery.

Behind towering walls only the palm trees were visible. As I passed the gates I saw the domes and turrets of the necropolis. On the other side of the street, young boys — hustlers — stood in doorways or sat at bus stops watching cars with violent intensity. As I drove between the whores and the cemetery I thought of Jim Pears for whom death and sex had been in even closer proximity. When I came to Highland, brightly lit and busy, I felt like one awakening from the beginnings of a bad dream.

□

The theater was surprisingly small, a dozen rows of folding wooden chairs broken into three sections in a semi-circle ascending from the stage. Larry and I sat third row center, arriving just as the lights began to dim. There were few other people around us. One of them was a woman with a familiar face. She glanced at me and then turned away.

"That's Irene Gentry," I said, more to myself than to Larry.

He looked over at her and nodded.

The house lights went out around us and I looked at the stage. A remarkably handsome man stood in the lights holding a piece of paper — it was Edward's lover, Gaveston. He lifted it toward his eyes and said:

> My father, old Edward, is dead. Come quickly
> Gaveston, and share the kingdom with your
> dearest friend, King Edward the Second.

There followed a scene in which Gaveston was approached by two itinerant soldiers who offered him their service. He mockingly refused and one of them cursed him to die at the hands of a soldier. The three of them then stepped into the shadows. Five other men emerged. One was Edward.

"Where's Zane?" I whispered to Larry.

"The blond."

I looked. "His hair—" I began, remembering that on the TV show he had had black hair.

"This is natural color," Larry said. "They made him dye it for the series because Houston is also blond. Or was, rather, twenty years ago."

"He's short," I said. Zane looked no taller than five-seven.

"He wears lifts in front of the camera," Larry explained. He looked at me and smiled. "Poor Henry, this must be terribly disillusioning."

Someone shushed us and I returned my attention to the stage. Beneath the glare of the stage lights, Zane's face lost the magic that the camera conjured up. He was still handsome but his face was oddly immobile; I diagnosed a case of the jitters. He delivered his first line, "I will have Gaveston," as if requesting his coffee black.

Midway through the play two things were apparent. First, as Larry had warned me, Tom Zane could not act. Second, the cast that surrounded him had been carefully directed to disguise Zane's disability as much as humanly possible. All except Gaveston. I glanced at my program. The actor playing Gaveston was named Antony Good. While the other actors covered Zane's fluffed lines, Good stared at Zane in open amazement as he raced through yet another speech, spitting it out like sour milk. The other actors underacted assiduously when playing a scene with Zane, but Good threw himself into the role of Gaveston in open competition with the star. It was a one-sided contest. Good was superb, bringing to the character of Gaveston the pathos of the street outside the theater.

Zane, by contrast, lumbered through these scenes like a wounded animal dragging itself to a burial ground. Sweat soaked his underarms and he sprayed spittle across the stage. Once or twice he simply stopped mid-speech and gasped for air. Then, frowning with concentration, he would begin again, devastating Brecht's elegant lines. I looked around to Irene Gentry. She sat, motionless, eyes facing the stage.

When the house lights went on at intermission, she was already gone.

Larry looked at me and said, almost irritably, "Whatever possessed him to do this play?"

"It is terrible, isn't it?"

"No," Larry replied. "He's terrible."

We got up to stretch.

"Gaveston is excellent, though," I said.

"Mm. It's a role Tony Good's played in his life."

"You know him?"

"Oh, yes," he said in a curious voice.

"Meaning?"

"Tony sometimes offers his services as an escort to men of a certain age."

"Have you ever taken him up on it?"

Larry shook his head. "No. I'm going outside to get some air. You coming?"

We went out.

□

In the first scene of the second half of the play Gaveston was killed. Tom Zane's performance began to improve at once. In the final scenes, where Edward is dragged from castle to castle alone except for his jailers, Zane was transformed. His delivery was still awkward but the suffering he conveyed was authentic. Not just Zane's expressions, but the contours of his face and his body changed so that he seemed a different man from the one who first stepped upon the stage. I began to believe that he was Edward the Second.

The culmination of his performance came in the assassination sequence. In the play, Edward has been locked in a cell in London, into which the city's sewage drops upon him. Drums are pounded to keep him from sleeping. The assassin, Lightborn, is let into Edward's cell.

The scene began in darkness. Slowly, a blue light glimmered from a corner of the stage where a man stood, arms loose at his sides, face tilted upward toward the light. His hair was matted and his body covered with filth. This was Zane. In the flickering blue light it took me a moment to see that, other than a soiled rag that cupped his genitals, he was naked. Zane had a first-class body. He said:

> This hole they've put me in is a cesspit.
> For seven hours the dung of London
> Has dropped on me.

A ladder of rope dropped from above the stage and an immense, powerfully muscled black man climbed down. Lightborn. At once, Zane accused him of being his murderer. Lightborn denied it.

Zane answered, "Your look says death and nothing else."

The drums that had been heard from the beginning of the scene were suddenly still. Lightborn went to a brazier where he lit a coal fire. Zane watched impassively. An amber light was added to the stage. Then, approaching the king as he would a lover, Lightborn coaxed him to lie down on his cot and sleep. Zane resisted.

Pulling away, Zane turned to face Lightborn and again accused him of being sent as his murderer.

Lightborn touched his fingers to Zane's filthy hair, picked out a bit of straw and repeated, "You have not slept. You're tired, Sire. Lie down on the bed and rest a while."

Zane turned to face the audience. Lightborn quietly approached him from behind and lifted his powerful arms which he wrapped around Zane's chest as if intending to squeeze the life from him. Zane did not resist. Lightborn released his arms and once again urged the king to sleep.

Zane replied:

> The rain was good. Not eating made me full. But
> The darkness was the best. . . .
> Therefore let
> The dark be dark and the unclean unclean.
> Praise hunger, praise mistreatment, praise
> The darkness.

Lightborn led Zane by the hand to a cot and Zane lay down. Looking at Lightborn he said, "There's something buzzing in my ears. It whispers: If I sleep now, I'll never wake. It's anticipation that makes me tremble so." He delivered these lines softly, as if speaking in a dream. I thought of Jim Pears. I glanced at Larry and wondered what he was thinking.

Lightborn kissed Zane on the lips. Then there was silence. Zane's breath grew light and rapid as he slipped into sleep. The cot creaked as he turned on his stomach. Lightborn raised his hand into the air and caught a metal poker tossed down from where the ladder had come. He placed the tip of the poker in the brazier. The blue light flickered out, leaving only the amber which slowly changed to deep red.

Lightborn stood above Zane holding the poker a foot or two above Zane and aimed it directly between his legs, upward toward his anus. He flexed his powerful arms. The light went out.

Zane's shriek rent the darkness.

It was only then that I remembered that the poker scene was not in Brecht's play.

— 14 —

The actors took their bows and filed off the stage. Larry and I got up and made our way to the aisle. Sandy Blenheim, wearing pleated black leather pants and a voluminous white shirt, stopped us. He grabbed Larry's hand and said, "You made it."

"Hello, Sandy," Larry replied, disengaging his hand. "You remember Henry Rios."

"Hello," I said.

Blenheim took me in with a reptilian flick of his eyes.

"You were that kid's lawyer," he said. "Too bad about him. It would have been a great movie." To Larry he said, "Wasn't T. Z. fabulous?"

"He got better toward the end," Larry replied.

"The last scene," Blenheim went on. "Perfect. You know it was his idea to do it with just the jock strap."

"That last scene wasn't in Brecht," I said. "Brecht has Lightborn suffocate Edward."

"T. Z., again," Blenheim replied. "Someone told him that's how the guy really died, so he wanted to do it that way." He looked at me. "It's kinda sexy, huh?"

"Yes," I allowed. "It was."

Blenheim smiled again as if confirming something about me. I could imagine what it was. I knew a tribesman when I saw one. So, it seemed, did he. He wagged a finger between Larry and me. "You two dating?"

Larry cut him off. "We're friends, Sandy."

"Well, why don't you and your friend come over to Monet's. Tom and Rennie are having a little party."

'Henry?"

"Sure," I replied, thinking that I might meet Irene Gentry there.

"That's great," Blenheim said. "Maybe you and me and Tom can get together about that contract, Larry."

"Okay," Larry replied without enthusiam.

"See you there," Blenheim said. He favored me with another narrow smile, and bounced off shouting the name of his next victim.

"Who's Rennie?" I asked.

"Irene Gentry. The name Irene doesn't really lend itself to abbreviation, but everyone calls her Rennie."

"Rennie," I repeated.

"Let's go meet her."

☐

The sky was clear but starless. Only a trickle of water in the gutters gave any clue of the day's rain. Santa Monica Boulevard was clogged with traffic — brake lights flared in the darkness, wheels squeaked to a halt — and the air was choked with exhaust fumes. Larry cadged a cigarette from a passerby and lit it.

"Monet's isn't far," he said. "Let's walk it."

It was Friday night and the bars were doing brisk business. Country-western music blared from one in which, through smoked windows, male couples did the Texas two-step. Outside another bar a gaggle of street kids offered us coke. At a fast food shack, painted bright orange and lit up like a birthday cake, Larry stopped to buy a pack of cigarettes. A boy with stringy hair downed the house specialty, a pastrami burrito. I found the phone and called Josh Mandel. He answered on the second ring.

I explained that I was going to a party. "If you still want to get together," I added, "I could meet you in about an hour." I wanted him to say yes.

"Okay," he said. "That's fine."

"Your place?"

"Where are you now?" he asked.

I stuck my head out of the booth and looked in vain for a street sign. "On Santa Monica," I replied. "There's a Mayfair market across the street."

After a moment's pause he said, "Oh, King's Road. There's a bar just east of Fairfax called the Hawk. South side of the boulevard. I could meet you there."

"All right. In about an hour."

"Mr. Rios?" he began, awkwardly.

"Yes, Josh?"

"It's a gay bar."

Larry came up and tapped on the phone booth.

"I've got to go now," I said. "I'll see you then."

I hung the phone up and stepped out of the booth.

"Josh Mandel is gay," I told Larry as we resumed walking down the street.

"The guy who testified against Jim?"

"The star witness," I replied.

☐

Monet's was a squat windowless building painted charcoal gray next to a porn shop. Marble steps led up from the filthy sidewalk to double wooden doors presided over by a man in a red jacket. He opened the door for us. Inside, at a plexiglass lectern, stood another red jacket. A huge Motherwell hung on the wall behind him. Two halls led off from the small foyer. The familiar sounds of a restaurant were absent. Instead, expensive silence reigned.

"Gentlemen?" the red jacket inquired.

"Zane party," Larry said.

"Very good," he said, just like in the movies, and summoned a third red jacket. "The Morgan Room."

We were led down one of the halls. In the coppery light I saw that the walls were marble.

"What is this place?" I asked Larry.

"A membership restaurant," he replied, lighting a cigarette and flicking the match to the carpeted floor. "You come in and you're assigned a private dining room."

"Is the point privacy?"

"No," Larry said. "The point is status."

We came to a door. The red jacket opened it and stepped aside to let us pass. The room looked like the conference room of a particularly stodgy law firm; all dark paneling and copper fixtures, Winslow Homer paintings on the walls and even brass spittoons. There were a lot of people inside, including some of the cast members, milling around with the provisional air of people waiting for a party to begin.

"This is going to be business for me," Larry said. "You mind being on your own?"

"No. I'm leaving in about an hour anyway."

"Come and find me on your way out."

I went over to one of two tables set with food. A dark-haired waiter asked me what I'd like. All that the various dishes had in common was that they were fashionable. There was sushi, crepes, antipasto, pasta salads, rolled sandwiches in pita bread, crudites, ham and smoked turkey, cheeses, and breads. I ate a bit of sushi. It wasn't fresh.

Beside me a woman said, "Stick to the raw vegetables."

I looked around. "Hello," I said.

The woman who had spoken to me smiled. She had a round, pretty face. Her dark hair was streaked with two colors, burgundy and red. She was not, perhaps, as young as she looked.

"You were in the play," I said. "You played Edward's wife."

"You came in with Larry Ross," she replied, helping herself to a radish.

"You know him?"

"Only by reputation. He's out of my league. Are you a lawyer, too?"

"Yes, but not that kind."

"Expensive?" She bit into the radish with preternaturally white teeth.

"No, entertainment. I practice criminal defense."

She drew in her cheeks a bit. "Who's in trouble?"

"I'm not here on business," I replied.

"Don't be absurd. Everyone here's on business. My name is Sarah."

"Henry," I replied. "You were very good as Anne."

"I hope you're a better lawyer than a critic," she said, examining a piece of cauliflower. Suddenly there was applause around the door. The Zanes entered with Sandy Blenheim hard on their heels. As they swept past me, Irene Gentry and I caught each other's eyes. She seemed to smile.

"The Macbeths," Sarah said, dryly. She dropped the unfinished radish back on the tray and joined the Zanes' entourage.

I turned my attention to Irene Gentry. In a black cocktail dress she moved across the room like an exclamation mark. Her long hair was swept over a bare shoulder. There were diamonds at her neck. Blenheim directed her and Tom Zane to a little group dominated by a white-haired man in a tweed jacket who was making a big show of lighting a meerschaum pipe. I moved closer to watch her. She laid a hand lightly on the man's wrist as he spoke and his shoulders seemed to inflate. Her husband, meanwhile, had backed himself against the wall with a pretty girl. Blenheim watched them for a moment, then broke them up and brought Zane back into the group.

I was standing behind the man to whom Irene Gentry was speaking. She looked past his shoulder at me. Our eyes met and her face formed a question. A moment later she excused herself and came over.

"I know you, don't I?" she asked in her famous voice.

"I wish I could say you did, Miss Gentry."

"My friends call me Rennie." She gazed at me intently and without embarrassment.

"Weren't you the lawyer for Jim Pears?" she asked.

"Yes. Henry Rios. How did you know that?"

She smiled. "Sandy was very interested in buying the rights to the story as a property for Tom. Didn't he approach you?"

"Yes," I replied, "but he didn't say who he was working for."

"Tom's his biggest client," she said, absently.

"Well," I replied, "I don't know anything about acting but your husband seems a bit old to play Jim Pears."

She seemed puzzled for a moment, then laughed. "I think the idea was for Tom to play you."

"Me?"

"The boy's lawyer," she replied. "Of course, we didn't know it was going to be you until we saw it on the news." She glanced around the room. "It's odd to find you here."

I explained that I had come with Larry Ross.

"Oh, Larry," she said. "He's our—" She looked at me, as if

for help. "Who was the Greek who carried the lamp looking for an honest man?"

"Diogenes," I replied, guessing that she'd known that all along.

She said, "I'm not making fun of him, Henry. I admire him. More now than ever."

I felt the heat rising to my face from my neck. "I don't understand."

She looked at me, tenderly. "Of course I know he's ill," she said. "We all know." Her glance swept across the room.

"He doesn't know that."

She laid her hand across my wrist. "He won't find out from me."

"Thank you."

"Did you enjoy the play?" she asked, dropping her hand, her voice light.

"Toward the end, especially."

"Not because you thought it was ending, I hope." She moved a bit closer. She smelled of roses.

"Your husband seemed to get his bearings in the second half."

"Tom's not a stage actor," she replied. "But on the whole I don't think he did too bad a job of it."

"You would have been perfect to play Anne."

Her smile was charming and wise. "Discretion is often the better part of marriage."

Her skin glistened, faintly, as if moistened by dew. I felt an overwhelming desire to touch her. I took her hand. "Do you mind?"

"Of course not," she replied, but then I suppose she was used to men wanting to touch her. "Tell me about Jim Pears. What will happen to him now?"

"The charges against him were dismissed," I said. "He'll never regain consciousness. Eventually, he'll die."

She studied me silently, then said, "You have the face of a man who feels too much."

As there was nothing to say to this, I said nothing.

She tugged at my hand. "Come and meet Tom."

Tom Zane stepped forward from the people he had been talking to and said to his wife, "You're trying to make me jealous."

This close, he looked to be in his mid-thirties. Small lines puckered the edges of his eyes and lips. His skin, still tanned, was faintly freckled. Clusters of broken veins had begun to surface around the edges of his nostrils, the sure sign of a drinker. He gave off the scent of an expensive cologne. His eyes were a deep, serene blue. Though he cast a blond's golden glow it was diluted by his hard, false cheerfulness.

Irene said, "Tom, this is Henry Rios. Jim Pears's lawyer."

Zane looked at me blankly for a moment, then said, "Oh, the gay kid. Sandy talked to you."

"Briefly."

Zane smiled. "You're too good-looking to be a lawyer. You look more like a wetback gigolo."

"I was at the play," I said, ignoring the comment. "Your last scenes were very moving."

"Or maybe a diplomat. Come on, Rennie," he said, and took her from me.

"Join us, Henry," she said, as her hand slipped from my fingers.

A circle of well-wishers formed around us and I stood at the edge of conversation as the Zanes received them. Irene — Rennie — handled them as skillfully as a politician and it appeared that she truly did not forget faces. Or names, or names of spouses, children, or dogs. She told funny stories on herself and listened to less funny stories which she made comic by her superbly timed reactions. Now and then, she'd lift her eyes and smile at me as if we shared a secret.

Tom Zane, on the other hand, seemed talented only at being admired. When he wasn't being praised he looked off with a vague smile to the other side of the room. He drank three glasses of champagne and was about to take a fourth when Sandy Blenheim intercepted it. Tom surrendered the glass with a shrug. He nibbled at a plate of food that Blenheim brought him. He seemed both bored and bewildered. I excused myself to look for Larry.

"Don't leave without saying goodbye," Rennie said.

"I won't."

Larry was talking to Tony Good, the actor who had played Gaveston. Tony Good was drunk. I complimented him on his performance.

"It's not easy playing against T. Z.," he said. "He's lousy. Who are you anyway?"

"Henry Rios," I said.

"Oh, yeah. Another gay lawyer? You're kinda cute, Henry. You gotta lover?" He reached for a glass of champagne from a passing waiter and tipped the tray, spilling the drinks on himself. The room was momentarily still.

"Shit," he said. A red jacket rushed over with a napkin and tried to dry Good's shirt. "Never mind the shirt," he said. "How about another drink."

Larry said, "You're drunk enough, Tony." To me he said, "I'm going to drive him home."

"Fine."

"Come on, Tony," Larry said. "It's time to go."

Tony Good smiled. "Will you tuck me in?"

"Not if you're still charging by the hour," Larry replied.

"Bitch," Tony said. To me he said, "You come, too. We'll make it a threesome."

"Another time," I said.

"Lemme give you my number," Tony said.

"I'm sure Larry has it," I said.

"No," Tony said. "Just take a minute." He scribbled a number on the back of a card that he fished out of his pocket and shoved it at me.

"Thanks," I said, accepting it.

"Call me," he shouted as Larry hustled him out the door.

Remembering the hangovers I got from champagne, I felt very sorry for Tony Good. I checked my watch; I had already overstayed the hour I had allowed myself. I looked around for Rennie to say goodbye, but neither she nor Zane were in the room. Sandy Blenheim was standing at the bar talking to the bartender. I approached them.

"Hello, Sandy," I said.

He glanced at me with annoyance. The bartender looked relieved and slipped away.

"Hi," he said. "Enjoying yourself?"

"The party's fine but I've got to go. I wondered if you'd say goodbye to Miss Gentry for me."

"Yeah, I saw you talking with her," he said. "You two know each other?"

"Not before tonight."

He picked up a tall glass from the bar and drank. When he set it down he wiped his mouth with the back of his hand. "What did you talk about?"

"This and that," I replied, disliking him.

"Yeah," he said. "You're gay, right?"

"I don't make a secret about it."

"Just making sure," he said. "Tom's the jealous kind."

Having seen Zane in action earlier with another woman, I doubted this, but said, "He has nothing to worry about from me."

"So," Sandy said, lowering his voice, "what are you doing later?"

I smiled. "I've got a date."

"And after that?"

"Just say goodbye to Rennie for me," I said.

"Sure," he replied, already losing interest. His glance drifted back to the bartender. "Hey, Nick, another drink."

On my way out I stopped at the men's room. As I stood at the urinal I heard the door open. When I went to wash my hands I found Tom Zane stooped over the marble counter that held the wash basins. He lifted his eyes to the mirror and saw me.

"It's the ambassador," he said. He inhaled a line of coke, straightened up, tilted his head back and sniffled. "Want some?"

"No thanks." I turned on the tap and ran my hands beneath the water. He did another line.

"Is that safe to do here?" I asked.

"Are you gonna tell?"

"No."

"Good." He did a third line and stood up, putting his arm

around my shoulder. "As long as you're not one of Sandy's spies."

"I'm not."

"He says you're gay. Is that right?"

"Yeah," I replied.

Zane dropped his arm to just above my waist and we looked at each other in the mirror. In the dim light he looked almost as he had in the last scene of the play: heroic, dissipated, and beautiful.

"We should get together sometime," he said.

Before I could think of an answer to this, the door opened again. He dropped his arm to his side and stepped away. I dried my hands. Sandy Blenheim came in, looked at us and scowled.

"Listen, T. Z., there's some important people out there wanting to meet you."

"Don't I get to take a leak?"

"What's he do," Blenheim said, pointing at me, "hold your dick?"

I said, "Looks to me like that's your job, Sandy."

"That's telling him, Ambassador."

"Come on, T. Z., you're wasting time." Blenheim grabbed Zane's arm and dragged him out.

I watched them go, then finished drying my hands. I looked at myself in the mirror. Zane's proposition hadn't meant anything more than Tony Good's or Sandy Blenheim's had. They were empty gestures, the kind it was beginning to seem that these people were full of. As I adjusted the knot in my tie, I tried to imagine Tom Zane as me, and burst out laughing.

— 15 —

The Hawk occupied a space in a row of stores between a deli and a manicurist. A blue awning over the entrance was the bar's only distinguishing feature. I parked on the street and made my way over to the bar. A couple of men in 501s and flannel shirts were standing at the entrance drinking from bottles of Budweiser. I was wearing a gray suit, a maroon tie, and wingtips. We exchanged friendly nods as I pushed through the upholstered door.

The front room was a long, narrow rectangle with the bar running the length of it. Opposite the bar, stacks of beer boxes were pushed up against the wall. The room was packed and there was only a small aisle between the men lined up against the bar and those leaning against the beer boxes. The place smelled of spilt beer and cigarettes and was lit in red by spotlights above the bar. Dolly Parton was belting out a song from the overhead speakers and everywhere mouths moved, singing along with her. I wedged my way down the room looking for Josh Mandel.

There was a pool room behind the bar. A green-shaded light hung over the pool table. A thin boy with a bad complexion waited while his opponent, a lumbering bear of a man, calculated a shot. Josh Mandel was sitting on a bar stool beneath a chalkboard that listed the order of players. He wore jeans and an old white button-down shirt and his glasses dangled out of his pocket. A red sweater was spread across his knees. He was smoking a cigarette with one hand while the other grasped a bottle of beer. He looked too young to be either smoking or drinking. I came around the room until I was standing beside him.

"Josh?"

He jerked his face toward me. "Mr. Rios."

"Henry," I replied. "I'm sorry I'm late."

"That's okay." He smiled at me. "You want a drink?"

"I don't drink. Is there somewhere quiet we can talk?"

"There's a patio out back," he said, and hopped off the bar stool. "Come on."

He led me out to a small fenced-in courtyard in the center of which was a big firepit. It was dark except for a couple of lights above the exit and the glow of the fire. We sat down on a bench beneath the feathery leaves of a jacaranda tree. Josh put on his glasses and the red sweater.

"I guess you figured out I'm gay," he said.

"I assume that's why you told me to meet you here."

He nodded. "You knew when you saw me in court the first time."

I remembered the odd jolt of recognition I'd felt that day when I had looked at him. I said, "I'm not sure. Maybe."

He finished his beer. A waiter came by and Josh asked for a screwdriver. I asked for mineral water.

"Did Jim know about you?" I asked.

"No one does," he said. "You probably think I should be more out."

"That's not my business."

"I just mean, you're out and everything."

"I learned pretty early on that I'm not a good liar. That's all there is to my being out."

He lowered his eyes. "It's not like I like lying," he said, softly.

"I didn't mean it that way."

"You don't have to like me, Henry," he said, suddenly. Our eyes met and I felt his sadness. Or maybe I felt my own. "You didn't come to talk about me, anyway. You want to know about Jim."

The waiter brought our drinks. I paid for them over Josh's protests. "What about him?"

He churned his drink with a straw. "It's something I found out after he tried to kill himself. I was hanging around the bar at the Yellowtail one night and the bartender asked me to dump the trash. He gave me the bar key to the back door. It was new."

"New?" I echoed.

"Uh-huh. I asked him what happened to the old one and he said it had disappeared months ago. The next day I went through work orders and stuff and I found this." He pulled his wallet out of his back pocket and extracted a piece of paper, handing it to me.

I examined it. It was a receipt from a locksmith for the making of a key. The receipt was dated less than a week after the night Brian Fox was murdered. I handed it back to Josh.

"You think the missing key has something to do with Brian's death?"

He folded the paper. "You'd need it to get out," he said.

I thought about this. "You think there was someone back there before Brian came in?"

He nodded.

"Kind of a strange coincidence," I said.

"There's a strongbox down in the manager's office," Josh said. "Someone could've cleaned it out and let himself out through the back door."

"A burglary?" I was interested, suddenly, in the missing key. "And Brian just happened to be there. Had the strongbox been tampered with?"

Josh shook his head. "That doesn't mean they didn't try." He shivered and pulled a pack of cigarettes from his shirt pocket. The fire cast a flickering light on his face.

"The problem is that they found Jim with the knife," I said. "There doesn't seem to be any way around that."

"Oh, that's right," he said too quickly and gulped his drink.

I looked at him. He hadn't asked me here to tell me about the key. Then why? To let me know about himself?

"Still," I said, "I'll have my investigator look into it."

"That skinny black guy?"

"Yes. Freeman Vidor. He talked to you, didn't he?"

Josh frowned. "Yeah. I'm going to get another drink. You want one?"

"No." He got up and started for the bar. "Josh," I said, "are you trying to get drunk?"

He sat down again and looked at me. "I could've told you about the key on the phone," he said, then added awkwardly, "I just really wanted to see you again."

I looked at him. "Why?"

"I've seen you before," he said.

"I beg your pardon?"

"Two years ago you gave a speech at a rally at UCLA against the sodomy law. Remember?"

"I gave so many speeches that year," I said apologetically.

He smiled. "I remember. Afterwards I came up and shook your hand." The smile faded and he looked at me gravely. "You gave me the courage to be who I am. But it didn't last."

"Few of us come out all at once," I said, gently. "It's not the easiest thing to do."

He shook his head and frowned. "I never came out at all."

"We are at a gay bar," I said.

"It's easy to come out in a bar," he said, "or in bed." A shadow crossed his face.

"Are you all right?"

He stared down at his hands and said, "No."

There was a lot of pain in the little word. He grabbed my hand, clutching it tightly.

"What is it, Josh?" I asked.

He drew a shaky breath. "My life's a lie," he said. "No one knows who I really am, not my friends or my folks. I can't live this way anymore."

Suddenly I thought of Jim Pears. "Don't say that," I said sharply.

He let go of my hand and looked away from me.

"I'm sorry," he said in a voice at the edge of tears. "I admire you so much. I wanted you to like me."

"I didn't mean to snap at you. It's just when you said you couldn't live this way, it made me think of Jim."

"If it wasn't for me, he would be all right," Josh said.

"You're taking the blame for a lot," I replied.

"If I'd told him I was gay—" he began.

"It wouldn't have made any difference," I said. "His denial was too deep."

Josh tipped his head back against the fence. The light from the doorway of the bar shone on his face and cast a sort of halo around his hair.

"Is that true?" he asked.

"Yes."

He inclined his face toward me. "But you still don't like me."

"You lied to me about where you were the night Brian was killed."

Someone dropped a glass and it shattered near the firepit.

"I wasn't anywhere near the restaurant," he said.

"But you didn't tell me the truth."

He rose from the bench and stood irresolutely. "I told you," he said, looking toward the bar. "My life's a lie."

He made a move to go.

"Wait," I said.

His look was disbelieving. "You want me to stay?"

"You asked me here to come out to me," I said. "That couldn't have been easy. I did a lot of harm to Jim by not listening to him. I don't want to make the same mistake with you."

He sat down.

"So," I continued, "you want to talk?"

He shook his head. "No, I want you to come home with me."

I smiled. "You need a friend, Josh, not another trick."

"It doesn't have to mean anything to you to mean something to me."

"That's not the point."

He touched my hand. "Are we really going to sit here and talk about this?

I looked up at him, saw my face reflected in his glasses and saw past my reflection into his eyes. A waiter came up and asked us if we wanted another drink.

"No," I said. "We're leaving."

☐

Josh lived in Hollywood on a decayed street lined alternately with boxy apartment buildings and little stucco houses whose front yards doubled as driveways. The squalor was softened by the big elm trees that lined the road and the wild rose bushes still putting forth their flowers four weeks before Christmas. I lowered my window as I followed his car down the street. Mariachi music blared from one of the houses where four men squatted on the front lawn guzzling beer. Lights were on in every house, though it was now near two in the morning.

Josh flicked his signal and turned into the carport of a two-storey apartment building. I pulled up along the curb and got out of my car. He met me at the sidewalk. It was cold. Behind us, in the Hollywood Hills, the lights flickered like distant stars. The big emptiness of the night was like a stage as we stood in the grainy light of a streetlamp looking at each other. In the darkness, I smelled jasmine.

"This is it," he said, nervously.

I put my arm around his shoulders, and felt the tension in his neck seep out as he leaned into me.

"You're cold," I observed, touching his face with the back of my hand.

"Let's go upstairs."

He led me around to a tall gate, through it, and up a concrete staircase to the second floor landing. "The place is kind of a mess," he said, unlocking the door.

He held the door open for me. The room I found myself in was, in fact, quite tidy. There was a fake Oriental rug on a fake parquet floor. A shabby couch flanked by two sling armchairs, and a glass-topped coffee table furnished the place. One wall was taken up by wooden bookshelves crammed with books. A stereo and a small TV were set on a couple of orange crates filled with records.

Josh stood beside me. "Can I get you something to drink?"

"No, thank you."

"Excuse me, then," he said, and went into a small kitchen.

The far wall was curtained. I went over and lifted the curtains, revealing a small patio behind a sliding glass door. I sat down on the couch. There was a fish bowl filled with change on the coffee table and next to it a photograph in a heavy bronze frame. The photograph showed a handsome middle-aged couple, two pretty girls, and a smiling Josh. He came back into the room holding a glass of milk.

"Your family?"

He nodded and sat down beside me. "My dad's a CPA," he said.

"Where do they live?"

"Sherman Oaks." He set the glass down on the table. "Are you comfortable?"

I loosened my tie.

Smiling faintly, Josh asked, "Is that as relaxed as you get?"

"It's been a long time."

"For me, too," he said. "I don't want you to think I spend all my time at bars or anything."

"I know."

"This feels like the first time for me," he said, then smiled nervously. "That's the wrong thing to say, isn't it?"

I held him. "No," I said. "My first time was almost twenty years ago. We thought we had invented love."

He kissed me. His mouth tasted of milk and his skin beneath my fingers was smooth and firm. He drew back and unknotted my tie, sliding it from my collar, and unbuttoned my shirt. I removed my jacket and tossed it aside. Sinking into the couch, I pulled him against me.

"What happened to him?" Josh asked.

"To whom?"

"Your first time."

"She got married."

He lifted his head and looked at me. "It was a girl?"

"Yes," I replied.

"Were you gay?"

"I've always been gay, Josh. I just happened to be in love with a girl." I kicked off my shoes and smiled at him. "You can't always specialize."

His dark eyes were unhappy. "Do you still go out with them?"

"Women? No," I said. "She was the only one."

He smiled. "That cuts down the competition."

"Don't worry about that. It's a buyer's market."

"We'll see," he said with a lewd flicker in his eyes.

Some time later we lay on the couch, facing each other, our clothes discarded, bodies touching.

I watched my face form in Josh's eyes. "You called me the night Jim tried to kill himself," I said.

He was surprised. "How did you know it was me?"

"Just a feeling. I wish you hadn't hung up."

"I lost my nerve," he replied and smiled. "Are you tired?"

I pressed him against me. "In a minute."

☐

It was cold. I opened my eyes and found that Josh had rolled himself into the blankets and now slept contentedly at the edge of the narrow bed. A light shone from beneath the bathroom door. He had carefully arranged my suit on a chair, leaving his own clothes in a little pile beside it. I gently unwound the blankets from him and lay against his back, putting my arm across his chest. He smelled of sweat and soap and semen. I lowered my hand to his firm belly, cupped his genitals and laid my hand, finally, between his thighs. He moved his head a fraction and I knew he was awake. He pressed his rump against my groin. I raised my hand along his torso to his nipples and grazed them with my palm. He sighed and pushed harder.

"Do you want to?" he whispered.

I raised myself on my elbow and said, "Of course I do, but I haven't carried rubbers with me since I was sixteen."

"Just this once," he said. "You could pull out before — you know."

I squeezed his neck between my fingers. "No," I said softly. "There's AIDS, Josh. It's not worth the risk."

Abruptly he drew away to the edge of the bed and lay on his back, looking at the darkness.

"I didn't mean that the way it sounded," I said.

"I know what you meant," he said in a flat voice. "You're right. It's not worth it."

He drew himself rigidly apart from me as if daring me to make a move across the channel of darkness between us.

"That's not what I meant at all," I said, reaching for him. He jerked away. "I said it didn't have to mean anything to you, Henry."

I lay back in the bed. "You've been awfully rough on yourself tonight, Josh. I'd like to know why."

"Does it really matter to you?" he asked, more in pain than defiance.

But I had long ago stopped issuing blank checks on my emotions and I waited a moment too long to answer.

"That's what I thought," he said.

"What's this about, Josh?"

Instead of answering, he turned away and quietly began to weep.

— 16 —

When he stopped crying, I asked, "Does this have anything to do with Jim?"

"Please hold me," Josh said. I moved myself against him and took him in my arms, feeling the dull thud of his heart against my ribs. "I don't want to talk now."

I opened my mouth to speak but thought better of it. After a few minutes, Josh slipped into sleep. A long time later, I did, too.

When I woke Josh was standing beside me, dressed in jeans and a UCLA sweatshirt. He squinted at me through his glasses. It was plain that he was seeing a stranger.

"I'll make you some breakfast," he said, politely.

"Coffee will be fine."

He nodded and left. I stretched my neck, shaking off the little aches that seemed to accumulate there as I got older, wiping the sleep from my eyes. The bathroom was steamy and smelled of Josh. A thin, suspicious face formed in the mirror. Deepening lines and graying hair foretold the coming of middle-age, what the French called — ironically, in my case — the age of discretion. I rinsed my mouth, showered, put on the clothes I had worn the night before, and followed the smell of coffee into the kitchen.

Josh stood at the stove scrambling eggs. He looked at me and said, "You should eat something."

"Whatever you're having." I poured coffee into a mug from Disneyland and leaned against the counter, watching him.

"Do you ever stop thinking?" he asked.

"I did last night," I replied. He stirred the eggs savagely.

"Lowered your standards, you mean."

"That's not what I mean."

"Don't worry about it." He shut off the flame beneath the skillet and faced me.

"What were you going to tell me last night?"

"Nothing."

I set my cup on the counter. "We shouldn't start out by lying to each other."

He jammed his hands into his pockets. "Sometimes I don't think there is any love, just a kind of envy." He looked at me. "I want to be who you are. What do you want from me, to be twenty-two again?"

"I think I'd better be on my way," I said.

He started to say something but then simply nodded. I let myself out. I told myself I didn't want to buy into his troubles, but I felt heavier going down the steps than I had coming up.

☐

There was a black Mercedes parked in front of Larry's house. The plate read GLDNBOY. I pulled into the driveway and went into the house. Tom Zane, Irene Gentry, and Sandy Blenheim were sitting in the big front room with Larry. The coffee table was littered with papers, coffee cups, and empty glasses. A half-empty bottle of Old Bushmill's sat near an ashtray filled with cigarette butts.

"Excuse me," I said.

Larry gave me a look that made me acutely aware that I was in the same clothes I had worn the night before. "I think you know everyone," he said.

"Looks like someone got lucky last night," Zane said.

"I don't mean to interrupt," I said, and headed up the stairs without looking back. I changed clothes and called Freeman Vidor. He was surprised to hear from me.

"Read about you in the paper today," he said. "D.A. dumped the Pears case."

"Justice triumphs again," I replied. Downstairs someone burst into loud laughter.

"You don't sound like a happy man."

From the window I watched shadows of clouds gather on the surface of Silver Lake. "It wasn't exactly an acquittal."

"He wasn't exactly innocent."

"There's something I'd like you to look into."

"We still talking about Pears?"

"Yes."

"I don't do *pro bono*," he said.

"I'll pay you the same rate we originally agreed on."

"Go ahead."

I told him about the missing bar key.

"That's it?" His voice was incredulous. "You think someone broke in, slashed the Fox kid and left the knife in Pears's hand?"

"I'm less interested in the bar key than I am in Josh Mandel," I replied after a moment's hesitation.

"What does that mean?"

"I think he's concealing information about the case," I replied. "I'd like you to find out what it is without approaching him."

"I'm an investigator, Henry, not a psychic."

There was more laughter from downstairs. "Then do what you have to do," I replied.

"What do you think he knows?"

"I have no idea," I said, irritably. "That's what I'm hiring you to find out."

"Uh-huh. You don't want to talk to him because, why? You think he'll run or ... " The sentence trailed off.

"I slept with him last night."

Vidor said, "I'm glad I'm not your boyfriend."

"Go to hell."

"I'll be in touch," he replied. I set the phone down with a clang.

I was lying on the bed flipping through the pages of a mystery called *The Vines of Ferrara*. As I began the same paragraph for the fifth time, my attention wandered to the wall where, inexplicably, the shadows of the tree outside the window reminded me of Josh Mandel. That and everything else. What was this? Second adolescence? I picked up the book again and examined the cover.

There was a knock at the door. Expecting Larry, I hollered, "Come in."

Irene Gentry stepped in. I hopped off the bed, buttoning my shirt.

"Sit down, Henry," she said. She wore a suit in winter whites tailored to her body. It was quite a good body. "Do you mind if we visit for a while?"

"Of course not. Here," I said, bringing a chair up to the bed. "Sit down."

She arranged herself in the chair and extracted a silver cigarette case from her pocket. "May I?"

"Let me find you an ashtray." The best I could do was the soap dish from the bathroom. I held it out to her. She smiled and set it at the edge of the bed.

She puffed on her cigarette like a stevedore and said, finally, "I hate Sandy Blenheim."

"Any reason in particular?"

"It's so obvious that Tom's nothing to him but a meal ticket." She stubbed out her cigarette. "He pushes Tom to take whatever crap's offered to him. Anything to bring in money." She paused and looked at me. "I suppose you wonder what Tom is to me."

"It's not my business to wonder that."

She smiled without amusement. "I'll tell you anyway, Henry, since you're bound to hear rumors. I love him."

In the musty stillness of the room, the words were startlingly clear. Rennie studied my face and said, "You seem surprised."

"I'm sorry if I do."

"We all love according to our natures," she continued. "You, of all people, should understand that."

"I don't doubt you," I replied.

"Scoot over," she said, and kicked off her shoes. She climbed up on the bed beside me. "Larry says you're from San Francisco."

"Close enough," I replied, and explained that I actually lived in a small university town on the peninsula.

"Linden University? Did you go to school there?"

"Yes."

"That's wonderful," she replied, shifting her weight so that our bodies touched. "The closest I ever came to higher education was doing summer stock in Ann Arbor."

I put my arm around her. Today she smelled faintly of lilac.

"May I ask you something?" she said, tipping her face toward mine.

"Sure."

"Are you and Larry lovers?"

"No," I replied.

"Oh," she said perplexed. "I thought that's why you were here, to take care of him."

Since she had told me she knew Larry was sick, it didn't seem worth being evasive. "Larry's not the type to allow himself to be taken care of."

"You don't seem the type either," she said. "Frankly — and I don't mean this badly — that always surprises me in gay men. They often seem so needy."

"Larry and I are just the other extreme," I replied. "It's a kind of psychological machismo. Not really much better than being constantly in need, when you get right down to it."

"And then there's Sandy," she said, her shoulders stiffening. "He defies types. I wish I knew why Tom keeps him around." She relaxed and said, "Is it really true that you don't need anyone?"

Perhaps because I had been thinking of Josh, the question tugged at my guts.

She must have seen it in my face. "Have I touched a sore spot?" she asked gently.

"It's just that I met someone."

"Last night?"

I nodded.

She closed her hand around mine. "Then shouldn't you be happy?"

"I don't think it's going to work out."

"The unlikeliest matches do, you know," she murmured. Someone shouted her name from downstairs.

"Time to go," she said, swinging her legs over the edge of the bed. "Will you come and have lunch with me day after tomorrow?"

"I'd love to," I replied.

She put her shoes on, stood up and staightened her skirt. "Good, make it around noon. Larry can tell you where I live." She leaned over and kissed my cheek. "He's a fool if he lets you go," she said.

"Larry?"

"You know who I mean. Goodbye, Henry."

"Goodbye, Rennie," I replied and listened as she made her way down the stairs. I got up and went to the window. The Zanes were getting into the black Mercedes, Tom in front and Rennie in back. Sandy Blenheim got into the driver's seat. Sandy Blenheim was Gldnboy? Only in Hollywood, I thought, and watched as the car pulled away.

A few minutes later, Larry came in.

"They're gone," he announced, pacing the room.

"I heard them leave. I thought you weren't taking new clients."

He sat down. "I'm not. That was just a little consulting."

"It looked like the IBM litigation to me."

He picked up the soap dish that Rennie had used as an ashtray and lifted an eyebrow. "You and Mrs. Zane have a nice chat?"

"I like her," I said, taking exception to his tone.

"That's allowed, I suppose."

"You don't?"

He stood up and paced to the doorway of the study. "In this business it doesn't pay to like anyone very much." He ran his hand across a dusty bureau.

"That's very cynical," I said.

He smiled at me, wiping his dusty fingers on his trousers. "Are you going to tell me where you spent the night?"

"With Josh Mandel," I said, amazed at how lightly I was able to speak his name.

"The waiter-witness?" Larry asked. "That's a surprise."

"To me, too," I replied, not wanting to pursue it.

"Doesn't the canon of ethics proscribe screwing witnesses? Except on the witness stand, I mean."

"There is no case," I snapped.

"Sorry," he said. He looked at me. "Was it that good, Henry?"

"Can we talk about something else?"

"Evidently, it was," he said as if to himself. "Forgive me, I'm just jealous."

"You needn't be," I replied. "I don't expect I'll be seeing him again."

He sat at the foot of the bed. "I'm sorry," he said firmly. "I'm being a bitch." He held out his hand to me. "Friends?"

I took his hand and smiled. "Friends."

"Let me take you to lunch."

"Okay."

He stood up and looked around. "I haven't been up here in a long time," he said. "Never did like this room. Come get me when you're ready."

Only after he left did I remember that his lover, Ned, had killed himself here.

— 17 —

It was one of those winter days in Los Angeles when the wind has swept away the smog and the air is clear and the light still and everything has the immediacy of a dream. I parked on a street called Overland in the Hollywood Hills. It was lined with white-skinned birch trees. Their nude branches shimmered against the sky. Tattered yellow leaves clogged the gutters and the air was scented with the rainy smell of eucalyptus. There were no cars on the street and the houses were barely visible behind walls and fences and sweeping lawns that had never been trod upon except by gardeners.

I pressed the intercom button on a white wall. A moment later Rennie asked, "Henry?"

"Yes, it's me."

"You're on time," she observed.

"A bad habit of mine."

There was a buzz and I pushed a wooden door and found myself in a courtyard paved with cobblestones and lined with pots that bore flowering plants and miniature fruit trees. I crossed to the house, where a door formed of planks opened. Rennie stood in the doorway. Her hair was pulled back from her head. She wore black pants and a loose silk blouse the color of the sky. Three strands of pearls hung around her neck.

"Come inside," she said, after kissing me lightly on the lips.

We entered a long rectangular room. The ceiling was crossed with beams of rough pine. The walls were blindingly white and the tiled floor the color of dried roses. The furniture was Mexican country antiques. Over the fireplace was one of

Diego Rivera's lily paintings. Above a long sofa was a tapestry that looked like a Miro. A big round crystal vase on a table held a dozen long-stemmed white roses and stalks of eucalyptus.

"Lunch is almost ready," she said. "How about a drink?"

"Mineral water," I replied.

She went to a bar and poured a glass of Perrier and a small sherry and brought them to the sofa where I was sitting. I took the Perrier from her. She settled in beside me.

"*Salud,*" she said, and we touched glasses. "I'm glad you came."

"So am I," I said. In the silence she seemed distant. I tried to think of things to say and settled, finally, on admiring her house.

"Thank you," Rennie replied. "It's my weakness. I bought it ten years ago with the only money I ever made in Hollywood."

"From movies?"

She laughed. "Oh, no. Real estate investments. I never made a cent out of the movies."

Just then, a squat Mexican woman in a lime-green frock appeared at the archway that led into the dining room and said, "Señora, lunch is ready."

"Thank you, Fe," Rennie said, and turning to me added, "It's so gorgeous out, I thought we'd eat on the patio."

She led me through the dining room onto a patio built around a small pool. The pool was fed by a stream that trickled from a concrete wall set into a hillside garden. Near the pool was a table set for two.

"Your husband?" I asked.

"He's at an interview," she said nervously. "He may show up later."

We sat down and I looked at her. The light picked out the lines that fanned from beneath her eyes. She looked tired.

"Is everything all right?" I asked.

"I'm sorry, Henry," she replied. "It has nothing to do with you. There was a scene with Sandy this morning."

"About what?"

"What else, Tom's career." The maid brought out salads and set them before us, a mix of sweet and bitter greens. She lifted her fork, then put it down again. "Tom is an actor who can't act," she said. "My solution is for him to learn. Sandy's solution is for him to make all the money he can before he's found out."

The maid reappeared and poured Rennie a glass of wine. I shook my head as she tipped the bottle toward my glass.

"What's Tom's solution?" I asked, cutting a piece of lettuce.

"It depends on who talked to him last," she replied, grimly.

"Who's been responsible for his success?"

"He has," she said, abandoning any pretense at eating. She produced her cigarette case and lit a cigarette. "Some people are just so beautiful that life seems to speak to us through them — they're vital, radiant. Tom is like that. It's more startling in men than women, I think, because we don't usually let ourselves think of men that way. But Shakespeare knew. Remember the sonnets? 'Shall I compare thee to a summer's day,' was written to another man."

"Golden boy?" I offered.

"Something like that." The maid removed our salad plates and replaced them with plates of spinach pasta in a cream sauce. "I'm a fool for beautiful men," she added. "No doubt there are psychological explanations."

"To appreciate beauty?"

"It's more than that," she replied, tilting her head back to reveal the pouched skin beneath her chin. "I always wanted to be beautiful."

I began to speak but she cut me off.

"Don't say it, Henry. I'm not fishing for a compliment." She crushed her cigarette in a heavy marble ashtray. "I'm forty-seven years old. I look into the mirror and see my mother. When a woman reaches that point, she loses whatever illusions she has about being beautiful."

"Is it so important?"

She finished her wine. "It's life and death," she replied, "if you're not. You, of course, are."

I couldn't think of a reply that didn't sound wildly immodest or incredibly smug. "Thank you."

"You're embarrassed," she said, smiling.

"It's not something I think about."

"I thought homosexuals did," she said.

"I suppose that depends on which homosexuals you know," I replied.

The maid made another pass at the table, pouring more wine, bringing us plates of veal and baby carrots.

I heard tires squeal and then a door in the house slammed shut. The maid appeared with a frantic look on her face.

"Señora—" she began.

Rennie looked at her and then at me. "Henry, Tom's—"

Suddenly Tom Zane appeared at the doorway, drinking from a bottle of champagne. His face was flushed beneath his tan and his golden hair was disheveled.

"It's the ambassador," he said, recognizing me. "And, of course, my lovely wife."

He swayed above the table. The maid brought him a chair.

"Sorry I missed lunch," he slurred. "How's about a little apres-lunch drinky." He attempted to pour champagne into Rennie's wine glass. She moved it away and the champagne sloshed onto the table. He blotted it with the sleeve of his coat.

"I think you better eat something," Rennie said mildly and told the maid to bring him a sandwich.

"It's all right. I ate breakfast." He had trouble getting his mouth around the last word. The maid brought him a ham sandwich. He wolfed it down and asked for another.

"How was the interview?" I asked.

"The reporter was a dyke," he said. "She spent the whole goddamn time giving the eye to some broad at the next table." He looked genuinely injured as he related this. Another sandwich was brought to him.

"Was Sandy there?" Rennie asked.

"Hell," he said, his mouth full. "He was after the busboy. This town's a regular Sodom ... Sodom and..." He looked at me for help.

"Gomorrah," I said.

"That's right, gonorrhea. You ever had the clap, Ambassador?"

I shook my head.

"Smart man," he said. "Keep your peter in your pocket. But you're queer, huh?"

Rennie said, "Tom, stop that."

"It's okay," Zane said. "I'm a little queer myself." He held up his hand and measured an inch between his thumb and forefinger. "Maybe this much." He shone a beautiful smile on me. "Maybe more."

"I think all people are basically bisexual," Rennie said, irrelevantly.

"That right?" Zane asked. "You ever made it with a dyke, honey?"

"You know I haven't," she replied.

"What about you, Ambassador? You fuck girls, too?" He looked at me, smiling. "I bet you're not even a real queer. I bet it's just a line. Does it work?"

"All the time," I replied.

He lowered his voice to a stage whisper. "You try it with Rennie?"

Rennie said, sharply, "You're drunk, Tom, and you're embarrassing my guest. Stop it."

He attempted a smile that withered under her gaze. "Io me he said, "Sorry. Too much to drink." He rose, stumblingly, from the table. "I need some sleep. Excuse me." He looked at Rennie who was lighting a cigarette. "I'm just tired, honey."

"I know," she said. "It's all right."

His face relaxed into a grin and he made his way into the house.

Rennie looked at me and shrugged. "Tom drinks too much," she said.

"I see that."

"There's nothing I can do about it."

"Probably not."

We talked for a few more minutes but it seemed her attention was wandering toward the direction of the house. I got up and excused myself. She walked me to the door.

"I'm sorry about all this," she said. "Can I see you again?"

"Of course," I replied. "Any time."

She kissed me and I headed across the courtyard to the street.

I had just opened the door to my car when I heard my name being called. I looked back at Rennie's house. Tom Zane was hurrying toward me.

"Let's go somewhere," he said. His breath was eighty proof.

"What are you talking about?"

"Come on, let's just go."

Rennie had appeared at the gate.

"You need to sleep it off," I said.

"Yeah, but not here."

I looked back at Rennie. Her arms were folded across her chest. She lifted her hand and waved at me. I looked at Tom. It would probably be a favor to her to take him away.

"Where to?"

"My house. On the beach."

"Get in," I said.

He got in and scooted across the driver's seat to the passenger side.

"Where are we going?"

"Malibu," he said.

Rennie had gone back into the house. I started up the car, made a U-turn and headed down to Sunset. By the time I got there Tom was asleep.

— 18 —

When we reached the ocean, I woke him.

"Where do I go from here?"

He sat up and got his bearings. "Right on the Coast Highway. Wake me up again when we get to Malibu." He shut his eyes and went back to sleep.

The blue sea glittered in the deep light of the winter afternoon. A few surfers in black wetsuits paddled out into the water and rode the slow waves back in, like children who dared the sea by wading a few feet into the surf and running back.

We reached Malibu, a strip of fast food places, surf shops, and bars. I woke Tom. He directed me off the highway down a narrow two-lane road that cut between meadows where horses grazed in the shade of big oaks. Here the light had a nimbus of gold and poured like a stream through the silty air. Tom had me turn down a dirt driveway to a small stucco house hidden from the road by a row of overgrown Italian cypresses. He stretched and opened the door.

"What's this?" he asked, picking up a card from beneath his leg. I glanced at it. It was the card that Tony Good had given me with his phone number.

"An admirer," I said.

He inspected the card, tossed it aside and got out of the car. I followed him to the door of the house. He fumbled with some keys and then let us in.

The living and dining rooms were combined into a single space. There was a counter along one wall, revealing the kitchen. A corridor led off from the main room to bedrooms and bathrooms. The place smelled of old fires and the fireplace held the charred remains of the last logs burned in it. The concrete floor was covered by threadbare carpets. A few sticks of old furniture were scattered haphazardly through the room. On the whole, the house was dark, chilly and quiet.

"Tom looked at me and grinned. "What do you think?"

"Not exactly what I expected."

"I like to be comfortable. Rennie's house is like a museum." His nap had sobered him up. I said as much.

"Booze doesn't have a big effect on me," he said as if he believed it. "It's warmer outside."

We went into the kitchen. He opened the refrigerator and pulled out a half-full bottle of Chardonnay. He led me outside to a covered patio. Weightlifting equipment was lying here and there, as were pieces of driftwood, sea shells, empty bottles of wine and beer. A bike leaned against a wall next to a battered surfboard and a wetsuit. A jock strap hung from a nail above a pile of firewood. Tom sat down on a canvas chair and invited me to pull up a chair next to him.

"I should get back to L.A.," I said.

"You can stay for a little while."

I pulled up a chaise longue and sat. An orange cat appeared at the far end of the yard and watched us.

"That your cat?"

"Only when she's hungry." He took a swallow of wine and passed the bottle.

"I don't drink."

"Never?"

"I'm an alcoholic."

Tom grinned at the cat and said, "Isn't that the point?"

The cat loped across the yard and came to the edge of the patio. She yawned and began to groom herself with quick, fastidious flicks of her tongue. Tom leaned forward, pulled off his blue polo shirt, and then sank back into his chair. His skin was as tawny as the little cat's fur. Even at rest, his elegant muscles seemed to quiver. He was kin to the little calico licking her paws at the edge of the patio; a great golden cat. He rolled his head toward me, lazily, and sketched the faintest smile at the corners of his lips. I imagine Narcissus had watched that smile form on the surface of a lake.

"It's quiet here," I said, to say something. "You come here to think."

"Thinking's not what I do best. That's Sandy's job. All my brains are in my face."

"Rennie doesn't much like Sandy," I observed.

He smiled distantly. "Sandy's all right. He knows what I am."

"And what's that?"

"A hustler," he replied. "Like Gaveston. You don't need brains to be a whore. Just a little luck and good timing."

"Rennie must see something else in you."

His face seemed to darken. "She knows, too," he said, then added, mockingly, "but she forgives me." He picked up his wine bottle and drank some more. "Poor Rennie," he muttered. "She brought me out here to shove me in the face of every producer who ever told her that she didn't have the looks to be a star. I've got the looks," he said, more to the cat than to me.

"She thinks she can turn you into an actor."

He set the wine bottle between his legs. "Who the hell cares."

"You did the play."

"I knew a guy like Edward," he said, lifting the bottle and drinking. "Someone I met in the joint." He studied my face and grinned. "Don't look so surprised, you're a lawyer — don't you know an ex-con when you see one?"

"Not always."

He tossed the empty bottle at the cat. She scampered but it caught her broadside. With a shriek, she hopped into the underbrush.

"I knew this guy," he continued, "only he wasn't a king, more like a queen, understand? A real lady." He laughed. "She was pretty and proud, like Edward."

"Were you lovers?"

He lurched forward in his chair. "Hell, no. I was just a punk trying not to get raped in the showers." He looked at me. "That's another story. But this queen was married to this big white dude."

"What happened to her?"

"The niggers got her," he said. "Beat the shit out of her, raped her, just to get back at her old man. She walked around for days like she had a broken bottle up her ass. Her old man didn't want her anymore. He said she led the niggers on. She never complained, never said anything bad about anyone." He stroked his chest, fitfully. "She just bought some pills and went to sleep."

"Suicide?" I asked.

"Yeah," he said, looking at me. "Like that kid you were defending. What's his name, Pears."

"He wasn't successful," I replied.

"That's a shame," Tom said. "I'd kill myself before I went back to the joint."

"What were you in for?"

"Being young and dumb," he said. "I'm going to get some more wine." He stood up.

"I've got to get back into town," I said, also standing. "You want a ride?"

"What's your hurry?" he asked, moving toward me. "You don't think I brought you out here just to talk?"

He unbuttoned my shirt and laid his hand against my chest. I stepped away. His hand dropped to his side.

"Don't you want me?" he asked.

"I wouldn't much like myself afterwards."

"That doesn't matter."

"It does to me."

He looked at me and then yawned. "You don't know what you just turned down."

"I think I do," I replied and walked away.

□

I pulled out of the long, dusty driveway and Tom's house disappeared behind the screen of trees. I rolled down the windows and the air poured in, blowing the card with Good's number across the seat to the floor. At the traffic light, I picked up the card and examined the drunken scrawl. There wasn't much to choose between Tom Zane and Tony Good, I thought, remembering Good's come-on at the party.

"You're kinda cute, Henry. You got a lover?"

No, that's what Josh Mandel said over the telephone the night Jim tried to kill himself. I looked up at the light as it flashed from red to green. That seemed wrong. Even drunk, Josh would never have said something as obvious as that. I crossed the intersection and merged into the traffic on the Coast Highway. And then I remembered something. There had been three calls that night. I had answered two of them. The third caller hung up before I could reach the phone. A car horn blared behind me. I glanced at the speedometer and saw that I had slowed to twenty. But my mind was racing, and, suddenly, I understood.

☐

I stopped at the first phone I could find, which was in a bar called "Land's End." The receptionist at the Yellowtail informed me that Josh had called in sick and would give me neither his prognosis nor his home phone number. According to information, his number was unlisted. The cheerful male voice that gave me this data was sympathetic but would also not give me his number. The next call I made was to Freeman Vidor.

"I tried to call you," Freeman said, after the preliminaries. "That Mandel kid has run off."

"What do you mean, run off?" I asked, pressing a hand against my ear to drown out the background whine of Tammy Wynette.

"Hey," Freeman said impatiently. "He's gone, man."

"You're sure?" A thin woman in a halter and blue jeans smiled at me suggestively from her bar stool. I looked away.

"He was going to meet me this morning to tell me about that key," Freeman said. "He didn't show. The restaurant said he called in sick."

"Yeah, I talked to them." The halter had moved herself back into my line of vision. She gave me the finger.

"I went over to his place and looked around."

"You broke in, you mean."

"Whatever," Freeman said.

I glanced at my watch. "I want you to meet me at his apartment in about a half-hour."

"You don't believe me," he said, with mock offense.

"There might be a clue to where he's gone."

Now, truly offended, Freeman said, "You think I wouldn't pick up on that?"

"It's not just what you see," I said. "It's what you know."

"If you think screwing the guy gives you better insight—" Freeman began.

"I'm sorry, Freeman. I want to look around for myself, okay?"

"It's your money," he said, unmollified. "Thirty minutes."

"Right."

On my way out, the halter stopped me. She was drunk. Even in the black and red bar light she looked bad. "You talking to your boyfriend, honey?" she sneered.

"That's about the size of it," I answered.

— 19 —

Driving back from Malibu I got caught in a traffic jam on Sunset just west of UCLA and arrived at Josh's apartment twenty minutes late. Freeman was leaning over the railing on the second floor landing tipping cigarette ash into a potted plant. When he saw me, he made a show of consulting his Rolex.

"Traffic," I explained, coming up the stairs.

The door to the apartment was open. "And here I thought you were just being fashionably late."

"Is anyone home?" I asked, indicating the door.

"Come in and see for yourself," he said, and led the way. As soon as we stepped in, he disappeared into the kitchen. A moment later he came back with a bottle of beer. "You go ahead," he said. "I'll take notes."

There was a cigarette butt in the ashtray on the coffee table. Not a Winston, Josh's brand, but a Merit — what Freeman smoked. Otherwise the living room looked just as it had two nights earlier. Freeman followed me into the bedroom. The bed had been hastily thrown together, a blue blanket slipping to the floor beneath a red comforter, but this looked to be its normal condition. I sat down and examined the contents of the night stand. They consisted of a paperback edition of *Siddhartha*, fourteen pennies, a pack of matches from the Yellowtail, and an empty water glass smudged with fingerprints, some of them, doubtless, mine.

Freeman picked up the book and said, "I never could get into this."

"You just weren't a hippie."

"Can't say that I was," Freeman agreed pleasantly.

I went through the bureau. The sock and underwear drawers were cleaned out but another drawer held a few shirts. A couple of other shirts hung in the closet along with some slacks and a herringbone sportscoat.

"He plans to come back," I said.

"Good sleuthing," Freeman replied, behind me.

I walked into the bathroom. A moment later I came back out into the bedroom smiling.

"Don't tell me," Freeman said. "He's in the shower just like Bobby Ewing."

"He took his dirty laundry with him."

"Huh?"

"His dirty laundry. It was in a hamper in the bathroom. The hamper's empty."

Freeman took a slow swallow of beer, brought the bottle down and smiled. "He's gone home to his mama," he said.

◻

It was a quiet house on an unremarkable suburban street. I brought my car to a stop and looked at the place. Above it, the enormous, urban sky was darkening as sunset broke apart like colored smoke and drifted upward to where a few stars already shone. The house's stucco facade was faced with beams of polished wood, giving it a vaguely Elizabethan look. In the yard, a big willow trickled yellow leaves. I got out of my car and walked to the door. A small, dark-haired woman with a face shaped like a heart responded to my knocking.

"Mrs. Mandel?"

"Yes," she said, her forehead worried.

"Is Josh here?"

"No," she lied. "Who are you?"

"I'm his friend," I said. "Please, I have to see him."

"Really," she began, but a hand appeared on the edge of the door above her head and pulled the door back. Josh was wearing his red sweater.

"It's okay, Mom," he said. "This is just my friend, Henry."

"Can I talk to you Josh?"

"Come on in," Josh said.

He led me back to a big, well-lit room that smelled of furniture polish and rosewood. A pot of yellow chrysanthemums matched the blaze in the fireplace. The television was tuned to a football game and there was a bowl of popcorn on the seat of the armchair from which Josh had been watching the game. Mrs. Mandel had followed us into the room.

"Mom, we need to talk alone."

"Joshua, who is this man?"

"I told you, he's my friend. He's here to help me. Right, Henry?"

"Yes." I looked at Mrs. Mandel. "I'm a lawyer, Mrs. Mandel. I'm working on the Jim Pears case. Are you familiar with it?"

"That was the boy at the restaurant."

"I'm his lawyer. I need to ask Josh a few questions."

She looked back and forth at us. "I'll make you some tea," she said, decisively.

"Thank you."

She fluttered out of the room, closing the door behind her.

"She seems nice," I told Josh.

"She is," he replied and looked at me stonily. "How did you find me?"

"This is the third house I've been to," I replied. "There are a lot of Mandels in Sherman Oaks."

He tried not to smile.

"Why didn't you go meet Freeman?"

"You think I killed Brian, don't you?"

I drew a deep silent breath and asked, "Did you?"

There was a lot working on Josh's face. I was relieved to see that most of it was anger. "No," he snapped.

"I believe you, Josh."

"To hell with what you believe, Henry."

It was only when he dropped into an armchair that I realized we'd both been standing. I sat down on the sofa. He stuck his hand into the cushions and brought up a grungy pack of Winstons. He lit one.

"Tell me where you were the night Brian was killed."

He blew a shaky smoke ring with all the nonchalance of a ten-year-old and said, "I was with someone."

"Who?"

"Am I supposed to remember all their names?"

"Stop it, Josh. I know you're not like that."

"Doug," he said. "He lives in a split-level condo on King's Road and he has a hot tub on his deck. We sat in the hot tub and drank a bottle of wine and then he fucked me." He glared at me.

"Is that the terrible secret you wouldn't tell me the other night?"

"Don't talk down to me," he said, his fingers quivering. "And no, that's not the terrible secret. Does it really matter to you?"

This time I knew the right answer. "Yes," I said.

He put the cigarette out and all the hardness slipped from his face. "Three months ago I got this little rash at the base of my — penis," he said. "I panicked. I was sure it was AIDS, so I ran out and took the antibody test. The rash was just a rash — going too long without wearing shorts or something. But the test came back positive."

"You know that test isn't completely accurate," I said, to cover the sudden pounding in my ears. "And anyway it only means you've been exposed to the virus, not that you'll get AIDS." My heart slowed down. "Half the gay men in California test positive."

"Did you take the test?" Josh asked, glaring at me.

"Yes."

"Did you test positive?"

"No," I said, but added, "There are false negatives, too, Josh."

"Is that supposed to make me feel better?" he snapped.

"I guess not." I looked at him. "Look, Josh—"

"That's why I ran away," he interrupted, "because I didn't want to have to tell you. Because I didn't tell you." He paused. "Before we made love."

"We didn't do anything risky," I replied.

"No," he said scornfully, "it wasn't worth it."

"Jesus, Josh, did you want to infect me?"

He lowered his eyes. "I'm sorry, Henry. I don't know what I'm saying."

"Then be quiet and listen to me," I said.

He reached for his cigarettes.

"And don't light another one of those."

He dropped his hand. "Sorry," he said.

"I've been driving all over L.A. looking for you," I said, "and it wasn't because I thought you killed Brian. Not really." I ran my hand through my hair. "I'm thirty-six years old, Josh. You have no idea how old that sounds to me, especially when I wake up in the morning alone." I paused. This was going to be harder than I thought. "I just have these feelings for you. . ." And then I couldn't think of anything else to say.

He looked at me. "I love you, too."

I nodded. "Then come here." He rose from his chair and joined me on the couch.

He sniffed. A trickle of snot glistened under his nose. I gave him my handkerchief. He blew his nose gravely.

"I'm so scared," he whispered, and began to cry.

I pulled him close and held him until I could feel the heat of his body through his sweater. I thought of all the rational things I should say but heard myself tell him, "I won't let anything happen to you."

He pulled away and looked at me, lifting his sleeve and wiping his nose. His eyes searched mine, slowly. I didn't look away. We both knew that what I'd just said was, on one level, impossible and, therefore, untrue. And yet we both knew I meant it, which made it true on a different level, the one that mattered between us now.

He brought his face forward and we kissed.

Just then the door opened. I saw Mrs. Mandel out of the corner of my eye. Behind her came a man who I recognized from the picture at Josh's apartment as Mr. Mandel.

"Joshua," Mr. Mandel said, "what is this?"

We moved apart. Josh said, "Mom, Dad, you'd better sit down. There's something I have to tell you."

□

Over the next eight hours, Josh not only told his parents that he was gay but that we were lovers and about the result of the antibody test. Mr. Mandel ordered me out of the house, relented, and alternately screamed at and wept for his son. Mrs. Mandel seemed to have been rendered catatonic.

Then, after the hysterics came the hard talk. Josh's sisters were called, one in Sacramento and one in Denver, and consulted. They came out heavily pro-Josh. His father brought down the Bible and read to us the passage in Leviticus that condemns homosexuality. That led to a long, rambling discussion about biblical fundamentalism which ended, predictably, in a stalemate.

Mrs. Mandel mourned for her unborn grandchildren. Josh said that he planned to have children. This silenced her. Silenced me, too. We talked for a long time about Jim Pears and how having to hide being gay had probably led him to kill someone. We talked about AIDS. This was the hardest part for all of us.

I argued that AIDS wasn't divine retribution on gay people any more than Tay-Sachs disease was God's commentary on Jews. Mr. Mandel bristled at the analogy but his wife diffused the tension with a series of surprisingly well-informed questions about AIDS. It occurred to me then that she had known Josh was gay all along. Even so, they both remained worried and frightened. So was Josh. So was I.

In the middle of all this, Mr. Mandel ordered pizza and we had an involved argument over the relative merits of anchovies. He and I wanted them. Josh and Mrs. Mandel resisted. The three of them went through a bottle of wine while I guzzled Perrier.

And then it was three o'clock in the morning and Mr. Mandel was apologizing for being sixty-two and needing his sleep.

Knees creaking and head throbbing, I got up to leave. "I need my coat," I said to Josh who was sitting on it.

"Wait," he said, amazement in his eyes. "You're not going to drive all the way back to Silver Lake now, are you?"

A long complex silence ensued.

"It's not that far," I said.

"Come on, Henry. You're exhausted." Josh looked at his parents. "You can't let him go out at this hour. The roads are full of drunks."

"Joshua," his father began.

"Dad," he said in a whine he must have perfected as a child. "It's just a matter of common courtesy. Let him sleep on the couch down here. Mom?"

"Silver Lake is — far away," she said, tentatively, looking at her husband. Then, more confidently she added, "The sofa folds out and there's a bathroom down here."

"Well, I'm going to bed," Mr. Mandel said "You want to stay Henry, stay."

"Thank you," I said to his back.

Mrs. Mandel opened a closet and pulled out some sheets and blankets. She put them on the couch.

"It folds out," she said.

"Thanks."

We looked at each other, then she looked at Josh. "Go to bed, Josh."

"In a minute, Mom," he said. "I'll just help Henry with the couch."

Defeated, she murmured her good-nights and slipped out of the room. We listened to her footsteps as she climbed the stairs.

"What a little brat you are," I said.

"It isn't over yet, you know," Josh said.

"I know. I know."

"It might go on forever."

"One day at a time," I said and nuzzled him. "I'm really tired."

"Do you mind us not sleeping together?"

"This is their house," I said. "Let's make it easy on them. They're probably upstairs awake as it is."

"How do you know that?" he asked, smiling.

"Years of legal training," I replied and kissed him. He kept his lips closed. "Josh, that's not how to kiss."

"My saliva," he said, biting his lower lip. "It might carry the virus."

"In negligible amounts, if at all," I replied. "Let's not let this thing run our lives."

We kissed again, properly.

"Go to bed, Josh, and let your parents get some sleep."

He pulled himself up from the floor and said, "You know what's really going to drive them crazy, is when it sinks in that you're not Jewish."

I smiled, then, remembering, asked, "Josh, the night Jim tried to kill himself and you called me, you didn't actually speak to me, did you?"

He shook his head. "No, I hung up before you answered. Why?"

"Because someone else called, too," I said, "and I now know who it was."

"Is it important?"

"Could be," I replied. "Good night, Josh."

"I love you," he said, and slipped quietly from the room. I watched the last embers spark and burn themselves out. When I finally arranged myself on the couch, my last conscious thought was not of Josh but of Jim Pears.

— 20 —

I heard someone rattling around in the next room and sat up on the couch. It was eight in the morning and I felt as close to hungover as I had in two years. I put on my trousers and shirt and followed the noise into the kitchen where I found Mr. Mandel pouring himself a cup of coffee. He seemed startled to find me still there.

"You want a cup?" he asked.

"Thank you." I studied him. Short and slender, he so resembled Josh that it was like looking forty years into the future.

"You want some cake?" Mr. Mandel asked, unwrapping a crumb cake.

"No thanks," I replied. It made my teeth ache just to look at it.

He caught my expression. "I have a sweet tooth," he said. "So does Joshua."

"He likes chocolate," I volunteered, remembering a box of chocolate cookies I'd seen at his apartment.

"Anything chocolate," Mr. Mandel agreed. "And marzipan. He likes that."

He brought two cups of coffee to the table and then went back to the counter for his piece of cake. We sat down. He blew over the top of his coffee before sipping it. I noticed the thin gold wedding band he wore. The kitchen was filled with light and papered in a light blue wallpaper with a pattern of daisies. Copper aspic molds decorated the walls. All the appliances — refrigerator, microwave, dishwasher, Cuisinart — were spotlessly clean and new-looking. We were sitting at a little pine table.

"Your house," I said, tentatively, "is very nice."

"Selma," he replied, referring to his wife, "puts a lot of work into it. She wallpapered this room by herself."

"It looks professional."

"You sure you're not hungry? There's cereal, eggs."

"No, I don't eat much."

He looked at me appraisingly. "You are on the thin side. So, you live up in San Francisco."

"Not exactly. I live in a little town down the bay. It's where Linden University is located."

"Yes, Linden University," he said, impressed. "You go to school there?"

"Law school."

"Good," he said, taking a bite of his cake. "I wish I could get Joshie interested in something like law school."

"He's still pretty young."

This was the wrong thing to say. Mr. Mandel glared at me and then pressed the bottom of his fork into the little crumbs of sugar that had fallen from the cake to the plate.

"Mr. Mandel," I began.

"Listen," he said wearily. "We talked enough last night. We'll talk again. For now, let's just enjoy our coffee."

"Sure."

We enjoyed our coffee for five tense minutes. At the end of that time Mrs. Mandel came in, wearing a padded floral bathrobe and black Chinese slippers. She said her good-mornings and offered me breakfast.

"He doesn't eat," her husband informed her.

"But you should," she said. "You're so thin."

Our discussion of my weight was cut short by Josh's appearance. He was wearing a ratty plaid bathrobe, the original belt of which had apparently been lost and was replaced by a soiled necktie. His hair was completely disheveled, his glasses sat halfway down his nose and he cleared his throat loudly. Ignoring us, he poured himself a cup of coffee. He cut a piece of crumb cake which he ate at the counter, and then announced, "I'm starving."

The rest of us, who had been watching him, transfixed, came back to life.

"Good morning, Josh," his father said acerbically.

"Good morning," he replied crankily.

"What do you want, Joshie?" his mother asked.

"Scrambled eggs," he said, "with cheese. And matzoh brei. And sausage."

"Sausage he wants with matzoh brei," Mr. Mandel said, smiling at me. I smiled back, feeling like a complete intruder.

Josh smiled at me, too. That smile packed a lot of meaning and it was lost on no one. "How did you sleep, Henry?"

"Fine," I replied.

"Not me," he said. "I missed you."

Mr. Mandel said, "You say this to hurt your mother."

"Shut up, Sam," Mrs. Mandel snapped. "Get me the eggs out of the refrigerator, Josh." She turned to me and said, in a quavering voice, "You eat, too, Henry. You're too thin."

Mr. Mandel rose noisily from the table and left the room. Somewhere in the house a door slammed shut. Mrs. Mandel looked at us and said, "He's — it's going to take time." Then she began to weep.

□

I called Tony Good, got his answering machine, and left a message that I wanted to see him. Josh came into the room and sat on the ottoman at the foot of my chair.

"Who was that?" he asked.

"Business," I replied, not wanting to have to explain Tony Good to Josh. There were enough Tonys in the world — Josh would encounter one of them eventually. "You're full of little surprises," I added.

"You mean about not sleeping well."

I nodded.

"They have to get used to the idea," he replied, but his eyes were uncertain.

"You're right." We looked at each other. "I have a confession to make "

"What?"

"I never told my parents."

He cocked his head and stared at me. "You didn't? Why not?"

"I guess the easy answer is that they died before I got around to it," I replied. "But the honest answer is — I was afraid."

·154·

He scooted forward on the ottoman so that our knees touched and said, "I can't believe you're afraid of anything."

"No? Well, I try to stay outraged and that keeps me from being afraid. But—" I put my hand on his leg, "—I don't think that's going to work with how I feel about you."

He put his hand on mine. "You're not afraid of me."

"Not of you," I replied, "for you. I can't stand the idea that anyone or anything might hurt you."

He smiled and seemed, suddenly, older, quite my equal. "Don't think of me as a job, Henry. You don't need a reason to love me."

☐

Just as I got to the door of Larry's house, it opened and I found myself face-to-face with a young woman carrying a clipboard.

"Excuse me," she said, and stepped aside to let me pass. Larry was standing behind her with two mugs in his hand. "Goodbye, Larry," she told him. "I'll call you tomorrow."

"Thanks Cindy."

"Goodbye," she said to me in a pleasant tone.

"Goodbye," I answered, puzzled. When she left I asked Larry who she was.

"My travel agent," he said, heading into the kitchen. I followed him. "Where have you been?"

"Are you going somewhere?"

"My question gets priority," he replied, rinsing the mugs in the sink and setting them in the dish rack. In his Levis and black turtleneck he looked spectrally thin.

"It's sort of a long story."

"Tell me while I fix myself something to eat. Do you want anything?"

Mrs. Mandel's ponderous breakfast was sitting in my stomach. "No."

I told Larry about the previous night's proceedings while he constructed an omelet. He brought it to the table where I joined him. Before he ate, he swallowed a fistful of vitamins, washing them down with cranberry juice. He cut an edge of the egg and ate it, chewing slowly but without much apparent pleasure.

"Josh sounds like a very smart boy," he said when I related

Josh's parting comment to me.

"Don't say boy. It makes me feel like a child molester."

Larry smiled. "Twenty-two is several years past the age of consent," he replied. "And you should stop thinking of yourself as an old man."

"I suppose. Anyway, I'm relieved that Josh didn't have anything to do with Brian Fox's murder."

Larry set down his fork. "You're still thinking about that?"

"Do you remember the night Jim Pears tried to kill himself?" I asked.

"How could I forget," he replied, grimly.

"The phone rang three times. The first time it was a drunk who told me that Jim was innocent. The second time it was the jail. The third time the caller hung up before I could answer." I poured myself a cup of coffee from the pot on the table. "I thought that the first caller was Josh."

"Why?" Larry asked, finishing his meal.

"I'd talked to him earlier and it was clear he wasn't telling the truth about where he'd been when Brian was killed. I just thought, I don't know, that he was trying to relieve his guilty conscience, but—" I sipped the coffee, "—this guy flirted with me."

"Really?" Larry asked, amused.

"It was strange in the context. But I still thought it was Josh. Well, Josh did call that night, but he was the third caller, the one who hung up before I could answer the phone."

Larry's eyebrow arched above his eye. "Do you know who the first caller was?"

"I think it was Tony Good," I replied.

Larry looked at me closely and said, "Why?"

"Something he said at the Zanes' party as you were leaving with him. Some words he used were the same words the first caller used," I said, remembering that on both occasions Good had said, *You're kind of cute, Henry. You gotta lover?* "And the way he insisted that I take his number. What I don't understand, though, is why Tony Good would know anything about Brian Fox's murder."

Larry lit a cigarette. He squinted slightly as the smoke rose into his eyes and said, "It was Tony."

"How do you know that?"

"He called again that night," Larry replied, tapping an ash into his plate.

"Why didn't you tell me then?"

He shook his head. "I didn't know he'd called before," he said, "and I wouldn't have had any reason to think he'd be calling you."

"But he would call you?" I asked.

Larry nodded. "I've known Tony for a long time," he said, smiling without humor. "And in many capacities. A drunken call in the middle of the night is about par for the course."

"What did he tell you?"

"Nothing," Larry said. "I mean nothing about you or Jim Pears. We just talked." He looked at me guiltily.

"You're sure?"

"Believe me, Henry, I had no idea." He pushed his plate away. "I told him I was sick." He shrugged. "That's what we talked about." He paused. "He went on a crying jag, but I'm sure he didn't mean anything by it."

"You didn't answer my question about whether you're taking a trip."

He picked up his plate and took it to the sink. "As a matter of fact," he said, sticking his cigarette beneath the tap, "I'm going to Paris on Friday."

"Day after tomorrow?"

He nodded, his back still turned to me.

"Why?"

"To check myself in at an AIDS clinic," he replied, coming back to the table.

"Isn't this kind of precipitous?"

He rolled up one sleeve of his turtleneck and held his arm out. There was what appeared to be a purple welt on his forearm, but it wasn't a welt. It was a lesion. I stared at it.

"Kaposi?" I asked.

"That's right," he said. "The first one appeared two weeks ago."

He covered his arm and slumped into a chair.

— 21 —

The kitchen clock had rattled off a full minute before I spoke. "Why Paris?"

"Anonymity," Larry answered, resting his chin on his hands. "And for treatment, of course. It's one of the centers of AIDS research."

"Then why anonymity?"

He rubbed a patch of dry skin at the corner of his mouth. "That's just my way," he said. "I've always done things in secret."

"But you're out," I replied. "You've been out for five years."

He looked at me with a helpless expression. "Henry," he said, "you don't understand. This has nothing to do with being out. This is about dying."

"No," I said, "I don't understand. Everyone who loves you is here."

"In this room," he replied, and looked at me. "You're all there is. Ned is dead. My family..." he shrugged dismissively. "My dying would be grist for the gossip mill but no one would really care. I couldn't stand it, Henry. Not the curiosity-seekers." His lips tightened. "Not to be an object lesson. I want some privacy for this. Some dignity."

"By crawling back into the closet to die?"

He winced.

"I'm sorry," I said.

"It's okay. I didn't expect you to understand. You're young and healthy and in love."

I felt as if I'd been cursed.

"Don't go," I pleaded.

"I'm afraid I—" The phone rang. Larry reached around and picked up the receiver. A moment later he said, "It's for you."

I took it from him. He got up and lit another cigarette.

"Hello," I said.

"Hi, handsome." It was Tony Good, returning the message I'd left on his machine.

We made arrangements to meet that night at ten at a bar in West Hollywood. I got up from the table and put the phone back. Larry was in his study, going through a pile of papers. Watching him, it occurred to me that I hardly knew him at all. It was as if all these years I'd been seeing him in profile and now that he turned his face to me, it was the face of a stranger.

"I have a million things to do before I leave," he said. "Some of them I'm going to ask you to finish for me once I'm gone."

"Sure. Of course."

He sat down behind his desk. "Don't take all this so hard."

"We're friends," I replied.

He didn't answer but picked up a folder, flipped through its pages, and withdrew a sheaf of papers.

"This is a copy of my will," he said, handing me the papers. "You're my executor. Take it, Henry."

Numbly, I accepted.

□

Freeman Vidor stepped into the Gold Coast wearing a pair of hiphuggers, a pink chenille pullover and about a dozen gold chains. He sauntered toward me, stopping conversation with each step.

"Jesus," I said, when he reached me. "This is a gay bar, not the Twilight Zone."

Freeman looked around the bar. There were a lot of Levis and flannel shirts, slacks and sweaters, even the odd suit, but his was the only chenille sweater to be seen in the place.

"Back to R. & D.," he said. "Is Good here yet?"

"No, I doubt if he'll be here any sooner than eleven," I replied. "Ten o'clock was just a negotiating point."

"How about a drink?"

"Sure. Pink lady, okay?"

"Screw you," he said, and in his deepest voice ordered a boilermaker.

"I want to talk to Good alone for a while," I said, when the drink came. "Then you join us."

"What am I supposed to do in the meantime?"

I looked at him and said, "Mingle, honey."

Tony Good walked in the door at five minutes past eleven. I watched him stand unsteadily, just inside the doorway, and swing his head around. I raised my hand and he nodded. He made his way through the crowded room until he was beside me. He was even better looking than I remembered. Black hair, blue eyes. Model perfect features. Only his teeth spoiled the package. They were small, sharp, and yellow. He climbed up onto the bar stool next to mine and ordered a Long Island Iced Tea. The bartender started pouring the five different liquors that went into the drink.

"You're not drinking?" Tony asked, indicating the bottle of mineral water in front of me.

"No," I said. "You go ahead." I paid for his drink.

"Here's looking at you, kid," he said in a tired Bogart voice, and knocked off a good third of the drink in a single swallow. "So," he said, crumpling a cocktail napkin, "is this a date or what?"

"You wanted to see me, Tony."

He squinted at me for a second, then said, "You called me, remember?"

I looked away from him and poured some mineral water in my glass. "Not the first time," I replied.

He took a sip of his drink. "You're cute, Henry, but not cute enough to play games."

"The first time you called," I said. "Back in October. You told me that you knew who killed Brian Fox."

Tony had worked his way down to the bottom of his drink. The bartender, without asking, starting pouring him another.

"Who the hell is Brian Fox?" he asked.

"Now you're playing games," I said, looking at him. I flicked my head and Freeman came across the room until he stood behind Tony. Tony looked over his shoulder and got an eyeful of pink chenille.

"Jesus, what's this?" he asked.

"Don't ask me to show my badge," Freeman said in a low voice. "It's bad for business."

Tony looked at Freeman and then at me. I waited for him to call Freeman's bluff. Instead, he picked up his drink, gestured to the bartender and told me, "Pay the man."

I paid for the drink. "So who was it, Tony?"

He churned his drink with a swizzle stick and answered, "Sandy."

"I want details," I said.

"First we gotta make a deal," he said. "I tell you what I know but it stays here, between us. You nail him some other way." He looked defiantly at Freeman and me.

"Okay," I said. "Go ahead."

"It was back about a year ago. We were in rehearsals on *Edward*. I came out back for a smoke and saw this kid hanging around the parking lot."

"Fox?" I asked.

He took a swallow of his drink and nodded. "Yeah, but he didn't say his name. He was kind of cute, so I started talking to him. I asked him what he was doing there, thinking maybe he was a hustler. He goes, 'I'm waiting for Goldenboy.'"

"Goldenboy?" Freeman asked.

"That's what I said," Good continued. "He points to Sandy's Mercedes. He's got this license plate on it—"

"It spells out Goldenboy," I said.

"You've seen it," Good said. "He tells me he's got to talk to Goldenboy, so I go, 'Don't you know his name?' The kid says 'Yeah, it's Sanford Blasenheim.'"

"Is that Sandy's real name?" I asked.

"Does that sound like a stage name to you?" Tony asked, smiling snidely. "Anyway, I know this kid doesn't know Sandy 'cause no one calls him by his real name."

Freeman asked, "So how did Fox know it?"

Tony had finished the drink and signaled the bartender for a third. "This is thirsty business," he said to me.

"How did Fox know?" I asked.

"He gave me some bullshit story about breaking into DMV's computer and running the license plate," he said.

I looked at Freeman. "Is that possible?"

"The kid knew his computers," Freeman said, "but that sounds like too much trouble. All's he had to do was call DMV and say he was in a hit-and-run with Blenheim's car and ask them to run the plate."

"DMV's pretty generous with their information," I observed.

"They don't get paid enough to care," Freeman replied.

Tony, who had been listening, broke in, "But how did he know about the license plate? He wouldn't tell me that."

"The parking lot," I said, still speaking to Freeman. "When he followed Jim and Sandy out to the car, he saw the license plate." I turned back to Tony. "What else happened, Tony?"

"Nothing," he said. "I tried to make a date with the kid, but he says he wasn't gay. So I told him, then you don't want to know Sandy, 'cause you're just his type. After rehearsal I came back outside and the kid was in the front seat of Sandy's car with Sandy. Then they took off."

"Is that the last time you saw Fox?" I asked.

"I saw his picture in the paper," Good said, slowly, "the day after he was killed."

"Why didn't you go to the cops?" Freeman asked.

Tony looked at me. "You saw me in the play. What did you think?"

"You were good," I said.

"Damn right," he said, easing himself off the bar stool. "I'm a fucking good actor. All I need is a break." He picked up his drink, took a gulp, then put it down. "I started out in that play as one of the soldiers in the first scene. Big fucking role. Two lines, two minutes. And I had to fuck Sandy to get even that. That pig."

"But you ended up as Gaveston," I answered. "You fuck Sandy for that, too?"

He smiled, showing his jagged little teeth. "Yeah, you could say that. I told him I knew about the kid. I told him what he could give me to keep my mouth shut."

I nodded. "Then why did you call me?"

He set the drink on the counter with the over-delicate movements of a drunk. "'Cause I wanted someone else to know," he said, "and put the pig in jail where he belongs." He looked at his watch. "This has been lots of laughs, Henry, but I've got a client waiting for me."

He started away.

Freeman and I followed a few minutes later and stood in front of the bar.

"Do you still have friends at L.A.P.D.?" I asked.

Freeman half-smiled and replied, "You told that guy you'd keep the cops out of it."

I thought of Jim Pears whom I had not believed when he told me he was innocent. "I lied," I said.

Freeman said, "There's still a lot to explain. Pears was in the room. He was the only one."

"I know," I replied. I shrugged. "Maybe nothing'll come of it, but if it helps Jim it's worth it."

"Nothing's going to help Jim," Freeman said. He shivered from the cold.

"Get ahold of your cop friend in the morning," I said. "We'll get together and visit Tony. By the way, where did you get that sweater?"

Freeman laughed. "My ex-wife."

□

It was after midnight when I got to Larry's. I pulled into the garage and sat for a moment in the darkness. It was perfectly still. I began to fit things together.

Brian Fox had not gone to the restaurant to see Jim, but to meet Blenheim. It was Fox who took the back door key from the bar. He used it to let Blenheim inside. Then what? I closed my eyes and reconstructed the layout of the restaurant in my head. They went downstairs. Blenheim killed Brian. But without a struggle? How? I listened to my breathing, and rolled down the window. That part I didn't know yet.

I had to get Jim down into the cellar, too. Could it be that he and Blenheim had killed Brian together? The garage creaked. A breeze swept through like a sigh. Or had Jim come down after it was done? Blenheim would have heard the steps from the kitchen floor overhead. Steps. I opened my eyes. There were footsteps in the garage. I pulled myself up in my seat and glanced into the rearview mirror. A dark figure merged into the shadows and was coming up beside me.

Slowly, I opened the glove compartment and got out the flashlight. I prepared to flash the light in the intruder's eyes and push the door open on him. Now. I swung the light around and clicked it on, reaching, at the same time for the door handle. Then I stopped as the figure backed up against Larry's car.

It was Rennie.

— 22 —

"Henry!"

I clicked off the light and got out of the car. "It's all right."

"I thought you had a gun," she said, recovering her breath.

"I'm a lawyer, not a cowboy," I replied. "I can hardly see you in here. Let's go outside."

I reached for her hand, found it, and led her back out where the streetlamp illuminated the quiet street. Although she wore an overcoat, she was still shivering. I put my arm around her.

"Where did you come from?" I asked.

"My car," she answered, pointing to a white Mercedes parked at the curb just past the house. "I've been waiting for you."

"Why didn't you wait inside?"

"I needed to see you alone," she said. "I didn't want Larry to know."

Her shivering subsided. In the bright white light her face was tired but seemed much younger, sharper. This is how she looks on stage, I thought.

"Come back to my car with me," she half-pleaded. I followed her to the Mercedes and got in. The car reeked of cigarettes. The dashboard clock read 12:30.

"Tom's in trouble," she said abruptly.

"Go on."

She stared out into the street. "I was at home, alone, when there was a call from someone — male, asking for Tom. He wouldn't tell me who he was. I hung up." She glanced at me. "I know it's rude but the strangest people somehow get our number, fans, salesmen, you name it."

She was getting off the point. "What happened next?" I prompted.

"He called again. He demanded to talk to Tom. I told him Tom wasn't in and he said—" Shallow lines appeared across her forehead. "—that if I was lying it wouldn't save Tom, and if I wasn't, he would find him."

"That's it?"

"Yes," she nodded.

"But you must be used to crank calls," I said. "Why did this one bring you to me?"

She fumbled with her cigarette case and extracted a cigarette. I rolled down the window when she lit it. "I know I'm not being clear," she said. She exhaled, jerkily, a stream of smoke. "Tom goes to bars. Homosexual bars. He meets men, has sex with them, and comes home. He doesn't do it often. It's a part of his life we don't discuss."

"But you know about it."

She dug into the pocket of her overcoat and came up with a handful of matchbooks. "It's these," she said.

I examined them. They were all from local gay bars.

"He leaves them for me to see," she said, softly.

Some of the matchbooks had names and phone numbers written in them. "That seems cruel," I commented.

"To an outsider," she said, stubbing her cigarette out. She smiled, faintly, ironically. "Tom is — he doesn't lie very well. He can't bring himself to talk about this with me, but he won't lie about it, either. These," she nodded toward the matchbooks, "are his way of letting me know."

"Why?" I asked. "Aren't you the one who told me that discretion is the better part of marriage?"

"I'm more his mother than his wife," she said as if giving the time. "He depends on me to look after him. And I have a mother's intuition about him — when his hurts are real, when they're not," she continued with a sort of mocking tenderness. "When there's danger."

"Lawyers have a kind of intuition, too," I said, "and my intuition tells me that there's something you're holding back."

She was silent for a moment, then said, "I lied about the call. It wasn't anonymous."

"Who was it?"

"Sandy," she replied.

"Why would he threaten Tom?"

She shook her head. "I honestly don't know. There's something going on between them. Sandy's been completely out of control. He and Tom had a big fight a couple of days ago and Tom finally threw him out of the house. Then this." She shuddered. "I'm afraid, Henry. He's crazy. Help me find Tom."

I put aside the questions I wanted to ask her about Tom and Sandy. They seemed irrelevant when I remembered that Sandy Blenheim was a killer.

"You think he's at one of these places?" I asked, holding up the matchbooks.

"I don't know where else to look," she replied.

◻

Last call had been called five minutes earlier but no one was moving. I walked around the bar again, the last in Tom's matchbook collection. The other three had also been like this, dark and out of the way, far from the glittery strip of Santa Monica Boulevard known by the locals as Boys Town with its trendy bars and discos.

This bar, The Keep, was on a Hollywood side street that had disappeared from the maps around 1930. There wasn't much to the place: a bar lined with stools where customers could sit and watch their reflections blur in the mirror as the night wore on, a small dance floor bathed in blue light, a few tables lit by orange candles. Posters of beefy naked men covered the walls. Many of the patrons were middle-aged or older, and the level of shrieking was pretty high. Definitely a pre-Stonewall scene.

I leaned against the wall and looked around. Half a dozen of the bar stools were occupied. A handsome man's reflection smiled at me. I smiled back and continued inspecting the other customers. Tom Zane was not among them.

As I started out the door, I heard someone say, "Ambassador."

I stopped. "Zane," I replied.

The skinny bartender jerked his head toward me, his long earring dangling against his cheek.

"You say something?" he asked me.

I shook my head and walked back to where I had been standing. The man in the mirror was still smiling. He wore a plaid shirt beneath a black leather jacket. He had dark hair and a moustache. His eyes were brown.

Holding his eye in the mirror, I stepped forward until I stood directly behind him. His smile widened.

"Zane?"

"Ambassador," he replied, and swung around on the bar stool until he faced me.

"I didn't recognize you at all."

"Were you trying to?"

"As a matter of fact, I was. Rennie sent me to find you."

He frowned. "Rennie?"

"There was a call tonight, threatening you. She brought your matchbook collection to me and sent me looking for you."

"Goddammit," he breathed. "What's wrong with her?"

"She was worried, Tom. The caller was Sandy."

He narrowed his eyes. "What did she tell you about Sandy?"

"That you had a fight and kicked him out of your house."

"Let's get out of here," he said. He dropped a ten dollar bill on the bar and we went out to the street. It was drizzling. The bar was in a warehouse district and, as we headed down the street toward Cahuenga, a Doberman sprang out from a fenced-in lot and barked. A woman in the tatters of a coat hurried by, stopped, and screamed invectives at the dog. We reached Cahuenga and Tom's car, a red Fiat Spider with a plate that read "Drifter."

"Where are you parked?" Tom asked.

"Just down the street."

"I think you should forget any of this happened," he said,

reaching to the moustache and pulling it from his face. I watched, fascinated.

"What about the eyes?" I asked.

"Brown contact lenses. The hair's just a colored mousse. Washes right out," he smiled. "It's Hollywood, Henry."

"Seems like a lot of trouble just to have a drink at a place like that."

"Haven't you ever wanted to be invisible, Henry?" he asked, opening the car door.

I shook my head.

"No," he said. "I guess you wouldn't miss what you haven't lost. Me, I can't walk down the street without some girl throwing her tits in my face or some fag groping me. Don't get me wrong. It's not like I'm down on sex, but I like to choose the time and the place." He got into the car and smiled. "You heard what I said about forgetting about tonight."

"I heard," I said, "but Sandy's about to have some other problems."

"Don't tell me anything," he said, starting up his car. "I'm finished with Sandy."

I looked at him. "Then you know," I said.

He shook his head. "I don't know anything. See you around, Henry." He put the car in gear and skidded off down the wet black street toward Sunset and, I hoped, home. I stood there for a minute, as if on an empty stage, and then started back to my car.

□

It was two-thirty-five when I knocked at the door to Josh's apartment. There was some noise from within and then he opened the door, drawing his robe around him. His hair was a sleepy tumble and his eyes beneath his glasses were tired.

"Hi," he said as I stepped into the warm room. There was a lamp on over the sofa and an open book on the floor.

"I'm sorry I'm so late."

"That's okay," he said and kissed me. "I'm happy you're here. I was just reading."

I took off my coat and tossed it to the sofa. The day had begun in the Mandels' kitchen, included Larry's revelation that he had contracted Kaposi, took in Tony Good's allegation that Blenheim killed Brian Fox, and ended in a Hollywood bar where a man with brown eyes watched me in a mirror. Images drifted across my brain with a lot of darkness between them.

"I'm exhausted," I said, smiling at Josh who watched me with dark, serious eyes. "How are you? How did things go with your folks after I left?"

He smiled, wearily. "As soon as you left they started in on me."

"I'm sorry, Josh," I said, and held him.

"It's okay," he replied uncertainly.

I kissed his warm cheek, feeling the faint stubble there against my lips. "Do they think I corrupted you?"

"It's not fair. I was gay before I met you."

"You can't expect them to be fair."

"Don't defend them," he said, momentarily annoyed.

"Sorry, Henry. I'm just tired."

"Let's go to bed then."

He yawned in agreement and we went into the bedroom. He got into bed while I undressed and washed my face and mouth at the bathroom sink. I slipped into bed beside him and we reached for each other, pressing the lengths of our bodies, one against the other, everything touching, foot, groin, belly, chest. In my mind — my relentless mind — I pictured our embrace, my exhausted thinness against his young sumpture, like a Durer etching of the embrace of youth with middle age. Thirty-six: that's middle age, isn't it? Midway down the road of life?

"You're thinking again," Josh whispered into my ear. "I can tell because your whole body gets stiff except one part."

I relaxed.

□

This dream I entered unwillingly because I knew where it would take me. I was sitting at the bar of The Keep, as thirsty as I had ever been. The bartender with the dangling earring refused to serve me because he said that I had stopped drinking. I looked into the mirror behind the bar. A stage illuminated by three blue lights formed in it.

As I watched I saw Tom Zane, naked, doing the last scene from *Edward the Second*, but instead of the black actor, Sandy Blenheim played the part of Lightborn. Blenheim was hugely fat, flesh almost dripping from his body, and wore only a jock strap. The scene was so grotesque I began to laugh.

"You think I'm funny?" Blenheim shrieked. "Then watch."

Suddenly he was holding a poker, with a red hot tip. He began to insert it into the anus of the body lying on the pallet on the stage. It should have been Zane, but it wasn't. It was Jim Pears, comatose and unable to protect himself.

"Stop it," I shouted. "Stop it!"

"Isn't this funny, isn't this funny," Blenheim yelled back.

I turned away from the scene to another part of the mirror. There, instead of my own reflection, I saw Larry's cadaverous face.

"Why is this happening?" I demanded of the bartender.

He looked at me. Now he had Mr. Mandel's face and he said, "Because you're a queer. A queer. A queer."

The last thing I remembered was ordering myself to wake up.

I opened my eyes. Josh, wide-eyed, had lifted his face above mine.

"Henry," he said.

I expelled a gust of pent-up breath. "It's all right. Bad dream."

He held me. I smelled his smells, felt his skin beneath my fingers and his hair against my face. At that moment, he was the only real thing in the world.

— 23 —

I left Josh the next morning and returned to Larry's house. I found him sitting at his desk writing checks.

"Did you see Tony last night?" he asked in response to my greeting. In the watery morning light he looked haggard but formidably alive, not at all the cadaver I had dreamt of the night before.

"Yes," I said, sitting down across from him. "He says Sandy Blenheim killed Brian Fox."

"That's unbelievable," Larry said.

I recounted for Larry the story that Good had told me. When I finished he nodded but his face remained skeptical.

"It sounds plausible," he said, finally.

"A plausible lie?" I asked.

He shook his head. "No, that's not it. Tony only lies to his advantage. I can't see how this would help him." He looked thoughtful. "And it's true about Sandy's taste for young boys."

"But you're not convinced."

"I still think Jim did it," he said quietly.

I stared at him. "Didn't you bring me down here to prove Jim's innocence?"

He smiled wanly. "Not exactly," he replied. "I wanted you to get him acquitted." He picked up a crystal paperweight from his desk and ran his fingers across its surface. "Look, I know what's bothering me about this Sandy business. It's that everyone knows Sandy's gay. The fact that he was caught having sex with a kid would have been embarrassing but not especially damaging." He set the paperweight down. "Not in this town, anyway. And another thing, Henry, don't you think the way Brian Fox was killed showed incredible rage?"

Remembering the pictures I had seen of the body, I nodded.

"Would Sandy Blenheim have that much anger inside of him?" he asked.

"How well do you know him?" I countered.

Larry shrugged. "Not very," he conceded.

"Well, someone who knows him better told me that she thinks he's crazy."

Larry squinted at me. "Who?"

"Irene Gentry."

He was silent for a moment. "Maybe," he said. "She would know, if anyone does, what he's really like. He practically lives with Tom and her."

"You want to believe it was Jim," I said. "Why?"

He looked away from me and said, slowly, "Because I want to believe that he was capable of fighting back."

"But not that way, Larry. Not by killing someone."

"You have strictures about killing that I don't share," he replied.

This seemed odd coming from a dying man.

"And anyway," he rubbed his eyes, "I loved him and you didn't."

"Who? Jim?"

He nodded.

"You never met him."

"I know," he said and looked past me to the window with its still view of the lake. "It's ridiculous, isn't it? A sick man's fantasy. I dreamed of bringing him here to live with me. I thought we could heal each other. How absurd."

"No," I said. "It isn't."

As if he hadn't heard, he said, "Does God give us life to want such things? It seems cruel."

"To love someone?"

"To fall in love with a picture in the newspaper," he said, "and to lie in bed at night like a schoolboy, unable to sleep because of it. To ask you to put your reputation on the line in the hope that you could work a miracle."

"But you were right," I said, fiercely. "Jim didn't do it."

"You don't understand, Henry," Larry said. "I wanted him to have done it, and I wanted the world to understand why."

"Meanwhile someone's dead," I answered.

"And how many of us have died at the hands of people like Brian Fox?" he demanded.

I glanced at the bills on his desk, from the newspaper, the utility companies, his gardener. Across the top of each of them he had written, "Discontinue service." I remembered he had told me that he was willing to trade his life for Jim's. At the time it had merely seemed like impassioned rhetoric. Now I knew he had meant it.

"I'm sorry," I said. "I'd like to agree but it goes against everything inside of me."

Larry smiled. "It's all right," he said. "I know you, Henry. You believe in the law the way other people believe in God. Not me. I'm dying. I only believe in balancing the accounts."

I went into the kitchen to call Freeman Vidor. He wasn't at his office. A moment after I hung up, the phone rang. It was Freeman.

"I'm at Tony Good's apartment with the L.A.P.D.," he said. "You better get over here."

"What happened?"

"He's been murdered," Freeman said. "Someone took a knife and rammed it up his guts."

"Up his—" I began to say, then I understood. "My God."

☐

Over Tony Good's bed was a framed poster that showed James Dean walking down a New York street in the rain. On the bed were sky-blue sheets soaked with blood.

"He bled to death," a small man in wire-rimmed glasses was telling me. I wasn't sure who he was, the medical examiner maybe. There was a faint chemical smell in the air. Tony had been using poppers. My stomach heaved.

"Someone stuck him," I said, to say something.

"A twelve-inch blade," the little man said, "inserted into the anus."

I turned and hurried from the room into the kitchen where

Freeman was sitting at the table with Phillip Cresly, the L.A.P.D. detective assigned to the case. Cresly glanced at me without much interest as I pulled up a chair.

"You satisfied?" Cresly asked. He was a tall man with light brown hair, eyes that had been chiseled from a glacier and a twitchy little mouth. I thought I had seen his face before and then I remembered the picture in Freeman's office of the three young cops. A long time ago Cresly had been one of them.

"The bed was soaked with blood," I replied. "How can you say he didn't struggle?"

"Position of the body," Cresly replied as if reading from a list. "Nothing disturbed in the bedroom. Neighbors didn't hear anything."

"You really think he took a knife up his rectum without fighting?"

The ice-cube eyes considered me. "Vidor says the guy told you he was going to meet a client after he left the bar."

It took a moment for me to understand what he was implying. "You think that this is something gay men do?" I asked, unable to keep the astonishment out of my voice.

"I used to work vice," he said. "I seen movies where guys took fists up their ass. Jesus, I mean, right up to the elbow." He made a sour face. "A little knife is nothing."

I glanced at Freeman. A warning formed on his face. I ignored it.

"A little knife is nothing," I repeated. "You learn that at the academy?"

"I'm paid to do my job, Rios," he said, the mouth twitching. "But I don't have to like it."

I stood up. "What about Blenheim?"

"He's gone," Cresly said.

"You looking for him?"

"We'll find him," he said, smugly. "You have anything else to tell me?"

Freeman stood up, quickly, and pulled at my arm. "Come on, Henry," he said. I let him lead me from the room.

"That jerk," I sputtered as soon as we were outside in front of Good's apartment building.

Freeman lit a cigarette. "The man's set in his ways," he said, mildly, "but he's a good cop, Henry. He don't like open files."

Two young men came down the sidewalk carrying an immense Christmas tree. They passed us with shy, domestic smiles.

"No struggle," I said, more to myself than to Freeman.

"Look," Freeman said, "the guy was drunk when we saw him. And he was probably dusted, too."

"PCP?" I said. "How do you figure?"

"I smelled ether in the bedroom," he said. He blew smoke out of the side of his mouth. "They use it to cover the smell."

"I know," I replied. "But that wasn't ether. It was amyl nitrite."

"Poppers?" Freeman shook his head. "I don't think so."

"What does it matter," I said. "He was obviously on something, but I can't believe it was enough to knock him out."

We got to Freeman's battered Accord. The license plate read, PRIVT I.

"It had to be Blenheim," I said.

"Yeah, that's what I figure. How do you think he found out that Good talked to us?" He leaned against the car, dropped his cigarette and crushed it.

"Maybe Good told him," I said. "Maybe he was Good's client last night, only the appointment wasn't for sex but a little more blackmail."

"Kinda stupid," Freeman observed.

"I doubt that Tony Good ever got any prizes for brains," I replied.

"What a way to go," Freeman said.

"Yeah. I think I better go pay a call on the Zanes."

"You think Blenheim will be going after them next?"

I nodded. "I bet Tom Zane knows everything."

"Poppers," Freeman said softly, tossing his cigarette to the ground. "Is it true that they make sex better?"

I shrugged. "All I ever got from them was a headache."

Freeman snickered. "Figures," he said. "You ain't exactly one for the wild side, are you Henry?"

"Not exactly," I agreed.

The Zanes were at home. Rennie, in a gray silk robe, arranged herself in a chair near the fire. The maid brought her tea. Tom was having his morning pick-me-up, a tall Bloody Mary that he mixed himself. He brought his drink into the living room and sat in the chair beside his wife. The two of them, blond, handsome, could have been brother and sister. They watched me with still, blue eyes. A fire crackled in the fireplace, releasing the scent of pine into the air. A Christmas tree had appeared in the corner, near the Diego Rivera, with expensively wrapped gifts piled beneath it.

I told them about Tony Good and Sandy Blenheim's disappearance. They said nothing though Rennie blanched when I described the manner of Tony's death.

I looked at Tom. "You knew Sandy killed Brian Fox," I said.

"How do you figure?" he asked, a lazy smile curling the edges of his lips.

"You produced the play," I said. "Blenheim couldn't have given Tony the part of Gaveston unless he cleared it with you. Isn't that right?"

He took a swallow of his drink. "You're a smart man," he said.

"You knew," I repeated.

He set the drink down and said, "Yeah, I knew all about Sandy's troubles."

"Why didn't you turn him in?" I asked. "The man's a murderer."

Rennie set her tea down with a clatter. "Don't say anything, Tom," she said. "Not without a lawyer."

"Henry is a lawyer," Tom replied. To me he said, "So it's like talking to a priest. Right?"

"If you tell me you've committed a crime, then I'd advise you to turn yourself in, but I wouldn't do it on my own."

"See, Rennie," Tom said, smiling. "These lawyers got all the angles covered." Tom looked at me. "I told you I did time in the joint, well, I was there more than once. It was a bad scene. I would kill myself before I went back there again."

I remembered he had told me the same thing that afternoon at Malibu a few days earlier. "Go on," I said.

"They picked me up for burglary," he said. "I managed to make bail." He picked up his drink and drank from it. "I split."

"Where was this?"

"A little town in Oklahoma," he said. "Shitsville. I did some hard years there, Henry. That's not important. The important thing is, I jumped bail." He finished his drink. "Sandy knew."

"He blackmailed you," I said.

"Yeah, that's about the size of it," Zane said, rising. He walked over to the bar and poured himself vodka and lime. Rennie lit a cigarette.

"But you're on TV," I said. "Aren't you afraid of being recognized?"

"It was fifteen years ago," Tom said, walking to the window that faced the terrace. "Hell, I could walk down the streets of that town and my mama wouldn't know me." For the first time I heard a twang in his voice.

"How old were you?" I asked.

He turned from the window. "Twenty-two." He smiled, bitterly. "I already done two years by then at a state pen. Got raped every night for the first six weeks till I married me some protection — a guy with a forty-inch chest and biceps I could swing from. That's how I stayed alive."

I glanced over at Rennie. Her cigarette had burned down to the filter and a chunk of ash dropped to the floor. She stared at the wall, her face without expression.

"You could use some protection now," I said. "You're Sandy's last hope. He'll be back looking for you."

"We can't very well go to the police," Rennie said, suddenly. She dropped the remnant of her cigarette into an ashtray.

"I understand that," I said, "but—"

"But nothing," Tom said. "I'll take care of Sandy if he comes back. In the meantime, Henry, you just don't worry about us. We'll be all right."

He stepped behind the chair where Rennie sat and rested his hands on her shoulders.

I stood up to leave. "You weren't Tom Zane, then," I said.

"No. I used to be Charlie Fry," he replied. "Poor little Charlie. He never had a chance."

— 24 —

Josh's vw was parked in front of Larry's house. I found them at the kitchen table, talking quietly over the remains of lunch, and sat down.

"I guess you've met," I said.

Josh said, "I hope you don't mind that I came here."

"Not me. Larry?"

Larry smiled. "I'm glad I finally met you, Josh." He looked at me. "What happened this morning?"

I summarized what I had seen at Tony Good's apartment and gave them an edited version of my conversation with the Zanes. I concluded, saying, "Blenheim could be anywhere. They may never catch him."

"Well, I guess I was wrong," Larry said.

Josh looked puzzled.

"Larry didn't think it was Blenheim," I said.

"Who did you think it was?" Josh asked.

"Jim," Larry said.

"But you've been helping him," Josh said.

Larry smiled at him. "Have Henry explain it to you sometime, Josh." He looked at me and said, "I'm closing up the house tomorrow. Of course you can stay as long as you want, Henry, but I imagine you'll be wanting to stay with Josh, anyway."

"You're really going through with it, then?" I asked.

"Yes," Larry said.

Josh looked back and forth between us. "What's going on?"

"I'm going on a trip," Larry said brightly, "to Paris."

"Great," Josh said enthusiastically.

Larry looked at me, then stood up. "Excuse me." He picked up their plates and carried them to the sink.

"Is something wrong?" Josh asked.

Larry rinsed the plates, set them in the dishwasher and said, "I'm going to Paris for treatment, Josh. I have AIDS."

Then he left the room.

Josh stared at me. "Is that true?"

"Yes."

"You can't let him go." His voice was spooked.

"I can't stop him," I replied.

He started to speak but said nothing. I could tell he was thinking about himself, about us. Finally he asked, "Would you let me go?"

"It won't come to that," I said firmly.

"But if it did?" There was fear in his face.

"No." I put my arm around him.

"I'm sorry about Larry," he said.

"I know," I replied. We sat in silence for a minute. "Josh, after Larry leaves, I'm going home."

He nodded. "I'm going with you," he said.

☐

The next morning we drove Larry to the airport. He gave me the number of the clinic in Paris where he would be staying and a list of errands he had been unable to finish. We walked him to the gate. I remembered that all this had begun at another airport, in San Francisco. As the crowd swirled around us, we stood and looked at each other, not knowing what there was left to say.

He turned to Josh and said, "Take care of him."

"I will," Josh replied. "Goodbye, Larry."

They embraced like old friends.

Then he looked at me and said, "And you take care of Josh."

I knew I would never see him again. "Goodbye. I love you."

We embraced. "I love you, too," he said, and his lips brushed against my cheek. "Goodbye."

When we got back to Josh's apartment, I called Freeman Vidor and told him that I would be leaving for San Francisco in a couple of days.

"I have one last job for you, though," I added.

"What's that, Henry?"

"I want you to keep your eye on Tom Zane for a few days, make sure nothing happens to him."

"You think Blenheim will be looking for him?" Freeman asked.

"If he's anywhere close."

"He could be in Tahiti by now," Freeman replied. "That's what the cops think."

"But just in case he's not."

"Sure, Henry," he replied. "Give me a number where I can reach you up there."

I gave him both my office and home numbers. "Listen, Freeman," I said, "it's been good working with you."

I could almost see him smile. "I travel, too," he said. "Anywhere, anytime. You just call."

"I'll do that."

☐

We left Los Angeles one week before Christmas, choosing to drive up the coast in Josh's vw. We had made no plans about how long he would stay with me; he simply arranged to be away from the restaurant for a couple of weeks. Although things were vague, I wasn't worried because it seemed to me that the decision to be together had already been made and the mechanics would work themselves out.

As we drove out of L.A., my sense of belonging with Josh grew keener. It was partly the departure itself because, unlike other cities, one leaves Los Angeles by increments, from the crowded central city, over the canyons, through thickets of suburbs, until the tracts of houses thin into the remotest outskirts and then there are hills and sky and the freeway narrows to a two-lane road lined by eucalyptus, and the L.A. radio stations fade in and out, and it becomes possible to hear birds and smell the sea.

We stopped at a roadside produce stand and bought apples and oranges. Back in the car we drank coffee from a thermos and were silent, my hand in his when I wasn't shifting gears. The sky was clear and cold and the sun cast a rich winter light. Josh whistled under his breath, fidgeted in his seat, read to me from the L.A. *Times*, yawned, peeled an orange, carefully dividing the sections between us, closed his eyes, napped. I glanced up in the rear-view mirror and saw that I was smiling. I felt his eyes on me, looked at him. His lips parted slightly, and his forehead was creased by shallow lines. I tightened my hand around his and returned my attention to the road.

"I used to play a driving game with Larry," I said, "back when we were traveling around the state speaking against the sodomy law."

"What's the game called?" he asked.

I rolled my head back and forth to relieve the tension. "We called it 'Classic or Kitsch.' You know what kitsch is?"

"Sure," Josh answered. "My aunt's rhinestone glasses."

"Perfect example," I said. We were coming into San Luis Obispo. The traffic was heavier and the sky was clouding over. "The way it's played is, one of us chooses a category, like movies, and gives the name of the movie and the other one says if it's classic or kitsch."

Josh stretched and yawned. "What if you don't agree?"

"Then you have to say why." I glanced at him. "That's really the point of the game, the disagreements. You can learn a lot about someone that way. For instance, Larry and I argued all the way from Sacramento to Turlock about whether *All About Eve* was a classic or kitsch."

Josh looked at me. "What's *All About Eve?*"

"Are you serious?" I asked, turning my head to him.

He nodded. "Is it a movie?"

"Twenty-two," I muttered under my breath, grinning. "I can see your gay education has been sadly neglected."

"You mean there's more to it than—"

"Don't, Josh, I'm driving."

He moved his hand. "No, really, the game sounds like fun."

"Why don't you find a radio station," I suggested as i began to drizzle.

He fiddled with the radio until he found one that was audible above the static. He had tuned in the tail-end of a news broadcast and moved to find another channel. Then the announcer said, "... in other news, accused killer James Pears died today in an L.A. area hospital."

"Turn it up," I said.

The announcer's unctuous voice filled the little car as he continued. "Pears, a nineteen-year-old, was accused of killing another teenager, Brian Fox, almost a year ago today. Fox reputedly threatened to expose Pears as a homosexual. Last October, Pears attempted suicide before he could be brought to trial and he had been in a coma since that time. He died today of natural causes. Closer to home..."

Josh clicked off the radio. I turned on the windshield wipers and tried to focus on the road, but all I saw was Jim's face and all I heard was his voice, telling me he was innocent.

Josh said, "I can't believe it."

"This will make his parents' lawsuit more valuable," I replied, bitterly.

"What lawsuit?"

I shook my head. "Nothing."

"It's my fault," Josh said, miserably.

I glanced over at him. "Don't be ridiculous, Josh." It came out harder than I'd intended. "If anyone's to blame, it's me."

"That's not true."

"This isn't getting us anywhere."

We drove on in an unhappy silence. Finally Josh asked, "Why are you mad at me, Henry?"

Without taking my eyes off the road I said, "I'm not mad at you."

"Don't bullshit me," he said tensely.

I looked at him. He was staring straight ahead.

"I'm not mad," I repeated, more gently. "It's just not always easy for me to talk about what I feel."

"Is that why you've never said you love me?" he asked, abruptly. His eyes left the road and he looked at me. His mouth was grim. "You never have, you know."

"Joshua..."

He cut me off. "Don't call me that," he said irritably. "That's what my dad calls me when I'm about to get a lecture."

·183·

The rain had stopped. In the dying light of late afternoon I could see a smear of rainbow above billboards advertising motels and restaurants.

"We're both feeling bad about Jim," I said. "Let's not take it out on each other."

There was a long silence from his side of the car. Finally, he said, "Okay."

A few minutes later I looked over at him again. He was asleep.

"Will you be patient with me?"

He didn't say anything for a long time but finally put his hand on mine.

□

The day before Christmas I was leaning against a post at Macy's in Union Square watching Josh try on leather jackets. He had already gone through half a rack of them and had long ago stopped asking my opinion since I thought he looked good in all of them. This one though — dark brown in buttery leather — nearly inspired me to unsolicited advice but then I heard my name. I looked around. The man approaching me was smiling in the faintly supercilious way he used to disguise his shyness.

"Grant," I said, embracing him.

Grant Hancock pulled me close, crushing his costly overcoat, smelling, as he always did, of bay rum.

We released each other. His yellow hair had darkened and there were folds beneath his eyes and deepening lines on either side of his mouth but, generally, time made him more elegant rather than simply older. It had been a long time since I had seen him last.

"This is the last place on earth I would look for Henry Rios," he said, "so, of course, I find you here."

"And, when did you start buying off the rack?"

A salesman rushed by and jostled me. Over the din, I heard the slow movements of Pachelbel's Canon in D, a piece of music I had first heard in Grant's apartment when we had been law students together.

"We just ducked in for the ladies' room, actually," he said, apparently not hearing the music. I caught the "we." Grant had married two years earlier and was, I had heard, the father of a baby son.

"How is Marcia?" I asked.

"She's fine. We're parents now," he added, with a smile that ended at his eyes.

"Yes, I heard. Congratulations. What's your son's name?"

"William," he replied.

"After your father?" I asked.

"Yes. I'm surprised you remembered his name."

"I remember."

We stood looking into each other's eyes. The occasion — former lovers meeting after a long time — seemed to demand that something significant be said. But there wasn't anything to say, really, except that I was glad to see him and hoped he was happy. So I said it.

Before he could answer I noticed that Josh was standing before the mirror watching us. He slipped off the jacket he was wearing, tossed it over the rack, and walked over to us.

"Hi," he said, to me, and then to Grant.

"Josh, this is an old friend of mine, Grant. Grant, Josh."

They shook hands, murmuring pleasantries.

Grant said, "Those are very nice jackets you were looking at."

"Yeah," Josh said, "but a little out of my price range." Wordlessly, he snifted his weight so that our bodies touched and slipped his arm around my waist. "So," he said with unmistakable hostility, "how do you know Henry?"

"We went to law school together," Grant said, barely able to keep the amusement out of his voice. "And how do you know Henry?"

Josh said, "He's my lover."

"Well, you're very lucky, Josh," he said smiling. "Excuse me, I'd better go collect my wife. Give me a call sometime, Henry. Nice meeting you, Josh."

After he'd gone, Josh said, "Was I a schmuck?"

"If that word means what I think it does, the answer's yes."

"I'm sorry," he said. "I was jealous."

I put my arm around his shoulders. "Come on, I'll buy you dinner."

Outside the store I told Josh that I had to make a phone call and went back in. When I returned ten minutes later I was jamming a sales receipt into my pocket but Josh, who was talking to the Goodwill Santa Claus, didn't notice.

Over coffee, Josh said, "I guess we should be getting back home."

The waiter returned with my change. I tucked it into my pocket and said, "We're not going home."

"What do you mean?"

"Trust me," I replied.

□

The immense wreath on the door of the inn on South Van Ness was composed of aromatic pine branches twisted and laced into a shaggy circle and bound by a red velvet ribbon. From outside we could see the big Christmas tree that dominated the drawing room. A bearded man on a ladder was hanging gold ornaments on the topmost branches while a woman strung ropes of popcorn and cranberries around the bottom of the tree. Another woman, gray-haired and aproned, opened the door to let us in.

"Merry Christmas," she said, smelling of cookies and lavender. "Are you Mr. Rios and Mr. Mandel?"

"Yes," I said, as we stepped inside to the companionable heat. "Is the room ready?"

"Just come in and sign the register," she replied.

"Come on, Josh," I said, taking his hand. We followed her to a little counter where I signed us in. She handed me a heavy brass key.

"Second floor," she said. "Room 209. Come down later for carols and eggnog."

"Thank you," I said.

On the stairs Josh stopped me and said, "What is this, Henry?"

"A Hanukkah gift," I replied.

"This is great," he murmured as I led him up the stairs.

Our room had a fireplace. I knelt down in front of it and started a fire. The only other light was cast from the Tiffany lamps and the discreet overhead light above the mammoth four-poster bed. Wings of eucalyptus branches fanned out beneath the mantle of the fireplace, dispersing their rainy fragrance into the room.

This was one Victorian whose rooms fulfilled the promise of its beautifully restored facade. Our walls were papered in deep green with marbled swirls of pink and blue, as if abstracted from a peacock's feathers. The period furniture was comfortably arranged around the oval of the room. High above us in the dusky region of the ceiling, embossed brass caught the glint of the fire and lamplight. Our window looked out upon downtown's brilliant spires and a distant prospect of the Golden Gate.

From the bathroom Josh said, "Henry, look at this bathtub."

I went in. The big porcelain tub was supported by clawed feet The faucet, set into the wall, was a golden lion's head.

"Let's try it out," I said, putting my hands on his shoulders as he knelt inspecting the lion.

He looked up, smiling a little lewdly, and nodded.

We lit the bathroom with candles ordered up from downstairs and stuck them in the sink, on the toilet, at the edges of the tub. Josh lay with his back against me, dividing the water with his fingers. I kissed his bare shoulder, lay my hands lightly on his groin and felt the jerky movements of his penis. From downstairs we heard singing.

"I guess we missed the carols," I said later.

"And the eggnog." He pressed more deeply against me. "Thank you, Henry."

"The water's getting cold," I observed.

"Do we have to get out?" he asked.

"There's still the bed," I said.

"You're right," he replied, and pulled the plug to let the water drain.

While he was still in the bathroom, I pulled the package from beneath the bed and put it on the comforter. He emerged from the bathroom, drying himself, pushed his glasses up his nose and, with a half-smile, inspected the brightly wrapped box.

"More?" he asked.

"One more," I replied, sitting in a wing chair, drawing my robe around me. "Open it."

He tore into the package. "That's why you went back into

the store," he said, holding up the leather jacket that I had most admired him in. "It's beautiful, but Henry, it cost so much."

"Indulge me."

He slipped the jacket on. The deep brown caught the fading firelight and shone against his skin. But I wasn't really looking at the coat.

"It looks great on you," I said. My voice sounded unfamiliar to me.

He took the jacket off and carefully laid it across a chair. "I have a present for you, too," he said.

"What?"

He got his wallet out of his pants pocket and extracted a package from it. "Merry Christmas," he said.

I took the package and laughed. It was a pack of condoms decorated with a picture of Santa Claus.

☐

I was awakened by the phone. I groped for it, picked up the receiver and mumbled a groggy hello.

It was Freeman Vidor. I listened to him for a few minutes, and then sat up in bed. "Are you sure?"

"Yeah," he said, "I'm sure. You better come down."

Josh reached out and stroked my leg. "Henry, who is it?"

"Shh," I said. "Not today, Freeman. Give me until tomorrow. Have you told Cresly?"

"I don't know if he'd buy it," Freeman replied.

"We need the cops," I said, swinging my legs over the edge of the bed. "We'll need all the help we can get."

He spoke for another couple of minutes and then, wishing me a Merry Christmas, hung up.

Josh was wide awake. "What's wrong? Is it Larry?"

"No," I replied. "It's about Jim. We have to get back to L.A."

— 25 —

Although I could not see his face, I knew that the man coming out of the men's room at the Texaco station had different color eyes than when he had gone in. In the front seat, Freeman nudged Cresly who was pressing the side of his face against the window, eyes closed. Sitting in the back, I watched Tom Zane get into his Fiat. A moment later, the Fiat's headlights flashed on and he slipped into the traffic on Highland Boulevard, heading north. Freeman started his car and we got in behind Zane.

Freeman said something to Cresly that I missed.

Cresly replied, "Yeah, let's bust him for using the toilet without buying gas." He lit a thin brown cigarette and rolled down the window. "Ain't this like old times," he said to no one in particular.

"You and Freeman were partners?" I asked, as we squealed to a stop just below Sunset.

"That's right," he said, "and even then Vidor got these hunches and dragged my ass all over town. Right, Freeman?"

"Hey, you're here, aren't you," Freeman replied, as we accelerated forward.

"Maybe," he said, "depending on what happens. If nothing happens, I was never here. This isn't police business yet."

The night sky was a dull red and there wasn't a flicker of natural light to be found in the heavens. Though New Year's Eve was four nights away, it was warm and gritty. We turned east on Hollywood Boulevard, a couple of cars behind the Fiat which now turned onto a side street and into the parking lot for the

Chinese Theater. Freeman followed but went past the lot, pulled up to the curb and parked. A couple of minutes later, Zane emerged from the lot and walked back toward the boulevard.

"You're sure he'll be coming this way?" I asked.

Freeman said, "He did before."

He switched on the radio to a classical music station. Cresly tossed his cigarette out the window and whistled beneath his breath. The dark, palm-lined street was deserted. The city looked like a gigantic backlot for *Day of the Locusts*. All that was needed was for someone to say "Action."

Headlights appeared in the rear-view mirror as a car crossed Hollywood Boulevard. When it passed, I saw it was an Escort bearing the sticker of a car rental agency on its back window.

"That's him," Freeman said, cutting off the last movement of Brahms's Third Symphony.

Cresly, who had been whistling the melody, sat up. "What are you waiting for?"

"This ain't a parade, Phil," Freeman replied.

Cresly spat out the window and muttered, "Feets don't fail me now."

When the Escort crossed the first intersection, Freeman started after it. At Santa Monica Boulevard, we turned right. Santa Monica was brightly lit and there was heavy traffic on the sidewalks, young men and boys standing on either side of the street, at bus stops and in doorways, watching the passing traffic. The Escort took a left at La Brea. Freeman let a couple of cars pass before he followed.

Our next turn was left onto Willoughby, a big street about four blocks south of Santa Monica. There were houses on the south side of Willoughby, but on the north side were the gloomy backs of industrial buildings.

"What's in there?" I asked, pointing at them.

"Office buildings," Freeman said. "Warehouses. Lots of dark places and no one around. That's where Zane takes his pick-ups."

"We're in West Hollywood now," Cresly said.

"This is a crazy place," I replied. "One minute you're in L.A.

and then you cross the street and you're in West Hollywood, but if you jog north you're back in L.A."

"L.A. surrounds West Hollywood," Cresly said, "and it's the sheriffs' turf."

At Highland, the Escort turned left, back up toward Santa Monica Boulevard, and, at Santa Monica, took another left back toward La Brea.

"He's going in circles," Cresly said.

"He's cruising," Freeman replied. He pulled off Santa Monica at Orange, the last cross-street before La Brea, and parked.

"Why are we stopping?" I asked.

"No point in getting him suspicious," Freeman answered. "He'll go around again, to get a good look at what's available, then he'll make his move."

I looked out the window. Two boys in tank tops sat on the bottom step of the entrance to a bank. Their collective age didn't add up to mine. One of them looked back at me, then at Freeman and Cresly. He nudged the other kid. They talked, got up and started moving away.

I pointed them out to Cresly. "They must think we're cops," I said.

"Probably they just think we're trouble," he replied. "Shitty life they got."

"Yeah," I said. "If Zane's been out here beating people up, wouldn't word spread?"

Freeman glanced at me over his shoulder. "He uses a different car. And he knows how to disguise himself."

"Anyway," Cresly added, "these kids come in by the busload every day, it seems. There's always some poor fucker willing to take a chance."

"There he is," Freeman said. I looked out the window to the other side of the street. The Escort was coming to a stop at the corner across from us. A dark-haired boy in tight jeans and a black jacket paced in front of a recording studio. He wasn't wearing a shirt beneath the jacket and when the Escort stopped, he flexed his arms, exposing his torso. He was a nice-looking kid. His dark hair made me think of Josh.

The boy stuck his head into the window of the Escort. A

minute later, he straightened himself, opened the door and got in. Zane signaled a right turn onto Orange. When he completed it, Freeman turned his key in the ignition. The engine whined, sputtered and died.

"Jumping Jesus," Cresly said.

I looked across the street. The rear lights of the Escort were just visible as Zane signaled a left turn into the warehouse district. Freeman grunted and turned the key again. There was a low roar and then nothing. The third time he tried the key, all we heard was a click.

"You flooded the goddam thing," Cresly snapped. He swung his head around to me. "Come on, Rios, let's go." He opened the door. "You," he barked at Freeman, "try to get this coonmobile working."

"Fuck you," Freeman shouted as we got out of the car. When there was a lull in the traffic we ran across the boulevard to the corner where Zane had picked up the hustler. We ran down Orange.

"He turned right at the first street," I said. A yellow junkyard dog sprang out of the shadows from behind a wire fence and chased us, barking and snarling. We reached the intersection and stopped. The street was empty.

We were surrounded by low, dark buildings, fenced-in yards filled with machines, trucks, and stacks of wooden pallets, deserted parking lots and narrow alleys. Scattered streetlamps drizzled yellow light into the darkness. As we stood there, the loudest noise I heard was Cresly's labored breathing. He was in pretty bad shape for a thin man.

"Let's split up," he sputtered, and started walking down the street we had come to. I started off in the opposite direction. I glanced at my watch. It was a little after midnight.

Ten minutes later I was walking through an alley, checking the dumpsters and piles of lumber for the kid's body. Out of the darkness beside me, I heard a car start up. I looked toward the direction of the noise and saw a covered garage, open at either end, running the length of a brick building. At the far end of the garage the headlights of a car flashed on and it rolled toward me. I threw myself against the wall into the shadows and watched the car roar into the alley, skid a turn and race out. It was the Escort. There was one person in it. Zane.

When the Escort turned out of the alley I ran down the garage to where the car had been parked and found another dark street. Hearing footsteps behind me, I turned, my hands clenched into fists. It was Cresly.

"You hear a car?" he called, running toward me.

"Yeah, it was parked here."

We stood on the spot and looked around. There was an ivy-covered wall in front of the photo processing lab across the street. The iron gate set into the wall was slightly ajar. I glanced over at Cresly. He was also staring at the gate.

"Over there," he said in a soft voice.

We crossed the street to the gate and pushed it open. Between the wall and the building behind it, there was a grassy courtyard centered around an elm tree. A body lay beneath the tree, a male body, clad only in a black coat. As we approached him, a strong chemical odor drifted toward us. I had smelled the same odor, though fainter, in Tony Good's bedroom. I'd been wrong. It wasn't amyl nitrite.

"Smell that," I said to Cresly.

"Yeah," he replied, sniffing the air. "Ether."

The boy lay on his stomach. Cresly extracted a pen light from his pocket and flashed it as we knelt down beside the kid. Blood and semen trickled from his anus down his thigh. Cresly pressed his thumb into the front of the boy's neck.

"He's alive," he said, "just knocked out. Let's turn him over."

We rolled him over and Cresly focused the light on the boy's face. Close up, he had a faint resemblance to Josh. His lips were bloody and a slight discoloration was beginning to show beneath his right eye. A shallow gash bisected his chest below his nipples. Cresly opened the boy's jacket and with unexpected delicacy pressed his fingers along the boy's sides.

"No broken bones," he grunted and stood up. "Shit, what a mess."

"We've got to get him to a hospital," I said, also standing.

Cresly switched off the pen light.

"Did you hear me?" I said.

"Yeah, I heard." Cresly looked around and walked away, returning with the boy's pants and shoes. He set them on the grass beside the boy. "Help me get his pants on him."

We struggled with the jeans until we got the boy dressed. Cresly unbuttoned the flannel shirt he was wearing, took it off, and told me to help him get the boy into it. When we finished, Cresly said, "If we go to a hospital I'll have to flash my badge around to get him admitted."

I looked at him, shivering in his undershirt. "So?"

"I want to know there's been a crime before I do that."

I stared at him, slack jawed. "Rape?" I suggested. "Battery? ADW?"

"The kid's a whore."

"Goddammit, are you telling me that this is just an occupational hazard?"

"I'm telling you," he said, "that I'm not about to accuse the star of a fucking cop show of anything until I talk to the kid."

"That's the craziest thing I've ever heard," I said.

"You don't have to like it," Cresly said. "That's the way it is."

"You want to just leave him here, then?" I demanded.

Cresly shook his head. "Your buddy lives around here, doesn't he?"

"Josh? Yeah "

"Let's take the kid there. I'll get a statement and then decide about a hospital "

"He needs a doctor now."

"Yeah, I'll take care of that." He dusted off the knees of his trousers. "You stay here. I'll go see if Vidor got that car started." He started out the gate. "Trust me," he said.

"Sure," I muttered.

□

The boy's name was Robert and he claimed to be twenty, but I would have staked my bar card that he was no more than seventeen. We got him into bed at Josh's apartment where he was examined by an unshaved and slightly inebriated coroner — the only medical type to whom Cresly had ready access — who pronounced him alive and, except for superficial wounds and bruises, in good shape.

Robert said that after Zane picked him up "we drove around and smoked some grass. Then he parked and started getting all lovey, you know. Deep-kiss, that shit. I didn't go for that 'cause I'm not a queer but he said it was his money, so..." He sipped some water. "Then he goes, there's a place around here where we can go. We went to that place where you found me. He tells me to take down my pants 'cause he wants to suck me off. But he wants them all the way off. I'm getting kinda nervous 'cause this guy's way too good-looking to be a trick. I'm thinking he's a cop or something so I tell him, let's just forget it, man. Then he punches me, real hard, and knocks me on my ass. Next thing I know he's sitting on top of me with this switchblade, big mother, too."

Robert's hands trembled as he lifted the water glass to his lips and then set the glass down again. "He goes, shut your fucking mouth or I'll kill you Sure, I go, just don't hurt me. Then he cuts me here," the boy touched the scar across his chest. "He says, take off your pants. I take them off, still lying there on the ground. Then he goes, turn over. The next thing I know he's fucking me, not using any lube or nothin', just sticking it in. Jesus, that hurt, but if I scream or something he stops and pushes the knife into my neck, so I just bite my lip." The boy bit his bruised lips, flinched, and then continued. "He's really hurting me. It's like he's just fucking me to hurt me, not to get off or anything. I guess he came or something 'cause he was lying there on top of me. Then he starts saying these crazy things like, I'm going to cut off your balls, and, I'm going to shove this knife up your ass. Shit like that. But it sounds like he's gonna do it, really. So I start crying." Robert stopped and looked at us. "He turned me over, still sitting on me and he's got the knife and I'm telling him, don't hurt me, don't hurt me."

I heard Josh's quick breathing beside me. "He reaches into his pockets and pulls out this smelly rag. Next thing, he shoves it on my face and it's all wet and cold and then..." He broke off and wiped his face with the back of his hand. "I woke up in your car."

The boy lay his head back into the pillows. "I'm real tired," he said. "Are you guys the cops?"

Cresly nodded. A few minutes later, Robert was asleep.

— 26 —

We were at the kitchen table. Cresly and Freeman were deep into a six-pack of Bud while I drank coffee. Josh sat with his back against the wall, quietly watching us. The little apartment was still except for the ticking of the clock above the stove and, from the bedroom, the faint, ragged noise of Robert's breathing.

Cresly said, "If the kid sticks to his story, we got an ADW." He rubbed his icy eyes. "You tell me how we turn that into Tony Good's murder."

"Zane killed Fox and Blenheim, too," I said, hearing the tiredness in my voice. "He killed them all."

Cresly lit a cigarette. "One thing at a time."

"I asked Freeman to keep an eye on Zane," I began, "because I thought that Blenheim might try something. That's when I still believed that it was Blenheim who killed Fox and Good. But then Freeman — you tell him."

Freeman covered a yawn. "I tracked him for a week," he said. "Three times he went out to pick up a hustler. I didn't think I had to go make sure he got what he paid for, so I just hung around Santa Monica waiting for him to finish." He sipped his beer. "Third night I noticed that he always came back by himself. I got curious, so I drove around looking for the kid he'd picked up that night. I found him. He was holding up a wall, spitting out pieces of his mouth. He split when he saw me. Can't say that I blame him." He smiled wanly at his bottle.

"Everybody needs a hobby," Cresly said in a flat voice. The cold eyes were thawing — from exhaustion, I thought.

"When Freeman told me," I said, picking up the story, "it got me to thinking about Zane and Blenheim. They both liked boys." I glanced at Cresly, who frowned. "But everyone knew about Blenheim," I said, echoing what Larry Ross had told me. "If it had been Blenheim who picked Jim Pears up, the fact that Fox saw them wouldn't have been that serious. Probably not serious enough to make Blenheim a target for blackmail, much less to give him a motive to murder. But Zane, if it had been Zane in the parking lot that night . . . "

"In Blenheim's car," Cresly said, and reached for another beer. "That what you're thinking?"

I nodded. "The rented cars, the disguises. It all fits. Zane took Blenheim's car that night to go cruising. He got lucky at dinner with Pears, and took him to the car. Then Fox found them, got the license plate and traced it to Blenheim."

"That's how Blenheim found out," Freeman said. "When the Fox kid came to the theater looking for Goldenboy. He musta known it wasn't Blenheim—"

"No confusing Sandy Blenheim and Tom Zane," I added, picking up the cup of cold coffee.

"Blenheim figured it was Zane," Freeman said. "Talked to Zane about it. Zane told him to arrange the meeting with Fox."

"Fox met him at the restaurant," I said. "Let him in through the back. They went down to the cellar. That smell tonight, ether, you said. In the transcript of Pear's prelim the waitress who found Jim with Fox's body said the room they were in smelled like someone had broken a bottle of booze. It was ether. Zane knocked Fox out, then killed him.

"Jim Pears, meanwhile," I continued, my exhaustion gone, "thought that Fox was there to see him."

"Why?" Cresly growled.

"That's another story," I replied. "Just listen to me. I've been in that cellar. You can hear footsteps when someone is walking in the kitchen overhead. Zane heard the footsteps, knew someone was coming. He hid himself. When Jim Pears came down, he knocked him out like he knocked out Fox and the kid tonight."

"With the ether," Cresly said, sounding interested in spite of himself.

"Right. Then he saw it was Pears," I said. "He dragged Pears into the room where he had killed Fox, smeared Pears with blood, put the knife in his hand, and let himself out through the back door." I paused, remembering another detail of Andrea Lew's testimony. She'd said she'd looked for Jim out back. That meant the door had been left unlocked — by Zane. In that detail was the whole story, if only I'd paid attention. "Jim came to and then the waitress found him," I continued. "Jim claimed he didn't remember anything. The reason was because there was nothing for him to remember. But that didn't occur to anyone, so we all wrote it off as traumatic amnesia."

From his silent corner, Josh whispered, "He *was* innocent."

We all turned to look at him. "That's right," I said. "Innocent but with no way of explaining why."

"So that's Pears," Cresly said. "What about Good and Blenheim?"

"Blenheim first," I said. "Blenheim knew everything. Irene Gentry — Zane's wife — told me that Blenheim was acting crazy toward Zane just before Good's murder. She was lying, mostly." I stopped and the implications of what Rennie knew sank in for the first time. I pushed it aside for now. There would be time to think it all out later, but there was no denying that it hurt. "But there was some truth in it — Blenheim was probably pushing Zane around, a kind of blackmail, to get Zane to do things that would line Blenheim's pockets."

Cresly squinted. "What, taking money from him?"

I shook my head. "No, working him. Milking Zane for all he was worth because Blenheim got his cut, and it was probably more than ten percent."

"So Blenheim had to go," Freeman said. "But first Zane set it up so that it looked like it was Blenheim who killed Fox and who killed Good."

"Zane and his wife," I corrected. "She came to me the night Good was killed, saying Zane was in terrible danger. I chased through Hollywood looking for Zane while he was taking care of

Blenheim and Good. I was part of the alibi."

Cresly smiled, nastily. "Zane's wife, huh? You bi, or what?"

I let it pass.

"Zane had the motive to kill," I said, "and when Freeman told me that he liked to beat up his pick-ups, well, then it seemed like he had the capacity, too."

Cresly belched, softly. "No way to prove any of this unless Zane or his wife start talking. They won't," he added with dead certainty. "Even if we bust him for what he did tonight. Why should he?"

By the look on Freeman's face, I could see that Cresly's questions had stumped him, too.

"Nope," Cresly continued, picking up his beer. "Old Zane'll hire someone like you, Rios, to cut a deal with the D.A. If he pleads to anything, he'll walk with probation. Or maybe just continue the case until our victim there," he jutted his chin in the direction of the bedroom, "disappears."

He drained his beer and set the bottle down with a thud.

☐

After Freeman and Cresly left, Josh and I made up the couch in the living room and got into it. We lay there in the dark. I thought of Jim Pears who said he was innocent, and was, and Irene Gentry who pretended to be, and wasn't. Depending on what she knew she was an accomplice to at least two of the murders.

Now I let myself think about Rennie. She had played me for a fool with consummate skill. It was a flawless performance. Her task had been formidable: the seduction of a gay man. Since sex, the most direct avenue, was closed to her, she had had to resort to other methods. But she was a brilliant actress, keenly observant of the emotional states of those around her and capable of seemingly profound empathy. She understood me immediately from our first meeting when she told me I had the face of a man who felt too much. A born do-gooder. A rescuer. All she had to do was play a lady in distress.

Her role jibed with what she and Zane had planned from the outset, to divert the suspicion to Blenheim. They must have worked it all out months earlier, when I first came to town to defend Jim Pears. When Blenheim approached me about buying the rights to Jim's story, what he really wanted was to find out how much Jim remembered and what I knew. The three of them had conspired together at first.

Then, later, Rennie and Zane saw their chance to get rid of Blenheim and close the book on the Fox murder once and for all. So Rennie made Blenheim out to be the bad guy. Fortunately for her I disliked Blenheim enough to be an easy convert. After that, it was just a matter of timing.

But now things had unraveled. Why? Rennie was fearless but Zane proved to be the weak link. Another fragment of remembered conversation passed through my head, the actress at the cocktail party who referred to the Zanes as the Macbeths. There was a crucial distinction, though. Lady Macbeth goaded on her husband out of her own ambition. Irene Gentry acted from love. The only time I had ever seen her break character was the day she told me she loved Zane. What a terrifying love that must be to lead her into such darkness.

"You're thinking," Josh said.

"I know. I can't sleep."

"Me neither," he replied. There was a pause. "Do you want to make love?"

I kissed his forehead. "I don't really feel like it."

"Okay," he said. "What are you thinking about?"

I couldn't think of a way to tell him about the darkness, not yet, anyway, so I said, "Tom Zane told me he skipped out on a court appearance fifteen years ago. There's a warrant for his arrest out somewhere. I'll have to tell Cresly about it."

There was a long silence and then Josh said, "Is that all you were thinking about?"

"No." I turned and faced him, trying to make his face out.

"It's about Jim, isn't it?" he asked. "You feel bad because you didn't believe him."

I held him close, not answering.

"I feel the same way," he whispered. "I feel terrible about him."

"Not your fault," I murmured. Then we were quiet again, each with his own thoughts. A long time later we slept.

☐

Someone was tugging at my shoulder. I opened my eyes to Josh's worried face and a sunny room.

"Robert's gone," Josh said.

I pulled myself up and stared at him. "What?"

"I got up and went into the bedroom to get to the bathroom. He's gone."

"Shit." I swung my feet over the edge of our makeshift bed to the floor. I got up and walked into the bedroom. The bed was disheveled but empty. "What time did you come in here?"

"Just now. I mean, ten minutes ago," Josh said, coming up behind me. "He took some things, too."

I looked at Josh. "What?"

"All the money in my wallet. Some clothes." He paused and sucked in air. "The leather jacket you gave me."

"I'm sorry, Josh," I said.

Josh attempted a smile. "He left me his."

"Great." The boy's jacket, cheap vinyl, was tossed across a chair. "I'd better call Cresly. They might be able to find him."

"They won't," Josh said, softly.

I nodded and went to make my call.

☐

Cresly and Freeman arrived just before noon. I put down the tuna sandwich I was eating and answered the door. Their faces were grim.

"No luck?" I asked, as they came into the kitchen.

Cresly's eyes were at their iciest. "I can't believe the kid just fucking walked out of here," he said.

"We were asleep," I said.

"Yeah," he replied, accusingly. "Asleep."

"Look, Cresly, if you'd put him in a hospital instead of bringing him here—" I began.

"Cut it out," Freeman snapped. "The kid's gone."

"What about the warrant?" I asked, having earlier told Cresly about Zane's flight from the robbery charge in Oklahoma.

He shook his head. "Oklahoma went on computer just a couple of years ago with warrants," he said. "For fifteen years back they have to do a hand search. Could take weeks, if they still got the records."

"So now what?" I asked.

Cresly and Freeman exchanged a look. I didn't like it.

Freeman cleared his throat. "The cops want to set up a decoy," he said. "Bust Zane in the act."

"Put someone out on Santa Monica?" I asked.

"Yeah," Freeman said.

"Those boys don't wear many clothes," I said. "You won't be able to wire them for sound. Especially if Zane likes to cuddle before he beats them up."

"That's what the cops figure," Freeman said. "Besides, they're not going to get those kids to cooperate."

Cresly, who had been ominously silent, added, "Yeah, look at the kid who was here last night."

"So use cops," I said.

"We plan to," Cresly said, "but you know how it is. Put a cop in jeans and a tank top, teach him how to mince and lisp and he still looks, walks, and smells like a cop."

I glared at him. "Do you think this stuff up in advance or does it just come to you?"

"He's got a point," Freeman said.

"What's going on here, Freeman?"

"Maybe you noticed how much that kid last night looked like Josh," he said.

"Oh, no," I replied, shaking my head. "Absolutely not."

Freeman said, "Look, Henry. I've watched Zane in action. Josh is exactly the type he goes for."

"The cops get paid for it."

"You want to get Zane or what?" Cresly said.

"Not that much."

"Maybe Josh should decide," Freeman said quietly. "Where is he?"

As if on cue, the front door opened and Josh walked in wearing the black jacket that Robert had left. He smiled, uneasily, and tossed the mail on the coffee table.

"What's up?" he asked.

□

"I'll do it," Josh said, simply, after Freeman and Cresly finished their pitch. We were sitting around the kitchen table again. The ashtray had filled with butts as the afternoon wore on.

"No," I said, quietly. "You won't."

"I want to help," Josh said, looking at me with his dark, serious eyes.

I shook my head in response. The others were silent.

"I owe it to Jim," Josh said.

"Getting yourself killed won't be doing him any favors," I replied.

Cresly said, "No one's gonna get killed here."

I turned on him. "We're dealing with a guy who's already killed three people."

Cresly lit a cigarette. The smoke curled upward into the frosty winter light. "We don't know that he killed anyone yet," he said. "Anyway, he don't kill his dates. And we'll be there."

"How?" I demanded. "You can't wire Josh."

"We'll wire the car Zane rents," Cresly said, exhaling a snaky stream of smoke. "As soon as they get out of the car, we'll be there."

"See, Henry," Josh said.

"Bullshit."

Freeman said to Cresly, "Let's go for a walk, Phil. Let them talk."

Cresly smirked, but got up from the table. "Yeah, you guys talk," he said, "but let me give you something else to think about, Rios. Something washed up on Venice Beach last night. It used to be Sandy Blenheim."

He stalked out of the room.

"We'll be back in a while," Freeman said, following him out.

"You can't do this, Josh," I said. "Cresly's using you. I don't trust him."

"How else are they going to catch Zane?"

"There are other ways," I insisted.

"Like how?" he asked, lighting a cigarette.

"The warrant."

He smiled, wanly. "Cresly says they might never find it."

"Cresly could tell me the sun was going to set tonight and I'd still want a second opinion."

"Why do you hate him?" Josh asked, flicking a bit of ash from the sleeve of his sweater. "'Cause he's a homophobe? The world's full of them," he continued, and added, "I was one. I called Jim Pears a faggot, just like the other guys at the restaurant." He looked at me, his lips a tight line. "I owe him."

"Not that much, Josh."

"If they had asked you, you'd do it. Wouldn't you?"

I didn't have to say anything because we both knew the answer.

— 27 —

Two nights after New Year's, I was sitting in an unmarked police car on Santa Monica Boulevard with Cresly, Freeman, and an officer named Daniels. The strip of the Boulevard between Highland and La Brea, usually packed with hustlers, was almost empty, the result of an earlier sweep by the L.A.P.D. The only hustlers left were actually cops with one exception . . . Josh. He stood at the same corner where Robert had stood, wearing tight jeans, a polo shirt and the black vinyl jacket that Robert had left behind. He ran a hand through his hair and shifted his weight from one foot to the other.

A flat male voice described Zane's progress from Hollywood Boulevard, where he had just rented a Chevette rigged for sound. We and three other cars in the area would be able to monitor what went on in the car within a four block radius. Now there was nothing to do but wait.

'He looks real good out there," Cresly said, referring to Josh.

The radio crackled. "Subject is approaching on Sycamore. You should have him in sight momentarily."

Daniels said, "There."

I looked to where he was pointing. The Chevette turned right and started, slowly, toward La Brea. Cresly fiddled with the monitoring device and the next thing we heard was a rock song.

"What's that?" Freeman asked.

I listened. "Talking Heads."

Freeman looked at me blankly. Zane made three passes on the boulevard between Highland and La Brea, coming in and out of the range of the radio. Each time he seemed to slow a little when he passed Josh. The fourth time he signaled a turn onto the side street where Josh stood, turned, and pulled up at the curb. I watched Josh walk over to the car, just as Robert had, and stick his head into the window.

Josh said, "Hi. How's it going?"

"Can't complain," Zane replied, his voice watery from drinking. "You waiting for someone?"

There was silence.

Zane spoke again. "You wanna go for a ride? I've got some grass here."

"Sure," Josh said. My stomach clenched. I looked up and watched as he climbed into Zane's car. We heard the engine start up and then the Chevette drifted lazily down the street.

A match was struck. We heard someone sucking in air and then, in a tight voice, Zane said, "Take it."

More sucking noises. Cresly said to Daniels, "Follow them."

We pulled a turn across four lanes of traffic and drove down the street where the Chevette had gone. The only noises we heard were of the joint being smoked. A moment later, we got the Chevette in sight. It pulled over to the curb. We passed it. I resisted the temptation to glance over at Josh.

"So," we heard Zane say, "what's your name?"

Josh said, "Josh. What's yours?"

"Charlie," Zane said. "What are you into, Josh?"

We turned up the first street and headed back to Santa Monica, then turned back, making a circle, toward the Chevette. Cresly instructed Daniels to park just before we got to the street where the Chevette was parked.

Josh was saying, "Whatever, you know. Anything you want."

Cresly glanced at me without expression.

There was a movement in the Chevette. Josh laughed. "That tickles," he said.

Zane said, "Does this tickle?"

There was squeaking, rapid breathing, silence, then a slow breath and a sigh.

Daniels asked, "What's going on in there?"

"They're making out," I said. Daniels stared at me.

"Gross," he muttered.

Zane said, "That was nice. How come I haven't seen you around before?"

"I just got into town," Josh replied.

"I know someplace around here we can go," Zane said. "I'll give you a hundred bucks if you let me—" A sudden wave of static drowned out the rest of his sentence.

"Okay," Josh said.

We heard the engine start up. Cresly told Daniels, "Go around again."

We edged up to the intersection of the street where the Chevette was parked. Just as we turned, and the Chevette started moving, a black-and-white appeared from still another street.

"What the fuck," Cresly said, and yanked the transmitter from the radio, trying to signal the black-and-white It passed beneath a streetlight as it slowly approached the Chevette. It wasn't L.A.P.D. but the county sheriffs who had, apparently, drifted across the county line into the city. A flashlight flared from within the black-and-white as it pulled up beside the Chevette.

Zane said, "Shit." He gunned the motor and made a run for Highland. The black-and-white's red lights flashed and we heard it order Zane to pull over.

We pulled out behind the sheriffs. Cresly was screaming into the radio trying to stop them from giving chase.

"Clear out!" Cresly was yelling. Abruptly, the black-and-white stopped. Over the radio, someone was asking for clarification. The Chevette, however, was gone.

We came up beside the sheriffs. Cresly rolled the window down and continued screaming at the driver. A couple of minutes later he slumped into the seat, breathing hard. He picked up the transmitter and canvassed the other L.A.P.D. cars in the area. Finally, he turned to me and said, "We lost them."

"What!"

"I said we lost them, goddammit. Put out an APB," he snapped at Daniels.

I listened as Daniels gave an urgent description of the Chevette and its passengers.

Cresly looked at me again. "Where would he go, Rios? Home?"

"Not likely if his wife is there," I replied, trying to keep my panic in check. "Maybe he'll just drop Josh off and call it a night. You might have someone watching the car rental place."

"That's covered," he said. "Anywhere else you can think of?"

"He has a place in Malibu," I said, finally.

"What's the address?"

"I don't know. His wife, she would know. I think I could get us in the neighborhood, though."

Cresly's mouth twitched. "All right," he said. "You tell us how to get there. I'll send a car to his wife and get the address to alert the sheriffs in Malibu. Can you think of anywhere else he might go?"

I shook my head.

Cresly ordered a car to go to Zane's house and get the Malibu address from Irene Gentry. Freeman, who had been stone silent, said, "I'm sorry, Henry."

"Let's hope you don't have anything to be sorry about."

"Where do we go?" Cresly asked.

"Out Sunset to the Coast Highway," I said, "then go north into Malibu."

"You heard the man," Cresly snapped at Daniels. He reached to the floor and came up with a siren which he stuck to the top of the car. We shot into the darkness, the siren whining and utter silence between us.

□

We sped through the city, its lights exploding around us like landmines. As we passed through UCLA, the radio crackled. I could not make out what was being said but a moment later, Cresly looked at me over his shoulder.

"We got an address from Zane's wife," he said. "Twenty-eight hundred Sweetwater Canyon Road. That sound right?"

"I never knew the address," I replied, "but I should be able to recognize the house."

Cresly relayed the address to the sheriffs in Malibu, who had already been alerted to what was happening.

"They'll probably beat us to him," Daniels, the other cop, said. He sounded disappointed.

I sat back in the seat. Freeman lit a cigarette. We passed a row of luxury condominium buildings lit up against the darkness of the January sky like ocean liners. A helicopter swept through the red skies. Traffic yielded in our wake and soon we were at the end of Sunset, facing the dark ocean at the end of the land. We turned onto the Coast Highway.

I considered the possibilities. If we found them at Malibu and Josh was unharmed, then there would be no reason to arrest Zane and no chance to link him to the murders he had committed. But if Josh was hurt — I stopped myself. If they were there at all. They could be anywhere in this catacomb of a city and anything could be happening. My body grew cold.

I looked out the window to the ocean. The last time I had been out here, the sea was alive with light. Now it swagged against the shore illuminated only by car headlights as they flickered, briefly, across the ocean's oily darkness. I thought of Sandy Blenheim, who had been disgorged by the sea only a few days earlier, and it was with relief that I turned away from the water as the highway twisted inland. Soon, the honky-tonk business district of Malibu sprang up around us. We passed the bar where I had stopped to call Freeman. The woman who had flipped me off might be there now, getting herself comfortably drunk.

Without warning, a seismic shiver worked its way up my spine. When it passed I found myself balling my hands into fists.

Freeman, sitting beside me, asked, "You okay?"

We skidded across an intersection. There was a Texaco station at the southwest corner and a road beside it that led off into darkness. Suddenly, I knew that that was the road that led to Zane's place.

"We're going the wrong way," I said.

Cresly said, "What?"

"The road where Zane lives. We just passed it."

"Sweetwater Canyon's up a ways," Daniels said tentatively.

"Don't you understand?" I said impatiently. "She lied to us."

"You sure?" Cresly asked, skeptically.

"I remember the gas station back there. That's where I turned."

There was silence in the front seat.

"We're wasting time," I snapped. "Cresly..."

Almost at that instant, the radio flared up. This time I could hear what was being said. Twenty-eight hundred Sweetwater Canyon Road was a vacant lot next to a trailer park.

"Turn around," Cresly said.

Daniels pulled a U-turn in a flurry of lights, squealing brakes and horns. Two minutes later we were back at the road by the gas station.

Cresly looked over his shoulder. "Where to?"

"It's not far," I said. "Kill the siren. You don't want him to panic."

"Right."

The dark trees swayed like ghosts along the road as the sea wind ripped through them. Out beyond the lights of Malibu, it was dark as a tomb. The landscape passed as if in a dream and yet I could feel we were coming to the place. The house behind the cypress. The ginger-colored cat. The charred wood in the fireplace. The trees came into view.

"There," I said. "There's a house behind those trees."

Daniels pulled into the driveway and we came to a lurching stop, just missing the white Mercedes that blocked the Chevette ahead of it.

"Someone beat us to him," Freeman said.

"That's his wife's car," I replied

Our headlights caught a dark-coated figure at the door. It was Rennie.

"That's her," I said. Daniels killed the lights and we were in total darkness but for a faint orange light coming from behind the curtain of one of the windows at the front of the house. The curtain seemed to sway a bit as if the window were open.

As we got out of the car, Cresly said to Freeman, "You armed?"

Freeman grunted an assent.

To Daniels, he said, "Radio Malibu. Tell them where we are. Is there a back way out, Rios?"

"Yeah," I said, opening my door.

"Go around the back when you're finished, Daniels. Take your rover, but don't shine any lights. If he's armed, we don't want to give him a target." Cresly picked up his own rover — a handheld radio — and got out of the car. Our feet crunched the gravel as we made our way to the back of the Mercedes.

"What's she doing?" Cresly asked as we strained to see through the darkness. She made a movement. Cresly drew his gun.

"Mrs. Zane," he said, "I want you to move back here, move away from the door."

"Who are you?" she demanded.

"The police, Mrs. Zane."

He's listening to us, I thought, watching the fluttering of the curtain at the window. Zane was inside listening. Suddenly, the light went out and then there was an explosion. A bullet sizzled through the darkness, within inches of where I stood. I dropped to my knees.

Daniels, kneeling beside me, said, "Draw his fire, while I get around back."

"No," I said. "Josh might be in there. You'll endanger him. And her."

Cresly said, "Move around the cars, Daniels. Just go slow."

"Tom! Tom! Let me in!" Rennie pounded on the door, shattering the stillness. Daniels scurried around the cars and quickly eased himself over the fence at the side of the house. Rennie screamed to be let in.

From within the house, Zane shouted. "Get back, Rennie! It's all over. Just get away."

She seemed to collapse against the door. I started toward her.

"Rios, stop," Cresly said in a fierce whisper.

Ignoring him, I squatted and darted to the porch. She sat with her back against the door, her face barely discernible in the darkness but when I whispered, "Rennie," she looked up at me, her eyes glittering.

"It's Henry. Come on." I reached my hand for her and she slapped it away.

"They'll kill him," she sobbed.

I half-lifted, half-dragged her up to her feet. "There's no time for this," I said. "The cops are here and more are on their way. You'll get caught in the crossfire. Let's go."

She struggled for a moment longer. "He won't let me in," she cried, then she let me pull her back toward the cars. I sat her down on the ground. Freeman was there, his gun drawn, looking into the darkness.

"Where's Cresly?"

"Out there," he said, nodding at a shadowy flicker of movement between a couple of trees.

"What's he doing?"

"He's gonna draw Zane's fire while Daniels breaks in through the back."

"Josh is in there," I said.

Just then, we heard Cresly from the other side of the yard say, "Zane. If the boy's in there with you, let him come out."

He was answered with another shot.

"Is that his evidence?" I demanded. I started toward Cresly, but Freeman pulled me back.

"You can't go out there, man."

"We don't know whether Josh is in there or not."

"Then ask her," Freeman said, jutting his chin at Rennie.

I knelt beside her. Her hair was disheveled and a silvery line of snot ran from her nose to her upper lip. Her face was slack and she looked old. Older than I had ever seen her before.

"Is Tom in there alone?" I asked.

She looked at me without apparent recognition and swayed her head back and forth.

I grabbed her by the shoulders. "Listen to me. Who's in the house?"

She turned her head away from me, lay her cheek against the car and muttered, "What does it matter. They're going to kill him."

Cresly yelled out, "Let the boy go, Zane. If he's okay we don't have anything on you."

I dug my hands deeper into her shoulders and shook her. "Tell me!"

She drew a long, shaky breath. "Is what he said true?"

"Yes," I said. "They know about the murders but they don't have any hard evidence. Tonight was a set-up. The boy was bait. If he's all right, they can't charge Tom with anything."

Even as I spoke I heard sirens, far off, but approaching.

"I heard another voice," she said. "Male."

I released her shoulders and crawled over to Freeman. "She says she heard Josh in there. I've got to tell Cresly."

"I'll go," Freeman said. "Watch her."

The sirens were coming closer. "Hurry, before the sheriffs get here. They'll scare him into something stupid."

"Zane?" he asked, confused.

"Cresly. Go on."

Freeman jumped into the darkness and disappeared, with only the crackle of grass, leaves, and twigs to mark his path. I returned to Rennie. The sirens. If Zane couldn't hear them by now, he soon would. I thought of Daniels alone in the back of the house.

"Did you just lie to me, Henry?" Rennie asked, in a semblance of her old voice.

"I'm just trying to avoid any more killing," I said.

She wiped her nose on her sleeve and said, "What hate you must feel for me."

"The boy in there is my lover," I replied, "and right now I don't feel anything about anyone except for him."

"But how—" she began.

"There's no time to explain." From their sirens, I guessed the sheriffs had found the road. "But if anything happens to him, I'll—"

"You don't have to threaten me," she said. "I understand."

I nodded. Someone tugged at my elbow. I swung around and found Cresly beside me.

"What the hell's going on here?" he demanded.

"She says she heard Josh in there."

"Bullshit." He bit off the word. "If he was in there, or still alive, Zane woulda used him to buy his way out. I'm sending Daniels in."

"You can't," I said, but he was reaching for his radio.

Then, three things happened, separated by only a matter of seconds yet seeming to span an eternity. The sirens screamed in my ears. I looked around and saw the first sheriff's car flash through the trees. Then, I turned back to Cresly who had lifted his rover to his mouth and swung at him wildly, knocking the radio to the ground. He looked up at me, fury and amazement spreading across his face. As he reached for the radio, there was a shot from within the house. We swiveled around. Rennie screamed. There was another shot and then, as its echo faded, doors slammed, voices cried out and the yard was full of cops moving toward the house, guns drawn.

"Don't shoot," Cresly shouted. "I got a man in there."

The sheriffs stopped in their tracks. A deputy hurried over to us. "What is this?"

"Keep your men back," Cresly said and picked up his radio. "Daniels."

"I'm right here," Daniels answered. "Out back. Something's going on in there."

We all looked toward the house. The porch light flashed on. Cresly stood up and shouted, "This is your last chance before we start shooting. Come out with your hands on your head."

Slowly, the door opened. My breath caught in my throat as someone stepped out onto the porch, hands raised high over his head. It was Josh. I breathed.

☐

We were sitting on the porch steps. I had wrapped my coat around Josh's shoulders and put my arm around him, but he could not stop shivering or talking, even as he cried. He simply talked through his tears.

"It happened so fast," he said. "He had me sitting by the fireplace with the gun on me. Then we heard the sirens and he looked out the window. Just for a second. I grabbed the poker and just swung. It was dark and I couldn't see very well but I must have hit his hand because the gun went off and then I heard it hit the floor. I went for it and when I got it I just started shooting — I just..." He broke off, sobbing.

I held him closer. "It's all right, Josh."

"But I killed him, Henry."

"He had the poker," I said.

"But I couldn't see that," Josh said. "I didn't wait to see what would happen."

"Thank God for that," I said. He buried his face in my chest. I looked above his head into the room behind us. A sheriff knelt beside Zane's body. Someone laughed. Someone sipped from a cup of coffee.

Irene Gentry stood with her back against the wall. Cresly walked up to her and said something. She shook her head slowly, again and again, until he shrugged and walked away. After he'd gone, she lifted a slender hand and, almost contemptuously, wiped the tears from her face. As if aware she was being watched, she looked slowly around the room and then out the door until our eyes met. I tried to read their expression but she was far away. I heard her ask for a cigarette and she passed out of my view.

Josh asked, "What will happen to her?"

"If they can prove the murders, she could be indicted as an accomplice. If not," I shrugged. "I doubt that anything worse can happen to her than happened tonight."

He was quiet in my arms. Nothing worse could happen to her. She told me once that we each loved according to our natures and her nature had brought her to an empty place, where it was as easy to die as to love. I looked down at Josh. The light shone off his face. His eyes were full of questions to which I had no answer but one. But that one I could finally give.

"I love you, Josh," I said.

HOW TOWN

For Sasha Alyson

ACKNOWLEDGMENTS

My thanks to Katherine V. Forrest, Jed Mattes, Larry Ashmead and Eamon Dolan for sweating this one out with me.

HOW TOWN

1

The road to my sister's house snaked through the hills above Oakland, revealing at each curve a brief view of the bay in the glitter of the summer morning. Along the road, houses stood on small woodsy lots. The houses were rather woodsy themselves, of the post and beam school, more like natural outcroppings than structures. Wild roses dimpled the hillsides, small, blowsy flowers stirring faintly in the trail wind of my car. Otherwise, there was no movement. The sky was cloudless, the weather calm and the road ahead of me clear.

Earlier, coming off the Bay bridge I'd taken a wrong turn and found myself in a neighborhood of small pastel houses. Grafitti-gashed walls and a preternatural calm marked it as gang turf. The papers had been full of gang killings that month. When I drove past, a child walking by herself flinched, ready to take cover. None of that was visible from these heights.

This was like living in a garden, I thought, and other associations came to mind: Eden, paradise, a line from "Sunday Morning" that I murmured aloud: "Is there no change in paradise?" I couldn't remember the rest. Elena would know. And she would appreciate the irony. She and I had grown up in a neighborhood called Paradise Slough in a town called Los Robles about an hour's drive from here.

There had been little about our childhood that could be described as paradisiacal. Our alcoholic father was either brutal or sullenly withdrawn. Our mother retaliated with religious fanaticism. As she knelt before plaster images of saints, in the flicker of votive candles, her furious mutter was more like invective than prayer. Their manias kept my parents quite busy, and Elena and I were more or less left to raise ourselves.

This should have made us allies, but it had the opposite effect. We lived in adjoining bedrooms and occasionally as I lay awake listening to one of my father's drunken rampages, and the wail of my mother's prayers, I was aware of Elena next door, also awake, also listening. It never occurred to me to seek shelter with her, though she was five years older and so, by my lights, almost an adult. What she made of all this, I had no idea, as we never discussed what went on in our house. Elena and I were united only in our unspoken determination to show nothing of what we felt about this embarrassment of a life that our parents had visited upon us. In this we succeeded. To the outside world we were simply quiet children, good at school, not very social, a little highstrung.

Consequently her friends and teachers were completely unprepared for her decision to enter a teaching order of nuns after she graduated from high school. I, on the other hand, understood perfectly. She didn't have a vocation. Our mother had ruined us both for religion. What had happened was that our father forced her to refuse admission to Berkeley on the grounds that she had had enough education for a woman. The Church offered her the one way she could defy him. After he died, Elena left her order, got her master's in American literature and took a job at St. Winifred's College, a girls' school where she had now taught for nearly twenty years. She never again referred to the four years she lived as Sister Magdalan, her bride-of-Christ moniker, and since it had all been faintly embarrassing to me—"my sister, the Sister," I called her, never to her face—I didn't raise the subject.

As long as my mother was alive, we maintained the fiction of being a family and I would see Elena once or twice a year. And then, ten years ago, Mother died, and we returned to Los Robles for the funeral. I was startled by how old Elena appeared; the five years she had on me looked more like twenty. If her appearance was due to grief over our mother's passing, it seemed excessive. My mother died of stomach cancer, and her last days on earth were ghastly.

So I could not understand why Elena seemed insensible with pain. On the way back from the cemetery, trying to do my brotherly duty, I took her hand and muttered consoling platitudes. She pulled her hand away, lit a cigarette and told me not to be a fool. We closed up the house and I went back to finish law school.

A few months later I called her on her birthday. The phone was answered by a woman who identified herself as Elena's roommate. When I asked Elena about her, she was evasive and then peremptory, but it was clear that her mood had lightened considerably since the funeral. In later phone calls, the roommate went unmentioned but every now and then Elena would slip pronouns from "I" to "we," and at some point it occurred to me that this woman was her lover.

I wouldn't have assumed this so quickly had I not been in the process of finally accepting my own homosexuality. By turns terrified and euphoric at the discovery that I wasn't crazy but only queer, I couldn't keep my mouth shut about it. I thought it would be wonderful if Elena was also gay, a final joke on our parents. When I told her about myself there was an appalled silence at her end of the line and then a sputtered, vehement lecture, complete with biblical citations, on the evils of homosexuality. Furious, I accused her of hypocrisy, spelling out exactly what I meant. She hung up on me. I did not talk to her again for a year and a half, until we ran into each other in San Francisco.

After that we had fashioned a kind of truce, careful to call each other just often enough so that nothing too dire could be read into periods between. For many years we'd lived within thirty miles of each other, she in Oakland and I on the peninsula. Our calls would terminate in a vapor of promises to meet for lunch or dinner, but we never did. Since moving to Los Angeles a year earlier, I'd not heard from her at all outside of a Christmas card and a note on my birthday. And then there'd been her urgent call two days earlier, the very day that I was leaving for San Francisco to attend a wedding.

I slowed down, searching for an address by which to orient myself. An old-fashioned mailbox on the side of the road bore the name of her street, and its number indicated I was approaching her house. An even clearer sign was the tumble of sensation in my stomach. Although I was acutely attuned to the emotions of those around me, this was merely a skill I'd developed as a defense against being lied to by my clients: very few people evoked my own feelings. Elena was one of them. Toward her I felt—what?—regret? No, nothing quite as settled as that. The truth was, I didn't know what I felt but it was strong enough to bring me here on a mysterious summons against every inclination.

I had never been to her house. I drove across a little wooden bridge that forded a stream, past a windbreak of pine, and came to a stop in front of a brick and redwood split-level perched on the side of a hill. As I got out of the car, it occurred to me just how much time had passed since that summer afternoon in San Francisco when I'd last seen her. She would be 42 now, and I, whom she'd last seen as a stripling of 28, a freshly minted lawyer, was now 37 and had been in some bad neighborhoods since then, and it showed.

I pushed the doorbell. Melodious chimes sounded from within the house. I found myself face to face with my sister. We looked at each other and for a moment it seemed as if we might embrace, but the moment passed.

"Hello, Henry. Come in."

"Hello, Elena."

I stepped into the cool hall. On a small wooden table was an earthenware pot filled with daisies, and above it a mirror in which I saw the back of her tidy head and my own expressionless face.

She shut the door behind me and said, "You look well, Henry."

"You, too."

She smiled briskly. "I don't change, I just get older."

We started down the hall. I said, "It has been a while. We look more alike than ever."

She nodded. "Yes, I noticed that, too."

As children there'd been a sort of generic resemblance between us; we shared our father's dark coloring, his black hair, teary brown eyes, and we each had the same high rounded cheekbones that had led to our grade school nickname, "*los chinitos.*" We no longer looked Chinese. There was a truer, more exact resemblance in the way our faces had thinned out with age, revealing the basic structure.

"I can offer you coffee, or would you like a drink?" Elena asked, leading me into a sparsely furnished room that looked out upon a patio and, beyond that, the bay. "Which?"

"Coffee is fine."

I hadn't told her I no longer drank, because I was unwilling to make the admission of weakness that that would imply to her.

While she made coffee in the kitchen I walked to the window. A regatta of sailboats drifted across the water like a cloud. Looking around the room, I observed the clean, hard

Nordic surfaces of Elena's surroundings. Even here, in her own home, she worked hard at revealing nothing about herself beyond conventional good taste, but there were clues about her past. A crucifix. A wave-shaped chunk of glass that, on closer inspection, was a stylized Madonna.

An oil painting of a nude above the fireplace showed a desiccated woman with a flat Indian face, standing with her hands at her breasts, as if to protect herself. There was nothing soft about her nudity; its graphic, painful clarity denied any sensuality—she was a Madonna for whom giving birth had been an act of self-obliteration. I wondered if this represented our mother to Elena.

Behind me, glass chinked against glass and I turned to find Elena setting cups and saucers, sugar bowl, creamer and spoons on the coffee table.

"Joanne's work?" I asked, indicating the painting. One of the few things I knew about Elena's roommate was that she taught art at St. Winifred's.

"Yes, that's right." Her tone warned me off that conversational trail. "You take your coffee black?"

"That's fine." I lowered myself into a chrome and leather contraption and watched her measure out a teaspoon of cream into her own cup, like Prufrock, measuring out his life with coffee spoons.

I was reminded of the poem I thought of driving up. "It's so beautiful up here," I said, "I was thinking of that Stevens poem, 'Sunday Morning.' What's the line after, 'Is there no change in paradise?' "

"You're misquoting, Henry." She got up and walked to the bookshelves at the far end of the room, returning with a volume that she flipped through knowingly. In a clear, low voice she read, " 'Is there no change of death in paradise? Does ripe fruit never fall? Or do the boughs hang always heavy in that perfect sky . . .' " Shutting the book, she looked up at me. "He makes it sound so dull."

"Don't you think it would be? Everyone sitting around gazing at God for eternity like reporters at a presidential press conference. Even Dante couldn't work up much enthusiasm for paradise."

"You're as cynical as my students, Henry. But they at least have the excuse of being young."

The coffee smelled of hazelnut. I sipped it. "Nice," I said. "You've become quite elegant, Elena."

"And you've been a lawyer too long. Everything you say sounds like innuendo." She reached into a silver case on the table and extracted a long brown cigarette. Putting it to her lips, she asked, "What is this wedding you're here for?"

I lit her cigarette with a crystal lighter. "Two friends," I replied, "a cop and a criminal defense lawyer. It's a little like a gathering of the Hatfields and the McCoys."

"Is he with the San Francisco police?"

"She," I replied, "is an assistant chief. He's the lawyer. I introduced them."

She drew lazily at her cigarette. "Are they marrying in a church?"

I shook my head. "A civil ceremony. They've rented out a bed-and-breakfast place on Alamo Square. Josh and I are staying there."

At the mention of my lover's name, she gazed down at the milky surface of her coffee. "Will you be staying long?"

"Until Monday," I said, adding deliberately, "Josh has to get back to school. He's at UCLA."

Brushing the tip of her cigarette against the edge of an ashtray, she said, "Yes, I think you mentioned that once." As if to forestall further discussion of Josh, she asked, "Do you like Los Angeles?"

"Most of the time. Our house is on a hill, too, like yours. I can see the Hollywood sign from the kitchen window. The other day Josh spotted a pair of deer in the underbrush. It's not at all what I expected."

"Deer," she repeated. "That's interesting."

"Do you ever get down to LA?" I asked.

"No," she replied. "I have no reason to."

I thought about that for a moment and let it pass. Tactless remarks were part of the price we paid for remaining strangers. That, and a finite store of small talk. I'd exhausted mine.

"You said you wanted to see me on a professional matter. Something going on?"

She set her cigarette down. "Not with me," she replied. "Do you remember Sara Bancroft? We grew up together."

A dim image formed in my head of a tall, blonde, unlikable girl. "Vaguely."

"She married Paul Windsor. I think you knew his brother Mark."

I remembered Mark Windsor well, his younger brother Paul less well. The Windsors were local gentry in Los Robles. Mark and I had run track in high school. Miler, we called him, after his event. I had been infatuated with him. Paul had just been someone who got in the way when I was trying to be alone with Mark, little good that that did.

"I remember them."

"Paul's been arrested for murder."

This got a startled "Really?" out of me.

"Apparently he needs a lawyer," she said, without a trace of irony. "I told her I'd talk to you."

"Do they still live in Los Robles?"

"Yes."

"There isn't a town in California that's too small not to have too many lawyers," I said, "including Los Robles. I suggest they start there."

Elena stroked her throat, a nervous gesture that went far back into our childhood. "Sara insisted on you."

"Why?"

She put out her cigarette decisively and said, "I don't know very much about it, Henry. Sara was upset, and she'd been drinking when she called me. The man Paul's supposed to have killed was involved in child pornography. The police are saying it was because he was blackmailing Paul. Sara denied it. She—"

"Wait," I said. "Back up. What's the connection between Paul Windsor and child pornography?"

Her fingers tugged her throat. "A few years ago Paul was arrested for—I don't know what it's called—child molesting?" She forced her hand down. "The girl was fifteen, I think, but it had been going on for some time."

"Are you telling me that Paul Windsor is a pedophile?"

"I don't know what that word means."

I had heard her use that tone before. It implied that her ignorance was grounded in superior morality.

"It's a technical term," I replied, "denoting someone who is sexually attracted to children. The street term is 'baby fucker.' "

Her face darkened. "That was cheap."

I shrugged. "Was he convicted?"

"I don't know," she said, "but he didn't go to jail." Clearly uncomfortable, she fiddled with her coffee cup. Elena had arranged her life as tastefully as she had this room. All this talk of murder and child molesting must have been as unpleasant for her as discovering a bowel movement in the center of her coffee table. I felt a tiny bit of pleasure at her discombobulation. Maybe, as she'd said earlier, I'd been a lawyer too long. In any event, I was used to cleaning up other people's shit.

"When did all this happen?" I asked.

"A week, ten days ago."

"Is he in jail?"

"Yes," she said.

"Then he's already been arraigned," I said. "He must've had a lawyer for that."

Elena looked doubtful. "I really don't know the details, Henry. Sara called three days ago. She said she'd read about you in the papers last year when you had that case in Los Angeles. That busboy."

Jim Pears, I thought, a boy who'd been accused of murdering a classmate who had threatened to expose Jim's homosexuality. The case had never gone to trial because Jim killed himself, but I had still been able to establish his innocence. Then it occurred to me why Sara Windsor might have insisted that I defend her husband.

"Does she think that because I'm gay I have some special insight into pedophiles?"

She cast a cool look at me and said, "Not everyone judges people by their sexual practices. Maybe she just thinks you're an able lawyer."

"What do you think, Elena? She's your friend."

"I hadn't spoken to her in years before she called."

I have a good ear for lies, and I'd just been lied to. Elena was apparently embarrassed by her old friendship with the wife of a child molester. It made me think less of her.

Acidly, I said, "Sexual deviance isn't a virus, Elena. It's not catching."

"What are you talking about, Henry?"

"Loyalty to one's friends."

Her face reddened again. "Why else would I have asked you up here?"

"Touché." I picked up my now cold cup of coffee. The faint flavor of hazelnut had soured as it cooled. "I don't defend child molesters."

"That's not what Paul's accused of," she pointed out.

"From what you've told me, his pedophilia would very likely come up in trial."

She reached into the silver box for another reedy brown cigarette and lit it impatiently. Her brand was popular in the ghettos because it could be dipped in PCP without showing a stain. She asked caustically, "Do you always make such fine moral distinctions?"

"Morality doesn't have much to do with it. I choose not to add to the popular delusion that all gay men are pedophiles by defending them."

"You don't want to be tarred with the same brush, is that it?"

"Don't patronize me, Elena. I don't give a damn what you think of me or how I live, or what my principles are."

"I never thought you did."

We stared at each other, puffed up and ready to strike.

"And what about Sara?" she demanded. "Are you going to tar her with the same brush?"

"That's touching considering that you haven't spoken to her for years."

"What would you say to Mark Windsor if he walked into the room and asked you for help, Henry?" she asked quietly.

"There are some old friends one does not refuse."

I was disarmed. Elena had never before acknowledged that she understood what I'd felt for Mark. Even more astounding was the implication of what she'd felt for Sara. I searched her face to see whether the implication was intended but her expression revealed nothing.

"All right, Elena. I'll talk to her."

"Thank you."

She got up and went over to a small desk where she consulted an address book and wrote something on a slip of paper. She handed it to me and I glanced down at the name and number.

"I've never asked you for anything before," she said, evidently bothered by incurring the debt.

I reassured her. "It's not a big deal." I extracted myself from the chair. "It was nice to see you, Elena."

"I'll walk you out to your car."

The heat had become a bit denser and the light a little dustier as the fragrant morning waned. Birds called from the surrounding trees and the low burble of water sounded from the stream that ran through Elena's property. Against this blurred and languid landscape, she seemed too sharp, too definite to belong.

"This is heaven," I said, opening the car door.

She smiled, deepening the lines around her mouth. "Have you ever read Primo Levi?"

"No."

"He has a passage in his book about concentration camp

survivors—to the effect that those who have once been tortured go on being tortured. Heaven's not possible for people like that."

I was startled by the vehemence of the analogy—if that's what it was—to our childhood and said, "You have a long memory."

"I'm older than you," she replied. "I have more to remember. Good-bye, Henry."

"Good-bye," I said, from my car, and rolled out of the driveway.

She waved, briefly, folded her arms in front of her and watched me go.

2

Josh wasn't in the room when I got back into the city though there were telltale signs of his recent occupancy—clothes scattered on the floor, the bathroom faucet left dripping, an open book left facedown on the bed. The book was called *Healing AIDS Through Visualization* and I picked it up and read a paragraph. The author urged his readers to imagine their bloodstreams were filled with anti-HIV commandos on search-and-destroy missions. It was the kind of thing that, privately, I felt he read far too much of. I preferred to place my trust in science. But given the shameful record of the medical establishment on AIDS I had to admit sometimes that my trust was perhaps as misplaced there as was his in New Age naturopathy. I upbraided myself for my negative thinking. Josh wasn't sick, after all, though the previous summer his T-cell count had fallen to the point that he'd been put on a combination of drugs, including AZT.

His health had precipitated our move back to Los Angeles from the Bay Area, to allow him to be close to his parents. The move had not been easy for either one of us. I had given up a going law practice and roots that went far back in a town that had been my home since I'd left my parents' house at seventeen. What Josh had surrendered was not as tangible but equally important. To him the move back had represented a step back from the adult independence which, at 25, meant so much to him. It had also awakened the nightmare of mortality for both of us. He wouldn't have done it except that his parents were old and the bond between them and their only son powerful. For their sake, we had moved, and yet I knew we both wondered if it had been the right thing to do.

As always when he was gone I felt a tiny tremor of apprehension, like a second, fainter heartbeat that never seemed to stop.

I forced myself to think about Elena. Having told her I would call Sara, I now felt reluctant to do so. Although Los Robles, Sara, even Elena, were in the past, the past was a thin layer of ash over embers that could still burn. Overcoming my resistance, I sat in the rocking chair by the bay window, pulled the phone into my lap and dialed Sara Windsor's number. After a moment of long-distance static, the phone rang and was answered, and a woman's voice ventured a tentative "Hello."

"Mrs. Windsor?"

The voice was cautious, remote. "Yes."

"This is Henry Rios. I've just been to see my sister. She said you wanted to talk to me."

"Hello, Henry. Thank you for calling. I didn't know how long it would take Elena to talk to you." She paused. "Did she explain the situation?"

Fencing with Elena had used up all my verbal delicacy. Abruptly, I replied, "Your husband's in jail for murder and you want to hire me to defend him."

When she spoke again, she matched my abruptness. "Yes, that's right."

I put my feet up on the bed and glanced out the window toward Alamo Square, the small park that gave the inn its name. A couple of joggers came to a slow stop. One of them was Josh and the other was Kevin Reilly, the bridegroom-to-be. Josh stripped off his blue singlet and even from here I could see how thin he was.

"Henry?"

"I'm sorry Mrs. Windsor, I didn't hear you."

"I was asking whether you were available."

"I practice in Los Angeles now," I said, looking away from the window. "Unless there's some special reason you want to hire me it would be inconvenient for all of us."

"There isn't a lawyer in town who'll touch the case."

"Why not? The Windsors aren't exactly sharecroppers."

"It's not a matter of money," she replied contemptuously. "They don't have the guts to stand up to the publicity."

"Has there been that much? I'd think that the family could contain it."

"You have a very exaggerated idea of the family's influence," she said tartly. "And you don't understand what's going on here."

"Then you'd better explain it," I said, impatient with her peremptory tone.

"I don't know exactly where to start," she said more softly. "Paul's been arrested before, did Elena tell you that?"

"Yes, on child molesting charges."

"That's right," she said quickly. "The charges were dropped because the—girl wouldn't testify. Everyone thought we pressured her but that isn't true. Anyway, the whole thing was a scandal. When Paul was arrested this time, all that came up again. But it's even more complicated than that."

"What else?" I asked, hearing Kevin and Josh's voices in the hall.

"Paul's father owned a construction company."

"Yes, I remember," I replied. Windsor Construction was big business in our little town.

"Mark took it over and expanded it into development. You wouldn't believe how much the town has grown," she added. "A lot of it's Mark's doing. There's always been talk about whether he was going about it in a strictly legal way."

"Mark?" I was incredulous.

"You've been away a long time," she replied dryly. "People here are beginning to debate whether all this growth is good. Mark's a major developer and that makes him the enemy to quite a few people, including the editor of the *Sentinel*."

The door was thrown open and Josh bounded into the room, saw that I was on the phone and froze for a second, then tiptoed toward me and kissed my forehead, dripping sweat on my shirt. He moved away but I reached out and gripped his arm. He looked back, smiled and pointed toward the bathroom. I let him go. A moment later I heard him run the shower.

"What does this have to do with Paul?"

"As I said, the editor of the paper is antidevelopment," she replied. "He led a campaign to put a no-growth proposition on the ballot in November. I guess he sees his best way of winning is to turn it into a vote against the Windsors, but first they have to make us out to be monsters. You'd think," she said scornfully, "we were the Marcoses or the Duvaliers."

"And Paul is caught in the cross fire."

"Yes. The funny thing is that Mark and Paul have their own problems. Or did you already know they hate each other?"

"What I know about the Windsors is twenty years out of date."

"We need your help, Henry. Can you see that?"

I could hear the fatigue in her voice, and what I saw was the makings of a first-class mess. "He's already been arraigned, hasn't he? Who was his lawyer for that?"

"A man named Robert Clayton," she said. "He's the company's lawyer."

"I don't remember anyone named Robert Clayton."

"He's not a native," Sara explained. "He's already told Paul that he won't be his lawyer if there's a trial, not that Paul wants him. Bob says he doesn't know enough about criminal law."

"You don't believe him."

"I've become an expert in excuses," she said bitterly. "Like your excuse, that it's too far to travel."

As we'd spoken, my recollection of Sara had become clearer. She was one of the bright, sharp-tongued girls that Elena seemed to surround herself with in high school. She'd carried herself as if she were coiled up and ready to strike. An unlikely match for Paul Windsor, who had to be several years younger than she. But then, if Paul was a pedophile, any match would have been unlikely. I wanted to hear more.

"I'm in San Francisco for a couple of days," I said. "Can you come down here to talk to me?"

"Tell me when."

"Day after tomorrow, for lunch. Do you know the city?"

"We have a place in Pacific Heights," she said, dryly.

"Meet me in front of the St. Francis at twelve-thirty," I said.

"Yes, all right. Thank you."

"I'm not agreeing to anything, Sara."

"So you do remember my first name," she said sardonically. "Good-bye, Henry. I'll see you Monday."

"Who was that?" Josh asked, stepping out of the bathroom wrapping a towel around his waist.

"A friend of my sister's. You went running with Kevin?"

"Ouch," he said, standing at the wardrobe in front of the mirror, untangling his curly hair with a three-pronged metal Afro pick.

From where I sat I could see him in profile and, simultaneously, full-faced in the mirror, and the two views told different stories. The face in the mirror was the face he was born with, roundish, unlined, with a child's softness to it, but in profile his fine bones asserted themselves just beneath the skin and I could see the man he was becoming, handsome, stubborn, fearless. I loved both the boy and man, but I didn't always know which one I was dealing with. This made for complications I was unused to, and having lived alone until I met him, I sometimes wanted to run from the complexities. Sometimes I tried, but he had entered the bone and marrow of my life, making all such efforts futile.

"You're just getting over a cold, Josh. Don't push yourself."

His back stiffened. "I feel fine, Henry."

"You took your medicines?"

"Shit," he snapped, ostensibly at the long lock of hair he was extricating from a mass of others. "I need a haircut."

"How far did you run?" I asked, getting up from my chair. I picked up his levis, underwear and shirt from the floor, folded them, put them on the bed, and lay down, watching him.

"To the wharf," he replied. "I was going to pick those clothes up. What did your sister want?"

I told him about my visit with Elena. He finished with his hair, shucked the towel and put on a pair of gray corduroys. He rummaged through his suitcase, retrieving a pink Oxford cloth shirt that I recognized as one of mine.

"Are you going to take the case?"

"I don't know. It would probably mean being away from LA for long periods at a time."

Josh flopped onto the bed beside me and stuffed pillows beneath his head. "Why not, Henry? You don't seem all that busy."

This was true. I had limited the number of cases I was taking so I could spend as much time as possible with Josh. In fact, I'd been exploring teaching at a local law school and shutting down my practice altogether.

"It's me, isn't it?" he asked. "You're afraid to leave me by myself."

I turned to him. "That has something to do with it."

"There's a really neat invention called the telephone," Josh said. "You pick it up and you push some buttons and then you can talk to the person at the other end of the line."

I laid my hand on his pink shoulder. "Sarcasm is not your strong point."

"The more we give into it, the more it's going to take over." It. AIDS. "We already moved to LA because of it. Now all I want is a normal life."

"I understand that."

Briskly he asked, "Then why are you afraid to leave me by myself?"

The question cornered me. There was nothing to do but tell the truth. "Because I worry."

"Well, then, stop." He shook off my hand. "Just stop. I know what I have to do to take care of myself." He folded his arms across his chest. "How do you think it makes me feel having you treat me like I was already dead."

"That's a cruel thing to say, Joshua."

"But I'm right," he insisted. "I'm alive right now, Henry. Right now." He put out his hand. "See?"

I closed my hand around his. "There's a difference between living with a disease and denying it."

He pulled his hand away again. "Well, you're the expert on that."

"What are you talking about?"

"You know."

And I did. Six months earlier, having been sober for four years, I'd gone on a binge following an especially bad fight with him and had spent a month at an alcohol rehab clinic. Now, whenever I raised the subject of his health, he had a ready answer. I didn't like it.

"Are you saying that because I made a stupid decision about my health, you should be able to make stupid decisions about yours? The consequences in your case are a lot more serious."

"Bullshit," he snapped, hopping off the bed. "You'd be

just as dead from drinking yourself to death as I'd be from AIDS. And who the hell are you to assume that the only decisions I can make about my health are stupid ones? Why don't you give me a fucking chance."

"And why don't you give me a break? Are you going to hold this over my head for the rest of my life? Look, I'm sorry that you had to discover I'm human, Josh." I climbed off the bed.

"Where are you going?"

"For a walk."

"Can we just stop this, now?"

"You tell me." I opened the door.

"Wait, Henry—"

I slammed the door on him and immediately regretted it but, too ashamed to apologize, I couldn't bring myself to go back.

I leaned against the hallway wall and breathed. Inside my head familiar voices assailed me, telling me what a shit I was for fighting with him. Immediately, another voice attacked me for my guilt, saying that I felt it only because he was right, that I treated him as if he might die at any second. Beyond these voices was the silence of fear. Fear that he would die and I would be left alone. Until I'd met him I had never felt this fear because I had never expected to be anything other than alone.

"Stop feeling sorry for yourself," I said, aloud.

Well if you don't, who will? I heard myself answer silently. Who else cares enough?

He does.

Well that's the whole problem, isn't it? The first time you've ever loved anyone and he's not only thirteen years younger than you are but—

But, what?

Dying.

I heard a noise at the end of the hall and looked up. Terry Ormes, the bride-to-be, was standing there, the door to her room open behind her. She carried a brush in her hand, and her red hair spilled, half-combed, around her angular, intelligent face. Cool gray eyes regarded me and she raised a questioning eyebrow.

I'd first met Terry five years earlier, when she was a homicide detective in the small town on the peninsula where I was then in practice. Now she was a captain in the San Francisco Police Department, assistant to the chief and, in general, a big deal. I'd introduced her to Kevin Reilly, a fellow criminal defense lawyer, at a Christmas party a couple of years earlier, and now they were marrying. As a yenta, I was batting a thousand.

"I thought it was bad luck to see the bride before the ceremony." I said, shutting up the voices as I approached her.

"That only applies to the bridegroom," she replied, subduing her hair with three quick strokes. "I heard a commotion in your room. Are you all right?"

"Josh and I were having a fight."

"Come in and have a cup of coffee with me and tell me all about it. I need some diversion or I'll hyperventilate."

I followed her into her room, a bigger and more ornately furnished version of mine. A brass peacock spread its tail feathers in front of the fireplace. The mantle was green marble. Near the four-poster bed, a silver coffee service and a plate of sweet rolls were laid out on a linen-covered tray. I helped myself to a cinnamon roll and a cup of coffee and we sat on the two wing chairs in front of the fireplace.

Inclining her red-haired head toward me, she said, "I thought I'd have to break down the door and make an arrest."

"I didn't realize we were that loud."

"Anything serious?"

"No, nothing serious."

She smiled uncertainly, revealing the small gap between her two front teeth. "You looked kind of pale out there in the hall."

"The last thing you want to hear about now is what happens after happily ever after."

21

"Try me."

I tried to form a complicated explanation of what I was feeling, but what finally came out was, "What if he dies?"

"If you're living in the 'what ifs,' you've lost him already," she replied briskly, being as unsparing of her friends as she was of herself.

"He said something like that, too."

In a gentler voice she said, "His 'what ifs' must be even scarier than yours."

"He's brave."

"So are you. A gay public figure, a criminal defense lawyer and a Chicano—you didn't choose the easy road, either."

"I didn't have any choice, Terry."

"Of course you did," she said, decisively. "You could have stayed closeted and gone for the big money on Montgomery Street as some huge firm's token minority partner."

"And drunk myself to death before I was forty. See, no choice."

Impatiently, she said, "Stop belittling yourself, Henry. Josh doesn't have a thing on you when it comes to courage. Now eat something. You'll feel better."

I ate a roll while she told me about how she and Kevin had spent the morning trying to figure out seating arrangements to avoid combustion between the cops and the lawyers.

"What did you do?"

"We decided to hell with it," she said, laughing. "Let them fight. Thank God we wrote our own service. Can you imagine what would happen if the judge asked whether anyone objected to us being married?"

"Fifty lawyers would rise as one."

"And the cops, too. Where've you been today?"

"Visiting my sister in Oakland. She has a job for me."

"I didn't know you had a sister. Is she in trouble?"

I shook my head and explained why I'd gone to see Elena.

"How does she know these people?"

"Childhood friends," I replied, and told her about my conversation with Sara Windsor.

"When was the last time you were home?" she asked.

"For my mother's funeral, ten years ago. All I ever wanted from Los Robles was to get out as fast and as far away as possible."

She refilled my cup and placed another roll on my plate. "Was it so terrible?"

"Stultifying," I replied. "You know there's a poem by E. E. Cummings called 'anyone lived in a pretty how town.' It's about two lovers in a little town populated by narrow-minded people so oblivious to passion they're not even aware of this love story unfolding around them."

I shut my eyes and tried to remember stanzas that I'd committed to memory as an undergrad.

> "women and men (both little and small)
> cared for anyone not at all
> they sowed their isn't they reaped their same
> sun moon stars rain . . ."

"That's lovely," she said, "is there more?"

"Yes, something about . . . 'someones married their everyones,' what's the rest—

> "laughed their cryings and did their dance
> (sleep wake hope and then) they
> said their nevers they slept their dream."

"What does that have to do with you, Henry? Were you in love?"

I thought about Mark Windsor. "I thought so at the time, but it was one-sided. No, it wasn't because I was in love that I hated the place; it was because I was filled with so much—" I paused and wondered, what had I been filled with? "So much feeling that never got expressed." I smiled, shrugged. "I was burning up from the inside and no one ever noticed."

"Well," she said, "if you never bothered to tell anyone, you can't blame them for not noticing."

I smiled at her. "You're pitiless."
There was a knock at the door. "Maid," a woman called.
"I was going for a walk," I said, "do you want to come?"
"You bet," she said. "It's my last morning as a free woman. Maybe we can make Kevin jealous."

3

The wedding was set for eight o'clock that night. While the other guests had drinks in the dining room before the ceremony, Josh and I, at peace again, inspected the parlor. All the chairs in the inn had been pressed into service: straight-backed wooden kitchen chairs, Art Deco armchairs, leather library chairs with brass studs, even an ottoman and a piano bench. They were arranged into a half-dozen rows, the wide aisle between covered with a white silk runner leading out of the parlor to a small antechamber, which was dominated by a triptych of tall leaded glass windows. In front of the center window was an antique wooden music stand, on either side of it two tall vases filled with white gladioluses. The windows caught the flicker of reflected light from candles burning on every available surface in both rooms as well as the light from antique brass and porcelain lamps. On the mantel over the fireplace, pink roses in a crystal bowl spilled a dry, sweet scent through the parlor.

"This is like a waiting room to heaven," I said.

Josh settled into a high-backed plush thronelike chair and announced, "This is where God sits."

In his tuxedo, tie slightly askew, he looked less like God than like an errant seraph. I reached down and straightened his tie.

"I haven't been to a wedding since the last time my sister got married," he said. "Was your sister ever married?"

I sat down. "No," I said, "we Rioses are not the marrying kind."

He elbowed me. "So what am I, chopped livah?"

"You know what I mean."

Other people trickled into the room. The guest list seemed about equally divided between cops and lawyers, animosities temporarily suspended. A burly white-haired gentleman and his diminutive wife—part of the cop contingent—took the chairs beside us, all smiles and eau de Cologne. Soon, everyone was seated and, like a theater audience waiting for the house lights to dim, we readied ourselves, hands folded into well-dressed laps, handkerchiefs tucked into sleeves, and all eyes fixed on the front of the room. From somewhere a tape played music—classical, but lively rather than solemn—and Kevin slipped into place with his best man, both dressed in thirties-style double-breasted tuxedos, handsome as movie stars. The judge whom Kevin and Terry had chosen to conduct the service also took her place. A small, white-haired woman, she wore an ivory-colored gown and a strand of pinkish pearls around her neck. She smiled warmly at Kevin as he fiddled with the music stand to adjust it to her height but her eyes had the rather reptilian cast not uncommon among judges—the stigmata of power.

The music changed to the traditional bridal processional and there was the rustle of silk behind us. We all turned round oohing and aahing as Terry made her way up the aisle, attended by her only living parent, her mother. Terry's gown, which I'd got a preview of when we'd returned from our walk that morning, was a pale sea-green, with an Empire waist and lace at the neckline and sleeves. Her red hair, normally tied back, fell loosely at her shoulders, gleaming in the candlelight. She rejected a veil, insisting on entering her marriage open-eyed. As the two tall women passed, I saw that her hand trembled in her mother's hand. Her odd, small smile was directed, as far as I could tell, at Kevin and Kevin alone. He, in a change from his habitual expression of slightly rancid good humor, was dumbstruck.

The woman beside me murmured, "Beautiful, beautiful," like someone awakening from a dream.

I glanced at Josh, whose eyes were getting rather moist, and put my arm around him.

The actual ceremony was brief. The judge welcomed us and then Kevin recited a poem by Donne. She answered him with one of the *Sonnets from the Portuguese*, reciting it with a schoolgirl gravity that made me briefly but intensely jealous of Kevin. They exchanged vows and there was a small comic moment as the best man dug through his pockets for the ring and then the judge invoked her civil authority and declared them married.

The music started up again as they walked down the aisle. It wasn't until they were almost out of the room that I recognized it as a Mantovani version of "Respect," and had to bite my lip to keep from laughing.

That night, Josh and I lay in the tumble of our bed watching sheer white curtains flutter in the breeze like a ghost. It was late and we would doze for a few minutes, awaken and talk for a bit, sip water, kiss, lie still.

"I'm glad I came with you," Josh said, laying his hand on my chest. A moment later he added, "I want to marry you."

"Honey, I thought you'd never ask," I joked through a yawn.

"I'm serious."

"I know." I stroked his hair. "But in the end it's all the same, you know. The two of them, the two of us."

He propped himself up on an elbow and looked gravely down on me. "But if something happens to me—"

I pressed my hand over his mouth. "Let's put aside the 'what ifs' for now."

He kissed the palm of my hand and I moved my fingers across his mouth and down to the hollow of his neck.

He said, "I think about what might happen and I get scared."

"I'll take care of you."

He lowered his face to mine. His breath filled me as his tongue slid into my mouth. My hand slipped to the small of his back and I felt his cock lengthening against my thigh. I closed my eyes.

A little later, his beeper went off and I woke him to take his dose of AZT, which he did, complaining of the cold and that he was sleepy.

"Don't be such a baby," I said, drawing the comforter over us.

"Baby, baby," he muttered pulling me against him, and then we both slept.

The next morning, after putting Josh on a plane for Los Angeles, I drove back into the city. Parking beneath Union Square I positioned myself in front of the St. Francis to await Sara Windsor. After two unusually clear days, summer had returned to San Francisco, overcast and cold. Tourists coming out of the hotel in shorts and thin shirts took one look at the sky and went back in or scurried across the square to Macy's to stock up on sweaters. I was glad I'd packed my blue wool suit—it not only had a calming effect on my clients but was warm, too. As twelve-thirty approached, and the crowd thickened, it occurred to me that not having seen Sara Windsor in twenty years, I had no idea of what she looked like now, so I made myself as conspicuous as one can in a blue suit.

"Henry?"

The voice came from across my shoulder and belonged to a tall red-faced woman. Her dress had been made for someone smaller and her bulk pressed against the seams. Two deep lines enclosed her mouth in parentheses and similar lines were stitched across her forehead, making her appear annoyed—accurately, it seemed. She complained, "The traffic was unbelievable."

"Hello, Sara." I put out my hand. She glanced at it uncertainly, then shook it, damply.

"I could use a glass of wine."

"The place I had in mind for lunch is just across the square," I said, surreptitiously wiping my palm on my pants."

"Maiden Lane?"

"Yes, that okay?"

"Any place," she replied.

Lips pursed, Sara moved swiftly and rudely through the crowd of midday shoppers as we crossed the square. Sara'd been thin as a girl, but no more. Not quite fat, but the extra weight she carried blurred her features. Pouches of flesh had gathered beneath her eyes and her chin. Damp circles stained her armpits and the seat of her dress was deeply wrinkled. Her makeup was hit-and-miss and she had the look of someone who no longer cared much about her appearance.

We reached Maiden Lane, a small pedestrian alleyway lined with expensive shops, and went into an Italian delicatessen. When we were settled with food and drink, she appraised me.

"You've become handsome," she said, disbelievingly.

"Thank you."

"You were so skinny as a boy that it was hard to tell what you would look like." She took a deep swallow from her wine.

"I'm surprised you gave it any thought."

Through a mouthful of spinach salad she said, "I didn't until I saw a picture of you in the paper last year. I hardly recognized you." She studied me. "Your eyes haven't changed. They still keep your secrets."

I shook my head. "I got rid of all my secrets when I left Los Robles. Did you know Paul was a pedophile when you married him?"

"You just launch into it, don't you?"

I said nothing. The direct approach often startled people into telling the truth.

She buttered a roll, slowly, buying time. "Paul," she said, as if announcing the title of a book. "I knew Paul was rich, younger and desperate to get married, but, no, I did not know that Paul was a pedophile."

"When did you find out?"

"The day the police came to arrest him." She put a piece of bread into her mouth. "The first time, I mean. Why are you asking me about this?"

"I understand the police think Paul was being blackmailed by the man who was killed."

She lifted her wineglass and tipped it back and forth, watching the wine wash against the sides of the glass. "The police are idiots," she said, quietly, stilling the glass. "Everyone knew about Paul. There was nothing to blackmail him with."

"Then why do they think it?"

She finished the wine. "He had a lot of money with him the night he went to see—McKay's the man's name—the victim," she said scornfully. "Naturally the police assumed it was to pay him off."

"What was it for?"

She flagged the waiter down. "Another glass," she said. "It was the Chardonnay." She looked at me. "I can't be called to testify against him, can I?"

"No, the marital privilege applies."

"And if I tell you?"

"Another privilege, lawyer-client."

"The money was to make a purchase," she said, after a moment's silence. "There was a little girl." She stopped, looked at me. Her eyes were empty. "Does that shock you?"

The waiter delivered her wine, setting it down so hard that it sloshed onto the table. We both looked up at him, but he was at the next table, his face frantic, reeling off the specials.

"I don't quite understand."

"I'm not able to have children," she said, "that's one reason I didn't marry sooner. There didn't seem to be any point. Early on, we considered adoption, but after Paul's arrest that was out of the question, of course. Some time ago Paul told me that he'd read about a black market in babies. He said he'd done some investigating and that it was possible to buy children who'd been abandoned or just sold by their parents. Of course, I thought it was crazy." She sipped her wine hurriedly. "I put it out of my mind, but Paul would bring it up every now and then."

"In what context?"

"Oh, when there were children around, he would start talking about how much he had hoped to have a family."

"That seems rather tactless."

"I tried not to pay attention." She smiled bitterly. "Not paying attention is my basic marital skill. Anyway, after he was arrested, he told me that this man, McKay, had offered to sell him a child. That's why he'd gone to the motel that night, and why he had so much money on him."

"You believed him?"

"If it will help him," she replied coolly.

Frowning, I asked, "Why did he go there, really?"

"I told you, Henry, I tried not to pay attention."

"Why didn't you just leave him?"

The question seemed familiar to her. "And do what?"

"You said you married late. You must have had a life before then."

"I taught high school," she replied, wearily. "I couldn't go back to that after all the publicity. You forget how small Los Robles is."

"There are other places."

"There are other places if you're a man," she replied, "or have money. I'm not and I don't." She gripped the stem of her glass with long, pale fingers. "Don't presume to judge me."

"I'm only trying to understand." I said.

"Is that absolutely necessary?" Her tone was corrosive.

31

"Let's get back to the murder. Tell me what happened."

She loosened her grip on the glass. "He went to meet McKay at a motel at the edge of town the night McKay was killed," she said. "A few days later the police came with a warrant to search the house and Paul's car. They found the money and arrested him. Then I got the story from him about where he'd gone and why."

"How did they find him?"

"Bob Clayton said they found Paul's fingerprints in the room."

"Is that all?" I asked.

She looked at me, surprised. "Isn't that enough?"

"To place him in the room, maybe," I said, "but that's hardly enough to indict him for murder. Was a weapon recovered? Did he make any statements to the police?"

She shook her head. "No. He asked to call Bob and Bob told him not to say anything. I don't know anything about a weapon."

I thought for a moment. "In other words, as far as you know, the only evidence the police have connecting Paul to McKay's murder is that he went to see him that night with some money and they had a common interest in—children."

"Yes," she said doubtfully.

"And they would have had even less than that for a search warrant," I said, more to myself than her. "They wouldn't have known about the money."

We were both still. I didn't know what Sara was thinking but what went through my mind was to wonder what kind of judge would issue a search warrant on such a faint showing of probable cause.

"Bob Clayton is the lawyer who represented Paul at the arraignment?" I asked.

She nodded.

"Who is he, again?"

"He represents the company, Windsor Development. He's Mark's lawyer, really. What are you thinking, Henry?"

"Unless there's something you haven't told me, or that you

don't know about," I said slowly, "there doesn't seem to be much of a case against Paul at the moment."

"I've told you everything I know," she said, and finished her wine. "Maybe you should talk to Bob."

"Yes, definitely," I said. "On the phone it sounded like you didn't have much confidence in Clayton."

She smiled unpleasantly. "He has a—what do you call it?—conflict of interest."

"What do you mean?"

"A couple of years ago, Mark bought out Paul's interest in the company. Right after that, the business took off like crazy. I don't know all the details, but Paul thinks that Mark didn't tell him the whole story when the sale went through and paid him less than what his share was worth." She lifted her glass, saw it was empty and looked around. The waiter was nowhere to be seen, so she continued. "Last time they talked about it, they had a big blowup and Paul told Mark that unless they settled it, he would sue."

I filled in the blank. "And in that case, Bob Clayton would represent Mark."

"Yes, exactly. Paul, of course, is convinced that Mark is somehow behind his arrest."

"Is there that much bad blood between them, Mark and Paul, I mean?"

"Oh, yes," she said. "That's why it's so ironic, that the newspaper is using Paul's arrest to get at Mark. It's probably the one thing in this whole mess that makes it bearable for Paul."

"Is it just this business about the sale?" I asked.

She shook her head. "No," she said, signaling the waiter with her lifted glass. "They've hated each other for years."

"Yes, you said that over the phone, but you didn't say why."

"I only know Paul's side of it, that Mark bullied and humiliated him when they were kids because Mark thought—" she paused delicately.

"Because Mark thought what?"

33

"That Paul wasn't quite a man."

"I see."

"I don't mean that he thought Paul was a homosexual," she said, her vinous breath drifting across the table. "Just that he never thought Paul was tough enough. Apparently toughness matters a lot to Mark, but you probably know that better than I do."

I said nothing. It was news to me.

4

As I entered Los Robles Valley, bare brown hills gave way to long unbroken stretches of farmland that ranged toward far-off bluish mountains in the east, the Sierra Nevada. The sky was flat and close. Straggly lines of cottonwoods marked distant watercourses and irrigation ditches flashed silver in the still light. I passed a group of farmworkers drinking water from a metal container at the back of a battered truck, a vast tomato field behind them. A billboard flashed the time and temperature: 8:30, 80 degrees. Nothing moved, not birds in the sky, nor a breeze through the great oaks that gave the valley its name, and the stillness had a heft as if everything, to the last blade of grass, had been fixed in place forever at the moment the earth was made.

Approaching the city, however, I noticed that, perhaps, one or two things had changed since Creation and even since

I'd last been on this road: housing tracts erupted on the landscape like geologic carbuncles, rows and rows of pastel boxes lining wide streets that emptied onto the surrounding fields or curled among themselves in a labyrinth of what nearby billboards advertised as "the good life." Clarendon Estates, the Oaks Condominiums, La Vista—the sonorous names promised a posh, worry-free, cable-ready existence on easy credit terms. But behind unnaturally green lawns, most of these places appeared uninhabited. Apparently the market for the good life had dried up or maybe it took too much imagination for the average consumer to picture it here, in these houses, amid the emptiness, beneath the suffocating sky.

Many of the same billboards shouting out their promises also listed Windsor Development as the developer. And then I was crossing a causeway above rice fields and there, in front of me, shimmering in the heat, was the prim skyline of Los Robles.

Every Californian knows that the real California can be found in the Central Valley, a great dish of land in the middle of the state, dotted by dour farm towns that bake in the summer and freeze in the winter. The city of Los Robles is the largest of those towns. Two broad, slow rivers, the Los Robles and the Oeste, flow into the city and merge there. Their wandering courses mark the city's northern and western borders; to the south and east is country. Within that quadrant is a town of 150,000.

The city's history is negligible. The only excitement in its hundred-and-forty-year existence had been the gold rush, which took place in the foothills east of the city. That mania swelled its population, making it the largest settlement between San Francisco and the Oregon border. When the gold rush played itself out, many prospectors remained. Pining for the Midwestern towns they'd left behind, they'd constructed a larger version of them here, wide, treelined avenues featuring gingerbread Victorians, Queen Anne cottages, shuttered Colonial Revival mansions, gloomy Romanesque and neo-Gothic churches, Federal-style public buildings. In short a very pretty town that bore no relation at all to the city's preceding hundred years of colonial rule under Spain and then Mexico.

True, that rule had touched lightly here, but even those traces had been almost entirely eradicated, leaving only the Spanish place names to inform the curious that time had not begun with the arrival of the first former resident of the Midwest. Along with the Spanish place names, there also remained many of the town's original Mexican families. In time, they and their descendents and others who had joined them in making the long trek north from Mexico were relegated to the neighborhood south of the main Southern Pacific line called Paradise Slough.

A ship was passing on the Los Robles River when I got to the bridge that led into town. Traffic stopped while the bridge was raised to let the vessel pass. Directly ahead of me was River Parkway, the main street into the city. Bright new buildings rose on either side of it, in a style I'd come to think of as neo-Corporate, the only distinction lying in the type of glass, black, green or mirrored, used in their construction. The river front, formerly skid row, was in the process of being transformed into an "Old Towne." Brick warehouses and former flophouses now housed boutiques and restaurants. The ubiquitous oaks lined the wooden walkway at the river's edge.

North of downtown was a wealthy old suburb called River Park. The Windsors had lived there, in an antebellum mansion. Built by Mark and Paul's father, it hinted at graceful Southern antecedents, but Herb Windsor was a Dust Bowl Okie. His wife, on the other hand—"the former Lydia Smith," as she was referred to in the society page of the *Sentinel*—was a local banker's daughter. I bore an ancient grudge against her, arising from her having banned me from the family swimming pool one summer after learning that I lived in Paradise Slough. Mexicans and Anglos didn't mix; each was "they" to the other. I remembered all this vividly as the bridge was lowered and I drove into town.

* * *

My first stop was at the law firm of Clayton and Cummings. I'd alerted Robert Clayton that I would be arriving to talk to him about Paul's case that morning and he'd agreed to a nine-thirty meeting. The address he'd provided turned out to be one of the glassy boxes on the Parkway. To the strains of "Scarborough Fair" a dimly lit elevator carried me to the fourth floor, depositing me at the end of the long airless corridor. Beige walls, deep green carpet, low lights and brass lettering on mahogany doors—a factory for the white-collar proletariat.

"My name is Henry Rios," I told the receptionist in Clayton's office. "I have an appointment with Mr. Clayton."

"One moment."

I sat down in a leather wing chair and tried to interest myself in a three-week-old issue of *Business Week*. An article worried that the Japanese were buying up the Western world. Let them have it, I thought, they couldn't do a worse job with it than its current masters. I was reminded of Gandhi's reply when he was asked what he thought of Western civilization: "I think it would be a good idea."

"Mr. Rios?" The short, fat, bearded man beamed at me, obviously mistaking my private smile over Gandhi's remark for amiability.

I extended my hand. "Mr. Clayton?" I was surprised, having expected a typical waistline-conscious Yuppie.

He shook his head and my hand with equal enthusiasm. "No, I'm Peter Stein."

I remembered the name from the door outside, near the bottom of the list, an associate.

"Bob had to cover a deposition at the last minute. He should be back soon. In the meantime, he thought you might want to review the Windsor file."

"How long is 'back soon'?"

"Well, by noon at the latest. Come on back."

I followed Stein past the receptionist into the hall behind her and then into his cramped office. He wedged himself into the chair behind his desk and picked up an accordion file, handing it to me. I glanced at the label: WINDSOR, PAUL, STATE OF CALIFORNIA V., and a series of numbers beneath it I assumed to be the firm's internal file number.

"This is it," he said, adding, "Have a seat. Can I get you coffee?"

I sat. "Why not? Black."

He placed an order for two coffees over the phone and continued to beam at me. "It's a real pleasure to meet you," he said. "I read your profile last month in the *Daily Journal*."

I nodded. The LA legal newspaper had run a profile of me on the front page after an unexpected victory in the state supreme court reversing a death penalty case. Unexpected only because the current reactionary governor had managed to stack the court with right-wing judges.

"You have an interest in criminal law?" I asked.

"Bob hired me out of the DA's office," he replied. Our coffees arrived via a Chicano boy who grinned at me, one *vato loco* to another. I grinned back.

"Really," I said to Stein. "Finding it hard to make the transition from criminal to civil?"

"Bob's been a real help there. He had a two-bit practice before he lucked into the Windsors." He smiled, his head bobbing like a manic balloon.

I felt sorry for him. He seemed to be one of those fat people who'd been tagged jolly at an impressionable age. "Is there someplace quiet I can go over this?" I plucked at the edge of the folder.

"At the end of the hall there's an empty office," he replied. "My predecessor. Couldn't cut it," he confided, and I detected a tremor of anxiety in his tone. Maybe the transition wasn't going so smoothly after all.

"Thank you, Peter," I said, rising. "Will you let Mr. Clayton know that I'm here?"

"Sure thing."

Stein's unfortunate predecessor had left only a dying rubber plant to mark his tenancy in the otherwise stark office. I dropped the folder onto the desk and looked out the window. The tinted glass cut the glare, but from the lack of movement on the street below I could tell that the heat had set in. It was not unusual for the temperature to rise to three digits by noon and stay there until evening when it dropped to the tolerable eighties. While it lasted, the heat produced a glacial calm, white and still, during which even breathing was exhausting. As a boy I had taken shelter from the heat at one of two places—the river and the library. The river was not much of an escape, as it was impossible to remain underwater all day and, at any rate, the water itself was bathtub tepid and sludgy. The library, on the other hand, was air-conditioned and offered the added diversion of books from which I first became aware of a world beyond the valley.

I spotted the roof of the central library not far away. I sometimes had trouble remembering what my mother looked like, but I could picture, to the last wattle beneath her chin, the woman at the check out desk. Mrs. . . . Mrs. . . . Stop this, I told myself, and went back to the desk and WINDSOR, PAUL, STATE OF CALIFORNIA V.

I disliked Robert Clayton on sight and the feeling appeared to be mutual. He was as slim and fashionable as his peers on Montgomery Street or Wilshire Boulevard, a briskly tailored seersucker suit his sole concession to the weather. It wasn't his tailoring I minded as much as his air of self-containment. He was a locked box and proud of it. I immediately set out to pick a fight.

We were in his tasteful office. He was saying, "Yes, I looked at the search warrant." He shrugged. "I specialize in real estate transactions, so I'm a little out of my element in crime."

"Mmm," I replied. "Not to insult you, Bob, but even a first-year law student would've recognized the absence of probable cause in the affidavit." I withdrew the bulky document from the file. "Half of it is a paean to the superior investigative skills of the affiant, a detective named Morrow. Then there's a lengthy reference to Paul's prior arrest for child molestation, and an equally lengthy account of the kiddie porn recovered at the motel room where they found McKay." Ignoring Clayton's frown I continued. "He then gets to the heart of it—Paul's fingerprints were found in the room. Ergo, he concludes, Paul was in the room. Well, that doesn't take a genius. From there he jumps to the spectacular conclusion that probable cause exists to connect Paul to the murder, justifying a search of his house and car for, *inter alia*, the murder weapon." I looked up at him. "This might pass muster in, say, Chile—"

"I'm not a jury, Henry. What's your point?"

"I don't see a motion in here to quash the warrant."

"Well, that's your job, isn't it? There hasn't even been a prelim yet. You have all the time in the world to make your motions."

I looked at him. "Meanwhile, Paul's in jail. If it had been brought to the attention of the arraigning judge that Paul was being held on the basis of this—" I stabbed at the warrant "—he might not have been so quick to deny him bail."

"The arraigning judge," he replied, "was the same judge who signed the warrant."

"Well, this is a one-horse town."

"And," he added, "is the same judge who'll hear the prelim."

"That's unlawful," I replied. "I'll move to disqualify him."

Clayton leaned forward slightly, gripping the edge of his desk with shapely fingers. "We're not in Los Angeles, Henry. There are only four muni court judges up here, and they don't like it when an attorney papers one of them."

"How much don't they like it?"

"I don't think you want to find out," he replied, releasing the desk. He tried out a grin on me. "You're right about the warrant, of course, but Paul had already told me that he wanted someone else to represent him. I didn't see the point in antagonizing Judge Lanyon. I thought I'd leave that to you. From what I've seen, you're probably better at pissing off judges than I am."

"Sara said you're the one who bailed out on the case."

He shrugged. "It was mutual."

"And the fact that you represent Windsor Development had nothing to do with it, I suppose?"

"Are you accusing me of something?"

"Just whose interest is being served by Paul remaining in jail?"

He smiled to mask his anger. "Even for a lawyer you have a suspicious mind, Henry. The reason I don't want to defend Paul is simple, I think he did it. I think the police are right. He went to McKay with the intention of paying him off, but McKay must have said something that made Paul realize he would be paying for the rest of his life, so he killed him." Indifferently, he added, "It's like Paul to panic and act stupidly."

"What about Paul's explanation of why he went to see McKay?"

He eyed me with interest. "What explanation?"

Apparently, he had not been taken into Paul's confidence. I feinted. "He must have one."

"Not that I know of." He rolled his head, slowly, from side to side, working out the tension. "Look, Henry, you don't think he's innocent, do you?"

"I haven't formed an opinion," I replied, "but I do know that any lawyer with even a little criminal experience would've acted a lot more aggressively than you did to at least get him out on bail."

"Don't lecture me," he snapped. "Paul barely speaks to me. You can't help someone who doesn't trust you."

"And why wouldn't he trust you?"

Stiffly, he said, "I've been instructed by Mark to cooperate with you, but you're making it awfully hard. You can work out of the office, use my secretary, the paralegals. Stein, if you want him. Just don't treat me like a hick. And stay out of my business."

I backed off. "That's generous of you. Sorry if I'm blunt. That's my way."

"I'm trying to appreciate that."

"When's the arraignment?"

"Two weeks from today. What do you need?"

"I understand from Sara there's been quite a bit of publicity about the case."

He smiled, grimly. "To put it mildly."

"Tell me about it."

"Paul was never tried on those child molest charges."

I nodded. "Sara said the girl wouldn't testify."

"That's right. It's commonly believed that the Windsors paid her family off. The mother was Paul and Sara's maid."

"I didn't know that."

"She'd worked for them for years. So there was that. And then the *Sentinel*'s been skewering Mark for years over his development deals. It's always been just this side of libel. They couldn't come right out and say he's done anything criminal, but they sure got close."

"And has he?" I asked.

"Anyone in his business is going to run afoul of some regulatory agency somewhere. It's the cost of doing business."

"I see."

"I doubt it," he said, sharply. "Anyway, the *Sentinel* is antigrowth. They got this proposition on the ballot that was going nowhere. Then Gordon Wachs came up with the bright notion that it's easier to run against a person than an idea."

"Wachs?"

"The new publisher. He bought out the Storey family about ten years ago. He's not a native." Not a native, the ultimate Los Roblean insult. "When Paul was arrested, they dredged up the molestation case as well as every infraction of every code that Mark was ever fined on and turned the election into a referendum on the Windsors."

"I'd like to see those stories."

"Sure," he said, "but why?"

I tapped the file. "I'm beginning to have my doubts about the quality of justice in Los Robles. Maybe the best thing I can do for Paul is get the case moved out of here."

"A motion to change venue?" he asked skeptically. "Good luck." He jotted a note and asked, "When do you want it?"

"I'm flying to LA after I see Paul and I won't be back until next week. Could you have it for me tonight?"

He lifted an eyebrow. "My people aren't used to big-city hours." He thought. "I'll give it to Peter. He's a hot dog."

Rising, I said, "Thanks."

"Henry," he said, stopping me at the door. "A word of advice."

"I'm listening."

"Don't push old friendships too hard."

"Does that come from Mark?"

"I think I can speak for him."

Too many years of living in temperate climates had cost me my tolerance for the heat. I took off my tie and jacket and rolled up my sleeves as I walked to my car. The Parkway had once been lined by trees. These had apparently been uprooted to widen the street. As a result, the grim blocks stretched shadelessly into town. I got into my rented car and the vinyl rose up to meet me, grabbing at the seat of my pants and the back of my shirt. I drove to my next stop, lunch with Sara Windsor.

The address she'd given me was in River Park, but wasn't the white wedding cake house that Herb Windsor had built for his family. Instead, these lesser Windsors lived in a rambling structure that looked like a Norman farmhouse on steroids. I pulled up to the curb, got out and crossed a wide lawn, past flower beds, low hedges and the three oaks that shaded the front of the L-shaped mansion. Where the two wings broke was a kind of turret where a heavy, paneled door, sporting a lion's-head knocker, provided entrance. I dropped the lion against the door. A moment later, a brown-skinned woman with plaited hair, wearing a servant's frock, eyed me suspiciously.

Without thinking, I addressed her in Spanish. "*Quiero ver la Señora Windsor, por favor.*"

Her expression grew sharper and I pictured myself in her eyes, a tall, sweaty Mexican in a not-too-clean white shirt and wrinkled trousers, demanding in Spanish to see *"la señora."*

"I'm Mr. Windsor's attorney, Henry Rios," I said, in English.

"Who's there?" I heard Sara ask. "Carrie?" She came up behind the maid. "Oh, Henry. Come in. It's all right, Carrie."

The maid let me pass. Carrie? I thought, looking into that broad, dark face.

"Carrie?" I asked Sara as she led me to an opulent living room.

"Caridad," Sara said, moving toward an antique credenza crowned by rows of bright glasses. "Do you want a drink before lunch?"

"No, thank you."

She poured bourbon into a tumbler and directed me to sit. "Lunch will be ready in a minute. Have you seen Paul yet?"

"No, I got tied up at Clayton's office." I sank into a large white chair. Sara sat across from me on a sofa about the length of an Olympic-sized swimming pool. Between us was a lacquered table on which I could have napped. It was a lot of house for two people but then again, based on what I knew about these two people, maybe not.

"Was he helpful?" Her dry tone was its own answer.

"I'm not sure."

"I know what you mean," she said. "He's absolutely convincing until you try to remember what he said to you."

I smiled. She seemed to be in good spirits, spirits being the operative word. The whiff of liquor I caught on the air-conditioned breeze seemed to emanate from her pores. Still, in loose-fitting linens she looked more relaxed than she had in San Francisco the day before.

"You sure you won't join me?" she asked, raising the glass to her lips.

"A glass of water."

"I'm sorry. Carrie?" she called. Caridad, Charity, appeared. "Would you bring Mr. Rios a glass of ice water."

As she left I wondered whether she was the same maid whose daughter Paul had molested. When she returned with the water, she looked at me without visible expression but I perceived the hostility in her eyes. Or maybe it was just my guilt at mixing with the rich Anglos.

"What did you think of Bob?" Sara was asking.

I said, "I would imagine he's in a real predicament. On the one hand, Paul's arrest for murder certainly weakens his hand in his dispute with Mark. On the other hand, it doesn't do much for the family's reputation. If Clayton's the loyalist he seems to be, he must be having a hard time deciding whether to help me or stonewall. Today he did a little of both." I sipped the icy water. "He doesn't seem to be in any hurry to see Paul get out of jail."

She'd finished her drink. I could see her trying to decide whether to get another right away or to wait. I'd been in similar conundrums myself.

To distract her, I said, "He seems convinced of Paul's guilt."

Rising decisively, she headed to the credenza, returning with another drink. "That's absurd."

"Is it?"

Swiftly, she walked to the windows at the far end of the room. "Come here, Henry."

I got up and went over to her. She parted the heavy curtain, revealing rows and rows of roses. "Paul made this."

Like an Impressionist painting the still roses seemed to blend their colors in the afternoon heat and I could almost smell their heavy scent on the motionless air. She dropped the curtain.

"An aptitude for gardening doesn't rule out an aptitude for murder," I remarked.

"Don't be stupid," she replied and went back to the couch.

"All right," I said, following her. "Who do you think did it?"

"That girl's brother," she replied tightly.

"What girl?"

She settled into her drink. "Ruth Soto. Her mother worked for us. Not Carrie, before her. Ruth used to come and help her. She liked the roses." She cradled her glass. "I thought it was sweet that Paul taught her about them. Really sweet." She took a drink, wiping her lips with her fingers. "If you want the details you'll have to ask him," she said, too loudly. "It went on for three years until she got pregnant." Quickly she added, "She was fifteen. Obviously, her family found out about it and went to the police."

"The charges were dropped because she wouldn't testify," I said. "Do you know why?"

She shook her head. "Everyone thinks we paid her off. We didn't. We—" She stopped herself.

"You what?" I pressed.

"It was her own decision. The day the case was dropped her brother showed up in the courtroom with a gun, threatening to kill Paul. The police stopped him. He was the one who ended up going to jail."

"What happened to Ruth?"

"I don't know. I suppose she still lives here somewhere, in Paradise Slough."

"And the baby?"

"I don't know about that either."

"Why would her brother have killed McKay?"

"Maybe it was a mistake," she said, her voice unsteady from the bourbon. "Maybe he meant to kill Paul."

"There are some steps missing here."

"Ask Paul to fill them in."

Before I could answer Caridad appeared at the doorway and announced lunch.

After lunch, Sara excused herself, saying she needed a nap, and gave me the run of the house. I washed up to go to the jail. On my way out, I looked for Caridad, and found her outside, in the rose garden, cutting roses with a pair of pinking shears and dropping them into a canvas bag. The heat and fragrance made me dizzy. "*Señora,*" I called.

She turned slowly, looked at me. Despite the heat, her skin was dry. "*Señor?*"

In Spanish, I said, "Do you know a family named Soto who live in Paradise Slough? They have a daughter named Ruth."

She looked at me for a long time. "No," she said, finally, adding, as she returned to her work, "*Con su permiso.*" I watched her stoop among the roses, thinking what a marvelous language Spanish was that she could convey so much contempt in a single polite phrase.

5

The city jail was down by the train station, on a shady street otherwise occupied by bail bondsmen and fly-specked, window-front law offices advertising in both English and Spanish. This bilingualism was new. There had only been one public language when I was growing up, creating a kind of linguistic apartheid. One of my earliest memories as a child was going around with my grandmother at the end of the month to translate for her at the bank, the social security office and the utility company. Over the years, I had lost my fluency in Spanish though I could still make myself understood, albeit ungrammatically. And there were some things that existed for me only by their Spanish names, private things, small things—hands would always be *manos* to me and God, to the degree that he existed for me at all, would always be known by my grandmother's loving diminutive, *Diosito*.

This nostalgia was not without its bitter edge. When I had left this place I had closed my mind to it because I could not think about Los Robles without confronting the furious ghost of my father. Still, in those moments when the present opened a crevasse beneath me and I had no idea of who I was, it was because I had chosen to go through life without memory.

I had come to a stop. Shaking myself, I made my way through the doors of the jail, grateful, for once, for the usual din and traffic: uniformed cops and their handcuffed charges, brilliant white lights and a scruffy green linoleum floor, the click of typewriters and shouts from the drunk tank. It was only a few degrees cooler inside than out.

I explained my purpose to the cop at the front desk, a skinny black man named Robertson. While he arranged for me to see Paul I leafed through the police report, studying the box that described the victim. John McKay, Caucasian, age forty-eight, driver's license showing a Glendale address, registered owner of a seven-year-old Honda Civic. I turned the pages looking for a rap sheet, which seemed a logical addendum considering his occupation, and was mildly surprised not to find one. Perhaps the cops had decided that he'd played his part in the case by getting killed. I made a mental note to look into it further.

"Counsel."

I looked up at Robertson who jerked his head toward another officer standing at a metal door, which Robertson buzzed open as I approached. I and the other cop went through and I was taken down a corridor to a small room. Inside, at a wooden table, Paul Windsor sat in an orange jumpsuit. The officer led me in and left, stationing himself at the door outside.

Contrary to popular belief, crime has no physiognomy. Paul was proof of that. His mild, bony face would've looked perfectly natural above a cleric's collar or in a gas jockey's coveralls. Of course, he was neither of those things. He was a pedophile and an accused murderer. I pulled out a chair and sat down.

"Hello, Paul."

"Hello, Henry." Something flickered in his eyes. Amusement? "You look like you went swimming in your clothes."

I glanced at the grimy cuff of my shirt. "Swimming in the heat is more like it."

He plucked at the collar of his jumpsuit. "You should wear one of these. They're very cool and always in style."

"But not generally available to the public."

"That's so," he replied, smiling. "I appreciate you taking my case."

"How are you doing?"

"Fine. Jail isn't a new experience for me," he said lightly. "They even gave me back my old cell. I'm in what they call high power. You know what that means, don't you?"

"Isolation?"

He nodded. "Child molesters have a life expectancy of about five minutes in here. Even reformed child molesters." His tone was bantering.

"I wouldn't be quite so free about tossing that around."

"Everyone knows about me, Henry. Hide the kids, Uncle Paul is coming to visit."

His calm made me wary. "That's not why you're here this time, of course."

His face grew serious. "No, it's not. Well, not directly, anyway, but we both know that if I hadn't been arrested before I wouldn't be here now."

"I don't know what you mean."

"Isn't it obvious? Someone kills a dealer in kiddie porn and the cops 'round up the usual suspects.' "

"You were there the night he was killed," I pointed out.

"That's not a crime," he said flatly.

"Therein lies our defense," I replied.

"The real crime is that I have to defend myself at all."

I said, "The police think you had a motive to murder John McKay. Blackmail."

He grinned. " 'Police think' is an oxymoron. They don't think any more than sides of beef think."

"Nonetheless you were carrying quite a bit of money with you."

A little irritably, he said, "I thought Sara explained all that to you."

"She told me what you told her," I replied. "That you'd gone to see McKay to purchase a child."

He laughed. "Does that sound like something I'd make up?"

"I don't know you well enough to answer that, Paul."

He got serious. "The only thing I'm guilty of is being different."

For now, I wanted to skirt that issue so I said, "Were you serious about buying this child, Paul?"

"Why do we have to go into that?"

"It could come out in trial."

"Only if I testify. Surely, you're not going to put me on the witness stand," he said caustically.

"It's a little early to decide that," I replied. "After the prelim we'll have a better idea of the strength of the prosecution's case."

He wasn't listening. "You just don't want to talk about it, do you?" he sputtered.

"About what, Paul?"

"You're talking as if there's some truth to what they're saying. I've been set up for one reason and one reason alone, because of what I am." He glared at me. "This is bullshit."

I let a moment pass before I answered so it wouldn't appear that I was arguing with him.

"Maybe you're right, Paul, I don't know. It wouldn't be the first time the cops have taken the easy way out on a difficult case. But here you are and, like it or not, there's only one way to get you out that I know of. We go into court, we listen to their evidence, we show that it's insufficient to prove the charge." I allowed myself a faint, disparaging shrug. "It's tedious. You won't feel vindicated. But you will be free."

In a calm, bitter voice, he replied, "Do you give that speech to all your clients?"

"In one form or another. To orient them."

Rubbing his eyes, he said, "This is different."

"How so?"

"You're assuming I'll be treated fairly here. I won't. Mark will see to that."

For all his apparent intelligence and self-possession, it occurred to me that maybe Paul really was paranoid. That would certainly complicate his defense.

"Paul, it's asking too much of me to believe that Mark arranged this murder to set you up."

He shook his head derisively. "That's not what I said. I didn't say he had McKay killed. He read about the murder and made some calls. Maybe money changed hands—it wouldn't be the first time he bribed a bureaucrat—and I'm arrested."

"No one fabricated your fingerprints in McKay's room," I pointed out.

"I'm not denying I was there," he said angrily. "That's what gave Mark the idea. But I didn't kill McKay."

"Someone did."

He turned his face away in contempt.

"I want you to tell me about McKay," I said. "How you came to know him, what happened that night. Everything."

Tight-lipped, he stared at me for a moment, then began. "I didn't actually know McKay, not the way you think. I mean, we never discussed *Lolita* over drinks, or anything like that. I talked to him over a computer bulletin board used by people who have my particular interests. He was a dealer in certain materials that appealed to me, and I bought things from him occasionally."

"Pornography?"

"If you like." He paused, eyes roaming the room for a moment before they rested on my face. "You of all people, Henry, should understand that sexuality is more than a matter of wiring."

"You might as well know now that I have the same biases as most people when it comes to pedophilia."

He smiled, fleetingly. "Maybe I can change your mind."

"I doubt it."

"I want you to understand anyway," he said. "Society tells a lot of lies about children, but the biggest one is that they're not sexual. They are, and it's the purest kind of sexuality because they haven't learned it's dirty." He pointed a finger, lecturing me. "When one is with a child sexually, one becomes a child, too. Everything's immediate, every sensation is the first sensation. I can't begin to describe how it feels." His face was utterly naked. "They taste different, they smell different. . . ."

"Stop it," I said, surprising myself with my vehemence.

Startled, he gaped at me, then said, reproachfully, "You disappoint me, Henry."

"That's to my credit, I think."

"Henry, Henry," he said, shaking his head sadly. "Are you going to tell me that a child can't consent to sex? Don't you think they have sexual fantasies?"

"A thirteen-year-old's sexual fantasy is different than a thirty-year-old's," I said. "A child can't fantasize adult sexual activity. You can't talk about consent in that situation."

"Someday you're going to meet a very pretty boy, Henry, who will change your ideas radically."

"We were talking about McKay."

"You're anxious to change the subject," he said. "Maybe I've said something that strikes home."

"Maybe you're full of shit, Paul."

He shrugged. "McKay was not a nice man. He lacked my refinement and his own tastes ran to boys." He made a face. "He was always going on about his latest twelve-year-old conquest. It's not that I begrudged him his boys but," he smiled again, "I'm straight. Anyway, we talked from time to time, and then, a couple of months ago, he told me about a girl. It seems that she'd been sold by her father when she was nine but she was too old for the man who'd bought her."

"How old was she?"

"Thirteen," he said. "A delicious age in a girl."

"This isn't a circle jerk. Let's confine ourselves to McKay. So he offered to what? Be the middleman?"

"Yes, exactly. It was all arranged. She would be delivered to him and he would bring her to me. He was asking twenty thousand dollars. That was reasonable, I thought. So I went to the motel. No girl. Just a seedy man in a seedy room. He said there'd been a problem with delivery but he expected her in a day or two. Meanwhile, he wanted half the money, to show my good faith." He laughed at the recollection.

"Evidently, you didn't believe him."

"You only had to look at the man to see he was lying. He was a tub of lard with all his brains in his balls."

"What happened then?"

"I left," he said.

"What time?"

"I got home at around one, so I must've left there no later than midnight."

"The police estimate the time of death between midnight and three."

"He was alive when I left him," Paul said. "Maybe he went out and picked someone up. That's another disadvantage of being attracted to boys. Sometimes they put up a fight."

"The coroner says McKay's head was bashed in. And his testicles had been crushed, probably while he was still alive. Someone was very disappointed with him. How disappointed were you not to find the girl there?"

That wiped the smile off his face. "You can't believe that I killed him."

"If I disliked you enough I could," I said. "If I was a juror with a child, a daughter, I might convince myself no matter how weak the evidence is."

"You're like everyone else," he said bitterly.

"Right now we're not talking about me. We're talking about the judge who'll try this case and the jurors who'll decide it. They're not going to regard pedophilia as normal, much less something to be proud of, and they'll be fighting against their sense of decency to put you back on the streets. So let's not make it any harder than it is."

"What kind of a faggot are you?" he shot back.

I smiled. "One with no illusions, Paul. I tell my gay clients the same thing I've just told you, and my black and Latino clients, too, for that matter. You don't need to invent a conspiracy against you by Mark. Society is a conspiracy and everyone who's different is its target."

"So you admit that you and I are the same," he said.

"I only admit that people in the mainstream don't cut very fine distinctions about those of us who aren't. I do."

"In order to feel superior to me?" he asked, smugly.

With some asperity, I said, "No. I acquired my values through trial and error. There isn't much margin for feeling superior when you do it that way. Now, let's get back to work."

"What do you want me to do?"

"I want you to keep your mouth shut about little girls and the joys of pedophilia."

His face flared red, but he nodded.

"Now, the preliminary hearing's in two weeks. I'm flying back to Los Angeles tonight to settle some business and free myself up. Do you have questions?"

He shook his head, sullenly.

"All right. By the way, when was the last time you saw Ruth Soto?"

He stared in surprise. "What?"

"Sara seems to think Ruth's brother may be mixed up in all this."

"I haven't seen her since that day in court when she wouldn't testify."

He was lying. "You're sure."

"I just said it, didn't I?"

I got up to leave. "Well, if you change your mind, let me know. Good-bye, Paul."

My thoughts were jumbled as I left the jail. The long summer day seemed to be going on and on. I made my way across the street to a Winchell's, ordered a cup of tea and wedged myself into an uncomfortable, sticky booth. The tabletop was littered with bits of sugared glaze and bright-colored sprinkles, like confetti. At another table sat the inevitable cops, a tall fair one and a bulky dark one. They glanced at me and then went back to their crullers and coffee.

I thought about Paul Windsor. The intelligence and charm he'd shown at the beginning of our interview were clearly in the service of something darker. Evidently, he belonged to a breed of pedophiles who not only defended their proclivity but proselytized on its behalf. Could this aggressive obsession have led him to murder McKay in a rage of disappointed lust? Or was I just reflecting my biases?

A woman I'd once worked for—an excellent lawyer—used to say that the best lawyers were guided by ethics, not morality. What she meant is that since moral judgments are by nature absolute, once you've made one, you're stuck with it and that doesn't leave you much room to do your job. Ethics, on the other hand, are boundaries, not judgments; they allow you to be impersonal without becoming inhuman.

Sipping tepid, bitter tea, I thought about boundaries and sex. I heard Paul saying, "They taste different, they smell different. . . ." And then another fragment of conversation drifted through my mind, the first man I'd ever had sex with telling me, "It takes a man to know what a man likes." Both statements of sexual chauvinism, but were they really comparable? I found myself staring at the dark cop. For all his bodybuilder's bulk, he had a child's round, large-eyed, pretty face. I looked away, quickly. "They taste different, they smell different. . . ." What I'd meant when I told Paul my values were acquired through trial and error was that they were learned, not given, and came out of my own experience. I was not a pedophile, nor had I ever consciously entertained those fantasies, but I was a sexual being and for a moment in the jail I'd felt Paul's excitement and it terrified me.

6

My day wasn't over yet. I still had to pay a call at the district attorney's office. I walked over to the county building and was directed by a janitor to the third floor. There, I told the girl at the counter that I wanted to talk to the DA assigned to the Windsor case. She disappeared for a moment and then told me to go back to Mr. Rossi's office.

Dominic Rossi was one of the two names painted on the frosted glass of a door halfway down the corridor. I knocked.

"Come in."

I opened the door and looked in. The office was standard government issue, square, windowless, walls painted an indeterminate pale color; two fake wooden desks, rotary phones, a girlie calendar on one wall and an autopsy picture on the other; bright lights overhead and a scuffed linoleum floor at my feet. The sole occupant of the room was a portly man in a rumpled blue shirt, skinny tie at half-mast. A big styrofoam cup of coffee sat on the desk in front of him with wadded-up pink Sweet 'N Low packets surrounding it.

"Mr. Rossi?"

"Dom," he said, taking the card I extended across the desk. His round, pale face was distinguished by a thick mustache and heavy glasses. His thin hair gleamed with sweat. "Henry Rios," he said, "I've heard of you."

"I'm substituting in on the Windsor case," I said, lowering myself into a naugahyde chair.

"I bet Bob Clayton's glad to be rid of that sucker," he said, tossing my card onto a stack of papers. "So what can I do you for?"

"I wanted to talk to you about discovery."

He blinked. "Discovery?"

"Am I going to have to file a motion or can we handle it informally?"

He half-smirked. "Do I look like the U.S. attorney?" he asked, grabbing a legal pad. "You tell me what you want and I'll get it to you."

"I have the complaint, the police report, the search warrant and affidavit," I replied. "I don't have the complete coroner's report . . ."

"Okay," he said, jotting a note.

"I'd also like a list of your witnesses, the investigating officer's notes, any other reports prepared in the case, the . . ."

"Wait a sec." He scribbled madly.

"Any forensic or toxicological reports," I continued, "any and all written statements by any witnesses, a list of all property seized during the search, are you getting this?"

"Mmm," he replied, still writing.

"A list of any other evidence and the file on Windsor's previous arrest."

He looked up, stopped writing. "That's not really kosher, Mr. Rios."

"Henry," I replied. "It could be relevant."

"How's that?"

"I won't know until I see it."

I could tell by his expression he wanted to give me an argument, but then he smiled and said, "Sure, why not." He made a final note. "I'll have the IO put together a packet."

"Who is the investigating officer?" I asked.

"Dwight Morrow. Good cop."

"Meaning what?"

"His arrests are clean and they stick."

"Morrow," I mused. "He's the cop who got the search warrant, isn't he? Good cop?" I shook my head. "I've never seen a search warrant issued on so little probable cause, and if you take away the money, all you've got are fingerprints. What kind of case is that?"

"So are you here to make a deal, or what?"

"No deals," I said. "I want a straight dismissal or a trial."

His attempt at gravity made him look like a pouting infant. "We take our crime a little more serious here than in the big cities," he replied.

"Speaking of that," I ventured, "I understand people were pretty upset when the charges were dropped against Paul in that child molest case a few years back."

"You could say that," he replied. "I was the DA on the case."

"You nursing a grudge?"

"I'm strictly a nine-to-five kind of guy, Henry."

"What happened on that case?"

"The judge wouldn't drop the charges. Made us put the girl on the stand and threatened to hold her in contempt if she wouldn't testify."

"But she didn't."

"Nope. Just sat there, crying. Judge still wouldn't dump the case. The DA had to come into court and ask for dismissal."

"Who was the judge?"

"Burton K. Phelan," he said. "Tough son-of-a-bitch."

I pocketed the information. "Clayton told me the prelim's in front of the same judge who issued the search warrant. Judge Lanyon."

"Yeah, luck of the draw. Not lucky for you, maybe, but you know the prelim's just a dog-and-pony show anyway." He picked up his coffee cup, sipped, made a face.

"You know as well as I do that it's unlawful for the same judge who issues a search warrant to hear the prelim."

"Tell him."

"You're not going to make this easy for me, are you?"

Cradling the cup between his hands, he said, "Like I said, Henry, we take our crime serious around here."

"What about procedure? You take that seriously, too?"

"You ought to talk to a couple of defense lawyers before you plan anything fancy," he said. "They'll tell you that kind of stuff doesn't sit well here."

"Frontier justice, huh?"

He put the cup down. "You want to watch your attitude, too."

I got up. "No offense intended, Dom. Thanks for the cooperation. Should I pick the stuff up from you?"

"Nah. Just go down to central and ask for Morrow. He'll have it. Pleasure meeting you, Henry. Let's have some fun with this case."

"Pleasure meeting you, Dom," I replied, and let myself out of his office.

After a final stop at Clayton's office to pick up the packet of *Sentinel* articles about the case, I drove to the airport at the edge of town. Within the hour I was looking down at the baked landscape, declining a cocktail and wondering what I'd let myself into.

Morning found me at my office, a shabby suite of rooms in a nondescript office building on Sunset and La Brea I'd picked up cheap. Our only neighbors were a publicist named Ronnie Toy and an actors' agent who called himself Marc-Alan. An OFFICE SPACE FOR LEASE sign was a permanent fixture on the door to the building; we were the commercial equivalent of the motels that lined that part of Sunset and rented by the hour to the prostitutes who negotiated their deals alfresco on the street below. My secretary, Emma Austen, a regal black woman, had once demanded a raise on the grounds that she was entitled to at least as much money per hour as the hookers made.

I was sitting in the conference room going over the *Sentinel* articles that Clayton had given me when I heard the radio start up in the next room. A moment later, Emma breezed in, swathed in a sort of filmy white caftan, her braided hair bright with blue and gold beads, carrying a mug of coffee in one hand and a stack of pink telephone message slips in the other.

"Are you trying to hide from me?" she asked, setting the messages at my elbow.

I glanced at the pile. "Make them go away."

She placed the mug in front of me. "I can't, honey, but I did bring you coffee to make them easier to swallow."

"Thanks."

"Don't go getting used to it," she replied, faint traces of the South in her accent. She glanced over my shoulder. "What are you reading, Henry?"

"These are articles from my hometown newspaper about a case I'm taking." I lifted the sheet I'd been looking at and handed it to her.

"The *Los Robles Sentinel*," she read. " 'Windsor Arrested in Killing of Kiddie Porn King. Suspect Is Brother of Developer; Was Once Arrested for Child Molestation.' " She shook her head, beads clattering. "Oh, my. 'Paul Windsor, brother of developer Mark Windsor, was charged with the brutal murder of John McKay, a dealer in child pornography who was found bludgeoned in a motel room early Monday morning.' " she read. " 'Windsor, 32, was arrested at his home in exclusive River Park yesterday. Four years ago, he was arrested in a child molestation case that was dismissed when the victim, a 15-year-old girl, refused to testify, allegedly due to the pressure of the Windsor family.' " She handed me the paper. "Who is this creep?"

"The brother of a boyhood friend of mine," I replied.

"Exclusive River Park home," she said. "Are you doing this for the money?"

"I'm doing it as a favor to my sister. Paul's wife is a friend of hers."

"Wife?" she said, incredulously. "Poor woman. Did he do it, Henry?"

"I don't know. He's not admitting to it and the case is weak. His creep quotient is pretty high but that doesn't make him a killer."

She sat down. "Did he molest the little girl?"

I nodded.

"He should have had his balls cut off," she said, decisively.

"Speaking as one who knows," I replied, "sexuality doesn't originate in the balls. It starts here." I tapped my head.

Rising, she said, "Then he ought to have his head chopped off. Or examined, anyway."

Her remark gave me an idea. "Do you remember that psychiatrist we used in the Castillo trial?"

"Uh-huh, the gorgeous one, Nick Trejo?"

"Find his number, would you? I'd like to talk to him."

"Sure," she said. "Why are you reading these articles? You already know what the case is about."

"There's some question about whether Paul can get a fair trial in Los Robles with all this publicity," I said. "If it gets that far."

"I'll call Nick," she said. "Mmm, that man. Even his voice is good-looking."

"He's gay, Emma."

"Any man that pretty would have to be."

The fact that there hadn't been much hard news about Paul's case hadn't deterred the *Sentinel* one whit. The stories quickly branched out to other transgressions by the Windsors, culminating in a three-part article called "An American Family."

"American Gothic" would have been an apter title. I learned a lot about the Windsors, most of it damning, none of it relevant to the murder charge against Paul. In exposé style, the writer informed his audience that, among other things, their mother, Lydia Windsor ("nee Lydia Smith"), was an alcoholic, Herb Windsor was a strikebreaker allegedly with ties to "the underworld," and Mark had been twice divorced and the defendant in a paternity suit, and, of course, dwelt on Paul's prior arrest for child molestation, repeating allegations that the Windsors had somehow pressured the victim into refusing to testify. Side by side with the last installment of the article was a front-page editorial urging the voters to approve Proposition K, the no-growth ordinance, necessary, the editor opined, to curb the excess of unscrupulous (and unnamed) developers.

I put the articles back into the folder. Over the years, I'd seen more and more of this kind of sensationalism in the media's coverage of criminal cases. "The court of public opinion" had become more than just a First Amendment platitude. It was actually the forum in which many serious criminal cases were tried and, usually, lost. So, as deplorable as the *Sentinel*'s coverage was, in any other city it might not be enough to persuade a judge that it had effectively tainted the minds of prospective jurors. Los Robles wasn't just any other city, however. In the first place, the *Sentinel* was the only general circulation paper in the entire county. In the second place, the *Sentinel* was doing more than just prejudging Paul's case. It was deliberately using his arrest to promote its editor's political agenda on the no-growth issue, which was one of the great public controversies in California.

Maybe the combination of things would be sufficient to convince a judge that Paul could not get a fair hearing in Los Robles. This assumed we could find a judge in Los Robles who'd give us a fair hearing on whether we could get a fair hearing.

I ran through the rest of my notes and saw the question about McKay's rap sheet. Reaching for the phone, I called my investigator, Freeman Vidor. A moment later I was explaining the situation to him.

He said, "The Los Robles PD don't seem too interested in the victim."

"He's definitely a bit player," I agreed. "Paul Windsor seems to be the star."

"You got a plan?" he rumbled.

"Plan A is to get him off at the prelim," I said.

"You better have a plan B," Freeman said, knowing as well as I did that virtually all preliminary hearings, the purpose of which was simply to determine whether there was sufficient evidence to support the charges against a defendant, were pro forma.

"Plan B is to argue that the prosecution can't make reasonable doubt," I said, referring to the requirement that the prosecution prove its case beyond a reasonable doubt. "As long as they can't prove Paul did it, it doesn't matter who killed McKay. But I have a bad feeling about the way they do justice in my hometown, so I want a plan C. I want to know if there's anything in McKay's background I could use to argue that someone had it in for him."

"Someone else besides Windsor, you mean," he said.

"That's my first preference," I replied, dryly. "Of course, if it turns out to be Paul, that's also useful information."

"You think he's lying to you."

"Being lied to is a way of life in this business."

"I'll be in touch," Freeman said.

From her desk, Emma called, "Henry, Nick Trejo is on line two. He wants to talk to you."

"One second," I said, giving myself time to collect my thoughts before talking to the psychologist. "Nick?"

"Hello, Henry. Emma was telling me about this case you have. Another winner?"

She was right about Nick's voice. It was good-looking.

"The bills have to be paid."

"So, what do you want to know?"

"My client is a self-proclaimed pedophile. I guess I want to know if a pedophile is more likely to commit a crime of violence because of his pedophilia."

"Does he have a history of violence?"

"Not that I know of," I replied, making a note to find out.

65

"On the other hand, he's really very aggressive about his pedophilia, and he was also real quick to shift the blame to other people for what was happening to him. It made me think that here's a man who lives by his own rules. Could it be that murder is not outside of those rules?"

"Tell me everything you know about him," Nick said.

"He's the younger of two sons," I said. "His brother, whom he hates, has always overshadowed him. The mother was an alcoholic, the father a very successful businessman." I thought for a moment. "He was very quiet as a kid."

"Is this someone you knew?"

"I was friends with the older brother," I replied. "Paul was the kind of a nuisance I never paid much attention to. He's evidently pretty bright. Articulate. Married a woman much older than he is. She told me he was desperate to get married."

"What's she like?" he asked.

"A victim, a drinker."

"What about his pedophilia?"

"Paul was arrested for molesting the daughter of their maid. It went on for several years until he got her pregnant. She wouldn't testify against him so the charges got dropped. The man he's accused of murdering was a dealer in child pornography. Paul said the guy offered to sell him a little girl, that's why he went to see him the night he was killed. Paul says the guy turned out to be a fraud. I'm afraid that's pretty much all I know. What do you think, Nick?"

Nick hesitated. "You know I don't like making this kind of spot analysis but off the top of my head, I'd say there's a lot going on with your guy. Between an alcoholic mother and a go-getter father, there probably wasn't much attention paid to the kids. If his brother was the star, your guy—Paul?—probably didn't even get any of that. It would be interesting to know what his sexual experience was as a child."

"Why's that?" I asked, scribbling notes.

"The one truism about pedophiles is that almost every one was himself molested as a child. Let's assume that Paul was pretty isolated and ignored as a kid. That would make him a ripe target for sexual abuse."

"I don't get it."

"Kids want attention, Henry. They need it and if it doesn't come from their families, it puts them at risk."

"Wouldn't a kid draw the line at sex?"

"Not necessarily," Nick said. "If a kid's very young he might not understand what's being done to him. If he's older, he may decide it's just part of the bargain."

"That comes awfully close to saying he'd consent."

" 'Awfully close' isn't the same thing. Let's say he puts up with it, even if he feels it's wrong. You can imagine the kind of damage that does."

"Paul's not exactly guilt-ridden about his preference for little girls," I remarked.

"Haven't you heard of rationalization? Particularly if he's bright, he'll have learned to mask his pain."

"His what?"

"Pain, Henry," he repeated, quietly. "Wouldn't you feel hurt if you woke one day and realized that you'd been used by someone you thought cared for you? Inside, Paul may still be trying to make sense of it."

"By molesting little girls?"

Nick said, "He acts out what happened to him as a way of giving himself power over a situation where he was powerless. Plus, kids are a lot less critical than other adults. He can feel in control."

"What does he feel for the kid he molests?"

"If you ask him, he'd probably tell you affection, and that may be true to some extent, but, basically, he's a narcissist, so intent on getting what he wants that he is incapable of empathy with his victim, or with anyone, for that matter."

I stopped writing and digested what Nick had told me. Soft rock drifted in from the radio on Emma's desk, the Eagles singing about "Hotel California."

"A sociopath," I said.

Nick chided me. "Let's not get sloppy with our labels.

Compulsive behavior isn't the same thing as an inability to distinguish right from wrong."

"Would he kill?"

"Well," Nick said, "if there's no history of violence I don't think the fact he's a pedophile is any indicator that he'd be more likely to kill than anyone else. And I don't really see much provocation in what you've told me about the circumstances of the murder."

"Disappointment at not getting the girl?"

"Pedophiles don't have a lot of trouble finding kids. Well, that's' your quarter's worth from me, Henry. An equivocal 'I don't think so.' "

"You guys are worse than lawyers."

"You flatter yourself," he replied. "You know," he added, "there is one thing that's kind of interesting."

"What's that?"

"You said you were friends with Paul's brother. A close friend?"

"I guess we were best friends. I had a crush on him."

"And Paul hates his brother, you said."

Uncomfortably, I asked. "What are you getting at?"

"Paul must enjoy having his brother's best friend defending him in a kind of case that's bound to be a real embarrassment to the family. You think?"

"Never talk to a therapist. They always end up by turning on you."

"You owe me lunch, counsel. I'll call to collect."

I put down the phone full of sour admiration for Paul Windsor.

7

When I came home that night, Josh was in the kitchen, standing at the sink, looking out the window.

"Josh?"

"Shh," he whispered. "Come here, Henry. Look."

I came up behind him and looked. Not more than twenty feet from us in the wooded slope of the hill that descended down to a ravine at the end of our property two deer grazed in the underbrush. One of them lifted its head and seemed to look back at us. It nudged its partner, who also looked, and then they moved off into the dusk like figures from a dream.

"How long have you been watching them?" I asked.

"Five, ten minutes," he said, turning to me.

"Where do they come from, I wonder?"

He put his arms around my waist. "You look tired."

"There was lots to catch up on. Do you want to do something tonight? Dinner? A movie?"

He kissed me. "No," he said. "I'll make us dinner—later. Unless you're hungry now."

I shook my head, and put my arms around him. "Have you ever thought about sexual attraction, Josh?"

"I'm thinking about it now," he said, nuzzling me, his beard brisk on my neck.

"I'm serious."

"Me, too." He let go of me and smiled, wearily. "Okay, tell me about sexual attraction."

"Do you think part of it is that we're trying to recapture something?"

"Is this your idea of foreplay?"

"I was wondering why an adult would want to have sex with a child."

His smile faded. "That's rape, not sex."

"Sex is part of it."

He shook his head vigorously. "It's just plain violence, Henry, with a dick instead of a gun."

I thought about this. "If that's right, then maybe a pedophile would be more inclined to violence than the average person. On the other hand, if I'm right, and sexual attraction is partly nostalgia, then maybe not."

Josh hoisted himself onto the kitchen counter. "What are you nostalgic for, with me?"

I looked at him. "I didn't mean it personally."

"But as long as you brought it up."

I laid my hand on his thigh, touching taut muscle beneath the fabric of his jeans. "I was almost nineteen when I had my first sexual experience."

He laid his hand over mine. "So?"

"But I'd been in love for years before that, with my best friend. Was it like that for you?"

He cracked a smile. "I chose my friends better than you did, Henry. I had sex with my best friend when we were ten."

"Slut."

"You knew I had a past when you married me. So are you saying that I remind you of your best friend? Little Tom, Dick or Harry?"

"His name was Mark," I said, thumping his leg. "And no, you've never consciously reminded me of him, but you are a lot younger than I am." I looked up at him, feeling vaguely ashamed. "That was part of the excitement for me."

"I should be taping this."

"Does that mean I have pedophile tendencies?" I asked, joking at my discomfort.

"Henry, I was twenty-two when I met you."

"I don't think I want to talk about this anymore."

He hopped off the counter. "Good. Let's go upstairs."

"Sex maniac."

He grabbed my hand. "Given half the chance."

We had a peaceful week until Sunday, the day I was to fly back to Los Robles. I was edgy about leaving Josh alone for a couple of weeks, and prodded him to call his parents, and me, and take his medicines, until he just exploded. Self-righteously, I blasted back. The drive to the airport was chilly and silent. Getting out of the car, I said, "Look, I'm sorry if I provoked you this morning. I just—"

He glared. "Stop it, okay? Your way of saying I'm sorry always ends up making it sound like it was my fault."

"Suit yourself." I closed the door a little more forcefully than suggested in the owner's manual. He opened the trunk from the inside and I got my bags. As soon as I closed the trunk, he drove away.

"Well, fuck you, too," I muttered, startling the skycap who'd come up to give me a hand. I brushed him away and went into the airport, only to discover that the plane was delayed. I checked in and roamed the corridors. I paused in front of a cocktail lounge. The TV was showing an old movie, and I thought maybe I could kill some time that way. I was over the threshold when I stopped myself. Who was I trying to fool? Instead, I found a phone and made a call to a friend in AA. Talking to him helped, but I was still in a foul mood when I checked into the Los Robles Hyatt a few hours later. I called Sara Windsor to let her know I was back in town.

"Henry," she slurred, adding something which it took me a moment to decipher as, "Mark's been trying to reach you."

"What's his number?" I asked, irritably.

She had to repeat it twice.

"Sara," I said, "there's a chance you may have to testify at Paul's trial. Do you think you could do it sober?"

There was a pause, and then the dial tone.

"Nice work," I told myself. I looked at the paper with Mark Windsor's phone number on it. My first impulse was to call immediately, but in my present frame of mind I wasn't capable of carrying on a rational conversation. Instead, I unpacked, took a shower, and gazed out my eighth-floor window.

In the late summer dusk, the sky was an enormous rose, unfolding slow, pink petals. I thought of Paul's garden and of Sara drinking her way through another night. I knew all about nights like that. I put the image aside and continued looking. From where I stood I could see the river, silver in the coming dark, seemingly motionless between densely wooded banks. I found myself wishing that Josh were here to show this to. It never ceased to amaze me how easily anger could alternate with tenderness in our dealings with each other.

The phone rang. I picked it up hopefully. "Josh?"

"Uh, Henry Rios?" The voice was vaguely familiar.

"Yes."

"This is Mark. Mark Windsor."

I sat down on the edge of the bed. "Hello, Mark. I'm sorry I didn't recognize your voice right away."

"It's a little deeper," he said, laughing. He was right. "Sara called me and told me you were here. Can we talk?"

"Sure. Where are you?"

"Downstairs in the bar," he replied, and I could hear barroom music in the background. "Why don't you come down and have a drink with me?"

"Okay. I'll be right down. Uh, you look pretty much the same?"

He laughed again. "Above the neck."

I saw what he meant when I got down to the bar. In khakis and a red Ralph Lauren polo shirt, he no longer had the body of the fastest miler in Los Robles Valley. He was still in pretty good shape, respectably Nautilusized in the chest and arms and shoulders, though his waist had thickened and, as Josh had once said about me, grabbing my butt, his center of gravity was shifting. His face had changed least of all. Though his blond hair had darkened it was still lighter than his blunt eyebrows, a combination that immediately called attention to his eyes. They were hazel, shading to green when his mood was light, brown when it wasn't, a barometer of his emotions. His face was fuller, once-incipient lines had deepened, skin coarsened, but he was still beautiful. Only now he seemed to know it, as he hadn't when we were kids. He turned a perfectly shaped smile on me as I approached him at the bar.

"Hi," I said, extending my hand.

He grabbed me in a bear hug. "God, it's good to see you. You look great."

Not wanting to embarrass either of us with my fledgling erection, I got away. "You, too."

"How do you manage to keep your weight? Still running?"

I shook my head. "In LA running's a slow form of suicide. It's my metabolism, I guess. Luck of the draw."

He pinched his waist. "I'm fat."

"You look wonderful, Mark, really." Was that a faggy thing to say? I wondered. "You work out?"

"When I can. Let's get a booth, okay, where we can talk."

I followed him to the back wall, away from the bright lights over the bar, to a booth illuminated by a recessed light and a candle in a green glass. The wall was papered with hunting scenes. In the distance I could make out a row of antlers. Beneath it was a glass case displaying rifles.

"What's this place called?" I asked. "The Abattoir?"

He looked at me blankly, then followed my gaze to the rifles and the moose. "The what?"

"Slaughterhouse," I said, self-consciously. Every time I opened my mouth, I seemed to take another notch out of my masculinity. It didn't help when, a moment later I heard myself ordering a diet Coke to his scotch-and-soda, adding gratuitously, "I don't drink."

"That's smart," Mark replied. He dug a pack of Marlboros out of his pocket. "You smoke?"

I shook my head, barely preventing myself from apologizing. What's going on? I wondered, as he lit up. Then it came to me: I had never told Mark I was gay, except in a letter, long ago, which he had never answered, or even acknowledged. With him, I was still pretending, still passing.

"When I came out," I said, lightly, "I figured that was enough of a vice for one lifetime."

Even this sounded apologetic.

"When you what?" he asked, smiling, wanting to share the joke.

"When I accepted being gay."

"Oh," he said, the smile went off like a light.

"I'm homosexual, Mark."

"I know what it means, Henry," he said, impatiently. "I don't care," he added without conviction.

Our drinks arrived. The waiter fussed with our cocktail napkins and I glanced up at him. The tone of his answering smile was unmistakable.

"Well, cheers," Mark said. He tapped my glass and knocked back half his drink. He was nervous, too. "Listen, I want to thank you for taking Paul's case."

For a minute, I considered pressing the point of my homosexuality with him, but I was too unclear about what I wanted from him, so I dropped it, too. "It's how I make my living."

"He's done stupid things all his life," Mark continued, "but this is by far the stupidest."

I set my glass down. "You think he killed the man?"

"Don't you?" he replied, eyes going from green to brown.

"I don't think the evidence is very persuasive."

"Shit, Henry. Paul is a fucking madman. You know about the trouble he got into with that girl." His eyes completed their transformation.

"Yes," I said. "That doesn't mean he'd kill someone."

He shrugged. "You're his lawyer. I guess you have to think that way. Now me, I know my brother. He's crazy."

"Actually, I don't think one way or the other about whether he did it except as it affects the way I defend him," I replied, "but I'm curious about why you think he's guilty."

Mark finished his drink and said, slowly, "He took twenty thousand dollars to pay the guy off," he said, "and when he got there, the guy let him know it was just the first installment. So Paul went nuts and bashed him."

"The problem with the blackmail theory," I replied, "is that after his last arrest, everyone knew that Paul was a pedophile, so what was the point of buying the man's silence?"

"What's a pedophile?" he asked, signaling for another round.

"An adult who's sexually attracted to kids. It's no secret that that's what Paul is."

Mark shook his head. "It's no secret that Paul knocked up a fifteen-year-old, but as far as anyone knew that was the only time he got into that kind of trouble. Now this guy was a whatchamacallit himself."

He interrupted himself to accept his drink. The waiter looked at me expectantly. I shook my head.

"Pedophile," I said.

"Yeah. And he obviously knew something about Paul that the rest of us didn't. That's what Paul wanted to keep a secret."

This sounded plausible, more plausible than Paul's story about taking the money to buy a little girl. "You've worked this out," I said. "Do you have any evidence?"

He snorted derisively. "What evidence, Hank? Do you think it's something Paul would talk to me about? He hates my guts."

I hadn't been called Hank in twenty years. Hearing it, I felt a surge of sentimental affection toward Mark. Paul, as he had when we were kids, receded into the distance, an unwanted nuisance.

"He mentioned that," I said. "He thinks you robbed him when you bought out his share of your business."

Mark leaned toward me, smiling. "He's full of shit. He thinks I had lined up all these contracts without telling him but he doesn't know anything about the business, Hank. Sure, I was negotiating those deals but they were like sand in my hand, you know. They could've fallen through this fast." He snapped his finger. "Then you would've heard him whining about that. No, it's not business. He hates me. Always has."

"Why?"

He lowered his eyes for a moment, studying the backs of his hands. The light turned the small hairs on his wrists to gold. He looked up at me, meeting my eyes. "You never really knew my dad, did you?"

"No, it was your mother I had the pleasure of meeting," I replied, still smarting from the swimming pool incident, twenty-five years later.

From the abrupt darkening of his eyes, I could tell that Mark also remembered how his mother had banned me from the pool, apparently out of fear that my brown skin would soil the water.

"She was a drunk," he said brutally.

"I know about drunks," I replied. "What about your father?"

"He wasn't a drunk, just an asshole. He was on us from the day we were born. Remember that time in Sacramento I ran a four-minute mile?"

I nodded. That had been a wonderful day.

"When I got home and told Dad he said, why couldn't you break four." He shook his head. "Same thing with Paul. He'd come home with straight As and Dad would tell him, I bet you can't do that next time or, these are pussy courses. There was no pleasing him, ever. The difference between Paul and me is that I stopped taking it after a while. Dad and me had some real knock-down, drag-out fights, but I stood my ground. Not Paul. He'd cry and go running to Mom, but she was always too drunk to give a shit. So he just got worse, afraid and nervous all the time, locked himself up in his room. I tried to help him but he was—I don't know how to say it, too much into himself, you know?"

"Yeah, I think so."

We'd fallen into our adolescent habit of whispering conspiratorially to each other and the tops of our heads almost touched above the table. I could smell cologne, scotch and sweat.

"I know you know," Mark was saying. "You had some trouble with your old man, too."

"How do you know that?"

"Your sister talked to Sara. She told me. She said you and your old man used to get into it, too. I wanted to say something but," he shrugged, "I don't know. I didn't want you to think I felt sorry for you. I didn't, you know. I thought you were tough and I respected you for it."

"Our fathers went to the same school of child rearing," I said. "My dad used to call me *el lloron*, the crybaby. He tried to toughen me up. Didn't take, I guess."

Mark's eyes, green now, were full of admiration. "You seem pretty tough to me. And you're a big-time lawyer. Success is the best revenge, isn't it?"

Our hair touched and I felt drunk. Half a phrase drifted into my mind—"the friends we make in youth"—no doubt mawkish in its entirety and probably untrue as well. Still, at that moment I wanted to reach across the table, touch his face and tell him how much I loved him. But a letter written when I was nineteen, and never answered, stopped me. I only allowed one rejection per person, per lifetime, thank you very much. I pulled back to my side of the booth. He looked at me, puzzled.

"I guess I never thought of it that way," I said.

He leaned back, exhaling fumes of scotch. "I do. I wanted to be bigger than my dad ever was, and I am."

"By hook or by crook?" I asked.

He lit a cigarette. Sometime between when he struck the match and touched it to tip of his cigarette, the spell was broken.

"What are you talking about, Hank?"

"Paul thinks you set him up, Mark. He thinks you made some calls to the police or the DA, maybe even bribed them, to get him arrested."

"I told you he was crazy, Hank."

"Henry," I said. "My friends call me Henry, now."

"Henry," he echoed, his eyes asking what had just happened between us.

"I have to investigate every possibility."

He drew on his cigarette. "It's a dead end," he said flatly. "You shouldn't take Paul too serious, that's what I wanted to tell you."

"I appreciate the advice."

He rattled the ice in his glass. "I've got to go, Henry. I've got a date." He smiled, putting a lot of charm into it. "Dating at my age, can you believe it?"

"You're not married?"

"I'm between wives." He scooted to the edge of the booth, took out his wallet and laid a twenty on the table. "Bob Clayton taking care of you?"

"Yeah."

He got up. "I'm still at the old place. Come by sometime. For a swim."

"Maybe."

"I'll barbecue." He looked at me, his expression bemused. "You know it's funny, Hank—Henry."

"What's that, Mark?"

"You being gay. I'd have figured that for Paul, not you. Well, I guess he became something even worse."

His parting smile turned him into a stranger.

After he'd left, the waiter came back by, picked up the twenty and said, "Can I get you another Coke?"

I shook my head.

"It's on the house."

I looked at him. He was a nice-looking kid, maybe a couple of years older than Josh.

"No thank you," I said, "but I appreciate the offer."

He nodded. "If you change your mind, I'll be here until closing."

"Thank you," I said, and got up to go.

8

When I called Dom Rossi the next morning about whether the discovery packet was ready, he again directed me to Dwight Morrow, the investigating officer on the case. I ventured out into the morning heat and made my way to police headquarters, already irritable from too little sleep. The heat only made my mood worse.

After talking to Mark, I'd spent much of the night in the kind of "what if" ruminations that served no particular purpose except to depress me. The only constructive notion my insomnia yielded was that maybe the whole purpose of the meeting was to allow Mark to minimize his involvement with Paul and his troubles. This naturally aroused my suspicions and I made a mental note to find out more about Mark's legal problems with Paul, perhaps from Peter Stein, Clayton's amiable associate.

I was, at any rate, in a foul mood when I stepped into the office of Detective Morrow. Phone pressed to his ear, he looked me up and down in the vaguely accusatory way cops do and motioned me to sit down. Clearing a stack of papers from the only available chair, I sat and waited for him to finish his conversation. He sat ramrod straight, clearly a man who confused posture with morality, as if being upright in one carried over to the other.

I looked around his glass-enclosed cubicle for something to break the monotony of its drab bureaucratic decor, settling, finally, on Morrow himself. Despite the Anglo name his looks were mostly Indian: the flat face, square jaw, beaky nose, russet-colored skin and black, almost Asiatic eyes. Any lingering doubt about his ancestry was dispelled by a framed caricature on the wall behind him, depicting him in headdress and loincloth, tomahawk in hand. Next to that was a picture of him crossing the finish line in a footrace, muscled torso straining with effort. A final picture concluded this triptych. It showed a row of boys in sweatsuits with the letters PAL printed across their chests. Morrow stood at the end in jeans and a windbreaker lettered COACH.

Only in this last picture did his face show any animation at all. He was almost smiling—the lips curved upwards, but the eyes still looked as if they were examining autopsy photographs—and almost handsome. I felt something of a shock when I concluded from this picture that he was probably a few years younger than I.

"Okay," he said, "I'll get back to you," and hung up. He directed his unsmiling attention to me.

"I'm Henry Rios," I said. "I'm representing Paul Windsor. Dom Rossi said you had something for me, some discovery."

"It was on the chair." His unfriendliness seemed impersonal.

I lifted the stack of papers from the floor and examined the first sheet. It was a page from the medical examiner's report.

"This is all of it?" I asked.

He was curt. "Rossi gave me a list. I filled it."

"Fine," I replied, with equal disdain. It has never taken much for me to dislike a cop. My automatic assumption that most of them are assholes is seldom disappointed.

"Sign the receipt." He pushed a piece of paper across his desk toward me.

I scanned it. It acknowledged full compliance with my discovery request. It wasn't normally the sort of thing I argued about, since it had no real legal effect, but I didn't care for Detective Morrow's broomstick-up-the-ass machismo.

"I can hardly say you've complied until I examine the packet."

"So examine it."

"When I have the time," I said, rising.

He looked up at me and said quietly, "I'm doing you a favor by giving you this stuff without a court order. In my book, you owe me a favor back."

I shook my head. "Discovery in a criminal case isn't a matter of favors, Detective, it's a matter of right. Now," I rattled the sheet of paper, "I'm not waiving any of my client's rights until I'm good and sure that you've given me everything I asked for."

His expression, unfriendly to begin with, turned actively hostile. In another moment he'd be giving me my Miranda rights. "Rossi warned me you'd be a smart ass."

I shrugged. "Well, he told me you were a good cop. I guess he was wrong about both of us."

He reached for the receipt. "Get out of here."

I gathered up the papers. "I appreciate your cooperation."

"You're not going anywhere with those."

I glanced at the papers in my hand. "Rossi and I had a deal."

He picked up the receipt. "This is part of it. You don't want to sign, you can leave the papers until you get a court order."

I moved toward the door. "Rossi didn't say anything about signing a waiver."

"Vega," he shouted, looking past me. A moment later a

bulky uniformed cop appeared in the doorway. His face was familiar—the cop I'd seen in the Winchell's a few days earlier, the Schwarzenegger with the baby face. "This guy is trying to walk out with police records," Morrow told him. "What are you going to do about it?"

The big cop looked at me in confusion.

I said, "This is what you might call a test of your manhood, Officer, but you better be sure of your grounds before you do anything."

"I asked you a question, Vega," Morrow said.

The boy mumbled, "You want me to arrest him?"

I was feeling better by the second. Confrontations with cops always had a tonic effect on me.

"On what charge? Doing my job? You wouldn't be the first cop who wanted to." I sat down. "I tell you what, why don't you call Rossi and talk this over with him before you give me more ammunition to cross-examine you on."

He stared angrily as he dialed the phone. As he explained to Rossi what had happened—putting himself in the best light, of course—and then listened to Rossi's reply, his anger was replaced by petulance.

He clanged down the phone. "I thought I told you to get out of here," he snapped.

I got up and made my way to the door, where the other cop still stood, his expression troubled as I edged past him.

"Uh, what should I do?" he asked Morrow.

"Let him go."

"Thanks, kid," I told the cop. "See you at Winchell's."

Mention of Winchell's reminded me about breakfast, so I headed over to the doughnut shop, where I bought a large coffee and a sugary bran muffin and sat down to leaf through the packet I'd extorted from Morrow. I'd just finished the medical examiner's report—rather well-written, considering the subject matter—when someone said. "Hi."

I looked up. It was the young cop, cruller and coffee in hand.

"Hello."

He smiled tentatively. "You sure pissed Morrow off."

"You helped."

The kid shrugged. "He gets like that sometimes. He don't mean nothing by it."

"Did he tell you to follow me?"

"It's my regular break."

It looked like he planned to stand there until I asked him to sit down, so I did. "What's your name, again?"

He squeezed into the chair across from me. "Ben Vega," he said, setting his breakfast down. He extended a hand flaked with sugar.

"Henry Rios," I replied. His palm sported a weightlifter's calluses. "What did Morrow tell you?"

"He didn't—"

"Come on, Ben. Cut the crap."

He got points for grinning instead of affecting indignation. "He told me to keep an eye on you, that's all. He's just pissed, is all. He won't even remember by the time I get back."

"You seem to know him pretty well."

"We've known each other since high school." He tapped the papers. "What's this?"

"*People versus Windsor*. You know about the case?"

He nodded. "Sure, everyone does. He's the child molester. How can you defend a guy like that?"

"If I had a nickel for every time someone asked me that question I'd be retired by now," I replied. "So do you really want an answer or were you just asking so you can feel superior to me?"

Startled, but game, Vega said, "Yeah, I want an answer. Really."

"Well, the answer changes depending on the case," I replied. "Sometimes I defend someone because I think he deserves a break, or maybe just because I like him. And sometimes I do it because, whatever the guy's done, worse has been done to him." I grinned. "And sometimes I do it for money. And sometimes I do it because no one else will. Like this case."

"A guy like that don't deserve a defense," Vega said, biting into his cruller.

I shrugged. "Well, there you are, the bottom line difference between cops and lawyers." I sipped my coffee. "Is Morrow always so cranky?"

Talking as he chewed, Vega said, "He arrested Windsor the last time."

"In the child molest case?"

Vega nodded. "Before he was Homicide he worked Sex Crimes." He gulped some coffee and took another bite of cruller, eating with a child's avidity. "He was pissed off when the DA dumped the case. I guess he took it personal and . . ." He trailed off, flustered. "Listen, you're Windsor's lawyer. Maybe I shouldn't be talking to you."

"You haven't told me anything I wouldn't have found out anyway, Ben. Finish your doughnut."

He munched away, scattering sugar across his shirt. "You like being an attorney?"

"I've been at it so long I've stopped thinking about whether I like it or not. It's just part of who I am. What about you? You like being a cop?"

"It's okay," he said, hesitantly. "I liked it better when I was on patrol."

"You're not now?"

"They got me working the counter, doing paperwork and like that. I pulled a muscle in my back, that's why," he explained.

"Lifting weights?"

He looked at me as if I were telepathic. "How did you know?"

"Wild guess," I replied, then felt guilty at making fun of him. "You look like a weightlifter."

He preened. "I'm okay now, you know, but the department don't want me back on patrol until the union doctor says its okay." He made a face. "And he don't care. He figures I like being cooped up in an office. It drives me nuts, you know? The first thing I do when I get off is go for a long run."

"You run?"

"I lettered in track in high school."

I smiled. "Me, too. Before you were born, probably."

"You ain't that old," he replied, finishing off his doughnut. "What's your event?"

"I was a distance runner. You?"

"Speed," he replied. "I used to be a lot smaller. Where'd you go to high school?"

"Right here," I replied. "Los Robles High. You?"

"Nueces," he said, smile broadening. Nueces was a small town about fifteen miles away. "We compete with Los Robles."

"Yeah, I know. We used to beat you like clockwork."

"Maybe in your day," he retorted.

I sipped my coffee, enjoying the first friendly conversation I'd had in Los Robles since returning to the town. Cop or not, Vega was a nice kid. Not a genius, but nice.

"You still run?" he was asking.

"Not for a while."

"We should go sometime."

"In this weather?"

He shook his head. "It cools off at night. You look like you still got some distance in you."

"Thanks, I think."

"Where you staying?"

"The Hyatt. You'd run me ragged."

He glanced at his watch. "Gotta go. See you later, Mr. Rios." He stood up, brushing crumbs from his uniform. "Maybe I'll come by sometime, take you running."

"See you, Ben," I said, and watched him walk away, swaggering a little for no better reason than that he was young and healthy. I went back to my reading. A few minutes later I looked up at where he'd sat, thinking perhaps I'd underestimated him. His name appeared in the prosecution's witness list—he had been one of the officers who searched Paul's house and it looked like he'd struck gold.

* * *

Paul watched me warily as I sat down across from him. I opened my briefcase and took out a legal pad. His weeks of incarceration had given him a jailhouse pallor and his face seemed a little bloated today.

"I talked to Mark last night," I said, uncapping a black felt pen. "He had an interesting theory as to why you may have killed McKay."

"For Christ's sake, you believe him over me."

"Let me just run it by you," I replied. "Mark goes along with the blackmail angle. I didn't think it was very plausible because, as Sara pointed out to me when I first talked to her, after all the publicity over your first arrest it didn't seem likely that you could be blackmailed over being a pedophile. What Mark said was that, except for that incident, you don't have any other record. He suggested that McKay had something on you of—more recent vintage."

Paul made a dismissive noise.

"The reason I bring it up," I went on, "is that it sounds a whole lot more believable than your story about going off to see McKay to buy a child from him."

"It's a lie."

"What's a lie?"

"What Mark told you is a lie. Look, I don't know if there was a girl or not, but that's why I went there."

I persisted. "What did McKay have on you?"

"I just told you . . ." His face was red.

"I heard you," I replied calmly. "I spent most of the morning reviewing documents I got from the cops. One of those documents is a list of evidence taken from their search of your house and your car. One of the things they recovered from the car was a roll of film. What's on it, Paul?"

He turned his face from me.

"Something you got from McKay?"

"It doesn't have anything to do with McKay," he said in a subdued voice.

"Then what is it?"

He faced me. "Pictures of her."

"Who?"

"Ruth."

"Ruth Soto?" I was really surprised. "When did you see her again?"

"I've never stopped thinking about her," he said, quietly. "I followed her around one day, and took pictures, that's all. Pictures of her and my son."

"She had the baby."

He nodded. "A little boy. His name is Carlos, I looked it up in the baptismal registry. Her last name, of course. Carlos Soto."

It was dusk when I arrived at Sara's house. Stone-faced Caridad opened the door.

"*Quiero hablar con la señora,*" I told her.

She let me in. "*Esta en la jardin.*"

"Drunk?" I asked.

"*Como siempre,*" she replied. As always.

I made my way through the big rooms, to the back, where I found Sara Windsor sitting beneath a willow tree, glass in hand, looking at nothing in particular. She saw me and said nothing. I lowered myself to the ground beside her.

"I have to ask you something," I said.

"Don't you want to wait until I'm sober?"

I was tired of her, and the Windsors generally. "I don't have that long."

"You don't talk to me that way," she said, slurring and sibilant. "You may be successful now, but I knew you when you were just a skinny little nothing from the wrong side of town, mooning over Mark like a girl. God, how you embarrassed your sister."

This was news to me, but I wasn't here to reminisce. "The police have a roll of film they removed from Paul's car the day they searched it. Paul says it contains pictures of Ruth Soto he took the Saturday before McKay was murdered. Did he go out that day?"

She raised her hands to her mouth and breathed shakily through her fingers.

"This is important."

She reached blindly for her drink, spilling it on the grass. "That bastard."

"Was he out that day?"

She glared at me with red-rimmed eyes. "It's all a dirty joke now." The drink seeped through the grass to the edge of her skirt. "A nasty little joke."

"Why are you so shocked, Sara? You're the one who implied that he was still seeing her."

"I didn't know." She stumbled to her feet. "He can go fuck himself."

She blundered her way back into the house. I got up to follow, but then thought better of it. She wasn't any use to me drunk, and I still felt the barb about my sister. I could imagine them together, giggling about me and Mark. No, giggles weren't Elena's style—pursed lips and perdition were more in keeping with her character. Around me, the heavy fragrance of the roses spilled into the dusky air, absurdly romantic. I walked to the edge of the garden to a sundial, a circle of brass set into a marble pedestal. In the center of the dial were inscribed six lines:

> Come near, come near, come near—Ah, leave me still
> A little space for the rose-breath to fill!
> Lest I no more hear common things that crave;
> The weak worm hiding down in its small cave,
> The field mouse running by me in the grass,
> And heavy mortal hopes that toil and pass . . .

9

"All rise. Department Three of the Los Robles Municipal Court is now in session, the Honorable Richard Lanyon presiding."

A fiercely red-haired man about my own age passed behind the clerk and ascended the couple of steps to the bench, arranged himself in the high-back wooden chair and reached into his robe for his reading glasses. As he busied himself with the file in front of him, I looked around the courtroom.

The courthouse had been built in the thirties by the WPA and the room reflected the populism of the times. On the walls was a mural depicting, as far as I could tell, great moments in legal history—if that wasn't an oxymoron—including scenes from the Constitutional Convention, Chief Justice Marshall delivering the *Marbury v. Madison* opinion and Daniel Webster arguing the Dartmouth case. Directly above Judge

Lanyon's head, Lincoln was signing the Emancipation Proclamation.

I sat at counsel table with Paul beside me, in a suit instead of his jail jumper. Dom Rossi sat at the other end, mopping up sweat from his forehead. Behind us in the gallery were the prosecution's witnesses and the press. We were there for the preliminary hearing to determine whether there was enough evidence to warrant putting Paul on trial. Normally, the proceeding was a formality and its main usefulness to the defense was to preview the prosecution's evidence, and it didn't make much difference which judge presided. However, the penal code prohibited a judge who had issued a search warrant from hearing the prelim. Lanyon had issued the search warrant and so I'd filed a routine motion asking him to disqualify himself.

Judge Lanyon glanced down at us. "*People versus Windsor.* State your appearances."

"Henry Rios for the defendant, Your Honor."

"Dominic Rossi for the People."

"Let the record reflect that the defendant is present," Lanyon said, directing his comments at the reporter, a pale, middle-aged man who recorded the proceedings on a stenographer's machine.

"Today is the day set for the preliminary hearing, however, I understand the defense wishes to make a motion."

I got to my feet. "Your Honor, as you know the penal code prohibits a judge who has issued a search warrant in a case from presiding over the preliminary hearing in the same case. Since you did issue the warrant in this case, I think we should be sent out to another department for today's proceeding."

Without looking up, he said, "Your motion is denied."

"I beg your pardon."

He now looked at me. "Your motion is denied, Counsel."

"Judge Lanyon," I said, "the words of the statute are mandatory."

"I can read, Mr. Rios," he replied. "And I don't care what

the Legislature says. There are only four municipal court departments in this judicial district and each of those judges has a full docket. I'm not going to disrupt some other judge's schedule."

His expression dared me to challenge him. I had run into other Judge Lanyons in my time, tin-pot judicial despots, and there was only one way to deal with them.

"Your Honor, the statute requires you to disqualify yourself. Putting that aside, it's our position that you should disqualify yourself anyway, for bias."

He drew himself up rigidly. "Based on what?"

"The defense believes that the search warrant you authorized was based on an inadequate showing of probable cause. Given that, we question whether you can fairly evaluate the evidence in this hearing much of which was obtained from that search."

"Counsel," he said, coldly, "I see no motion to quash the warrant or to suppress evidence."

"It's our intention to make those motions after the prelim, if this case gets that far. And I don't think it would—in another court."

"I really take exception to that, Mr. Rios."

"Judge, I take exception to the fact that this court is prepared to disregard a mandatory statutory directive."

Although we'd both kept our tone conversational, there was no mistaking the belligerence in the air. I glanced over at Paul who looked puzzled and alarmed, and smiled reassuringly. Rossi, at the other end of counsel table, was watching me with an expression that hovered between admiration and pity.

Lanyon spoke. "Anything more, Mr. Rios?"

"No, Judge. I submit." I sat down.

Rossi stood up. "If I may . . ."

Lanyon thundered, "Sit down, Mr. Rossi. The court doesn't need to hear from you on this matter."

Rossi sat down, bewildered by Lanyon's ire, but I was delighted. It had been my intention to provoke Lanyon by accusing him of bias so that any response he made other than granting my motion would lend substance to the charge. It helped that in this case I had the law on my side, although for this tactic it was not indispensable. All one needed was a choleric judge and the willingness to spend the night in jail on contempt charges.

"The court will grant the motion—" Lanyon began. Rossi sputtered. In a slightly louder voice, Lanyon continued, "—if the defendant agrees to continue the preliminary hearing for eight weeks—"

Paul grabbed my arm, but I waved him off. "Let me hear this."

Lanyon was saying, "—because I find that the condition of the court's calendar is such that another judge will not be available to conduct hearing until then." He looked at me, smiling almost imperceptibly. "Well?"

I had to give him points for being smart, but I was by no means done.

"Your Honor," I said, rising from my chair, "in that case I would ask the court to set reasonable bail."

His bland expression was momentarily ruffled. "Well, Counsel, if I grant the motion and disqualify myself it will be for all purposes, including whether bail should be set."

"In that case," I replied, "I'd ask that the case be transferred to another department immediately for the limited purpose of a ruling on bail."

He frowned. "As I just indicated to you, Mr. Rios, there's no court available . . ."

"To conduct the prelim," I said, jumping in to keep him off balance, "but a bail application wouldn't take more than a few minutes."

He glanced around the court, as if for inspiration. It came in the rotund form of the DA, who now rose to his feet.

"Your Honor," he said, "the People consider Mr. Windsor a definite threat to public safety. That's why we opposed bail when he was first arrested, and that's why bail was denied. If he wants to renew the request, we'll want a full-scale evidentiary hearing, and that's going to take time."

"I don't think—" I began.

Lanyon cut me off. "The People have the right to call witnesses in a bail hearing."

"Be that as it may, this is nothing more than a delaying tactic."

Lanyon said, sternly, "Your client is charged with murder, Mr. Rios. There's almost a presumption that he poses a threat to public safety."

"Accused murderers are let out on bail all the time."

"Not in this county," Lanyon replied, sharply. In the same tone he said, "I'm giving you what you want, Counsel. You can take it or leave it, but let's not waste any more time."

I fired my last, feeble volley. "The court's condition of an eight-week delay violates my client's right to a speedy trial."

"You can take that up with the Court of Appeal," he said, coldly, "after you give me an answer."

"I'd like five minutes to discuss this with my client."

"Court is in recess for five minutes. You can talk to your client in the tank," he said, adding acerbically, "We'll wait for you here."

The bailiff led Paul and me to the holding cell off the courtroom. As soon as he left, Paul asked, "What the hell's going on out there?"

"I think I may have offended the judge's pride," I said, and explained the choice that Lanyon had given us. "The bottom line is that we can do the prelim today in front of a very angry judge, or wait eight weeks for another court to open up."

Paul paced the cell. "What difference does it make?"

"It could make a lot of difference on how he conducts the hearing, how he rules on my objections, what he lets Rossi get away with, and I can promise you that you will be held to answer."

He stopped pacing. "They're going to hold me to answer no matter where we go. They're not going to dismiss the complaint."

"Probably not," I agreed, "though with a case this thin, we'd have a fighting chance in another court."

Paul balled his hands into fists. "I'm not sitting in that fucking cell for another eight weeks. Why won't he give me bail?"

"You're too unpopular to get bail."

He glared at me. "It couldn't be any worse if I had killed the son-of-a-bitch."

"We've got to go back in, Paul. What do you want to do?"

"Let's just do it."

"I think you're making a mistake."

"I've had lots of practice."

"Well?" Lanyon asked, when Paul and I had resumed our seats at counsel table.

"The defense withdraws its motion, Your Honor," I said. "We would like to proceed with the hearing."

"Fine," he said, with the narrowest and briefest of smiles. "People call their first witness."

"The People call Robert Doyle."

Doyle was the medical examiner with the literary flair. As he made his way to the witness stand, I watched Lanyon, who glanced back at me once as if I were a fleck of dust on his robe, and I settled in for what promised to be a long day.

On the stand, Doyle, without much prodding from Rossi, essentially repeated what he'd put in his report.

McKay had been killed between midnight and three in the morning. He'd been bound to a chair and gagged. The cause of death was blunt force trauma—a series of blows to the head by an instrument unknown. The same instrument had also been used to crush his testicles. Offhandedly, Doyle remarked that McKay had also suffered partial asphyxiation.

Rossi asked, "What caused that?"

"He swallowed his gag," Doyle said.

"Do you have an opinion on why he might have done that?" Rossi asked.

"Objection, relevance. Asphyxiation was not the cause of death."

Lanyon brushed my objection aside with a curt, "Overruled."

Doyle said, "It was a fear reflex."

"He suffered?" Rossi asked solicitously.

"Yes. This wasn't a quick or painless death."

"Nothing further," Rossi said.

Lanyon looked at me. "Mr. Rios?"

I got up. There had been some murmuring in the gallery as Doyle sketched the gruesome details of the murder, but now there was silence as if everyone was wondering how I could turn his testimony to the defense's advantage. Sitting up late the night before, going over Doyle's report and examining the autopsy pictures, I'd wondered the same thing myself. The key lay in the passionate nature of the killing: this death made a statement.

"Mr. Doyle," I said, making my way to the podium at the end of counsel table. "Do you have any idea of what kind of object was used to kill Mr. McKay?"

He smiled. "Well, it was bigger than a swizzle stick."

I smiled back, as if this was nothing more than an exchange of pleasantries. "More on the order of a baseball bat?"

"Something like that."

"And do you have any idea of the kind of force that was used on the victim?"

"I don't understand," he replied.

"The skull is a pretty hard thing, isn't it?" I asked, tapping my head.

Rossi said, "Objection, vague."

Lanyon looked at Doyle. "Can you answer the question?"

"Sure," he said agreeably. "The skull is a pretty hard thing. It does take a certain amount of force to shatter it."

"Do you have an estimate of how long it actually took between the first blow and last blow to the victim's head?"

"They were fairly close in time."

"Fairly close?" I echoed. "Five seconds? Five minutes? An hour?"

He turned his eyes upward for a second and his lips moved silently. "I'd say ten minutes, maximum."

"So, Mr. Doyle, what we have is someone striking another person with a baseball bat for a ten-minute period with sufficient force to shatter the victim's skull, is that right?"

He smiled, again, having apparently caught the drift of my questioning. "Are you asking me whether your client was strong enough to do it?"

"Or sufficiently motivated."

Rossi and Doyle spoke simultaneously. "Objection." "I can't answer that."

"I have nothing further," I said.

Doyle was excused. Lanyon said. "Your next witness, Mr. Rossi?"

"The People call James Mitchell," Rossi said.

James Mitchell was the first officer called to the scene of the motel the morning after the murder. He testified that there was no evidence of forcible entry. He had searched the grounds of the motel for a weapon without success. What he did find, in McKay's suitcase, were pictures of nude teenage boys, engaged in sexual acts with each other and adult men. Over my relevance objection, the photos were admitted into evidence. With that, Rossi concluded his examination.

"Officer Mitchell," I said, rising, "what was the condition of the room when you entered it?"

Rossi said, "Objection, vague."

"Sustained."

"Was there blood in the room?" I asked.

Rossi stirred in his seat but said nothing.

"Yeah, there was blood, all right," Mitchell replied.

"Where?" I asked, approaching him.

"All over."

"On the walls?"

"Yes."

"On the bed?"

"Yes."

"On the floor around the chair where Mr. McKay was bound?"

Impatiently, he said, "Yeah. All over the room. Even on the windows."

"And how far were the windows from the chair?" I asked. "Your best estimate."

Thoughtfully, he said, "Five, eight feet."

"In other words," I concluded, "would it be a fair statement that when Mr. McKay was struck, his blood sprayed across the room?"

"Yeah, I guess."

I smiled. "No guessing, just answer based on what you saw."

"Yes," he said, fidgeting.

I returned to counsel table and scribbled a note: "blood everywhere—why no bloody clothes from paul. no blood in car. ask sara if she saw him that night."

"Now, Officer," I continued, looking up at him. "You testified there were no signs of forcible entry into the room, is that right?"

"Yeah, it looked like he let the guy in."

"Well, was the door unlocked when you arrived at the scene?"

He looked at me blankly. "The maid was there."

I scribbled a note to track down the maid.

"But you don't know whether the door was locked or unlocked the night McKay was murdered, do you?"

"I wasn't there."

"So," I continued, "as far as you know the door could've been unlocked."

"Objection," Rossi said, "calls for speculation."

Lanyon said, "Sustained."

"Your Honor, if I may be heard."

Lanyon glanced down at me. "Save it, Counsel. I think we all see what you're driving at."

I shrugged. I'd made my point—if the door had been left unlocked by McKay his murderer could have entered the room at any time with or without his consent.

"Officer Mitchell, did you observe any signs of a struggle in the room?"

He thought about it for a moment. "The room was a mess but . . ."

I pressed him. "But what?"

"I don't know what you mean by struggle," he said, petulantly.

"Well, Officer," I said, "McKay was gagged and bound when you found him. Were there any signs he resisted?"

He repeated, "The room was a mess."

"What do you mean by that?"

He drew a deep breath. "The bed wasn't made. His suitcase was open and there was stuff all over."

"Officer, are you sure that wasn't just bad housekeeping?"

There was laughter in the courtroom. Rossi objected.

Humorlessly, Lanyon said, "Sustained. The statement is stricken."

"Nothing further," I said.

"Step down," Lanyon directed the officer. "Your next witness, Mr. Rossi."

"The People call Calvin Mota."

Mota was the fingerprint man. His testimony was crucial to the prosecution's case because it provided the only evidence that Paul had been in McKay's room. A bespectacled, civil-servant type, Mota began his testimony with a professorial calm that doubtless went over well with juries.

Rossi got him to lay out his professional qualifications and was asking him to explain the process by which he made fingerprint comparisons. He asked, "Now, you've used two words, latent prints and inked prints. What do those terms mean?"

Mota could probably have replied by rote, but he managed to put a little animation into it. "The latent fingerprints are usually those prints which are lifted at the crime scene and submitted to evidence for checking against a suspect. The comparison is made with an inked print. These are rolled at booking stations and kept on file cards in the sheriff's bureau of identification."

"Tell me what produces a latent fingerprint," Rossi said.

On the bench, Lanyon stiffled a yawn. It was getting near to noon.

"Well," Mota was saying, "latent prints are the result of certain body fluids that are secreted through the pores at the tips of the fingers, the palms of the hand and the soles of the feet. These fluids contain salts and fatty acid, amino acids, and also water. Sweat, in other words. Now of course, the other part of this is that you have to have a surface capable of recording the print . . ."

He droned on, explaining how prints were developed, lifted and transferred to evidence cards. He explained how comparisons were made between the latent prints and inked prints by looking for points of similarity between the two. When there were enough such points—seven was what he looked for—he would make an identification.

"Now," Rossi said, his voice becoming brisker, "do you know whether the sheriff's bureau of identification has an inked print of the defendant?"

"Yes, it does," Mota said.

"And do you know how that print was acquired?"

I broke in. "Your Honor, we stipulate that such a print exists. I don't think it's necessary to go into how it was acquired."

"Yes, go on, Mr. Rossi."

"Mr. Mota, you've heard testimony about a murder committed on Tuesday, July twenty-fifth, at the Little King Motel. Did you lift any fingerprints from that location?"

"Yes," Mota said. "On July twenty-fifth, in the morning."

"Did you compare any of those prints with the defendant's inked print?"

"Yes, I did."

"And what were the results?"

"I was able to identify eleven of the prints at the crime scene as the defendant's fingerprints."

Next to me, Paul balled his fingers into his palms.

"Relax," I whispered.

Mota was saying that Paul's prints had been lifted from the metal toilet handle, a glass, the doorknob and McKay's suitcase. Only the last location seemed at all suspicious and

I made a note to ask Paul about it. After a couple of follow-up questions, Rossi finished.

"Do you have any questions on this witness?" Lanyon asked.

"One or two, Your Honor," I rose. "Mr. Mota, were you able to lift any fingerprints off the victim's body?"

"No."

"What about the chair where he was sitting?"

"No, I wasn't, Counsel."

"Now, Mr. Mota, you're not able to tell at what time these prints were made, are you?"

"Do you mean, what? Day? Weeks?"

"Well, in any twenty-four-hour period, you couldn't tell by looking at it whether a print was made at twelve noon or at twelve midnight, isn't that right?"

"Yes, that's true."

"Nothing further."

Lanyon dismissed the witness and said, "It is now near noon. We will be in recess until one-thirty."

Paul whispered, "Why didn't you ask him any more questions?"

We rose while Lanyon left the bench. I turned to Paul and said, "Well, they were your prints, Paul. But all they prove is that you were there sometime before McKay was murdered. That's not enough."

"What's not enough?" Rossi asked, coming up behind us, all smiles.

"Your evidence."

"We're not done yet."

The bailiff tapped Paul on the shoulder. "Lunchtime."

"I'll see you after lunch," I said, as he was led away.

Rossi rested his considerable butt against the edge of the table. "I like the way you took on Lanyon."

"Thanks," I said, "I keep waiting for him to take his revenge."

Rossi got up. "Don't worry about that, Henry. He will."

10

"Henry, how about lunch?"

I looked around and saw Sara standing at the rail that separated the gallery from the well of the court. I hadn't seen or spoken to her since the night in her garden. Her smile was tentative, worried.

"Sure," I said.

We stepped out of the courthouse into the blazing noontime heat. Men in shirtsleeves and women in sleeveless blouses poured from the nearby office buildings, faces hidden behind dark glasses, walking quickly to nearby fast-food places. Sara stopped and fished her own sunglasses out of her purse, adjusting them on her face, pushing stray, brittle hairs away from her face.

"I know a nice place not far from here," she said, "if you can stand the heat."

"Lead on," I replied. We walked beneath the motionless branches of the sycamores from the civic center to the old streets of downtown. Untouched by urban renewal, these streets were lined with squat brick buildings and canopied entrances to vacant storefronts.

The restaurant she'd chosen was a cubbyhole of prosperity in an otherwise fading neighborhood. It billed itself as a café on the big window that looked into it from the street but the starched white tablecloths, gleaming flatware and handsomely attired waiters belied the modest claim. Inside, the air, the paneled walls, the clatter of footsteps on parquet floors and the murmur of expense-account conversation bespoke unhurried affluence. We were led to a table in the back of the big dining room.

"Would you care for something to drink?" the waiter asked.

"Perrier," she said, without looking at me.

"Water," I said. When he walked away, I watched her carefully remove her sunglasses. "How long were you in court?"

"I was there from the start," she said. "Doesn't it bother you, Henry?"

"What?"

"Murder," she replied. "The way he was killed was horrible," she added, grimacing. "Or don't you think about that?"

"Oh, yes," I answered. "I think about it, but not in the same way you do. I can't afford to be shocked because then I don't learn anything."

"What do you mean?"

"It's hard to know the mind of a murderer," I said, and paused to sip the glass of water which a busboy had discreetly deposited on the table. "Talking to them doesn't help much. Their explanations of why they killed are often incredibly banal."

"That surprises me." she said. "I mean, it's so—"

"Dramatic?" I offered. "Exactly. And horrifying. So, of course they retreat into banalities. They can't focus on the horror any more easily than we can. The only way I can reconstruct their mental states is to study how the killing was done."

"You make it sound so scientific," she said edgily.

"A little detachment helps." I sipped more water.

"That's appalling."

I said, "One of the things I do in Los Angeles is draft wills for people with AIDS. Sometimes I'm the last person they see besides doctors and nurses. Everyone else has written them off, even the people they leave their things to. Now that's true detachment."

We ordered lunch.

I managed a few minutes with Paul in the holding tank before the noon recess ended. He sat against the wall, head tipped up, eyes closed, listening to my assessment of how the morning had gone. When I finished, he asked, "I saw Sara in the courtroom?"

"Yes, I had lunch with her."

He lowered his head. "She hasn't come to visit in a few days. It's because you told her that I'd seen Ruth, isn't it?"

"I don't know, Paul. Maybe."

"Maybe," he said softly. "It's funny, Henry, this is the first time since we been married that I actually need her."

"Maybe you can learn to make a virtue out of necessity."

He stood up. "What's going to happen in court?"

"The cops will testify, and they'll put the things they took during the search into evidence. The money. The pictures from the film."

"Did they develop it?" he asked, tensely.

"Yes," I replied. "I called Rossi and asked him about it and he told me they had the pictures. When I asked to see them, he said he couldn't break the evidence seal except in open court. I asked him if he'd seen them and he said only Morrow had. Morrow told them they were pictures of a girl."

Paul nodded. "I didn't want to get her involved in this."

"Well, they're not really relevant so maybe we keep them out of the trial."

The bailiff came in and said, "The judge is about to take the bench."

"The People call Benjamin Vega."
Ben Vega made his way to the stand and perched there nervously while the oath was given to him, whispering an almost inaudible, "I will."
"Who is he?" Paul asked.
"The officer who took the film from your car."
Paul shifted in his seat, straining forward to listen. Vega was being asked, "And how long have you been a police officer?"
"Two years," he said, eyes riveted on Rossi.
"Officer Vega, did you take part in a search of the premises at 6537 La Tijera Drive on the evening of July twenty-seventh of this year?"
"Yes, sir, I did," he replied with, I thought, unnecessary servility.
"What exactly did you do?"
Vega took a deep breath and said, "Well, there were six of us assigned to the search. Detective Morrow took four officers into the house and me and Officer Mitchell, we were told to search the car."
"Describe the car."
"A black Mercedes sedan. Brown leather interior. It was parked in the driveway."
"Was it unlocked?"
"The lady, Mrs. Windsor, I guess, she unlocked it for us after Morrow showed her the warrant."
"The warrant authorized a search of the car?"
"Yes, sir."
"And what, if anything, did you recover from the car?"
"I found a roll of film on the floor of the front seat, on the passenger's side."
I leaned over to Paul. "Is that right?"
He shrugged. "I don't remember."
"And what did you do with the film, Officer Vega?"

105

"I took it into the house and gave it to Detective Morrow."
"And did you see what Morrow did with it?"
"Yes, sir. He put it in a baggie."
"No further questions."
Lanyon said, "Mr. Rios."
Ben Vega looked over at me nervously.
"I have no questions of this witness."
"You're excused, Officer Vega."

The prosecution's next witness was the criminalist from the forensics lab who had developed the pictures. His testimony was limited to establishing that the film which Vega had given to Morrow, Morrow had then given to him. He had developed the film and returned it and the pictures to Morrow. This was called establishing the chain of custody, a necessary foundation before physical evidence could be introduced into a proceeding. Although I might find reason to try to pick the chain apart at trial, for now I was only interested in seeing the pictures. Rossi had the witness identify the envelope into which he'd placed the pictures and when it was my turn to examine him I passed.

"The People call Dwight Morrow."
Morrow stalked to the witness stand, took the oath, folded his hands on his lap and stared out at us with expressionless black eyes.

"Detective Morrow, what is your current occupation?" Rossi asked, leaning against the podium.
"I'm a detective with the Los Robles Police Department," he said stonily, "assigned to Homicide."
"And how long have you had that assignment?"
"Two years."
"And prior to that, what was your assignment?"
"I worked in Sex Crimes."
Rossi drew a breath. "And when you were assigned to Sex Crimes," he said, "were you ever involved in an investigation relating to the defend—"
I was on my feet. "Objection, this is completely irrelevant."

Lanyon bestirred himself from his postprandial daydreams and asked the reporter to read back the question. When this was done, he said, "Will you approach the bench, Counsel."

"With the reporter," I added, making my way across the well of the court.

"You, too, Barry," he said to the reporter.

The three of us arranged ourselves at the sidebar. Lanyon, his breath faintly alcoholic, said to Rossi, "How about an offer of proof, Mr. Rossi."

"Your Honor," he chirped, "this is foundational."

"To what?" I asked.

"Let's give him a chance to tell us," Lanyon lectured.

"By showing that the defendant is a pedophile, the People will establish why he was at the victim's room as well as why he may have had a motive to murder Mr. McKay."

"What motive?" I demanded.

"The People will show that the defendant was being blackmailed by the victim."

Lanyon looked at us, drowsily. To me, he said, "We could cut this short if you'd stipulate your client was previously arrested on child molest charges."

"I still object to relevance."

"That objection's overruled," he said, "and the question is whether you want the gruesome details to come out."

"We will stipulate that Mr. Windsor was arrested, but not convicted, of those charges," I said, carefully, "for the purposes of this hearing only."

"Mr. Rossi?"

"Fine," Rossi said.

"Okay, so stipulated," Lanyon said, "now let's get on with this."

We went back to our respective places. Lanyon said, "For the record, counsel has stipulated to the matters which Detective Morrow had begun to testify to."

"What matters?" Paul whispered fiercely.

I whispered back an explanation of what had just occurred.

"... assigned to investigate the murder of John McKay?" Rossi was asking.

"Yes," Morrow replied.

"And in connection with this investigation, did you execute a search warrant on the defendant's home and vehicle on the night of the July twenty-seventh?"

"I did."

"What, if anything, did you recover in that search?"

"Well," Morrow said, "in the defendant's study I recovered a briefcase that contained cash."

"And how much cash?"

"I later determined it to be twenty thousand dollars," he said. "Also, there was a roll of film."

"You recovered this film."

"No," Morrow said, "the film was given to me by Officer Vega, who found it in the defendant's car."

"Detective, what did you do with the money?"

"I booked it into evidence, sir."

"Why did you do that, Detective?"

Morrow shifted slightly in his seat. "Well, based on the circumstances, I formed the belief that the large amount of cash might have been used for some illegal purpose."

I got to my feet. "Your Honor, there's no foundation to this testimony. I move to strike."

Rossi said, "If I may ask a follow-up question."

Lanyon nodded.

"What circumstances are you referring to, Detective?"

"Well, first the fact that the victim dealt in child pornography, and, second, the fact that the defendant is a known pedophile . . ."

"Objection. We stipulated precisely to avoid this characterization of my client."

Lanyon's look let me know that we'd reached the moment of settling scores. "Overruled. Go on, Detective."

"Is a pedophile," Morrow repeated, emphatically, "and he had been at the victim's motel room, all this led me to believe that the money may have been to make some kind of payoff, or—"

"I renew my objection. This is the flimsiest foundation I've ever heard for the admission of this kind of evidence."

Lanyon looked straight through me. "Overruled."

"What did you do with the film, Detective?" Rossi asked.

"When I got back to the station, I booked it into the evidence locker where it remained until I took it to forensics for developing."

"And when was that?"

"That was the next day."

"And was the developed film returned to you at some point, Detective?"

"Yes, within the day."

Rossi reached down to counsel table for the sealed envelope. "Your Honor," he said, "I have in my hand an envelope sealed with an official seal of the Los Robles Police Department, and marked with an evidence number. May I approach the witness?"

"You may."

He walked over to Morrow and handed him the envelope. "Do you recognize this, Detective?"

"Yes, it's the evidence envelope that I used to put the pictures in."

"Is it sealed in exactly the same way you sealed it?"

"Yes."

"With the court's permission," Rossi said, "I'd like Detective Morrow to open the envelope."

"Fine." He threw me an acerbic look. "Mr. Rios, you may want to watch this."

"Thank you," I replied with equal sarcasm. I went over to the witness stand and watched Morrow tear open the envelope. He turned it upright, tapped the end, and a stack of pictures slid out. I caught a glimpse of the first one, which, as advertised, was a picture of a girl, no older than thirteen, lying nude on a bed. A man's head and naked back lay between her spread legs.

Her eyes were wide open and absolutely vacant.

11

The remaining dozen photographs were of the same girl in positions intended to be lascivious, but which, instead, ranged from the near comic to the terrifying. She was a little rag doll of a girl, neither exceptionally pretty nor homely; not exceptionally anything but young. Her eyes were glazed—drugs, terror, boredom, it was hard to tell which. In all the pictures she was on the same bed, a big, lumpy-looking thing covered by a deep blue comforter that showed off her pale, skinny body. On the wall above the bed was the bottom half of a painting of ocean waves, the kind of mass-produced art that decorated the walls of a million motel rooms. An edge of a nightstand was also visible, a part of a phone, a glass of something red, wine, maybe. And that was all there was by way of a setting. No pretense at fantasy. Just the stick figure of a girl who, in one picture, was being sodomized and in another performed fellatio.

The man in the pictures was carefully photographed so that only his profile showed once or twice. He was, like Paul, Caucasian, slender, fair-haired, without any distinguishing marks on his body. He could have been any youngish white man, Paul included; it was impossible to tell. All this I concluded in the couple of minutes it took Morrow to shuffle the pictures to Rossi, who handed them to me, who gave them to Lanyon. Lanyon glanced at them impassively and stacked them neatly on the corner of the bench.

"I want to move these into evidence," Rossi said, his voice unsteady and faint.

"Where are the negatives?" I asked quietly.

"They're in the envelope."

"I want an order from the court requiring an independent lab to process the negatives."

"Let me see them," Lanyon replied.

Morrow tapped the envelope again, and a smaller envelope, also sealed, slid out. He unsealed it and handed it to the judge, who opened it and removed the negatives. One by one, he held them up to the light.

"They appear to be the same pictures, Mr. Rios. I don't see the point of spending county money to put another set of these into circulation." He slipped them back into the envelope. "Do you have any objections to my receiving these into evidence?"

"I want the criminalist back on the stand," I said. "I want him to testify under oath that these were the pictures he developed."

Lanyon glanced at Rossi. "Where is he, Dom?"

"In the hallway."

Lanyon ordered his bailiff to bring the criminalist back into the courtroom, and he was escorted to the sidebar with the rest of us.

Handing him the pictures, Lanyon asked, "Are these the photographs you developed from the roll of film that Detective Morrow gave you?"

He hurried through them. "Yes, sir."

Lanyon inclined his head toward me. "Satisfied?"

"I renew my objection on other grounds," I said quickly.

"State them," the judge said.

"Your Honor, is this supposed to be my client in these pictures? That's ridiculous. You never see his face. Any resemblance is too vague to put these into evidence."

Lanyon looked at the top picture. "For the purpose of this hearing, Mr. Rios, I think the resemblance is sufficient. I will admit them."

"Your Honor, I'd ask that you clear the courtroom before allowing any further testimony about these pictures," I said, clutching at straws. "This could ruin whatever chances my client has of getting an impartial trial."

Lanyon smiled grimly, his revenge complete. "This is a public proceeding, Counsel. Your request is denied."

"I'd like to show them to my client," I said.

Lanyon shrugged. "Okay. Let's mark them and I'll call a recess."

Rossi said, "The People ask that these twelve photographs be marked in order, as People's exhibits 1 through 12."

"They will be so marked."

"I would move them into evidence."

"I object for the reason I stated at the bench."

Lanyon said, "Objection noted and overruled. The photographs are received. We will take a fifteen-minute recess."

He handed me the photographs and left the courtroom.

We'd been huddled around the bench, audible only to the reporter. I took the pictures and walked back to Paul. He looked angry and puzzled.

I sat down. "Do you recognize these?"

He went through them quickly, without expression. When he got to the last one, he turned it over on top of the others.

"No," he said, quietly.

"Are these pictures of you?"

"No."

"Did you get this film from McKay?"

"No," he said, a third time, in the same level tone. "Is that what they say?"

"That's what they're leading up to."

"It's a lie."

I turned to him and said, "You have to tell me the truth."

"I didn't take any film from McKay," he replied. "These pictures were not developed from the film in my car. That's not me in them. Is that plain enough?"

"Yes."

He muttered, "This is a fucking nightmare."

When court resumed, Morrow took the stand again and described the pictures. There was dead silence in the court as he droned on without emotion, describing each one until he reached the last, which was the first picture I'd seen: "This one is the same female child. Again, there is a nude white male in the picture and he's uh—he appears to be committing an act of cunnilingus on the girl."

"Thank you, Detective," Rossi said. "I have nothing further."

"Mr. Rios?"

"Good afternoon, Detective," I said, picking up my legal pad and making my way to the podium.

He did not reply to my greeting.

"Detective, you were in charge of the search of Mr. Windsor's house on the evening of July twenty-seventh, is that right?"

"That's right."

"And, in fact, you were the officer who sought the warrant, is that right?"

"Yeah."

"Now, Detective, isn't it also true that you were the investigating officer when my client was charged with child molestation four years ago?"

Rossi said, "Objection. Relevance."

I addressed Lanyon. "It goes to this witness's bias."

Lazily, Lanyon said, "Sustained."

"You knew Mr. Windsor prior to being assigned to investigate these charges against him, didn't you?"

I'd barely got the question out before Rossi objected.

"Sustained," Lanyon said.

"Your Honor, I'd like to make an offer of proof," I replied. Gimlet-eyed, Lanyon looked at me. "I can't conceive of any offer you could make that would change my mind. The objection's sustained, Counsel. Ask your next question."

"Detective, how long were you and your men at the Windsor residence the night you executed the warrant?"

Suspiciously, Morrow said, "About three hours."

"Can you give the exact times?" I asked glancing up at him. "Do you need to look at your report?"

"I got a copy," he said, and flipped through some pages. "We arrived at 5:13 P.M. and we left at 8:30."

"And while you were there you searched the entire house?"

He set the report down on the ledge of the stand. "Every room."

"Thoroughly?"

He cast a bemused looked at Rossi, and then answered. "I'd say so, yes."

"And you didn't find a weapon, did you?"

"No."

"Now you heard the testimony of Officer Mitchell this morning describing the scene of the murder, didn't you?"

"I did."

"And you heard him talk about the amount of blood that was present in the room, didn't you?"

"Yes."

"Now Officer," I said, leaning toward him across the top of the podium, "you didn't find any traces of blood anywhere in the Windsor house, did you?"

"No, I didn't," he said, adding quickly, "He had two days to—"

I cut him off. "Excuse me, Detective. I'm sure Mr. Rossi will give you a chance to explain your answers. Now, did you obtain fiber samples from the carpet in Mr. Windsor's car?"

He looked a little worried as he said, "We didn't do that."

"No? Well, would it have been useful to take such samples to have them analyzed for traces of blood?"

Grudgingly, he said, "Maybe."

"Now, did you talk to the clerk who was working registration the night that Mr. McKay was murdered?"

"I sent someone out to interview him."

"With pictures of Mr. Windsor and his car, correct?"

I could feel the tension rising between us. "That's right, Counsel. It's in the police report."

"And it's also in the report that the clerk failed to identify either Mr. Windsor or his car, isn't it?"

"Yes."

"Now was there someone, a guest, in the room adjacent to Mr. McKay's room the night he was murdered?"

"Yeah, he lives in Oregon."

"And you haven't been able to contact him, isn't that right?"

"That's right."

"Even though you've had almost six weeks now to do it?" Morrow scowled.

I scowled back. "Detective?"

"We haven't contacted him."

I paused, pretending to make a note. "What time did Vega give you the film?"

"I don't remember. Not long after we got there."

"More than an hour?"

"No. Half-hour maybe."

"Half-hour," I repeated. "So, before six?"

"Something like that," he allowed tensely.

Carefully, I asked, "And what time did you book the film into evidence?"

He shot Rossi another look, this time of disbelief.

"I'm going to object," Rossi said, struggling to his feet.

Quizzically, Lanyon asked, "On what basis?"

"It's—" he cast about. "It's irrelevant."

"Overruled on that ground. Answer the question."

"I booked it that night, when we got back to the station," Morrow said. "I don't remember when, exactly."

115

I pressed him. "Then give me your best estimate."

Morrow worked his brow for a moment. "I can't tell you without looking at the log in the evidence locker. It was before midnight."

"Before midnight," I repeated, this time actually jotting a note, to obtain a copy of that page of the log. "So you may have had the film in your possession for as long as six hours after it was given to you?"

I spoke quickly, anticipating an objection. I was not disappointed.

"Your Honor," Rossi said, "this is improper cross-examination. We established chain of custody without objection. He can't go into it now."

Lanyon pretended to give the matter some thought. "Yes, I'll sustain the objection."

"I'd like to be heard," I said.

"I'm listening," Lanyon said.

"The detective testified in direct examination that he booked the film into evidence. Asking for details is well within the scope of cross-examination."

"The objection is sustained," he replied.

There's an expression lawyers use, when they find themselves in out-of-town courts where everyone tends to close ranks against outsiders. They say they've "been hometowned." I was being hometowned, but good.

"I have no further questions."

"Mr. Rossi?"

Laboriously, Rossi set about rehabilitating Morrow's testimony, trying to imply through his questions that Paul would have had two days during which to destroy any evidence that might link him with McKay's murder. I spent another half-hour going through the various forensic techniques that the Los Robles Police Department had at its disposal for the analysis of physical evidence, few of which had been used in the McKay investigation. Rossi got another ten minutes worth of re-redirect, and then it was over. Morrow stepped down. The prosecution rested. The defense rested.

We didn't waste much time on argument. Lanyon's evidentiary rulings had made clear what the outcome would be.

"The court finds the evidence is sufficient to hold the defendant to answer. Trial is set in the superior court, Judge Phelan, in three weeks. The defendant is remanded into custody until then. Court is in recess."

Phelan, the judge who had refused to dismiss the child molestation charges against Paul three years earlier. It was Lanyon's parting shot.

"I'll talk to you back at the jail," I told my exhausted client as the bailiff led him out of the court. I scanned the room for Sara, but she'd already gone. As I was gathering up my papers, Rossi came over to me.

"Nice job, Henry."

"For a Star Chamber," I replied, shutting my briefcase. "You and Lanyon hometowned me there when I was taking Morrow on chain of custody. I want a copy of the evidence locker log, by the way. I'll get a court order if necessary."

Rossi put up a pudgy hand. "Hey, hey, relax, man. You don't need a court order. I'll get it to you tomorrow." He sat in the chair that Paul had occupied. "Why don't we get down to dealing, Henry."

I stopped my fidgeting. "No deals, Dom."

"Even with the pictures? Or do you think Judge Phelan's going to keep them out?" He smiled. "Phelan makes Lanyon look like William O. Douglas. He's a hanging judge, Henry."

I didn't think he was bluffing. "I'm obligated to communicate any offer to my client," I said, "if you have one."

"Manslaughter," he replied.

"Manslaughter?" I repeated. "You must think less of your case than I do."

"I'd say my chances of winning are about even," Rossi said, loosening his tie. "Those are decent odds for me. Not so good for you." He got up. "Think it over, Henry."

"My client says he's innocent."

Rossi smiled. "That's why I asked you to think it over."

12

"I'm missing dinner," Paul said as I sat down across from him at the table in the jail room where we talked. The J. Press sack suit he'd worn at the hearing had been replaced by jeans and a blue work shirt, transforming him from the superannuated college sophomore he'd seemed in court to a tired-looking con.

"I figured you might," I replied, opening my briefcase. I extracted two cans of 7-Up, some candy bars and packets of crackers and cheese and arranged them on the table between us. I'd had to threaten to obtain a court order to get the sheriffs to let me bring the food in.

He smiled wearily. "Are you trying to set up a Twinkie defense?" he asked, choosing a Mars bar and a bag of M&M's. Holding up a red M&M, he added, "I thought they'd stopped making these."

"Someone started a letter-writing campaign and got the candy company to start making them again." I opened a 7-Up and took a swig. It was as warm and thick as the air in the room. "It's funny what people get themselves worked up about."

He ate the candies one at a time. "Did it go as bad as you thought it would?"

"Pretty much," I replied. "Lanyon let the DA get away with a lot, but with those pictures I don't think the outcome would have been different anywhere else."

He stopped eating. "Why didn't you argue that they were faked?"

"The criminalist testified at the bench that those pictures were the same ones he developed from the film Morrow gave him," I said.

"He could've switched the film," Paul insisted.

"Without knowing what was on it?" I asked. "That's a stretch. Paul."

"You really don't think much of me, do you, Henry?" he asked, slowly opening a packet of cheese and crackers. "You probably never have." He bit into a cracker. "I remember when I was a kid I used to try to tag along with you and Mark when you'd go running. As soon as you guys saw me, you'd take off so fast that I couldn't keep up." He dropped the uneaten part of the cracker to the table. "I bet you never knew how hard I tried."

"You want me to apologize for things I did when I was fifteen?"

"I want you to understand," he said roughly. "You believe that I lied to you about why I went to see McKay because Mark told you so, so naturally you're going to believe the cops over me about the pictures. You're still running ahead of me, Henry. You and Mark. You and the cops and the DA and the judge. You're still running with winners." He smiled contemptuously. "But maybe you've forgotten something. You're a queer. Queers aren't winners. Not in their book. In their book, you and I are the same."

"And so I'm supposed to believe whatever bullshit story you tell me, one pervert to another? One loser to another? Is that it, Paul?"

He brought his fist down on the table, scattering M&M's like tiny billiard balls. "One man to another. Is that too fucking much to ask?"

"Tell me about the pictures," I said.

"I told you about the pictures."

"Then tell me how I can prove they're not you."

He jerked his chair away from the table and stood up. "Talk to her. Maybe she saw me."

"Ruth Soto?"

He nodded brusquely and walked to the other side of the room, slumping against a wall, arms folded across his chest. "I took them in the park from my car. She knows my car."

"Where does she live?"

"Paradise Slough, with her mother. On La Honda Road. It's a yellow house near the end of the street. You'll recognize it from . . ." He hesitated, drawing upon a memory. "From the roses. There are some bushes in front of the porch. I planted them."

Nodding, I said, "All right, Paul, I'll go see her tomorrow."

He dropped his hands to his sides. "Yeah, do that. And tell her I'm sorry."

"Sorry?"

"To get her involved." He came back to the table and sat down. "I wanted to keep her out of it. She's already done enough for me."

"What do you mean?" I asked.

"When she wouldn't testify," he said. "She did that for me, because . . ." He shrugged. "You wouldn't understand." Bitterly, he added, "Your biases won't let you."

The security guard at the building where Clayton had his office wasn't going to let me upstairs. I stood at his desk bickering with him, a skinny, crew-cut geezer, who kept saying he didn't know me from Adam. The feeling I got was that in his book a Mexican in a suit and tie was still a Mexican and probably up to no good. Our voices ricocheted off walls of polished granite in the big, cold foyer.

"Look," I said, "why don't you call Mr. Clayton. He'll tell you that it's okay."

He moved his head slowly from side to side. "We ain't supposed to disturb the tenants unless it's an emergency."

"Well, is anyone up there?"

He moved a finger across the pages of a sign-in log. "Someone named Stein," he said, finally, "but I ain't . . ."

"Never mind," I snapped, and went back outside into the humid September night. I walked up and down the Parkway until I found a phone and dialed Clayton's office. After a dozen rings, someone picked up and said, "Law offices."

"Peter?"

"Yeah," he said cautiously. "Henry?"

"Yes, it's me. Look, Peter, I wanted to come up and do some work but I can't get past the security guard. Could you call down and tell him it's okay?"

"I'll come down and get you," he said.

"Great, I'll meet you in the lobby."

When I got back to building, Stein was joking with the guard. He saw me coming in, smiled and waved me over. "Hey, Henry. I guess you met Mr. Johnson."

"I had the pleasure," I replied.

The guard said, "I'm sorry, Mr. Rios. We ain't supposed to let strangers in."

"No problem," I said, and started moving toward the elevators.

"Uh, sir. Mr. Rios?" the guard called. "You gotta sign in, sir."

I went back and scribbled the name in his log. "Remember my face, would you, Mr. Johnson. It'll save us both some wear and tear."

On the way up in the elevator, I pointed at Stein, who

was wearing jeans and a yellow polo shirt, and said, "You're out of uniform."

"I came back after dinner," he replied. "Bob's got me cross-indexing some depos. Real fun."

The elevator came to a stop and the doors slid open. As we exited, I said, "It must be big case. That's usually paralegal work."

Stein grimaced. "It's not a big case." He unlocked the office door and let us in. "And you're right, it's shit work."

"Trouble in paradise?" I ventured, as we walked down the hall toward my office.

Stein stopped. "You want to know the truth, Henry? I'm sorry I ever left the DA." He jabbed his chest. "Man, I was trying major felonies but here they don't trust me to try a little slip-and-fall."

"Is there any coffee?"

He shook his head. "I'll make some."

"Do that," I said, "and then come on in and kibitz."

A big smile split his face. "Funny, you don't look Jewish."

I tossed my briefcase onto my desk and dialed Sara Windsor's number. She answered on the second ring and I was relieved to find that she was more or less sober.

"I wanted to talk to you after court," I said.

"I was trying to escape the reporter from the *Sentinel*," she replied. "Have you seen the paper?"

"No. What does it say?"

Paper rustled on her end of the line. "The headline is 'Pornographic Pictures Link Windsor to Murder,' " she read and then asked, anxiously, "Was it Paul in the pictures?"

"The man's face wasn't visible," I replied.

After a moment's silence, she asked, "Is that a 'no'?"

"Paul says no," I replied. "He insists the pictures he took were pictures of Ruth Soto."

"But what do you think?"

"I really don't know."

In the pause that followed I heard the clink of ice against glass. "I wanted to ask a question, Sara," I said. "The night

McKay was killed. What did Paul look like when he came in? Did you see any signs that he'd been in a struggle?"

"Was he drenched in blood?" she asked caustically.

"Yes, for starters."

"I don't remember."

"Come on, Sara. How can you not remember what he looked like?"

"I just don't," she said dismissively.

"You're bailing out, aren't you?"

"I have to go now," she said, hanging up.

I put the phone down and jerked my tie loose, fumbling with my top shirt button. Plan A, getting the complaint against Paul dismissed at the prelim, was history, and plan B, attacking the prosecution's evidence as insufficient, looked a lot worse than it had when I'd awakened that morning. I was mulling over the prosecution's offer to allow Paul to plead to manslaughter when Peter Stein came in with mugs of coffee. He set one in front of me and sat down.

"So," he said, cheerfully, "I was watching the six o'clock news tonight. Sounds like you got nuked at the prelim."

"That's a fair assessment," I replied. I sipped the coffee, scalding my tongue. "You're an ex-DA," I said, "let me run a few things by you."

Peter threw a heavy leg over the arm of his chair. "Shoot."

"Do you know Dwight Morrow?"

He shook his head. "Yeah, I tried some cases with him as my investigator."

"Like him?"

"He's a regular bloodhound," Peter replied, "but not the friendliest guy in the world. Why?"

"Well, if he wanted to nail someone, how far would he go?"

Peter looked a little less friendly at this question, the prosecutor in him showing. "What do you mean. Henry?"

"Would he perjure himself?"

He shook his head. "Not Morrow. He plays by the rules."

"Always?"

"What are you getting at?"

I explained the situation about the pictures—that Paul claimed the film had been switched, with the likeliest candidate being Morrow, who had taken part in the unsuccessful prosection of Paul for molesting Ruth Soto.

"What did you expect Paul to say?" he asked shortly. "Come on, Henry, he's a con. He'll say anything to get off."

I nursed my scalded tongue, aware of how naive I must sound to Peter but also keeping in mind Paul's challenge to me to believe him. There'd been enough truth in his accusations of how easily I'd discounted his protestations of innocence to make me wary.

"What if I came up with a witness to corroborate him?"

Peter assessed me. "Someone who says he took pictures of the girl?"

I nodded, but in a little spasm of paranoia—he *had* been a DA—didn't say my potential witness was Ruth.

"Then it's straight credibility," he said, "and take my word for it, Henry, ain't no one in this town that's gonna believe Paul Windsor or any of his witnesses over the cops."

I decided to level with him. "Even if it's the girl?"

He smiled happily. "Now that would be fun."

"You still think the jury would believe the cops?"

He drank some coffee, thinking it over. "The thing is," he said, finally, "people around here believe that the Windsors paid her off last time not to testify. If she testifies for him, they're likely to believe she was paid off again."

Reluctantly, I nodded. "I see your point. Let me ask you something else. Why would the DA be offering me a manslaughter on this case?"

His eyes widened. "Did Dom do that?"

"Right after the prelim."

"The case *is* thin," he said tentatively. "Maybe second-degree thin, but manslaughter?" He looked at me with puzzled eyes. "Might be Mark."

"Mark?" I said, incredulously.

"Might be that Mark cut a deal with the DA—not Rossi, someone higher up."

"Why?"

"The case is an embarrassment, Henry," he said, decisively. "The Windsors, Mark anyway, are still pretty well entrenched with the local powers . . ."

"Not the *Sentinel*," I said quickly.

"They don't give a damn about the *Sentinel*," he said. "To them, Gordon Wachs is just a pushy Jew." He smiled. "Like me. Mark's money in the bank."

I let this information sink it, recalling Paul's theory that Mark had been behind his arrest in the first place. "Would it also be to Mark's advantage to have his brother safely in prison so that he couldn't muck around with Windsor Development?"

Peter raised his shaggy eyebrows. "Paul sold out his interest."

"He thinks Mark cheated him by not telling him about the development deals he was lining up that would have increased the value of his interest," I replied. "Sara told me he was threatening to sue."

"Well, well," Peter said.

I took a slug of coffee. Even my skin was tired. "What do you think?"

"I think maybe I'll review some client files," he replied. "Partner."

I smiled. "What about your loyalty to Clayton and Cummings?"

"This sounds like too much damn fun to pass on. You going to be around here tomorrow?"

"At some point."

"Good, I'll talk to you, then." He looked at me. "You really look beat, man. Go home, get some sleep."

"Not yet," I said, "I want to do some research on a change of venue motion. If there is going to be a trial, I'd prefer it to take place far away from Los Robles."

"What about Rossi's offer?" he asked.

"I haven't told Paul about it, and I won't until I investigate his corroboration."

Peter got up to go. "Okay. You know I did a lot of research on venue when I was a DA. I've probably still got it somewhere. It's opposition, but it might give you some case to get you started."

"I'd appreciate that, Peter."

"There's a condition," he said. "You go get some rest, and I'll get them to you tomorrow."

Wearily, I nodded. "Okay. Thanks."

He smiled. "No, thank you. This is the most excitement I've had in months."

On my way out of the office, I stopped by the receptionist's desk to check for phone messages and found a folder that had been delivered earlier in the evening. Tearing it open, I found a Xeroxed copy of a log with a note scrawled on a slip of paper attached to it. The note, from Rossi, said it was a copy of the evidence locker log showing the time that Morrow had booked the film. The log showed that he'd booked the film at 10:45. I thought back to his testimony and calculated that this meant he would have driven back to the police station, filed his report for the search warrant and booked the film within two hours of the search. That didn't seem unusually long, considering the paperwork that must have been involved. Disappointed, I folded the paper and slipped it into my coat pocket.

There was also a phone message, from Josh. Calling him back from the hotel gave me something to look forward to as I headed out the door.

As I walked down the Parkway toward the hotel a black man wearing a dirty red kerchief around his head, eyes downcast, stumbled toward me, stopped and asked for a quarter. He looked younger than I, and it was clear from his ruined physique that he'd been a big man once. Now his skin hung from him like a dirty, oversized coat. His shoulders stooped as if they'd been broken and he stank of the rankest alcohol.

"What's your name?" I asked him.

Startled, he glanced up at me. "James. James Harrison."

"Nice night, isn't it, James."

"Homeless people don't have no nice nights," he replied.

"The Bible says the meek will inherit the earth."

"Shit, ain't gonna be worth having when rich people done with it."

"Yeah, you're probably right," I said, reaching for my wallet to give him a dollar. All I had were tens and twenties. Somehow, turning him down because I didn't have change seemed wrong so I gave him a ten.

He looked at the bill and asked, "What's your name?"

"Henry," I replied.

"Got a brother Henry."

I smiled. "Where's he?"

"Folsom." With that, he nodded and headed down the street toward the neon sign. I went off in the other direction.

Entering the hotel, I found another message from Josh and a second message from Ben Vega, asking me to call him. Too tired to speculate on why the young cop might have called, I tucked both messages into my pocket and headed toward the elevators with nothing more ambitious on my mind than a hot shower and a sitcom. As I pressed the elevator button, a hand clamped my shoulder. I shook it off and turned around.

"Josh, what the hell are you doing here?"

He wore khaki shorts and a blue button-down shirt, open to expose the crystal he'd taken to wearing on a leather loop around his neck.

"Waiting for you," he said wearily. "I've been here since nine but they wouldn't let me up into your room. I tried to call."

"I know. It's been a long day. I'm glad to see you," I said, embracing him. The elevator door slid open and a middle-aged couple stared awkwardly for a moment and then passed around us.

"Henry," he said, smiling, "don't you know what day it is?"

"What do you mean?"

He let go of me and laughed. "September fourth."

It took me a moment to get it. September 4. My birthday.

13

"I think someone's at the door," Josh whispered into my ear, waking me. I opened my eyes to the alarm clock on the nightstand.

"It's not even six."

"I'll see who it is."

I rolled over onto my back and watched him pull on a pair of boxer shorts. "If it's the grim reaper, tell him he's a couple of years early."

A moment later he returned to the room smirking. "Henry, there's a guy named Ben here."

"Ben," I repeated. Vega? "A cop?"

"It's hard to tell. All he's got on is running shorts and a T-shirt."

I got out of bed, pulled on my bathrobe and went to the door. Ben Vega stood there awkwardly studying the carpet.

"Hi, Ben," I said.

"I guess you didn't get my message," he said.

"Come in, Ben." He stepped into the hall and stood there trying not to look into the room. "I got the message, but I just didn't get around to calling you back."

"I thought you might want to go running," he said, his face reddening. "I shoulda called from downstairs."

"That's okay. Why don't I take a rain check."

"Yeah, sure Mr. Rios." He smiled embarrassedly. "Sorry to disturb you."

From behind me, Josh said, "Hi, I'm Josh."

"This is my friend, Josh," I added unnecessarily. "This is Ben."

Josh stepped forward, still clad in his underwear and smiling impishly. "Nice to meet you, Ben."

Ben stuck out his hand. "Nice to meet you."

Shaking his hand, Josh said, "You can have him tomorrow, unless, you know, you want to join us."

I glared at him.

Face clenched like a fist, Ben said, "I better get going. It heats up real early. See you."

" 'Bye," I said.

Closing the door, I turned to Josh and said, "That was really unnecessary."

"Come on," Josh said with a smile, "he liked it."

"That must explain why he looked like he wanted to arrest us."

He shook his head. "Henry, he had a hard-on."

"Please," I said skeptically.

Josh shrugged and walked back into the bedroom. "Okay, don't believe me, but I don't see how you could miss it in those little shorts of his."

We got back into bed. I turned to him. "Did he really?"

"Really, and it wasn't for me."

"You know how to make an old man feel good," I said, and for the next hour gave no further thought to Ben Vega or anyone else.

* * *

Later, while Josh showered I finally pulled myself out of bed and searched for my watch among the debris on the top of the bureau on which Josh had emptied his pockets. There, amid laundry claim checks, crumpled dollar bills, his plane ticket and his beeper was a green poker chip on a small chain. On one side the chip had the words "30 days" and on the other side it said "Keep coming back."

I picked it up and took it into the bathroom where Josh was now standing at the mirror putting in a contact lens.

"Josh, where did you get this?" I asked, holding the chip up for him to see.

He squinted at it. "Oh, that. I almost forgot. Freeman gave it to me yesterday to bring up to you. He said he found it in that guy's apartment, the one that was killed. McKay?"

"Is that all he said?"

"No, he said you'd know what it was and to call him." He got the lens in and blinked, then started on the other eye. "Do you know what it is?"

"Oh, yes," I said, slipping the chip into the pocket of my bathrobe. "I have quite a collection of these myself."

I went back into the bedroom and picked up the phone, dialing Freeman's home number. The phone rang and rang. Finally, he picked it up and, in a voice that sounded like he'd been gargling with toxic waste, said, "Yeah."

I looked at the clock. It was seven-thirty. "It's Henry," I said. "Did I wake you?"

"Do I sound like I was in the middle of aerobics?" he replied, grumpily. In the background, a female voice sleepily asked who was calling. He said something to her, then asked, "You in Los Robles?"

"Yeah," I said, digging the chip out of my pocket. "What's this chip all about?"

"You know what it is, don't you?" Freeman asked, awakening.

"You get them at AA for thirty days of sobriety. So?" I

dangled the chip in front of me. I kept mine in my desk at work.

"There was a whole bunch of those chips in McKay's apartment," Freeman said through a yawn. "Not much else. Landlord didn't waste any time getting rid of his stuff. Said it was bad luck to keep a murdered man's things around."

"You say there was more than one?"

"Yeah, five or six."

Someone knocked at the door. Josh came out of the bathroom, naked, opened it and stood back. A waiter came in wheeling a trolley with covered plates. He glanced at Josh, then me, and looked away, resolutely. Josh went back into the bathroom.

"Were there any chips with sixty or ninety days on them?" I asked Freeman, watching the waiter set up the small table near the window.

"Nope. Why?"

"Looks like McKay's what we call a slipper." I tossed the chip onto the bed.

"What's that?"

"It's an AA expression for an alcoholic who can't stay sober—someone who slips. I still don't understand the significance of McKay being an alcoholic."

"That's the only thing I been able to find out about him that wasn't in the police report," Freeman replied. "No rap sheet, nothing from DMV. Neighbors couldn't tell me squat."

"He wasn't exactly Mr. Rogers, Freeman. There must be something."

Grumpily, he replied, "I don't have contacts in NAMBLA, Henry."

I smiled. NAMBLA was the North American Man Boy Love Association, an organization of pedophiles. "No, I wouldn't think that was your neighborhood."

The waiter finished and left, quickly.

"What I figure," Freeman was saying, "is that maybe we could get a lead from some of these AA meetings he went to."

I frowned. "Even if that's true, you're an outsider, Freeman. Most of the meetings are closed."

"You're not an outsider," he replied.

"It's called Alcoholics Anonymous for a reason," I said. "You don't repeat what gets said at those meetings."

"It's the first break I've had," he growled.

"There'll be others. The guy was dealing kiddie porn, after all. What about your contacts with LAPD? They must keep track of people like McKay. Or the FBI, they're always busting guys who send stuff through the mail."

He sighed. "Okay, it's your money. When are you coming back up here?"

"Next weekend, probably."

"If I find anything out before then I'll call you."

We hung up.

I got up from bed and wandered over to the table lifting the lids of the plates. French toast, maple syrup, marmalade—Josh ate dessert even for breakfast. Fortunately, there was also ham and a couple of plain biscuits. I poured two cups of coffee and carried them into the bathroom where I found Josh standing at a full-length mirror, examining his inner thigh. I set his cup of coffee on the counter.

"When did you order breakfast?" I asked.

"While you were sleeping." He smiled at me briefly in the mirror and went back to his leg.

"What are you doing, baby?" I asked, running the palm of my hand across his back. He was smooth as stone, but a lot warmer.

"Looking for lesions," he replied, carelessly, straightening himself up.

I studied the beautiful body in the mirror, speechless for a moment. "Why, Josh? You haven't—I mean, there's no reason to think—"

He interrupted my sputtering. "I look every morning." He pivoted on the balls of his feet and turned around, penis flopping. "Top to bottom." As if to emphasize the point, he bent forward, spread the cheeks of his buttocks and inspected the mirrored image of his anus. "It's just something I do," he added, standing up.

"Since when?" I asked, trying to be as casual as he.

"Since I started on the Retrovir." He picked up the cup of coffee, and studied his mirrored back for a moment. "I usually wait until you've gone to work."

I didn't know what else to say. Moments like this brought home to me that no matter how well I thought I knew him, how much I loved him, we were on different sides of the fence that separated the infected from the uninfected. I could see a little way over to his side, but he lived there. Not only did I feel helpless, I was afraid to tell him so, to give him the burden of my anxiety in addition in his own. Then it occurred to me—he had wanted me to see him doing this.

"Is everything all right, Josh?" I asked, propping myself against the counter.

He put on his bathrobe. It was made of cotton, striped gray and white, and made him look like an Old Testament angel. "The doctor wants to start me on some new treatment, pentamidine. It's supposed to help prevent PCP."

I nodded. Repeated bouts of pneumocystis had killed my friend Larry Ross, and many others with AIDS. "When?"

"As soon as possible." He came up and put his arms around me, laying his head on my chest. "No biggie, right?"

I held him and said nothing. My memory, a trash heap of lines from poems I'd loved as an undergrad, produced this one: ". . . in a country as far away as health."

We ate breakfast, discussed the limited possibilities for tourism that Los Robles offered and went back to bed, shooing the maid away when she banged at the door an hour later. We both needed the break, I from the case and Josh from a frantic school-and-job schedule that had me worried about his health. Around noon, though, we both got restless.

"There must be something to see around here," Josh insisted, idly flicking through TV channels with the remote control.

"Cut that out, it gives me a headache."

"Look, Henry, it's Tom Zane," he said, pointing the remote at the screen.

I watched the late Tom Zane in a rerun of the cop show in which he'd starred. "Turn the channel," I commanded.

But Josh was mesmerized by the sight of the man who had held him at gunpoint and whom he had ended up killing. I took the remote away and switched channels to an aerobics program.

"I still think about him sometimes," Josh said.

"So do I," I replied.

He scooted toward me. "That was the last case of yours I helped you with."

"Thank God for that." I put my arm around his shoulders and we watched a spandexed starlet with big hair dance frantically across the screen. His mention of cases had got me thinking about Paul and what I still needed to do. "There's someone I need to talk to today. A possible witness."

"You're not going to leave me here," he complained.

I considered whether there would be any risks to him if I took him along while I talked to Ruth Soto. "Why don't you come with me? I'll show you the neighborhood where I grew up."

"And show me the manger where you were born?"

There was a Southern Pacific railroad line across the top of one side of the levee that ran along Paradise Slough, a tributary of the Los Robles river. A wooden bridge forded the slough and led into the neighborhood which had been given its name. We came over the bridge slowly and I glanced out the window to the water, almost hidden by the thick underbrush and tall oaks and cottonwoods at its banks. Spores of cottonwood drifted across the windshield. We came down the other side of the bridge on Los Indios Way, the main road through Paradise Slough. Having just come out of River Park, the change in the character of the neighborhood was immediate and dramatic.

"This is where you grew up?" Josh asked, disbelievingly.

I looked at the houses along the road, some little more than wooden shacks with corrugated metal roofs. There were no sidewalks, and the front yards were littered with hulks of cars, stoves, busted-out TVs and doorless refrigerators. Chickens wandered through the yards with stilted dignity.

"This is one of the worst streets," I replied. "And it's not really as bad as it looks."

He turned to me. "It isn't?"

"Look at the gardens."

Almost every house had its little garden and in them were not only beautiful flowers but also vegetables and herbs. These, and the flocks of chickens, provided many families with some of their food. When I was growing up, people had even kept cows and goats. These seemed to be gone now, victims of zoning ordinances, I imagined.

"I was joking about the manger," Josh said. "It's hard to believe people live this way."

"Have you been to Watts lately? Believe me, there are worse ways."

He glanced at me. "Sorry, Henry, I didn't mean. . . ."

I squeezed his hand. "That's okay. It's a reflex, from growing up around here and having people give me that look that poor people get when I said I was from Paradise Slough."

"What look?" he asked.

"The look that says, if you're poor, there must be something wrong with you." An old dog decided to lope its way across the road and I came to a skidding stop. "Sometimes I think what people really want is to criminalize poverty. Not that the law doesn't already do that, in a way."

I let up on the brake and drove on. We turned off Los Indios to La Avia and, as I'd told Josh, the houses here were more durable. Paradise Slough, like everywhere else on earth had its better addresses. These interior streets were not as bad as the streets around the fringe of the community, which got the heaviest traffic, and were, for that reason, undesirable and transient. Here, the yards were better maintained, the houses not so much in need of repairs and there were fences, the universal symbol of affluence. In fact, some of these houses were scrupulously maintained, as if each mowed blade of grass was a hedge against the encroachment of poverty.

Like the house we were coming up to, visible behind a chain-link fence to which the owner had somehow attached a border of barbed wire across the top. The house was L-shaped, on a large lot that was part orchard. An almond orchard. Painted white with green trim and with striped awnings above the windows, the place was as much a monument to bourgeois aspiration as it was a residence. The shade that the awnings cast over the windows gave them a defiant opacity. It was a very private place.

"That's where I grew up," I told Josh as we drove past the place.

"Wait! Stop!"

"Why? None of my family lives there anymore."

He craned his head around looking as the house flickered in the side mirror and was gone. "It looked nice, Henry."

"The walls are paneled with slats of oak inside," I said, "and there's a chandelier in the dining room. My father built that house, almost by himself, room by room. He was prouder of it than anything else."

"He must have been proud of you," Josh ventured.

I shook my head. "He could build a house but he couldn't raise children. In the end, he just gave up."

Josh looked at me, expectantly, but I had nothing further to say.

14

I turned onto La Honda Road, driving slowly until I came to a house that fit Paul's description: a yellow house, rosebushes growing in front of the porch. I parked beneath an apple tree spotted with small red fruit and we got out of the car. Children's toys were scattered across the wan grass. The rosebushes were weedy and uncultivated, far different from the symmetrical look of Paul's rose beds. The few remaining flowers were overblown, as if the buds had skipped the intermediate stages and simply exploded one morning.

With Josh hovering behind me, I knocked at the door. From inside there was the scampering of small feet and a female voice shouting something in Spanish, and then the doorknob turned and the door opened. A tiny, gray-haired woman blinked at me from behind thick glasses.

"*Señores,*" she said tentatively.

"*Estoy buscando la señorita Ruth Soto,*" I said.

"*Pues, yo soy su madre,*" she replied. A little dark-haired boy in green overalls wrapped his thin arms around her legs and looked up at me, smiling happily.

"*Me llamo Henry Rios,*" I said, "*y este es mi amigo, Josh Mandel. Soy un abogado representando señor Paul Windsor.*" When she heard Paul's name, her expression lost what little animation it had had. "*Es muy importante que hablo con su hija.*"

"*No esta en casa,*" she said, already closing the door.

Gently, but firmly, I gripped the edge of the door above her head and held it open. "*Señora Soto, por favor, llame su hija y pregunta a ella si quiere hablar con me. Si ella dice no, me voy.*"

She looked at me, taking in my suit, my briefcase, the indicia of authority. "*Bueno, esperate aqui, por favor.*"

I nodded.

She picked up the little boy and hobbled away from the door, leaving it ajar. I caught a glimpse of a sunny room and shabby furniture. A TV broadcast snatches of Spanish soap opera dialogue.

Josh said, "What's going on?"

"She claimed Ruth wasn't home. I told her if Ruth didn't want to talk to me, I'd leave."

"The little boy is cute."

"Ruth's son, I think."

From the back of the house the shadowy figure of a young woman emerged, walking slowly toward me. Dark hair framed a round, pretty face. She wore jeans and a pale pink sweatshirt and was large-breasted and thick-hipped, not at all the little girl I'd been imagining. But perhaps, like the roses, the change had been sudden because she carried herself a little awkwardly, as if unaccustomed to her body.

"I can't see you right now," she said, coming to the door. Her large, brown eyes were frightened. "Can you come back later?"

"Your mother told you who I am?"

She nodded. "There's something I have to do." She was nearly pleading.

"When can I come back?"

"In an hour," she said, closing the door softly. "Please."

We went and had lunch at the only restaurant in Paradise Slough, a drive-in called Emma's Taqueria. Exactly one hour later we presented ourselves at her doorstep and I knocked, half expecting that no one would answer, but she came to the door and let us in, silently.

"Thank you for talking to me," I said. "This is my friend, Josh Mandel."

She shook his hand, limply. "Please, sit down."

Dust drifted up from the couch when we sat down. She settled nervously into an armchair and said, "What do you want to talk to me about?"

At that moment, the little boy whom we'd seen earlier came running into the room with his grandmother a few steps behind him. He threw himself into his mother's lap, squealing.

Ruth looked at her mother. "It's okay, Mom. I'll watch him."

The old woman shrugged, then said, to Josh and me, "*Quieren algo a beber? Una coca o café?*"

"Coffee," I said. "Josh?"

He nodded. "Thank you."

She wandered off into the back of the house. The little boy had righted himself and sat in his mother's lap, looking at us.

"This is my son, Carlos," Ruth said.

I said "Hello, Carlos."

But the boy ignored me and smiled at Josh, whom he apparently took for a large child of approximately his own age. He climbed off his mother's lap and sat down on the floor where there was a collection of plastic trucks. He began playing with them, glancing now and then at Josh. Josh smiled and joined him. Carlos handed him a red truck and they began to race their cars across the floor.

Ruth and I watched them crawl into the dining room. She looked at me and said, "He's not usually like that with strangers."

"He must think Josh is just another kid."

"Your friend is nice. My mother said you work for Mr. and Mrs. Windsor." There was a tiny note of deference in how she said their names.

"Did you know he's in trouble?"

Her smile was unexpectedly sophisticated. "Again," she said.

"Yes, again. He's accused of murder. I represent him."

She nodded, pressing her lips together.

"When the police arrested him," I continued, "they found a roll of film in his car. He said it was pictures of you and Carlos that he'd taken without you seeing him, but the pictures the police showed the judge were . . . of someone else."

"Who?"

There seemed no way to be delicate about it. "A girl and a man, having sex. Paul says it wasn't him."

"Are you sure?" she asked with sudden bitterness.

"That's why I'm here."

We were interrupted by Mrs. Soto, who brought me a cup of coffee. From the dining room we heard giggling. Mrs. Soto smiled at me as she left the room.

"I don't understand what you mean," Ruth said nervously.

"Paul says the police switched the film," I replied, "but it's his word against the police. Paul says he took the pictures from his car while you and Carlos were in the park over on Dos Rios. It would have been around six weeks ago." I paused. "He thought you recognized his car."

She looked past me. "Does he still have that black car? That Mercedes?"

Hope building, I nodded.

"I try to take Carlos to the park every day," she said, wistfully, "but it's so bad there with drugs. I have to watch him real careful. One time I found him playing with a rubber." She scowled. "We didn't go back for a long time after that."

"Did you see the car?" I asked.

"I'm trying to remember," she replied. "Like I said, I got my hands full with Carlos." She rubbed the palms of her hands against her thighs. "What would happen if I said I seen him?"

"I would ask you to testify at his trial," I replied. "To show that the pictures that Paul took weren't the same pictures that the police have."

Now she fussed with the ends of her hair. "What if I don't testify?"

"Well," I began, "I could try to force you to but I guess you already know there's only so much that can be done if you don't want to."

She glanced at me sharply. "Like the last time I was in court."

"It would be different," I said. "The last time when you decided not to testify, the case was dismissed and Paul went free. This time, if you did see him that day, and you didn't testify, there's a good chance he would be convicted."

"Would he go to jail?" she asked quietly.

"Yes."

She exclaimed, "Good. That's where he belongs." Then, as if astonished by her own vehemence, she drew back and bit her lip.

"If you feel that way," I asked, "why didn't you testify against him?"

"I didn't want to have to tell my son that I made his father go to jail," she said, after a moment's hesitation. "That would have been on me. But this time—"

"You did see the car, didn't you?"

"There ain't many cars like that in Paradise Slough," she replied, her tone curving toward bitterness again.

From the other room, I heard Josh laughing and looked over. Carlos was crawling all over him, pounding his small fists against Josh's back and head.

"So," I asked, in the tone I reserved for cross-examination, "it's all right with you if he goes to prison for something he didn't do because that lets you off the hook with Carlos?"

She looked at me angrily, but said nothing.

"In a way, Ruth, you'd still be sending him to prison."

She shook her head. "No."

"What he did to you was wrong. I'm not defending him. But this is different. Not even Paul should be punished for something he didn't do."

She pressed her lips together again. "He's a bad man."

"I'm not saying he isn't," I replied. "I'm just saying this is different. This is something he didn't do."

Her anger was giving way to confusion.

"I just want him to leave us alone," she said.

"When this is over," I replied, "I can help you with that. We can get the court to order him to stay away from you."

She shook her head slowly. "The court don't care. They put my brother away for trying to defend me."

"I can help you," I said. "When this is over."

"I have to talk to Elena," she whispered.

"Your mother?" I asked.

"Your sister, Mr. Rios," she said. "I have to talk to your sister."

"How do you know my sister?" I demanded.

She bit her lip. "I thought you knew," she said. "When I got pregnant, the social worker said I should get an abortion but we're Catholic and I wanted my baby. But my father, he said the social worker was right. Then Elena called me. She told me I should keep my baby if I wanted him. She talked to my father. She gave us money for the hospital and let me come and stay with her and finish school where nobody knew what happened."

My mind was racing. "When?"

"I came back home last June," she said, "after I graduated. Now I'm in junior college. I want to be a nurse." Frightened, now, she began to cry. "I thought you knew."

Awkwardly, I reached out and touched her hand. "It's okay," I said. "It's okay. I guess Elena just forgot to tell me that she knew you. But how *does* she know you?"

"Mrs. Windsor told her what happened, and she called me."

I nodded. Out of my confusion, one or two things were beginning to fall into place. "Let me talk to Elena," I said. "Okay?"

She nodded.

"Give me your phone number," I added, "and I'll call you after I've talked to her."

She nodded again and gave me the number. I jotted it down, then called Josh. He came in carrying Carlos.

"We have to go now," I said.

In the car, he asked, "Henry, what's wrong?"

"I'll explain it to you later. Right now I need to go see someone, alone."

"Sure," he said.

I dropped Josh off at the hotel and drove to Sara Windsor's house. She was in the garden, clipping dead roses from the bushes, her face shadowed by a big straw hat, a glass of iced tea beside her.

"We have to talk," I said.

She put the shears down and picked up her tea. "Let's go inside." As we entered the house, she took off the hat, tossed it on a table and asked, "Is something the matter, Henry?"

"Yes," I said, angrily, "something is the matter. I'm being played for a fool by you and my sister."

"What are you talking about?" she asked impatiently.

"I just saw Ruth Soto. She told me that my sister came to her rescue after Paul was finished with her. What the hell is going on here, Sara?"

She sat down. "Why did you see Ruth?"

"She saw Paul's car the day he was taking pictures of her. Those pictures the cops had in court, they're not the ones he took. Now, tell me about my sister."

"Sit down, Henry, you make me nervous, standing there." I remained on my feet. She shrugged. "Then have it your way. I didn't ask her to come to Ruth Soto's rescue," she said coolly. "That was her own idea."

"Why? Why should she care about what happens to Ruth Soto?"

Sara combed a stray, limp hair from her forehead with her fingers. "Why should you care about the men you help make out their wills? You think you've cornered the market on compassion?"

"Why didn't she tell me?"

"You cut her off a long time ago."

"It was mutual."

Sara shook her head. "You and she seem to have compassion for everyone but each other. Maybe it's time you talked."

15

After I left Sara's house, I drove to Clayton's firm, shut myself up in my office and called my sister. I got her answering machine and left an awkward message. I thought about what Sara had said, how Elena and I had compassion for everyone but each other, and I also remembered Elena's terrifying comparison of our childhood to a concentration camp.

At the time it had seemed extreme, but now, as I thought about it, it reminded me of something I had always known about myself: what kept me alive as a child was a tiny spark of hope I managed to preserve in that crazy, violent household. But alongside that hope was a belief, irrational and profound, that what I had suffered—the beatings, the neglect—I had in some way deserved. Even now, I saw how those feelings persisted, hope alternating with guilt. It made for a conscientious lawyer, but not a particularly happy man. What had Elena said? Those who have been tortured go on being tortured. I wanted my sister at that moment in a way I had never wanted anyone.

Someone was knocking at the door. "Come in."

Peter Stein pushed the door open, carrying a stack of papers in his hand. "Hey, Henry, I thought I saw you coming in."

"Hello, Peter," I replied, swiveling in my chair to face him.

"Are you feeling okay?" he asked. "You look a little pale."

"I'm fine. What do you have there?"

"That research I told you about on changing venue." He sat down and plopped the papers down in front of me. I pretended to read them.

"These will help," I said, stacking them.

"I got some other news that might interest you," he said, dropping his voice. "About Mark."

"Yes, go on. I'm listening," I replied, completing the difficult transition from my private thoughts to this conversation.

"Do you know about S&Ls?"

"Savings and loan associations? Just that a lot of them are failing."

Peter nodded. "Including one here called Pioneer S&L. The feds are on the verge of taking it over."

I tried to appear interested. "What does that have to do with Mark?"

"He owns it," Peter replied. "Not in his own name. He's got other people fronting for him. The reason it's going down the tubes is that it made a lot of risky loans, mostly on shopping malls and condos."

I nodded, waiting for the punch line.

"As it happens, most of those deals involved Windsor Development."

"I thought Mark was doing well," I said.

"He was in too much of a hurry to expand," Peter said. "He put up things that no one wanted to get into and he did it with Pioneer's money. The worse it got for him, the more ready cash he needed, and the more money he took out of Pioneer." He tapped the desk. "That's against the law. The feds call it looting."

I was beginning to get the picture. "And when Pioneer started failing, the feds came in and took a look at the books."

"They're about to run an audit," he said. "They don't know what I've told you, yet. I got it from reading some very confidential memorandums in a special client file."

"How did you find it?"

He smiled. "You know how lawyers are, there's copies of everything if you look hard enough. There was a copy of the file in billing. The way I look at it, Henry, Mark's not concerned about what happens to Paul. He's about to have enough on his hands just trying to keep himself out of jail."

"Poor Mark."

"Well," he said, rising heavily, "if someone has framed Paul, this at least eliminates Mark. Hey, did you talk to your corroboration?"

I nodded. "Yes. She saw Paul's car the day he said he was out taking pictures of her. It backs up his story that the film was switched."

"Maybe," he cautioned. "Maybe he had two rolls."

"Yes, that's possible, but it's the kind of coincidence that makes the DA's case look a little less compelling."

"True," he allowed. "So who does that leave?"

"The cops," I said. "If someone switched the film, it would have had to be Morrow."

"That's mighty hard to believe, Henry."

I shrugged. "Maybe he really wanted to nail Paul on the child molest thing and saw his chance."

"I don't know," he said doubtfully. "Cops get cases dismissed on them all the time and they get over it. Unless he had special reason to be interested in the girl. Family friend, maybe."

"That's a possibility I hadn't thought about," I said, jotting myself a note.

"Listen," he said, at the doorway, "just out of curiosity, did she tell you why she wouldn't testify?"

"She said she didn't want to have to explain to her son that she put his father in jail," I replied. "I can't blame her. She's going to have enough to explain to him as it is."

He nodded.

"Peter," I said, "I appreciate your help but I don't want you to get into trouble around here."

"I'll tell you a little secret, Henry. When I was snooping around I found another file, a personnel file. There's a memo from Clayton to Cummings saying that I don't seem to be working out. They're getting ready to fire me, I guess."

"I'm sorry, Peter."

"They'll be doing me a favor."

After Peter left, I tried calling Elena again, but this time didn't even get her machine. There was no answer at Ruth Soto's house, either. Finally, I packed up my papers, called Josh and told him I was on my way.

Josh insisted on taking me to dinner for my birthday so we went off to Old Towne and a French restaurant which he had read about somewhere. Having worked in them from the time he was thirteen, Josh knew something about restaurants and food. At one point he'd considered going to cooking school, but he'd put the idea aside because he didn't think anyone would hire a chef who was HIV-positive. No one would take the chance that he might accidentally cut himself and bleed into the food. There was a certain logic in this, but it pained me when he imposed limits on himself like that.

He ordered for both of us. Living with him, I'd begun to overcome my indifference to food, but presented with more than two choices I invariably ordered whatever my dining companion was having. Josh diagnosed this as a form of ahedonia, a word he'd picked up from God knows where that purportedly meant an indifference to pleasure.

Over the grilled lamb chops he'd ordered for me, I told him what I had learned about my sister that afternoon. He listened intently, and when I finished said, "Why didn't she ever tell you?"

"We're not close," I replied. The answer sounded inadequate even to me.

"I bet you have secrets you've never told her."

I shrugged. "Being born into my family was like being thrown into an accident. Elena and I went our own ways, no questions asked."

He sipped some wine. "I'd like to get to know her."

"So," I said, "would I."

Josh left for LA the next morning and, after taking him to the airport, I went to my office. I worked until noon drafting a motion to change the venue of Paul's trial from Los Robles to San Francisco, the nearest big city. Peter had left me the points and authorities he'd used when he was a DA opposing a similar motion. I was pleasantly surprised at how thorough and well written they were. Criminal law is a courtroom practice, and few of us, on either side of the table, have much talent for the written word.

Motions to change venue are rarely granted since their premise is that pretrial publicity has prejudiced a defendant's ability to get a fair trial by tainting the pool of prospective jurors. A court must be convinced of the "reasonable likelihood" that this has occurred. It's a vague standard that gives the court a lot of room in which to move and with my hometown disadvantage I knew I'd have to work doubly hard to box the court in.

I gathered up my notes and went down to Peter's office. As I walked down the hall, Mark Windsor emerged from Bob Clayton's office. We hadn't seen each other since the night we'd talked at the hotel.

"You look pretty official there," Mark said, with a crinkly smile.

"What's going on, Mark?" I asked, stopping.

"Just counting my money," he replied.

"Well, everyone needs a hobby." I started past him.

"I thought you were going to call me," he said.

I stopped again and looked at him. Maybe the crinkles around his eyes weren't good humor but worry. After what Peter had told me, I could imagine Mark had good cause for concern.

"Your brother's kept me busy," I said.

"You've gotta eat, right? Relax? Come over some night."

It sounded casual enough but I could hear him struggling to connect.

"I promise."

"Good. See you later, Hank."

Peter was at his desk, with a half-eaten sandwich before him, dictating something. He clicked off his tape recorder when I came in. I dropped into a chair and said, "I just ran into Mark."

Peter nodded. "He's been here all morning. I think the feds have caught his scent. So how's the motion going?"

"Great, thanks for your Ps and As. You're a pretty good lawyer, Peter."

With a sidewise smile, he said, "Go tell that to Bob."

"Can you give me some more help on this?" I asked, laying the motion on the desk.

"Just let me cancel my appearance before the Supreme Court," he replied. "What do you need?"

"I can handle the legal research part but what I need is someone to do some fact gathering to support my argument."

"Like what?"

"Well, I'd like to know the *Sentinel*'s circulation in the county, both by subscription and at vending machines. Also, I want to know how jurors get drawn around here . . ."

"Voter registration rolls," he said.

"What about DMV registration? I want a clear idea of how big the pool is in relation to how many people the *Sentinel* reaches. Also, I'd like some kind of analysis of the amount of coverage that Paul's case had received in the paper compared to other murders it's reported in, let's say, the last eighteen months."

Peter had been taking notes. He stopped and said, "You're really serious about this."

I nodded. "And what about TV and radio coverage? Can we get transcripts or something, and the dates of broadcast? I want to be able to say that there isn't anyone in Los Robles County who hasn't heard of Paul Windsor."

"That doesn't mean anything if you can't show possible prejudice," he pointed out.

"I know that. But look, one thing the court considers is the notoriety of the crime. Here we've got a brutal murder plus a connection with pedophilia and a defendant with a famous name. This is not a routine homicide for Los Robles."

"Let me play the DA," Peter said. "You can't say that just because the case involves a couple of child molesters people around here can't be fair. They've heard of McMartin. They're just as bombarded as everyone else is about abused kids."

"True," I allowed, "so here's my trump card. It's not just the way the *Sentinel*'s covered the case, it's how they've used it to try to get at Mark Windsor. It's turned this case into part of its political vendetta against the Windsors on the no-growth issue. Paul's trial isn't just about his guilt or innocence, it's a referendum on big developers in general, and his family in particular."

"Well, it's a novel argument," Peter said. "I don't know how convincing it is."

"It's what I've got."

"So when do you want all this stuff?"

"I'd like to file the motion next Monday. That gives you four days."

He grinned. "You're counting the weekend."

"You mind?"

He looked around his file-littered room and said, "What else do I have to do?"

Back in my own office, I called Ruth Soto. From the way she answered my greeting I knew that she wasn't happy to hear from me. I didn't blame her a bit. It was one of those times when it seemed to me that my job consisted of getting people to do what they didn't want to.

"Have you had a chance to think about what we talked about yesterday?" I asked her.

"I been busy," she said with schoolgirl surliness. "I don't remember everything you said."

"I'm talking about whether you're willing to testify at Paul's trial."

There was silence at her end. "I want to talk to Elena."

"Have you called her?"

"She don't answer her phone," Ruth said. "I'm really busy with school starting, and Carlos . . ."

"Ruth, the trial won't be for weeks, at least," I replied, cutting off her evasions.

"I don't know," she said, her voice getting faint. "I want to think about it."

"Okay," I said, letting it go for now. My appeal to her sense of fairness had evidently failed, and I could understand why. How fairly had Paul treated her? I would have to devise another approach. "I'll call you tomorrow. If you talk to Elena, tell her . . ." but I couldn't think of what I wanted Ruth to tell her. "Tell her I tried calling her, too."

I put down the phone and contemplated the irony of Paul's defense lying in the hands of the one person in the world who had the least reason to want to help him. This case seemed to be generating its own peculiar brand of karma.

On the street, a jogger braved the early afternoon heat, heading toward the river on the Parkway. I thought of Ben Vega, and that brought me around to another thread in this mystery, the possibility that the cops had fabricated evidence to convict Paul.

I turned away from the window and considered the pile of documents on my desk generated by the Windsor prosecution. Idly, I flipped through them, coming to the police reports of Paul's previous arrest for child molestation. I studied the signature of the investigating officer, Dwight Morrow.

Morrow. Was it really a coincidence that he was also the investigator on the McKay case? Ben had told me how angry Morrow'd been when Paul got away the first time. Despite Peter's defense of him, to me Morrow had the look of a cop who always got his man.

Always? I wondered, as I picked up the phone.

16

The phone rang just as I'd finished lacing my brand-new Nikes. "Hi. Ben?"

"Yeah, I'm downstairs in the lobby. It's real nice running weather."

I glanced out the window. It was just getting to be dusk. "Still hot?" I asked.

"Not too bad. It'll be nice and fresh by the river."

"Give me five minutes."

He was downstairs, looking nervously out of place in his black running shorts and Los Robles Police Department singlet. He smiled when I appeared, and I was again struck by the contrast between his heavily muscled body and round, little boy's face—he looked like he'd stuck his head through one of those muscleman cardboard cutouts.

"You ready, Mr. Rios?"

"If we're going to parade down River Parkway half-naked," I said, "you're going have to stop calling me Mr. Rios. Try Henry."

"Sure, Henry. Ready?"

It had been months since I'd run. "As ready as I'm going to get."

We walked the few blocks from the Hyatt to the river's edge.

"Where's your friend?" Ben asked abruptly as we approached Old Towne.

I glanced at him, but he looked intently ahead. "Josh? He went back to LA." I hesitated, then added, "Listen, about that crack he made, Ben. I'm sorry if it embarrassed you."

"Different strokes for different folks," he said, with forced nonchalance.

I couldn't think of an appropriate platitude with which to answer him and we walked on in a faintly uncomfortable silence, stopping when we got to the river.

A bike path went upriver from the newly renovated waterfront to a park about seven miles away. I figured I was good for three.

"Let me stretch," I said. While he stood watching, I went through my stretching routine waking slumbering joints and muscles. They weren't gracious about being called back into service, but slowly, and sullenly, they responded. "Okay."

We started at a slow warmup trot, passing the T-shirt shops and fast-food restaurants that now occupied the brick structures that had been the original city. It was warmish, still, and the air was thick with light the color of honey. Briefly, a motorboat shattered the green surface of the river. Soon we were out of Old Towne and into a wooded area between the river and a levee.

Away from the cars and businesses and people, the air was fresher, and the odor different, mixing the smell of the muddy earth and anise, and some underlying scent of vegetable decay that I'd never smelled anywhere other than by the banks of this river. Stands of bamboo obscured the river at points, but then we would pass an open space and it reappeared, leaves and spores of cottonwood glancing its surface. The sky was beginning to change, darken, and the sun was slipping out of view in a slow smoke of red and orange and violet.

Our pace had steadily increased and now, as we passed a wooden mile marker, I felt my breath deepen, my legs relax and my arms develop a rhythm instead of simply jerking at my side. We'd been running abreast but I knew that if Ben increased the pace I'd have to drop behind. I found myself remembering my boyhood runs along the river with Mark Windsor.

Except for the methodical rasp of our breathing, Mark and I had run in silence. Occasionally one of us would see something at the side of the trail, a covey of quail or a skunk or some hippie's marijuana patch, and would nudge the other to alert him to the sight. Mostly, though, we just ran, side by side as if yoked together, and I had the absolute certainty that everything I was seeing, Mark was seeing at the same moment with the same eyes. I'd never felt so much a part of another person as I did then; it was what sex was supposed to be like but, as I discovered soon enough, seldom was.

When we stopped one of us would say, "Good run," or "Hard run," and we'd strip off as much of our clothing as we thought we could get away with and dash into the river. There for the rest of the afternoon we'd swim and float, sit on the bank, again not saying much. In fact, I never knew what Mark was actually thinking or how he felt. I just assumed that he was as happy to be with me as I was with him. At twilight we'd get dressed and go to our respective houses for dinner and I wouldn't see him until the next day. Sometimes it was only the thought of the next day's run that got me through those tense and silent meals.

Ben and I were coming up on two miles. I was still holding my own, but I could hear the rattle at the end of my exhalations. It seemed as good a time as any to get on with my purpose in having suggested this outing.

"What did you think about the prelim?" I asked.

Ben glanced over at me, sweat beading at his hairline. "It was real interesting. I never testified before except one time for drunk driving."

"I was real surprised by those pictures. Had you seen them before?"

He worried his brow. "Hey, should we be talking about this?"

"What's the harm?" I panted. "Everything was laid out at the prelim." I jogged a couple of steps before adding. "Wasn't it?"

"Yeah, sure." He speeded up a little, forcing me into overdrive.

"The pictures surprised me, that's all. Makes me kind of wonder if the DA has anything else up his sleeve."

"Don't know," he replied, uncomfortably. Eyes forward he added, "I don't know much about the case. They just brought me in on the search."

"I know," I said. It was getting harder for me to keep up my end of the conversation as we passed the two-mile mark. "Getting a conviction's not too hard in most criminal cases, it's making it stick."

He looked at me. "What do you mean?"

I slackened our pace. "The DA has to win fair," I said, "or it's no good. I figure I've already got three or four grounds to appeal if Paul gets convicted."

We slowed even more. "Like what?" he asked, intently.

"There's that bogus search warrant," I replied, "and then the way the judge ran all over me at the hearing. But the biggest thing is those pictures. Paul says he didn't take them. He says that roll of film had pictures of something else." We were trotting now. "I have a witness who'll back him up."

"Uh-huh," Ben said, and quickened the pace. "Who?"

"I'm afraid I can't say. It gets into his alibi." For a few minutes we ran in silence. My knees were complaining. To shut them up, I said, "I believe my witness. So I also have to believe that someone switched the film you took from Paul's car with the film those pictures at the prelim came from."

"Uh-huh," he repeated, increasing his speed again. Sweat ran down his face, and soaked his singlet.

"Can we slow down?" I asked.

"Sure," he said, but didn't.

"Are we at three miles yet?"

"Just about."

"Let's turn around."

"One more mile."

"There's still three miles back, Ben."

"One more," he said, and spurted off.

Watching his fierce legs pumping, I muttered, "Jesus," took as deep a breath as I could and pushed on, managing to stay a few draggy paces behind him. Now, though, it was painful to breathe and my legs were cramping. Meanwhile it was also getting dark and there were small eruptions of sound from the riverbank, crickets, frogs, muskrats slithering across the mud and into the water. We passed a lacy railroad bridge, unused for decades.

"This is it, Ben," I shouted, when we got to four miles. "I'm heading back."

He looked at me over his shoulder. "Two miles to the park," was all he said.

"Asshole," I thought and prepared to turn around and start back. I figured this was his macho revenge for my having impugned the integrity of the cops. The sight of his broad back as he stripped off his singlet enraged me. I'd been running this trail when he was still in grade school and I was damned if I was going to give up. Fueled by anger, I pushed on, waiting for that moment when my body'd go into overdrive and break through the pain. It had been a long time since I'd called upon it to break that barrier and I wasn't sure I could do it anymore. But I carried less bulk than he did and I'd been at this for a lot longer. Long enough to know that he had speed but no strategy for a long run. Stategy was all I had left.

At about four and a half miles, just when I seemed to be losing sight of him in the darkness and the distance, my breath evened itself out and the pain in my legs subsided. Up ahead, his pace slackened, all that muscle weighing him down. Resisting the impulse to spend everything in a sprint to overtake him, I increased my speed just to the edge of pain and kept it there, testing that limit, accustoming my body to it.

At five miles I was close enough to see that his running was getting sloppy and wayward. A moment later I was alongside of him, listening to his shaky breath. Glancing over I saw sweat pouring down his chest, the strain in his face. Although I knew that it must be almost chilly now, my skin was so hot that I dried up my own sweat.

And then the pain lifted and I saw with incredible clarity the pavement beneath my feet, the curl in Ben's fingers, the dark leaves in the bushes along the trail, the moon rising above the levee. I felt myself smile and with a choppy breath surged forward a step, then two, then three, until I was running ahead of him, high on the euphoria of the effort. It no longer mattered whether he caught up or not, or how long I ran or that my body was knotted in pain just beneath the euphoria—I was ready to run until I dropped.

At mile six I turned around and could no longer see him. Ahead was the entrance to the park. I came in at a jog and then slowed to a walk. Tomorrow would be torture but at that moment I was sixteen again. A few minutes later, Ben shuffled in, veered off toward some bushes and threw up.

He came up to me, wiping his mouth on his singlet.

"Good run," I said. "Are you ready to head back?"

Panting, he said, "Let's flag down a patrol car."

When he'd recovered, we walked up the levee road and stood there shivering in the darkness. On the other side of the levee a field stretched away into the night beneath the moon. Although my knees ached and my chest was wracked with pain each time I drew a breath, I still felt wonderful.

"You okay?" I asked Ben. His face was tense.

"You run pretty good for an old man," was all he said. A moment later, a black-and-white came down the road and he flagged it down. It took us back to the Hyatt.

Outside the hotel I asked, "Where did you park, Ben?"

"In the lot," he said, "downstairs."

"I'll go down with you."

We went into the lobby and took the elevator to the parking lot, saying nothing. I walked him to his car, an old Chevy lovingly cared for. He leaned against the driver's door and grinned at me.

"Man, you're a ringer."

"Were you trying to kill me out there?"

"I guess I got kind of pissed off at you when you was talking about those pictures." He wiped sweat from his forehead. "Anyway, it don't make sense, about switching the film. Morrow booked it right away."

"Two hours after the search," I corrected him.

"It takes that long to do the paperwork."

I didn't want to admit that I'd also thought of this. A car skidded around the corner. "I just wanted to give you something to think about."

"Why me?" he asked. "Morrow's the one you should talk to."

"I know. I was talking about Morrow."

He frowned. "I told you, Morrow's my compadre," he said, using the Spanish expression that described a friend whom one thought of almost as kin.

I persisted. "Morrow was the investigator the last time Paul was arrested. You're the one who told me he was pissed when Paul got off. Maybe he's trying to make up for that."

"I don't know nothing about that, Henry."

"I just want you to think about it," I replied, shivering in the chilly subterranean air.

Ben opened the door of his car, reached in and pulled out a sweatshirt. "Here," he said, handing it to me.

"Thanks," I said, putting it on. It was too big by half.

He stood irresolutely for a moment. "Can I ask you something, Henry?"

"Yeah."

"When I came up to your room the other day, and that guy answered the door. What was going on?"

"We were sleeping."

He looked at me. "Together?"

"Uh-huh."

He nodded, slowly. "I thought maybe he was joking when, you know, he said that thing about me joining you guys."

I studied his expression. He seemed neither particularly upset nor even especially embarrassed. "He was joking, Ben."

"You know what I mean."

"Well, like you said, different strokes for different folks."

He opened the door to his car again. "I got to go."

"Here," I said, taking off the sweatshirt.

"You can give it back to me next time," he said, getting into the car. He rolled down the window. "Thanks for the run."

"See you, Ben."

"Yeah, see you."

I stood aside and let him back out. He waved and drove off. I waved back and headed up to my room, thinking I owed Josh an apology. Standing next to the car, talking about Josh and me, Vega'd had an erection.

"Hiya, pal."

I glanced over in the direction of the bar and saw Mark standing half in, half out of the doorway with a tall glass in his hand. From the way he was holding himself, it didn't look like his first drink of the evening. I went over to him.

"Mark. What are you doing here?"

He held out his glass. "Happy hour. You want to join me?"

"I'm not really dressed for it."

A sloppy smile slid across his mouth. "I guess not. You been out running, huh?"

"Yeah, a lot farther than I wanted to. I need to go upstairs and clean up."

"How 'bout some company?"

"You alone?"

"I was kind of waiting for you, Hank. Henry."

His eyes were streaked with red, and I could've got drunk

just by breathing the same air. It wasn't the way I wanted to remember him. "I'll have to take a rain check, Mark. I'm really beat."

He opened his mouth to say something, but then just nodded.

"I'll call you."

"Yeah, do that. Do that."

The rest of the week passed quickly. Peter and I worked around the clock to put together the motion to change venue. It was in good shape by Friday, and I left Peter to finish it up, then went to see Paul before catching a flight to LA for the weekend.

Though I'd talked to him on the phone a couple of times, I hadn't seen Paul since the prelim. Over the phone he'd been listless, barely interested in what I'd had to say. The longer he was jailed, the more the jauntiness and defiance he'd displayed the first time I'd spoken to him had slipped away. Even so, I was still shocked by his appearance. He seemed to have aged ten years—ten bad years. He had a fatigued jailhouse pallor, bluish-white, and the lines around his eyes and mouth puckered sourly.

"Have you been sick, Paul?" I asked.

He shook his head.

"You look like it," I continued. "I think maybe we should have a doctor take a look at you."

In a low, tired voice, he said, "I don't need a doctor, I know what's wrong. This place is killing me." He shut his eyes briefly. "Fucking guards. All day long it's 'Hey, pervert,' 'Hey, asshole.' The cons are even worse."

I frowned. "I thought you were in high power."

He shook his head. "They moved me out after the prelim. I got my own cell but it's on a regular cellblock. This big Mexican said to me last night, 'I hear you like to fuck with little girls. Wait till lights out and I'll fuck with you.' I told the guard, the decent one, and he put me in another cellblock."

"I can get you moved back into isolation."

He shook his head. "And go crazy by myself?" Rubbing his eyes, he said, "I'll take my chances. Last time I was here it wasn't this bad. Of course, I bailed out after a couple of weeks. Now it's been what, six, eight weeks. I lost track of time. So what's going on, Henry?"

"I'm going to file a motion to transfer venue on Monday. If we win, they'll move you down to San Francisco. If we lose, I'll go up on appeal."

Grimly smiling, he said, "And I get to remain a guest of the state no matter what, right?"

"I'll make another bail application."

"In front of Phelan?" he asked. "He's the one who wouldn't drop charges last time. I've got a feeling that I'm just where everyone wants me." He yawned. "Sorry, didn't sleep much last night."

"I bet."

He half-smiled. "I wasn't worried about getting raped. What happened is that they brought in this kid a couple of days ago, maybe eighteen, nineteen, kind of pretty if you go for that. Someone did, last night." He bit a nail, spat it out. "You know what's happened to me in here, Henry? I heard that kid and did I call for the guards?" He shook his head. "No, I beat off." He looked away from me. "Can you believe that? I don't even like boys. When I get out of here, I'm going to take what's left of me and kill it."

"This won't last forever."

"Yeah?" he said caustically. "You think I won't be remembering this the rest of my life?" A moment later he said, "I haven't seen Sara since the prelim."

"I'm sorry."

He shrugged. "Who the fuck can blame her, married to a fuckup like me."

"You just make it worse for yourself, talking that way."

"Positive thinking doesn't work in here, Henry," he said. "It's the real world in here. Eat or be eaten. Have you talked to Ruth again?"

I nodded. I'd been calling her almost every day but she was still being evasive about whether she'd testify. Apparently Elena hadn't come down on the side of truth and justice.

"Is she going to testify for me?"

"She's still thinking about it," I said, adding, "You know I can still subpoena her whether she wants to testify or not."

"We both know how much good that's going to do," he replied. "If I could just talk to her."

"I think that would be a mistake right now." I got up. "I have a plane to catch to LA. I'll be back on Monday. Will you be all right?"

"Yeah, I'll be fine."

"I'll see you then," I said. He didn't reply.

17

I got into LA shortly after noon. I'd arranged for Emma to pick me up in my car, so that I could drop her off back at the office and go directly to the Criminal Courts Building downtown, where I had an appearance at one-thirty. Stepping to the curb outside the United terminal, I saw her lounging against my triple-parked Prelude, deep in conversation with an airport cop, who had his citation book on the top of the car, pen poised in the air. She laid a languid hand on his shoulder, bent close and whispered something. He straightened up, looking at her skeptically and slowly put the book away.

"Hello," I said, approaching, "is there a problem?"

Emma looked at me, and I saw myself doubled in her sunglasses. "No problem, Henry. Is there, Officer?"

He smiled. "No Ma'am," and moved down to the next car.

Getting into the car, I asked, "What was that all about?"

She started the car up. "He wanted to give me a ticket but I just told him what a bother it would be if my father had to call his supervisor and straighten things out."

We bumped forward in the heavy traffic. "Your father?"

"The mayor," she replied. "Thank God all us black people look alike to white folk. He didn't know if I was shittin' him or not, then you showed up just in time."

"Your father the mayor," I said. "You're going to get into trouble someday."

"So what? I know a great lawyer." She glanced at me. "You look tired, Henry."

"It's been a long week." I rubbed my eyes. "Any emergencies?"

She leaned on the horn at the Mercedes that had just cut us off. "Freeman wants you to call him when you're finished in court."

The sky was steel gray, not from clouds but from smog, and the air was almost as hot here as it had been in Los Robles that morning. My stomach complained about not having been fed and I felt a headache coming up. I wanted to blame someone for the lousy way I felt but the only available candidate was my secretary and I knew better than to tangle with her, so I lapsed into churlish, silent self-pity.

"You're going to be late," she said, as we bounded down Century Boulevard. "You better call."

I picked up the car phone and dialed the court. The phone was a concession to the distances I had to travel getting around to the various courthouses in the city. My day would sometimes begin in Pasadena and end in Santa Monica. I reached the clerk and explained the problem.

"Don't worry," he said. "The judge went out for a birthday lunch. He won't be back before two."

We turned sharply, and I bumped my head against the window. I looked at Emma. "Do you mind?"

"Sorry, I'm just trying to get you to court on time."

* * *

The hearing downtown was for sentencing in a felony driving-under-the-influence case. My client was a Westside doctor who had dipped once too often into his own pharmaceuticals and then driven home. He'd struck an old man, seriously injuring him. In fact, the old man would probably have died if my MD hadn't had enough of his wits left about him to render emergency first aid. This, a stack of testimonials, and self-commitment into a drug-treatment center kept him out of jail, for the time being. The judge told us to come back in three months for a progress report and final sentencing.

My client thanked me effusively. If I'd been thinking straight I would have presented him with my bill then and there while he was in the white heat of gratitude. But I didn't. I accepted his thanks, told him to stay sober until at least the next hearing and called my investigator, Freeman Vidor.

Once we'd got past the preliminaries, he said, "Why don't you come over to my office."

I glanced at my watch. It was three-thirty. "Let's make it lunch," I replied. "I haven't eaten today."

"How about the Code Seven."

"If you insist."

"It's convenient."

"It's lethal," I replied. "Oh, all right. Ten minutes."

"See you there."

Code Seven is police argot for a meal break and was also the name of a dark, smoky bar-and-grill on First Street that served as a watering hole for LA's finest. Freeman's lingering affection for the place dated to the time when he'd been a cop. Never having been a cop I didn't share his enthusiasm. Coming into the Code Seven out of the afternoon glare was like crawling into the earth. The brightest thing in the room was a glass-enclosed display of badges and shoulder patches from various police agencies mounted on the wall near the entrance. After that the going got pretty murky. I found a booth, ordered a hamburger and a cup of coffee and waited for Freeman to show up.

Patsy Cline crooned from the jukebox while a couple of guys, off-duty cops by their postures, sat at the bar getting drunk. One of them had reached that contemplative state in which song lyrics begin to sound really deep. The other was putting the sauce away pretty grimly, a man in the process of self-medication. Watching them brought back entirely too much of my own history and I was relieved when Freeman slid into the booth, removed his Porsche sunglasses and ordered a boilermaker from the used blonde who slammed my burger and coffee on the table like a woman who had something to say.

"Enjoy," she sneered. I inspected the food—this was not a likely possibility.

"So how's your weenie wagger up in Los Robles?" Freeman asked.

I swallowed the bite of burger in my mouth. "We got screwed seven ways from Sunday at the prelim." Briefly, I filled him in.

Our blonde brought him his booze and he knocked back the whiskey. "Signal Hill justice."

The allusion was to the murder of a black prisoner by members of the police department of a nearby town and the subsequent cover-up.

"Something like that." I sipped my coffee. "Paul thinks his brother set up the prosecution, but this is a little too deep for a civilian to pull off."

"What do the cops have against him?"

"He got out of that child molest case," I said. "The same cop who investigated that case is investigator on this one. Same DA. It's supposed to be tried by the same judge. None of them were happy when charges were dismissed last time. Maybe they want to be sure he doesn't get away."

Freeman looked skeptical. "When I was a cop," he said, "I saw a lot of my arrests go to shit when they got into court. You just figure on that happening to a certain percentage of them and you don't take it personal."

"Los Robles isn't Los Angeles. The DA probably wins every

case he takes to trial. Cops are a bigger deal up there, too."

He sipped his beer. "You know what I don't understand about this case?"

"No, what?"

"McKay's part. Was it just a coincidence that he was in Los Robles? Was it just a coincidence that he was killed?"

"You think he was murdered as part of a frame-up?"

"Unless Paul Windsor did it."

I abandoned my food. "I'm prepared to believe that the cops fabricated evidence," I said, "but killing the guy?"

"It sure would help if we knew more about him."

"That's your job," I said.

"I've been drawing blanks," Freeman said. "LAPD never heard of him. Neither have the feds. That alone seems real suspicious. Fifty-year-old man who we know is a pedophile, deals porn, procures kids for his friends, with no record at all." He shook his head. "Now maybe he was very, very careful and discreet, but I doubt it. These guys are on a crusade to make the world safe for baby fucking, plus, it's risky to date eleven-year-olds. Someone gets suspicious."

"Do you have a theory about Mr. McKay?"

"Yeah," Freeman said, lighting a Winston. "Maybe his name wasn't John McKay."

"If he has any kind of rap sheet it would be cross-indexed by his aliases," I pointed out.

"Only if the cops knew about them."

Our waitress came by, glanced at my empty coffee cup and splashed more coffee into it. She slammed down a check.

"Yes, that's true."

"The only thing we got is those AA chips."

"I told you, Freeman, if he said anything at those meetings, it was confidential. That's the whole point of anonymity."

"Hey," he said, holding up his empty shot glass to the waitress. "The point's to protect the identity of the guy talking, not the guys listening, right?"

"So?"

"Well this guy's dead, so who are you protecting except maybe the man who killed him?"

The waitress slopped another shot on the table. Freeman lifted it to his lips, tasting it. Mechanically, I raised my coffee cup and drank.

"Am I right, Henry?"

I nodded. "There's still a little problem of logistics," I said. "There are almost two thousand meetings a week in the LA area."

"He lived in Glendale," Freeman said, "and I bet he went to gay meetings."

"He was a pedophile, not gay," I said, by rote. "But you're probably right. I can't imagine him speaking up in a straight meeting full of moms and dads. AA unity has its limits." I ran my mental map of LA through my head. "The nearest gay meetings from Glendale would be in Silver Lake."

Freeman smiled. "There's one at six o'clock."

"Your research has been thorough," I remarked.

"And then there's one at eight, and one at eleven."

"Well, I needed a meeting, anyway."

"My name is Todd and I'm an alcoholic."

This announcement was greeted by a chorus of "Hi, Todd," from the dozen or so men, including myself, sitting around a table behind candles set into orange pear-shaped jars covered with plastic netting. They were the kind of candles found only at economy-minded Italian restaurants and meetings of AA. The speaker, a tall, dark-haired man in his mid-twenties with a guileless face, opened a notebook and began to read.

"Alcoholics Anonymous is a fellowship of men and women who share their experience, strength and hope with each other that they may solve their common problem and help others to recover from alcoholism. The only requirement for membership is a desire to stop drinking. There are no dues or fees for AA membership . . ."

My mind wandered as Todd continued reading the preamble. This was the tenth meeting I'd been to in two and a half days. I'd stopped at home only to eat, sleep and catch up on pending cases. I'd called Peter and instructed him to file our motion. I was due back in Los Robles on Friday for the hearing.

I hadn't gotten anywhere with McKay until I'd run into Todd just before this meeting started. Todd was someone I'd seen around before, one of those AA types who make it their mission to talk to backbenchers like me. I didn't mind him the way I did other self-appointed guardians of sobriety; he had a lighter touch than most. I'd run into him coming in tonight and we'd talked for a few minutes catching up. I'd mentioned John McKay's name without much expectation of response and been surprised when he said, "John M. I know him."

Before he could tell me more, it was time for the meeting and, as he was leading it, we couldn't dawdle. He suggested we get coffee afterwards.

"I have stated that I am an alcoholic," Todd was saying when I channeled him in again. "Are there any other alcoholics present?"

Along with everyone else in the room, I raised my hand, something that came easy to me now, but had been excruciating the first few times I'd been at a meeting.

"The format of this meeting," Todd was saying, "is that the leader shares on a topic of his choice for twenty to thirty minutes and then it's open up questions or comments from the group." He smiled shyly. "Tonight the topic I've chosen is staying serene." The smile flickered, disappeared. "When I had to come up with a topic last week for this meeting, staying serene was the first thing that came into my mind. I didn't know why. Well, yesterday I got the results of my test. It was positive, so I guess I need all the serenity I can get.

"At the end of my drinking," he went on, "I wanted to die. I was trying to kill myself." He smiled. "In slow motion, because I'm a coward like all the rest of you." We laughed. "But when I came into these rooms it was because I had had

171

that moment of clarity where I knew that I wanted to live." He passed his hand above the candle, making the flame flicker. "I am here to live. That's what I thought when the doctor gave me my test results. I am here to live." He looked at me, his eyes bright. "I accept my life. That's how I stay serene. But before we get to the happy ending," he added, "first I get to tell the gory details. How it was, what happened and what it's like now."

An hour passed. After Todd finished, half a dozen others spoke. I wasn't among them. Todd said, "That concludes this meeting. After a moment's silent meditation for the alcoholic who still suffers I'd like," he looked at me, "Henry R. to lead us in the Lord's Prayer."

One did not decline the request. I bowed my head, forming the words silently to make sure I remembered their proper order. Usually I mumbled along without thinking because I was pretty sure if I listened to what I was saying I'd choke on my skepticism.

Someone cleared his voice and I looked up. Todd was smiling at me, waiting.

"Uh, our father," I began and, when other voices joined me, I lapsed into a mutter, grateful to reach "Amen."

"I'm sorry to hear about your test results," I told Todd as we sat over coffee at a restaurant off on Sunset near the gay bookstore he managed.

"I knew it was coming, Henry. My ex died a year ago. PCP." He poured sugar into his coffee. "I was with him five years, drunk or stoned most of the time. Safe sex? What's that." He stirred vigorously. "I'm grateful to be asymptomatic and I'm happy to be alive and sober." He smiled, jaggedly. "Do I sound like Betty Ford, or what? How are you, Henry R.?"

"I'm all right."

He cocked his head, skeptically, "Yeah?"

"Yes," I said, not rudely, but firmly.

"I haven't seen you around lately," he persisted.

"I've been out of town on a case. That's what I wanted to talk to you about."

"As long as you're okay," he said, his dark eyes ironic.

"Would I lie to you, Todd?"

He gave me his best grin, a heart melter. "What drunk doesn't?" He stopped a passing waitress and got us refills. "It's a disease of denial. But okay, we'll do it your way. What do you want to know about John M., or," he added theatrically, "should I say, Howard T.?"

"Howard T.?"

"He called himself both," Todd explained. "He liked mystery. He said he was 'on the lam' and kept hinting about a deep, dark secret."

"Do you know what it was?" I asked. "His secret?"

"He was a schoolteacher and he dicked one of his kids and got caught." He lit a cigarette. "Who knows if it was true."

"Why do you say that?"

"Like I said, he was a total drama queen. He liked the attention."

"Where did this supposedly happen? In LA?"

"Nah. Someplace up north. That's why he was quote on the lam unquote. He said he ran out on probation or something. I kinda lost interest the eighth time I heard it."

On a hunch, I asked, "Was it a place called Los Robles?"

Todd blew out a stream of smoke and shook his head. "No, that wasn't it."

"What was his last name, the one he used when he called himself Howard?"

"I just know 'T,' " Todd said. "We're anonymous, remember?"

"You asked me my last name the first time you met me," I pointed out.

He smiled. "I thought you were single, that's why. I didn't care what Howard T.'s status was. Why are you so interested in him? He's never been able to get more than a little sobriety going. Seems like every time I see him he's taking a thirty-day chip."

"He's dead, Todd. He was murdered two months ago in Los Robles. I've been hired to defend the man who's accused of killing him."

"Jesus," he whispered, visibly shocked. "Who'd want to kill John? He's just a blowhard. He never hurt anyone."

"He did once," I said.

The next morning I was sitting in Freeman's dark little office on Grand Street listening to a bulldozer pound through the walls of a nearby building. I'd just finished telling him about my conversation with Todd.

"I told you those chips were good luck," he said.

I shrugged. "That remains to be seen."

He shook his head. "No satisfying some people. You got," he said, ticking off the points on his bony fingers, "the guy's real name, that he was a teacher, that he screwed around with one of his students, that he got caught, that he was on the run. What else do you want?"

"We have," I replied, "a first name and a last initial. He claimed he was a teacher, but we've just got his word for it, and that he came from somewhere outside of LA, which covers a lot of distance in this state. As for molesting a student, well, it's probably true he molested someone."

"How come you're so skeptical?"

"Because Todd's right," I replied. "Drunks are not the most credible people."

"Well, it's better than nothing."

"Marginally."

"Let's establish some parameters."

I raised an eyebrow. "Some what?"

"Hanging out with lawyers plays hell with my vocabulary," he said. "Let's assume he has a conviction as Howard whatever, for child molest. How long did Windsor know him?"

"Four or five years," I replied.

"So, he was McKay for at least that long. His conviction could be five, ten years old."

I nodded, having done a similar calculation myself. "Maybe

longer," I replied, "but let's say twenty as the outside date."

"He's on somebody's system," Freeman said. "Somebody up north. You know any cops up there who like a challenge?"

I thought for just a second. "As a matter of fact, I do. If she's back from her honeymoon."

She was. I reached Terry Ormes later that day and explained the situation. She said she would do what she could which, from previous experience, I knew meant that she would do everything short of manually searching every child molest complaint filed in the last twenty years in every town and hamlet in the state. As an afterthought, she told me she and Kevin enjoyed Maui, particularly the ride-along with the Honolulu police. Kevin, she said, had almost been inducted into a lineup.

"Sounds romantic," I said. "It makes me want to run right out and marry the first cop I see."

"Listen," she said, "if you and Josh ever break up, there's a real sweet guy in Homicide who'd just love to meet you."

18

On Friday I was back in Los Robles, before Burton K. Phelan, the superior court judge assigned to try *People v. Windsor*, to argue the motion to transfer venue that Peter and I had put together. Entering the courtroom I was surprised to see Peter there, his bulk arranged precariously on the edge of the bailiff's table, talking in to the young Latino bailiff. He called me over.

"Hey, Henry, I want you to meet Eddie Ramirez. Henry's a compadre of yours, Eddie."

"Hello, Eddie," I said, extending a hand.

"Hi, Henry. You know this clown?"

"Eddie knew me when I was a dog-meat DA," Peter said.

"Hey, man, you're gonna break my table," the bailiff replied. A light flickered on his phone. He picked it up, waving us off, and I heard him say, "Yes, Your Honor, the defense lawyers are here . . ."

Moving toward counsel table I asked, "What are you doing here?"

"I busted my ass on this motion," he replied. "You didn't think I was going to miss seeing how it turns out, did you?"

There was already a briefcase at the defense end of the table, with the faded monogram I,-HpbsH,-I worked into the battered leather.

"Besides," he added, as we seated ourselves at the table, "you could use a local in your corner."

"I am a local."

He flicked the bottom of my Ralph Lauren rep tie. "You're too smooth by half, Henry. When I was cite-checking your papers I thought, This guy is thinking two steps ahead, to the Court of Appeal."

"I am."

"Maybe if you backed off a little you could win it here."

"That's unlikely, isn't it? Phelan's the same judge who wouldn't dismiss charges against Paul the last time around."

"So you assume he'll jerk you around this time," Peter said. "And that's how you're going to come on to him, and leave him no choice but to do it."

Stung, I snapped, "Get to the point."

"Think about what you're asking him to do here," Peter said, dropping his voice low as the DA swung through the railing and dumped his briefcase at the other end of the table. "You're saying, There's no way my guy can get a fair trial in this town. Maybe in the city a judge can hear that without taking it personally, but not here. Don't blame the people, Henry. And don't," he whispered urgently, coffee on his breath, "don't even think of blaming the court. Dump on the *Sentinel*. Gordon Wachs isn't a native and the *Sentinel*'s pretty liberal for these parts. Phelan's a very conservative guy. And another thing," he added, "you're going to have to eat some shit. Tell him how reluctant you are to have to bring the motion, how you know the community has a stake in this trial . . ."

"That's going a little too far," I said.

Peter shook his big head. "It's like you said, Phelan thinks Paul weaseled out of the molestation case, and so do a lot of other people. Acknowledge it." He jerked his head toward the DA, who watched us warily. "Don't let Rossi be the one who brings it up. You've got to take the curse off it." He sat back in his chair. "That's the bad news."

"There's good news?" I asked skeptically.

"Yeah," Peter said. "Phelan's been on the bench forever. He doesn't think he has to answer to anyone, except himself. That makes him a little unpredictable. Sometimes he even does the right thing."

"Peter." We both looked toward Rossi, who approached and laid a chummy hand on Stein's shoulder.

"Hey, Dom," Peter said. "How's it going?"

"Just great," he said, looking past Peter to me. "Morning, Henry."

"Morning."

"Peter giving you pointers?" he asked genially.

"Something like that," I replied. "He helped me draft the motion."

He clucked at Peter, "You've really gone over to the other side, pal."

"I wanted to even out the fight," Peter replied.

A buzzer sounded in the room and Rossi scurried back to his side of the table. Behind the bench, a door opened and Burton K. Phelan stepped grimly to his seat, stopped and glared at us. He was tall, well over six feet, and probably in his early sixties. There seemed to be too much flesh for his face and it hung in bags and folds beneath his eyes, at his jowls, under his chin. I found myself staring at his hair; it covered his head haphazardly in splotchy patches of gray and brown. I'd seen that pattern of baldness recently, making out a will for someone with AIDS who had been battling Kaposi's sarcoma. The hair loss was a side effect of chemotherapy.

"He has cancer," I whispered to Peter as we rose to our

feet. He looked at me, startled, but said nothing.

The bailiff was saying, "Department Two of the Los Robles Superior Court is now in session, the Honorable Burton K. Phelan presiding."

"Be seated," Phelan commanded. *"People versus Windsor.* Is the defendant in court?"

It had occurred to me that it might not be a good idea to have Paul unnecessarily facing his old nemesis. I stood up. "Your Honor, Henry Rios for the defendant who waives his presence for his proceeding."

Peter was suddenly standing beside me, "And Peter Stein, for the defendant, Your Honor."

Phelan looked puzzled. "I see no association of counsel, Mr. Stein."

"I apologize," Peter said. "I haven't filed it yet, but I don't plan to argue."

Grumpily, Phelan said, "Very well. Your appearance is noted but file the association before the end of the day."

"Yes, sir," Peter said, sitting down.

I sat down bedside him and whispered, "Does Clayton know about this?"

He smiled his round, fat man's smile. "Fuck Clayton."

". . . Rossi for the People, Your Honor," Rossi was saying.

On the bench, Phelan folded his hands beneath his chin and looked at me. "The defendant has filed a motion to transfer venue and I have read and considered both the defendant's points and authorities and those of the People. I will hear Mr. Rios."

Rising again, I pressed my fingers against the edge of the table to keep them from quivering. It used to bother me that I could still get nervous in court but I'd come to see that it was only because I still believed that what I did here mattered.

Despite the day-to-day cynicism of criminal practice, the casual epithets with which the most horrifying behavior is described and the popular belief that trials are a game, for me a courtroom is a place of serious purpose. If I ever really thought otherwise, it would be time to find another line of work.

"Your Honor," I began, "I won't repeat the legal argument which I have set forth in papers. Instead, I want to reduce this motion to its barest elements." I paused and looked down. My fingertips were white. "Paul Windsor is no stranger to this court." Rossi stirred at his end of the table. "Several years ago he was accused of a very serious crime. The truth or falsity of the allegations against him were matters of grave interest not only to Mr. Windsor and his family, but to the entire community." I looked at Phelan, who looked back, curious. "As Your Honor knows, that matter never went to trial." His mouth a grim line, Phelan nodded. "It's perfectly understandable that there was some dissatisfaction in this community with how that case was resolved but, Your Honor—" I raised my voice, slightly "—the point that I want to make is that it was resolved."

Phelan rumbled, "You're not suggesting, are you, that that dismissal was the same as an acquittal?"

"Absolutely not, sir. It was neither an acquittal nor a conviction, but it was a disposition and a perfectly lawful one." I considered my next few words carefully. "And I think it's fair to say that once the case was dismissed the legal system had no further claim on Paul Windsor on those charges."

Sotto voce, Peter whispered, "Cool it."

"It's my opinion," Phelan said, "that the legal system worked pretty poorly in that case."

"Yes, I understand that," I said, "and I understand that many, many people hold the same opinion, but again, the system ran its course in that case. Now, Paul Windsor is accused of a different crime, equally serious, but it isn't the charge that this court dismissed, however reluctantly, three years ago."

I lifted my hand from the table and gestured toward him. "I have no doubt at all that this court understands that and could give Mr. Windsor a fair trial. Also I have no doubt that, given half a chance, the people of this community could also be fair. But the point of our motion today is that the people have not been given half a chance." I raised my voice again. "Paul Windsor had been tried and found guilty on the pages of the *Los Robles Sentinel*. But my client is not guilty, Your Honor. My client is presumed innocent." Walking toward the end of the table, I continued, "Now, Your Honor, over the years I've been in practice it's been my observation that the press has little understanding, and, too often, no regard, for what the presumption of innocence means. It's been my observation that the press treats presumption of innocence like small print at the bottom of a contract, as something of no importance. But we know differently." I met Phelan's scowl and continued. "We tell prospective jurors at the beginning of every trial that they must presume a defendant innocent and that if they have the slightest reservation about that, then they cannot serve. We tell them that because we know that the whole system of criminal justice is based upon that presumption."

I eased up a little. "Now I don't pretend that potential jurors aren't biased against criminal defendants. If the police have gone to the trouble of arresting someone for a crime and the prosecutor has gone to the trouble of charging him, it's only natural for a potential juror to think there's something to it. But that doesn't invalidate the presumption of innocence. On the contrary, it makes it all the more vital because it's the only way we have to try to neutralize that natural bias and give the defendant a fighting chance. But in this case, Your Honor, my client doesn't have a chance." I reached into my briefcase and pulled out a stack of *Sentinel*s and read selected passages from a half-dozen stories. When I'd finished, I said, "Even I would have a hard time judging my client objectively after this kind of reporting."

To my surprise, Phelan nodded, but then he said, "Mr. Rios, even if I agree that the press has treated your client unfairly, what makes him different from other defendents the media gets its hands on?"

I saw my opening. "I'll tell you, Your Honor. What makes it different is the reason that my client has been tried on the front page of the only newspaper of general circulation in this county. It has nothing to do with his innocence or guilt. The reason is that the paper has a political position to push, banning new development in the city, which can be furthered by embarrassing the Windsor family. I don't think that the merits of any political controversy should be decided on the back of a criminal defendant. It just isn't right. And I am truly sorry that the *Sentinel*, and other members of the media, have made it impossible to give Paul Windsor a fair trial in this town because we would like nothing better. But it is impossible and that's why we're asking you to grant our motion."

I sat down. "Too much silk?" I whispered to Peter.

"Just enough," he whispered back.

The judge looked over at Rossi. "Counsel?"

"Your Honor," Rossi said, getting to his feet. "Paul Windsor is entitled to a jury by his peers but he doesn't want to face his peers. That's the only reason for this motion. He knows he's guilty and he'd rather take his chances somewhere else . . ."

"Mr. Rossi," Phelan rasped, "if the state has the evidence to prove the man's guilty, it doesn't matter whether he's tried here or in Timbuktu. That's not what we're about here. We're talking about whether he can get twelve impartial jurors. Or are you telling me," he said, eyes narrowing, "that the prosecution's case is so thin you need a biased jury to convict the man?"

"Absolutely not," Rossi yelped. "But look, Judge, there's a quarter-million people in this county. The defendant can't tell me every last one of them is prejudiced against him."

"He doesn't have to," Phelan snapped. "He just has to convince me that the press has fixed it so that there's a reasonable probability of prejudice. Address that point and maybe we'll get somewhere."

And so it went. Rossi would get in a couple of sentences

and then Phelan would interrupt with a question or comment. These got sharper as the DA, who was obviously unprepared for this reception, muddled through defensively. For the first time in this case I felt hopeful. Phelan was clearly not going along and Rossi was panicking. Finally, he concluded his argument and sat down, breathing hard.

Phelan rubbed his eyes. "Submitted?" he barked.

"Submitted," I said.

Rossi echoed, "Submitted."

"This is a complicated motion," Phelan said. "And I have to tell you both, it's very close. Very close. I'm taking it under submission until further notice."

"Your Honor, the defense has applied for bail," I began.

Phelan looked at me sourly. "Denied, for now. You'll get my ruling within a week. Court will stand in recess."

Abruptly, he stood up and got off the bench, leaving us half-rising.

I sat back down and turned to Peter. "What did you mean when you said Clayton could fuck himself?"

With studied nonchalance, he said, "That memo I told you, how Clayton said I wasn't working out? He gave me notice this morning. Three weeks."

"I'm sorry, Peter."

He shrugged. "It's the best thing that could've happened to me."

"Good job, Henry," Dom Rossi said from the other end of the table.

"Thanks, you, too."

He grimaced and looked away.

To Peter, I said, "What will you do now?"

"Hang my shingle, I guess."

"Why don't you come in on this case, officially, I mean."

He smiled, "I thought you'd never ask. By the way," he said, handing me my stack of *Sentinel*s, "the feds have begun their audit of Pioneer. You may have another Windsor client before long."

"When did all this happen?"

"Last week, sometime. Why, you seen Mark?"

I nodded. "Yeah, but I didn't talk to him."

"Going back to the office?" Peter asked.

"No, I have to track down a witness," I replied. "Ruth Soto."

19

I stepped out of the courthouse into the mid-September heat. An acrid vapor of smoke hung in the air, the result of the annual burning of rice fields outside the city. Combined with the continuing heat, the sour, sooty air made the city unbearable, as bad as the worst days of smog in LA. But soon, around the beginning of October, the heat would break, the air clear and the temperature drop for the brief season of autumn that preceded the long winter rains. With any luck, I would be long gone by then, trying this case in San Francisco.

I drove to Paradise Slough, rehearsing yet another little speech about justice and morality to persuade Ruth Soto to testify on Paul's behalf. I hadn't called her while I was in LA and I hoped the respite had given her time to do some serious thinking. More and more, I saw that she was Paul's best chance at acquittal. She wasn't the typical alibi witness, a friend or family member of the defendant whom a jury could assume had a reason to lie. Nor was her testimony the usual alibi testimony. She wouldn't claim to have been with Paul when McKay was murdered. Her testimony was far more devastating because it shifted the focus from Paul to the cops, which was exactly where it had to be if I was going to undermine the evidence they'd gathered against him. That might not play so well in Los Robles but in a big city like San Francisco, cops weren't revered in the same way.

I pulled up in front of her house and went to the door. I knocked and waited for a couple of minutes, then knocked again. Finally, the door opened and Mrs. Soto frowned at me.

"*Puedo hablar con Ruth?*" I asked.

"*Ya se fui,*" she said sharply. Her tone suggested that Ruth had gone for more than the afternoon.

"*Adonde?*"

"*Para ver su hermana,*" she replied.

"My sister," I said in English. "When?"

"*Hace tres dias, señor,*" she said, closing the door. "*Buscala allá.*"

"Thank you," I mumbled.

Back at the hotel I called my sister and got an answering machine, again. I asked Elena to call me and hung up, speculating on Ruth's sudden decision to visit Oakland. Before I could get too far in my speculations the phone rang. I grabbed it.

Terry Ormes said, "I have some news for you."

"About Howard T.?" I asked, reaching for a legal pad.

"Howard Thurmond," she replied. "T-h-u-r-m-o-n-d," she added with typical thoroughness. "He was convicted of PC 288 thirteen years ago here in the city. Sentenced to two years at Folsom, did ten months, came back here and then moved to LA about eight years ago."

Penal code section 288 was lewd conduct with a child fourteen years of age or younger, an offense that required the convicted defendant to register with the local department as a sex offender. "Was he registered with LAPD?"

"Come on, Henry," she said. "Why do you think he moved in the first place and changed his name?"

"Point taken. What about a superior court case number?" I asked.

She rattled off a number while I scribbled. "Wait," she said. "That's funny, there's another one." She read it to me. "I wonder why that is?"

I looked at the two numbers. Each had seven digits, but one began with the letter A while the other began with the letter R. "What are you reading from, a rap sheet?"

"Yeah, a CII printout," she replied, referring to the statewide criminal computer network.

"Who was the arresting agency? San Francisco?"

She grunted. "How could I be so dumb? It's not us, it's something listed as WCSO. Look, let me run down abbreviations for police departments statewide and call you back."

"It might be faster if I could get a look at the court file. Let me call Kevin. Is he in the office or in court?"

"At the office, I think," she replied. "In the meantime, I'll check out that abbreviation."

"Henry," Kevin said when I reached him at his office, "where are you calling from?"

"Los Robles," I said.

"Terry said you had a case up there. What a pit."

"It's my hometown," I replied.

"Well wipe the cow shit off your shoes next time you come to visit. What's going on?"

"I need a favor."

"Yeah, go ahead."

"I wonder if you could drop by the superior court clerk's office and take a look at a case file for me. It's an ancient 288 conviction. I'd like a copy of the complaint and the police report."

"I can't get to it until morning. That okay?"
"Yeah."
"What's the case number?"
I read him both numbers.
"Two numbers," he said. "So it came from someplace else?"
I looked at the numbers, feeling a little stupid. "Why didn't I figure that out?" I said. "Which one is San Francisco, the A number, right?"
"Right."
"Any guesses on the R-number?" I asked.
"LA?"
"No," I said, "they use G. What about Oakland, the East Bay courts?"
"F," he said. "Well, shit, Henry, there are fifty-eight counties in California and we could be here all night trying to figure out which one it is. Let me check it out in the morning and get back to you."
"Thanks, Kev."
After hanging up, I went to my breifcase, took out the complaint against Paul and looked at the case number. It started with the letter *S*. Thurmond's case had not been filed in Los Robles.

I tried Elena and got the machine again. I left another message and dialed Clayton's office to check if I'd had any calls there. Someone knocked. Putting the phone down, I shouted, "Come in."

Ben Vega pushed the door open slowly and slipped into the room. "Hello, Henry," he said.

"Hello, Ben."

He closed the door behind him and stood doubtfully at the edge of the room.

"Have a seat," I said. "You on your way to work?"

He shook his head. "It's my day off." He walked over to the window. "You got a nice view from here. I can see the river."

"You want something to drink?" I asked, picking up the phone to call room service.

He shook his head quickly. "I don't want nobody to know I came up here."

"Okay," I said, hanging up. "Why did you come here?"

He sat down at the bed. "To tell you that you're wrong about Morrow."

"How would you know that?"

"After what you said about those pictures, I decided to look around."

"Look around where?" I asked.

"His locker, to begin with," Ben said. "His truck. His apartment. He's clean."

"How did you get into those places?"

"I told you, Morrow's my compadre." His tone became hostile. "There ain't no other film."

"Did you really expect to find it, if it existed? Morrow's not going to keep something like that lying around."

"Goddammit, you don't know him," Ben said fiercely. "You're calling him a thief and a liar and it's not true."

Calmly, I replied, "I have a witness who can testify that Paul Windsor shot a roll of film three days before you found the film in his car."

"What witness?" he demanded. "Let me talk to her."

"Her? How do you know it's a her?"

For a second he was flustered, but then he said. "It's his wife, huh? That's your witness."

"No," I said. "It's not his wife." I looked at him. "And you didn't mean his wife, did you?"

Abruptly, he stood up and took a couple of steps toward me. "Don't run that bullshit about Morrow at the trial."

"Are you threatening me, Ben?"

He shook his head. "He's good people, Henry. A hell of a lot better than that rich fucker you're working for." He backed off a step. "You grew up here," he said. "You're Mexican. What did those people in River Park ever do for you? You're one of us, Henry. We gotta stick together."

"It's not that simple, Ben."

"Don't be a traitor, man. Don't be a fucking *bolino*."

I hadn't heard that expression in years, the Spanish word for coconut, brown on the outside, white on the inside; it was the local equivalent to Oreo, the word that blacks used to describe a brother or sister who'd sold out.

"I don't pick my clients by the color of their skin," I replied, stiffly. "I don't think Paul Windsor killed McKay. I think someone set him up, and I think it was Morrow. And that's what I'm going to try to prove."

"Man, you're disgusting," he said, in a tone of disbelief. "But I shoulda known about you when I saw that kid in here. You're just like Windsor. A fucking queer."

I shook my head. "Paul's straight."

Ben snorted, turned on his heel and strode out of the room, slamming the door behind him. I got up and locked it.

Lying on the bed later I played the scene with Ben through my head. How much had been planned and how much improvised was hard to tell but it was obvious that the purpose of his visit wasn't to clear Morrow but to persuade me to ease up on him. That removed the last doubt I had over whether Morrow had switched the film. I'd already figured out how he'd developed the film that Vega took from Paul's car. The solution had come to me over the weekend, in LA. Josh had sent me on an errand to pick up some pictures he'd taken at a friend's birthday party. They'd been developed at a place that boasted one-hour service.

Morrow would've had just enough time to find someplace like that in Los Robles, have the film developed, see it consisted of pictures of Ruth and substitute another roll of film, filched from a file in Sex Crimes, his last assignment before Homicide. I was sure that a check among photo labs in the area would uncover someone who remembered Morrow bringing the film in, but I was saving this for trial.

If there was a trial. Morrow was getting nervous, sending Ben to see me. Nervous enough to do something stupid, maybe. Or maybe he already had. Ben had slipped when he referred to my witness as "her." I knew, and he knew, that he didn't mean Sara. The more I thought about it, the clearer it seemed that he and Morrow had figured out that I'd talked to Ruth. It fit with her sudden disappearance. She'd been warned off, or threatened.

Reaching to the night table I switched on the light and looked at my watch. A little after one. I sat up and pulled the phone over, dialing Elena's number. I got the same damned answering machine on which I'd already left two unanswered messages. Apparently, Elena was screening her calls. This fit, too. I left another message, telling her that it was urgent that I speak to Ruth.

A few minutes later, the phone rang. I picked it up, expecting Elena at the other end.

"Mr. Rios?" It was an unfamiliar male voice.

"Yeah."

"This is Don at the desk downstairs," he said it on a rising inflection, as if he had some question about his own identity. "I'm sorry to bother you but someone just called you when you were on the phone. He said it was urgent. Mark Windsor?"

"Did he say what he wanted?" I asked sitting up in bed.

"Just that it was urgent. He left a number."

"What is it?"

Don, at the desk, enunciated the number slowly. I immediately recognized it as Sara's.

"Are you sure it was Mark Windsor?" I asked. "Not Sara?"

"It was a guy," Don said, "and that was the number he left. Do you want me to call?"

"Please."

The phone rang twice at the other end before someone picked it up. "Callahan."

"I'm sorry," I said, in a complete fog, now. "I'm trying to reach Mark Windsor."

"Yeah," he said and I heard a thump as the receiver hit a hard surface. There were a lot of voices in the background. My first thought was that there was some kind of party going on, but that seemed bizarre. More thumps and then someone else, Mark, said, "Hello."

"Mark, this is Henry Rios. What the hell's going on?"

With preternatural calm he said, "Sara's dead, Henry. Could you come here, please?"

20

I hadn't really noticed the pool before, but then I hadn't ever ventured much beyond the rose garden and had no idea of how extensive the grounds were behind the house. The pool was east of the roses, where the yard descended. All that was visible from the back of the house was the arched wall that ran along the poolside. Between the arches and the water was a cobblestone terrace furnished with wrought-iron lawn chairs and tables painted white. One of the chairs had been upturned. An almost empty bottle of Sauvignon Blanc, the glass still sweating, stood on a tabletop. The wineglass from which the wine had been drunk lay at the bottom of the pool, not far, Mark was telling me, from where they'd recovered Sara's body.

The lights beneath the water illuminated its still depths. The body had been removed and everyone was gone now, or leaving—the cops, the paramedics, the neighbor whose sleep Sara had disturbed for the last time. She, the neighbor, had heard a scream and shouting but had not been able to make out any words. The noise had frightened her into calling the police. When they arrived, they found the doors locked, the house undisturbed and Sara Windsor at the bottom of the pool. They'd come to the unremarkable conclusion that she'd drunkenly fallen into the water, become disoriented and drowned.

"Why out here?" I asked, standing at the edge of the pool, near where the cobblestones were still drenched.

Mark tossed the match he'd used to light his cigarette and shrugged. "Who knows. She was drunk. When she was drunk, she wandered."

I looked back at him, where he stood between two arches, the moon fading at his back, and noticed he was wearing his high-school letter jacket, blue and white, the big I,-HIrH,-I stitched into one side. For a moment, in the shadowy light, he could have been sixteen again, but then he moved and the illusion was destroyed. He looked a sleepless, puffy thirty-odd, the same as me.

"Paul know?" I asked, approaching him.

He shook his head. "I'll go see him tomorrow."

"You want me to come with you?"

"Thanks, but I think I should go by myself." He yawned. "Listen, I could use a drink. What about you?"

"Some coffee, maybe."

"Let's go inside. It's cold out here."

He was right. A thin vapor drifted off the surface of the water and I felt the autumn damp through my shirt. We made our way back to the house and into the kitchen. He set about fixing coffee while I sat at the table watching him, piling up the day's events in my head; Ruth's disappearance, Ben's visit to me, Sara's death. Two of the three I was pretty sure were related. Although I couldn't fit Sara into the equation, I couldn't add it up without her.

Pouring two cups of coffee, Mark said, over his shoulder, "You take anything in it?"

"Black."

He excused himself and left the room, returning a moment later with a bottle of Jameson. He poured some into his cup and brought both cups to the table, setting them down delicately. He pulled out a chair and sat down. Closing tired eyes, he took a drink.

He shuddered, drank some more and reached back to the counter for the bottle. Pouring another slug into his cup, he glanced at me and said, "I've got a taste for the stuff, too. Not as bad as Sara though."

"No one starts out a drunk," I replied.

"That why you stopped?" he asked.

"Yeah. It got out of control."

He smiled, wanly. "I can't imagine you ever out of control, Hank."

Remembering the last time I'd detoxed, I said, "Trust me. This is good, Mark."

"Coffee and fried egg sandwiches," Mark said. "The Mark Windsor cookbook. You cook?"

"Sometimes." We settled into an awkward silence.

"Sara could be a real bitch," Mark said abruptly, his eyes darkening, "but I couldn't blame her, not after what she went through with Paul. It's to her credit that she stayed with him."

Cynically, I said, "For the money?"

He smiled sourly. "You wouldn't ask if you'd ever been through a divorce."

"Well, from what I saw of her and Paul, money sounds more probable than love."

He brooded over his cup. "You never seem to love the people you're supposed to." He ran a fingertip around the rim of his cup. "Like with Paul. He's my brother, but I've never loved him. Or my dad." He pushed his cup back and forth. "That's not true. I did love my dad, even if he was an asshole, even if he couldn't care less for me."

"What is it about Paul that you despise so much?" I asked. "That he didn't stand up to your father? It's not his fault he wasn't as strong as you. He was just a kid, Mark."

He worked the muscles in his face. "I need another drink for this," he said, finally, and filled his cup. "There was just the four of us." He sipped the whiskey. "There wasn't anyone else to talk to except Paul about what used to happen. Like the time Mom got so drunk at dinner she threw up and Dad made us sit there and keep on eating, like nothing had happened. I had to count on Paul." He took another drink, and when he spoke again, his voice had thickened. "But Paul was worse than them. They were just pretending nothing was wrong. Paul really believed it. Really." He looked at me, his eyes like flares. "I think he made himself kind of crazy so that he didn't have to deal with it. And that left me alone."

My first thought was that self-pity seemed to run deep in the Windsor sons, but then I thought of Elena and me. The only difference between the children of the Rioses and the Windsors was the dimension of our isolation from each other.

"Except you," Mark muttered. "There was you, too. You don't have to believe this," he said, "but when I heard you were back in town, I was really happy. It had been too long."

"I wrote you once," I said. I would have sounded less like the offended lover had I not been as tired as I was. But then again, it was an exhausting conversation, after all these years. For Mark, too. He was white with fatigue.

"Yeah, I still have that letter somewhere," he said. "Telling me you were queer." He clenched his fingers around the handle of the cup. Angrily, he asked, "What did you want me to do? Send you flowers? Tell you it didn't make any difference? It sure as hell did, Hank. I trusted you, man, and you . . . I'm not that way, not like you."

"You think all I wanted was to fuck you?"

For a second, he recoiled from me. Then, in a low, furious voice, he said, "You said in that letter that you loved me. What else was I supposed to think?"

"I did love you," I said just as angrily. "I counted on you the same way you counted on Paul, to understand me." I watched him trying to work it out in his head, and plunged on, having waited twenty years for this moment. "It wasn't about sex. Well," I relented. It was urgent that I be honest. "Not mainly about sex. I could have lived with you saying no to sex. But when you didn't answer, you said no to everything, to being friends, to the only happiness I had ever had."

"That's how I felt when I got that letter," Mark said, not yielding an inch to my anger. "I already knew I was a freak, Henry, growing up in that house. Being your friend was the most normal thing I ever did, but that letter changed it."

"Well, what the hell did you feel for me?"

The question caught him off guard and I watched the anger evaporate from his expression. Finally, he said, "You were my brother."

"Don't brothers love each other?"

"Jesus," he muttered, but I couldn't tell whether the tone was revelation or resignation.

"Don't they?" I asked again, quietly.

Setting his hand on the table, he nodded. "I loved you," he said.

The sourness in my mouth wasn't the coffee or lack of sleep. And it sure as hell wasn't victory. It was the twenty years' worth of regret. "Do you have any more cigarettes?"

"Sure," he said, surprised. He fumbled in his coat pocket for his pack of Winstons, took two out, handed me one and lit them. "I thought you didn't smoke."

"Not since law school," I replied, tasting the acrid smoke.

We smoked in silence for a few minutes. I thought about Sara, whom I'd completely forgotten about for the past half-hour. Yet it was only the proximity of death, her death, that let Mark and me say these things to each other.

"I think I understand now," he said, finally.

"Good. I'm glad."

He put out his cigarette in his coffee cup. "I'm broke, Hank, and I'm probably going to go to jail."

"I know," I said. "Stein told me. He read some memo in Clayton's office."

He yawned. "Well, at least I won't have to worry about how I stand with you."

"I'll represent you, if you want."

He got up from the table. "Thanks, but I don't think I'm going to be able to afford you."

"I didn't say I'd charge you."

He patted my shoulder. "I'm proud of you, Hank, have I told you that?" He yawned. "I guess we should clear out."

"I'd better drive you home."

"No," he said. "I'll walk. It's not far and it'll sober me up. What time is it, anyway?"

I glanced at my watch. "Almost five."

"Geez, if I was twenty years younger or just a little drunker, I'd go out for a run."

We locked up the house and he walked me to my car. The sky was turning smoke gray as the first light of day edged slowly along the horizon and the air was fresh and damp. Good running weather.

"See you," he said.

"Mark, what did you want to talk to me about the other night at the Hyatt?"

"Nothing that I didn't tell you tonight," he replied. " 'Bye."

"See you."

He walked up the street with a drunkard's fragile gait, whistling tunelessly, and I didn't think I'd be getting that call from him when the time came. He'd made his way through life alone and he'd see it through alone, not taking handouts, not trading on an old friendship. Maybe he was just a garden-variety neurotic and no doubt he'd hurt a lot of people to build the business that was now collapsing around him. Still, I had loved so infrequently I felt a debt to those whom I had, for the reprieve from solitude. It was the weight of what I owed that I felt as I watched him round the corner.

The phone woke me at noon. Reaching blindly, I knocked the receiver to the floor and fumbled with it. I pressed the cool plastic to my ear and shut my eyes against the glare from the windows.

"Yeah," I managed.

"Catch you at a bad time, sport?"

"Was asleep, Kev."

"Is that cow town in a different time zone or did you have a rough night?"

"My client's wife drowned last night," I said.

"Ah." He paused. "Have you figured out how you're going to get it into evidence?"

"Don't be an asshole," I replied, awakening. "You're calling about the file, I assume. Did you have a chance to look at it?"

"Couldn't do it, old man. The record was ordered sealed."

I sat up. "Why?"

"My guess is that it was to protect the identity of the victim."

Yes, that would make sense since the victim was a minor. "How quickly could we get a court order to unseal it?"

"Well," he said, slowly, "if I went in ex parte today we might get a hearing in a week."

"Too long. You have any chips you can cash in with a judge down there? How about the one that married you?"

"Frances Flynn?" he asked on a note of rising incredulousness. "You don't know what you're asking me to do."

"It's really important. There are some very heavy things going on in this case, including this woman's death last night. I need to see that file."

"Well, you know your business," he said. "I might be able to get us on calendar tomorrow afternoon, but I'd just as soon that you came down and handled it."

"Sure, I have to go to Oakland anyway."

"No one has to go to Oakland," he replied. "Let me see what I can do and I'll call you back."

"Thanks," I said.

I threw back the covers and got out of bed, wandering through the room, waking myself. When my head cleared I ordered up a pot of coffee and prepared myself for the task of going to see Paul.

Mark had already been by, but even before then Paul had known about Sara's death. One of the cops at the scene had called the jail. Paul had been awakened at three and told that his old lady had killed herself. It was evident from the way he looked that he hadn't slept after that. He sat across the table from me, unshaven and disheveled. His eyes were manic but he spoke without affect. In his exhaustion I saw, for the first time, the family resemblance to Mark.

"You don't know it was suicide," I said, for the third or fourth time, but he remained unpersuaded. "It could have been an accident." I wasn't really convinced of this myself, but it was dangerous to fuel either his guilt or his paranoia.

"How do you know, you weren't there when it happened."

"Paul, I talked to her last week. She seemed fine."

"You don't understand what I put her through, what I took away from her. She didn't have any friends. She didn't have any life. Just the booze."

I shook my head. "Will you stop feeling sorry for yourself?"

He bristled, but said nothing.

"You're not God, Paul," I continued. "You don't control other people. You don't give them reasons to live or reasons to die. Sara was tough, she'd survived a lot, you know that better than I do. Don't take that away from her."

Raggedly, he began to cry. His hand strained across the table for mine and clutched my wrist. "You don't know."

"Didn't you hear me?"

"She hated me," he said, looking up red-eyed. "She wanted to hurt me."

I pulled my hand away. "Don't you ever think about anyone else, Paul?"

He wiped his face on his sleeve. "You don't understand me."

"I guess you're right," I said. "Your wife's dead and you're crying for yourself. I don't understand."

"I've suffered," he said, bitterly. "You don't know what it was like when I was a kid."

"I've heard it from Mark," I replied. "It was rough. I sympathize but you're thirty-two years old, Paul. You're too old to be blaming Mom and Dad."

"Fuck you. What do you know about my parents?"

"Mark said—"

"I fucked her, Henry," he yelled. "She made me."

"What are you talking about?"

"She was a drunken slut. I was so happy when she died. I thought she took the feelings with her, but then I met Ruth."

"Who are you talking about?"

"My mother," he whispered. "My mother."

21

Paul said, "I'd just come in from the pool and I heard her banging around the house, drunk as usual. No one else was home, maybe the maid was there, I don't know. I heard her talking to herself outside my room and then she came in, carrying a can of my dad's talc." For a moment he talked about his father, but circled back and continued. "I was standing there in my bathing suit and she started shaking the powder all over me. In my eyes. I couldn't see. Saying crazy stuff. 'My baby,' that's what she said. My baby."

He interrupted himself again. "I never told anyone this. Well, Sara. I told Sara." He started crying again. "I pushed her away but she kept on coming. Then I was on the bed and she was rubbing me. She was laying on top of me. She stank. Her hair, her skin. She didn't clean herself when she was drinking. Jesus, Henry, say something."

"I'm sorry, Paul. I'm sorry that it happened."

"She got her hand down into my bathing suit. Squeezing my balls until I wanted to scream." He rubbed the side of his neck, inflaming the skin. "She started jerking me off. She stuck her tongue in my mouth, it tasted like gin. That was her drink." He paused in his rubbing. "Sara liked gin, too. Just like Mom. 'Get me G and T while you're up, Herb.' That was Mom's motto."

"You don't have to tell me any more," I said.

"I want to! She was kissing me, she was jerking me off. Look, I was thirteen, you know. I walked around with a hard-on." His breathing was quick and nervous. "It began to feel pretty good. I pulled down my bathing suit." He glanced at me and then looked away. "Make it easier for her."

"You must have been terrified."

He nodded. "I flashed between that and, well, the physical sensation. How the hell else was I supposed to react with someone jerking me off?"

"I understand, Paul."

"Do you?" he asked bitterly. "She lifted her dress up and she . . . I couldn't believe what was happening. It was like being swallowed. And then I came. She didn't come. Not that time."

"It happened again?"

He calmed himself. "Off and on, until I went to college. She was always drunk. In blackouts."

"Always?"

He shrugged. "Well, we never talked about it."

"Have you ever thought of getting help?"

"When it was over, it was over," he said.

"What about Ruth?"

"Yeah, I know. I've read the goddamned literature, Henry. I know all about pedophiles. I know all about how it works. Well, believe me, it's not that simple. I wasn't passing on what my mother taught me. My feelings for Ruth were real."

"But you must know there's a connection."

"What am I supposed to do, just say no?" He got up. "Hate myself? Kill myself? Fuck that."

"Get help," I replied.

"Thanks," he said, moving toward the door. "Thanks a lot."

Back at the hotel there was a message from Kevin.

"What's going on?" I asked when I'd been put through to him.

There was a moment's pause. "You sound worse than you did this morning, pal."

"It's been a long day."

"We're on the one-thirty calendar at Judge Flynn's court tomorrow," he said. "On your motion to unseal the records. I put one together pretty fast. What I said was that it might reveal evidence material to the case you're on now. Does that sound about right?"

"Yeah." Outside, dusk gathered in the sky. The thought of another night in Los Robles was unbearable. "Listen, if I drive down to the city tonight can you and Terry put me up?"

"Sure. What time will you be in?"

"If I leave right away I should be there by eight."

"Sounds good. You sure you're all right?"

"Yeah. I'll see you in a couple of hours."

I hung up, stared at the phone for a minute, and then dialed my number in LA. It rang twice and then Josh picked it up.

"Hi," I said.

"Hi, I was thinking about calling you."

It felt awkward to be talking to him, having so much going on without any coherent way of saying it. "Sara Windsor was killed last night."

"What happened?"

"Cops think she got drunk and fell into the pool."

"You don't."

Wearily I said, "I don't know what I think. I just wanted to hear your voice."

"Henry." His voice was low with worry. "Are you okay?"

"I miss you."

"I think I should come up there."

"In a couple of days, maybe. I have to go to San Francisco tonight. And to Oakland. I'm not sure when I'll be back."

"Do you always have to carry everything by yourself?"

"I'm trying not to. That's why I called."

"Call me tomorrow, okay?"

"I promise."

I pulled into the driveway at Terry's house on Noe and parked. I'd no sooner gotten my bag out of the trunk than I heard the door opened and looked up to see Kevin at the top of the stairs, wineglass in hand, still in his suit, but barefoot.

"Howdy, you need a hand?"

I made my way up the stairs, shaking my head. "You just get home?"

"Yep. Terry's meeting us at the restaurant." He moved aside to let me pass. I put my bag down in the hall. "You want a Coke or something?"

"Coffee?"

"There's some left from this morning. Come on up."

I followed him into the kitchen. A French door led outside to a deck that overlooked China Basin.

"Our reservation's not till nine," he explained, pouring me a mug of coffee. "Come outside."

I followed him out to the patio and watched him roll a joint on the railing. He lit it and inhaled.

"Too bad you've given up intoxicants," he wheezed. "I brought this back from Maui."

"Does Terry . . ."

He exhaled. "Nope. She leaves the room when I light up." He shrugged. "You look like you had a hard day, Henry."

"I heard a pretty scary story this morning."

He took another hit and nodded. "Yeah? I like scary stories."

"My client was raped by his mother."

He lifted an eyebrow. "That's what I like about this business. If you stick around long enough, you'll hear everything."

"Sometimes I can't believe what people do to each other."

"Believe it," he said. "There's nothing that hasn't been done by someone to someone. People settling scores is what keeps us in business."

I nodded. "Maybe that's why the cops have fabricated evidence against my client."

"That only happens on *L.A. Law*," he replied, and took another toke from the joint.

"Come on, Kev, it happens every day. You get a cop on the stand in a supression motion after your client's just finished telling you they broke down the door and held him at gunpoint and you ask, 'Now Officer Jones, isn't it true that you broke down the door' and what's he going to do, admit it? No, he'll say 'We knocked and the defendant let us in.' They know who the judge is going to believe."

"That's different from making up evidence. Isn't that what you mean by fabricating?"

"It's only different in degree." I watched a brightly lit ship make its way up the bay. "It's just a matter of what they think they can get away with. In a small town like Los Robles where everyone's tight, they can get away with a lot."

"Why did they do it?"

"A few years ago my client was charged with child molest. The case was dismissed because the victim wouldn't testify. The same cop and the same DA on that case are on the murder case. Maybe they're trying to administer some rough justice."

He put out the joint and tossed the roach into the tangled garden below the deck. "I hope you have a fallback position."

"That's why I want a look at that file tomorrow."

"Terry says the case is fifteen years old," Kevin replied. "What do you expect to find?"

"I don't know."

"Good luck, compadre. We better get going."

We walked down to the restaurant on Twenty-Fourth Street, an Italian place that you could smell a block away. Terry was already at the table, briskly examining a menu when we came in.

"Ten minutes late," she said, without looking up.

"You know how long it takes guys to get ready to go out," Kevin said, kissing her cheek.

She said, "I ran down the arresting agency on Thurmond's rap sheet, Henry."

"What did you find?"

She dug around in her purse and came up with a computer printout. "There's four possibilities."

I took the paper and examined it. West Covina Sheriff's Office. Westminister Sheriff's Office. West Valley Sheriff's Office. All these agencies were in the LA area, but then I saw the final entry—Woodlin County Sheriff's Office.

"This one," I said, pointing at it. "Definitely."

Kevin glanced down. "Where's Woodlin County?"

"Right next door to Los Robles County," I replied.

The next morning I drove to my sister's house. Coming up the winding road, I saw that it had changed since I'd last been there two months earlier. The leaves were turning colors, and the road was dustier. Only a few roses remained along the road, stray petals hanging tenuously from the buds. I crossed the small bridge to Elena's yard and was surprised to find her car parked there. I'd assumed she'd be teaching.

I went to the door, pushed the bell, listening to the rainy chime within, and waited. After a moment, the door opened and Elena frowned, seeing who it was.

"I have to talk to Ruth," I said.

"She isn't here."

"She is here, Elena," I replied, wedging my foot in the door. "This is important."

She looked down at my foot disdainfully. "Don't make a scene. Just go."

I played my trump card. "Sara Windsor is dead."

She jerked her head up. "That's a vicious thing to say."

"It's the truth."

She looked at me for a long time. Slowly, she opened the door. "Come in."

I followed her inside. The cool, austere living room was

flooded with morning light. On the floor, near the coffee table, were toy trucks. On the couch was an open book, face-down. I glanced at the title, *Selected Poems* by Elizabeth Bishop. Next to it was a yellow legal tablet, the top sheet filled with small, precise script, and a black enameled pen.

"Sit down," she said. In the hard light her face was puckered with deep lines and the gray in her hair seemed white. "What happened?"

"I need to talk to Ruth."

She drew her lips into a line of contempt. "Don't bargain with me."

"I don't see that I have any choice."

"She's out, with Joanne. They should be back soon. You can talk to her then. Now tell me about Sara."

"Two nights ago she drowned in her swimming pool. The police think she was drunk and fell in." I paused to let her take it in.

"Go on." Her face was unreadable.

"That's it," I said.

"That's it? What about a funeral?"

"I suppose Mark's seeing to that, or does she still have family?"

"It's like you not to know," she said, sourly, "or to care. Yes, she has family. Her mother, some brothers. My God," she said, abruptly.

"I'm sorry, Elena. I know she was a friend."

"Why didn't you call me before?"

"I left messages."

"You didn't say anything about Sara."

"It's not the kind of message you leave on an answering machine."

Grudgingly, she nodded. After a moment, she said, "What do you want with Ruth?"

"I want to know why she came here."

"To get away from you," she said. "To keep you from making her relive something that she's trying to put behind her."

"Whose idea was it for her to come here? Not hers."

"I know what you can be like when you get an idea in your head to do something," she said. "Ruth's just a girl. No match for you."

"But you are," I said sharply, irritated by her hostility and self-righteousness. "You knew Ruth might get dragged into the case, so you suggested to Sara that she hire me to be Paul's lawyer, to give yourself some strings to pull."

She reached for her cigarettes. "What strings? We've hardly spoken in ten years."

"We grew up together, remember? Alcoholic father, crazy mother? You knew I'd feel sorry for Ruth. You hoped I'd protect her. But you couldn't quite trust me, could you? So you brought her here."

From behind a veil of smoke, she said, "You wanted her to testify. I'm not about to let anyone hurt her."

"But it's all right if Paul goes to jail for something he didn't do."

"Paul's done quite enough to deserve jail."

"There's not much scope to your compassion."

She jabbed out the cigarette. "It doesn't encompass child molesters, if that's what you mean."

"Or *male* homosexuals."

She slapped me, hard, jerking my head back. "You contemptible son-of-a-bitch."

I grabbed her wrist. "Do you think I care whether you're a lesbian?"

She yanked her hand free. "So you pry out of disinterested cruelty?" she demanded. "Does that make it all right?"

"Elena, I'm here because you brought me into this case. Why?"

She massaged her wrist. "I was curious about you," she said. "I wanted to know what kind of man you've grown up to be."

"You didn't give me much of a chance to show you."

She shrugged. "Maybe I also wanted you to find out about me, Henry."

"I have," I said. "You're a decent human being. The rest is unimportant."

"Thank you," she said. "Thank you for saying that."

"Now let me show you that I am, too."

Just then, the door opened, and Carlos ran into the room, shrieking, "Grandma, look what I have."

He saw me and froze. Ruth came in behind him and, behind her, a heavy middle-aged black woman. Joanne, the famous roommate.

"Who are you?" she demanded.

"Joanne, this is my brother, Henry."

I stood up. "Hello."

"Hello," she said, ignoring my outstretched hand. To Elena she said, "What is he doing here?"

"He came to tell me that Sara Windsor is dead," she replied.

Moving swiftly to Elena she said, "I'm so sorry, honey. What happened?"

Elena reached up and took Joanne's hand. "I'll tell you later. Henry wants to speak to Ruth now."

Ruth had sat down in a chair, and was staring at me. Carlos went over to her and clutched her knee.

"Mrs. Windsor's dead?" she asked.

I nodded. "Ruth, why did you leave town?"

She looked at me for a moment, then said. "The detective told me I had to leave."

"Who? Morrow?"

She bit her lip and nodded. "Until the trial was over, he said. He said if I left you couldn't make me testify."

"Did you tell him I'd talked to you?"

"No, he already knew."

Vega, I thought. Vega. He must have told Morrow that I had a surprise witness and Morrow had figured it out.

Ruth demanded, "What does this mean, Henry?"

"It means the police are trying to convict Paul for a murder he didn't commit."

22

Promptly at one-thirty, Kevin Reilly and I presented ourselves in the courtroom of Judge Frances Flynn just in time to hear her sentence to state prison, for the highest term possible, a man convicted of robbery who had no prior record.

I leaned over to Kevin and said, "Does she always sentence like that?"

He whispered back, "The public defenders call her Frying Flynn."

"*People versus Thurmond*," she said, then with a baffled look turned to her clerk. "What's this here for, Luis?"

"A motion to unseal the record, Your Honor," the little Latino answered. "Mr. Reilly is the attorney."

"Oh, is that why Mr. Reilly is here," she said with a relenting smile.

Kevin got up and grabbed me. "Come on," he said. We went through the railing to counsel table and Kevin said, "Good morning, Your Honor. Kevin Reilly on the motion, and my associate, Henry Rios."

"Oh, yes," she said, warmly, "I've heard of you, Mr. Rios, but I don't think I've ever had the pleasure of having you in my court before."

"The pleasure's all mine."

"So, let me see what we have here." She glanced down, occasionally making a comment. " 'Material evidence' . . . 'related prosecution' . . . 'possible alibi.' " She looked up. "I don't see any opposition by the district attorney."

"This is an ex parte application, Your Honor," Kevin said.

She frowned. "You didn't serve this on the People?"

"We did, Your Honor. If you'll look at my declaration you'll see that I talked to the attorney who prosecuted the case and he indicated that he would not oppose the motion."

Judge Flynn read along, muttering to herself. "Well, I don't really like these ex parte matters but since the People aren't opposing it, I'll grant the motion."

"Your Honor, could that order be forthwith so that we could take it down to the clerk's office?"

"Yes, all right." She wrote something and then handed the sheet of paper to her clerk. "How is Mrs. Reilly?"

"She sends her regards, Your Honor," Kevin said, his voice mysteriously acquiring an Irish lilt.

"Yes, tell her I said hello, will you?"

"Thank you very much, Your Honor," Kevin said.

"Nice to see you, Mr. Reilly, and you, too, Mr. Rios."

When her clerk finished writing up the order, I grabbed it and we went down to the court's records office where Kevin and I parted company. I went in and laid the order on the counter, explaining to the young, indifferent woman what it was. She stared at it as if it were a Dead Sea scroll, then took it and wandered off into a room behind the counter.

A few minutes later, she returned. "You want the file, right?"

"That's right."

"That file's sealed."

I smiled, tightly. "Yes, I know that. That's why I got this order from Judge Flynn, to unseal the record."

"I never heard of nothin' like that."

I was about to educate her as crudely as possible when her supervisor appeared. "What's the problem?" he asked.

I tapped the order. "I would like to see this file."

He read it. "So, what's the problem?"

"There won't be one if you'll bring it to me," I snapped.

He bunched his eyebrows together ominously. "Greta, get the file."

She again retreated into the bureaucratic tundra, emerging with a surprisingly slim file sealed with a piece of tape that read, "Not to be opened except upon order of the court." Her supervisor took it and, with great ceremony, cut the seal.

"Satisfied?" he asked, handing it across the counter.

"Thank you."

I opened it up to the complaint. It was in eight counts. Five alleged a violation of penal code section 288, lewd and lascivious conduct with a child under the age of sixteen. The remaining three alleged sodomy and oral copulation. The child-victim was identified simply as "B, a child under the age of 16." The last two counts identified the victim as "D., a minor."

Digging further, I found two minute orders from the Woodlin County Superior Court. The first recorded that the defendant, Thurmond, was held to answer on all charges and bound over for trial. The second recorded the transfer of the action to San Francisco following the granting of a motion to change venue. I searched the file for either the preliminary transcript or the motion to learn the identity of the victims but neither was to be found. I mentioned this to the clerk.

"Geez, I don't know why they didn't send it," she said.

"Maybe there's more to the file."

She shook her head. "That was it. They probably just kept that stuff at the other court."

"Well, could you just check to see if there's another file?"

Grudgingly, she wandered off while I went through what remained of the San Francisco file. There were various form motions, discovery, suppression of evidence, which I recognized as the work of the San Francisco public defender's office, but none of these mentioned the victim's name. Finally, there was a minute order recording that the defendant pled to three counts of the complaint and was sentenced to five years in state prison and ordered to register as a sex offender upon his release.

The clerk came back. "That's it."

I made copies of the complaint and the Woodlin court minute orders and went out to a pay phone. I asked the Woodlin court clerk's office whether they had a file for the case. The clerk went off to look, and when he came back on the line he told me the file had been sealed by order of the court.

I went downstairs to the court cafeteria for a cup of coffee and to think. I was stymied. It seemed unlikely that I would prevail in a motion to unseal the Woodlin court file as easily as I had here. I flipped through the complaint and read, "B., a child under the age of 16," and "D., a minor." The distinction was that D. could have been as old as 17 while B. was under 16.

B. D. Woodlin County. Fifteen years ago.

And then I got it.

The county seat of Woodlin was the little town of Nueces. It had a main street called Main Street. There was a cemetery at one end of the street, and a grammar school at the other. I parked my car near the school and got out. There wasn't anything Norman Rockwellesque about Nueces. The small businesses that lined Main Street traded more in nostalgia than chattels; behind flyspecked storefronts many were vacant, violated, fixtures torn from the walls, empty shelves gathering dust, linoleum floors cracked and faded. The only place that seemed to be doing any business was a bar called

La Cabaña. Mexican ballads drifted out from behind its doors. Down the street was a restaurant called El Faisan. I pushed open the door, setting off a tinkling bell. The place had a couple of booths upholstered in orange vinyl, some tables and a counter that looked into the kitchen. A plump-faced Mexican woman standing at the counter smiled at me.

"Any place," she said.

I went over to her. "I'm looking for the high school."

She came out from the kitchen, wiping her hands on a flowered apron. A thin greasy smell hung in the air, familiar to me from my mother's kitchen, refried beans, stewed meat, onions.

"Es that way," she said flapping her hand behind me. She looked at me, and added, *"Detras del cemetario, en la calle Walnut. Acercita."*

"Muchas gracias, señora. Smells good in here."

She smiled broadly at the compliment, gold shining dully in her mouth. *"Pues, cuando acabas en la escuela vuelves aqui y comes algo."*

I went back out and followed her directions, walking alongside the cemetery to Walnut Street. I could see the school from the corner, an Art Deco building. Around it square concrete bunkers huddled like a squatter's camp.

School was out for the day. The corridors smelled of chalk and Lysol. In the registration office I asked to see the principal. The woman to whom I spoke raised ribboned glasses from her ample breasts, fixed them on her face and looked at me, then got up and went into an adjoining room. A minute later, she reappeared with Santa Claus in tow.

Santa said, "I'm Mr. Hendricksen, did you want to see me?"

"Yes, my name is Henry Rios. I'm a lawyer."

The silver-haired, red-faced fat man looked alarmed. "Why don't you come into my office, Mr. Rios." He held open a swinging door to let me in behind the counter.

I sat down and surveyed the room. Faded pep posters on the wall and drawn blinds gave the place a look of indescribable sadness. Slats of light glanced across the cluttered desk and dusty bookshelves. Atop one of the bookshelves was a framed picture of football team, circa 1950-something.

Observing my interest in the picture, Hendricksen said, "That was the year we were number one in the valley."

"You in that picture?"

He smiled, creasing his double chin. "Running back." He patted his gut. "That was a long time ago. So what can I do for you, Mr. Rios?"

"I'm interested in Howard Thurmond. I think he used to teach here."

He narrowed his eyes. "Is that right?"

"Mr. Hendricksen, I'm a criminal defense lawyer," I said. "I represent a man in Los Robles named Paul Windsor. Maybe you've heard of him."

He nodded. "I read something about it in the papers. He killed someone, didn't he?"

"So they say," I replied. "What's important is that I believe the dead man was Howard Thurmond."

Hendricksen stared at me. In the other room, someone was sharpening a pencil.

"That's not the name I saw in the paper," he said, finally.

"No, he changed his name, because of what happened here fifteen years ago. I don't think my client killed him," I said. "I think someone else did. I think he was killed by the boys he molested."

"If it was them," he said, "it served him right."

"Maybe so," I replied, "that's not for me to say. I'm just interested in clearing Paul Windsor. If you'll help me informally I can be discreet, but if I have to start subpoenaing records and witnesses, people could be hurt all over again."

After a moment's thought, his face formed a decision. Slowly, he picked up the phone, pushed a button and spoke. "Get me a 1973 yearbook." Phone still in hand, he asked, "You want some coffee, Mr. Rios? We might be here awhile."

"Yes, thank you."

He pushed another button and said, "Mary, bring me a

pot of coffee and two cups. Cream, sugar. Any cookies left from lunch? Bring those too."

A few minutes later, a cafeteria worker brought in a tray with a pot of coffee, a couple of mugs and a plate of thick brown cookies.

"Help yourself," Hendricksen said.

I poured a cup of coffee and picked up a cookie. "These bring back memories," I said. I bit into it and nearly choked.

Hendricksen grinned. "It helps if you dip 'em," he said, demonstrating.

"I'll pass," I replied. "Nueces doesn't look like it's prospering these days."

"Useta be there were a lot more people, with the braceros and all," he said. "Now all the big farms are mechanized and they don't need as many workers. Plus, a lot of the canneries have shut down. We're drying up. We've closed classrooms."

"What about those bunkers outside?"

He swept crumbs from his shirt front. "They went up in the sixties when the place was packed with kids." He squinted at me. "I guess that woulda been your generation, Mr. Rios. The whole bunch of you were smart-ass troublemakers and I never thought I'd miss those days, but I do." He poured me more coffee. "You kids were alive. Nowadays, the students, they seemed kinda depressed."

"It's a harder world to be young in," I said.

"I won't have to worry about it after next semester. I'm retiring."

The woman from the counter bustled in and laid a large book on Hendricksen's desk. He thanked her, opened it and flipped through the pages until he found the one he wanted. He passed it across the desk to me, saying, "The top picture."

A group of boys, arranged according to size, stood in a semicircle facing the camera. Some of them wore track suits and others running shorts and singlets with Woodlin High Track printed across their shirt fronts. United in their extreme youth, their faces were almost indistinguishable, one from the other, and they looked out, startled, self-conscious, at the camera. I could imagine the photographer trying to coax smiles out of them, but they were having none of that; smiling was for sissies. I searched the faces and found the dark visage of a seventeen-year-old whom the caption identified as D. Morrow. Standing in front of him was a much younger boy, with the face of a Caravaggio cherub. B. Vega. And then I saw the man, standing at the end of the first row, almost completely eclipsed by a tall senior, only part of his face showing. I glanced at the caption: Coach Thurmond.

I handed the book back to Hendricksen. "What grades do you have, here?" I asked. "Nine through twelve?"

He shook his head. "We combine junior and senior high. From seven to twelve."

"So how old were Ben and Dwight?"

He looked at the picture. "Dwight was a senior, maybe seventeen, maybe eighteen. Ben was in eighth grade, so he was what? Thirteen? Fourteen?"

"That's kind of young for the track team."

"He was a sprinter, fastest little guy I ever saw. I know because back then I was head of athletics. The other kids called him Speedy Gonzalez, some kind of cartoon character, I guess."

"A mouse," I volunteered. "How did he know Dwight?"

Hendricksen broke a corner of the last cookie and put it in his mouth. They were neighbor kids, I understand. Ben's father was kind of a drifter and there was a whole passel of little Vegas for mom to take care of. Dwight's dad was no prize, either, a crazy, drunk Indian, but that boy was real responsible. Went to school, worked, always had time for younger kids." Decisively, he picked up the rest of the cookie and took a bite out of it. "The way I understand it, Dwight stepped in and became like an older brother to Ben. He's the one that got Ben started on running."

"And Thurmond?"

He tilted his head back, narrowing his eyes, remembering. "Howard," he said, finally. "Howard was a model teacher, Mr. Rios. He taught English, coached track, chaperoned dances, was faculty advisor to the student council, to the Honor Society. He couldn't do enough for the kids. Nights and weekends, he was always out there doing something." He rolled his big head back toward me. "Of course, it didn't seem strange at the time that most of the kids he spent time with were the boys. Seemed only natural—a male teacher who hung around girls, now that would have caused a stir. I never gave it a second thought when I heard that Howard liked to take some of his boys up to the Sierras for weekend campouts. It just seemed like another good-hearted thing he was doing, especially since he chose kids like Dwight and Ben, kids who didn't have dads to do that kind of stuff with them."

"How was he found out?"

It was getting dark in the office. Hendricksen switched on a desk lamp, illuminating a sagging, pale face as soft as dough.

"Ben showed up with some cankers in his mouth," he said, "and one of his teachers sent him to the nurse. Turned out to be gonorrhea. Had it in his anus, too."

"And Dwight Morrow?"

Hendricksen rubbed his eyes. "Now that's the funny part, Mr. Rios. Seems like there was something going on between him and Howard for a couple of years, but he never said anything until it came out about Ben. Then he wanted to kill Howard."

"You think he didn't know about Ben and Thurmond?" I asked.

"That's what I think," he said, nodding. "He maybe thought he was the only one Howard was pulling that stuff with. It must have hit him pretty hard when he found out about Ben, because he was the one that got Ben together with Howard in the first place."

"What happened?" I asked. "I mean, I know the trial was eventually moved to San Francisco, but what happened before that?"

Grimly, Hendricksen said, "You can see this is a small

town. We tried to keep things quiet, but the story got out. The boys got it almost as bad as Howard. Not Dwight so much because he could take care of himself, but Ben was still a little guy. He got called queer for a long time after it was over."

"But Thurmond was convicted," I said. "Didn't that count?"

"He pled guilty without a trial as soon as they moved it down to San Francisco." He smiled without humor. "They had to get him out of town, for his own safety, but it was a bad deal for Ben. The other kids didn't understand why there wasn't a trial. Too much Perry Mason, I guess. They figured it meant Howard was innocent. Kids have dirty minds. You can imagine what they called Ben." He sighed. "I think about those boys sometimes. I wonder what became of them."

23

It was dusk when I left the school and headed back to my car. The few shop lights on Main Street only drew attention to those shops that remained darkened, and the gorgeous sunset in the big sky only made the town seem poorer. One of the places lit up was the café where I'd sought directions. The woman I'd spoken to was taking an order from a table of straw-hatted, plaid-shirted laborers. She nodded at me as I entered. The four men at the table looked me over, taking in my suit, and went back to their Tecates. I sat down at the counter. The woman came over and laid a soiled, hand-typed menu in front of me.

"*Algo a beber?*" she asked.

"A Coke," I replied. Scanning the menu quickly, I added. "*Un plato de pozole.*"

She grinned her golden grin. "*Muy bien.*"

A few minutes later she brought the bowl of pozole, a stew of grits and pork, some tortillas, and my Coke. I thanked her and set about eating a dish I'd last tasted years ago in my mother's kitchen. My mother was a wonderful cook, but there had always been too much of everything. Even then I understood that this was how she apologized and so I ate very little, no matter how hungry I was, pretending an indifference to food that in time became real. Eating the stew reminded me of her and touched a tiny corner of forgiveness somewhere.

I thought about my interview with Hendricksen. The question in my mind was how to use the information he had given me. I could spring it on the prosecution at trial, but this would implicate Morrow and Vega, and I wasn't sure how I felt about that. As I'd told Hendricksen, my job was to get Paul acquitted, not bring McKay's killers to bay. That function belonged to the police, the courts and other lawyers. But then there was Sara. Had her drowning really been accidental? Could Morrow and Vega have had something to do with that? Yet, even if they had, Paul's trial would not be the proper forum to uncover facts about her death.

That brought me to a second option, to confront the DA with what I'd learned and bargain for a dismissal. If I could persuade him, Paul would not have to stand trial and face the possibility, however slight, that we might lose. At the same time, the DA would have to at least investigate Morrow and Vega, and that might yield information about Sara's death. I paid my bill, thanked the proprietor for the meal and walked out to my car, still undecided.

On my way back to Los Robles, I drove past the motel where McKay had been murdered, and pulled into the parking lot. Across the street, in an otherwise vacant lot, was a billboard advertising soup. Another piece of the puzzle slipped into place.

When I got back to the hotel, the registration clerk gave me three message slips, all from Peter Stein. I called from the lobby.

A woman answered the phone. I asked for him and she put him on the line.

"Peter? This is Henry. Was that your wife?"

"Yeah," he said. "Where have you been, Henry?"

"I had to go down to the city yesterday. I just got back. What's up?"

"Phelan called us into court this afternoon," he said. "He granted the motion."

It took a moment for this to sink in. "You mean he transferred the case?"

"That's right," Peter said, gleefully. "Said he was convinced that Paul couldn't get a fair trial up here and was ordering the whole kit and caboodle to San Francisco superior court. Rossi was shitting bricks. Congratulations."

"We need to talk, Peter," I said. "Can I come over?"

"Sure," he said. "Everything okay?"

"I'll tell you when I get there. Where do you live?"

Home for the Steins was a gray tract house just outside the city limits in a development called Fairhaven. Half the streets dead-ended into fields and there wasn't a tree to be seen for miles. I rang the bell and waited, smelling the earth in the air.

"Henry," he said, boisterously, opening the door, in jeans and a 49er T-shirt. "Come on in."

I stepped into a little foyer. Off to one side was an immaculate living room that looked seldom used. Off to the other side was a narrow kitchen where a slender, plain woman stood over the sink, tap water running, steam rising around her head.

"This is my wife, Gina," Peter was saying. "She's a court reporter."

The kitchen smelled of tomato sauce and garlic. Gina shut off the faucet and dried her hands on a kitchen towel.

"I'm glad to meet you," she said. "Peter's been talking about what a good lawyer you are."

"Thanks."

"Are you hungry?" she asked.

"No, thank you. I ate. Smells good, though."

She smiled. "It was Pete's night to cook. On my nights we eat Lean Cuisine." She poked his stomach. "He eats two."

"Come on into the den, Henry," Peter said, and steered me through the kitchen to the next room. Furnished with odds and ends of chairs and tables, a lumpy couch partly covered with an afghan, a bookshelf filled with legal treatises and a plain wooden desk, this room evidently was where the Steins did most of their living. A TV was going in the corner, the sound shut off. A rust-colored cat lay in front of it, watching.

Peter saw me looking at the cat. "That's Calico," he said. "She sits in front of the TV for hours, just like a kid. Her favorite channel is MTV. Have a seat."

On the screen, a man in red latex tights with big hair pranced around a stage, thrusting a microphone toward the camera like a penis. Calico was mesmerized.

"So, what's going on?" Peter asked.

"I know who killed John McKay," I replied. "And it wasn't Paul."

"I'm listening," he said, in a tone I'd come to respect.

I laid out my theory of the murder: telling him what I'd discovered about McKay in the last two days and about my conversation with the high school principal.

When I finished, he said, "Now it's my turn. Your first problem is explaining how they tracked McKay down."

"Yes, I've thought about that," I said. "And then I remembered that Paul first met McKay through a computer bulletin board for pedophiles. The cops monitor those things because they know if they wait long enough there's a pretty good chance that they'll come up with something illegal. Morrow worked Sex Crimes, remember? He'd have access to information all over the state about pedophiles."

"But how would he have known it was McKay?" Peter insisted. "Morrow knew him as Thurmond."

"You have to assume that finding McKay was an obsession

with Morrow and that he was willing to take whatever time it took. Working Sex Crimes gave him a perfect cover. Maybe he subscribed to some of the publications these pedophile organizations put out, maybe he went to their conventions."

"Conventions?" Peter asked incredulously.

"There's nothing illegal about an organization that advocates changing the age-of-consent laws, Peter. NAMBLA advertises in a lot of the gay papers. Finding McKay would have been difficult, but not impossible. Especially for a cop."

Gina Stein came in and went over to the desk, sitting down to a stack of transcripts. "Will it bother you if I work in here?" she asked.

Peter said, "Nope."

"Fine," I said, and picked up the thread of my thought. "At some point, Morrow found McKay."

"What about Vega?"

"From what I've seen of Ben, I doubt he's smart enough to have contributed much to the search. Maybe he came in later."

"You think he's the killer?"

I thought about Ben. "I don't know, Peter. I kind of hope not. I like the kid."

"Tell me how they got McKay up here."

"They tell him they have a kid," I replied.

"What kid?"

"The girl that Paul Windsor thought he was buying from McKay."

"That's really weird," he said.

From her corner, Gina said, "Honey, I just reported a case in district court where the defendant was bringing babies in from South America to sell to couples who got turned down for adoption."

"Think of the Steinberg case in New York," I added. "The little girl he murdered had been placed illegally. Look at the back of your milk carton. What do you think happens to some of those kids?"

"Yeah," he said thoughtfully. "What kind of world do we live in?"

"A world where both Paul and McKay thought they were dealing with a bona fide offer."

"Windsor will have to testify," he said, "and once he's done that, he's waived the Fifth and you'll open him up to the DA."

"Yes," I conceded, imagining how all this would sound to a jury. "That's a problem."

"What about the actual killing?" Peter asked. "How did they do it without being noticed?"

"That part was easy. Across the street from the motel where McKay was killed there's a lot that's empty except for a billboard. A cop car could park there all night, and all anyone would think was that it was a speed trap. My guess is that the night McKay was killed, Vega and Morrow were out there in a black-and-white. At the right moment, one or both of them went across the street and knocked on McKay's door."

" 'McKay, this is the police,' " Peter said. "That must've scared him shitless."

"No," I said. "I don't think they played it that way. What they did was tell him they'd be by with the girl, so he was expecting them. He let them in."

Peter nodded. "Yeah, I see your point."

"The other thing," I said. "You know how he was killed? Someone bashed his head in with something about the size of a baseball bat."

"A nightstick?"

I nodded. "That's why they never found a weapon."

We were quiet. The cat stretched and purred. I glanced toward the TV screen. A half-naked woman crawled on all fours toward a guillotine. The camera cut to the gleaming blade descending. The next image was a ratty-looking, potbellied singer in leather swinging a mannequin's head by her hair.

"How much of this can you prove?" Peter asked, diverting me from the screen.

"McKay's conviction," I said, "and the tie-in with Morrow and Vega. Paul can testify about why he was there. Maybe someone noticed a patrol car parked across the street from the motel." Listening to myself I realized how iffy this sounded. "All I've got to do is establish reasonable doubt."

"If the DA sits still for it," Peter was saying. "But he won't. He'll fight you tooth and nail."

"Then what do you think about going to the DA with it to bargain for a dismissal?"

"Rossi?" he asked incredulously.

"No, the head of the office."

"Joe Burke?" He thought for a moment. "Burke's a straight arrow."

"What does that mean?"

"It means he'd hear you out. It doesn't mean anything else."

I sighed. "I don't want to go to trial with this. Once I get started pointing the finger at Morrow and Vega, there's no turning back and if I can't come up with some really strong evidence, it could backfire. I mean, if you were Jane Juror, who would you believe? The DA doesn't have to believe. The only thing I have to convince him of is that I could make things very messy for the cops and his office." I looked at him, seeking confirmation.

"Do you believe what you've just told me, Henry?"

"About eighty percent."

He smiled. "I believe it about sixty percent. That would be enough for me to kick the case, and the higher up you go in the DA's office, the lower the percentage of belief has to be before someone'll dump the case, because the higher-ups are the ones who'll eat shit if Windsor's acquitted. Let's go see Burke."

"When?"

"Tomorrow. Technically, the case isn't even in the Los Robles judicial district anymore, so we have to move fast."

"Thanks," I said, getting up.

"You going?"

"I'm exhausted."

I said good-bye to Gina, and Peter walked me to my car. As I was getting in, he said, "Henry, if you're right about Morrow and Vega, you better be looking over your shoulder."

The first thing I did when I got back to the hotel was to change rooms.

The sign on the door said, 1,-Hjoseph burke, district attorney. Beneath it was the Los Robles county seal, an undecipherable device that involved a river, an oak tree and a Latin motto that, as near as I could translate, meant gift of the earth. Peter, who occupied the chair next to me, nervously tapped his foot.

"What's wrong?" I asked him.

"When I was a DA the only time you came in to see Joe Burke was to get your ass handed to you." He noisily unwrapped a stick of gum and stuffed it into his mouth.

"He have a temper?"

"Do bears shit in the woods?"

Burke's secretary looked up and hushed us with a frown. The door to the anteroom opened and Dom Rossi hurried in. Seeing us his expression curdled. He announced himself to the secretary, who was clearly unimpressed. She got up and went into Burke's office.

Rossi said, "What's this all about?"

"Henry wanted to meet the DA," Peter drawled. "Thought I'd oblige him."

He glared at us. Burke's secretary reappeared and told us to go in. Rossi pushed his way ahead of me and Peter followed.

Burke's office was big but sparsely furnished. Its windows overlooked the city eight stories below. The blond wooden paneling reflected the light, giving the place a sunny glow. The DA sat in shirtsleeves behind a long, narrow desk. There was nothing sunny about him. His face was deeply seamed and cragged, his silver hair plastered back. Before him was an open file. Sitting down, I glanced over and saw the complaint in *People v. Windsor*.

"You Rios?" he rumbled at me.

"Yes. Good morning."

He nodded unpleasantly. To Peter he said, "Private practice must agree with you, Pete, you're fatter than ever."

"Thank you," Peter mumbled.

"Rossi," he said, turning his attention to Dom, "when I assign a case I expect it to be handled by the deputy from start to finish."

"I didn't ask for this meeting," Rossi said, crouching down a little in his chair.

"This man"—he pointed to me—"must not think he can do business with you. That's not his problem, it's yours." He jerked his head toward me. "Let's get this over with."

"Mr. Burke, my client is accused of murdering a man named John McKay."

"I read the file," he said dourly.

"Good, then I'll come straight to the point. My client didn't do it. John McKay was murdered by members of the Los Robles Police Department."

Peter drew in his breath sharply. Rossi lurched forward and started to speak but Burke held up his hand. "I hope you can prove that," he said. "I surely hope you can."

For the next fifteen minutes I laid out the story of Howard Thurmond, Ben Vega and Dwight Morrow. Burke trained his eyes on me the whole time, motionless, but as I went on his expression shifted from hostility to something akin to interest. When I finished, the room was still. I noticed the plaque on the wall above Burke's head—District Attorney of the Year—presented by the California District Attorneys' Association two years earlier, and was absurdly heartened by it.

"This is the biggest pile of shit I ever heard," he said, quietly.

My insides collapsed.

"That's what I think," Rossi piped up, lurching forward.

"Shut the fuck up," Burke snapped. "I'll deal with you later."

Rossi dropped back in his chair.

"What you think and what a jury will think are two different things," I said to Burke, "particularly since the jury in question won't be composed of a lynch mob from Los Robles County. You said you read the file? Then you have to know that the case is being moved to San Francisco."

"Land of fruits and nuts," he commented. "What do you want, Rios?"

"Dismissal."

He made a contemptuous noise. "We don't dismiss cases up here."

I got up. "Then we don't have anything else to talk about."

"I guess not," he said.

The three of us, Peter, Rossi and I, headed for the door. Burke said, "Rossi, stay put."

On our way out of the office, we could hear Burke yelling at him.

Waiting for the elevator, I turned to Peter. "Well, that was a bust. All I've done is give away the defense."

"I'm not so sure," he said.

"What do you mean?"

The elevator came and we got on. There were other people on it. "Downstairs," he said.

Outside, he stopped on the steps and turned to me. "I think you might get your dismissal."

"How do you figure that?"

"Look, Henry, put yourself in Burke's position. He's hearing this stuff for the first time and he has no way of knowing whether it's true or not. Why should he take your word? You're the enemy. He needs to hear it from his own people." We took a couple of steps down to the sidewalk and started walking toward the office. "You did the important thing, you got his attention, and once you've got Joe Burke's attention, you've got his attention." He smiled. "I sure wouldn't want to be Dom Rossi."

24

Over lunch, Peter and I discussed trial strategy should the case get that far. When we got to dessert, I said, "It just occurred to me, Peter, you're working for me, now."

He dug into his banana cream pie. "What are you paying me?"

I smiled. "I'd like to say double what Clayton's been paying you, but I don't know what that is."

"I get billed out at fifty an hour," he said. "You manage that?"

"I bill myself out at a hundred and twenty-five," I said, adding, "when I can get it. I'm getting it from the Windsors. You're entitled to half."

He finished his pie. "I'll be sorry when it's over."

I had a revelation. "How deep are your roots up here?"

"Come again?"

"I need a partner," I said. "I've got more work than I can handle in LA plus, being the famous faggot lawyer that I am, I'm always getting requests to travel all over the countryside giving speeches, sit on panels, that kind of stuff."

Peter sipped some coffee. "I bet. But I'm not gay, obviously."

"I don't mind if you don't mind."

"Let me talk it over with Gina."

I headed back to the hotel, where I spent the rest of the afternoon on the phone to Los Angeles trying to direct my cases long distance. By the time I was done I was ready to offer Peter whatever it took to get him to LA.

My last call was to the jail to check in with Paul. When I asked the deputy to put him on the line, he said, "He's gone."

"I beg your pardon. What do you mean he's gone?" I asked, apprehensively. Even though the case had been transferred to San Francisco, I hadn't expected they would move Paul without informing me in advance.

"He was OR'd about an hour ago," the deputy said indifferently. "His brother picked him up."

For over two months, Paul had been denied bail on the theory that he was a danger to the community and now, suddenly, he was set free on his own recognizance, which amounted to little more than his promise to appear for trial and to behave himself in the interim. Moreover, this could have been accomplished only by a court order and, since the case had been transferred out of Los Robles, technically the local judge had no power to make any further orders on the matter.

"Who signed the order?" I asked.

I heard him rattle through some papers. "Judge Phelan."

"Today?"

"Yep."

"Thanks," I said, and hung up. Peter was right—Burke had been paying attention and whatever investigation he'd conducted had convinced him there was at least enough merit in my story to OR Paul out of jail. I doubted that he'd done this out of the goodness of his heart; he was just hedging his bets and trying to minimize the possibility of a false arrest action. The phone rang.

"Henry Rios," I said, picking it up.

"Mr. Rios," a woman said, "this is Mary Flores with the DA's office. I've been assigned the Windsor case."

I smiled to myself. "What happened to Rossi?"

"He's no longer on the case," she said, flatly. "I'd like to make an appointment with you to talk about a possible plea negotiation."

"I just called the jail," I replied, "and it seems my client was OR'd. It's customary to inform the defense attorney when that kind of action is taken."

Smoothly, she said, "I tried calling earlier but your line was busy. We didn't think you'd object. Are you busy tomorrow at, say, nine?"

"No, I'm not busy, but I've already stated my position on a plea bargain to your boss. We want a dismissal."

"I understand," she said. "I think we can work something out." She paused. "Of course, we'd have to take any disposition we work out to San Francisco."

"Of course," I agreed. I saw the DA's strategy: a quick, quiet dismissal far away from the local media.

"And," she continued, "if we did agree to a dismissal— and I'm not saying we would—we'd be looking for a quid pro quo."

"Such as?" I asked dryly.

A little nervously, she said, "Well, we can't ask your client to waive any civil action he might have against the city as a condition of dismissal . . ."

"That's right."

"But we are concerned about that possibility."

"You should be," I replied. "Just off the top of my head, I see a suit for false arrest and false imprisonment. If I did a little research I'm sure I could come up with a few other causes of action."

"We haven't agreed to dismissal yet," she reminded me. "If we have to, we'll go to trial."

"That would be interesting."

"Let's talk about this tomorrow," she said. "Nine? My office?"

"I'll be there. Oh, Ms. Flores?"

"Yes?"

"What about Vega and Morrow?"

After a moment's hesitation, she said. "That's a police matter, Mr. Rios."

"I see. Good-bye."

"Good-bye," she said. I smiled. This business about going to trial was bluster. Without Morrow's testimony there was no case against Paul. We'd won. But where was Paul? I called Mark.

"Oh, yeah, Henry," he said, when I got through. "Paul tried to call you but you were on the phone."

"Where is he now?"

"Upstairs, asleep. You want me to wake him?"

"No, let him sleep," I replied, "but let's get together for dinner. Say about eight."

"Sure," Mark said. "We'll come and get you."

"Tell him I think the case may be dismissed."

"He'll like that."

"How are you two getting along?"

"Same as always," he said. "Talk to you later."

A nap sounded good to me, too. I got undressed and under the sheets. Within minutes I was asleep, only to be awakened a half-hour later by the phone. I rolled over, picked it up and managed a groggy, "Henry Rios."

"I've got to talk to you."

Ben Vega's voice cut through the fog. "About what, Ben?"

"Not on the phone," he said. His voice was tight with anxiety. "I'm at a bar on the Parkway."

"I think you want to be talking to the cops."

"I want to talk to you," he said, edgily. "I've got to make you understand."

I sat up and switched on the light. The only noise in the room was the hum of the air conditioner. "I think I do understand, Ben. But I'm not the person you have to convince."

Vega rushed on. "I want you to defend me."

"Ben," I said softly, "I may be a witness against you."

"Then just listen," he whispered harshly. "He used to take me camping up in the mountains. Fishing. Like that." He paused. "He taught me how to shoot."

"He was your friend," I said.

After a moment's silence, he said, "Morrow says they're all like that, taking advantage. They prey on kids that don't have dads. My old man never had time for me. Coach always had time." He stopped and I heard the rasp of his breathing. "That time in the mountains it was just me and him, like a lot of other times. We hiked to a lake and went swimming bare ass. I didn't think nothing of it. We came back, made some dinner and talked for a long time. Then he goes, 'I forgot to pack my sleeping bag. We'll have to double up.'" He stopped again. "I was just starting to get wet dreams and I was all nervous that I might get one, so I kept trying to get away from him when we were in the bag. He got pissed and said, 'Settle down,' and kind of pulled me over to him. Then we went to sleep."

"I'm listening, Ben."

"When I woke up it was still dark and I felt something between my legs. It was his dick, man. I thought I was dreaming, then I figured, maybe he was asleep so I tried to move, but he held on to me. Then I knew he was awake and I wasn't dreaming." His voice broke. "He hurt me, man. He hurt me."

"I know, Ben. It was wrong. It wasn't your fault. There was nothing you could've done."

"He made me . . . he made me . . ." he sputtered.

"Ben?"

"A queer. I'm a queer."

"Where are you now?"

"At the bar, in the B of A building."

"I'll be there in fifteen minutes," I said.
In a choking voice he said, "Thank you."
"Ben, is Morrow with you?"
"I don't know where he is."

I got dressed and went downstairs. Outside, River Parkway was largely deserted. The office workers had already gone home, leaving only a few harried-looking stragglers and the street people who roamed among the glass towers looking for a companionable doorway in which to bed. The Bank of America building was at the far end of the Parkway, its sign lit in blue neon on the roof.

The streetlights flickered on, illuminating the broad road in a greenish light. A bus rumbled by, its brightly lit interior empty. The few cars on the road sped by, through a row of traffic lights flashing yellow overhead. I set out on foot, thinking about Ben Vega, the boy in the giant's body, and I understood that the muscles were armor against his horror at his own sexual nature.

I knew about the horror because I had felt it myself, at about the same age Ben was when McKay got to him. Twelve, thirteen. I remembered standing in the shower one morning and looking down startled and disturbed to see wisps of public hair on my groin.

More disturbing had been the midnight awakening to damp sheets and my underwear caked to my skin. I'd risen quietly, gone into the bathroom and scrubbed my underwear and then taken a washcloth back into my bedroom to work on the sheets. Without ever having been told, I knew this was something I didn't want my mother to discover. I never associated it with the dreams that preceded my awakening, nor did I remember the dreams very clearly. They seemed composed of sensations more than images: a deep rumbling sensation that began in the pit of my stomach and seemed to flood my chest and then my entire body, a seizure of emotion at once terrifying and thrilling. And somewhere, in all of that, were brief images of myself and a neighbor boy naked, about to dive into the river on a still, hot summer afternoon. I saw the long dense curve of his thigh, his lank penis swinging free as he jumped into the water, splashing me.

This, I knew, instinctively, was even a more dangerous secret than the damp sheets, the soiled shorts. For hours afterward I'd lie in bed trying not to think about it, praying to be free of these impure thoughts. But always, exhausted and confused, my mind wandered back to that picture and the weight of the sheets against my body became like the weight of another's body pressed against me. I hadn't understood what I was trying to tell myself, only that what I felt was physical, like hunger or fatigue, and there was more to it, a kind of wild loneliness and a deep, scary sense of being different.

Over the years I had learned that only a few of us come to accept that difference. Most of us struggle against our homosexuality and never learn to trust our natures. And if a John McKay comes into our lives, precisely at that moment when we first awaken to what we are, what chance would we have at all? I heard Ben saying, "He made me a queer." A child's sexual innocence isn't moral, it's literal: he has no context for it. From the adult who uses him sexually, he learns a context in which pleasure alternates with brutality, until the two begin to merge. Who wouldn't want to kill that horror? Was that what Ben had done?

I walked on, aware of my reflection in the dark glass of the building next to me. Someone was approaching. I smelled him before I saw him—a stooped-over black man with a soiled kerchief around the frayed explosion of his hair. He looked up at me with bloodshot, hopeful eyes. It was the panhandler I'd given money to weeks earlier. John? No, James.

"Spare change, mister," he said blocking my way. He looked at me without recognition.

"Hello, James," I said.

"I don' know you," he replied, alarmed.

"Yes, you do. My name's Henry, same as your brother up at Folsom."

Slowly, he smiled, revealing yellowing stumps of teeth.

"Oh, yeah. Sure, Henry. You got some spare change for me, Henry?"

I reached for my wallet and he put out a grimy hand. Suddenly, glass was blowing up behind us. I dropped the wallet as something hard went through my shoulder. In the same second, with shocking speed, James crashed into me, knocking me to the ground, glass flying around us. "Jesus, Jesus," he moaned. Then there was silence, total, dark silence. My shoulder throbbed. I worked my head around to see blood gushing through my sweater. James lay on me like a stone, his face inches from my face. He wasn't breathing.

I heard a siren and panicked. Morrow was coming. Vega . . . I'd been set up. The dead man pressed against me reeking of booze and piss as his bladder emptied. Blood and urine seeped through his clothes. I began to push him off me, then froze. What if they were still there? The siren got closer, and I heard footsteps running toward us. The blood kept coming from my wound. I laid my head against the pavement and closed my eyes and thought, first of Josh and then of Ben. Ben had set me up. All my fault, I thought, and slipped into the black.

25

I was wrong about Ben. He was waiting for me at the bar in the bank building. Hearing the sirens, he'd gone out to investigate. He saw what happened, figured it was Morrow and turned himself in to a fellow cop at the scene. He'd figured right about Morrow.

Morrow was the second person to die that night, after James Harrison. After he shot at us he kept driving, catching the I-80 east, toward Reno. A CHP car clocked him at eighty-five miles an hour and tried to flag him down. When he wouldn't pull over, the chippies gave chase. About twenty miles out of Los Robles, Morrow went through the median strip divider, skidded across four lanes of oncoming traffic and ran into the side of a granite hill. That wasn't what killed him, though. What killed him was the bullet hole through his head. Self-inflicted, the chippies swore.

Of all the characters in the cast of *People v. Windsor*, Morrow was the one I'd known the least and yet it was he who haunted me. I'd think about the two photographs I'd seen of him, pictured in a high school yearbook as a teenage jock and then, fifteen years later, with the kids in the Police Athletic League. Here was a man who had bleakly shouldered the blame for what had been done to him and spent his life in expiation. Had we ever been able to talk, I believe we would have understood each other.

I never did get to have my chat with Ben Vega. He was represented by a public defender in the criminal case against him for McKay's murder. He laid the blame on Morrow and, for whatever reason, maybe just to get the thing off the books, maybe because he believed in him, the DA let him plead to voluntary manslaughter, for a five-year term at Folsom. I'd written him a couple of times, but my letters had gone unanswered.

Meanwhile, the man everyone wanted in prison was free. The charges against Paul were dismissed, of course. Two weeks later he filed a suit against the city for conspiracy to violate his civil rights and a raft of other causes of action. Bob Clayton represented him. After a last appearance for the dismissal I didn't talk to Paul again. He seemed to harbor a resentment against me and I think he blamed me for not having figured things out earlier. I didn't lose much sleep over the loss of his friendship. I did have some problems with the thought that he might try to harass Ruth again so, before I left Los Robles, I put her in touch with a lawyer who got a permanent injunction against Paul, preventing him from coming within a thousand feet of her or Carlos.

Peter was able to obtain a copy of the coroner's inquest report on Sara. I went over the report carefully and could find no reason to quarrel with the conclusion of accidental death.

And that was how matters stood on *People v. Windsor* the third day of December, two months after I'd closed my file. My office was in chaos, half of it packed into boxes and the rest waiting to be packed. With Peter Stein coming into the firm, we'd had to find more space, so we were moving upstairs. Still, move or no move, there was work to be done and I was at my desk, poring over a toxicology report. I made a note and felt a twinge in my shoulder, a souvenir of my last encounter with Detective Morrow.

"Mail call," Emma said, flopping a stack of mail on my desk. "If you'd take the day off, Henry, the movers could get their work done a lot faster."

"I'm leaving in a few minutes," I replied without looking up.

I heard the chair squeak as she sat down. "You are?"

I looked up at her, smiling. "Josh goes in for some kind of new treatment. I'm taking him to the doctor."

She smiled pro forma and then, with worried eyes, asked, "Is he okay?"

"His T-cell count dropped again. This is all preventive. He was pretty cranky when I talked to him. That's a good sign."

She didn't look convinced. "Well tell him—" She stopped. "Tell him I care."

"He knows, and so do I. Thank you."

After she'd gone, I couldn't get back to work. I studied the picture of Josh I kept on my desk—who knew what the movers would make out of that. It wasn't a great picture; he was in midlaugh and, consequently, a little blurred. But he looked joyously happy and it was impossible to believe that anything bad could happen to him.

I picked up the mail, tossing the solicitations, the offers of computers and fax machines and luxurious office space in Century City. Emma had separated out the bills and fees—we'd go over those later. That left the usual handwritten pleas from the imprisoned asking me to take on some hopeless appeal or complaining, for pages and pages, about the quality of my representation. These would all have to be read, and some of them answered. Finally, there were two oversized envelopes. Christmas cards, I thought, tearing open the first one, which had no return address.

The cover featured a reproduction of a medieval painting

of the Nativity. The slender Virgin cradled a child who looked at her with ancient, knowing eyes. I opened the card: "May your holidays be blessed," it said, and was signed, "Elena." I weighed the card in my hand. It was as light and flimsy as the bond between my sister and me. But it was palpable, real. I set it aside and picked up the other envelope. This one came from the federal penitentiary at Lompoc and bore, in accordance with prison rules, a stamped "Previously Opened." The return addressee was prisoner number 2136534592-X, or, as he had been christened, Mark Lewis Windsor.

Mark. He'd done less well by the criminal justice system than Ben Vega. Indicted by a federal jury on charges arising from his looting of Pioneer Savings & Loan. The best he could do was a plea and eight years. He'd be out in two and a half if all went well. The envelope contained a cheap dime-store Christmas card with Santa on the cover. A folded sheet of plain white paper slipped from inside the card.

"Dear Hank," it began in the backhanded, slanting script I recognized from a long time ago. "Justice has been done, ha-ha, but maybe you already heard about that. I should've taken you up on your offer to defend me. This place isn't as bad as I thought it would be, but it's bad enough. The drill is, up at 6, slop for breakfast, work (I'm a clerk), lunch, some time in the yard, dinner, lights out at 9. My module's all so-called white collar criminals so it's pretty low-key. I'm getting to be friends with an ex-congressman. That kind of place. I'm getting in shape, lifting weights, they call it 'driving' around here. Pretty soon I'll be strong enough to break a hole through the walls. (Note to the censor: that's a joke.)"

I smiled and continued reading. "Still have too much time on my hands. I do a lot of thinking. If I had thought this much in high school I would've passed trig, but I never did catch on, even with your help. What I'm thinking is, maybe this is a break after all. It was like everything was out of control out there and it was all going down. I don't know, sometimes I feel like that, other times, I don't. You were a good friend to me, Hank. I just wanted to tell you that. Take care, Mark." Below his signature was a "P.S. Lompoc's not that far from LA."

I put the sheet down. He never did know how to ask for things directly. Well, Lompoc really wasn't that far from LA, and I made a note on my calendar to call about visiting hours.

Restless suddenly, I bolted up from my desk and put my jacket on. I walked out of my office as if I actually knew where I was going.

"Are you leaving, Henry?" Emma asked as I passed her desk.

"Yeah, I won't be back today," I said. "You pack it in too, if you want."

A ledger opened on her desk, piles of invoices and bills around her, she smirked. "Sure."

"Tomorrow," I said.

"You're not ready," I said, entering the bedroom, where Josh stood shirtless and with a sweater in either hand.

"I never know what to wear to the doctor's," he said. "This one." He held up a pink sweater. "Is it too gay?" He held up the other sweater, a black turtleneck. "Too butch?"

"Wear anything, Josh."

He smiled. "I guess you're right. They'll make me take it off anyway and put on one of those gowns." He pulled the pink sweater over his head. "How come hospital gowns let your butt hang out, Henry? Don't they know it's hard enough to be there in the first place without walking around mooning everyone?"

"We're going to be late."

He sat down at the edge of the bed and tied his shoelaces. "I hate hospitals."

I sat down beside him and put my arm around his shoulder. "Worried?"

He sat up. "Can't you tell? I'm babbling like an idiot."

"It'll be all right."

He held my hand and we sat in silence for a moment. "I called your sister."

"You called Elena? Why?"

"To wish her a Merry Christmas."

"What did she say?"

"She said thank you," he replied, "and wished me a Merry Christmas back. I told her I was Jewish and she said, so was Jesus." He smiled at me. "I like her, Henry, but of course I would. She is your sister." He took a deep breath. "I'm ready now."

He got up and held out his hands to me and pulled me up to my feet from the bed, like a child.

MICHAEL NAVA's novels include *The Little Death*, *Goldenboy*, *How Town*, *The Hidden Law*, *The Death of Friends*, *The Burning Plain*, and *Rag and Bone*. The recipient of the Bill Whitehead Award for Lifetime Achievement in Lesbian and Gay Literature, a five-time winner of the Lambda Award for best mystery, and a coauthor of *Created Equal: Why Gay Rights Matter in America*, Nava is a lawyer in San Francisco.